College accounting fundamentals

Chapters 1–29   SECOND EDITION

College accounting fundamentals

Chapters 1–29   SECOND EDITION

DOUGLAS J. McQUAIG
Wenatchee Valley College

HOUGHTON MIFFLIN COMPANY • BOSTON
Atlanta   Dallas   Geneva, Ill.   Hopewell, N. J.   Palo Alto   London

Credits

© Alan Oransky, 1980, pp. 1, 39, 123, 181, 215, 293, 527, 557
© Mike Malyszko, 1980, pp. 17, 95, 267, 409, 491, 651, 687, 751, 765
© Janice Fullman, pp. 67, 149, 373, 795, 821
© Paul Light, 1980, p. 237
© Carol Palmer, 1980, pp. 321, 439, 515, 693
Jennifer D. Cogswell/THE PICTURE CUBE, p. 351
George Bellerose/STOCK, BOSTON, INC., p. 465
Fredrick D. Bodin, p. 589
© Margaret Thompson/THE PICTURE CUBE, p. 623
© Andrew Brilliant, 1980, p. 717

Technical art by ANCO/BOSTON, INC.

Printed in U.S.A.

This text previously published in 1977 as *College Accounting Fundamentals*.

Library of Congress Catalog Card Number: 80-83573

ISBN: 0-395-29408-8

Contents

Preface

College Accounting Fundamentals provides students with a sound basic knowledge of accounting concepts and procedures, always taking into consideration the widely varying objectives that students have. When completed, a course of instruction based on this program will provide the following:

- Vocational preparation for students entering the job market in the field of accounting.
- A practical background in accounting for students embarking on various other business careers, such as clerical, secretarial, technical, sales, and managerial positions.
- Preparation and background for students planning more advanced studies in accounting.

In the preface of the first edition of the accounting program, I remarked that after 25 years of "chalk-in-hand" experience as a classroom teacher, I believed that there was a real need for a teachable accounting book: an accounting book aimed at students having widely different goals and written in a language they can understand. Apparently, many others agreed with me. Their acceptance of the program is a continuing source of satisfaction to me, and I vowed that in revising the book and its ancillary materials, I would not depart from my original approach.

College Accounting Fundamentals is designed for use primarily in first-year accounting courses and is based on the assumption that the reader has no previous accounting background. It presents the fundamentals of accounting in a logical, easy-to-understand manner, yet uses the most up-to-date accounting terminology. The text starts with simple descriptions and progresses to more complex topics. An appropriate, but not needless amount of repetition is provided to establish fundamental concepts clearly in the minds of the students, as well as to enable them to build up their confidence to handle more complex material. To encourage the transfer of learning, each chapter relates new topics to examples, concepts, and procedures presented previously. The book uses the analysis approach to introduce students to the subject matter and gives concrete examples of business papers and accounting stationery to illustrate each step of the accounting process.

While the approach is still the same, the present edition is markedly different from the first in several respects. In response to requests from many users, several chapters—particularly those relating to banking and payroll activities—have been shifted to provide greater unity. Many teachers have called for a grouping of chapters that would accommodate the full accounting cycle for a professional enterprise, and this new arrangement should well suit their needs. To meet other needs, a chapter on the statement of changes in financial position has been added. Payroll and tax data, as well as other information, has been updated to reflect the changes that have occurred in the real world. And the new book design, as well as the functional use of color, enhances student understanding of certain concepts and allows for more realistic examples of different types of accounting stationery.

Special features

In addition to providing an easy-to-understand approach to the fundamentals of accounting, *College Accounting Fundamentals* offers these other features.

Latest recognized accounting principles The accounting principles described here are those endorsed by the Financial Accounting Standards Board and its predecessor, the Accounting Principles Board of the American Institute of Certified Public Accountants. All package materials have also undergone numerous professional accuracy checks.

Illustrations Every effort has been made to accompany the introduction of each concept and procedure with an example. Diagrams and exhibits are used widely to portray illustrations of concepts.

Reviews To help the instructor sum up and reiterate important principles, the text provides reviews of T-account placement and representative transactions after Chapters 6, 10, and 15. Moreover, a practical review problem, given after Chapter 6, offers a mini-practice set that enables students to apply what they have learned in those first six chapters.

Ancillary material

College Accounting Fundamentals is the principal resource of the program. Each chapter of the text contains these teaching aids:
- Specific objectives, to tell the students what procedures they can expect to master as they work their way through the material.
- A summary, to reinforce new concepts, principles, and procedures.
- A glossary, to define terms introduced for quick and easy reference.
- Questions, to review the concepts and procedures presented.
- Exercises, to demonstrate understanding of chapter material.
- Problems (four regular and four alternate, of increasing difficulty), to apply the techniques just mastered.

Accounting stationery Three workbooks—*Accounting Stationery, Chapters 1–10, Accounting Stationery, Chapters 1–15,* and *Accounting Stationery, Chapters 16–29*—provide working papers on which students may solve the text problems. Each workbook also contains a two-page review section for each of the text chapters, and the workbooks for Chapters 1–10 and 1–15 also have reviews of business mathematics to help those students with a weak background in mathematics.

Practice sets Westside Lanes, a sole-proprietorship professional enterprise, is the setting for a practice set designed to be used after the completion of Chapter 10. Driscoe's Rugs offers realistic practice for a sole-proprietorship merchandising firm and may be used after the completion of Chapter 15. A third practice set, Cloverton Outdoor Store, uses a voucher system for a partnership merchandising business, and it would normally be completed after Chapter 22.

Instructional aids *College Accounting Fundamentals* is part of a complete instructional package that offers these teaching aids: annotated editions of the accounting stationery, which have the solutions highlighted in a second color; a complete instructor's manual, which contains suggestions for teaching, solutions to all test exercises and to the practice sets, final examinations, and selected transparency masters; and a set of overhead transparencies for projecting solutions of text problems for Chapters 1 through 15 on a chalkboard or screen.

Acknowledgments

I am still deeply appreciative of the assistance that was given to me by a number of people during the preparation of the first edition of this text. Chief among these were Professors Hobart W. Adams, University of Akron, and Joseph M. Goodman, Chicago State University, both of whom read and critiqued the entire manuscript; my colleague, Professor Heinz W. Pruss, and my students at Wenatchee Valley College, whose recommendations then and now have been most helpful; and the many others upon whose expertise in specific areas of accounting and business I have drawn in order to create realistic settings for the presentation of the various accounting principles and procedures.

Since the publication of the first edition of *College Accounting Fundamentals,* I have either corresponded or visited with many users of the program. Their constructive suggestions for its improvement are reflected in the changes that have been made, and for these contributions, I am especially grateful.

Finally, I would like to thank my family for their understanding and cooperation during the hours of my writing the original manuscript and the many years of preparing its revision. Without their support and patience, this program would not have been realized. The efforts of my daughter and son—Judith L. McQuaig, C.P.A., and John D. McQuaig, C.P.A.—are particularly appreciated.

Douglas J. McQuaig

1

Analyzing business transactions: asset, liability, and owner's equity accounts

objectives

After you have completed this chapter, you will be able to do the following:
- Define accounting.
- Record a group of business transactions, in columnar form, involving changes in assets, liabilities, and owner's equity.
- Present a balance sheet.

ACCOUNTING is often called the *language of business,* because when confronted with events of a business nature, all people in society—owners, managers, creditors, employees, attorneys, engineers, and so forth—must use accounting terms and concepts in order to describe these events. Examples of accounting terms are *net, gross, yield, valuation, accrued, deferred*—the list could go on and on. So it is logical that anyone entering the business world should know enough of the "language" to communicate with others and to understand their communications.

Some terms used in accounting have meanings that differ from the meanings of the same words used in a nonbusiness situation. If you have studied a foreign language, you have undoubtedly found that as you became more familiar with the language, you also became better acquainted with the country in which it is spoken, as well as with the customs of the people. Similarly, as you acquire a knowledge of accounting, you will also gain an understanding of the way businesses operate and the reasoning involved in the making of business decisions. Even if you are not involved directly in accounting activities, most assuredly you will need to be sufficiently acquainted with the "language" to be able to understand the meaning of accounting information, how it is compiled, how it can be used, and what its limitations are.

Definition of accounting

Accounting is the process of analyzing, classifying, recording, summarizing, and interpreting business transactions in financial or monetary terms. A *business transaction* is an event that has a direct effect on the operation of the economic unit and can be expressed in terms of money. Examples of business transactions are buying or selling goods, renting a building, hiring employees, buying insurance, or any other activity of a business nature.

The accountant is the person who keeps the financial history of an economic unit in written form. The term *economic unit* includes not only business enterprises, but also nonprofit-making entities, such as government bodies, churches, clubs, fraternal organizations, etc. All these require some type of accounting records. The primary purpose of accounting is to provide the financial information needed for the efficient operation of the economic unit and to make the information available in usable forms to the interested parties, such as owners, members, taxpayers, creditors, and so on.

Accountants follow rules in carrying out the various phases of the accounting process. In the United States, these rules or guidelines have been determined by an independent body called the Financial Accounting Standards Board (FASB) and its predecessors. The Financial Accounting Standards Board is composed of seven highly skilled accountants who are experienced in various areas of accounting.

Fields in which accounting is needed

A knowledge of accounting is most valuable in the following three fields:

Bookkeeping and accounting Those who plan to enter the field as a vocation naturally need training in accounting.

Business management Those aspiring to managerial positions must be able to understand financial reports, evaluate operations, and make logical decisions.

Personal recordkeeping Every person—even one who does not plan to be an accountant or a business manager—benefits from a study of accounting, because such a study enables one to keep better records, understand financial reports, engage in financial planning and budgeting, invest savings, and prepare necessary tax returns.

Bookkeeping and accounting

Considerable confusion exists over the distinction between *bookkeeping* and *accounting*. Actually the two are closely related, and there is no universally accepted line of separation. Generally, bookkeeping involves the systematic recording of business transactions in financial terms. When compared with bookkeeping, accounting is distinguished by level or degree. An accountant sets up the system by which business transactions are to be recorded by a bookkeeper. An accountant may supervise the work of the bookkeeper; the accountant may prepare financial statements and tax reports. Although the work of the bookkeeper is more routine, it is hard to draw a line where the bookkeeper's work ends and the accountant's begins. The bookkeeper must understand the entire accounting system, exercise judgment in recording financial details, and organize and report the appropriate information.

Career opportunities in bookkeeping and accounting

When it comes to career opportunities, accounting is commonly divided into three main fields, in the order of numbers of positions available.

Private accounting Most people who are accountants work for private business firms. The growing importance of accounting often provides opportunities for advancement into managerial positions, such as office managers, data processing supervisors, systems analysts, internal auditors, and controllers.

Governmental and institutional accounting Local, state, and federal government bodies employ vast numbers of people in accounting jobs, not only for recordkeeping but also for auditing private businesses and individuals whose dealings are subject to government regulation. Many accountants in the federal government work as internal revenue agents, investigators, and bank examiners; and at all levels of government, there are traditional accounting positions.

Public accounting Certified public accountants (or CPAs) are independent professional persons, comparable to doctors and lawyers, who offer accounting services to clients for a fee. There are approximately 140,000 CPAs and more than 550,000 noncertified public accountants in the United States today. Accounting is easily the fastest growing of all the professions; it is expanding, in fact, at twice the rate the economy is expanding. Factors responsible for the growth of professional accounting include the increasing size and complexity of business corporations, the broadening of income taxes and other forms of taxation, and the increase in government regulation of business activities.

The lay person's need for accounting

Anyone who aspires to a position of leadership in business or government needs a knowledge of accounting. Managers and supervisors often have to keep financial records, understand accounting data contained in reports and budgets, and express future plans in financial terms. A study of accounting gives a person the necessary background, as well as an understanding of an organization's scope, functions, and policies. People who have managerial jobs must be aware of how accounting information can be developed for use as a tool in the decision-making process, and they should also be acquainted with the recordkeeping and management functions of accounting.

Assets and owner's equity

Assets are properties or things owned by the economic unit or business entity, such as cash, equipment, buildings, and land. If there is no money owed against the assets, then the owner's right would be equal to the value of the assets. The owner's right or claim is expressed by the word *equity*, or *investment*. You often see these terms in the classified-advertising section of a newspaper, where a person wants to sell the ownership right to a property. Other terms that may be used include *net worth*, *capital*, or *proprietorship*.

Assets = Owner's Equity

Items or property owned by the business	Owner's right or investment in the business

Suppose that the total value of the assets is $10,000, and the owner does not owe any amount against the assets. Then,

Assets = Owner's Equity

$10,000	$10,000

Or suppose that the asset consists of a truck that costs $8,000; the owner has paid $2,000 down and borrowed the remainder from the bank. This would be shown as follows:

Assets =	Liabilities +	Owner's Equity
Items owned	Amount owed to creditors	Owner's investment
$8,000	$6,000	$2,000

We have now introduced a new classification, *liabilities,* which represents debts and includes the amounts that the owner owes his or her creditors or the amount by which the owner is liable to the creditors. The debts may originate because the owner bought goods or services on a credit basis, or borrowed money, etc. The creditors' claims to the assets have priority over the interest of the owner.

An equation containing these elements is called the *fundamental accounting equation.* We'll be constantly dealing with this equation from now on. If we know two parts of this equation, we can determine the third. Let us look at some illustrations.

Ms. Smith has $9,000 invested in her advertising agency, and she owes creditors $3,000; that is, she has liabilities of $3,000. Then,

Assets =	Liabilities +	Owner's Equity
?	$3,000	$9,000

We would find the amount of Smith's assets by adding her liabilities and her equity:

$ 3,000	Liabilities
+9,000	Owner's Equity
$12,000	Assets

The completed equation would now read

Assets =	Liabilities +	Owner's Equity
$12,000	$3,000	$9,000

Or take Mr. Jones, who raises geraniums to sell to florists. He has assets of $20,000, and he owes creditors $4,000; that is, he has liabilities of $4,000. Then,

Assets =	Liabilities +	Owner's Equity
$20,000	$4,000	?

We find the owner's equity by subtracting his liabilities from his assets:

$20,000	Assets
−4,000	Liabilities
$16,000	Owner's Equity

The completed equation would now read

Assets = Liabilities + Owner's Equity
$20,000 $4,000 $16,000

Mr. Anderson, who has an insurance agency, has assets of $18,000; and his investment (his equity) amounts to $12,000. Then,

Assets = Liabilities + Owner's Equity
$18,000   ? $12,000

In order to find Anderson's total liabilities, we subtract his equity from his assets:

$18,000 Assets
−12,000 Owner's Equity
$ 6,000 Liabilities

The completed equation would now read

Assets = Liabilities + Owner's Equity
$18,000 $6,000 $12,000

Recording business transactions

To reiterate: Business transactions are events that have a direct effect on the operations of an economic unit or enterprise and are expressed in terms of money. As one records business transactions, one has to change the amounts listed under the headings of Assets, Liabilities, and Owner's Equity. However, the total of one side of the fundamental accounting equation should always equal the total of the other side. The subdivisions under these three main headings, as we shall see, are called *accounts.*

Let us now look at a group of business transactions. Although these transactions illustrate a service type of business, they would also pertain to a professional enterprise as well. In these transactions, let's assume that Neil Singleton establishes his own business and calls it Neil's Cleaners.

Transaction (a) Singleton invests $16,000 cash in his new business. This means that he deposits $16,000 in the bank in a new, separate account entitled Neil's Cleaners. This separate bank account will help Singleton keep his business investment separate from his personal funds. The Cash account consists of bank deposits and money on hand. The business now has $16,000 more in cash than before, and Singleton's investment has also increased. The account, denoted by the owner's name followed by the word *Capital,* records the amount of the owner's investment, or equity, in the business. The effect of this transaction on the fundamental accounting equation is as follows:

Assets =	Liabilities +	Owner's Equity
Items owned	Amounts owed to creditors	Owner's investment
Cash =		Neil Singleton, Capital
(a) +$16,000 =		+$16,000

Transaction (b) Neil Singleton knows that his first task is to get his cleaning shop ready for business and that to do this he will need the proper equipment. Accordingly, he buys for cash $9,000 worth of equipment. It is important to note that at this point Singleton has not invested any new money; he simply exchanged part of his cash for equipment. As equipment is a type of property that is new to the firm, a new account, called Equipment, is created, and it is included under Assets. Because of this transaction, the accounting equation is changed as follows.

	Assets =		**Liabilities +**	**Owner's Equity**
	Items owned		Amounts owed to creditors	Owner's investment
	Cash +	Equipment =		Neil Singleton, Capital
Initial investment	$16,000	=		$16,000
(b)	−9,000	+$9,000		
New balances	$ 7,000 +	$9,000 =		$16,000

Transaction (c) Neil Singleton buys $2,000 worth of equipment on credit from Johnson Equipment Company.

The Equipment account shows an increase because the business owns $2,000 worth of additional equipment, and there is also an increase in liabilities, because the business owes $2,000 more than before. The liabilities account, Accounts Payable, is used for short-term liabilities or charge accounts, due usually within 30 days. There is now a total of $18,000 on both sides of the equals sign.

	Assets =		**Liabilities +**	**Owner's Equity**
	Items owned		Amounts owed to creditors	Owner's investment
	Cash +	Equipment = Accounts Payable +		Neil Singleton, Capital
Previous balances	$7,000 +	$ 9,000 =		$16,000
(c)		+2,000	+$2,000	
New balances	$7,000 +	$11,000 =	$2,000 +	$16,000

To continue the idea of equality, observe that the recording of each transaction must result in a balance by itself. For example, Transaction **(c)** resulted in a $2,000 increase to both sides of the equation, and Transaction **(b)** resulted in a minus $9,000 and a plus $9,000 *on the same side,* with nothing recorded on the other side.

Transaction (d) Singleton pays $500 to Johnson Equipment Company, to be applied against the firm's liability of $2,000.

In analyzing this payment, we recognize that cash is involved and that cash is being reduced. At the same time, the firm *owes* less than before, so it should be recorded as a minus under Liabilities.

	Assets =		Liabilities +	Owner's Equity
	Items owned		Amounts owed to creditors	Owner's investment
	Cash +	Equipment =	Accounts Payable +	Neil Singleton, Capital
Previous balances	$7,000 +	$11,000 =	$2,000 +	$16,000
(d)	−500		−500	
New balances	$6,500 +	$11,000 =	$1,500 +	$16,000

Transaction (e) Singleton buys cleaning fluids from Acme Supply Company for $200 on credit. Cleaning fluids are listed under Supplies instead of Equipment because a cleaning business uses up cleaning fluids in a relatively short period of time—as a matter of fact, in one or a few operations. Equipment, on the other hand, normally lasts over a number of operations.

	Assets =			Liabilities +	Owner's Equity
	Items owned			Amounts owed to creditors	Owner's investment
	Cash +	Equipment +	Supplies =	Accounts Payable +	Neil Singleton, Capital
Previous balances	$6,500 +	$11,000	=	$1,500 +	$16,000
(e)			+$200	+200	
New balances	$6,500 +	$11,000 +	$200 =	$1,700 +	$16,000

Accounting, as we said before, is the process of analyzing, recording, summarizing, and interpreting business transactions. In relating these elements to the transactions of Neil's Cleaners, we made an analysis to decide which accounts were involved and then determined whether the transaction resulted in an increase or a decrease in the accounts. Then we recorded the transaction. After one records each transaction, the equation should still be in balance, in that the totals of both sides are equal. This represents an introduction to *double-entry accounting*. We have demonstrated that each transaction must be recorded in at least two accounts and that the equation must always remain in balance.

Summary of transactions   Let us now summarize the business transactions of Neil's Cleaners in columnar form, identifying each transaction by a letter of the alphabet. To test your understanding of the recording procedure, describe the nature of the transactions that have taken place.

	Assets =			Liabilities + Owner's Equity	
	Cash +	Equipment +	Supplies	Accounts Payable	Neil Singleton, Capital
Transaction (a)	+16,000		=		+16,000
Transaction (b)	−9,000	+9,000			
Balance	7,000 +	9,000	=		16,000
Transaction (c)		+2,000 .		+2,000	
Balance	7,000 +	11,000	=	2,000 +	16,000
Transaction (d)	−500			−500	
Balance	6,500 +	11,000	=	1,500 +	16,000
Transaction (e)			+200	+200	
Balance	6,500 +	11,000 +	200 =	1,700 +	16,000

	Total			Total
Cash	$ 6,500			
Equipment	11,000	Accounts Payable		$ 1,700
Supplies	200	Neil Singleton, Capital		16,000
	$17,700			$17,700

The following observations apply to *all* types of business transactions:

1. Every transaction is recorded in terms of increases and/or decreases in two or more accounts.

2. The equality of the two sides of the accounting equation is always maintained.

The balance sheet

Earlier we listed summarizing as one of the five basic steps in the accounting process. To accomplish the summarizing step, accountants use financial statements. One of these financial statements, the *balance sheet,* summarizes the balances of the assets, liabilities, and owner's equity accounts on a given date (usually at the end of a month or year). The balance sheet shows the financial position of the company and is sometimes referred to as a *statement of financial position.* Financial position is shown by a list of the values of the assets or property, offset by the liabilities or amounts owed to creditors, and the owner's equity or financial interest. *Financial position,* as used in this accounting concept, means the same thing we would mean if we were to speak of the financial position of a person. It is a listing of what the person owns, as well as a listing of the claims of his or her creditors; and the difference between them is the person's equity or net worth.

Perhaps you might have noticed, in the back pages of a newspaper, the balance sheets of commercial banks and savings and loan associations. The law requires them to publish their balance sheets in daily newspapers at certain times of the year. The purpose of these financial statements is to show the financial positions of these institutions; the total of their assets listed must equal the total claims of the depositors plus the owner's equity.

In the next chapter the fundamental accounting equation will be expanded to include revenue and expense elements. For the moment, however, we may refer to the equation as the *balance sheet equation* because only the three elements that appear on the balance sheet—assets, liabilities, and owner's equity—appear in the equation. And instead of presenting the equation in linear form as

Assets = Liabilities + Owner's Equity,

we could now present it in the pyramid form in which it appears when one records the same balances in the balance sheet:

Assets
=
Liabilities
+
Owner's Equity

After Singleton records his initial transactions, the balance sheet for Neil's Cleaners as of June 15 would look like this:

Neil's Cleaners	
Balance Sheet	
June 15, 19—	
Assets	
Cash	6 5 0 0 00
Supplies	2 0 0 00
Equipment	11 0 0 0 00
Total Assets	17 7 0 0 00
Liabilities	
Accounts Payable	1 7 0 0 00
Owner's Equity	
Neil Singleton, Capital	16 0 0 0 00
Total Liabilities and Owner's Equity	17 7 0 0 00

Note some details about the format of this type of balance sheet, which is called the *report form:*

1. The three-line heading consists of the name of the firm, the title of the financial statement, and the date of the financial statement. The heading is centered at the top of the page.

2. The headings for the classifications of accounts (Assets, Liabilities, Owner's Equity) are all centered. The classifications are separated by the space of one line.

3. Dollar signs are not used except on typewritten statements. Then they are placed alongside the first entry and total under each heading.

4. Single lines (drawn with a ruler) are used to show that figures above are being added or subtracted.

5. Double lines are used under the totals in a column.

Summary

Accounting is often called the *language of business,* because recordkeeping and financial reports use the terms and concepts of accounting. This chapter has presented the definitions of accounting and of business transactions. The fundamental accounting equation, consisting of three elements, is

$$\text{Assets} = \text{Liabilities} + \text{Owner's Equity}$$

An accountant analyzes business transactions to determine which accounts are involved, then records them as increases or decreases in the appropriate accounts. After each transaction is recorded, the equation must always remain in balance. The balance sheet—which is a statement showing the balances of asset, liability, and owner's equity accounts—states the financial position of an enterprise.

Glossary

Accounting   The process of analyzing, classifying, recording, summarizing, and interpreting business transactions in terms of money.

Accounts   Subdivisions under the main headings of Assets, Liabilities, and Owner's Equity.

Assets   Cash, properties, and other things owned.

Balance sheet   A financial statement showing the financial position of a firm or other economic unit at a given point in time, e.g., June 30 or December 31.

Business entity   A business enterprise is considered to be separate and distinct from the persons who supply the assets it uses. Property involved in the business is an asset of the business. The owner is separated from the business and occupies the status of a claimant of the enterprise.

Capital The owner's investment or equity in an enterprise.

Economic unit Business enterprises; also nonprofit-making entitites, such as government bodies, churches, clubs, fraternal organizations, etc.

Equity The value of a right or financial interest in an asset or group of assets.

Liabilities Debts, or amounts owed to creditors.

Transaction An event affecting an economic entity that can be expressed in terms of money and which must be recorded in the accounting records.

Questions

1. What do we mean by an owner's equity?

2. What is the fundamental accounting equation? Why should the total amount on one side of the equation always equal the total amount on the other side of the equation?

3. List five examples of assets.

4. What effect will the purchase of supplies on account have on the fundamental accounting equation?

5. What is a business transaction? Give three examples of business transactions.

6. What does a double ruling across an amount column indicate?

7. What are the three sections of the body of a balance sheet?

Exercises

Exercise 1 Complete the following equations.

a. Assets, $20,000 = Liabilities, $4,500 + Owner's Equity, $_____

b. Assets, $_____ = Liabilities, $15,000 + Owner's Equity, $19,000

c. Assets, $28,000 − Owner's Equity, $11,000 = Liabilities, $_____

Exercise 2 Determine the following values.

a. The amount of the liabilities of a business having $29,614 of assets, and in which the owner has a $19,400 equity.

b. The equity of the owner of an automobile, costing $6,000, who owes $4,200 on an installment loan payable to the bank.

c. The value of the assets of a business having $4,720 in liabilities, and in which the owner has a $22,000 equity.

Exercise 3 Rita Jordan, a real estate broker, owns office equipment amounting to $8,600, a car, which is used for business purposes only, valued at $5,250, and other property that is used in her business amounting to $3,200. She owes business creditors a total of $1,600. What is the value of Jordan's equity?

Exercise 4 Describe the transactions that have been recorded in the following equation.

		Assets =		Liabilities + Owner's Equity	
	Cash +	Equipment		Accounts Payable	C. Lee, Capital
(a)	+8,000		=		+8,000
(b)		+2,000		+2,000	
Bal.	8,000 +	2,000 =		2,000 +	8,000
(c)	−1,500	+1,500			
Bal.	6,500 +	3,500 =		2,000 +	8,000
(d)	−600	+2,600		+2,000	
Bal.	5,900 +	6,100 =		4,000 +	8,000

Exercise 5 Dr. Leo Gallo is a chiropractor. As of April 30, he owned the following property that related to his professional practice: Cash, $720; Prepaid Insurance, $240; Professional Equipment, $10,600; Office Equipment, $3,560. As of the same date, he owed business creditors as follows: Pinkerton Supply Company, $1,980; Eastern Equipment Sales, $750. Compute the following amounts of the Balance Sheet Equation.

Assets _____ = Liabilities _____ + Owner's Equity _____

Exercise 6 Describe a business transaction that will do the following:

a. Increase an asset and decrease an asset.

b. Increase an asset and increase a liability.

c. Decrease an asset and decrease a liability.

d. Increase an asset and increase owner's equity.

Exercise 7 Dr. C. L. Mayer is a dentist. Describe the transactions that have been completed involving the asset, liability, and owner's equity accounts.

			Assets =		Liabilities + Owner's Equity	
	Cash +	Prepaid + Insurance	Dental + Equipment	Office Furniture and Equipment	Accounts Payable	C. L. Mayer, Capital
Bal.	1,964 +	280 +	19,628 +	4,620 =	8,016 +	18,476
(a)	+1,000					+1,000
Bal.	2,964 +	280 +	19,628 +	4,620 =	8,016 +	19,476
(b)	−928				−928	
Bal.	2,036 +	280 +	19,628 +	4,620 =	7,088 +	19,476
(c)			+468		+468	
Bal.	2,036 +	280 +	20,096 +	4,620 =	7,556 +	19,476
(d)	−1,000		+1,600		+600	
Bal.	1,036 +	280 +	21,696 +	4,620 =	8,156 +	19,476

Exercise 8 From Exercise 7, present a balance sheet, using the ending balances dated as of December 31 of this year. Use notebook paper.

Problems

Problem 1-1 The Mid-town Shoe Repair has just been established by the owner, Peter Abbott, who deposited $11,500 cash in the Southern State Bank in the name of the business. The transactions described below affect the asset, liability, and owner's equity accounts. (Use plus, minus, and equals signs.)

a. Abbott initially invested $11,500 in cash.

b. Bought equipment for use in the business, $4,000 in cash.

c. Acquired additional equipment for the business, $2,400 on credit.

d. Paid $1,400 in cash to creditors as part payment on account.

e. Abbott invested an additional $1,600 in cash.

Instructions **1.** Record the transactions in columnar form, using plus and minus signs, and show the balances after each transaction.

2. Prove that the total of one side of the equation equals the total of the other side of the equation.

Problem 1-2 The Suburban Insurance Agency has just been established by the owner, Agnes Segal. The following transactions affect the asset, liability, and owner's equity accounts.

a. Segal deposited $9,600 in cash in the Nevada State Bank in the name of the business.

b. Acquired office equipment for use in the business, $4,200 in cash.

c. Bought supplies consisting of stationery and business forms on account, $420.

d. Bought additional equipment for use in the business on account, $990.

e. Bought postage stamps and other supplies for use in the business, $91, paying cash.

f. Paid $500 to creditors as part payment on account.

g. Segal invested an additional $900 in cash in the business.

Instructions **1.** Record the transactions in columnar form, using plus and minus signs, and show the balances after each transaction.

2. Prove that the total of one side of the equation equals the total of the other side of the equation.

Problem 1-3 Douglas Dorsett owns Dorsett Insurance Agency. Balances of the assets, liabilities, and owner's equity accounts are shown at the top of page 15.

Cash	$ 960
Supplies	310
Office Equipment	4,680
Office Furniture	4,200
Building	28,000
Land	8,000
Accounts Payable	2,170
Douglas Dorsett, Capital	43,980

Instructions Prepare a balance sheet as of December 31 of this year.

Problem 1-4 California Cleaners is owned by Miriam Downey. The firm's books show the following balances in assets, liabilities, and owner's equity accounts.

Cash	$ 1,467
Cleaning Supplies	921
Office Supplies	106
Prepaid Insurance	180
Cleaning Equipment	10,460
Delivery Equipment	4,200
Office Furniture and Fixtures	3,760
Accounts Payable	1,768
Miriam Downey, Capital	19,326

Instructions Prepare a balance sheet dated July 31 of this year.

Alternate problems

Problem 1-1A Florida Cleaners has just been established by the owner, Jane Bryan, who deposits $8,400 cash in the First National Bank in the name of the business. Record the changes in assets, liabilities, and owner's equity accounts for the following transactions. (Use plus, minus, and equals signs.)

a. Bryan originally invests $8,400 in cash.

b. Bought equipment for the business, $5,600 on credit.

c. Paid $1,800 in cash to creditors as part payment on account.

d. Bryan invested an additional $3,000 in cash.

e. Bought additional equipment for the business, $700 in cash.

Instructions **1.** Record the transactions in columnar form, using plus and minus signs, and show the balances after each transaction.

2. Prove that the total of one side of the equation equals the total of the other side of the equation.

Problem 1-2A The Local Employment Agency has just been established by the owner, Randall Altman. Record the following transactions. (Use plus, minus, and equals signs.)

a. Altman deposited $9,200 in cash in the Citizens State Bank in the name of the business.

b. Bought office equipment for use in the business, $4,400 in cash.

c. Bought supplies, consisting of stationery and business forms, on account, $410.

d. Bought additional equipment for use in the business, $1,240 in cash.

e. Paid $84 in cash for postage stamps (supplies) to be used in the business.

f. Paid $320 to creditors as part payment on account.

g. Altman invested an additional $960 in cash in the business.

Instructions
1. Record the transactions in columnar form, using plus and minus signs, and show the balances after each transaction.

2. Prove that the total of one side of the equation equals the total of the other side of the equation.

Problem 1-3A Robert Brooks owns the Brooks Real Estate Agency. His books show the following balances in assets, liabilities, and owner's equity accounts.

Cash	$ 800
Supplies	290
Office Equipment	3,120
Office Furniture	3,600
Building	24,000
Land	6,000
Accounts Payable	5,780
Robert Brooks, Capital	32,030

Instructions Prepare a balance sheet as of July 31 of this year.

Problem 1-4A Kettering Photography Studio is owned by D. L. Porter. The firm's books show the following balances in assets, liabilities, and owner's equity accounts.

Cash	$ 2,150
Film	862
Office Supplies	216
Camera Equipment	7,600
Lighting Equipment	1,560
Office Equipment	1,900
Automobile	4,800
Accounts Payable	1,050
D. L. Porter, Capital	18,038

Instructions Prepare a balance sheet dated December 31 of this year.

2 Analyzing business transactions: revenue and expense accounts

objectives

After you have completed this chapter, you will be able to do the following:
- Record a group of business transactions in columnar form, involving all five elements of the fundamental accounting equation.
- Present an income statement.
- Present a statement of owner's equity.

IN CHAPTER 1, we analyzed and recorded a number of transactions in asset, liability, and owner's equity accounts and did so in a way that was consistent with the definition of accounting. In this chapter we shall introduce the remaining two classifications of accounts: revenues and expenses. We shall record business transactions involving revenue and expense accounts in the same type of columnar arrangement we used in Chapter 1. Again let us stress that, after each transaction has been recorded, the total of the balances of the accounts on one side of the equals sign should equal the total of the balances of the accounts on the other side of the equals sign. To illustrate, we shall continue to use transactions of Neil's Cleaners.

Revenue and expense accounts

Revenues are the amounts of assets that a business or other economic unit gains as a result of its operations. For example, revenues represent inflows of cash, or other assets, derived from fees earned for the performing of services, sales involving the exchange of goods, rent income for providing the use of property, and interest income for the lending of money. Revenues are *not* only in the form of cash; they may also consist of credit-card receipts or charge accounts maintained for customers.

Expenses are the amounts of assets that a business or other economic unit uses up as a result of its operations. For example, expenses represent outflows of cash, or other assets, for services received, such as wages expense for labor performed, rent expense for the use of property, interest expense for the use of money, and supplies expense for supplies used. When payment is to be made at a later time, an increase in an expense will result in an increase in a liability.

Recording business transactions

Soon after the opening of Neil's Cleaners, the first customers arrive, beginning a flow of revenue for the business. Let us now itemize further transactions of Neil's Cleaners for the first month of operations.

Transaction (f) Neil's Cleaners receives cash revenue for the first week, $300. Revenue has the effect of increasing the owner's equity; however, it is better to keep the revenue separate from the capital account until you have prepared the financial statements. So as a result of this transaction, the accounting equation would be affected as follows (PB stands for previous balance, and NB stands for new balance):

	Cash +	Equipment +	Supplies	=	Accounts Payable	Neil Singleton, Capital	+ Revenue
	Assets =				**Liabilities +**	**Owner's Equity**	
PB	$6,500 +	$11,000 +	$200	=	$1,700 +	$16,000	
(f)	+300						+$300
NB	$6,800 +	$11,000 +	$200	=	$1,700 +	$16,000 +	$300

Transaction (g) Shortly after opening the business, Singleton pays $200 monthly rent. Rent is the payment for a service—the privilege of occupying a building. Because this service will be used up in one month or less, we record the amount as an expense. If the payment covered a period longer than one month, we would record the amount under Prepaid Rent, which is an asset account.

Expenses have the effect of decreasing the owner's equity. We shall consider revenues and expenses later as separate elements in the fundamental accounting equation. However, through the medium of the financial statements they will be connected with owner's equity, and for this reason we are listing them under the heading of Owner's Equity as follows:

	Cash +	Equipment +	Supplies	=	Accounts Payable	Neil Singleton, Capital	+ Revenue	− Expenses
	Assets =				**Liabilities +**	**Owner's Equity**		
PB	$6,800 +	$11,000 +	$200	=	$1,700 +	$16,000 +	$300	
(g)	−200							+$200 (Rent)
NB	$6,600 +	$11,000 +	$200	=	$1,700 +	$16,000 +	$300 −	$200

Transaction (h) Singleton pays wages to employees, $120, June 1 through June 10. This additional expense of $120 is added to the previous balance of $200, resulting in a total deduction of $320, since the incurring of expense has the result of reducing the owner's equity. Now the equation looks like the following:

	Cash +	Equipment +	Supplies	=	Accounts Payable	Neil Singleton, Capital	+ Revenue	− Expenses
	Assets =				**Liabilities +**	**Owner's Equity**		
PB	$6,600 +	$11,000 +	$200	=	$1,700 +	$16,000 +	$300 −	$200
(h)	−120							+120 (Wages)
NB	$6,480 +	$11,000 +	$200	=	$1,700 +	$16,000 +	$300 −	$320

Transaction (i) Singleton pays $160 for a 2-year liability insurance policy. As it expires, the insurance will eventually become an expense. However, since it is paid in advance for a period longer than one month, it has value and is accordingly recorded as an asset. At the end of the year or financial period, Singleton will have to make an adjustment, taking out the expired portion and recording it as an expense. Generally accountants initially record expenses that are paid for more than 1 month in advance as assets.

	Cash +	Equipment +	Supplies +	**Assets = Liabilities +** Prepaid Insurance	Accounts Payable	Neil + Singleton, Capital	**Owner's Equity** Revenue −	Expenses
PB	$6,480 +	$11,000 +	$200	=	$1,700 +	$16,000 +	$300 −	$320
(i)	−160			+$160				
NB	$6,320 +	$11,000 +	$200 +	$160 =	$1,700 +	$16,000 +	$300 −	$320

Transaction (j) Neil's Cleaners receives cash revenue for the second week, $380.

	Cash +	Equipment +	Supplies +	**Assets = Liabilities +** Prepaid Insurance	Accounts Payable	Neil + Singleton, Capital	**Owner's Equity** Revenue −	Expenses
PB	$6,320 +	$11,000 +	$200 +	$160 =	$1,700 +	$16,000 +	$300 −	$320
(j)	+380						+380	
NB	$6,700 +	$11,000 +	$200 +	$160 =	$1,700 +	$16,000 +	$680 −	$320

Observe that each time a transaction is recorded, the total amount on one side of the equation *remains equal to* the total amount on the other side. As proof of this, look at the following computation.

	Total		**Total**
Cash	$ 6,700	Accounts Payable	$ 1,700
Equipment	11,000	Neil Singleton, Capital	16,000
Supplies	200	Revenue	680
Ppd. Ins.	160		$18,380
	$18,060	Expenses	−320
			$18,060

Let us now continue with the transactions.

Transaction (k) Neil's Cleaners receives a bill for newspaper advertising, $90, from the *Daily News*. Singleton has simply received the bill for advertising; he has not paid any cash. However, an expense has been incurred, and the firm owes $90 more than it did before, so this transaction must be recorded.

	Cash +	Equipment +	Supplies +	Ppd. Ins.	=	Accounts Payable +	Neil Singleton, Capital +	Revenue −	Expenses
					Assets = Liabilities +		**Owner's Equity**		
PB	$6,700 +	$11,000 +	$200 +	$160 =		$1,700 +	$16,000 +	$680 −	$320
(k)						+90			+90
									(Advertising)
NB	$6,700 +	$11,000 +	$200 +	$160 =		$1,790 +	$16,000 +	$680 −	$410

Transaction (l) Singleton pays $900 to Johnson Equipment Company, his creditor (party to whom he owes money), as part payment on account.

	Cash +	Equipment +	Supplies +	Ppd. Ins.	=	Accounts Payable +	Neil Singleton, Capital +	Revenue −	Expenses
					Assets = Liabilities +		**Owner's Equity**		
PB	$6,700 +	$11,000 +	$200 +	$160 =		$1,790 +	$16,000 +	$680 −	$410
(l)	−900					−900			
NB	$5,800 +	$11,000 +	$200 +	$160 =		$ 890 +	$16,000 +	$680 −	$410

Transaction (m) Singleton receives and pays bill for utilities, $110. Because Singleton had not previously recorded the bill as a liability, the accounting equation is affected as follows:

	Cash +	Equipment +	Supplies +	Ppd. Ins.	=	Accounts Payable +	Neil Singleton, Capital +	Revenue −	Expenses
					Assets = Liabilities +		**Owner's Equity**		
PB	$5,800 +	$11,000 +	$200 +	$160 =		$890 +	$16,000 +	$680 −	$410
(m)	−110								+110
									(Utilities)
NB	$5,690 +	$11,000 +	$200 +	$160 =		$890 +	$16,000 +	$680 −	$520

Transaction (n) Now Singleton pays $90 to the *Daily News* for advertising. Recall that he had previously recorded this bill as a liability. The equation is shown at the top of page 22.

	Assets			=	Liabilities +		Owner's Equity		
	Cash +	Equipment +	Supplies + Ppd. Ins.	=	Accounts Payable	Neil Singleton, Capital +	Revenue −	Expenses
PB	$5,690 +	$11,000 +	$200 + $160	=	$890 +	$16,000 +	$680 −	$520
(n)	−90				−90			
NB	$5,600 +	$11,000 +	$200 + $160	=	$800 +	$16,000 +	$680 −	$520

Transaction (o) Neil's Cleaners receives cash revenue for the third week, $415.

	Assets			=	Liabilities +		Owner's Equity		
	Cash +	Equipment +	Supplies + Ppd. Ins.	=	Accounts Payable	Neil Singleton, Capital +	Revenue −	Expenses
PB	$5,600 +	$11,000 +	$200 + $160	=	$800 +	$16,000 +	$ 680 −	$520
(o)	+415						+415	
NB	$6,015 +	$11,000 +	$200 + $160	=	$800 +	$16,000 +	$1,095 −	$520

Transaction (p) Neil's Cleaners signs a contract with Ace Rental to clean their for-hire formal clothes on a credit basis and cleans ten dress suits. Accordingly, Neil's bills Ace Rental for services performed, $40.

A firm uses the *Accounts Receivable account* to record the amounts owed by charge customers. Since Ace Rental owes Neil's Cleaners $40 more than before the transaction took place, it seems logical to add $40 to Accounts Receivable. Revenue is earned when the service has been performed, and hence the corresponding increase in revenue. When Ace pays the $40 bill in cash, Singleton should record this as an increase in Cash and a decrease in Accounts Receivable. He would not have to make an entry for the Revenue account, as he has previously recorded the amount.

	Assets				=	Liabilities +		Owner's Equity		
	Cash +	Equip. +	Supp. +	Ppd. Ins. + Accts. Rec.	=	Accounts Payable	Neil Singleton, Capital +	Revenue −	Expenses
PB	$6,015 +	$11,000 +	$200 +	$160	=	$800 +	$16,000 +	$1,095 −	$520
(p)				+$40				+40	
NB	$6,015 +	$11,000 +	$200 +	$160 + $40	=	$800 +	$16,000 +	$1,135 −	$520

Transaction (q) Singleton pays wages of employees, $195, June 11 through June 24.

	Cash +	Equip. +	Supp. +	Ppd. + Ins.	Accts. Rec.	=	Accounts Payable	+	Neil Singleton, Capital	+	Revenue	−	Expenses
						Assets = Liabilities +							**Owner's Equity**
PB	$6,015 +	$11,000 +	$200 +	$160 +	$40 =		$800 +		$16,000 +		$1,135 −		$520
(q)	−195												+195
													(Wages)
NB	$5,820 +	$11,000 +	$200 +	$160 +	$40 =		$800 +		$16,000 +		$1,135 −		$715

Transaction (r) Singleton buys additional equipment on account, $140, from Johnson Equipment Company. Because buying an item on account is the same as buying it on credit, both the expressions *on account* and *on credit* will be used to describe such transactions.

	Cash +	Equip. +	Supp. +	Ppd. + Ins.	Accts. Rec.	=	Accounts Payable	+	Neil Singleton, Capital	+	Revenue	−	Expenses
						Assets = Liabilities +							**Owner's Equity**
PB	$5,820 +	$11,000 +	$200 +	$160 +	$40 =		$800 +		$16,000 +		$1,135 −		$715
(r)		+140					+140						
NB	$5,820 +	$11,140 +	$200 +	$160 +	$40 =		$940 +		$16,000 +		$1,135 −		$715

Again, because the equipment will last over a number of operations, Singleton lists this $140 as an increase in the assets.

Transaction (s) Neil's Cleaners receives revenue from cash customers for the rest of the month, $480.

	Cash +	Equip. +	Supp. +	Ppd. + Ins.	Accts. Rec.	=	Accounts Payable	+	Neil Singleton, Capital	+	Revenue	−	Expenses
						Assets = Liabilities +							**Owner's Equity**
PB	$5,820 +	$11,140 +	$200 +	$160 +	$40 =		$940 +		$16,000 +		$1,135 −		$715
(s)	+480										+480		
NB	$6,300 +	$11,140 +	$200 +	$160 +	$40 =		$940 +		$16,000 +		$1,615 −		$715

Transaction (t) Neil's Cleaners receives $30 from Ace Rental to apply on the amount previously billed. Since Ace Rental now owes Neil's Cleaners less than before, Singleton should deduct the $30 from Accounts Receivable. He previously recorded this amount as revenue, so the equation looks like the one shown at the top of page 24.

	Cash +	Equip. +	Supp. +	Ppd. Ins. +	Accts. Rec. =	Accounts Payable +	Neil Singleton, Capital +	Revenue −	Expenses
	Assets = Liabilities +						**Owner's Equity**		
PB	$6,300 +	$11,140 +	$200 +	$160 +	$40 =	$940 +	$16,000 +	$1,615 −	$715
(t)	+30				−30				
NB	$6,330 +	$11,140 +	$200 +	$160 +	$10 =	$940 +	$16,000 +	$1,615 −	$715

Transaction (u) At the end of the month, Singleton withdraws $500 in cash from the business for his personal living costs. One may consider this transaction to be the opposite of an investment in cash by the owner.

	Cash +	Equip. +	Supp. +	Ppd. Ins. +	Accts. Rec. =	Accounts Payable +	Neil Singleton, Capital +	Revenue −	Expenses
	Assets = Liabilities +						**Owner's Equity**		
PB	$6,330 +	$11,140 +	$200 +	$160 +	$10 =	$940 +	$16,000 +	$1,615 −	$715
(u)	−500						−500 (Drawing)		
NB	$5,830 +	$11,140 +	$200 +	$160 +	$10 =	$940 +	$15,500 +	$1,615 −	$715

Because the owner is taking cash out of the business, there is a decrease in Cash. The withdrawal decreases Capital, because the owner has now decreased his equity. One does not consider a withdrawal as a business expense, since it is not money paid to anyone outside the business for services performed, or for materials received that would benefit the business.

Summary of transactions On the next page we have summarized the business transactions of Neil's Cleaners in columnar form, identifying the transactions by letter. To test your understanding of the recording procedure, describe the nature of the transactions that have taken place.

	Cash +	Equip. +	Supp. +	Ppd. Ins. +	Accts. Rec. =	Accts. Pay. +	Neil Singleton, Capital +	Revenue −	Expenses
	Assets = Liabilities +						**Owner's Equity**		
Bal.	6,500 +	11,000 +	200		=	1,700 +	16,000		
(f)	+300							+300	
Bal.	6,800 +	11,000 +	200		=	1,700 +	16,000 +	300	
(g)	−200								+200 (Rent)
Bal.	6,600 +	11,000 +	200		=	1,700 +	16,000 +	300 −	200
(h)	−120								+120

	Cash	Equipment	Supplies	Ppd. Ins.	Accts. Rec.	=	Accts. Pay.	Capital	Revenue	Expenses (Wages)
Bal.	6,480	+ 11,000	+ 200			=	1,700 +	16,000 +	300 −	320
(i)	−160			+ 160						
Bal.	6,320	+ 11,000	+ 200	+ 160		=	1,700 +	16,000	300 −	320
(j)	+ 380								+ 380	
Bal.	6,700	+ 11,000	+ 200	+ 160		=	1,700 +	16,000 +	680 −	320
(k)							+ 90			+ 90

(Advertising)

	Cash	Equipment	Supplies	Ppd. Ins.	Accts. Rec.	=	Accts. Pay.	Capital	Revenue	Expenses
Bal.	6,700	+ 11,000	+ 200	+ 160		=	1,790 +	16,000 +	680 −	410
(l)	−900						−900			
Bal.	5,800	+ 11,000	+ 200	+ 160		=	890 +	16,000 +	680 −	410
(m)	−110									+ 110

(Utilities)

	Cash	Equipment	Supplies	Ppd. Ins.	Accts. Rec.	=	Accts. Pay.	Capital	Revenue	Expenses
Bal.	5,690	+ 11,000	+ 200	+ 160		=	890 +	16,000 +	680 −	520
(n)	−90						−90			
Bal.	5,600	+ 11,000	+ 200	+ 160		=	800 +	16,000 +	680 −	520
(o)	+ 415								+ 415	
Bal.	6,015	+ 11,000	+ 200	+ 160		=	800 +	16,000 +	1,095 −	520
(p)					+ 40				+ 40	
Bal.	6,015	+ 11,000	+ 200	+ 160 +	40	=	800 +	16,000 +	1,135 −	520
(q)	−195									+ 195

(Wages)

	Cash	Equipment	Supplies	Ppd. Ins.	Accts. Rec.	=	Accts. Pay.	Capital	Revenue	Expenses
Bal.	5,820	+ 11,000	+ 200	+ 160 +	40	=	800 +	16,000 +	1,135 −	715
(r)		+ 140					+ 140			
Bal.	5,820	+ 11,140	+ 200	+ 160 +	40	=	940 +	16,000 +	1,135 −	715
(s)	+ 480								+ 480	
Bal.	6,300	+ 11,140	+ 200	+ 160 +	40	=	940 +	16,000 +	1,615 −	715
(t)	+ 30				−30					
Bal.	6,330	+ 11,140	+ 200	+ 160 +	10	=	940 +	16,000 +	1,615 −	715
(u)	−500							−500		

(Drawing)

	Cash	Equipment	Supplies	Ppd. Ins.	Accts. Rec.	=	Accts. Pay.	Capital	Revenue	Expenses
Bal.	5,830	+ 11,140	+ 200	+ 160 +	10	=	940 +	15,500 +	1,615 −	715

	Total			**Total**
Cash	$ 5,830	Accounts Payable	$ 940
Equipment	11,140	Neil Singleton, Capital	15,500
Supplies	200	Revenue	1,615
Ppd. Ins.	160		$18,055
Accts. Rec.	10	Expenses	−715
	$17,340		$17,340

The income statement

The *income statement* shows total revenue minus expenses, which yields the net income, or profit. This income statement pictures the results of the business transactions involving revenue and expense accounts over a period of time. In other words, it shows how the business has performed or fared over a period of time, usually a month or year. Other terms that are identical with the name *income statement* are *statement of income and expenses* or *profit and loss statement.* If the total revenue is less than the expenses, the result is a net loss.

The income statement shown here tabulates the results of the first month of operations of Neil's Cleaners. (This is a tentative income statement, in that adjustments have not been recorded; we shall discuss them in Chapter 5.)

Note that as in all financial statements, the heading requires three lines:

1. Name of company (or owner, if there is no company name).

2. Title of the financial statement (in this case, income statement).

3. Period of time covered by the financial statement or its date.

Neil's Cleaners					
Income Statement					
For month ended June 30, 19–					
Revenue:					
Income from Services				1 6 1 5 00
Expenses:					
Wages Expense	3 1 5 00			
Rent Expense	2 0 0 00			
Utilities Expense	1 1 0 00			
Advertising Expense	9 0 00			
Total Expenses				7 1 5 00
Net Income				9 0 0 00

The income statement covers a period of time, whereas the balance sheet has only one date: the end of the financial period. The revenue for June, less the expenses for June, shows the results of operations—a net income of $900. To the accountant, the term *net income* means "clear" income, or profit after all expenses have been deducted. Many accountants prefer to list expenses in declining order (the largest amount first, followed by the next largest, etc.). In this arrangement, if Miscellaneous Expense is present, it is placed last regardless of the amount. This procedure will be followed in the illustrations that will be shown in the text.

Statement of owner's equity

We said that revenue and expenses are connected with owner's equity through the medium of the financial statements. Let us now demonstrate this by a *statement of owner's equity,* which the accountant prepares after he or she has determined the net income in the income statement.

	Neil's Cleaners				
	Statement of Owner's Equity				
	For month ended June 30, 19—				
Neil Singleton, Capital, June 1, 19—				16 0 0 0 00
Net income for June	9 0 0 00			
Less: Withdrawals for June	5 0 0 00			
Increase in Capital			4 0 0 00	
Neil Singleton, Capital, June 30, 19—			16 4 0 0 00	

Balance sheet

Next, we prepare a balance sheet, recording the ending capital, which has been determined previously in the statement of owner's equity.

Neil's Cleaners		
Balance Sheet		
June 30, 19—		
Assets		
Cash		5 8 3 0 00
Accounts Receivable		1 0 00
Supplies		2 0 0 00
Prepaid Insurance		1 6 0 00
Equipment		11 1 4 0 00
Total Assets		17 3 4 0 00
Liabilities		
Accounts Payable		9 4 0 00
Owner's Equity		
Neil Singleton, Capital		16 4 0 0 00
Total Liabilities and Owner's Equity		17 3 4 0 00

This balance sheet is tentative, due to the fact that adjustments have not been recorded (see Chapter 5).

Any additional investment by the owner during the period covered by the financial statements should be shown in the statement of owner's equity, since such a statement should show what has affected the Capital account from the *beginning* until the *end* of the period covered by the financial statements. For example, assume the following for the C. E. Davis Company, which has a net income:

Balance of C. E. Davis, Capital, on April 1	$86,000
Additional investment by C. E. Davis on April 12	9,000
Net income for the month (from income statement)	1,500
Total withdrawals for the month	1,200

One can show this information in the statement of owner's equity.

C. E. Davis Company
Statement of Owner's Equity
For month ended April 30, 19—

C. E. Davis, Capital, April 1, 19—		86 000 00
Additional Investment, April 12, 19—		9 000 00
Total Investment		95 000 00
Net income for April	1 500 00	
Less: Withdrawals for April	1 200 00	
Increase in Capital		3 00 00
C. E. Davis, Capital, April 30, 19—		95 3 00 00

As another illustration, assume the following for the H. L. Spangler Company, which has a net loss:

H. L. Spangler, Capital, on Oct. 1	$70,000
Additional investment by H. L. Spangler on Oct. 25	6,000
Net loss for the month (from income statement)	250
Total withdrawals for the month	420

Again, one can show this information in the statement of owner's equity.

H. L. Spangler Company
Statement of Owner's Equity
For month ended October 30, 19—

H. L. Spangler, Capital, October 1, 19—		70 000 00
Additional Investment, October 25, 19—		6 000 00
Total Investment		76 000 00
Less: Net loss for October	2 50 00	
Withdrawals for October	4 20 00	
Decrease in Capital		6 70 00
H. L. Spangler, Capital, October 30, 19—		75 3 30 00

The importance of financial statements

The owners or managers of a business look on their financial statements as a coach looks on the scoreboard and team statistics, as showing the results of the present game as well as the team's standing. The income statement shows the results of operations for the current month or year. The statement of owner's equity shows why the owner's investment has changed. The balance sheet shows the present standing or financial position. The owner or manager can use the figures on the financial statements to plan future operations. Not only owners or managers are interested in financial statements. Creditors, prospective investors, and government agencies are also interested in the profitability and financial standing of the business. Financial statements are the medium through which one can take the pulse of the business, and consequently they are extremely important.

Summary

We have now defined the final two elements of the fundamental accounting equation: revenues and expenses. Business transactions involving the earning of revenue are recorded as increases in revenue; those involving the incurring of expenses are recorded as increases in expenses. The fundamental accounting equation always remains in balance. With all five elements it now appears as follows in relation to the financial statements we have discussed.

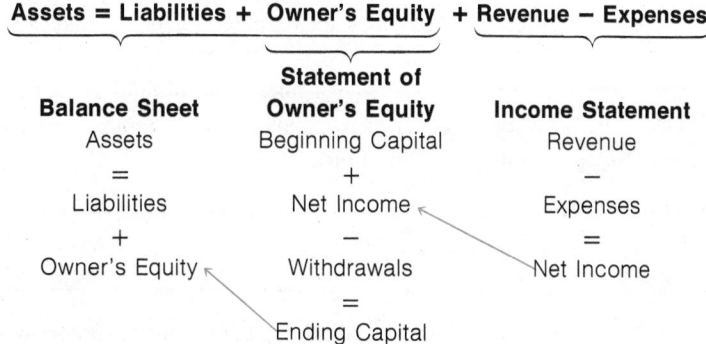

Assets = Liabilities + Owner's Equity + Revenue − Expenses

Balance Sheet	**Statement of Owner's Equity**	**Income Statement**
Assets	Beginning Capital	Revenue
=	+	−
Liabilities	Net Income	Expenses
+	−	=
Owner's Equity	Withdrawals	Net Income
	=	
	Ending Capital	

The income statement summarizes the results of operations condensed into one figure, either *net income or net loss*. The income statement is prepared first, so that the net income so determined can be recorded in the statement of owner's equity. The statement of owner's equity is prepared next, so that the ending capital so determined can be recorded in the balance sheet.

Glossary

Accounts Receivable Charge accounts or open-book accounts maintained for customers, representing credit usually extended for 30-day periods.

Expenses Cost of services or goods acquired which have been used up or consumed in the operation of the business or economic unit.

Income statement A financial statement showing the results of business transactions over a period of time: total revenue minus total expenses.

Revenue The total price charged for services rendered or goods sold during a period of time. It may be in the form of cash or receivables.

Withdrawal The taking of cash or goods out of a business by the owner for his or her own personal use. (This is also referred to as a *drawing*.) One treats a withdrawal as a temporary decrease in the owner's equity, since one anticipates that it will be offset by net income.

Questions

1. Define the term *expense*. Does every payment of cash by a business indicate that an expense has been incurred?

2. What titles might you select to describe the kinds of expenses a TV repair shop would incur in its operations?

3. What happens to the elements in the fundamental accounting equation when a sale of services is made on a charge-account basis?

4. What does an income statement show?

5. What is the difference between the headings required for statements of owner's equity and the headings required for balance sheets?

6. List two ways to increase owner's equity and two ways to decrease owner's equity.

7. List some groups other than the owner or owners of a business who would be interested in data contained in the firm's financial statements. What is the specific interest of each group?

Exercises

Exercise 1 Describe a business transaction that will do the following:

a. Decrease an asset and increase an expense.

b. Decrease a liability and decrease an asset.

c. Increase an asset and increase a revenue.

d. Increase a liability and increase an expense.

Exercise 2 From the following balances in the elements of the fundamental accounting equation, determine the amount of the ending owner's equity.

Assets	$32,000
Liabilities	10,000
Owner's Equity (beginning)	16,000
Revenue	24,000
Expense	18,000

Exercise 3 Describe the transactions recorded in the following equation.

	Cash +	Accounts Receivable +	Equipment =	Accounts Payable +	M. L. Roe Capital +	Revenue −	Expenses
(a)	+10,000		+ 4,000 =	+	14,000		
(b)	−800						+800
Bal.	9,200		4,000 =	+	14,000	−	800
(c)	+	2,100			+	2,100	
Bal.	9,200 +	2,100 +	4,000 =	+	14,000 +	2,100 −	800
(d)	−3,000		+12,000	+9,000			
Bal.	6,200 +	2,100 +	16,000 =	9,000 +	14,000 +	2,100	800
(e)	−1,600				−1,600 (Drawing)		
Bal.	4,600 +	2,100 +	16,000 =	9,000 +	12,400 +	2,100 −	800

Exercise 4 Woodward Shoe Repair has the following account balances. Using notebook paper, prepare an income statement for the month ended April 30 of this year.

Cash	$1,950
Supplies	860
Equipment	8,420
Accounts Payable	900
R. O. Woodward, Capital, April 1	8,590
Service Income	3,170
Rent Expense	700
Supplies Expense	620
Utilities Expense	70
Miscellaneous Expense	40

Exercise 5 From Exercise 4, present a statement of owner's equity and a balance sheet.

Exercise 6 Dr. S. L. Sharp is an optometrist. Describe the transactions that have been completed.

	Cash +	Accts. Rec. +	Supplies +	Equipment =	Accts. Pay. +	S. L. Sharp, Capital +	Revenue −	Expenses
Bal.	1,620 +	810 +	819 +	7,493 =	2,416 +	8,326		
(a)	+360	−360						
Bal.	1,980 +	450 +	819 +	7,493 =	2,416 +	8,326		
(b)	−418							+418 (Rent)
Bal.	1,562 +	450 +	819 +	7,493 =	2,416 +	8,326	−	418

(c)	+2,730					+2,730	
Bal.	4,292 +	450 +	819 +	7,493 =	2,416 +	8,326 +	2,730 −	418
(d)	−300				−300			
Bal.	3,992 +	450 +	819 +	7,493 =	2,116 +	8,326 +	2,730 −	418
(e)	−410							+410
								(Wages)
Bal.	3,582 +	450 +	819 +	7,493 =	2,116 +	8,326 +	2,730 −	828
(f)	−1,200					−1,200		
						(Drawing)		
Bal.	2,382 +	450 +	819 +	7,493 =	2,116 +	7,126 +	2,730 −	828
(g)	−875				−875			
Bal.	1,507 +	450 +	819 +	7,493 =	1,241 +	7,126 +	2,730 −	828

Exercise 7 From Exercise 6, present an income statement for the month ending September 30.

Exercise 8 From Exercise 6, present a statement of owner's equity and a balance sheet.

Problems

Problem 2-1 On April 1 of this year, Donald Pesara, D.D.S., established an office for the practice of dentistry. Transactions completed during the month were as follows.

a. Deposited $9,000 in a bank account entitled Donald Pesara, D.D.S.

b. Paid office rent for the month, $380.

c. Bought dental supplies for cash, $740.

d. Bought dental equipment consisting of a chair, electric drills, x-ray equipment, etc., $9,800 on account.

e. Bought a desk and chair for the reception room, $2,400, paying $400 down in cash and the remainder on account.

f. Earned $910 in professional fees, receiving cash.

g. Received and paid bill for utilities, $98.

h. Paid $600 to creditors on amount owed on dental equipment recorded previously.

i. Paid salary of assistant, $530.

j. Earned $1,428 in professional fees, receiving cash.

k. Pesara withdrew $760 in cash for personal use.

Instructions **1.** Record the transactions and the balances after each transaction, using the account headings shown at the top of page 33.

Assets =	Liabilities +			Owner's Equity

Cash + Supplies + Dental Equip. + Office Equip.   Accts. Pay.   Donald Pesara, + Revenue − Expenses
Capital

2. Prepare an income statement and a statement of owner's equity for March and a balance sheet as of April 30.

Problem 2-2 H. D. Curtis, a photographer, opened a studio for her professional practice on August 1. Transactions completed during the month were as follows.

a. Deposited $8,750 in a bank account in the name of the business, Curtis Photographic Studio.

b. Bought photographic equipment on account, $4,620.

c. Invested personal photographic equipment, $3,360. (Increase the account for Photographic Equipment, and include in the statement of owner's equity as Additional Investment.)

d. Paid $350 as office rent for the month.

e. Bought photographic supplies for cash, $526.

f. Paid premium for a 2-year insurance policy on photographic equipment, $72.

g. Received $578 as professional fees for services rendered.

h. Paid salary of part-time assistant, $335.

i. Received and paid bill for telephone service, $39.

j. Paid $274 to creditor on amount owed on the purchase of photographic equipment.

k. Received $986 as professional fees for services rendered.

l. Paid $36 for minor repairs to photographic equipment (Repair Expense).

m. Curtis withdrew $660 in cash for personal use.

Instructions **1.** Record the transactions and the balances after each transaction, using the following account headings.

Assets =	Liabilities +		Owner's Equity

Cash + Supplies + Ppd. Ins. + Photographic Equip.   Accts. Pay.   H. D. Curtis, + Revenue − Expenses
Capital

2. Prepare an income statement and a statement of owner's equity for August and a balance sheet as of August 31.

Problem 2-3 On May 1 of this year, W. C. Clark started the Clark Advertising Agency. During May Clark completed these transactions.

a. Invested $9,400 cash in the business.

b. Bought a car for use in the business for $6,800, paying $1,000 in cash with the balance due in 30 days.

c. Bought office equipment on account, $1,842.

d. Paid rent for the month, $360.

e. Cash receipts for the first half of the month from cash customers, $1,765.

f. Paid cash for property and public liability insurance on car for the year, $294.

g. Bought office supplies for cash, $124.

h. Received and paid heating bill, $39.

i. Received bill for gas and oil used during the current month for the company car, $76.

j. Billed customers for services performed on account, $317.

k. Cash receipts for the remainder of the month from cash customers, $1,791.

l. Paid salary of commercial artist, $984.

m. Clark withdrew $1,600 in cash for personal use.

Instructions **1.** Record the transactions and the balance after each transaction, using the following headings.

Assets =	Liabilities +	Owner's Equity
Cash + Accts. + Supplies + Ppd. + Car + Office Rec. Ins. Equip.	Accts. Pay.	W. C. Clark, + Revenue − Expenses Capital

2. Prepare an income statement and a statement of owner's equity for May and a balance sheet as of May 31.

Problem 2-4 An accountant determines the following account balances for the Lafferty-Soft-Water Service Company as of October 31 of this year.

Cash	$ 1,718
Advertising Expense	315
Income from Services	5,016
Wages Expense	3,207
Equipment	15,164
Accounts Payable	1,350
Rent Expense	390
Accounts Receivable	2,873
L. O. Lafferty, Capital, Oct. 1	18,819
L. O. Lafferty, Drawing	750
Miscellaneous Expense	154
Supplies	614

Instructions Prepare an income statement and a statement of owner's equity for October, and a balance sheet as of October 31.

Problem 2-1A On June 1 of this year, Cecil Shinn established a business under the name Shinn Realty. Transactions completed during the month were as follows.

a. Deposited $4,500 in a bank account entitled Shinn Realty.

b. Paid office rent for the month, $250.

c. Bought supplies consisting of stationery, folders, and stamps for cash, $126.

d. Bought office equipment consisting of desks, chairs, filing cabinets, and a calculator for $2,700 on account.

e. Received bill for advertising, $180.

f. Paid $400 to creditors on amount owed on purchase of equipment recorded previously.

g. Earned sales commissions, receiving cash $1,410.

h. Received and paid bill for utilities, $68.

i. Paid newspaper for bill recorded previously, $180.

j. Paid automobile expense, $115.

k. Shinn withdrew $485 in cash for personal use.

Instructions **1.** Record the transactions and the balances after each transaction, using the following account headings.

Assets =	Liabilities +	Owner's Equity
Cash + Supplies + Equipment	Accts. Pay.	Cecil Shinn, Capital + Revenue − Expenses

2. Prepare an income statement and a statement of owner's equity for July and a balance sheet as of July 31.

Problem 2-2A R. P. Kibby, CPA, opened an office for public accounting practice on September 1. Transactions completed during the month were as follows.

a. Deposited $7,000 in a bank account in the name of the business, R. P. Kibby, CPA.

b. Bought office equipment on account, $4,900.

c. Invested a professional library costing $1,900. (Increase the account for Library and the account of R. P. Kibby, Capital, and include in the statement of owner's equity as Additional Investment.)

d. Paid $320 as office rent for the month.

e. Bought office supplies for cash, $295.

f. Paid the premium for a two-year insurance policy on the equipment and the library, $62.

g. Received $820 as professional fees for services rendered.

h. Received and paid bill for telephone service, $76.

i. Paid salary of part-time receptionist, $320.

j. Paid automobile expense, $96.

k. Received $740 as professional fees for services rendered.

l. Paid $500 to creditor on amount owed on the purchase of office equipment.

m. Kibby withdrew $725 in cash for personal use.

Instructions   **1.** Record the transactions and the balances after each transaction, using the following account headings.

Assets =	Liabilities +		Owner's Equity
Cash + Supplies + Ppd. Ins. + Library + Equip.	Accts. Pay.	R. P. Kibby, + Revenue − Expenses	Capital

2. Prepare an income statement and a statement of owner's equity for September, and a balance sheet as of September 30.

Problem 2-3A   W. A. Berry started the Speedy Delivery Service on October 1 of this year. During October, Berry completed the following transactions.

a. Invested $8,000 cash in the business.

b. Bought delivery equipment for $7,500, paying $800 in cash with the balance due in 30 days.

c. Bought office equipment on account, $1,800.

d. Paid rent for the month, $300.

e. Paid cash for property and public liability insurance on delivery equipment for the year, $480.

f. Cash receipts for the first half of the month from cash customers, $2,400.

g. Bought supplies for cash, $180.

h. Billed customers for services on account, $245.

i. Paid cash for utilities, $75.

j. Received bill for gas and oil used during the current month, $210.

k. Cash receipts for the remainder of the month from cash customers, $2,790.

l. Berry withdrew $860 in cash for personal use.

m. Paid drivers' commissions, $935. (This is an expense.)

Instructions   **1.** Record the transactions and the balance after each transaction, using the following account headings.

Assets =	Liabilities +		Owner's Equity
Cash + Accts. + Supplies + Ppd. + Del'y + Office Rec. Ins. Equip. Equip.	Accts. Pay.	W. A. Berry, + Revenue − Expenses Capital	

2. Prepare an income statement and a statement of owner's equity for October and a balance sheet as of October 31.

Problem 2-4A The Holman Auto Parking Company hires an accountant, who determines the following account balances as of November 30.

Cash	$1,764
Wages Expense	1,400
Advertising Expense	126
Revenue from Parking	3,917
Equipment	3,974
Rent Expense	750
A. C. Holman, Capital, Nov. 1	4,820
A. C. Holman, Drawing	1,200
Accounts Receivable	721
Accounts Payable	1,424
Supplies	116
Miscellaneous Expense	110

Instructions Prepare an income statement and a statement of owner's equity for November and a balance sheet as of November 30.

3
Recording business transactions in ledger account form; the trial balance

objectives

After you have completed this chapter, you will be able to do the following:

• Record a group of business transactions for a service business directly in T accounts involving changes in assets, liabilities, owner's equity, revenue, and expense accounts.

• Present the fundamental accounting equation with the T account forms, the plus and minus signs, and the sides labeled as debit and credit.

• Determine balances of T accounts having entries recorded on both sides of the accounts.

• Prepare a trial balance.

UP TO NOW we have discussed the fundamental accounting equation in two places. In Chapter 1, we described it as *Assets = Liabilities + Owner's Equity.* Later, in Chapter 2, we introduced two more accounts—Revenues and Expenses—and then described the equation as *Assets = Liabilities + Owner's Equity + Revenue − Expenses.* With these two accounts, the fundamental accounting equation was brought up to its full size of five account classifications. There are only five; so, as far as you go in accounting—whether you are dealing with a small one-owner business or a large corporation—you can count on the fact that there will be only these five major classifications of accounts. These classifications relate to the principal financial statements as follows:

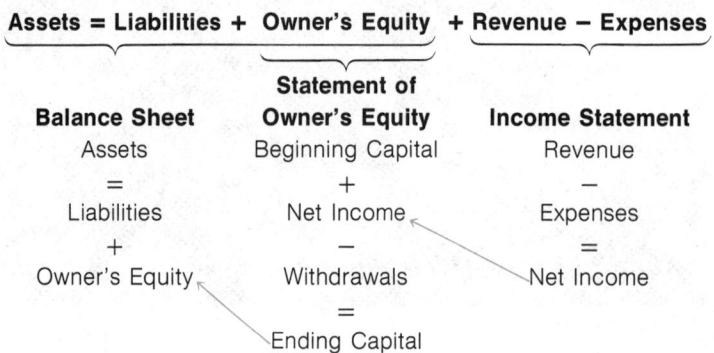

In this chapter we shall record in T account form the same transactions illustrated in Chapters 1 and 2, and we shall prove the equality of both sides of the fundamental accounting equation. We'll do this by means of a trial balance, which we'll talk about soon.

The T account form

In Chapters 1 and 2, we recorded business transactions in a columnar arrangement. For example, in the books for Neil's Cleaners, the Cash account column is as shown at the top of the next page.

Transaction (a)	16,000	**Balance**	6,480	**Balance**	5,600
Transaction (b)	−9,000	**Transaction (i)**	−160	**Transaction (o)**	+415
Balance	7,000	**Balance**	6,320	**Balance**	6,015
Transaction (d)	−500	**Transaction (j)**	+380	**Transaction (q)**	−195
Balance	6,500	**Balance**	6,700	**Balance**	5,820
Transaction (f)	+300	**Transaction (l)**	−900	**Transaction (s)**	+480
Balance	6,800	**Balance**	5,800	**Balance**	6,300
Transaction (g)	−200	**Transaction (m)**	−110	**Transaction (t)**	+30
Balance	6,600	**Balance**	5,690	**Balance**	6,330
Transaction (h)	−120	**Transaction (n)**	−90	**Transaction (u)**	−500
Balance	6,480	**Balance**	5,600	**Balance**	5,830

As an introduction to the recording of transactions, this arrangement has two advantages.

1. In the process of analyzing the transaction, you recognize the need to determine *which* account is involved. Next, from the viewpoint of the accounts, you must conclude that the transaction results in either an increase or a decrease in the accounts.

2. You further realize that after each transaction has been recorded, the balance of each account, when combined with the balances of the other accounts, proves the equality of the two sides of the Fundamental Accounting Equation.

The T form of account (that is, one shaped like the letter T) is the traditional form. It is also known as a *ledger account,* because the records of *all* the accounts are kept in the ledger. The ledger may be as simple as a loose-leaf binder or as complex as a whole filing system.

The T form, developed for convenience as a space-saving device, is subdivided into two sides: one side to record increases in the account and the other to record decreases. Let us now record those transactions just listed for Neil's Cleaners in the T form.

Cash

+			
(a) 16,000	**(b)**	9,000
(f) 300	**(d)**	500
(j) 380	**(g)**	200
(o) 415	**(h)**	120
(s) 480	**(i)**	160
(t) 30	**(l)**	900
17,605	**(m)**	110
	(n)	90
Balance → *5,830*	**(q)**	195
	(u)	500
Footings	*11,775*

After we record a group of transactions in an account, we add both sides and record the totals in small pencil-written figures called *footings.* Next, we subtract the amount of one footing from the other to determine the balance of the account. For the account illustrated above, the balance would be $5,830 ($17,605–$11,775).

We now record the balance on the side of the account having the larger footing, which, with a few minor exceptions, is always the plus (+) side. Consequently, the plus side of an account is the side that represents the *normal balance* of the account. The normal balance may, however, be either the left side or the right side of the account.

Plus and minus signs for T accounts

Each of the classifications of accounts consistently has the same placement of the plus and minus signs. For example, we presented the T account for Cash with the plus on the left side and the minus on the right side:

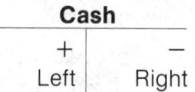

The T accounts for *all* assets are

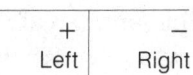

and so Cash, being an asset, would have the same arrangement:

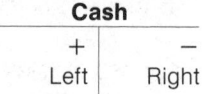

Let us now restate the fundamental accounting equation with the T forms and plus and minus signs for each classification of accounts. Remember that in Chapter 2, we stated the fundamental accounting equation like this:

Assets = Liabilities + Owner's Equity + Revenue – Expenses

We can now express this equation with T accounts in this way:

Assets		=	Liabilities		+	Owner's Equity		+	Revenue		–	Expenses	
+	–		–	+		–	+		–	+		+	–
Left	Right		Left	Right		Left	Right		Left	Right		Left	Right

Revenue has been treated as an addition to owner's equity, so the placement of the plus and minus signs is the same as in owner's equity. On the other hand, expenses have been treated as deductions from owner's equity, so the placement of the plus and minus signs is reversed. We shall use this form of the fundamental accounting equation throughout the remainder of the text.

Your accounting background up to this point has taught you to analyze business transactions in order to determine which accounts are involved and to recognize that the amounts should be recorded as either an increase or a decrease in the accounts. Now, when you are working with the T form, the recording process becomes simply a matter of knowing which side of the accounts should be used to record increases and which side to record decreases.

Generally speaking, you will not be using the minus side of the revenue and expense accounts, since transactions involving revenue and expense accounts usually result in increases in these accounts.

Recording transactions in T account form

Our task now is to convert to the recording of business transactions in the T account form. To facilitate this transition, let's use the transactions of Neil's Cleaners again, because we are familiar with them; and we can readily recognize the resultant increases or decreases in the accounts involved.

The fundamental accounting equation with T accounts for Neil's Cleaners is presented below. We have given specific account titles for revenue and expense accounts, as it is necessary to list each account separately in the income statement. The account "Neil Singleton, Drawing" has been set up to record withdrawals by the owner for his own personal use. As we said in Chapter 2, withdrawals by an owner are made in anticipation that they will be offset by net income, and hence are considered to be a temporary decrease in the owner's equity. Because of this temporary nature, they are recorded in a separate account; only permanent decreases would be recorded in the Capital account. The Drawing account is placed under the heading of owner's equity because it appears in the statement of owner's equity. The Drawing account is an exception and should be remembered specifically as a deduction from Capital. Consequently, the placement of the plus and minus signs is the reverse of that for Capital. To accentuate this fact, we have highlighted the Drawing account in color. When we want to treat one account as a deduction from another, our way of handling this is to reverse the plus and minus signs.

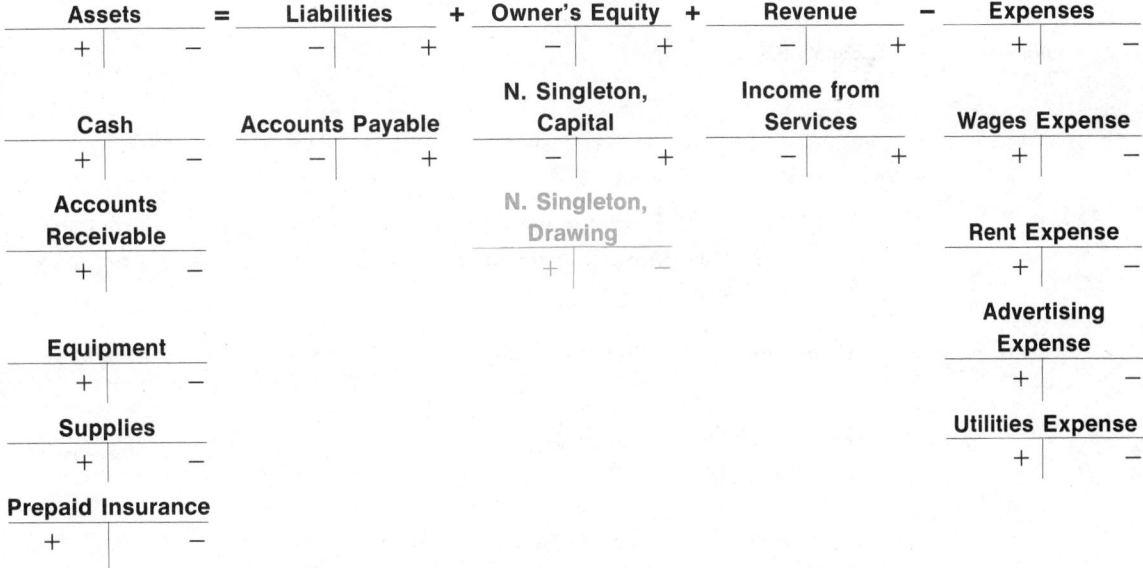

Transaction (a) Neil Singleton invests $16,000 cash in his new business. This transaction results in an increase in Cash and an increase in the Capital account, affecting the T accounts shown at the top of the next page.

Assets		=	Liabilities		+	Owner's Equity		+	Revenue		−	Expenses	
+	−		−	+		−	+		−	+		+	−

Cash			N. Singleton, Capital	
+	−		−	+
(a) 16,000				(a) 16,000

Transaction (b) Singleton buys $9,000 worth of equipment, paying cash. This transaction results in an increase in Equipment and a decrease in Cash.

Assets		=	Liabilities		+	Owner's Equity		+	Revenue		−	Expenses	
+	−		−	+		−	+		−	+		+	−

Cash	
+	−
	(b) 9,000

Equipment	
+	−
(b) 9,000	

Transaction (c) Singleton buys $2,000 worth of equipment from Johnson Equipment Company, on credit. This transaction results in an increase in both Equipment and Accounts Payable and is shown in T accounts as follows:

Assets		=	Liabilities		+	Owner's Equity		+	Revenue		−	Expenses	
+	−		−	+		−	+		−	+		+	−

Equipment			Accounts Payable	
+	−		−	+
(c) 2,000				(c) 2,000

Transaction (d) Singleton pays $500 to be applied against the firm's liability of $2,000. This transaction results in a decrease in Cash and a decrease in Accounts Payable.

Assets		=	Liabilities		+	Owner's Equity		+	Revenue		−	Expenses	
+	−		−	+		−	+		−	+		+	−

Cash			Accounts Payable	
+	−		−	+
	(d) 500		(d) 500	

Transaction (e) Singleton buys cleaning fluids for $200, on credit. This transaction results in an increase in Supplies and an increase in Accounts Payable.

Assets	=	Liabilities	+	Owner's Equity	+	Revenue	−	Expenses
+ −		− +		− +		− +		+ −

Supplies	Accounts Payable
+ −	− +
(e) 200	(e) 200

Summary of illustration

The transactions were recorded in separate accounts before but here is a restatement of the accounts after recording Transactions **(a)** through **(e)**. To test your understanding of the recording process, trace through the recording of each transaction and describe the nature of the transaction. Footings, or totals—remember always to write them in pencil—are included as a means of determining the balances of the accounts. The balances are inserted in the accounts on the side having the largest total.

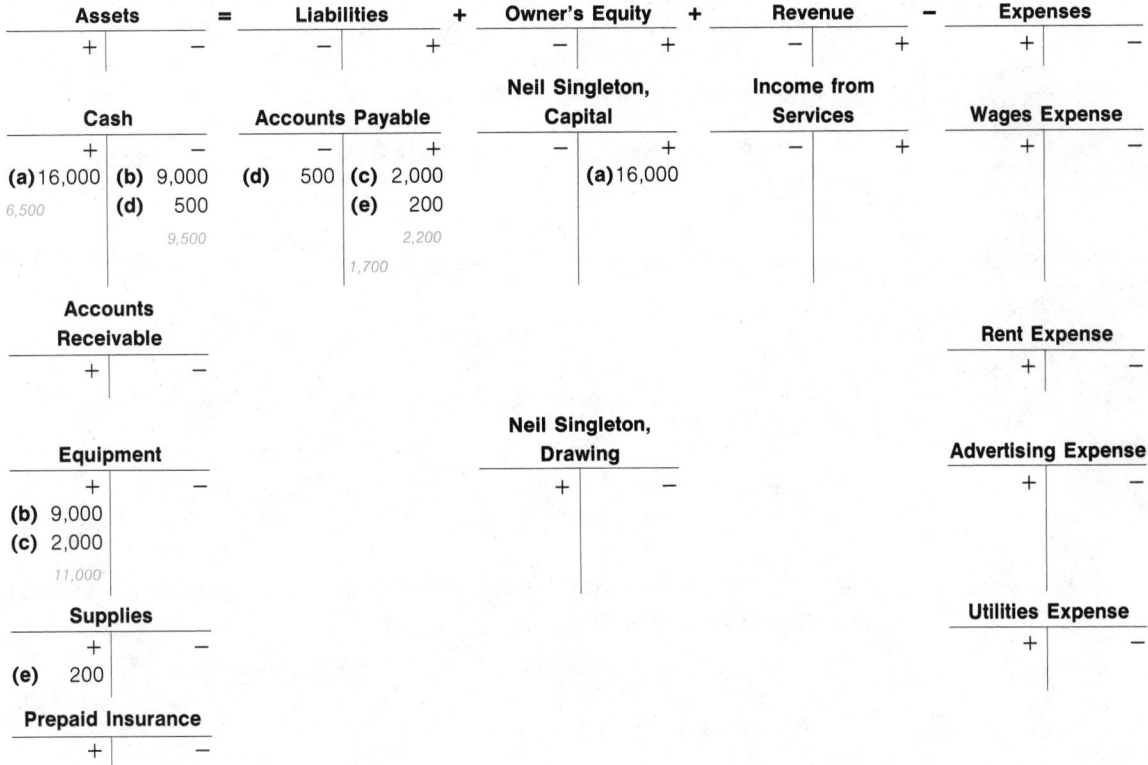

At this point let us pause to determine the equality of the two sides of the equation by listing the balances of the accounts as we have done in the illustration shown on the top of the following page.

Account Name	Accounts with the normal balances on the left side	Accounts with the normal balances on the right side
	Assets	Liabilities
	Expenses	Owner's Equity
		Revenue
Cash	$ 6,500	
Equipment	11,000	
Supplies	200	
Accounts Payable		$ 1,700
Neil Singleton, Capital		16,000
	$17,700	$17,700

Left equals right

In recording each transaction, we write the same amount that is on the left side of one T account, or accounts, on the right side of another T account, or accounts. This is *double-entry accounting.* The amount of each transaction *must* be recorded at least twice. As an illustration, let us review the recording of the preceding transactions.

Transaction (a) Singleton invests $16,000 cash in his new business.

Cash		Neil Singleton, Capital	
+	−	−	+
(a) 16,000			(a) 16,000

Transaction (b) Singleton buys $9,000 worth of equipment, paying cash.

Cash		Equipment	
+	−	+	−
	(b) 9,000	(b) 9,000	

Transaction (c) Singleton buys $2,000 worth of equipment from Johnson Equipment Company, on credit.

Equipment		Accounts Payable	
+	−	−	+
(c) 2,000			(c) 2,000

We observe from the foregoing that transactions are recorded in various combinations of pluses and minuses in the accounts. However, the important element is that:

The amount recorded on the left side of one T account, or accounts, must equal the amount recorded on the right side of another T account, or accounts.

Transaction (d) Singleton pays $500 to be applied against the firm's liability of $2,000. (Left side of Accounts Payable and right side of Cash.)

Cash		Accounts Payable	
+	−	−	+
	(d) 500	(d) 500	

Transaction (e) Singleton buys cleaning fluids for $200, on credit. (Left side of Supplies and right side of Accounts Payable.)

Supplies		Accounts Payable	
+	−	−	+
(e) 200			(e) 200

Transaction (f) Singleton's Cleaners receives $300 cash revenue for the first week. We write $300 on the plus, or left, side of Cash and $300 on the plus, or right, side of Income from Services. In other words, the firm has more cash than before, so we record $300 in the Cash account on the plus side (which happens to be the left side). Also, we recognize that there is an increase in income from services, so we record $300 in Income from Services on the plus side (which happens to be the right side).

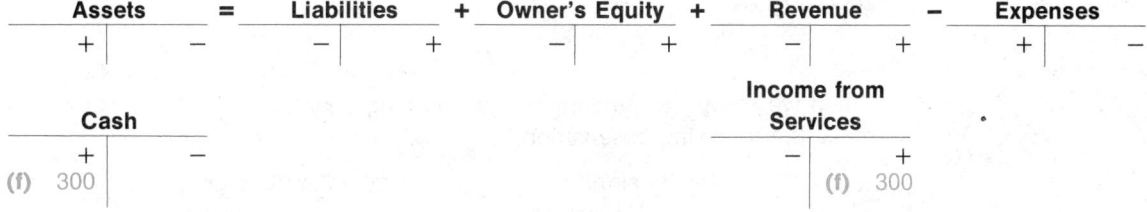

Assets		=	Liabilities		+	Owner's Equity		+	Revenue		−	Expenses	
+	−		−	+		−	+		−	+		+	−
									Income from				
Cash									**Services**				
+	−								−	+			
(f) 300										(f) 300			

Transaction (g) Singleton pays $200 for one month's rent on his shop. We write $200 on the plus, or left, side of Rent Expense. From the point of view of a running record of the Rent Expense account, there is an increase in this account. We also write $200 on the minus, or right, side of Cash.

Assets		=	Liabilities		+	Owner's Equity		+	Revenue		−	Expenses	
+	−		−	+		−	+		−	+		+	−
Cash												**Rent Expense**	
+	−											+	−
	(g) 200											(g) 200	

Transaction (h) Singleton pays wages to employees, $120. We write $120 on the plus, or left, side of Wages Expense and $120 on the minus, or right, side of Cash as illustrated on the following page.

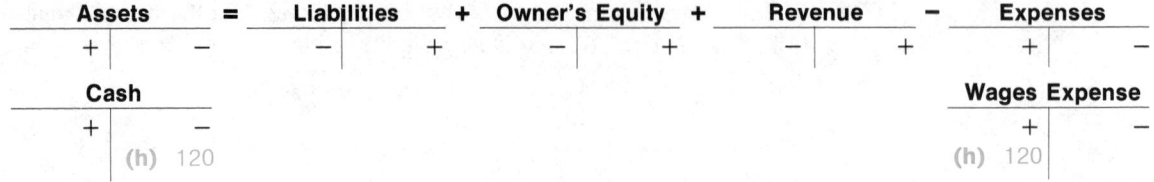

Assets		=	Liabilities	+	Owner's Equity	+	Revenue	−	Expenses	
+	−		−	+	−	+	−	+	+	−

Cash									Wages Expense	
+	−								+	−
	(h) 120								(h) 120	

Debit and credit sides

In accounting, the *left side* of a T account is called the *debit side;* the *right side* is called the *credit side*. To repeat the fundamental accounting equation with the T's as shown here:

Assets		=	Liabilities	+	Owner's Equity	+	Revenue	−	Expenses	
+	−		−	+	−	+	−	+	+	−
Left	Right		Left	Right	Left	Right	Left	Right	Left	Right
Debit	Credit		Debit	Credit	Debit	Credit	Debit	Credit	Debit	Credit

Note that the left side is always the debit side, regardless of whether it represents the plus or minus side of an account. One may use the word *debit* as a verb. If we debit Wages Expense for $120, for example, this means that we write $120 on the left side of Wages Expense. If the other half of the entry results in a credit to Cash for $120, this means that we write $120 on the right side of Cash.

Rules of debit and credit

When we study the fundamental accounting equation with the T's, we can make the following observation.

Debits signify		Credits signify	
Increases in	⎰Assets ⎱Expenses	Decreases in	⎰Assets ⎱Expenses
Decreases in	⎰Liabilities ⎨Owner's Equity ⎩Revenue	Increases in	⎰Liabilities ⎨Owner's Equity ⎩Revenue

Previously we said that when one records each business transaction, the amount placed on the left side of one account (or accounts) must equal the amount placed on the right side of another account (or accounts). Let us now state this rule in terms of debits and credits.

The amount placed on the debit side of one account, or accounts, must equal the amount placed on the credit side of another account, or accounts.

Now let's continue with the illustration of the transactions of Neil's Cleaners.

Transaction (i) Singleton pays $160 for a 2-year insurance policy. We write $160 on the plus, or debit, side of Prepaid Insurance, and $160 on the minus, or credit, side of Cash.

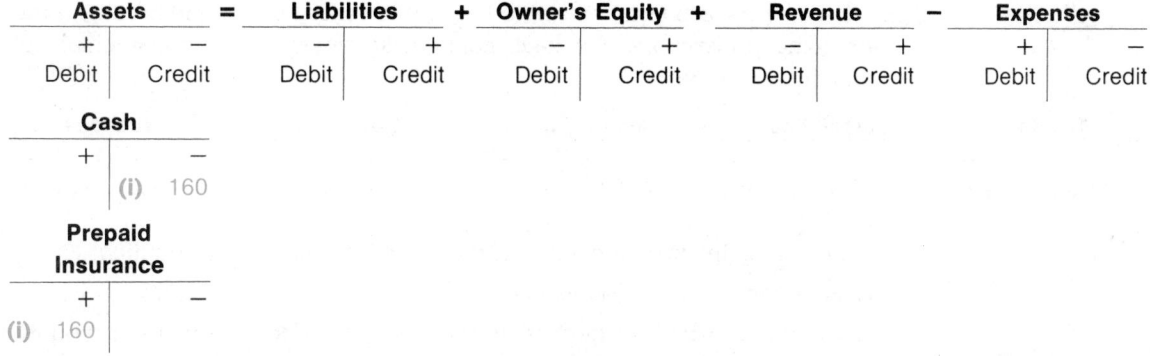

Assets		=	Liabilities		+	Owner's Equity		+	Revenue		−	Expenses	
+	−		−	+		−	+		−	+		+	−
Debit	Credit		Debit	Credit		Debit	Credit		Debit	Credit		Debit	Credit

Cash

+	−
	(i) 160

Prepaid Insurance

+	−
(i) 160	

Transaction (j) Neil's Cleaners receives cash revenue for the second week, $380. We write $380 on the plus, or debit, side of Cash, and $380 on the plus, or credit, side of Income from Services.

Assets		=	Liabilities		+	Owner's Equity		+	Revenue		−	Expenses	
+	−		−	+		−	+		−	+		+	−
Debit	Credit		Debit	Credit		Debit	Credit		Debit	Credt		Debit	Credit

Cash

+	−
(j) 380	

Income from Services

−	+
	(j) 380

Transaction (k) Neil's Cleaners receives a bill for newspaper advertising, $90. We write $90 on the plus, or debit, side of Advertising Expense, and $90 on the plus, or credit, side of Accounts Payable.

Assets		=	Liabilities		+	Owner's Equity		+	Revenue		−	Expenses	
+	−		−	+		−	+		−	+		+	−
Debit	Credit		Debit	Credit		Debit	Credit		Debit	Credit		Debit	Credit

Accounts Payable

−	+
	(k) 90

Advertising Expense

+	−
(k) 90	

Transaction (l) Singleton pays $900 to creditors as part payment on account. We write $900 on the minus, or debit, side of Accounts Payable, and $900 on the minus, or credit, side of Cash.

Assets		=	Liabilities		+	Owner's Equity		+	Revenue		−	Expenses	
+	−		−	+		−	+		−	+		+	−
Debit	Credit		Debit	Credit		Debit	Credit		Debit	Credit		Debit	Credit

Cash

+	−
	(l) 900

Accounts Payable

−	+
(l) 900	

In order to help you determine the way to record debits and credits in the foregoing transactions, we have continually repeated the fundamental accounting equation:

Assets		=	Liabilities		+	Owner's Equity		+	Revenue		−	Expenses	
+	−		−	+		−	+		−	+		+	−
Debit	Credit		Debit	Credit		Debit	Credit		Debit	Credit		Debit	Credit

Let us again stress the steps in the analytical phase of accounting:

1. Ascertain which accounts are involved.

2. Determine whether there is an increase or a decrease in the accounts.

3. Formulate the entry as a debit to one account (or accounts) and a credit to another account (or accounts).

For the last step, you must be able to visualize this last equation. It is so useful that you ought to engrave it in your mind so that it will become automatic to you. For example, in the analysis of Transaction (e), when you determine that the Accounts Payable account is involved, then you mentally classify Accounts Payable as a liability account. You should be able to picture in your mind the T account for Liabilities, with the minus (−) sign on the debit side and the plus (+) sign on the credit side. There is a decrease in Accounts Payable, so the entry should be recorded on the debit side. Without a doubt, this is the most important concept that you will ever learn in accounting. Accordingly, we strongly recommend memorizing the fundamental accounting equation with the T's and the plus and minus signs, as well as the accounts which represent exceptions, such as the Drawing account.

Now let's get back to the transactions of Neil's Cleaners.

Transaction (m) Singleton receives and pays bill for utilities, $110.

We write $110 on the plus, or debit, side of Utilities Expense, and $110 on the minus, or credit, side of Cash.

Assets		=	Liabilities		+	Owner's Equity		+	Revenue		−	Expenses	
+	−		−	+		−	+		−	+		+	−
Cash												**Utilities Expense**	
+	−											+	−
	(m) 110											(m) 110	

Transaction (n) Singleton pays $90 to a newspaper for advertising. (This bill has previously been recorded.) We write $90 on the minus, or debit, side of Accounts Payable, and $90 on the minus, or credit, side of Cash.

Assets		=	Liabilities		+	Owner's Equity		+	Revenue		−	Expenses	
+	−		−	+		−	+		−	+		+	−
Cash			**Accounts Payable**										
+	−		−	+									
	(n) 90		(n) 90										

Transaction (o) Neil's Cleaners receives cash revenue for the third week, $415. We write $415 on the plus, or debit, side of Cash, and $415 on the plus, or credit, side of Income from Services.

Assets	=	Liabilities	+	Owner's Equity	+	Revenue	−	Expenses
+ −		− +		− +		− +		+ −

Cash						Income from Services	
+ −						− +	
(o) 415						(o) 415	

Transaction (p) Neil's Cleaners signs a contract with Ace Rental to clean their for-hire rental clothes on a credit basis. Accordingly, we bill Ace Rental $40 for services performed. We write $40 on the plus, or debit, side of Accounts Receivable, and $40 on the plus, or credit, side of Income from Services.

Assets	=	Liabilities	+	Owner's Equity	+	Revenue	−	Expenses
+ −		− +		− +		− +		+ −

Accounts Receivable						Income from Services	
+ −						− +	
(p) 40						(p) 40	

Transaction (q) Singleton pays wages of employees, $195. We write $195 on the plus, or debit, side of Wages Expense, and $195 on the minus, or credit, side of Cash.

Assets	=	Liabilities	+	Owner's Equity	+	Revenue	−	Expenses
+ −		− +		− +		− +		+ −

Cash								Wages Expense	
+ −								+ −	
(q) 195								(q) 195	

Transaction (r) Singleton buys additional equipment from Johnson Equipment Company on account, $140. We write $140 on the plus, or debit, side of Equipment, and $140 on the plus, or credit, side of Accounts payable.

Assets	=	Liabilities	+	Owner's Equity	+	Revenue	−	Expenses
+ −		− +		− +		− +		+ −

Equipment		Accounts Payable					
+ −		− +					
(r) 140		(r) 140					

Transaction (s) Neil's Cleaners receives revenue from cash customers for the remainder of the month, $480. We write $480 on the plus, or debit, side of Cash, and $480 on the plus, or credit, side of Income from Services.

Transaction (t) Neil's Cleaners receives $30 from Ace Rental to apply on the amount previously billed. We write $30 on the plus, or debit, side of Cash, and $30 on the minus, or credit, side of Accounts Receivable.

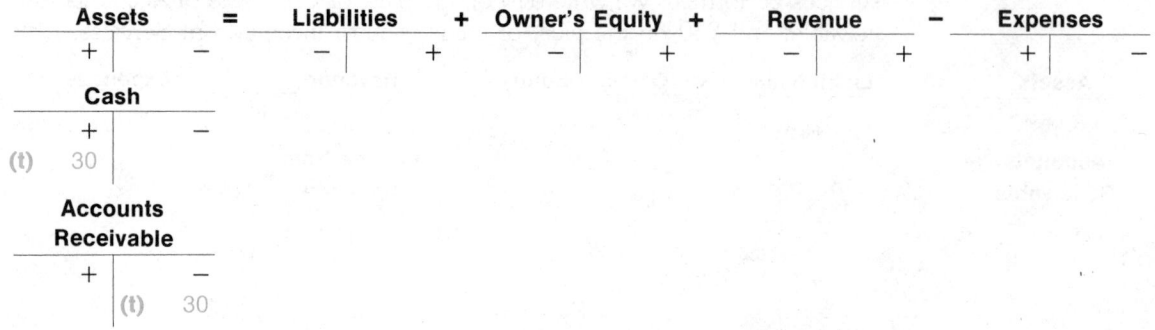

Transaction (u) At the end of the month, Singleton withdraws from the business $500 in cash for his personal use. We write $500 on the minus, or credit, side of Cash, and $500 on the plus, or debit, side of Neil Singleton, Drawing. Because the account, Neil Singleton, Drawing, is used to record personal withdrawals by the owner, and because an additional withdrawal has been made, it should be recorded on the plus, or debit, side of this account.

Assets		=	Liabilities		+	Owner's Equity		+	Revenue		−	Expenses	
+	−		−	+		−	+		−	+		+	−
Cash						**Neil Singleton, Drawing**							
+	−					−	+						
	(u) 500					(u) 500							

Summary of illustration On the following page are the transactions as they are ordinarily recorded in the accounts. Footings are shown in color. Note that, in the recording of expenses, one places the entries only on the plus, or debit, side. Also, in the recording of revenues, one places the entries on the plus, or credit, side.

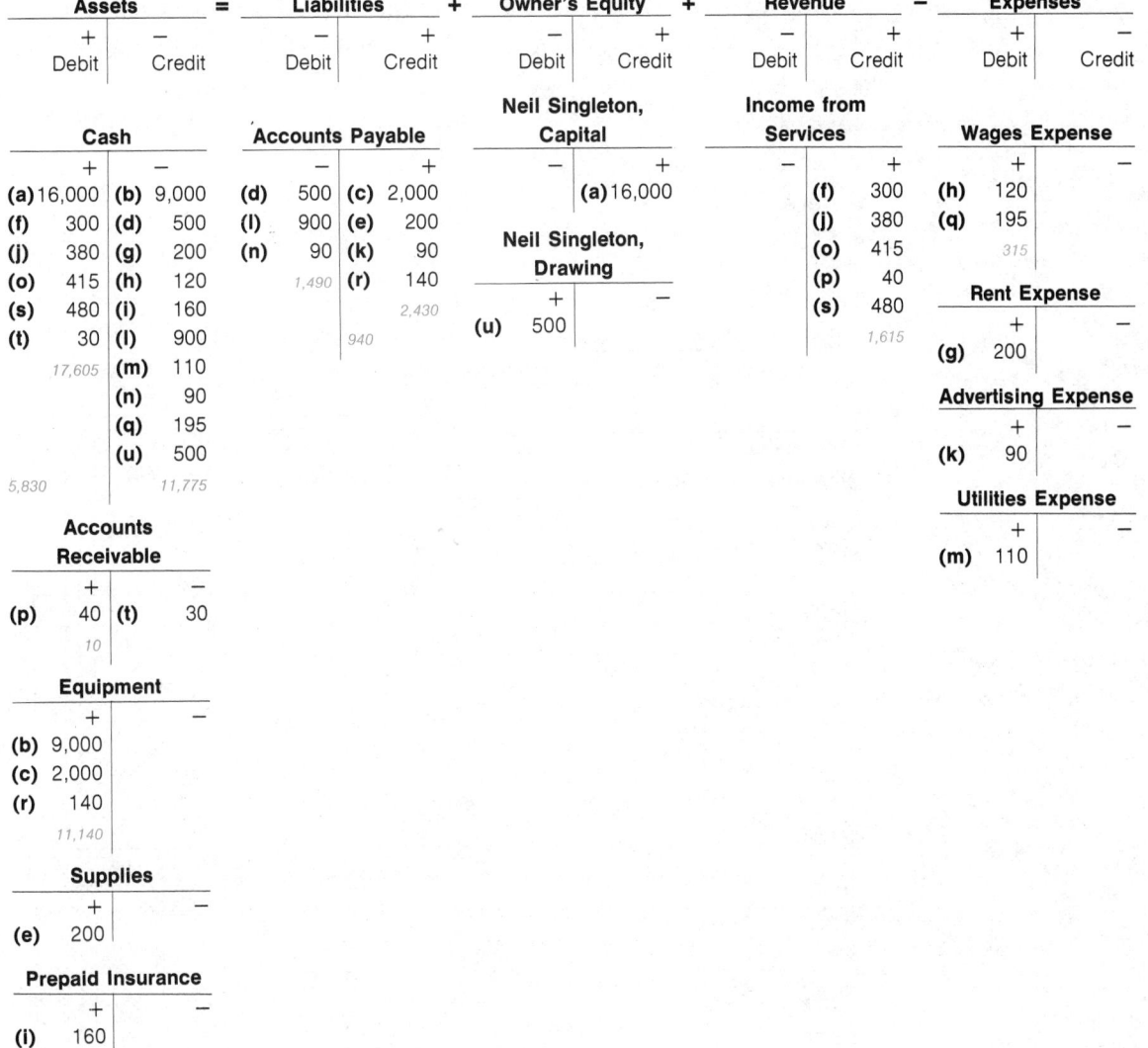

The trial balance

You can now prepare a *trial balance* by simply recording the balances of the T accounts. This is not considered to be a financial statement, but, as the name implies, it is in essence a trial run by the accountant to prove that the debit balances of T accounts equal the credit balances of other T accounts. This represents proof of the equality of both sides of the fundamental accounting equation. The trial balance is a prerequisite to the preparation of financial statements.

In preparing a trial balance, record the balances of the accounts in the order in which they appear in the ledger. This order follows the chart of accounts, where first balance sheet accounts and then income statement accounts are listed:

- Assets
- Liabilities
- Owner's Equity
- Revenue
- Expenses

Neil's Cleaners									
Trial Balance									
June 30, 19—									
Cash	5	8	3	0	00				
Accounts Receivable			1	0	00				
Supplies		2	0	0	00				
Prepaid Insurance		1	6	0	00				
Equipment	11	1	4	0	00				
Accounts Payable							9	4	0	00
Neil Singleton, Capital						16	0	0	0	00
Neil Singleton, Drawing		5	0	0	00				
Income from Services						1	6	1	5	00
Wages Expense		3	1	5	00				
Rent Expense		2	0	0	00				
Advertising Expense			9	0	00				
Utilities Expense		1	1	0	00				
	18	5	5	5	00	18	5	5	5	00

The normal balance of each account is on its plus side. Remember that when there is more than one entry in an account, we record the totals in footings, subtract one footing from the other to determine the balance, and record this balance on the side of the account having the larger footing. (Here we record the Drawing account balance in the debit column, however, because it has a debit balance and we don't deduct it from the Capital account at the time that we prepare the trial balance.) The table atop the next page summarizes where each of the account balances normally would be shown in a trial balance.

Trial Balance		
Account titles	Left or debit balances	Right or credit balances
	Assets	
		Liabilities
		Owner's Equity
	Drawing	
		Revenue
	Expenses	
Totals	XXXX XX	XXXX XX

Errors exposed by the trial balance

If the debit and credit columns are not equal, then it is evident that we have made an error. Possible causes of errors include the following:

- Recording only half an entry, such as a debit without a corresponding credit, or vice versa.
- Recording both halves of the entry on the same side, such as two debits, rather than a debit and a credit.
- Recording one or more amounts incorrectly.
- Making errors in arithmetic, such as errors in adding the trial balance columns, or in finding the balances of the ledger accounts.

Procedure for locating errors

Suppose that you are in a business situation in which you have recorded transactions for a month in the account books, and the accounts do not balance. To save yourself time, you need to have a definite procedure for tracking down the errors. The advisable method is to do everything in reverse, as follows:

- Re-add the trial balance columns.
- Check the transferring of the figures from the ledger accounts to the trial balance.
- Verify the footings and balances of the ledger accounts.

As an added precaution, form the habit of verifying all addition and subtraction. You can thus correct many mistakes *before* making a trial balance.

When the trial balance totals do not balance, the difference might indicate that you forgot to post half of an entry in the accounts. For example, if the difference in the trial balance totals is $20, you may have recorded $20 on the debit side of one account without recording $20 on the credit side of another account. Another possibility is to divide the difference by two; this may provide a clue that you accidentally posted half an entry twice. For example, if the difference in the trial balance is $600, you may have recorded $300 on the debit side of one account and an additional $300 on the debit side of another account.

Transpositions and slides

If the difference is evenly divisible by 9, the discrepancy may be either a *transposition* or a *slide*. A transposition means that the digits have been transposed, or switched around. For example, one transposition of digits in 916 can be written as 619:

$$
\begin{array}{r}
916 \\
-619 \\
\hline
297
\end{array}
\qquad
\begin{array}{r}
33 \\
9\overline{)297}
\end{array}
$$

A slide refers to an error in recording the decimal point, in other words, a slide in the decimal point. For example, $163 could be inadvertently written as $1.63:

$$
\begin{array}{r}
\$163.00 \\
-1.63 \\
\hline
\$161.37
\end{array}
\qquad
\begin{array}{r}
17.93 \\
9\overline{)161.37}
\end{array}
$$

Or the error may be a combination of transposition and slide, such as when $216 is written as $6.21:

$$
\begin{array}{r}
\$216.00 \\
-6.21 \\
\hline
\$209.79
\end{array}
\qquad
\begin{array}{r}
23.31 \\
9\overline{)209.79}
\end{array}
$$

Again, the difference is evenly divisible by 9.

Summary

There are only five classifications of accounts. These classifications are embodied in the fundamental accounting equation.

Assets		=	Liabilities		+	Owner's Equity		+	Revenue		−	Expenses	
+	−		−	+		−	+		−	+		+	−
Left	Right		Left	Right		Left	Right		Left	Right		Left	Right
Debit	Credit		Debit	Credit		Debit	Credit		Debit	Credit		Debit	Credit

Let us again stress the most important concept in accounting. When you are recording transactions, the amount you place on the left, or debit, side of an account (or accounts) must equal the amount you place on the right, or credit, side of another account (or accounts).

At the end of the month, to prove the equality of debit and credit balances, prepare a trial balance.

Accounting may be considered as a game of accounts and balances. If you know the rules and make the right moves, you can win the game. The rules are the fundamentals, and they are based on logical assumptions. The consequences of a move follow you throughout the game. Take it as a challenge! As a starter, concentrate on mastering the fundamentals.

Glossary

Compound entry   The recording of a transaction resulting in two or more debits and/or two or more credits.

Credit   The right side of a ledger T account; to credit is to record an entry on the right side of a ledger T account. Credits represent increases in liability, capital, and revenue accounts, and decreases in asset and expense accounts.

Debit   The left side of a ledger T account; to debit is to record an entry on the left side of a ledger T account. Debits represent increases in asset and expense accounts, and decreases in liability, capital, and revenue accounts.

Double-entry accounting   Recording the amount of a transaction in at least two accounts, with the total of the amounts recorded as debits equal to the total of the amounts recorded as credits.

Footing   The temporary total of one side of a T account, recorded in pencil.

Ledger   A book or binder containing all the accounts of an enterprise.

Normal balance   The plus side of any T account.

Slide   An error in the recording of the decimal point of a number.

T account form   A form of ledger account having one side for entries on the debit, or left, side, and one side for entries on the credit, or right, side.

Transposition   Interchanging, or switching around, the digits during the recording of a number.

Questions

1. List the five classifications of accounts. Which classifications are identified with the balance sheet? Which classifications are identified with the income statement?

2. Regarding the five classifications of accounts, indicate the normal balance (whether debit or credit) of each account classification.

3. Why are the rules for debit and credit the same for both liabilities and owner's equity accounts?

4. Does the term *debit* always mean increase? Does the term *credit* always mean decrease? Explain.

5. What is the reason for using a separate owner's drawing account?

6. What is a compound entry?

7. Give an example of (a) a transposition and (b) a slide.

Exercises

Exercise 1   On a sheet of paper set up the fundamental accounting equation with T accounts under each of the five account classifications, noting plus and minus signs on the appropriate sides of each account. Under each of the five classifications, set up T accounts—again with the correct plus and minus signs—for each of the following ledger accounts of the Reliable Telephone Answering Service: Cash; Accounts

Receivable; Supplies; Equipment; Accounts Payable; Dora Lewis, Capital; Dora Lewis, Drawing; Fees Earned; Rent Expense; Telephone Expense; Utilities Expense; Miscellaneous Expense.

Exercise 2 Using the ledger accounts prepared in Exercise 1 for the Reliable Telephone Answering Service, record the following transactions.

a. Bought supplies for cash, $73.

b. Billed customers for services performed, $575.

c. Paid rent for the month, $360.

d. Collected accounts receivable $468.

e. Purchased a new typewriter, $258, on account.

f. Paid $18 for advertising in a community brochure.

g. Dora Lewis withdrew $75 in cash for personal use.

Exercise 3 Steven Dillon operates the Dillon Delivery Service. The company has the following chart of accounts:

Assets
Cash
Accounts Receivable
Prepaid Insurance
Delivery Equipment
Office Equipment

Liabilities
Notes Payable
Accounts Payable

Owner's Equity
Steven Dillon, Capital
Steven Dillon, Drawing

Revenue
Fees Earned

Expenses
Wages Expense
Truck Expense
Telephone Expense
Utilities Expense
Miscellaneous Expense

On a sheet of ordinary notebook paper, record the following transactions directly in pairs of T accounts. (*Example:* Paid telephone bill, $38)

Telephone Expense		Cash	
+	−	+	−
38			38

a. Paid creditors on account, $285.

b. Paid $220 for liability insurance.

c. Paid electric bill, $36.

d. Paid $36 for advertising.

e. Received $411 from charge customers to apply on account.

f. Steven Dillon withdrew $96 in cash for personal use.

g. Paid gasoline bill for truck, $148.

Exercise 4 During the first month of operation, Rasmussen's Welding Shop recorded the following transactions. Describe transactions (a) through (k).

Cash		
(a) 2,600	**(c)**	63
(k) 840	**(e)**	320
	(f)	70
	(g)	1,000
	(i)	200
	(j)	71

Accounts Receivable	
(h) 795	

Welding Supplies	
(b) 290	

Welding Equipment	
(d) 3,800	
(g) 1,900	

Accounts Payable	
(b)	290
(g)	900

L. Rasmussen, Capital	
	(a) 2,600
	(d) 3,800

L. Rasmussen, Drawing	
(i) 200	

Income from Services	
	(h) 795
	(k) 840

Rent Expense	
(e) 320	

Utilities Expense	
(j) 71	

Bottled Gas Expense	
(c) 63	

Miscellaneous Expense	
(f) 70	

Exercise 5 From the accounts in Exercise 4, prepare a trial balance for Rasmussen's Welding Shop, dated September 30 of this year.

Exercise 6 The accounts (all normal balances) of the Dixie Taxi Service as of September 30 of this year are listed here in alphabetical order. On a sheet of notebook paper, prepare a trial balance listing the accounts in proper order.

Accounts Payable	$ 5,700
Accounts Receivable	8,100
Cash	1,100
Equipment	20,000
Fares Earned	22,000
Insurance Expense	300
Miscellaneous Expense	100
Prepaid Insurance	300
Rent Expense	2,100
Supplies	700
Supplies Expense	2,500
Utilities Expense	1,100
Wages Expense	11,900
C. E. Ludeman, Capital	21,100
C. E. Ludeman, Drawing	600

Exercise 7 From the trial balance prepared in Exercise 6, prepare an income statement for the month of September of this year.

Exercise 8 Assume that a trial balance has been prepared and that the total of the debit balances is not equal to the total of the credit balances. On a sheet of paper, note the amount by which the two totals would differ, and label which column is overstated or understated.

Error	Amount of difference	Debit or credit column overstated or understated
A $28 debit to Supplies was not posted.	$28	Debit column understated
a A $36 credit to Cash was not posted.		
b A $72 credit to Accounts Payable was posted twice.		
c A $90 debit to Prepaid Insurance was posted twice.		
d A $49 debit to Accounts Receivable was posted as $94.		
e A $54 debit to Equipment was posted as $540.		
f A $21 debit to Supplies was posted as a $21 debit to Miscellaneous Expense.		

Problems

Problem 3-1 During August of this year, S. C. Rolf established the Rolf Linen Supply Company. The following asset, liability, and owner's equity accounts are included in the ledger: Cash; Linen Supplies; Laundry Equipment; Office Equipment; Truck; Accounts Payable; S. C. Rolf, Capital. During August, the following transactions occurred.

a. Rolf invested $8,900 cash in the business.

b. Bought used washers and dryers for $3,680, paying cash.

c. Bought sheets and pillow cases from Virginia Textile Company for cash, $475.

d. Bought towels from Ohio Hotel Supply Company, $640, on account.

e. Bought a typewriter, desk, and filing cabinet for cash, $464.

f. Bought a used delivery truck for $2,900 from Westland Automotive, paying $500 down; the balance is due in 30 days.

g. Paid $150 on account to Ohio Hotel Supply Company.

Instructions **1.** Record the plus and minus signs under each T account, and label the sides of the T account as either debit or credit.

2. Record the amounts in the proper positions in the T accounts. Key each entry to the alphabetical symbol identifying each transaction.

Problem 3-2 Ronald Stevens established Steven's Garage during November of this year. The accountant prepared the following chart of accounts.

Assets

Cash
Accounts Receivable
Office Equipment
Shop Equipment
Truck

Liabilities

Accounts Payable

Owner's Equity

Ronald Stevens, Capital
Ronald Stevens, Drawing

Revenue

Income from Services

Expenses

Rent Expense
Utilities Expense
Wages Expense
Repair Parts Expense

The transactions listed below occurred during the month.

a. Stevens invested $7,200 cash to establish an auto repair business.

b. Bought an office desk and filing cabinet for cash, $140.

c. Bought an electronic analyzer for $3,600, paying $1,200 down; the balance is due in 30 days.

d. Paid $360 rent for the month.

e. Received $235 in cash for services rendered.

f. Bought used truck for $2,400, with $400 as a down payment; he agreed to pay the balance in 30 days.

g. Received bill for repair parts, $220.

h. Billed customers for repair parts, $840.

i. Received and paid electric bill, $72.

j. Paid bill for repair parts, billed previously under **g.**

k. Collected $720 from charge customers, billed previously under **h.**

l. Paid wages to employee, $390.

m. Stevens invested his personal tools in the business, $726.

n. Stevens withdrew $325 in cash for personal use.

o. Received and paid telephone bill, $16.

Instructions

1. Record the plus and minus signs under each T account, and label the sides of the account as either debit or credit.

2. Record the transactions in the T accounts. Key each entry to the alphabetical symbol identifying each transaction.

3. Prepare a trial balance, with a three-line heading, dated November 30.

Problem 3-3 Charlotte R. Singer, an attorney, opens an office for the practice of law. Her accountant recommends the chart of accounts presented at the top of the following page.

Assets	**Revenue**
Cash	Professional Fees
Accounts Receivable	
Office Equipment	**Expenses**
Office Furniture	Salary Expense
Law Library	Rent Expense
	Utilities Expense
Liabilities	Travel Expense
Accounts Payable	

Owner's Equity

Charlotte R. Singer, Capital
Charlotte R. Singer, Drawing

The following transactions occurred during June of this year.

a. Singer invested $8,400 cash in her law practice.

b. Paid $740 in cash for desks, chairs, and rugs.

c. Bought an electric typewriter for $480, paying $220 down; the balance is due in 30 days.

d. Billed clients for legal services performed, $785.

e. Singer invested her personal law books in the firm, $4,600 (additional investment).

f. Bought a set of filing cabinets for $180, on account (Office Equipment).

g. Received and paid telephone bill, $72.

h. Received $450 from clients billed previously in **d.**

i. Received and paid electric bill for heat and lights, $58.

j. Billed clients for $924 for additional legal fees.

k. Paid $96 on the filing cabinets purchased on credit in **f.**

l. Paid $104 in expenses for business trip.

m. Paid salary of receptionist, $415.

n. Paid $300 as rent on her office for the month.

o. Singer withdrew $750 in cash for her personal use.

Instructions

1. Record the plus and minus signs under each T account, and label the sides of the T account as either debit or credit.

2. Record the transactions in the T accounts. Key each entry to the alphabetical symbol identifying each transaction.

3. Prepare a trial balance as of June 30, 19—.

4. Prepare an income statement for June.

5. Prepare a statement of owner's equity for June.

6. Prepare a balance sheet as of June 30, 19—.

Problem 3-4 On June 1 of this year, Ray Baker opened a coin-operated dry cleaning service under the name Fast-Service Dry Cleaners. His accountant listed the following accounts for the ledger: Cash; Dry Cleaning Supplies; Prepaid Insurance; Dry Cleaning Equipment; Furniture and Fixtures; Accounts Payable; Ray Baker, Capital; Ray Baker, Drawing; Dry Cleaning Sales; Wages Expense; Rent Expense; Power Expense; Miscellaneous Expense. During June the following transactions were completed.

a. Baker deposited $11,700 in a bank account in the name of the business.

b. Bought used chairs and magazine stands for $155 cash.

c. Paid rent for the month, $360.

d. Bought machinery and equipment for $9,600, giving $1,600 cash as a down payment with the remainder due in 30 days.

e. Bought dry cleaning supplies on account, $196.

f. Received $820 from cash customers for the first half of the month.

g. Paid $140 cash for liability insurance for 12 months.

h. Received and paid electric bill, $106.

i. Paid $24 for license and other miscellaneous expenses.

j. Paid $160 as a partial payment on the equipment purchased in **d.**

k. Received $982 from cash customers for the second half of the month.

l. Paid wages to employee, $400.

m. Baker withdrew $385 in cash for his personal use.

n. Paid $150 on account for the dry cleaning supplies acquired in **e.**

Instructions **1.** Record the plus and minus signs under each T account, and label the sides of the T account as either debit or credit.

2. Record the transactions in the T accounts. Key each entry to the alphabetical symbol identifying each transaction.

3. Prepare a trial balance as of June 30, 19—.

4. Prepare an income statement for June.

5. Prepare a statement of owner's equity for June.

6. Prepare a balance sheet as of June 30, 19—.

Alternate problems

Problem 3-1A During January of this year, Roger T. James established the James Television Company. The following asset, liability, and owner's equity accounts are included in the ledger: Cash; Repair Parts and Supplies; Shop Equipment; Store Equipment; Truck; Accounts Payable; Roger T. James, Capital. The following transactions occurred during the month of January.

a. James invested $10,000 cash in the business.

b. Bought testing equipment for cash, $720 (Shop Equipment).

c. Bought resisters and other repair parts from Midvale Supply, $326; payment is due in 30 days.

d. Bought store fixtures for $760 from Newton Hardware; payment is due in 30 days.

e. Bought a used service truck for $2,700 from Logan Truck and Tractor, paying $500 down; the balance is due in 30 days.

f. Paid $250 on account for the store fixtures in **d** above.

g. James invested his personal tools and testing devices in the business, $740.

Instructions   **1.** Record the plus and minus signs under each T Account, and label the sides of the T account as either debit or credit.

2. Record the amounts in the proper positions in the T accounts. Key each entry to the alphabetical symbol identifying each transaction.

Problem 3-2A   Hubert Sheerer established Sheerer's Garage during October of this year. The accountant prepared the following chart of accounts.

Assets	**Revenue**
Cash	Income from Services
Accounts Receivable	
Office Equipment	**Expenses**
Shop Equipment	Rent Expense
Truck	Utilities Expense
	Wages Expense
Liabilities	Repair Parts Expense
Accounts Payable	

Owner's Equity
Hubert Sheerer, Capital
Hubert Sheerer, Drawing

The transactions listed below occurred during the month.

a. Sheerer invested $3,600 cash to establish his auto repair business.

b. Paid $450 rent for the month.

c. Bought an office desk and filing cabinet for cash, $155.

d. Bought an electric analyzer for $3,300, paying $1,400 down; the balance is due in 30 days.

e. Bought a used truck for $1,750, paying $250 down; the balance is due in 30 days.

f. Sheerer invested his personal tools in the business, $1,240.

g. Received $194 in cash for services rendered.

h. Received bill for repair parts, $198.

i. Received and paid electric bill, $67.

j. Billed customers for repair services, $789.

k. Paid bill for repair parts, billed previously under **h.**

l. Collected $638 from charge customers, billed previously under **j.**

m. Paid wages to employee, $440.

n. Received and paid telephone bill, $21.

o. Sheerer withdrew $280 in cash for personal use.

Instructions
1. Record the plus and minus signs under each T account, and label the sides of the T account as either debit or credit.

2. Record the transactions in the T accounts. Key each entry to the alphabetical symbol identifying each transaction.

3. Prepare a trial balance with a three-line heading, dated October 31.

Problem 3-3A Cynthia M. Baldwin, an attorney, opens an office for the practice of law. Her accountant recommends the following chart of accounts.

Assets	**Revenue**
Cash	Professional Fees
Accounts Receivable	
Office Equipment	**Expenses**
Office Furniture	Salary Expense
Law Library	Rent Expense
	Utilities Expense
Liabilities	Travel Expense
Accounts Payable	

Owner's Equity
Cynthia M. Baldwin, Capital
Cynthia M. Baldwin, Drawing

The following transactions occurred during May of this year.

a. Baldwin invested $8,200 cash in her law practice.

b. Bought a set of filing cabinets for $180, on account (Office Equipment).

c. Bought an electric typewriter for $410, paying $200 down; the balance is due in 30 days.

d. Received and paid telephone bill, $64.

e. Baldwin invested her personal law books in the firm, $5,620 (additional investment).

f. Bought desks, chairs, and rugs, $1,164, paying cash.

g. Paid $75 on the filing cabinets purchased on credit in **b.**

h. Billed clients for legal services performed, $838.

i. Received and paid electric bill for heat and lights, $56.

j. Paid expenses for business trip, $84.

k. Billed clients, $1,050, for additional legal fees.

l. Bought bookcases for $326, on account (Office Furniture).

m. Paid salary of receptionist, $485.

n. Paid $310 as rent on her office for the month.

o. Baldwin withdrew $620 in cash for her personal use.

1. Record the plus and minus signs under each T account, and label the sides of the T account as either debit or credit.

2. Record the transactions in the T accounts. Key each entry to the alphabetical symbol identifying each transaction.

3. Prepare a trial balance as of May 31, 19—.

4. Prepare an income statement for May.

5. Prepare a statement of owner's equity for May.

6. Prepare a balance sheet as of May 31, 19—.

Problem 3-4A On August 1 of this year, Gerry Bailey opened a coin-operated dry cleaning service called Fast-Service Dry Cleaners. His accountant listed the following accounts for the ledger: Cash; Dry Cleaning Supplies; Prepaid Insurance; Dry Cleaning Equipment; Furniture and Fixtures; Accounts Payable; Gerry Bailey, Capital; Gerry Bailey, Drawing; Dry Cleaning Sales; Wages Expense; Rent Expense; Power Expense; Miscellaneous Expense. During August the following transactions were completed.

a. Bailey deposited $12,500 in a bank account in the name of the business.

b. Bought used chairs and stands for $164 cash.

c. Paid rent for the month, $460.

d. Bought machinery and equipment for $10,400, giving $1,800 cash as a down payment with the remainder due in 30 days.

e. Acquired dry cleaning supplies on account, $282.

f. Received $924 from cash customers for the first half of the month.

g. Paid $102 cash for liability insurance for 12 months.

h. Paid $220 as a partial payment on the equipment purchased in **d.**

i. Received and paid electric bill, $115.

j. Paid $210 on account for the dry cleaning supplies acquired in **e.**

k. Received $1,040 from cash customers for the second half of the month.

l. Paid $36 for license and other miscellaneous expenses.

m. Paid wages to employee, $410.

n. Bailey withdrew $480 in cash for personal use.

Instructions

1. Record the plus and minus signs under each T account, and label the sides of the T account as either debit or credit.

2. Record the transactions in the T accounts. Key each entry to the alphabetical symbol identifying each transaction.

3. Prepare a trial balance as of August 31, 19—.

4. Prepare an income statement for August.

5. Prepare a statement of owner's equity for August.

6. Prepare a balance sheet as of August 31, 19—.

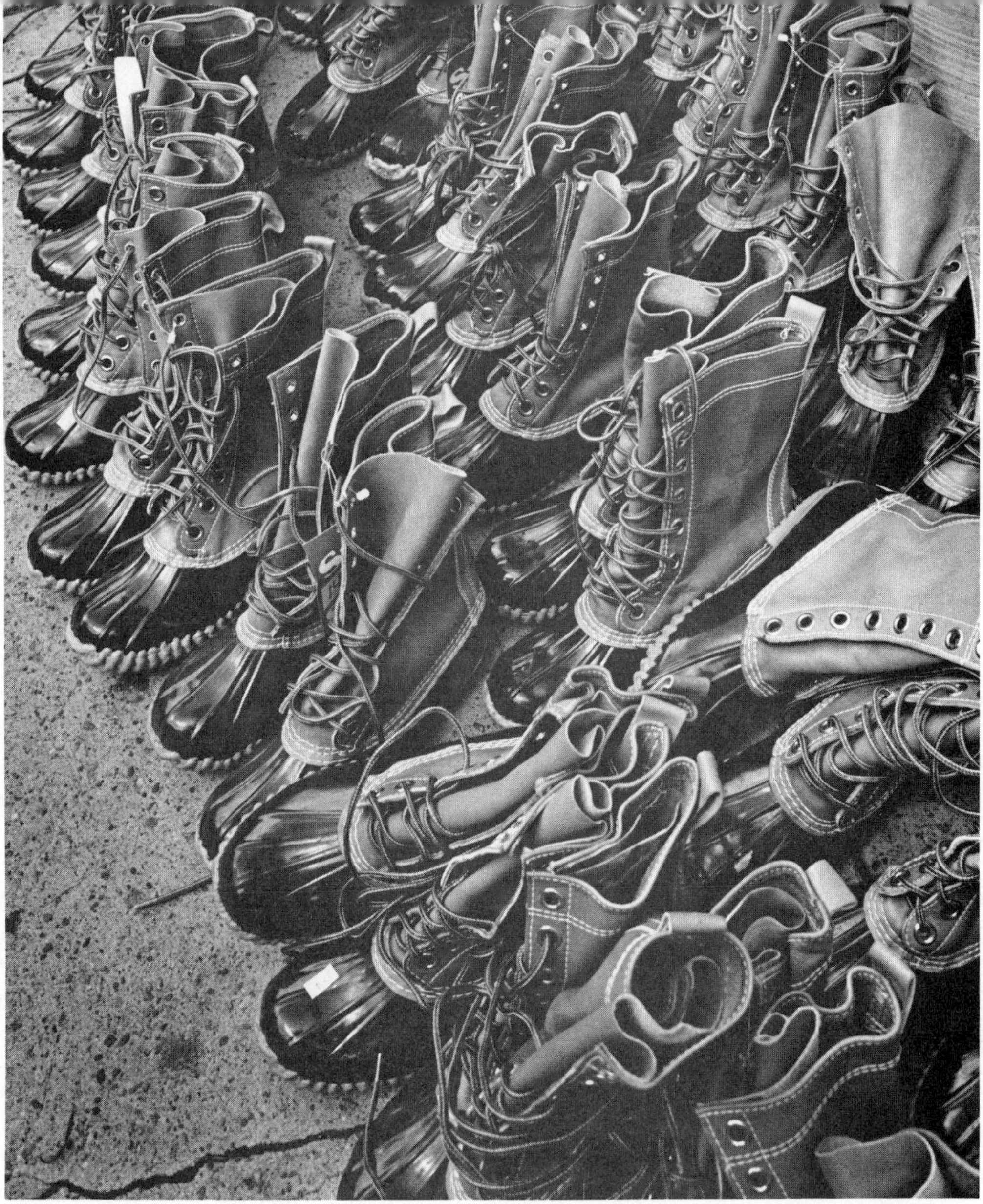

4 The general journal and posting

objectives

After you have completed this chapter, you will be able to do the following:
- Record a group of transactions pertaining to a service-type enterprise in a two-column general journal.
- Post entries from a two-column general journal to general ledger accounts.

IN CHAPTER 3 we recorded business transactions directly as debits and credits to T accounts. This enabled you to visualize the accounts and tell which should be debited and which should be credited.

The initial steps in the accounting process are as follows:

1. Recording business transactions in a journal
2. Posting to T accounts in the ledger
3. Footing the T accounts and determining the balances
4. Preparing a trial balance

Up to this time we have covered steps 2, 3, and 4. In our previous presentation, we introduced T accounts because, in the process of formulating debits and credits for business transactions, one has to think in terms of T accounts. Now we need to backtrack slightly in order to take up step 1, recording business transactions in a journal. Accordingly, in this chapter we shall present the general journal and the posting procedure.

The general journal

We have seen that an accountant must keep a written record of each transaction. One could record the transactions directly in T accounts; however, one would list only part of the transaction in each T account. A *journal* serves the function of recording both the debits and credits of the entire transaction. This journal is like a diary for the business, in which one records in day-by-day order all the events involving financial affairs. A journal is called a *record of original entry*. In other words, always record a transaction in the journal first, and from there record it in the T accounts. The process of recording in the journal is called *journalizing*. One obtains information about transactions from business papers, such as checks, invoices, receipts, letters, memos, etc. These documents furnish proof that a transaction has taken place, so we should identify them in the journal entry whenever possible. Later on we shall introduce a variety of special journals. However, the basic form of journal is the two-column *general journal*. The term *two-column* refers to the two money columns which are used for debit and credit amounts.

Journalizing business transactions

As an illustration, let's use the transactions for Neil's Cleaners, covering the transactions listed in Chapter 3. Each page of the journal is numbered in consecutive order. This is the first page, so we write a 1 in the space for the page number. And, of course, we must always remember to put the date of transaction. Now let's get on with the first entry.

Transaction (a) June 1: Neil Singleton deposited $16,000 in a bank account in the name of Neil's Cleaners.

We write the year and month in the left part of the date column. We don't have to repeat the year and month until we start a new page, or until the year or month changes. (The illustrations we show, however, may repeat the month simply to eliminate confusion.) We write the day in the right part of the date column, and repeat it for each journal entry.

✓ Balance Section

GENERAL JOURNAL   PAGE __1__

DATE		DESCRIPTION	POST REF.	DEBIT	CREDIT
19– Jun.	1				

Since we are familiar with the accounts, the next step is to decide which accounts should be debited and which credited. We do this by first figuring out which accounts are involved and whether they are increased or decreased. We then visualize the accounts mentally with their respective plus and minus sides, and thus we can make the debit and credit entries. Here is an example.

Cash is involved. Cash is considered to be an asset because it falls within the definition of "things owned," and assets are

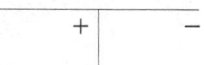

Cash is increased, so we debit Cash. Neil Singleton, Capital is involved; Neil Singleton, Capital is an owner's equity account because it represents the owner's investment, and Owner's Equity is

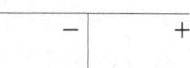

Neil Singleton, Capital is increased, so credit Neil Singleton, Capital.

As we said earlier, you perform this process mentally. Or, if the transaction is more complicated, then use scratch paper, drawing the T accounts. Using T accounts is the accountant's way of drawing a picture of the transaction. This is why we stressed the fundamental accounting equation, with the T accounts and plus and minus signs, so heavily in Chapter 3. You are urged to get in the T account habit.

Record the *debit* part of the entry first. Enter the account title—in this case, Cash—in the description column. Record the amount—$16,000—in the debit money column.

GENERAL JOURNAL   PAGE __1__

DATE		DESCRIPTION	POST REF.	DEBIT	CREDIT
19– Jun.	1	Cash		16 000 00	

Next, record the *credit* part of the entry. Enter the account title—in this case, Neil Singleton, Capital—on the line below the debit, in the Description column, indented about ½ inch. Do not abbreviate account titles, and do not extend them into the Posting Reference column.

GENERAL JOURNAL

PAGE __1__

	DATE		DESCRIPTION	POST REF.	DEBIT	CREDIT	
1	19– Jun.	1	Cash		16 0 0 0 00		1
2			Neil Singleton, Capital			16 0 0 0 00	2
3							3
4							4
5							5

You should now give a brief explanation, in which you may refer to business papers, such as check numbers or invoice numbers; you may also list names of charge customers or creditors, or terms of payment. Enter the explanation below the credit entry, indented an additional ½ inch.

GENERAL JOURNAL

PAGE __1__

	DATE		DESCRIPTION	POST REF.	DEBIT	CREDIT	
1	19– Jun.	1	Cash		16 0 0 0 00		1
2			Neil Singleton, Capital			16 0 0 0 00	2
3			Original investment by Singleton in Neil's				3
4			Cleaners.				4
5							5
6							6
7							7
8							8

In order for an entry in the general journal to be complete, it must contain (1) a debit entry, (2) a credit entry, and (3) an explanation. To anyone thoroughly familiar with the accounts, the explanation may seem to be quite obvious or redundant. This will take care of itself later; but in the meantime, let us record the explanation as a required, integral part of the entry.

Transaction (b) June 2: Singleton buys $9,000 worth of equipment, for cash.

Mentally select the accounts that are involved. Next classify them under the five possible classifications. Visualize the plus and minus signs under the classifications. Now decide whether the accounts are increased or decreased. When you use T accounts to analyze the transaction, the results are as illustrated at the top of the facing page:

Equipment		Cash	
+	−	+	−
Dr	Cr	Dr	Cr
9,000			9,000

Now journalize this analysis below the first transaction. For the sake of appearance, leave one blank line between transactions. Record the day of the month in the date column; remember that it is necessary to list only the day, because you don't have to record the month and year again until the month or year changes, or you use a new journal page.

GENERAL JOURNAL

PAGE ___1___

	DATE		DESCRIPTION	POST REF.	DEBIT	CREDIT	
1	19– Jun.	1	Cash		16 0 0 0 00		1
2			Neil Singleton, Capital			16 0 0 0 00	2
3			Original investment by Singleton in Neil's				3
4			Cleaners.				4
5							5
6		2	Equipment		9 0 0 0 00		6
7			Cash			9 0 0 0 00	7
8			Bought equipment for cash.				8
9							9
10							10
11							11
12							12
13							13
14							14
15							15

Transaction (c) On June 2 Singleton buys $2,000 worth of equipment from Johnson Equipment Company. In order to get organized, think of the T accounts first.

Equipment		Accounts Payable	
+	−	−	+
Dr	Cr	Dr	Cr
2,000			2,000

On the journal, skip one more line and record the day of the month and then the entry. In journalizing a transaction involving Accounts Payable, always state the name of the creditor. Similarly, in journalizing a transaction involving Accounts Receivable, always state the name of the charge customer as is done in the example on page 74.

DATE		DESCRIPTION	POST REF.	DEBIT	CREDIT
	2	Equipment		2 0 0 0 00	
		Accounts Payable			2 0 0 0 00
		Bought equipment on account from			
		Johnson Equipment Company.			

Transaction (d) On June 4, Singleton pays $500 to be applied against the firm's liability of $2,000. Mentally picture the T accounts like this.

Cash		Accounts Payable	
+	−	−	+
Dr	Cr	Dr	Cr
	500	500	

Cash is an easy one to recognize. So, in every transaction, ask yourself, "Is Cash involved?" If Cash is involved, determine whether it is coming in or going out. In this case we see that cash is going out, so we record it on the minus side. We now have a credit to Cash and half of the entry. Next, we recognize that Accounts Payable is involved. We ask ourselves, "Do we owe more or less as a result of this transaction?" The answer is "less," so we record it on the minus, or debit, side of the account.

DATE		DESCRIPTION	POST REF.	DEBIT	CREDIT
	4	Accounts Payable		5 0 0 00	
		Cash			5 0 0 00
		Paid Johnson Equipment Company on			
		account.			

Now let's list the transactions for June for Neil's Cleaners with the date of each transaction. The journal entries are illustrated on the following pages.

June   1   Singleton invests $16,000 cash in his new business.

         2   Buys $9,000 worth of equipment for cash.

         2   Buys $2,000 worth of equipment on credit from Johnson Equipment Company.

DATE		DESCRIPTION	POST REF.	DEBIT	CREDIT	
19– Jun.	1	Cash	111	16 000 00		1
		Neil Singleton, Capital	311		16 000 00	2
		Original investment by Singleton in Neil's				3
		Cleaners.				4
						5
	2	Equipment	121	9 000 00		6
		Cash	111		9 000 00	7
		Bought equipment for cash.				8
						9
	2	Equipment	121	2 000 00		10
		Accounts Payable	211		2 000 00	11
		Bought equipment on account from				12
		Johnson Equipment Company.				13
						14
	4	Accounts Payable	211	500 00		15
		Cash	111		500 00	16
		Paid Johnson Equipment Company on				17
		account.				18
						19
	4	Supplies	113	200 00		20
		Accounts Payable	211		200 00	21
		Bought cleaning fluids on account from				22
		Acme Supply Company.				23
						24
	7	Cash		300 00		25
		Income from Services			300 00	26
		For week ended June 7.				27
						28
	8	Rent Expense		200 00		29
		Cash			200 00	30
		For month ended June 30.				31
						32
	10	Wages Expense		120 00		33
		Cash			120 00	34
		Paid wages, June 1 to June 10.				35

June 4 Pays $500 to Johnson Equipment Company, to be applied against the firm's liability of $2,000.

4 Buys cleaning fluids for $200 on credit from Acme Supply Company.

7 Cash revenue received for first week, $300.

8 Pays $200 rent for the month.

10 Pays wages to employees, $120, June 1 through June 10.

	DATE		DESCRIPTION	POST REF.	DEBIT	CREDIT	
1	19– Jun.	10	Prepaid Insurance		1 6 0 00		1
2			Cash			1 6 0 00	2
3			Premium for 2-year liability insurance.				3
4							4
5		14	Cash		3 8 0 00		5
6			Income from Services			3 8 0 00	6
7			For week ended June 14.				7
8							8
9		14	Advertising Expense		9 0 00		9
10			Accounts Payable			9 0 00	10
11			Received bill for adv. from Daily News.				11
12							12
13		15	Accounts Payable		9 0 0 00		13
14			Cash			9 0 0 00	14
15			Paid Johnson Equipment Company on				15
16			account.				16
17							17
18		15	Utilities Expense		1 1 0 00		18
19			Cash			1 1 0 00	19
20			Paid bill for utilities.				20
21							21
22		15	Accounts Payable		9 0 00		22
23			Cash			9 0 00	23
24			Paid Daily News for advertising.				24
25							25
26		21	Cash		4 1 5 00		26
27			Income from Services			4 1 5 00	27
28			For week ended June 21.				28
29							29
30		23	Accounts Receivable		4 0 00		30
31			Income from Services			4 0 00	31
32			Ace Rental, for services rendered.				32
33							33
34							34
35							35

June 10 Pays $160 for a 2-year liability insurance policy.

14 Cash revenue received for second week, $380.

14 Receives bill for newspaper advertising, $90, from the *Daily News*.

15 Pays $900 to Johnson Equipment Company as part payment on account.

	DATE		DESCRIPTION	POST REF.	DEBIT	CREDIT	
1	19– Jun.	24	Wages Expense		1 9 5 00		1
2			Cash			1 9 5 00	2
3			Paid wages, June 11 to June 24.				3
4							4
5		26	Equipment		1 4 0 00		5
6			Accounts Payable			1 4 0 00	6
7			Bought equipment on account from				7
8			Johnson Equipment Company.				8
9							9
10		30	Cash		4 8 0 00		10
11			Income from Services			4 8 0 00	11
12			For remainder of June, ended June 30.				12
13							13
14		30	Cash		3 0 00		14
15			Accounts Receivable			3 0 00	15
16			Ace Rental, to apply on account.				16
17							17
18		30	Neil Singleton, Drawing		5 0 0 00		18
19			Cash			5 0 0 00	19
20			Withdrawal for personal use.				20
21							21
22							22
23							23
24							24
25							25
26							26
27							27
28							28
29							29
30							30
31							31
32							32
33							33
34							34
35							35

June 15 Receives and pays bill for utilities, $110.

  15 Pays $90 to the *Daily News* for advertising. (This bill has previously been recorded.)

  21 Cash revenue received for third week, $415.

  23 Singleton enters into a contract with Ace Rental to clean their for-hire

formal garments on a credit basis. Bills Ace Rental $40 for services performed.

June 24 Pays wages of employees, $195, June 11 through June 24.

26 Buys additional equipment on account, $140, from Johnson Equipment Company.

30 Cash revenue received for the remainder of the month, $480.

30 Receives $30 from Ace Rental to apply on amount previously billed.

30 Singleton withdraws $500 in cash for own personal use.

Posting to the general ledger

From this illustration, you can see that the journal is the *book of original entry,* meaning that each transaction must first be recorded in the journal in its entirety. Ledger accounts give us a cumulative record of the transactions recorded in each individual account. The general ledger is simply a book which contains all the accounts. The book used for the ledger is usually a loose-leaf binder, so that one can add or remove leaves. The process of transferring figures from the journal to the ledger accounts is called *posting.*

The chart of accounts

One arranges the accounts in the ledger according to the chart of accounts. The chart of accounts is the official list of accounts in which transactions may be recorded. Assets are listed first, liabilities second, owner's equity third, revenue fourth, and expenses fifth. The chart of accounts for Neil's Cleaners is as follows.

Chart of Accounts

Assets (100–199)
111 Cash
112 Accounts Receivable
113 Supplies
114 Prepaid Insurance
121 Equipment

Liabilities (200–299)
211 Accounts Payable

Owner's Equity (300–399)
311 Neil Singleton, Capital
312 Neil Singleton, Drawing

Revenue (400–499)
411 Income from Services

Expenses (500–599)
511 Wages Expense
512 Rent Expense
513 Advertising Expense
514 Utilities Expense

Notice that the arrangement consists of the balance sheet accounts followed by the income statement accounts. The numbers preceding the account titles are the *account numbers.* Accounts in the ledger are kept by numbers rather than by pages because it's hard to tell in advance how many pages to reserve for a particular account. When you use the number system, you can add sheets quite readily. The digits in the account numbers also indicate *classifications* of accounts: Assets start with 1, liabilities with 2, owner's equity with 3, revenue with 4, and expenses with 5. The second and third digits indicate the positions of the individual accounts within their respective classifications.

The ledger account form

We have been looking at accounts in the simple T form primarily because T accounts illustrate situations so well. The two sides, the debit side and the credit side, are readily apparent. As we have said, accountants trying to solve problems usually use the T form, because it's such a good way to visualize accounts. However, the T form is awkward when you are trying to determine the balance of an account, since it necessitates adding both columns and subtracting the smaller total from the larger. To overcome this disadvantage, accountants generally use the four-column account form with balance columns. As a comparison, let's look at the Cash account of Neil's Cleaners in four-column form and in T form. Temporarily, the Posting Reference column is left blank. The meaning and use of this column is described in the posting process which follows in the next paragraph.

GENERAL LEDGER

ACCOUNT _____ Cash _____ ACCOUNT NO. 111

DATE		ITEM	POST. REF.	DEBIT	CREDIT	BALANCE DEBIT	BALANCE CREDIT
19– Jun.	1			16 000 00		16 000 00	
	2				9 000 00	7 000 00	
	4				500 00	6 500 00	
	7			300 00		6 800 00	
	8				200 00	6 600 00	
	10				120 00	6 480 00	
	10				160 00	6 320 00	
	14			380 00		6 700 00	
	15				900 00	5 800 00	
	15				110 00	5 690 00	
	15				90 00	5 600 00	
	21			415 00		6 015 00	
	24				195 00	5 820 00	
	30			480 00		6 300 00	
	30			30 00		6 330 00	
	30				500 00	5 830 00	

Cash

+		−	
(a)	16,000	(b)	9,000
(f)	300	(d)	500
(j)	380	(g)	200
(o)	415	(h)	120
(s)	480	(i)	160
(t)	30	(l)	900
	17,605	(m)	110
		(n)	90
	5,830	(q)	195
		(u)	500
			11,775

The posting process

In the posting process, you must transfer the following information from the journal to the ledger accounts: the *date of the transaction,* the *debit and credit amounts,* and the *page number* of the journal. Post each account separately, using the following steps. Post the debit part of the entry first.

1. Write the date of transaction.

2. Write the amount of transaction.

3. Write the page number of the journal in the Posting Reference column of the ledger account.

4. Record the ledger account number in the Posting Reference column of the journal. (This is a cross reference.)

The transactions for Neil's Cleaners are illustrated below. Let's look first at the debit part of the entry.

GENERAL JOURNAL   PAGE __1__

DATE			DESCRIPTION	POST REF.	DEBIT	CREDIT
19– Jun.	1		Cash	111	16 0 0 0 00	
			Neil Singleton, Capital			16 0 0 0 00
			Original investment by Singleton in Neil's			
			Cleaners.			

GENERAL LEDGER

ACCOUNT __Cash__   ACCOUNT NO. __111__

DATE	ITEM	POST. REF.	DEBIT	CREDIT	BALANCE	
					DEBIT	CREDIT
19– Jun.	1	1	16 0 0 0 00		16 0 0 0 00	

And now we post the credit part of the entry, as shown at the top of the facing page.

	DATE		DESCRIPTION	POST. REF.	DEBIT	CREDIT
1	19– Jun.	1	Cash	111	16 000 00	
2			Neil Singleton, Capital	311		16 000 00
3			Original investment by Singleton in Neil's			
4			Cleaners.			

GENERAL LEDGER

ACCOUNT __Neil Singleton, Capital__   ACCOUNT NO. __311__

DATE		ITEM	POST. REF.	DEBIT	CREDIT	BALANCE DEBIT	BALANCE CREDIT
19– Jun.	1		1		16 000 00		16 000 00

Entering the account number in the Posting Reference column of the journal should be the last step. It acts as a verification of the three preceding steps.

The accountant usually uses the Item column only at the end of a financial period. The words that may appear in this column are *balance, closing, adjusting,* and *reversing.* We'll introduce all these terms later.

Follow the four steps in the recording of the second transaction.

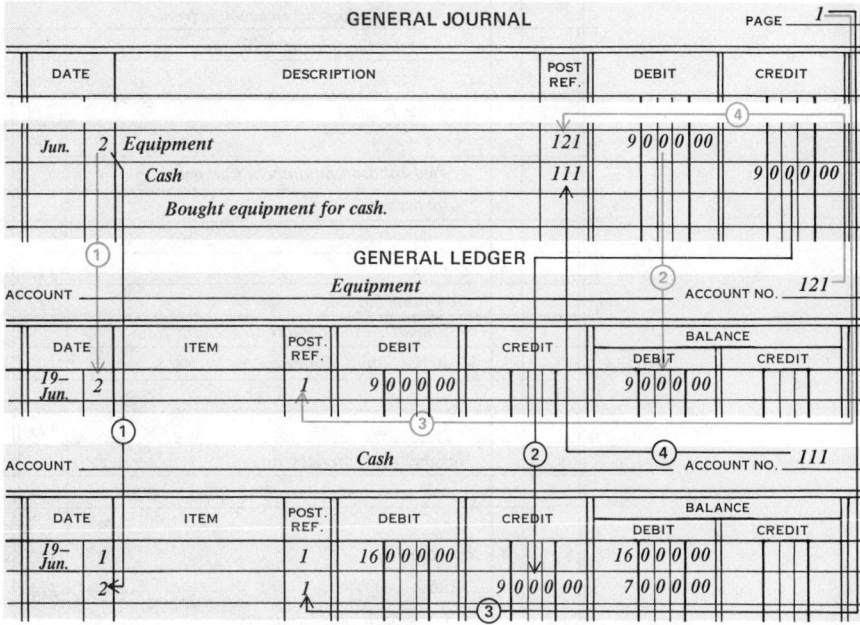

Let us now look at the journal entries for the first month of operation for Neil's Cleaners. As you can see from the general journal and general ledger on the following pages, the Posting Reference column has been filled in, since the posting has been completed.

For the purpose of journal illustrations in this textbook, assume that a full journal page permits 35 lines of entries. Remember that 1 blank line is left between complete entries and that entries are not broken up (that is, all 3 lines of a complete entry are shown on one journal page).

GENERAL JOURNAL   PAGE __1__

	DATE		DESCRIPTION	POST REF.	DEBIT	CREDIT	
1	19– Jun.	1	Cash	111	16 0 0 0 00		1
2			Neil Singleton, Capital	311		16 0 0 0 00	2
3			Original investment by Singleton in				3
4			Neil's Cleaners.				4
5							5
6		2	Equipment	121	9 0 0 0 00		6
7			Cash	111		9 0 0 0 00	7
8			Bought equipment for cash.				8
9							9
10		2	Equipment	121	2 0 0 0 00		10
11			Accounts Payable	211		2 0 0 0 00	11
12			Bought equipment on account from				12
13			Johnson Equipment Company.				13
14							14
15		4	Accounts Payable	211	5 0 0 00		15
16			Cash	111		5 0 0 00	16
17			Paid Johnson Equipment Company				17
18			on account.				18
19							19
20		4	Supplies	113	2 0 0 00		20
21			Accounts Payable	211		2 0 0 00	21
22			Bought cleaning fluids on account from				22
23			Acme Supply Company.				23
24							24
25		7	Cash	111	3 0 0 00		25
26			Income from Services	411		3 0 0 00	26
27			For week ended June 7.				27
28							28
29		8	Rent Expense	512	2 0 0 00		29
30			Cash	111		2 0 0 00	30
31			For month ended June 30.				31
32							32
33		10	Wages Expense	511	1 2 0 00		33
34			Cash	111		1 2 0 00	34
35			Paid wages, June 1 to June 10.				35

	DATE		DESCRIPTION	POST REF.	DEBIT	CREDIT	
1	19— Jun.	10	Prepaid Insurance	114	1 6 0 00		1
2			Cash	111		1 6 0 00	2
3			Premium for 2-year liability insurance.				3
4							4
5		14	Cash	111	3 8 0 00		5
6			Income from Services	411		3 8 0 00	6
7			For week ended June 14.				7
8							8
9		14	Advertising Expense	513	9 0 00		9
10			Accounts Payable	211		9 0 00	10
11			Received bill for adv. from Daily News.				11
12							12
13		15	Accounts Payable	211	9 0 0 00		13
14			Cash	111		9 0 0 00	14
15			Paid Johnson Equipment Company on				15
16			account.				16
17							17
18		15	Utilities Expense	514	1 1 0 00		18
19			Cash	111		1 1 0 00	19
20			Paid bill for utilities.				20
21							21
22		15	Accounts Payable	211	9 0 00		22
23			Cash	111		9 0 00	23
24			Paid Daily News for advertising.				24
25							25
26		21	Cash	111	4 1 5 00		26
27			Income from Services	411		4 1 5 00	27
28			For week ended June 21.				28
29							29
30		23	Accounts Receivable	112	4 0 00		30
31			Income from Services	411		4 0 00	31
32			Ace Rental, for services rendered.				32
33							33
34							34
35							35

	DATE		DESCRIPTION	POST REF.	DEBIT	CREDIT	
1	19— Jun.	24	Wages Expense	511	1 9 5 00		1
2			Cash	111		1 9 5 00	2
3			Paid wages, June 11 to June 24.				3

5	26	Equipment	121	1 4 0 00			5
6		Accounts Payable	211		1 4 0 00		6
7		Bought equipment on account from					7
8		Johnson Equipment Company.					8
9							9
10	30	Cash	111	4 8 0 00			10
11		Income from Services	411		4 8 0 00		11
12		For remainder of June, ended June 30.					12
13							13
14	30	Cash	111	3 0 00			14
15		Accounts Receivable	112		3 0 00		15
16		Ace Rental, to apply on account.					16
17							17
18	30	Neil Singleton, Drawing	312	5 0 0 00			18
19		Cash	111		5 0 0 00		19
20		Withdrawal for personal use.					20
21							21
22							22
23							23
24							24
25							25
26							26

GENERAL LEDGER

ACCOUNT _____ Cash _____ ACCOUNT NO. _111_

DATE		ITEM	POST. REF.	DEBIT	CREDIT	BALANCE DEBIT	BALANCE CREDIT
19– Jun.	1		1	16 0 0 0 00		16 0 0 0 00	
	2		1		9 0 0 0 00	7 0 0 0 00	
	4		1		5 0 0 00	6 5 0 0 00	
	7		1	3 0 0 00		6 8 0 0 00	
	8		1		2 0 0 00	6 6 0 0 00	
	10		1		1 2 0 00	6 4 8 0 00	
	10		2		1 6 0 00	6 3 2 0 00	
	14		2	3 8 0 00		6 7 0 0 00	
	15		2		9 0 0 00	5 8 0 0 00	
	15		2		1 1 0 00	5 6 9 0 00	
	15		2		9 0 00	5 6 0 0 00	
	21		2	4 1 5 00		6 0 1 5 00	
	24		3		1 9 5 00	5 8 2 0 00	
	30		3	4 8 0 00		6 3 0 0 00	
	30		3	3 0 00		6 3 3 0 00	
	30		3		5 0 0 00	5 8 3 0 00	

ACCOUNT _Accounts Receivable_ **ACCOUNT NO.** 112

DATE		ITEM	POST. REF.	DEBIT	CREDIT	BALANCE DEBIT	BALANCE CREDIT
19– Jun.	23		2	4 0 00		4 0 00	
	30		3		3 0 00	1 0 00	

ACCOUNT _Supplies_ **ACCOUNT NO.** 113

DATE		ITEM	POST. REF.	DEBIT	CREDIT	BALANCE DEBIT	BALANCE CREDIT
19– Jun.	4		1	2 0 0 00		2 0 0 00	

ACCOUNT _Prepaid Insurance_ **ACCOUNT NO.** 114

DATE		ITEM	POST. REF.	DEBIT	CREDIT	BALANCE DEBIT	BALANCE CREDIT
19– Jun.	10		2	1 6 0 00		1 6 0 00	

ACCOUNT _Equipment_ **ACCOUNT NO.** 121

DATE		ITEM	POST. REF.	DEBIT	CREDIT	BALANCE DEBIT	BALANCE CREDIT
19– Jun.	2		1	9 0 0 0 00		9 0 0 0 00	
	2		1	2 0 0 0 00		11 0 0 0 00	
	26		3	1 4 0 00		11 1 4 0 00	

ACCOUNT _Accounts Payable_ **ACCOUNT NO.** 211

DATE		ITEM	POST. REF.	DEBIT	CREDIT	BALANCE DEBIT	BALANCE CREDIT
19– Jun.	2		1		2 0 0 0 00		2 0 0 0 00
	4		1	5 0 0 00			1 5 0 0 00
	4		1		2 0 0 00		1 7 0 0 00
	14		2		9 0 00		1 7 9 0 00
	15		2	9 0 0 00			8 9 0 00
	15		2	9 0 00			8 0 0 00
	26		3		1 4 0 00		9 4 0 00

Neil Singleton, Capital — ACCOUNT NO. 311

DATE		ITEM	POST. REF.	DEBIT	CREDIT	BALANCE DEBIT	BALANCE CREDIT
19—Jun.	1		1		16 000 00		16 000 00

Neil Singleton, Drawing — ACCOUNT NO. 312

DATE		ITEM	POST. REF.	DEBIT	CREDIT	BALANCE DEBIT	BALANCE CREDIT
19—Jun.	30		3	5 00 00		5 00 00	

Income from Services — ACCOUNT NO. 411

DATE		ITEM	POST. REF.	DEBIT	CREDIT	BALANCE DEBIT	BALANCE CREDIT
19—Jun.	7		1		3 00 00		3 00 00
	14		2		3 80 00		6 80 00
	21		2		4 15 00		1 095 00
	23		2		40 00		1 135 00
	30		3		4 80 00		1 615 00

Wages Expense — ACCOUNT NO. 511

DATE		ITEM	POST. REF.	DEBIT	CREDIT	BALANCE DEBIT	BALANCE CREDIT
19—Jun.	10		1	1 20 00		1 20 00	
	24		3	1 95 00		3 15 00	

Rent Expense — ACCOUNT NO. 512

DATE		ITEM	POST. REF.	DEBIT	CREDIT	BALANCE DEBIT	BALANCE CREDIT
19—Jun.	8		1	2 00 00		2 00 00	

Advertising Expense — ACCOUNT NO. 513

DATE		ITEM	POST. REF.	DEBIT	CREDIT	BALANCE DEBIT	BALANCE CREDIT
19—Jun.	14		2	9 00 00		9 00 00	

ACCOUNT	Utilities Expense						ACCOUNT NO. 514	

DATE	ITEM	POST. REF.	DEBIT	CREDIT	BALANCE DEBIT	BALANCE CREDIT
19— Jun. 15		2	1 1 0 00		1 1 0 00	

A trial balance is presented below.

Neil's Cleaners

Trial Balance

June 30, 19—

	DEBIT	CREDIT
Cash	5 8 3 0 00	
Accounts Receivable	1 0 00	
Supplies	2 0 0 00	
Prepaid Insurance	1 6 0 00	
Equipment	11 1 4 0 00	
Accounts Payable		9 4 0 00
Neil Singleton, Capital		16 0 0 0 00
Neil Singleton, Drawing	5 0 0 00	
Income from Services		1 6 1 5 00
Wages Expense	3 1 5 00	
Rent Expense	2 0 0 00	
Advertising Expense	9 0 00	
Utilities Expense	1 1 0 00	
	18 5 5 5 00	18 5 5 5 00

Summary

The journal is a chronological record of the business transactions of a firm. The first step in the accounting process is recording the transactions in the journal. Each journal entry should be based on some material evidence that a transaction has occurred, such as a sales invoice, a receipt, a check, etc. The second step in the accounting process is posting to the T accounts in the ledger. This step consists of transferring the amounts to the debit or credit columns of the specified accounts in the ledger, using a cross-reference system. The ledger is the book in which all accounts are kept. Accounts are placed in the ledger according to the account numbers in the chart of accounts. After one has journalized and posted a group of transactions for a period of time, one prepares a trial balance to prove that the totals of the debit balances and of the credit balances of the ledger accounts are equal.

Glossary

Account numbers The numbers assigned to accounts according to the chart of accounts.

Chart of accounts The official list of the ledger accounts in which the transactions of a business are to be recorded.

Journal The book in which a person originally records business transactions; commonly referred to as a *book of original entry*.

Journalizing The process of recording a business transaction in a journal.

Posting The process of recording accounting entries in ledger accounts, the source of information being a journal.

Questions

1. What is the sequence of the accounts in the general ledger?

2. Is it necessary to add the columns of a two-column general journal?

3. What is a chart of accounts?

4. In the process of recording transactions in a journal, which is recorded first, the title of account debited or the title of the account credited?

5. Arrange the following steps in the posting process in proper order. (a) Write the page number of the journal in the Posting reference column of the ledger account. (b) Write the amount of the transaction. (c) Record the ledger account number in the Posting Reference column of the journal. (d) Write the date of the transaction.

6. What is the difference between a journal and a ledger?

7. What is meant by cross reference?

Exercises

Exercise 1 The accounts of Stutzman Realty on December 31 of this year are listed below in alphabetical order. Prepare a trial balance, with a three-line heading, and list the accounts in the proper sequence.

Accounts Payable	$1,400
Office Equipment	6,400
Commissions Income	9,800
Cash	1,000
Accounts Receivable	700
Advertising Expense	1,700
A. R. Stutzman, Capital	1,000
Rent Expense	2,400

Exercise 2 Record the balance of the ledger account shown at the top of the facing page, inserting the appropriate footings.

Accounts Payable

1,200	8,400
2,600	5,200
700	2,400
1,900	

Exercise 3 In the two-column general journal below, the capital letters represent parts of a journal entry. On notebook paper, write the numbers 1 through 8. Alongside each number, write the letter that indicates where in the journal the items are recorded.

GENERAL JOURNAL   PAGE _1_

	DATE			DESCRIPTION	POST REF.	DEBIT	CREDIT	
1	G H	I	J		M	O		1
2			K		N		P	2
3			L					3
4								4
5								5
6								6
7								7
8								8
9								9
10								10

1. Ledger account number of account credited

2. Month

3. Explanation

4. Title of account debited

5. Year

6. Day of the month

7. Title of account credited

8. Amount of debit

Exercise 4 Which of the following errors would cause unequal totals in a trial balance? Explain why.

a. An accountant recorded a $45 payment for advertising as a debit to Advertising Expense of $54 and a credit to Cash of $45.

b. An accountant recorded a withdrawal of $42 in cash by the owner as a debit to Miscellaneous Expense of $42 and a credit Cash of $42.

c. An accountant recorded an $83 payment to a creditor by a debit to Accounts Payable of $38 and a credit to Cash of $38.

Exercise 5 For the State Refrigeration Service, the accountant has recommended the following accounts to be used in recording transactions on the firm's books. On notebook paper, arrange the accounts in a chart of accounts. Use proper headings for each of the five account classifications.

312 A. P. Shull, Drawing
514 Advertising Expense
112 Accounts Receivable
121 Truck
111 Cash
515 Telephone Expense
311 A. P. Shull, Capital
113 Repair Parts
511 Wages Expense
212 Accounts Payable
411 Service Income
122 Shop Equipment
516 Miscellaneous Expense
211 Notes Payable
512 Payroll Tax Expense
513 Truck Operating Expense

Problems

Problem 4-1 The chart of accounts of the Meadowdale Laundry is given below, followed by the transactions that took place during April.

Assets
111 Cash
112 Accounts Receivable
117 Supplies
121 Equipment

Liabilities
211 Accounts Payable

Owner's Equity
311 H. C. Keller, Capital
312 H. C. Keller, Drawing

Revenue
411 Income from Services

Expenses
511 Wages Expense
512 Rent Expense
513 Utilities Expense
514 Repair Expense

April 1 Bought laundry soap on account, $52, from Neher Supply Company.

1 Sold services for cash, $256.

3 Paid rent for April, $250.

5 Received and paid electric bill, $98.

7 Billed Rolland Swim and Tennis Club for services performed, $246.

16 Paid wages to employees, $200, for two weeks.

April 16 Bought equipment on account, $480, from Boswell Equipment Company.

18 Received $220 from Rolland Swim and Tennis Club on account.

19 Sold services for cash, $369.

24 Paid $52 to Neher Supply Company, paying account in full.

26 Billed Hotel Duncan for services performed, $396.

27 Sold services for cash, $390.

30 Received bill for repairs to equipment, $46, Reed's Repair Shop.

31 Paid wages to employees, $260, for two weeks.

31 H. C. Keller withdrew $250 in cash for personal use.

Instructions Record the transactions in a general journal, including a brief explanation for each entry. Number the journal page 28.

Problem 4-2 The journal entries in the workbook relate to Neil's Cleaners for Neil Singleton's second month of operation. The balances of the accounts as of July 1 have been recorded in the accounts in the ledger.

Instructions **1.** Post the journal entries to ledger accounts.

2. Prepare a trial balance as of July 31.

Problem 4-3 Johnston Telephone Answering Service had the following transactions during June of this year. The chart of accounts is as follows.

Assets
111 Cash
112 Accounts Receivable
113 Supplies
121 Office Equipment

Liabilities
211 Accounts Payable

Owner's Equity
311 Jean Johnston, Capital
312 Jean Johnston, Drawing

Revenue
411 Income from Fees

Expenses
511 Rent Expense
512 Equipment Rental Expense
513 Advertising Expense
514 Telephone Expense
515 Utilities Expense
516 Miscellaneous Expense

June 1 Johnston transferred cash from a personal bank account to an account to be used for the business, $1,050.

2 Paid $120 as rental for telephone equipment.

4 Paid cash for stationery and other supplies, $82.

5 Paid rent for the month, $185.

5 Bought desk and chair on account, $165, from Aaron Office Supply Company.

June   7 Bought filing cabinet for cash, $39.

7 Billed charge customers for services rendered, $116.

9 Bought typewriter from Linden Equipment Company for $172. Paid $42 as a down payment; balance is due in 30 days.

11 Received and paid bill for newspaper advertising, $32.

14 Billed charge customers for services rendered, $159.

17 Paid Aaron Office Supply Company $82 to apply on account.

18 Paid $8 for delivery charges (Miscellaneous Expense).

23 Collected $86 from charge customers to apply on account.

28 Received and paid telephone bill, $81.

30 Billed charge customers on account, $410.

30 Received and paid electric bill for the month, $27.

30 Johnston withdrew $260 in cash for personal use.

Instructions **1.** Record the transactions in the general journal, giving a brief explanation for each entry.

2. Post the entries to the ledger accounts.

3. Prepare a trial balance dated June 30.

Problem 4-4. The chart of accounts of R. T. Niven, M. D., is given below, followed by the transactions that took place in September.

Assets
111 Cash
112 Accounts Receivable
113 Supplies
114 Prepaid Insurance
121 Equipment

Liabilities
211 Accounts Payable

Owner's Equity
311 R. T. Niven, Capital
312 R. T. Niven, Drawing

Revenue
411 Professional Fees

Expenses
511 Salary Expense
512 Laboratory Expense
513 Rent Expense
514 Utilities Expense

Sept.   1 Paid office rent for the month, $490.

2 Paid cash for property insurance policy for the year, $62.

3 Paid Nathan Medical Supply Company, a creditor, $696, on account.

6 Bought laboratory equipment from Woods Surgical Supply Company, $940, on account.

9 Received cash on account from patients, $2,842.

Sept. 11 Bought bandages and other supplies from Nathan Medical Supply Company, $112, on account.

14 Billed patients on account for professional services rendered, $1,648.

17 Received and paid bill for laboratory analyses, $184.

20 Received cash for professional services, $316 (patients not billed previously).

26 Received and paid electric bill, $89.

27 Part of the laboratory equipment purchased on September 6 was defective. Returned the equipment and received a reduction in the bill, $120.

29 Received and paid telephone bill for the month, $32.

30 Paid salary of nurse, $790.

30 Billed patients on account for professional services rendered, $1,210.

30 Dr. Niven withdrew $1,100 in cash for personal use.

Instructions **1.** Journalize the transactions for September.

2. Post the entries to the ledger accounts. (Because the professional enterprise was in operation previously, the balances have been recorded in the ledger accounts. A checkmark has been placed in the Post Reference column to represent the various pages of the journal from which the entries were posted.)

3. Prepare a trial balance as of September 30.

Alternate problems

Problem 4-1A The chart of accounts of the Oakland Laundry is given below, after which is a list of the transactions that took place in June.

Assets
111 Cash
112 Accounts Receivable
117 Supplies
121 Equipment

Liabilities
211 Accounts Payable

Owner's Equity
311 L. E. Ford, Capital
312 L. E. Ford, Drawing

Revenue
411 Income from Services

Expenses
511 Wages Expense
512 Rent Expense
513 Utilities Expense
514 Repair Expense

June 1 Sold services for cash, $354.

2 Paid rent for June, $360.

4 Received and paid electric bill, $107.

5 Bought laundry soap on account, $53, from Associated Supply Company.

June 7 Billed Townhouse Hotel for services performed, $304.

16 Paid wages to employees, $250, for two weeks.

19 Bought equipment on account, $515, from Newman Electric.

22 Received $250 from Townhouse Hotel on account.

24 Sold services for cash, $468.

25 Billed Thompson Motel for services performed, $194.

26 Paid $53 to Associated Suppy Company, paying account in full.

28 Sold services for cash, $468.

28 Received bill for repairs to equipment, $43, from Norlin Appliance Repair.

30 Paid wages to employees, $410, for two weeks.

30 L. E. Ford withdrew $325 in cash for personal use.

Instructions Record the transactions in a general journal, including a brief explanation for each entry. Number the journal page 36.

Problem 4-2A The journal entries in the workbook relate to Neil's Cleaners for Neil Singleton's second month of operation. The balances of the accounts as of July 1 have been recorded in the accounts in the ledger.

Instructions 1. Post the journal entries to ledger accounts.

2. Prepare a trial balance as of July 31.

Problem 4-3A Johnston Telephone Answering Service had the following transactions during May of this year. The chart of accounts is as follows.

Assets
111 Cash
112 Accounts Receivable
113 Supplies
121 Office Equipment

Liabilities
211 Accounts Payable

Owner's Equity
311 Jean Johnston, Capital
312 Jean Johnston, Drawing

Revenue
411 Income from Fees

Expenses
511 Rent Expense
512 Equipment Rental Expense
513 Advertising Expense
514 Telephone Expense
515 Utilities Expense
516 Miscellaneous Expense

May 1 Johnston transferred from a personal bank account to an account to be used for the business, $950.

2 Paid $92 as rental for telephone equipment.

3 Bought a filing cabinet for cash, $49.

3 Paid rent for the month, $175.

3 Bought desk and chair on account, $142, from Jacobs and Son.

May 6 Billed charge customers for services rendered, $132.

7 Paid cash for stationery and other supplies, $81.

10 Paid Jacobs and Son $142 in full of account.

10 Bought typewriter for $176; paid $46 as downpayment; balance is due to Harold's Office Supply in 30 days.

14 Billed charge customers for services rendered, $216.

19 Received bill for advertising, $63, from The Daily News.

23 Paid $6 for delivery charges (Miscellaneous Expense).

28 Received and paid telephone bill, $86.

29 Received and paid electric bill for the month, $29.

29 Collected $104 from charge customers to apply on account.

31 Billed charge customers for services rendered, $514.

31 Johnston withdrew $240 in cash for personal use.

Instructions **1.** Record the transactions in the general journal, giving a brief explanation for each entry. Number the page 1.

2. Post to the ledger accounts.

3. Prepare a trial balance dated May 31.

Problem 4-4A The chart of accounts of R. T. Niven, M.D., is shown below, followed by the transactions completed during September.

Assets
111 Cash
112 Accounts Receivable
113 Supplies
114 Prepaid Insurance
121 Equipment

Liabilities
211 Accounts Payable

Owner's Equity
311 R. T. Niven, Capital
312 R. T. Niven, Drawing

Revenue
411 Professional Fees

Expenses
511 Salary Expense
512 Laboratory Expense
513 Rent Expense
514 Utilities Expense

September 3 Paid office rent for the month, $535.

5 Received and paid bill for laboratory analyses, $196.

7 Paid cash for property insurance policy, $56.

9 Bought laboratory equipment on account, $928, from Browning Surgical Supply Company.

11 Received cash on account from patients, $3,168.

12 Billed patients on account for professional services rendered, $2,006.

September 14 Bought bandages and other supplies on account, $121, from Thompson Medical Supply Company.

19 Received and paid telephone bill for the month, $41.

23 Received cash for professional services, $363 (patients not billed previously).

24 Part of the laboratory equipment purchased on Sept. 9 was defective; returned equipment and received a reduction in bill, $52.

30 Billed patients on account for professional services rendered, $1,970.

30 Dr. Niven withdrew $1,200 in cash for personal use.

30 Paid salary of nurse, $820.

30 Received cash for professional services, $426 (patients not billed previously).

Instructions   **1.** Journalize the transactions for September.

2. Post the entries to the ledger accounts. (Because the professional enterprise was in operation previously, the balances have been recorded in the ledger accounts. A checkmark has been placed in the Post Reference column to represent the various pages of the journal from which the entries were posted.)

3. Prepare a trial balance as of September 30.

5 Adjustments and the work sheet

objectives

After you have completed this chapter, you will be able to do the following:
- Complete a work sheet for a service-type enterprise, involving adjustments for supplies consumed, expired insurance, depreciation, and accrued wages.
- Prepare an income statement and a balance sheet for a service-type business directly from the work sheet.
- Journalize the adjusting entries.

NOW THAT you have become familiar with the classifying and recording phase of accounting for a service-type enterprise, let's look at the remaining steps in the accounting procedure, to give you a feel for the scope of accounting operations, as embodied in the accounting cycle.

Fiscal period

The *fiscal period* or *year* is 12 consecutive months. It does not necessarily have to coincide with the calendar year. If a business has seasonal peaks, it's a good idea to complete the accounting operations at the end of the most active season. At that time the management wants to know the results of the year and how they stand financially. As an example, the fiscal period of a resort that is operated during the summer months may be from October 1 of one year to September 30 of the next year. Government, at all levels, has a fiscal period from July 1 of one year to June 30 of the following year. Department stores often use a fiscal period extending from February 1 of one year to January 31 of the next year. For income tax purposes, any period of 12 consecutive months may be selected. However, you have to be consistent and continue to use the same fiscal period.

The accounting cycle

The *accounting cycle* represents the steps that are involved in the accounting process. In Chapter 4 we summarized the first four steps in the accounting cycle. Here are the remaining steps and their placement in this text.

Step	Description	Text Placement
1	Record business transactions in a journal.	
2	Post to the accounts in the ledger.	Chapter 4
3	Prepare a trial balance.	
4	Compile adjustment data and record the adjusting entries in the work sheet.	Chapter 5
5	Complete the work sheet.	
6	Complete the financial statements.	Chapters 1, 2
7	Journalize and post adjusting entries.	Chapter 5
8	Journalize and post closing entries.	Chapter 6
9	Prepare a post-closing trial balance.	Chapter 6

First we shall complete the entire accounting cycle for a service type of business and for a professional enterprise, because the accounting involved in these types of economic units is fairly elementary. That is why we have talked about Neil's Cleaners (representing a service type of business). To show you the accounts for a professional enterprise, Chapter 7 will present the transactions of Dr. John A. Tanner. We'll go through the entire accounting cycle for each of these illustrations.

This summary has brought you up to date on what we have accomplished thus far, and what we hope to do in the future. The chapters that are not listed cover additional topics about the steps in the accounting cycle.

The work sheet

At the moment we are concerned with the *work sheet*. As we said in listing the steps of the accounting cycle, the work sheet is a prelude to the preparation of financial statements. Thus the work sheet serves as a medium for recording necessary adjustments and for furnishing the account balances for making up the income statement and balance sheet. We described the income statement and balance sheet that we looked at in Chapter 2 as being tentative, in that adjustments had not been recorded at that time. Often accountants refer to the work sheet as *working papers,* in the sense that the work sheet is a tool accountants use to bring all the accounts up to date. Accountants use pencil to make entries in the work sheet, since it is a working document.

For our purposes, we will use a ten-column work sheet—so called because two money columns are provided for each of the work sheet's five major sections. We will discuss the function of each of these sections, again illustrating our discussion with the accounting activities of Neil's Cleaners. But first, we will fill in the heading, which consists of three lines: the name of the company, the title of the working paper, and the inclusive period of the time covered.

Neil's Cleaners
Work Sheet
For month ended June 30, 19—

ACCOUNT NAME	TRIAL BALANCE		ADJUSTMENTS		ADJUSTED TRIAL BALANCE		INCOME STATEMENT		BALANCE SHEET	
	DEBIT	CREDIT	DEBIT	CREDIT	DEBIT	CREDIT	DEBIT	CREDIT	DEBIT	CREDIT

The columns of the work sheet

When using a work sheet, you do not have to prepare a trial balance on a separate piece of paper because you enter it in the first two columns of the work sheet. As usual, list the accounts as they appear in the chart of accounts. Thus, in abbreviated form, the accounts are listed in the Trial Balance section of the work sheet as follows:

Trial Balance	
Debit	**Credit**
Assets	
	Liabilities
	Owner's Equity
	Revenue
Expenses	

Entries in the Income Statement section would look like the following when shown in an abbreviated form:

Income Statement	
Debit	**Credit**
	Revenue
Expenses	

Revenue accounts have credit balances, so they are recorded in the Income Statement Credit column. Expense accounts have debit balances, so they are recorded in the Income Statement Debit column.

And in abbreviated form, the accounts in the Balance Sheet section would be recorded as follows:

Balance Sheet	
Debit	**Credit**
Assets	
	Liabilities
	Capital (Owner's Equity)
Drawing	

Asset accounts have debit balances, so they are recorded in the Balance Sheet Debit column. Liability accounts have credit balances, so they are recorded in the Balance Sheet Credit column. The Capital account has a credit balance, so it is recorded in the Balance Sheet Credit column. Because the Drawing account (debit balance) is a deduction from Capital, Drawing is recorded in the Balance Sheet Debit column (the opposite column in which Capital is recorded).

Now we combine all these in the work sheet. It is important that you know the placement of the classifications of accounts in the various columns. Observe that all five classifications are placed in the Trial Balance and Adjusted Trial Balance columns. The up-to-date balances are taken directly from the Adjusted Trial Balance columns, with the revenue and expense accounts in the Income Statement columns, and the assets, liabilities, and owner's equity accounts in the Balance Sheet columns.

Account Classification	Trial Balance		Adjustments		Adjusted Trial Balance		Income Statement		Balance Sheet	
	Debit	**Credit**	**Debit**	**Credit**	**Debit**	**Credit**	**Debit**	**Credit**	**Debit**	**Credit**
Assets	x				x				x	
Liabilities		x				x				x
Capital		x				x				x
Drawing	x				x				x	
Revenue		x				x		x		
Expenses	x				x		x			

Adjustments

Adjustments may be considered *internal transactions*. They have not been recorded in the accounts up to this time because no outside party has been involved. In the steps of the accounting cycle, as stipulated in Chapter 4, one determines the adjustments after the trial balance has been prepared.

The accounts that require adjusting are few in number, and after a limited exposure one can readily recognize them. They are applicable to service as well as merchandising businesses. To describe the reasons for—and techniques of handling—adjustments, let's return to the illustration of Neil's Cleaners. First, let's select the accounts that require adjustments. For the moment, we'll show the adjusting entries by T accounts; later on we'll record them in the work sheet and journalize them.

Supplies   In the trial balance, the Supplies account has a balance of $200. Each time Neil's Cleaners bought supplies, Singleton wrote the entry as a debit to Supplies and a credit to either Cash or Accounts Payable; so he recorded each purchase of supplies as an increase in the Supplies account.

But we haven't taken into consideration the fact that any business is continually using up supplies in the process of carrying on business operations. For Neil's Cleaners, the items recorded under Supplies consist of cleaning fluids. At the end of the month, obviously some of these supplies have been used. It would be very time consuming to keep a continual record of the exact amount of supplies on hand; so at the end of the month someone takes a physical count of the amount on hand.

Accordingly, Singleton takes an inventory on June 30, and he finds that there are $160 worth of supplies left. The situation looks like this:

Had	$200	(Recorded under Supplies)
− Have left	− 160	(Determined by taking an inventory)
= Used	$ 40	(The amount used is an expense of doing business. This is Supplies Expense.)

To bring the books up to date, Singleton has to make an *adjusting entry*. Let's look at this in the form of T accounts.

(a)

Supplies			Supplies Expense		
+		−	+		−
Balance 200	Adjusting 40		Adjusting 40		

Drawing T accounts on scratch paper is an excellent way of organizing the adjusting entry. By making this entry, Singleton has merely taken the amount used out of Supplies and put it into Supplies Expense. The new balance of Supplies, $160, represents the cost of supplies that are on hand and should therefore appear in the balance sheet. The $40 figure in Supplies Expense represents the cost of supplies that have been used and should therefore appear in the income statement.

Prepaid Insurance The $160 balance in Prepaid Insurance stands for the premium paid in advance for a 2-year liability insurance policy. One month of the premium has now expired, which amounts to

$$\underline{\quad\$\ \ 6.67 \text{ per month}\quad}$$
$$24 \text{ months})\$160.00$$

In the adjustment, Singleton deducts the expired or used portion from Prepaid Insurance and transfers it to Insurance Expense.

(b)	**Prepaid Insurance**		**Insurance Expense**	
	+	−	+	−
Balance	160	Adjusting 6.67	Adjusting 6.67	

The new balance of Prepaid Insurance, $153.33 ($160 − $6.67), represents the cost of insurance that is now paid in advance and should therefore appear in the balance sheet. The $6.67 figure in Insurance Expense represents the cost of insurance that has expired and should therefore appear in the income statement.

Depreciation of equipment We have followed the policy of recording durable items such as appliances and fixtures under Equipment, because they will last longer than one year. However, since these assets will eventually have to be replaced, we should systematically apportion their costs over the period of their useful lives. In other words, we write off the cost of the assets as an expense and call it *depreciation,* because such equipment depreciates, or loses usefulness. In the case of Neil's Cleaners, the Equipment account has a balance of $11,140. Suppose that we estimate that Singleton's dry cleaning equipment will have a useful life of 10 years and will have a trade-in value of $340 at the end of 10 years. Therefore, the total depreciation for the estimated useful life of the equipment is $10,800 ($11,140 − $340). The calculation of the depreciation for one month is given below.

$$\underline{\quad\$1,080 \text{ per year}\quad}$$
$$10 \text{ years})\$10,800 \text{ full depreciation}$$

$$\underline{\quad\$\ \ \ 90 \text{ per month}\quad}$$
$$12 \text{ months})\$1,080$$

One always records this as a debit to Depreciation Expense and a credit to Accumulated Depreciation. The adjustment in T account form would appear as follows.

(c)	**Depreciation Expense**		**Accumulated Depreciation**	
	+	−	−	+
Adjusting	90			Adjusting 90

On the balance sheet, the balance of Accumulated Depreciation is a deduction from the balance of the related asset account as illustrated below on the partial balance sheet for Neil's Cleaners.

Neil's Cleaners			
Balance Sheet			
June 30, 19—			
Assets			
Equipment	11 140 00		
Less Accumulated Depreciation		90 00	11 050 00

Accumulated Depreciation is contrary to Equipment, so we call it a *contra account*. To show the accounts under their proper headings, let's look at the fundamental accounting equation. (Brackets indicate that Accumulated Depreciation is a deduction from the Equipment account.)

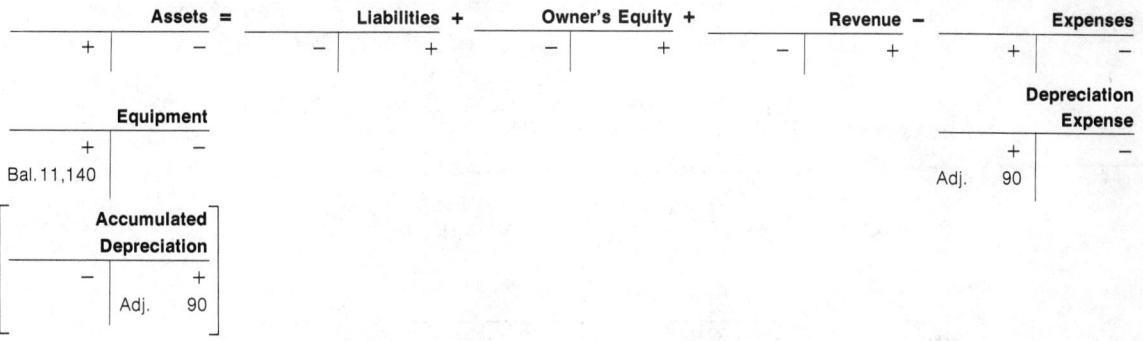

Incidentally, there are a number of legally acceptable ways of computing depreciation. The method illustrated here is the *straight-line method,* in which one apportions the cost of the asset, less any trade-in value, on an average basis over the useful life of the asset. Regardless of the method used, however, the accounts that are debited and credited are always the same. Accumulated Depreciation, as the title implies, is the total depreciation that the owner has taken since the original purchase of the asset. Rather than crediting the Equipment account, Singleton uses a separate account to keep track of the total depreciation that he has taken since he first acquired the asset. The maximum depreciation that he could take would be the cost of the equipment, which in this case is $11,140. So, month after month, the Accumulated Depreciation will increase at the rate of $90 per month, assuming that he hasn't bought any additional equipment. The *book value* of an asset is the cost of the asset minus the accumulated depreciation.

Wages expense Usually the end of the fiscal period and the end of the employees' payroll period do not fall on the same day. By diagram it looks like this.

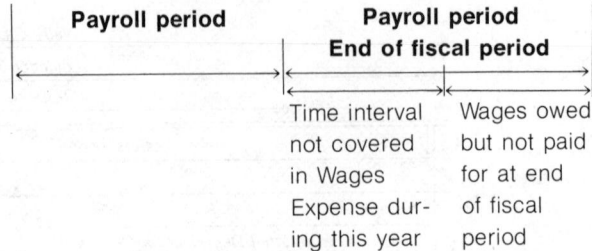

As an illustration, assume that a firm pays its employees a total of $200 per day and that payday falls on Friday throughout the year. When the employees pick up their paychecks on Friday, at the end of the work day, the amount of the checks includes their wages for that day as well as for the preceding 4 days. The employees work a 5-day week. And suppose that the last day of the fiscal period falls on Wednesday, December 31. We can diagram this as shown in the following illustration.

				Dec. 26	Dec. 29	Dec. 30	Dec. 31	End of fiscal year	Jan. 2
Mon	Tue	Wed	Thur	Fri	Mon	Tue	Wed	Thur	Fri
200	200	200	200	200	200	200	200	200	200

←————Payroll period————→ ←————Payroll period————→

Payday $1,000 (after Dec. 26 column)   Payday $1,000 (after Jan. 2 column)

December

S	M	T	W	T	F	S
	1	2	3	4	(5)	6
7	8	9	10	11	(12)	13
14	15	16	17	18	(19)	20
21	22	23	24	25	(26)	27
28	29	30	31			

— Paydays

In order to have the Wages Expense account reflect a more accurate balance, you should add $600 for the cost of labor between the last payday, December 26, and the end of the year, December 31 (for December 29, $200; for December 30, $200; for December 31, $200). Because the $600 is owed to the employees at December 31, you should also add $600 to the liabilities account, Wages Payable.

Wages Expense		Wages Payable	
+	−	−	+
Adjusting 600			Adjusting 600

Returning to our illustration of Neil's Cleaners: The last payday was June 24. Neil's Cleaners owes an additional $50 in wages at the end of the month. Accountants refer to this extra amount that has not been recorded at the end of the month as being *accrued.*

Wages Expense		Wages Payable	
+	−	−	+
Balance 315			Adjusting 50
Adjusting 50			

First we have to enter the adjustments in the work sheet. But before doing so, let's digress briefly to recapitulate the work sheet, with the addition of the drawing and accumulated depreciation accounts, as well as the net income. The drawing account looks like this:

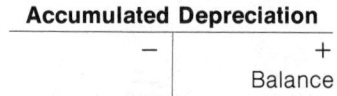

Neil Singleton, Drawing

+	−
Balance	

Drawing is a deduction from capital and is shown in the column opposite the normal balance of the capital account.

The accumulated depreciation account looks like this:

Accumulated Depreciation

−	+
	Balance

Accumulated depreciation is a deduction from the respective asset account; and, as we have said, it is shown in the column opposite the normal balance of the asset account. *Net income* is the difference between revenue and expenses. It is used to balance off the Income Statement columns; and, since revenue is normally larger than expenses, the balancing-off amount must be added to the expense side. Net income (or net loss) is also used to balance off the Balance Sheet columns. And, as in the statement of owner's equity itself, one adds net income to the owner's equity; similarly, one deducts net loss from owner's equity. The illustration at the top of page 104 shows these relationships in diagram form.

Account Name	Trial Balance		Adjustments		Adjusted Trial Balance		Income Statement		Balance Sheet	
	Debit	Credit	Debit	Credit	Debit	Credit	Debit	Credit	Debit	Credit
	A	L			A	L	E	R	A	L
	+	+			+	+			+	+
	E	Cap.			E	Cap.			Draw.	Cap.
	+	+			+	+				+
	Draw.	R			Draw.	R				Accum.
		+				+				Depr.
		Accum.				Accum.				
		Depr.				Depr.				
Net Income							NI			NI

On the other hand, if expenses are larger than revenue, the result is a net loss. One must add net loss to the revenue side to balance off the Income Statement columns. Also, because one deducts a net loss from the owner's equity, one includes net loss in the debit side of the Balance Sheet columns, thereby balancing off these columns. To show this, let's look at the Income Statement and Balance Sheet columns diagramed here.

	Income Statement		Balance Sheet	
	Debit	Credit	Debit	Credit
	E	R	A	L
			+	+
			Draw.	Cap.
				+
				Accum.
				Depr.
Net Loss		NL	NL	

Summary of adjustments by T accounts

To test your understanding, try to mentally form the reasons why the following adjustments are necessary. The answers are shown below the accounts.

Supplies			Supplies Expense	
+		−	+	−
(a) Balance 200	Adjusting 40		Adjusting 40	

Prepaid Insurance			Insurance Expense	
+		−	+	−
(b) Balance 160	Adjusting 6.67		Adjusting 6.67	

Depreciation Expense			Accumulated Depreciation	
+		−	−	+
(c) Adjusting 90				Adjusting 90

	Wages Expense	Wages Payable

	+		−	−	+
(d) Balance	315			Adjusting	50
Adjusting	50				

(a) To record the cost of supplies used during June
(b) To record the insurance expired during June
(c) To record the depreciation for the month of June
(d) To record accrued wages owed at the end of June

Recording the adjustments in the work sheet

As a means of explaining the handling of adjustments in the examples above, we have used T accounts. T accounts, as you are aware, represent a reliable method of organizing any type of accounting entry.

After the trial balance has been completed in the first two columns of the work sheet, enter the adjustments directly in the Adjustments columns.

Adjustments columns of the work sheet

When we enter the adjustments, we identify them as (a), (b), (c), and (d) to indicate the relationships between the debits and the credits.

Neil's Cleaners
Work Sheet
For month ended June 30, 19—

ACCOUNT NAME	TRIAL BALANCE		ADJUSTMENTS	
	DEBIT	CREDIT	DEBIT	CREDIT
Cash	5 8 3 0 00			
Accounts Receivable	1 0 00			
Supplies	2 0 0 00			(a) 4 0 00
Prepaid Insurance	1 6 0 00			(b) 6 67
Equipment	11 1 4 0 00			
Accounts Payable		9 4 0 00		
Neil Singleton, Capital		16 0 0 0 00		
Neil Singleton, Drawing	5 0 0 00			
Income from Services		1 6 1 5 00		
Wages Expense	3 1 5 00		(d) 5 0 00	
Rent Expense	2 0 0 00			
Advertising Expense	9 0 00			
Utilities Expense	1 1 0 00			
	18 5 5 5 00	18 5 5 5 00		
Supplies Expense			(a) 4 0 00	
Insurance Expense			(b) 6 67	
Depreciation Expense			(c) 9 0 00	
Accumulated Depreciation				(c) 9 0 00
Wages Payable				(d) 5 0 00
			1 8 6 67	1 8 6 67

Note that Supplies Expense, Insurance Expense, Depreciation Expense, and Wages Payable did not appear in the trial balance because there were no balances in the accounts to record. So we wrote them below the Trial Balance totals. Some people consider them to be new accounts, because they were never used during the fiscal period. But observe that they all have one thing in common: *They are all increased.* In other words, one brings a new account into existence in order to increase it; definitely not to decrease it. This hint can help you when it comes to formulating any adjusting entry. After the first fiscal period, Accumulated Depreciation will always have a balance, and consequently will be included in the trial balance.

Now we include the Adjusted Trial Balance columns, as shown below, bringing the balances of the accounts that were adjusted up to date.

Neil's

Work

For month ended

ACCOUNT NAME	TRIAL BALANCE		ADJUSTMENTS	
	DEBIT	CREDIT	DEBIT	CREDIT
Cash	5 8 3 0 00			
Accounts Receivable	1 0 00			
Supplies	2 0 0 00			(a) 4 0 00
Prepaid Insurance	1 6 0 00			(b) 6 67
Equipment	11 1 4 0 00			
Accounts Payable		9 4 0 00		
Neil Singleton, Capital		16 0 0 0 00		
Neil Singleton, Drawing	5 0 0 00			
Income from Services		1 6 1 5 00		
Wages Expense	3 1 5 00		(d) 5 0 00	
Rent Expense	2 0 0 00			
Advertising Expense	9 0 00			
Utilities Expense	1 1 0 00			
	18 5 5 5 00	18 5 5 5 00		
Supplies Expense			(a) 4 0 00	
Insurance Expense			(b) 6 67	
Depreciation Expense			(c) 9 0 00	
Accumulated Depreciation				(c) 9 0 00
Wages Payable				(d) 5 0 00
			1 8 6 67	1 8 6 67

After we get to the stage at which the Adjusted Trial Balance columns are completed, then we go through the mental process of classifying the accounts so that we know where to place the classifications in the various columns; and we enter each account balance in the appropriate column. We now carry forward the amounts in the Adjusted Trial Balance columns to the remaining four columns, recording each amount in only one column. The completed work sheet is shown on pages 108 and 109.

Accountants refer to accounts such as Supplies and Prepaid Insurance, as they appear in the trial balance, as being *mixed accounts*—accounts with balances that are partly income statement amounts and partly balance sheet amounts. For example, Supplies is recorded as $200 in the Trial Balance, but after adjustment this is apportioned as $40 in Supplies Expense in the Income

Cleaners
Sheet
June 30, 19—

ADJUSTED TRIAL BALANCE		INCOME STATEMENT		BALANCE SHEET		
DEBIT	CREDIT	DEBIT	CREDIT	DEBIT	CREDIT	
5 830 00						1
10 00						2
160 00						3
153 33						4
11 140 00						5
	940 00					6
	16 000 00					7
500 00						8
	1 615 00					9
365 00						10
200 00						11
90 00						12
110 00						13
						14
40 00						15
6 67						16
90 00						17
	90 00					18
	50 00					19
18 695 00	18 695 00					20

ACCOUNT NAME	TRIAL BALANCE DEBIT	TRIAL BALANCE CREDIT	ADJUSTMENTS DEBIT	ADJUSTMENTS CREDIT
Cash	5 8 3 0 00			
Accounts Receivable	1 0 00			
Supplies	2 0 0 00			(a) 4 0 00
Prepaid Insurance	1 6 0 00			(b) 6 67
Equipment	11 1 4 0 00			
Accounts Payable		9 4 0 00		
Neil Singleton, Capital		16 0 0 0 00		
Neil Singleton, Drawing	5 0 0 00			
Income from Services		1 6 1 5 00		
Wages Expense	3 1 5 00		(d) 5 0 00	
Rent Expense	2 0 0 00			
Advertising Expense	9 0 00			
Utilities Expense	1 1 0 00			
	18 5 5 5 00	18 5 5 5 00		
Supplies Expense			(a) 4 0 00	
Insurance Expense			(b) 6 67	
Depreciation Expense			(c) 9 0 00	
Accumulated Depreciation				(c) 9 0 00
Wages Payable				(d) 5 0 00
			1 8 6 67	1 8 6 67
Net Income				

Statement columns and $160 in Supplies in the Balance Sheet columns. Similarly, Prepaid Insurance is recorded as $160 in the trial balance, but is apportioned as $6.67 in Insurance Expense in the Income Statement columns and as $153.33 in Prepaid Insurance in the Balance Sheet columns. In other words, portions of these accounts are recorded in each section.

	ADJUSTED TRIAL BALANCE		INCOME STATEMENT		BALANCE SHEET		
	DEBIT	CREDIT	DEBIT	CREDIT	DEBIT	CREDIT	
1	5 8 3 0 00				5 8 3 0 00		
2	1 0 00				1 0 00		
3	1 6 0 00				1 6 0 00		
4	1 5 3 33				1 5 3 33		
5	11 1 4 0 00				11 1 4 0 00		
6		9 4 0 00				9 4 0 00	
7		16 0 0 0 00				16 0 0 0 00	
8	5 0 0 00				5 0 0 00		
9		1 6 1 5 00		1 6 1 5 00			
10	3 6 5 00		3 6 5 00				
11	2 0 0 00		2 0 0 00				
12	9 0 00		9 0 00				
13	1 1 0 00		1 1 0 00				
14							
15	4 0 00		4 0 00				
16	6 67		6 67				
17	9 0 00		9 0 00				
18		9 0 00				9 0 00	
19		5 0 00				5 0 00	
20	18 6 9 5 00	18 6 9 5 00	9 0 1 67	1 6 1 5 00	17 7 9 3 33	17 0 8 0 00	
21			7 1 3 33			7 1 3 33	
22			1 6 1 5 00	1 6 1 5 00	17 7 9 3 33	17 7 9 3 33	

Completion of the financial statements

We now prepare the income statement, the statement of owner's equity, and the balance sheet, taking the figures directly from the work sheet. These statements are shown on pages 110 and 111.

Note that one records Accumulated Depreciation in the asset section of the balance sheet as a direct deduction from Equipment. As we have said, ac-

Neil's Cleaners
Income Statement
For month ended June 30, 19—

Revenue:		
Income from Services		1 6 1 5 00
Expenses:		
Wages Expense	3 6 5 00	
Rent Expense	2 0 0 00	
Utilities Expense	1 1 0 00	
Depreciation Expense	9 0 00	
Advertising Expense	9 0 00	
Supplies Expense	4 0 00	
Insurance Expense	6 67	
Total Expenses		9 0 1 67
Net Income		7 1 3 33

Neil's Cleaners
Statement of Owner's Equity
For month ended June 30, 19—

Neil Singleton, Capital, June 1, 19—		16 0 0 0 00
Net Income for month of June	7 1 3 33	
Less: Withdrawals for month of June	5 0 0 00	
Increase in Capital		2 1 3 33
Neil Singleton, Capital, June 30, 19—		16 2 1 3 33

Assets			
Cash			5 8 3 0 00
Accounts Receivable			1 0 00
Supplies			1 6 0 00
Prepaid Insurance			1 5 3 33
Equipment	11 1 4 0 00		
Less Accumulated Depreciation		9 0 00	11 0 5 0 00
Total Assets			17 2 0 3 33
Liabilities			
Accounts Payable	9 4 0 00		
Wages Payable	5 0 00		
Total Liabilities			9 9 0 00
Owner's Equity			
Neil Singleton, Capital			16 2 1 3 33
Total Liabilities and Owner's Equity			17 2 0 3 33

countants refer to it as a *contra account*, because it is contrary to its companion account. The difference, $11,050, is called the *book value*, because it represents the cost of the assets after the Accumulated Depreciation has been deducted.

In the example of Neil's Cleaners, Equipment is the only type of asset that is subject to depreciation, so the related accounts are simply titled Depreciation Expense and Accumulated Depreciation. On the other hand, if Neil's Cleaners buys a building that is also subject to depreciation, Neil's would have to separate the depreciation taken on the equipment from the depreciation taken on the building. As a result, separate related accounts would be set up for each type of asset: Depreciation Expense, Equipment and Accumulated Depreciation, Equipment; Depreciation Expense, Building and Accumulated Depreciation, Building.

To illustrate the placement of these accounts in a balance sheet, let's use another example. Standard Travel Agency has the following balance sheet:

Standard Travel Agency		
Balance Sheet		
September 30, 19—		
Assets		
Cash		6 2 4 0 00
Supplies		2 0 0 00
Office Equipment	4 6 0 0 00	
Less Accumulated Depreciation	2 2 0 0 00	2 4 0 0 00
Building	26 7 0 0 00	
Less Accumulated Depreciation	1 4 0 0 00	25 3 0 0 00
Land		4 4 0 0 00
Total Assets		38 5 4 0 00
Liabilities		
Accounts Payable		2 8 0 0 00
Owner's Equity		
Stanley C. Clay, Capital		35 7 4 0 00
Total Liabilities and Owner's Equity		38 5 4 0 00

Land supposedly will last forever; consequently, land is not depreciated. Previously, in the work sheet separate adjustments would have been made for depreciation of office equipment and building.

Adjusting entries

In order to change the balance of an account, you need a journal entry as evidence of the change. Up to this time, we have been listing adjustments in the Adjustments columns of the work sheet only. Since this does not constitute a journal, you must journalize the entries. You can take the information of these entries directly from the Adjustments columns of the work sheet, debiting and crediting exactly the same accounts.

In the Description column of the general journal, write "Adjusting Entries," and this does away with the need to write explanations for each entry. The adjusting entries for Neil's Cleaners are shown atop page 113.

DATE		DESCRIPTION	POST REF.	DEBIT	CREDIT
		Adjusting Entries			
19– Jun.	30	*Supplies Expense*		4 0 00	
		Supplies			4 0 00
	30	*Insurance Expense*		6 67	
		Prepaid Insurance			6 67
	30	*Depreciation Expense*		9 0 00	
		Accumulated Depreciation			9 0 00
	30	*Wages Expense*		5 0 00	
		Wages Payable			5 0 00

When you post the adjusting entries to the ledger accounts, write the word "Adjusting" in the Item column of the ledger account. For example, the adjusting entry for Supplies is posted as shown below.

GENERAL LEDGER

ACCOUNT _____ *Supplies* _____ ACCOUNT NO. ___ 113 ___

DATE		ITEM	POST. REF.	DEBIT	CREDIT	BALANCE	
						DEBIT	CREDIT
19– Jun.	4		1	2 0 0 00		2 0 0 00	
	30	*Adjusting*	4		4 0 00	1 6 0 00	

ACCOUNT _____ *Supplies Expense* _____ ACCOUNT NO. ___ 515 ___

DATE		ITEM	POST. REF.	DEBIT	CREDIT	BALANCE	
						DEBIT	CREDIT
19– Jun.	30	*Adjusting*	4	4 0 00		4 0 00	

Summary

The steps in the accounting cycle that we have talked about up to this point are as listed here.

1. Record business transactions in a journal, from source documents.

2. Post to the accounts in the ledger.

3. Record the trial balance in the first two columns of the work sheet.

4. Record any adjustments in the work sheet.

5. Complete the work sheet.

6. Prepare the financial statements.

7. Record adjusting entries in the journal and post to the ledger accounts.

Adjustments are necessary to bring the accounts up to date. One first records adjustments in the work sheet, but in order to do so, one must know the classification of accounts that occupy the various columns of the work sheet. After the work sheet is completed and the financial statements are prepared, the adjusting entries must be journalized. This is accomplished by taking the information of these entries directly from the Adjustments column of the work sheet, debiting and crediting exactly the same accounts.

Glossary

Accounting cycle The steps in the accounting process that are completed during the fiscal period.

Accrued wages The amount of wages owed to employees for the time between the last payday and the end of the fiscal period.

Adjustments Internal transactions that bring ledger accounts up to date, as a planned part of the accounting procedure. They are first recorded in the Adjustments columns of the work sheet.

Book value The cost of an asset minus the accumulated depreciation.

Contra account An account that is contrary to, or a deduction from, another account; for example, Accumulated Depreciation entered as a deduction from Equipment.

Depreciation An expense, based on the expectation that an asset will gradually decline in usefulness due to time, wear and tear, or obsolescence; the cost of the asset is therefore spread out over its estimated useful life. A portion of depreciation expense is apportioned to each fiscal period.

Fiscal period The period of time covered by the entire accounting cycle, generally consisting of 12 consecutive months.

Mixed accounts The balances of certain accounts that appear in the trial balance that are partly income statement accounts and partly balance sheet accounts—for example, Prepaid Insurance and Supplies.

Straight-line method A means of calculating depreciation by taking the cost of an asset, less any trade-in value, and allocating this amount, on an average basis, over the useful life of the asset.

1. If it is agreed that there is a need to make adjusting entries at the end of a fiscal period, does this mean that errors were made in the accounts during the period? Explain.

2. Why is it necessary to journalize adjusting entries?

3. What is meant by a mixed account? Give an example.

4. What is a contra account? Give an example.

5. What is the nature of the balance in the prepaid insurance account at the end of the fiscal period (a) before the adjusting entry? (b) after the adjusting entry?

6. In which column of a work sheet (Income Statement columns or Balance Sheet columns) would the adjusted balances of the following accounts appear?

(a) Depreciation Expense   **(e)** Insurance Expense
(b) Prepaid Insurance   **(f)** Supplies
(c) Wages Payable   **(g)** Accumulated Depreciation
(d) Income from Services   **(h)** C. D. Jones, Drawing

7. At the end of the fiscal period, the usual adjusting entry to record supplies used was unintentionally omitted. What is the effect of the omission on (a) the amount of net income for the period? (b) the balance sheet as of the end of the fiscal period?

Exercises

Exercise 1   Journalize the necessary adjusting entries at June 30, the close of the current fiscal year, based on the following data.

a. The supplies account before adjustments on June 30 has a balance of $1,490. By taking a physical inventory, you now determine that the amount of supplies on hand is worth $290.

b. The last payday was June 26. From June 27 to 30, $680 of wages accrue.

c. The Prepaid Insurance account before adjustments on June 30 has a balance of $980. You now figure out that $400 worth of insurance has expired during the year.

Exercise 2   From the ledger accounts for Supplies, determine the missing figures.

a.

Supplies			
Balance	220	Used	(?)
Bought	914		
End Inv.	200		

b.

Supplies			
Balance	220	Used	730
Bought	868		
End Inv.	(?)		

c.

Supplies			
Balance	(?)	Used	316
Bought	460		
End Inv.	200		

d.

Supplies			
Balance	742	Used	900
Bought	(?)		
End Inv.	140		

Exercise 3 From the following ledger accounts, journalize the adjusting entries.

Wages Expense	
4,340	
127	

Supplies Expense	
517	

Accumulated Depreciation	
	2,614
	720

Prepaid Taxes	
930	310

Taxes Expense	
310	

Insurance Expense	
150	

Supplies	
927	517

Depreciation Expense	
720	

Prepaid Insurance	
600	150

Wages Payable	
	127

Exercise 4 Record the adjusting entry in each of the following situations.

Supplies	
+	−
Bal. 140	
Purch. 600	

Supplies Expense	
+	−

Ending Inventory, $120.

Supplies	
+	−
Bal. 300	
Purch. 960	

Supplies Expense	
+	−

Supplies used, $720.

Exercise 5 Using a form similar to the one shown, list the following in all the columns in which they appear in the work sheet, with the exception of the Adjustments columns: Liabilities, Drawing, Capital, Expenses, Accumulated Depreciation, Revenue, Net Income, Drawing. (*Example:* Assets)

Trial Balance		Adjustments		Adjusted Trial Balance		Income Statement		Balance Sheet	
Debit	Credit	Debit	Credit	Debit	Credit	Debit	Credit	Debit	Credit
Assets				Assets				Assets	

Exercise 6 Journalize the year-end adjusting entry for each of the following.

a. The supplies account had a $160 balance on January 1, the beginning of the year;

$400 of supplies were bought during the year; the year-end inventory shows that $200 worth of supplies are still on hand.

b. Five employees earn a total of $240 per day for a 5-day week beginning on Monday and ending on Friday. They all worked on Monday, December 30, and Tuesday, December 31.

c. The payment of the $360 insurance premium for 3 years in advance was originally recorded as Prepaid Insurance. Six months of the policy has now expired.

d. Depreciation of equipment was estimated at $4,800 for the year.

Exercise 7 If the required adjusting entries for Exercise 6 were not made at the end of the year, what would be the effect of the omissions on the net income?

Problems

Problem 5-1 Here is the trial balance for the C. N. Ruhl Insurance Agency as of April 30, after the firm has completed its first month of operations.

C.N. Ruhl Insurance Agency						
Trial Balance						
April 30, 19—						
Cash	2 5 1 6	00				
Accounts Receivable	1 2 0 8	00				
Prepaid Insurance	2 7 2	00				
Office Equipment	3 8 4 0	00				
Accounts Payable			9 6 2	00		
C.N. Ruhl, Capital			6 6 2 8	00		
C.N. Ruhl, Drawing	6 0 0	00				
Commissions Earned			1 4 9 0	00		
Rent Expense	3 0 0	00				
Advertising Expense	1 5 6	00				
Travel Expense	1 1 4	00				
Utility Expense	6 0	00				
Miscellaneous Expense	1 4	00				
	9 0 8 0	00	9 0 8 0	00		

Instructions

1. Record the trial balance in the Trial Balance columns of the work sheet.

2. Record the letters standing for the account classifications at the top of each column of the work sheet.

3. Complete the work sheet. Data for the adjustments: Depreciation expense of office equipment, $22; expired insurance, $23.

Problem 5-2 The Workbook presents the completed work sheet for C. E. Karns, Attorney at Law, for Karn's law practice for September.

Instructions 1. Prepare an income statement.

2. Prepare a statement of owner's equity.

3. Prepare a balance sheet.

4. Journalize the adjusting entries.

Problem 5-3 The trial balance of Napa Coin-Operated Laundry at December 31, the end of the current year, is presented below.

Napa Coin-Operated Laundry		
Trial Balance		
December 31, 19–		
Cash	2 4 6 2 00	
Laundry Supplies	2 9 1 3 00	
Prepaid Insurance	4 6 8 00	
Furniture and Equipment	32 8 2 4 00	
Accumulated Depreciation, Furniture and Equipment		9 7 6 0 00
Accounts Payable		3 2 9 00
S.D. Pavlof, Capital		24 3 7 8 00
S.D. Pavlof, Drawing	9 2 6 0 00	
Income from Services		29 8 1 7 00
Wages Expense	10 4 0 0 00	
Rent Expense	3 6 0 0 00	
Utilities Expense	1 5 7 0 00	
Advertising Expense	4 2 9 00	
Miscellaneous Expense	3 5 8 00	
	64 2 8 4 00	64 2 8 4 00

Data needed for year-end adjustments are as follows.

a. Inventory of laundry supplies at December 31, $943.

b. Insurance expired during the year, $242.

c. Depreciation of furniture and equipment, $1,720.

d. Wages accrued at December 31, $126.

Instructions 1. Complete the work sheet.

2. Journalize the adjusting entries.

Problem 5-4 The trial balance of Leisure Lanes, a bowling alley, as of December 31, the end of the current year, is as follows.

Leisure Lanes

Trial Balance

December 31, 19—

Cash	2 8 5 4 00	
Supplies	8 9 6 00	
Prepaid Insurance	6 5 0 00	
Bowling Equipment	88 7 2 0 00	
Accumulated Depreciation, Bowling Equipment		58 7 0 0 00
Furniture and Fixtures	8 6 0 0 00	
Accumulated Depreciation, Furniture and Fixtures		4 2 8 0 00
Building	82 8 0 0 00	
Accumulated Depreciation, Building		24 0 0 0 00
Land	9 0 0 0 00	
Accounts Payable		4 1 8 0 00
Mortgage Payable		56 0 0 0 00
T. L. Andrews, Capital		35 6 6 8 00
T. L. Andrews, Drawing	14 0 0 0 00	
Bowling Fees Income		42 7 2 1 00
Concession Income		6 1 4 2 00
Wages Expense	15 8 0 0 00	
Advertising Expense	3 9 6 0 00	
Repair Expense	2 2 7 8 00	
Utilities Expense	1 6 4 0 00	
Miscellaneous Expense	4 9 3 00	
	231 6 9 1 00	231 6 9 1 00

Data for year-end adjustments are as follows.

a. Inventory of supplies at December 31, $318.

b. Insurance expired during the year, $420.

c. Depreciation of bowling equipment during the year, $15,200.

d. Depreciation of furniture and fixtures during the year, $1,560.

e. Depreciation of building during the year, $2,840.

f. Wages accrued at December 31, $348.

Instructions **a.** Complete the work sheet.

b. Journalize the adjusting entries.

Alternate problems

Problem 5-1A The trial balance of the A. L. Cook Company as of November 30, after the company has completed the first month of operations, is as follows:

A. L. Cook Company																				
Trial Balance																				
November 30, 19—																				
Cash			3	8	2	7	00													
Accounts Receivable			6	2	1	4	00													
Office Equipment			4	8	2	0	00													
Accounts Payable											7	6	4	00						
A. L. Cook, Capital									12	1	3	8	00							
A. L. Cook, Drawing			1	4	0	0	00													
Commissions Earned											4	6	7	0	00					
Salary Expense				9	0	0	00													
Rent Expense				2	5	0	00													
Advertising Expense					9	5	00													
Utilities Expense					4	0	00													
Miscellaneous Expenses					2	6	00													
			17	5	7	2	00			17	5	7	2	00						

Instructions **1.** Record the trial balance in the Trial Balance columns of the work sheet.

2. Record the letters standing for the account classifications at the top of each column of the work sheet.

3. Complete the work sheet. Data for the adjustments: Depreciation expense of office equipment, $114; accrued salaries, $130.

Problem 5-2A The Workbook presents the completed work sheet for C. E. Karns, Attorney at Law, for Karn's law practice for September.

Instructions **1.** Prepare an income statement.

2. Prepare a statement of owner's equity.

3. Prepare a balance sheet.

4. Journalize the adjusting entries.

Problem 5-3A The trial balance of the Alexander's Beauty Salon as of December 31, the end of the current year, is presented below.

Alexander's Beauty Salon
Trial Balance
December 31, 19–

Cash	1 3 2 0 00	
Beauty Supplies	3 1 6 2 00	
Prepaid Insurance	3 2 8 00	
Shop Equipment	38 7 9 0 00	
Accumulated Depreciation, Shop Equipment		17 6 4 0 00
Accounts Payable		5 2 6 00
D. E. Alexander, Capital		24 1 4 4 00
D. E. Alexander, Drawing	11 6 0 0 00	
Income from Services		25 7 1 4 00
Wages Expense	9 6 0 0 00	
Rent Expense	2 4 0 0 00	
Utilities Expense	5 1 8 00	
Telephone Expense	1 2 0 00	
Miscellaneous Expense	1 8 6 00	
	68 0 2 4 00	68 0 2 4 00

Data for the adjustments:

a. Inventory of beauty supplies at December 31, $728.

b. Insurance expires during the year, $142.

c. Depreciation of shop equipment during the year, $1,680.

d. Wages accrued at December 31, $120.

Instructions **1.** Complete the work sheet.

2. Journalize the adjusting entries.

Problem 5-4A The trial balance for Play-time Miniature Golf at October 31, the end of the current year, is as shown on page 122.

Play-time Miniature Golf											
Trial Balance											
October 31, 19—											
Cash		1	8	6	8	00					
Supplies			4	1	7	00					
Prepaid Insurance			5	4	0	00					
Golf Clubs			7	4	9	00					
Field Equipment		28	7	6	0	00					
Accumulated Depreciation, Field Equipment							7	1	2	0	00
Lighting Fixtures		1	9	1	6	00					
Accumulated Depreciation, Lighting Fixtures								4	1	8	00
Accounts Payable								4	2	1	00
Notes Payable								9	4	0	00
L. C. Mayer, Capital							26	9	3	5	00
L. C. Mayer, Drawing			5	6	8	0	00				
Golf Fees Income							22	7	2	8	00
Concession Income								9	6	1	00
Wages Expense		16	7	5	0	00					
Repair Expense		2	0	8	4	00					
Advertising Expense			5	2	0	00					
Miscellaneous Expense			2	3	9	00					
		59	5	2	3	00	59	5	2	3	00

Data for year-end adjustments are as follows.

a. Inventory of supplies at October 31, $210.

b. Insurance expired during the year, $188.

c. Depreciation of field equipment during the year, $3,750.

d. Depreciation of lighting fixtures during the year, $410.

e. Wages accrued at October 31, $290.

Instructions   **1.** Complete the work sheet.

2. Journalize the adjusting entries.

6 Closing entries and the post-closing trial balance

objectives

After you have completed this chapter, you will be able to do the following:
- Journalize and post closing entries for a service-type enterprise.
- Prepare a post-closing trial balance for any type of enterprise.

IN THE ACCOUNTING cycle, after you have prepared the financial statements from the work sheet and journalized and posted the adjusting entries, the remaining steps consist of (1) journalizing and posting the closing entries, and (2) preparing a post-closing trial balance.

In this chapter we shall explain the functions and procedures for accomplishing these final steps in the accounting cycle.

Interim statements

Interim statements consist of the financial statements that are prepared during the fiscal year for periods of *less* than 12 months. For example, a business may prepare the income statement, the statement of owner's equity, and the balance sheet *monthly*. These statements provide up-to-date information about the results and status of operations. Suppose a company has a fiscal period extending from January 1 of one year through December 31 of the same year; it might have the following interim statements.

	Jan. 1	Jan. 31	Feb. 28	Mar. 31	Apr. 30
		Income statement for month ended Jan. 31	Income statement for month ended Feb. 28	Income statement for month ended Mar. 31	Income statement for month ended April 30	
Beginning of fiscal period		Balance sheet dated Jan. 31	Balance sheet dated Feb. 28	Balance sheet dated Mar. 31	Balance sheet dated Apr. 30

Income statement for 2 months ended Feb. 28

Income statement for 3 months ended March 31

Income statement for 4 months ended April 30

In this case, the company would prepare statements of owner's equity for the same periods as the income statements.

With respect to the accounting cycle, the work sheet and the financial statements would be completed. However, the accountant would perform the remaining steps—consisting of the journalizing of adjusting and closing entries and the preparation of the post-closing trial balance—only at the end of the fiscal period. Just for the sake of illustration and practice in the text, however, let's take a fiscal period, with the closing entries and post-closing trial balance, which consists of one month. We need to do this for practical purposes, so that we can thoroughly cover the material. Let us now proceed with these latter steps.

Closing entries

So that you will understand the reason for the closing entries, let us first repeat the fundamental accounting equation:

$$\text{Assets} = \text{Liabilities} + \text{Owner's Equity} + \text{Revenue} - \text{Expenses} - Drawing$$

We know that the income statement, as stated in the third line of its heading, is for a definite period of time. It consists of revenue minus expenses for this period of time only. So, when this period is over, we should start from zero for the next period. In other words, we wipe the slate clean, so that we can start all over again next period.

Purposes of closing entries

This brings us to the *purpose* of the closing entries, which is to close off the revenue and expense accounts. We do this because their balances apply to only one fiscal period. As stated before, with the coming of the next fiscal period, we want to start from scratch, recording brand-new revenue and expenses. Accountants also refer to this as *clearing the accounts*. For income tax purposes, this is certainly understandable. No one wants to pay income tax more than once on the same income, and the Internal Revenue Service frowns on counting an expense more than once. So now we have this:

$$\text{Assets} = \text{Liabilities} + \text{Owner's Equity} + \overset{(\text{closed})}{\text{Revenue}} - \overset{(\text{closed})}{\text{Expenses}}$$

The assets, liabilities, and owner's equity accounts remain open. The balance sheet, with its one date in the heading, merely gives the present balances of these accounts, and the accountant will carry them over to the next fiscal period.

Procedure for closing

The procedure for closing is to simply balance off the account, in other words, to make the balance *equal to zero*. This meets our objective, which is to be able to start from zero in the next fiscal period. Let's illustrate this first with T accounts. For example, suppose an account happens to have a debit balance; then, to make the balance equal zero, we *credit* the account.

We put the label *closing* in the Item column of the ledger account.

Balance	960	Closing	960

For another example, suppose an account happens to have a credit balance; then, to make the balance equal to zero, we *debit* the account.

Closing 1,200	Balance 1,200

Four steps in the closing procedure:

1. Close the revenue accounts into Income Summary.
2. Close the expense accounts into Income Summary.
3. Close the Income Summary account into the Capital account.
4. Close the Drawing account into the Capital account.

Every entry should, of course, have both a debit and a credit. So, in order to give us the other half of the entry, we bring into existence Income Summary. To illustrate the entries directly in T accounts, we again fall back on the accounts of our friendly neighborhood business, Neil's Cleaners. For the purpose of the illustration, assume that Neil's Cleaners' fiscal period consists of one month. We now have the following revenue and expense accounts.

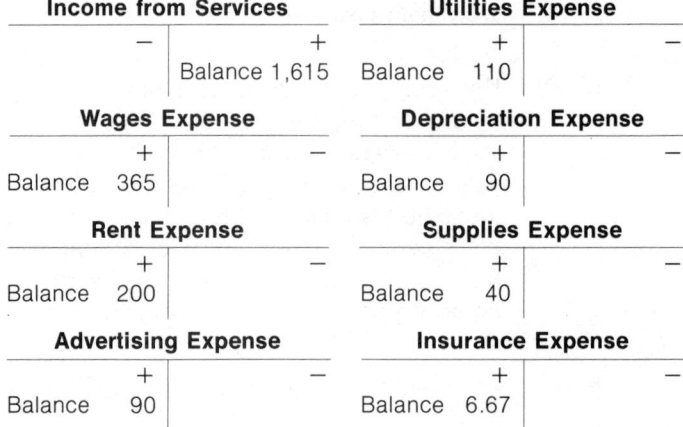

Income from Services

−	+
	Balance 1,615

Utilities Expense

+	−
Balance 110	

Wages Expense

+	−
Balance 365	

Depreciation Expense

+	−
Balance 90	

Rent Expense

+	−
Balance 200	

Supplies Expense

+	−
Balance 40	

Advertising Expense

+	−
Balance 90	

Insurance Expense

+	−
Balance 6.67	

Step 1 Close the revenue account, or accounts, into Income Summary. In order to make the balance of Income from Services equal to zero, we *balance it off*, or debit it, in the amount of $1,615. Because we need an offsetting credit, we now credit Income Summary for the same figure.

Income from Services

−	+
Closing 1,615	Balance 1,615

Income Summary

	1,615

In essence, the balance of Income from Services is transferred to Income Summary. To learn how to formulate the journal entry, let's look at the journal entry for this step.

DATE		DESCRIPTION	POST REF.	DEBIT	CREDIT
		Closing Entries			
	30	*Income from Services*		1 6 1 5 00	
		Income Summary			1 6 1 5 00

Writing *Closing Entries* in the Description column makes it possible to eliminate explanations for all the closing entries.

Step 2 Close the expense accounts into Income Summary. In order to make the balances of the expense accounts equal to zero, we need to balance them off, or credit them. Again the T accounts are a basis for formulating the journal entry. In essence, the balances of the expense accounts are transferred to Income Summary.

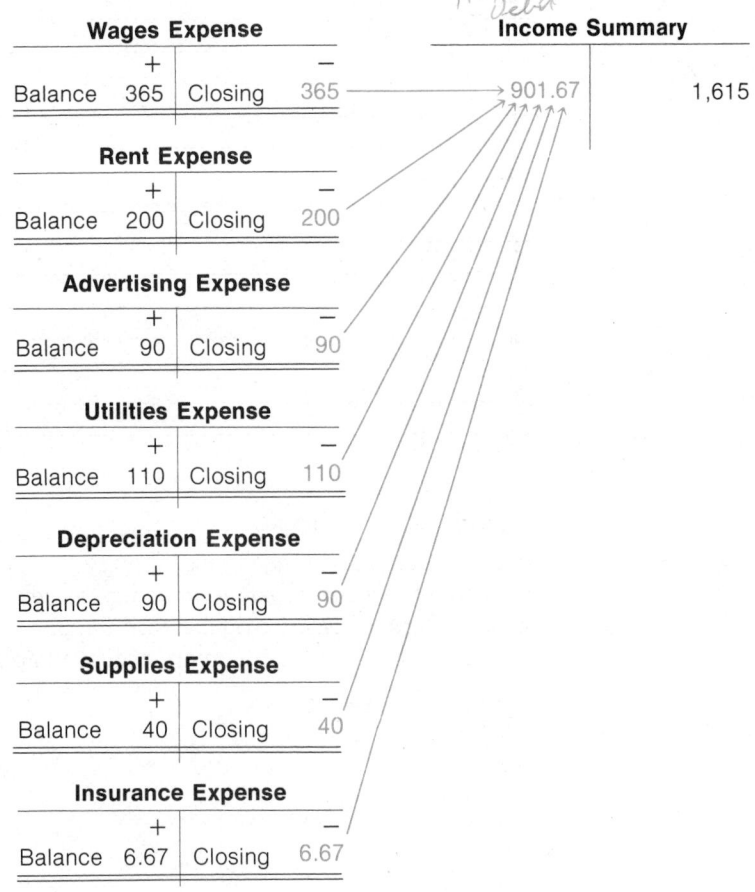

The journal entries look like this.

GENERAL JOURNAL   PAGE ___4___

DATE		DESCRIPTION	POST REF.	DEBIT	CREDIT
		Closing Entries			
	30	**Income from Services**		1 6 1 5 00	
		Income Summary			1 6 1 5 00
	30	*Income Summary*		9 0 1 67	
		Wages Expense			3 6 5 00
		Rent Expense			2 0 0 00
		Advertising Expense			9 0 00
		Utilities Expense			1 1 0 00
		Depreciation Expense			9 0 00
		Supplies Expense			4 0 00
		Insurance Expense			6 67

Step 3 Recall that we instigated Income Summary only in order to have a debit and credit with each closing entry. So now that it has done its job, we close it out. We use the same procedure as before, in that we make the balance equal to zero, or balance off the account. In essence, we transfer, or close, the balance of the Income Summary account into the Capital account.

Income Summary		Neil Singleton, Capital	
		−	+
901.67	1,615		Balance 16,000
Closing 713.33			(Net Inc.) 713.33

DATE		DESCRIPTION	POST REF.	DEBIT	CREDIT
		Closing Entries			
	30	Income from Services		1 6 1 5 00	
		Income Summary			1 6 1 5 00
	30	Income Summary		9 0 1 67	
		Wages Expense			3 6 5 00
		Rent Expense			2 0 0 00
		Advertising Expense			9 0 00
		Utilities Expense			1 1 0 00
		Depreciation Expense			9 0 00
		Supplies Expense			4 0 00
		Insurance Expense			6 67
	30	Income Summary		7 1 3 33	
		Neil Singleton, Capital			7 1 3 33

You should observe that Income Summary is always closed into the Capital account by the amount of the net income or the net loss. This can act as a check point or verification for you.

At the same time, it seems logical that net income should be added or credited to the Capital account, because in the statement of owner's equity, as we have seen, net income is treated as an addition. On the other hand, any net loss should be subtracted or debited to the capital account, because in the statement of owner's equity net loss is treated as a deduction. Here's an illustration of the closing of Income Summary of a net loss for J. Doe Company.

Income Summary		**J. Doe, Capital**	
(Expenses) 900	(Revenue) 700	(Net Loss) 200	Balance 30,000
	Closing 200		

For a situation involving a net loss of $200, the entry to close Income Summary into the Capital account would look like this.

DATE		DESCRIPTION	POST REF.	DEBIT	CREDIT
		Closing Entries			
	31	J. Doe, Capital		2 0 0 00	
		Income Summary			2 0 0 00

Step 4 Let us return to the illustration of Neil's Cleaners. The Drawing account, since it also applies to one fiscal period only, must also be closed. Because it appears in the statement of owner's equity as a deduction from the Capital account, it is closed directly into the Capital account. So we balance off the Drawing account, or make the balance of it equal to zero. The balance of Drawing is transferred to the Capital account.

Neil Singleton, Drawing			Neil Singleton, Capital	
+	**−**		**−**	**+**
Balance 500	Closing 500		500	Balance 16,000
				(Net Inc.) 713.33

The four journal entries in the closing procedure are presented below.

GENERAL JOURNAL   PAGE 4

DATE		DESCRIPTION	POST REF.	DEBIT	CREDIT
		Closing Entries			
	30	*Income from Services*		1 6 1 5 00	
		Income Summary			1 6 1 5 00
	30	*Income Summary*		9 0 1 67	
		Wages Expense			3 6 5 00
		Rent Expense			2 0 0 00
		Advertising Expense			9 0 00
		Utilities Expense			1 1 0 00
		Depreciation Expense			9 0 00
		Supplies Expense			4 0 00
		Insurance Expense			6 67
	30	*Income Summary*		7 1 3 33	
		Neil Singleton, Capital			7 1 3 33
	30	*Neil Singleton, Capital*		5 0 0 00	
		Neil Singleton, Drawing			5 0 0 00

These closing entries show that the owner has had a net income of $713.33, has withdrawn $500 for personal expenses, and has retained or plowed back $213.33 into the business, thereby increasing the capital investment.

One can gather the information for the closing entries either directly from the ledger accounts, or from the work sheet. Since the Income Statement columns of the work sheet consist entirely of revenues and expenses, one can pick up the figures for the closing entries from these columns. Here we see a partial work sheet for Neil's Cleaners.

ACCOUNT NAME	TRIAL BALANCE		INCOME STATEMENT	
	DEBIT	CREDIT	DEBIT	CREDIT
Cash	5 8 3 0 00			
Accounts Receivable	1 0 00			
Supplies	2 0 0 00			
Prepaid Insurance	1 6 0 00			
Equipment	11 1 4 0 00			
Accounts Payable		9 4 0 00		
Neil Singleton, Capital		16 0 0 0 00		
Neil Singleton, Drawing	5 0 0 00			
Income from Services		1 6 1 5 00		1 6 1 5 00
Wages Expense	3 1 5 00		3 6 5 00	
Rent Expense	2 0 0 00		2 0 0 00	
Advertising Expense	9 0 00		9 0 00	
Utilities Expense	1 1 0 00		1 1 0 00	
	18 5 5 5 00	18 5 5 5 00		
Supplies Expense			4 0 00	
Insurance Expense			6 67	
Depreciation Expense			9 0 00	
Accumulated Depreciation				
Wages Payable				
			9 0 1 67	1 6 1 5 00
Net Income			7 1 3 00	
			1 6 1 5 00	1 6 1 5 00

You may formulate the closing entries by simply balancing off all the figures that appear in the Income Statement columns. For example, in the Income Statement column, there is a credit for $1,615; so we debit that account for $1,615 and credit Income Summary for $1,615.

There are debits for $365, $200, $90, $110, $40, $6.67, and $90. So now we *credit* these accounts for the same amounts, and we debit Income Summary for their total.

Next, as usual, we close Income Summary into Capital, by using the net-income figure already shown on the work sheet.

We would of course have to pick up the last entry from the Balance Sheet columns to close Drawing.

Collectively, we call these accounts that are closed *temporary-equity accounts.* In this context they are temporary in that the balances apply to one fiscal period only, and in the last analysis they are closed into the Capital account.

We indicate that the accounts are closed by writing in the ledger, in the Item column, the word *Closing,* and by extending a line through both the debit and credit balance columns.

Posting the closing entries

After we have posted the closing entries, the Capital, Drawing, Income Summary, revenue, and expense accounts of Neil's Cleaners appear as follows.

GENERAL LEDGER

ACCOUNT _____ *Neil Singleton, Capital* _____ ACCOUNT NO. _311_

DATE		ITEM	POST. REF.	DEBIT	CREDIT	BALANCE DEBIT	BALANCE CREDIT
19— Jun.	1		1		16 00 00 00		16 00 00 00
	30		4		7 13 00		16 7 13 33
	30		4	5 00 00			16 2 13 33

ACCOUNT _____ *Neil Singleton, Drawing* _____ ACCOUNT NO. _312_

DATE		ITEM	POST. REF.	DEBIT	CREDIT	BALANCE DEBIT	BALANCE CREDIT
19— Jun.	30		4	5 00 00		5 00 00	
	30	Closing	4		5 00 00		

ACCOUNT _____ *Income Summary* _____ ACCOUNT NO. _313_

DATE		ITEM	POST. REF.	DEBIT	CREDIT	BALANCE DEBIT	BALANCE CREDIT
19— Jun.	30		4		1 6 13 00		1 6 13 00
	30		4	9 0 0 67			7 13 33
	30	Closing	4	7 13 33			

ACCOUNT _Income from Services_ ACCOUNT NO. _411_

DATE		ITEM	POST. REF.	DEBIT	CREDIT	BALANCE DEBIT	BALANCE CREDIT
19– Jun.	7		1		300 00		300 00
	14		2		380 00		680 00
	21		2		415 00		1 095 00
	23		3		40 00		1 135 00
	30		3		480 00		1 615 00
	30	Closing	4	1 615 00		—	

ACCOUNT _Wages Expense_ ACCOUNT NO. _511_

DATE		ITEM	POST. REF.	DEBIT	CREDIT	BALANCE DEBIT	BALANCE CREDIT
19– Jun.	10		2	120 00		120 00	
	24		3	195 00		315 00	
	30	Adjusting	4	50 00		365 00	
	30	Closing	4		365 00	—	

ACCOUNT _Rent Expense_ ACCOUNT NO. _512_

DATE		ITEM	POST. REF.	DEBIT	CREDIT	BALANCE DEBIT	BALANCE CREDIT
19– Jun.	8		1	200 00		200 00	
	30	Closing	4		200 00	—	

ACCOUNT _Advertising Expense_ ACCOUNT NO. _513_

DATE		ITEM	POST. REF.	DEBIT	CREDIT	BALANCE DEBIT	BALANCE CREDIT
19– Jun.	14		2	90 00		90 00	
	30	Closing	4		90 00	—	

Closing entries **133**

ACCOUNT _____ *Utilities Expense* _____ ACCOUNT NO. _514_

DATE		ITEM	POST. REF.	DEBIT	CREDIT	BALANCE DEBIT	BALANCE CREDIT
19– Jun.	15		2	1 1 0 00		1 1 0 00	
	30	Closing	4		1 1 0 00	—	—

ACCOUNT _____ *Depreciation Expense* _____ ACCOUNT NO. _515_

DATE		ITEM	POST. REF.	DEBIT	CREDIT	BALANCE DEBIT	BALANCE CREDIT
19– Jun.	30	Adjusting	4	9 0 00		9 0 00	
	30	Closing	4		9 0 00	—	—

ACCOUNT _____ *Supplies Expense* _____ ACCOUNT NO. _516_

DATE		ITEM	POST. REF.	DEBIT	CREDIT	BALANCE DEBIT	BALANCE CREDIT
19– Jun.	30	Adjusting	4	4 0 00		4 0 00	
	30	Closing	4		4 0 00	—	—

ACCOUNT _____ *Insurance Expense* _____ ACCOUNT NO. _517_

DATE		ITEM	POST. REF.	DEBIT	CREDIT	BALANCE DEBIT	BALANCE CREDIT
19– Jun.	30	Adjusting	4	6 67		6 67	
	30	Closing	4		6 67	—	—

The post-closing trial balance

After one has posted the closing entries, and before one goes on to the next year, it is wise to verify the balances of the accounts that remain open. Therefore, one makes up a *post-closing trial balance,* using the final-balance figures from the ledger accounts. This represents a last-ditch effort to make absolutely sure that the debit balances equal the credit balances.

The accounts listed in the post-closing trial balance are called *real accounts* (assets, liabilities, owner's equity, balance sheet accounts). The accountant carries forward the balances of real accounts from one fiscal period to another.

This is in contrast to temporary-equity accounts, which, as you have seen, are closed at the end of each fiscal period.

Neil's Cleaners						
Post-Closing Trial Balance						
June 30, 19—						
Cash	5	8	3	0	00	
Accounts Receivable			1	0	00	
Supplies		1	6	0	00	
Prepaid Insurance		1	5	3	33	
Equipment	11	1	4	0	00	
Accumulated Depreciation					9 0 00
Accounts Payable					9 4 0 00
Wages Payable					5 0 00
Neil Singleton, Capital					16 2 1 3 33
	17	2	9	3	33	17 2 9 3 33

Summary

The purpose of closing entries is to close off temporary-equity accounts. These accounts consist of revenues, expenses, Income Summary, and the Drawing account. In the closing process we balance off the account, or make the balance equal to zero. The four steps for closing are:

1. Close the revenue accounts into Income Summary.

2. Close the expense accounts into Income Summary.

3. Close Income Summary into the Capital account by the amount of the net income or net loss.

4. Close the Drawing account into the Capital account.

One writes the word *Closing* in the Item column of the ledger accounts, and extends lines through the balance columns, indicating that the balance of each account closed is zero.

A post-closing trial balance consists of the final balances of the accounts remaining open. It is the final proof that the debit balances equal the credit balances.

Glossary

Closing entry An entry made at the end of a fiscal period to intentionally make the balance of a temporary-equity account equal to zero. This is also referred to as *clearing the accounts*.

Interim statements Financial statements prepared during the fiscal period, and covering a period of time less than the fiscal period.

Post-closing trial balance The listing of the final balances of the real accounts at the end of the fiscal period.

Real accounts Assets, liabilities, and the Capital account in owner's equity, having balances which are carried forward from one fiscal period to another.

Temporary-equity accounts Revenue, expense, Income Summary, and Drawing accounts. This category may also be described as being all accounts except assets, liabilities, and the Capital account.

Questions

1. For the first two months of the year, what interim statements would you suggest for a restaurant which operates on fiscal year of January 1 through December 31?

2. Explain the functions served by the Income Summary account?

3. What is the difference between a real account and a temporary-equity account?

4. What is the closing entry required for a firm that made a profit for the fiscal period, and also for a firm that had a loss for the fiscal period?

5. List the four steps in the closing procedure.

6. What is the purpose of the post-closing trial balance?

7. What accounts appear in the post-closing trial balance?

Exercises

Exercise 1 From these accounts, prepare the closing entries in proper order.

Salary Expense		Income from Fees	
7,200			29,000

Rent Expense		C. O. Nolan, Drawing	
840		18,000	

Miscellaneous Expense	
160	

Exercise 2 Complete the posting of the closing entry for this account.

ACCOUNT _____ *Professional Fees* _____ ACCOUNT NO. *411*

DATE		ITEM	POST. REF.	DEBIT	CREDIT	BALANCE DEBIT	BALANCE CREDIT
19— Mar.	31		56		16 4 0 0 00		16 4 0 0 00
Jun.	30		71		18 4 6 0 00		34 8 6 0 00
Sep.	30		84		19 7 2 0 00		54 5 8 0 00
Dec.	31		96		13 1 7 0 00		67 7 5 0 00
	31		97	67 7 5 0 00			

Exercise 3 The Income Summary ledger account is as follows.

Income Summary

6.100	9.800

Total revenue is _____.

Total expenses are _____.

Net income is _____.

Exercise 4 After all revenues and expenses have been closed at the end of the fiscal period, Income Summary has a credit of $27,000 and a debit of $29,000. On the same date, C. L. Lerner Drawing has a debit balance of $6,000, and C. L. Lerner, Capital, has a credit balance of $46,000. On a sheet of paper, record the journal entries necessary to complete the closing of the accounts. What is the new balance of C. L. Lerner, Capital?

Exercise 5 The ledger accounts of M. E. Smith Company are as follows. Prepare a statement of owner's equity.

Income Summary

Dec. 31	60,000	Dec. 31	90,000
Dec. 31 Closing 30,000			

M. E. Smith, Capital

Dec. 31	24,000	Jan. 1 Bal.	67,000
		Dec. 31	30,000

M. E. Smith, Drawing

Mar. 31	6,000
Oct. 30	9,000
Nov. 30	9,000

Exercise 6 From the following ledger accounts, journalize the adjusting entries and closing entries that have been posted to the accounts.

Accumulated Depreciation

	1,900
	500

Prepaid Insurance

360	120
90	

Depreciation Expense

500	500

Insurance Expense

120	120

Income from Services

3,500	300
	2,900
	300

Wages Expense

800	1,670
800	
70	

Wages Payable

	70

Miscellaneous Expense

160	160

Income Summary

2,450	3,500

Exercise 7 With reference to a statement of owner's equity, determine the missing figures.

a. Net income for year $37,000
    Owner's equity at beginning of year   90,000
    Owner's equity at end of year   ?
    Owner's drawings during year   21,000
b. Owner's drawings during year   28,000
    Owner's equity at beginning of year   82,000
    Net income for year   ?
    Owner's equity at end of year   84,000

Exercise 8 The Income Statement columns of the work sheet of R. C. Johnson Company for the fiscal year ended April 30 contain the following.

ACCOUNT NAME	INCOME STATEMENT DEBIT	INCOME STATEMENT CREDIT	BALANCE SHEET DEBIT	BALANCE SHEET CREDIT
Income from Services		52 00 0 00		
Salary Expense	26 00 0 00			
Rent Expense	4 80 0 00			
Supplies Expense	1 20 0 00			
Miscellaneous Expense	1 00 0 00			

The Balance Sheet columns of the work sheet contain the following:

ACCOUNT NAME	INCOME STATEMENT DEBIT	INCOME STATEMENT CREDIT	BALANCE SHEET DEBIT	BALANCE SHEET CREDIT
R. C. Johnson, Capital				80 00 0 00
R. C. Johnson, Drawing			17 00 0 00	

Record the four closing entries.

Problems

Problem 6-1 The revenue, expenses, Income Summary, Drawing, and Capital accounts of W. E. Milner Advertising Agency are as follows.

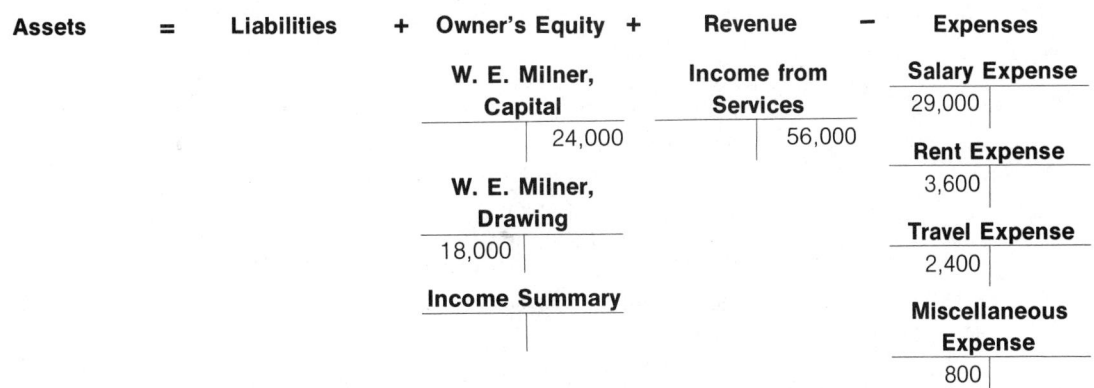

| Assets | = | Liabilities | + | Owner's Equity | + | Revenue | − | Expenses |

W. E. Milner, Capital
24,000

W. E. Milner, Drawing
18,000

Income Summary

Income from Services
56,000

Salary Expense
29,000

Rent Expense
3,600

Travel Expense
2,400

Miscellaneous Expense
800

Instructions Record the closing entries as of December 31,19—, with the four steps in order.

Problem 6-2 The partial work sheet for Precision Sign Painting for the fiscal year ending December 31 of this year is presented below.

ACCOUNT NAME	TRIAL BALANCE DEBIT	TRIAL BALANCE CREDIT	INCOME STATEMENT DEBIT	INCOME STATEMENT CREDIT
Cash	6 8 0 0 00			
Accounts Receivable	3 6 0 0 00			
Supplies	1 8 2 0 00			
Equipment	8 4 4 0 00			
Accumulated Depreciation, Equipment		5 2 0 0 00		
Truck	6 3 8 0 00			
Accumulated Depreciation, Truck		2 9 4 4 00		
Accounts Payable		1 2 8 0 00		
L. E. Morris, Capital		15 1 9 6 00		
L. E. Morris, Drawing	19 2 0 0 00			
Service Income		47 3 4 0 00		47 3 4 0 00
Wages Expense	16 8 4 0 00		16 8 4 0 00	
Rent Expense	4 8 0 0 00		4 8 0 0 00	
Truck Operating Expense	3 7 2 0 00		3 7 2 0 00	
Telephone Expense	3 6 0 00		3 6 0 00	
	71 9 6 0 00	71 9 6 0 00		
Supplies Expense			4 5 4 00	
Depreciation Expense, Equipment			6 5 2 00	
Depreciation Expense, Truck			9 6 4 00	
			27 7 9 0 00	47 3 4 0 00
Net Income			19 5 5 0 00	
			47 3 4 0 00	47 3 4 0 00

Instructions   Record the closing entries, with the four steps in order.

Problem 6-3   After the adjusting entries have been posted, the ledger of W. A. Schmidt, architect, contains the following account balances as of June 30, 19—.

Cash	$5,455.50
Office Supplies	285.00
Furniture and Fixtures	2,379.00
Accumulated Depreciation, Furniture and Fixtures	1,626.00
Accounts Payable	1,279.50
Salaries Payable	246.00
W. A. Schmidt, Capital	4,873.50
W. A. Schmidt, Drawing	1,800.00
Income Summary	0
Income From Professional Fees	5,730.00
Salary Expense	2,532.00
Rent Expense	312.00
Telephone Expense	36.00
Office Supplies Expense	631.50
Depreciation Expense, Furniture and Fixtures	324.00

Instructions   Record the closing entries with the four steps in order.

Problem 6-4   The trial balance section of the work sheet for Dependable Janitorial Service as of December 31, the end of the current fiscal year, is as follows.

ACCOUNT NAME	TRIAL BALANCE		ADJUSTMENTS	
	DEBIT	CREDIT	DEBIT	CREDIT
Cash	1 9 4 7 00			
Accounts Receivable	3 1 6 5 00			
Cleaning Supplies	6 3 9 00			
Cleaning Equipment	5 7 9 6 00			
Accumulated Depreciation,				
Cleaning Equipment		2 8 9 8 00		
Truck	4 4 7 0 00			
Accumulated Depreciation, Truck		3 1 8 0 00		
Accounts Payable		1 3 0 8 50		
D. L. Perron, Capital		2 7 5 8 00		
D. L. Perron, Drawing	16 2 0 0 00			
Service Income		37 2 6 0 00		
Wages Expense	12 9 6 0 00			
Advertising Expense	3 9 3 00			
Truck Operating Expense	6 3 6 00			
Utilities Expense	4 7 8 50			
Miscellaneous Expense	7 2 0 00			
	47 4 0 4 50	47 4 0 4 50		

Data for the adjustments.

a. Accrued wages, $174.

b. Inventory of cleaning supplies, $456.

c. Depreciation of cleaning equipment, $180.

d. Depreciation of truck, $444.

Instructions
1. Complete the work sheet.
2. Prepare an income statement.
3. Prepare a statement of owner's equity.
4. Prepare a balance sheet.
5. Journalize the adjusting entries.
6. Journalize the closing entries with the four steps in order.

Alternate problems

Problem 6-1A The revenue, expenses, Income Summary, Drawing, and Capital accounts of L. A. Dunne Insurance Agency are as follows.

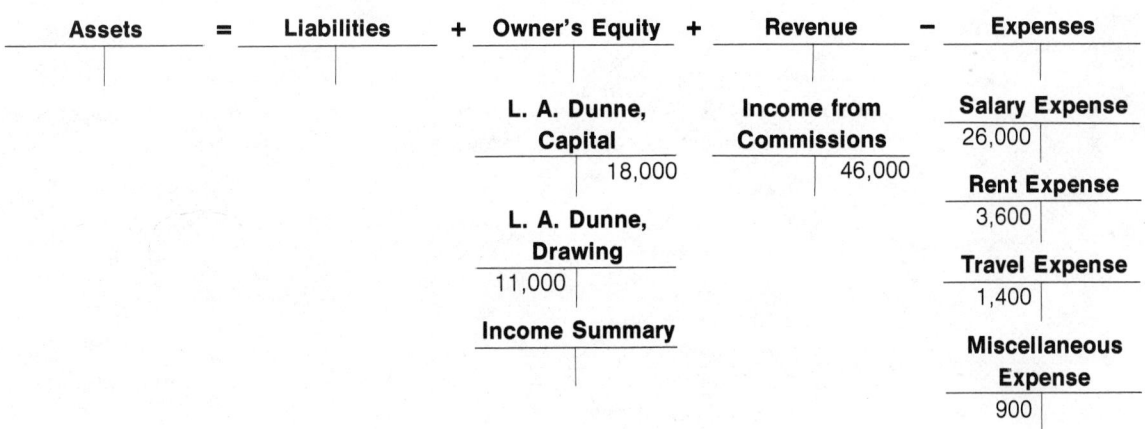

| Assets | = | Liabilities | + | Owner's Equity | + | Revenue | − | Expenses |

L. A. Dunne, Capital
| 18,000

L. A. Dunne, Drawing
11,000 |

Income Summary

Income from Commissions
| 46,000

Salary Expense
26,000 |

Rent Expense
3,600 |

Travel Expense
1,400 |

Miscellaneous Expense
900 |

Instructions Record the closing entries as of December 31, 19—, performing each of the four steps in order.

Problem 6-2A The partial work sheet for Foleen Rug Cleaning Service for the fiscal year ending December 31 of this year is shown in the illustration at the top of the following page.

ACCOUNT NAME	TRIAL BALANCE		INCOME STATEMENT	
	DEBIT	CREDIT	DEBIT	CREDIT
Cash	5 926 00			
Accounts Receivable	3 562 00			
Supplies	1 774 00			
Equipment	9 828 00			
Accumulated Depreciation, Equipment		6 596 00		
Truck	7 168 00			
Accumulated Depreciation, Truck		5 560 00		
Accounts Payable		1 652 00		
T. C. Foleen, Capital		7 798 00		
T. C. Foleen, Drawing	20 800 00			
Service Income		51 432 00		51 432 00
Wages Expense	14 840 00		14 840 00	
Rent Expense	4 800 00		4 800 00	
Truck Operating Expense	3 860 00		3 860 00	
Telephone Expense	480 00		480 00	
	73 038 00	73 038 00		
Supplies Expense			464 00	
Depreciation Expense, Equipment			624 00	
Depreciation Expense, Truck			880 00	
			25 948 00	51 432 00
Net Income			25 484 00	
			51 432 00	51 432 00

Instructions Record the closing entries, with the four steps in order.

Problem 6-3A After the adjusting entries have been posted, the ledger of S. E. Neilson, architect, contains the following account balances as of June 30, 19—.

Cash	$7,083.00
Office Supplies	706.50
Furniture and Fixtures	4,318.50
Accumulated Depreciation, Furniture and Fixtures	2,761.50
Accounts Payable	1,411.50
Salaries Payable	60.00
S. E. Neilson, Capital	6,600.00
S. E. Neilson, Drawing	1,620.00
Income Summary	0
Income from Professional Fees	7,594.50
Salary Expense	3.390.00
Rent Expense	525.00
Telephone Expense	78.00
Office Supplies Expense	180.00
Depreciation Expense, Furniture and Fixtures	114.00
Miscellaneous Expense	412.50

Instructions Record the closing entries with the four steps in order.

Problem 6-4A The trial balance section of the work sheet for Super Window-Washing Service as of December 31, the end of the current fiscal year, is as follows.

ACCOUNT NAME	TRIAL BALANCE DEBIT	TRIAL BALANCE CREDIT	ADJUSTMENTS DEBIT	ADJUSTMENTS CREDIT
Cash	2 5 2 4 50			
Accounts Receivable	2 6 8 5 00			
Cleaning Supplies	3 6 4 50			
Cleaning Equipment	4 4 5 5 00			
Accumulated Depreciation, Cleaning Equipment		2 7 9 0 00		
Truck	4 7 6 2 50			
Accumulated Depreciation, Truck		2 1 3 7 50		
Accounts Payable		9 4 0 50		
N. C. Mullin, Capital		4 9 9 8 00		
N. C. Mullin, Drawing	14 4 0 0 00			
Service Income		29 4 6 1 50		
Wages Expense	9 6 3 0 00			
Advertising Expense	3 9 6 00			
Truck Operating Expense	6 2 2 50			
Utilities Expense	3 3 0 00			
Miscellaneous Expense	1 5 7 50			
	40 3 2 7 50	40 3 2 7 50		

Data for the adjustments are as follows.

a. Accrued wages, $192

b. Inventory of cleaning supplies, $180

c. Depreciation of cleaning equipment, $337.50

d. Depreciation of truck, $570

Instructions

1. Complete the work sheet

2. Prepare an income statement.

3. Prepare a statement of owner's equity.

4. Prepare a balance sheet.

5. Journalize the adjusting entries.

6. Journalize the closing entries with the four steps in order.

Review of T-account placement

The following sums up the placement of T accounts covered in Chapters 3 through 6 in relation to the fundamental accounting equation.

Assets		=	Liabilities		+	Owner's Equity		+	Revenue		−	Expenses	
+	−		−	+		−	+		−	+		+	−
Dr	Cr		Dr	Cr		Dr	Cr		Dr	Cr		Dr	Cr

Cash		Accounts Payable		J. R. Doe, Capital		Income from Services		Rent Expense	
+	−	−	+	−	+	−	+	+	−

Accounts Receivable				J. R. Doe, Drawing		Professional Fees		Wages Expense	
+	−			+	−	−	+	+	−

Supplies				Income Summary		Commissions Earned		Advertising Expense	
+	−			Exp.	Rev.	−	+	+	−

Prepaid Insurance								Utilities Expense	
+	−							+	−

Equipment								Supplies Expense	
+	−							+	−

Accumulated Depreciation								Insurance Expense	
−	+							+	−

								Depreciation Expense	
								+	−

Review of representative transactions

The illustration on the facing page summarizes the recording of the various transactions described in Chapters 1 through 6. The illustration also summarizes the classification of the accounts involved.

Transaction	Accounts involved	Class.	Increase or decrease	Therefore debit or credit
Owner invested cash in business	Cash	A	I	Dr
	J. R. Doe, Capital	OE	I	Cr
Bought equipment for cash	Equipment	A	I	Dr
	Cash	A	D	Cr
Bought supplies on account	Supplies	A	I	Dr
	Accounts Payable	L	I	Cr
Bought equipment paying a down payment with the remainder on account	Equipment	A	I	Dr
	Cash	A	D	Cr
	Accounts Payable	L	I	Cr
Paid premium for insurance policy	Prepaid Insurance	A	I	Dr
	Cash	A	D	Cr
Paid creditor on account	Accounts Payable	L	D	Dr
	Cash	A	D	Cr
Sold services for cash	Cash	A	I	Dr
	Income from Services	R	I	Cr
Paid rent for month	Rent Expense	E	I	Dr
	Cash	A	D	Cr
Billed customers for services performed	Accounts Receivable	A	I	Dr
	Income from Services	R	I	Cr
Owner withdrew cash for personal use	J. R. Doe, Drawing	OE	I	Dr
	Cash	A	D	Cr
Received cash from charge customers to apply on account	Cash	A	I	Dr
	Accounts Receivable	A	D	Cr
Paid wages to employees	Wages Expense	E	I	Dr
	Cash	A	D	Cr
Adjusting entry for supplies used	Supplies Expense	E	I	Dr
	Supplies	A	D	Cr
Adjusting entry for insurance expired	Insurance Expense	E	I	Dr
	Prepaid Insurance	A	D	Cr
Adjusting entry for depreciation of assets	Depreciation Expense	E	I	Dr
	Accumulated Depreciation	A	I	Cr
Adjusting entry for accrued wages	Wages Expense	E	I	Dr
	Wages Payable	L	I	Cr
Closing entry for revenue accounts	Revenue accounts	R	D	Dr
	Income Summary	OE	—	Cr
Closing entry for expense accounts	Income Summary	OE	—	Dr
	Expense accounts	E	D	Cr
Closing entry for Income Summary account (Net Income)	Income Summary	OE	—	Dr
	J. R. Doe, Capital	OE	I	Cr
Closing entry for Drawing account	J. R. Doe, Capital	OE	D	Dr
	J. R. Doe, Drawing	OE	D	Cr

Practical review problem

The purpose of this problem is to get you to review and apply the knowledge that you have acquired in the preceding chapters. In accounting, the ultimate test is to be able to handle data in real life situations; the following will give you valuable experience.

You have been given the job of keeping the books for the Grandview Drive-In Theater. The owner, Frederick Baker, has formulated a chart of accounts.

Chart of Accounts

Assets

111 Cash
112 Accounts Receivable
113 Supplies
114 Prepaid Insurance
121 Projection Equipment
122 Accum. Dep., Projection Equipment
123 Screen and Speakers
124 Accum. Dep., Screen and Speakers
125 Office Equipment
126 Accum. Dep., Office Equipment
127 Buildings
128 Accum. Dep., Buildings
129 Land

Liabilities

211 Accounts Payable
212 Wages Payable
221 Mortgage Payable

Owner's Equity

311 Frederick Baker, Capital
312 Frederick Baker, Drawing
313 Income Summary

Revenue

411 Admissions Income
412 Concessions Income

Expenses

511 Film Rental Expense
512 Wages Expense
513 Advertising Expense
514 Utilities Expense
515 Interest Expense
516 Supplies Expense
517 Insurance Expense
518 Dep. Exp., Projection Equipment
519 Dep. Exp., Screen and Speakers
520 Dep. Exp., Office Equipment
521 Dep. Exp., Buildings
522 Miscellaneous Expense

You are to record transactions in a two column general journal. To get in a little more practice, assume that the fiscal period is 1 month, so that you will be able to complete all the steps in the accounting cycle.

When you are analyzing the transactions, think them through by mentally visualizing the T accounts or by writing them down on scratch paper. In the case of unfamiliar types of transactions, the book gives specific instructions for recording them. However, go ahead and reason them out for yourself as well.

The following transactions were completed during July of this year:

July 1 Baker deposited $39,200 in a bank account for the purpose of buying the Grandview Drive-In Theater.

July 2 Bought the Grandview Drive-In Theater in its entirety for a total price of $73,500. The assets include projection equipment, $8,400; screen and speakers, $4,900; office equipment, $2,800; buildings, $22,400; land, $35,000. Paid cash as a down payment, $25,200, and signed a mortgage note for the remainder. (Debit the assets, and credit Cash and the liability.)

2 Received and paid bill for newspaper advertising, $266.

2 Received and paid invoice for insurance on property and liability insurance, $672.

2 Received and paid bill for billboard advertising for month, $126.

2 Received bill for film rental, $854, from Intermountain, Inc.

2 Bought supplies on account, $154, from L. D. Ramsey Company.

2 Made a contract for leasing out the refreshment stand. The rental income is to be 12% of sales, payable in advance. Accordingly, received $200 in cash as advance payment for month. (Debit Cash and credit Concession Income.)

3 Paid cash for miscellaneous expenses, $37.80.

8 Received $2,240 in cash from admissions for week.

9 Bought office equipment on account, $123.20, from Jones Office Supply Company.

15 Paid wages expense for period ending July 14, $2,296.

16 Paid the bill for film rental previously recorded on July 2.

16 Baker withdrew $378 in cash for personal use.

16 Received $2,716 in cash from admissions for week.

17 Bought additional speakers on account, $735, from Ordway Electronics.

19 Received and paid bill for advertising brochures, $137.20.

20 Paid cash to L. D. Ramsey Company in full payment of account, $154.

22 Bought stationery and other supplies on account, $121.80, from Rambo Supply Company.

22 Received $2,884 in cash from admissions for week.

23 Returned some of the speakers purchased on July 17 and received full credit (a reduction in bill), $252.

24 Received bill for film rental, $1,344, from Intermountain, Inc.

26 Received and paid bill for electricity, $154.

29 Paid wages for period July 15 through 28, $2,492.

29 Paid bill for film rental previously recorded on July 24.

29 Paid cash to Ordway Electronics to apply on account, $336.

30 Received and paid telephone bill, $30.80.

31 Paid cash as an installment payment on the mortgage, $336. Of this amount, $245 is a payment on the principal; the remainder is interest. (Debit Mortgage Payable, debit Interest Expense, and credit Cash.)

31 Received and paid water bill, $28.

July 31 Sales for concession stand for month amounted to $2,400, and 12% of $2,400 equals $288.00. Since you have already recorded $200 as rent received in advance, list the additional $88 owed the Grandview Drive-In Theater by the concessionaire for July.

    31 Baker received $2,954 in cash from admissions for week.

    31 Baker withdrew $448 in cash for personal use.

    31 Received bill for film rental, $1,022, from Intermountain, Inc.

Instructions
1. Journalize the transactions beginning with page 1 of the general journal.
2. Post the transactions to the ledger accounts.
3. Prepare a trial balance in the first two columns of the work sheet.
4. Complete the work sheet. Data for the adjustments are as follows:
   a. Inventory of supplies at July 31, $205.80.
   b. Insurance expired during the month, $56.
   c. Depreciation of projection equipment for the month, $140.
   d. Depreciation of screen and speakers for the month, $154.
   e. Depreciation of office equipment for the month, $47.60.
   f. Depreciation of building for the month, $91.
   g. Wages accrued at July 31, $226.80.
5. Prepare the income statement.
6. Prepare the statement of owner's equity.
7. Prepare the balance sheet.
8. Journalize the adjusting entries.
9. Post the adjusting entries to the ledger accounts.
10. Journalize the closing entries.
11. Post the closing entries to the ledger accounts.
12. Prepare a post-closing trial balance.

7 Accounting for professional enterprises

objectives

After you have completed this chapter, you will be able to do the following:
- Define the following methods of accounting: cash-receipts-and-disbursements basis, modified cash basis, accrual basis.
- Record transactions for both a professional and a service-type enterprise in a combined journal.
- Complete the entire accounting cycle for a professional enterprise.

PROFESSIONAL ENTERPRISES include the practice of medicine, dentistry, law, architecture, engineering, optometry, and so forth. Naturally the knowledge of accounting procedures that you have acquired can be readily applied to professional enterprises. Generally, the accounting records for professional enterprises are kept on a modified cash basis. To obtain the background setting for this basis, we shall digress briefly in order to define the bases of accounting currently in use and officially recognized.

Accrual basis versus cash basis of accounting

Up to this time we have been dealing with the accrual basis of accounting, and therefore we shall look at it first in this section. When we use the accrual basis, we record revenue when it is earned and expenses when they are incurred. In this way, revenue and expenses are matched up with the appropriate fiscal period. For example, the books of Neil's Cleaners were recorded on the accrual basis; as proof, let us recall two transactions that we first looked at in Chapter 3.

Transaction (k) Received the bill for newspaper advertising, $90. The expense was recorded before it was paid in cash. The expense is matched up with the fiscal period in which it was incurred.

Advertising Expense		Accounts Payable	
(k) 90			(k) 90

Transaction (p) Entered into a contract with Ace Rental to clean their for-hire garments on a credit basis. Accordingly, we billed Ace Rental $40 for services performed.

Accounts Receivable		Income from Services	
(p) 40			(p) 40

The revenue was recorded before it was received in cash. The revenue is matched up with the fiscal period in which it was earned. Incidentally, accountants feel strongly that this accrual basis gives the most realistic picture of the revenue and expense accounts and hence the net income. (Net income equals total revenue minus total expenses.) We shall depart from the accrual basis temporarily because we are now concerned with professional enterprises and their accounting records. As we said, the books of professional enterprises are typically kept on a modified cash basis.

The *cash basis* is used primarily for convenience and simplicity. As a practical matter, it is divided into two types: the cash-receipts-and-disbursements basis and the modified cash basis.

Cash-receipts-and-disbursements basis

The term *disbursements* refers to cash payments. A firm which uses the cash-receipts-and-disbursements basis records revenue only when it is received in cash and expenses when they are paid in cash. The only type of business that could use this basis is a firm having practically no equipment. Consequently, no adjusting entries need be made. Actually, the cash-receipts-and-disbursements basis is used by most individuals in filing their personal income tax returns. Revenue in the form of salaries, wages, dividends, etc., is recorded in the year in which it is received. Likewise, expenditures—to be counted as employee business expenses or personal deductions—are recorded in the year in which they are paid.

Modified cash basis

Not only professional enterprises use a modified cash basis, but also many small business firms use it; in addition, it is useful in accounting for income from rental units. In Internal Revenue Service publications, the modified cash basis is referred to as the *hybrid method*. The modified cash basis is similar to the cash-receipts-and-disbursements basis in that revenue is counted only when it is received in cash, and expenses are ordinarily counted only when they are paid in cash. However, an exception is made in the case of expenditures for supplies, insurance, and equipment. The costs of these items must be spread out over their useful lives. Consequently, adjusting entries must be made for supplies used, insurance expired, and depreciation of equipment. No further adjusting entries are necessary, such as an adjustment for accrued salaries as well as a number of other adjustments that we shall introduce later.

Illustration: records of a dentist

To understand the accounting system used for a professional enterprise, let us look at the records of Dr. John A. Tanner, a dentist. The basic records used in his office are the appointment record and the patient's ledger record. The chart of accounts for the office is shown on the top of the following page.

Chart of Accounts

Assets
111 Cash
112 X-ray Supplies
113 Dental Supplies
114 Office Supplies
115 Prepaid Insurance
121 Dental Equipment
122 Accum. Dep., Dental Equipment
123 Office Furniture and Equipment
124 Accum. Dep., Office Furniture and Equipment

Liabilities
221 Notes Payable

Owner's Equity
311 J. A. Tanner, Capital
312 J. A. Tanner, Drawing
313 Income Summary

Revenue
411 Professional Fees

Expenses
511 Dental Supplies Expense
512 Dental Instruments Expense
513 X-ray Supplies Expense
514 Laundry and Cleaning Expense
515 Office Salary Expense
516 Laboratory Expense
517 Rent Expense
518 Insurance Expense
519 Office Supplies Expense
520 Dep. Exp., Dental Equipment
521 Dep. Exp., Office Furniture and Equipment
522 Telephone Expense
523 Utilities Expense
524 Repairs and Maintenance Expense
525 Miscellaneous Expense

Appointment record

The dentist's receptionist keeps a daily appointment record, showing the time of appointment and the name of each patient and gives a copy of the appointment record to the dentist the day before the scheduled appointments. An example appears on page 153.

Patient's ledger record

The dentist's receptionist also maintains a patient's ledger record card for each patient. One side of this card shows a daily record of the services performed, amount of any cost estimate given, plan of payment, information regarding collections, etc.; the card looks like the example shown on page 154.

The other side of the card contains a diagram of the patient's teeth and a space for personal information about the patient.

After Dr. Tanner has completed the work, he (or an assistant) records a description of the services performed and the amount of the fees in the debit column. The card is returned to the receptionist, who records on the original appointment record the services rendered and the fees charged.

When a patient sends in a payment, the receptionist records the amount in the appointment record on the day the payment was received and on the patient's ledger record in the credit column. Remember that the fees charged are not recorded in the Professional Fees account until they are received in cash. The record showing the amounts patients owe is much like Accounts Receivable, except that these amounts are not officially recorded in the books.

Hour	Patient	Service Rendered	Fees	Receipts
8 00	Donald Rankin			
15	Patricia Fischer			
30				
45	Cecil Hansen			
9 00				
15				
30				
45	Donna Heller			
10 00	C. F. Elliott			
15				
30				
45	Ralph Simons			
11 00	Peter Smithson			
15				
30				
45				
1 00	Donald C. Kraft			
15				
30	N. C. Byers			
45				
2 00	Mrs. N. D. Silversmith			
15				
30	John F. Piper			
45	Nolan F. Sanderson			
3 00				
15	Nancy Stacy			
30				
45	C. D. Harper			
4 00	Ardis Newell			
15				
30				
45				
5 00				
15				

This record does resemble Accounts Receivable in that debits mean increases in the amounts owed by patients and credits mean decreases in the amounts owed by patients. The balance columns show the final amounts owed by patients at the time of the latest entry.

The services to be performed may require a number of appointments. Some patients may make partial payments each time they have appointments. Others may pay the entire amount at—or after—the last appointment. Patients' bills are compiled directly from the ledger cards. The dentist or receptionist keeps a constant watch on the patients' ledger records to determine those accounts that are past due and to take the necessary measures to speed up collections. The statement shown at the bottom of page 154 was mailed to a patient at the end of the month.

Elliott, C. F.   365-2619
1629 S. W. Arbor St.
Denver

DATE		SERVICE RENDERED	TIME	DEBIT		CREDIT		BALANCE	
Jun.	15	#31 - M O D (4)	10:00	40	00			40	00
Jul.	4	Ck				40	00		
	16	#27 - D O (Amal.)	9:15	33	00			33	00
Aug.	5	Ck				33	00		
Sep.	24	#25 - P. J. C.	10:00	188	00			188	00
Oct.	6	Ck				75	00	113	00
	18	#24 - D (Porc.)	9:00	30	00			143	00
Nov.	3	Ck				75	00	68	00
	9	#18 - full gold crown	10:00	150	00			218	00
Dec.	1	B. W. X-rays (6)		42	00			260	00
		Impression upper 7/1		368	00			628	00
	1	C J.				90	00	538	00

PLAN OF SERVICE	PLAN OF PAYMENT	COLLECTION EFFORTS
1-2 surf. } amalgam	30-day basis	
2-3 surf. } 1 full gold crown	or $75 per	
1-1 surf.) 1 ceramic crown	month	
2 anterior porcelain		

ESTIMATE IF ANY

$273 upper denture (6 appt.)	$90 per month	

STATEMENT

C F ELLIOTT
1629 S W ARBOR STREET
DENVER CO 80232

Date	Professional Service	Charges	Payments	Balance
6/15	#31 - M O D (4)	40.00		40.00
7/4	Ck		40.00	—
7/16	#27 - D O (Amal.)	33.00		33.00
8/5	Ck		33.00	—
9/24	#25 - P J C	188.00		188.00
10/6	Ck		75.00	113.00
10/18	#24 - D (Porc.)	30.00		143.00
11/3	Ck		75.00	68.00
11/9	#18 - full gold crown	150.00		218.00
12/1	B. W. X-rays (6)	42.00		260.00
	Impression upper	368.00		628.00
12/1	C J		90.00	538.00

Pay last amount in Balance column ▲

Receipt of payments from patients

Depending on the size of the office, the person who receives payments may be the receptionist or the cashier in the accounting office. Whoever receives them issues a written receipt for all incoming cash, filled out in duplicate, sending the first copy to the patient and filing the second copy as evidence of the transaction. Receipts should be prenumbered, so that they can all be accounted for. The payment is recorded in the receipts column of the appointment record.

Date 12/1

Appointment Record

Hour	Patient	Service Rendered	Fees		Receipts	
8 00	Donald Rankin	Extraction	22	00		
15	Patricia Fischer	Three amalgam fillings DO (3)	68	00	16	00
30						
45	Cecil Hansen	Gold inlay filling	97	00		
9 00						
15						
30						
45	Donna Heller	Amalgam filling DO	18	00		
10 00	C. F. Elliott	Denture – full upper	410	00	90	00
15		(6 appointments)				
30						
45	Ralph Simons	Prophylaxis	24	00	24	00
11 00	Peter Smithson	Endodontia treatment	120	00	15	00
15						
30						
45						
1 00	Donald C. Kraft	Amalgam filling MOD	27	00	22	00
15						
30	N. C. Byers	Porcelain jacket crown	173	00		
45						
2 00	Mrs. N. D. Silversmith	Extraction	26	00		
15						
30	John F. Piper	Amalgam filling 1 surf.	12	00		
45	Nolan F. Sanderson	Prophylaxis and full-mouth				
3 00		x-ray (14)	27	00		
15	Nancy Stacy	Fixed bridge 3 units (Gold)	540	00	60	00
30		(5 appointments)				
45	C. D. Harper	Prophylaxis & bitewing x-rays	30	00		
4 00	Ardis Newell	Periodontal treatment	62	00		
15						
30						
45						
5 00						
15						
	Ronald T. McCaw				60	00
	Helen Bower				55	00
	Eugene Sampson				72	00
	A. Stacy Weeks				27	00
	C. D. Sanderson				100	00
	Roger Lindsay				27	00
	Gilbert Rae				40	00
			1,656	00	608	00

The above form is a typical appointment record for a day, showing services rendered, fees (recorded by the dentist on the patients' ledger records), and payments received (recorded by the receptionist). The receptionist deposits $608 in the bank.

1. Patients request appointments.

2. Receptionist records appointments on appointment record: date, time, and name of patient.

3. Receptionist furnishes dentist with appointment record for the day, plus the patients' ledger records.

4. Dentist performs services and records on each patient's ledger record descriptions of the services and the fees to be charged, in the debit column.

5. Receptionist accepts payments from patients both in the office and through the mail and records receipt of payments in the receipts column of the appointment record.

6. At the end of the day, receptionist deposits in the bank any cash received.

7. Receptionist records on the appointment record the description of services and the amount charged.

8. Receptionist records the payments received from patients on the patients' ledger records, in the credit column. The source is the appointment record.

9. The receptionist compiles monthly statements directly from the patients' ledger records.

This procedure may vary, depending on the size of the office staff. It could be further abbreviated by avoiding the repetition of description of services. For the sake of security or internal control, if the size of the office staff is sufficiently large, the function of accepting and depositing money should be separated from the function of recording payments.

Here is a list of Dr. Tanner's transactions for December, the last month of the fiscal period. To save time and space, the receipts of cash are recorded on a weekly basis.

Dec. 1 Paid rent for the month, $500.

1 Paid telephone bili, $16.

1 Paid electric bill, $33.

3 Issued check to Superior Printing for patient statement forms, $66.

5 Bought drills for cash, $127, from Anderson Dental Supply.

5 Total cash received from patients during the week, $2,762.

8 Paid bill for repair of office typewriter to Johnson Office Supply, $29.

9 Tanner withdrew $200 for personal use.

11 Paid Dan-Dee Building Maintenance Company for janitorial service, $60.

The entries for the first nine of these transactions are now recorded in general journal form as shown here.

	19–Dec.	1	Rent Expense				5 0 0 00				
			Cash						5 0 0 00	
			Rent for December.							
		1	Telephone Expense				1 6 00			
			Cash						1 6 00	
			Telephone bill for November.							
		1	Utilities Expense				3 3 00			
			Cash						3 3 00	
			Electric bill for November.							
		3	Office Supplies				6 6 00			
			Cash						6 6 00	
			Superior Printing for statement forms.							
		5	Dental Instruments Expense				1 2 7 00			
			Cash						1 2 7 00	
			Anderson Dental Supply for drills.							
		5	Cash				2 7 6 2 00			
			Professional Fees						2 7 6 2 00	
			For period December 1 through 5.							
		8	Repairs and Maintenance Expense				2 9 00			
			Cash						2 9 00	
			Johnson Office Supply, typewriter.							
		9	J. A. Tanner. Drawing				2 0 0 00			
			Cash						2 0 0 00	
			For personal use.							
		11	Laundry and Cleaning Expense				6 0 00			
			Cash						6 0 00	
			Dan-Dee Building Maintenance Company.							

Dec. 12 Total cash received from patients during the week, $921.

16 Paid Pacific Dental Supply for miscellaneous dental supplies, $216.

16 Paid salaries of dental assistant and receptionist, $490.

19 Bought new dental chair from Anderson Dental Supply, $617, $217 down, the balance to be paid in eight monthly payments of $50 each.

19 Total cash received from patients during the week, $310.

22 Tanner withdrew $260 for personal use.

23 Paid bill for laboratory expense to Rogers Dental Laboratory, $148.

Dec. 23 Paid Pacific Dental Supply $160 as a contract payment on dental equipment purchased in October.

27 Total cash received from patients during the week, $196.

29 Tanner wrote check to garage for repairing his car, $64 (to be recorded as Drawing).

31 Paid Anderson Dental Supply for miscellaneous dental supplies, $96.

31 Paid salaries of dental assistant and receptionist, $490.

31 Tanner withdrew $390 for personal use.

31 Paid $27 to Manson Publishers Service for magazines for the office.

31 Paid Quality Linen Supply for laundry service, $42.

31 Total cash received from patients up until last day of year, $133.

The combined journal

One can obtain more efficiency in the recording and posting of transactions by using a type of journal that is employed for both professional and service-type operations: a *combined journal*. The person keeping records may record each transaction on one line and use special columns that are set up to record transactions that occur frequently for a particular business. One can use the Sundry columns to record accounts for which special columns are not available. Compare the recording of the first nine transactions in the combined journal shown on pages 160–161 with the same transactions recorded in the general journal just shown. When you use a combined journal, you don't need any other journal.

After you have added all columns at the end of the month, prove on scratch paper that the sum of the debit totals equals the sum of the credit totals, as shown in the following example.

Column	Debit totals	Credit totals
Cash	$4,322.00	$3,631.00
Dental Supplies	312.00	
J. A. Tanner, Drawing	914.00	
Professional Fees		4,322.00
Laundry and Cleaning Expense	102.00	
Office Salary Expense	980.00	
Laboratory Expense	148.00	
Miscellaneous Expense	27.00	
Sundry	1,548.00	400.00
	$8,353.00	$8,353.00

Posting from the combined journal

The person who is keeping records posts items in the Sundry columns individually, usually daily. After posting the ledger account, the person records the ledger account number in the Posting Reference column of the combined journal. This procedure is similar to posting from a general journal. He or she puts a check mark ($\checkmark$) below the totals of the Sundry columns to indicate that the totals are not to be posted, because the amounts have previously been posted individually.

Special columns, used only for the debit or credit to specific accounts, are posted as totals. After posting the ledger account, the accountant records the ledger account number in the special column immediately below the total. The account number is placed in parenthesis. The total of the Cash Debit column in the illustration on page 161 may be used as an example. After the cash account in the general ledger has been debited for $4,322.00, in the combined journal, the account number of Cash (111) is placed in parenthesis below the total of the Cash Debit column.

A dash in the Posting Reference column indicates that individual amounts in the special columns are being posted as totals.

Determining cash balance

The cash balance may be determined at any time during the month by taking the beginning balance of cash, adding the total cash debits so far during the month, and subtracting the total cash credits so far during the month. For example, to determine the balance of cash on May 12:

Cash

May 1 Balance 6,000

COMBINED JOURNAL   PAGE _____

	DATE		OFFICE SALARY EXPENSE DEBIT	LABORATORY EXPENSE DEBIT	MISC. EXPENSE DEBIT	CASH DEBIT	CASH CREDIT	
1	19– May	4				1 6 0 00		1
2		5					2 0 00	2
3		7				4 0 00		3
4		8				7 0 00		4
5		8					1 0 0 00	5
6		8					1 2 0 00	6
7		10				9 0 00		7
8		12				3 0 00		8
9						3 9 0 00	2 4 0 00	9
10								10
11								11
12								12
13								13
14								14

Beginning balance (May 1)	$6,000
Add cash debits	390
Total	$6,390
Less cash credits	240
Ending balance (May 12)	$6,150

DATE		ACCOUNT NAME	POST REF.	SUNDRY		DENTAL SUPPLIES	J. A. TANNER, DRAWING
				DEBIT	CREDIT	DEBIT	DEBIT
19— Dec.	1	Rent Expense	517	500 00			
	1	Telephone Expense	522	16 00			
	1	Utilities Expense	523	33 00			
	3	Office Supplies	114	66 00			
	5	Dental Instruments Expense	512	127 00			
	5	Professional Fees	—				
	8	Repairs and Maintenance					
		Expense	524	29 00			
	9	J. A. Tanner, Drawing	—				200 00
	11	Laundry and Cleaning					
		Expense	—				
	12	Professional Fees	—				
	16	Dental Supplies	—			216 00	
	16	Office Salary Expense	—				
	19	Dental Equipment	121	617 00			
		Notes Payable	221		400 00		
	19	Professional Fees	—				
	22	J. A. Tanner, Drawing	—				260 00
	23	Laboratory Expense	—				
	23	Notes Payable	221	160 00			
	27	Professional Fees	—				
	29	J. A. Tanner, Drawing	—				64 00
	31	Dental Supplies	—			96 00	
	31	Office Salary Expense	—				
	31	J. A. Tanner, Drawing	—				390 00
	31	Miscellaneous Expense	—				
	31	Laundry and Cleaning					
		Expense	—				
	31	Professional Fees	—				
				1548 00	400 00	312 00	914 00
				(✓)	(✓)	(113)	(312)

Work sheet for a professional enterprise

Assume that Dr. Tanner's receptionist has posted the journal entries to the ledger accounts and has recorded the trial balance in the first two columns of the work sheet. Dr. Tanner uses the modified cash basis of accounting, recording revenue only when he has received it in cash, and recording expenses only when he has paid for them in cash. In addition, when Dr. Tanner buys an item that is going to last a number of years, he records this item as an asset and writes it off or depreciates it in the form of an adjusting entry made each year over the duration of its useful life. He also makes adjusting entries for expired insurance, as well as for supplies used.

PROFESSIONAL FEES CREDIT	LAUNDRY AND CLEANING EXPENSE DEBIT	OFFICE SALARY EXPENSE DEBIT	LABORATORY EXPENSE DEBIT	MISC. EXPENSE DEBIT	CASH DEBIT	CASH CREDIT	
						500 00	1
						16 00	2
						33 00	3
						66 00	4
						127 00	5
2762 00					2762 00		6
							7
						29 00	8
						200 00	9
							10
	60 00					60 00	11
921 00					921 00		12
						216 00	13
		490 00				490 00	14
						217 00	15
							16
310 00					310 00		17
						260 00	18
			148 00			148 00	19
						160 00	20
196 00					196 00		21
						64 00	22
						96 00	23
		490 00				490 00	24
						390 00	25
				27 00		27 00	26
							27
	42 00					42 00	28
133 00					133 00		29
4322 00	102 00	980 00	148 00	27 00	4322 00	3631 00	30
(411)	(514)	(515)	(516)	(525)	(111)	(111)	31
							32

Data for the adjustments are as follows:

a. Additional depreciation on dental equipment, $4,200.

b. Additional depreciation on office furniture and equipment, $760.

c. Inventory of x-ray supplies, $309.

d. Inventory of dental supplies, $808.

e. Inventory of office supplies, $98.

f. Insurance expired, $360.

ACCOUNT NAME	TRIAL BALANCE		ADJUSTMENTS	
	DEBIT	CREDIT	DEBIT	CREDIT
Cash	3 8 9 3 00			
X-ray Supplies	1 3 8 1 00			(c)1 0 7 2 00
Dental Supplies	2 7 4 0 00			(d)1 9 3 2 00
Office Supplies	6 5 4 00			(e) 5 5 6 00
Prepaid Insurance	4 2 4 00			(f) 3 6 0 00
Dental Equipment	42 6 1 7 00			
Accum. Depr., Dental Equip.		8 6 0 0 00		(a)4 2 0 0 00
Office Furniture and Equipment	3 9 0 0 00			
Accum. Depr., Off. Furn. & Equip.		2 1 0 0 00		(b) 7 6 0 00
Notes Payable		3 8 0 0 00		
J. A. Tanner, Capital		26 2 7 9 00		
J. A. Tanner, Drawing	16 6 4 0 00			
Professional Fees		56 0 1 2 00		
Dental Instruments Expense	9 9 1 00			
Laundry and Cleaning Expense	1 5 1 2 00			
Office Salary Expense	11 7 6 0 00			
Laboratory Expense	2 9 2 8 00			
Rent Expense	6 0 0 0 00			
Telephone Expense	2 0 6 00			
Utilities Expense	3 8 9 00			
Repairs and Maintenance Expense	4 4 4 00			
Miscellaneous Expense	3 1 2 00			
	96 7 9 1 00	96 7 9 1 00		
Depr. Expense, Dental Equipment			(a)4 2 0 0 00	
Depr. Exp., Off. Furn. & Equip.			(b) 7 6 0 00	
X-ray Supp. Expense			(c)1 0 7 2 00	
Dental Supp. Expense			(d)1 9 3 2 00	
Office Supp. Expense			(e) 5 5 6 00	
Insurance Expense			(f) 3 6 0 00	
			8 8 8 0 00	8 8 8 0 00
Net Income				

With these adjusting entries, the rest of the work sheet can now be completed as shown above and on the facing page. First the balances of the accounts that were adjusted are brought up to date in the Adjusted Trial Balance columns. Then these amounts are carried forward to the remaining columns.

ADJUSTED TRIAL BALANCE		INCOME STATEMENT		BALANCE SHEET		
DEBIT	CREDIT	DEBIT	CREDIT	DEBIT	CREDIT	
3 893 00				3 893 00		1
309 00				309 00		2
808 00				808 00		3
98 00				98 00		4
64 00				64 00		5
42 617 00				42 617 00		6
	12 800 00				12 800 00	7
3 900 00				3 900 00		8
	2 860 00				2 860 00	9
	3 800 00				3 800 00	10
	26 279 00				26 279 00	11
1 664 00				1 664 00		12
	56 012 00		56 012 00			13
991 00		991 00				14
1 512 00		1 512 00				15
11 760 00		11 760 00				16
2 928 00		2 928 00				17
6 000 00		6 000 00				18
206 00		206 00				19
389 00		389 00				20
444 00		444 00				21
312 00		312 00				22
						23
4 200 00		4 200 00				24
760 00		760 00				25
1 072 00		1 072 00				26
1 932 00		1 932 00				27
556 00		556 00				28
360 00		360 00				29
101 751 00	101 751 00	33 422 00	56 012 00	68 329 00	45 739 00	30
		22 590 00			22 590 00	31
		56 012 00	56 012 00	68 329 00	68 329 00	32
						33

Financial statements

From the work sheet, Dr. Tanner's accountant prepares the financial statements shown on pages 164–165.

In the case of Dr. Tanner, assume that the balance of J. A. Tanner, Capital did not change during the year (no additional investment). In preparing any

J. A. Tanner, D.D.S.

Income Statement

For year ended December 31, 19—

Revenue:		
Professional Fees		56 012 00
Expenses:		
Office Salary Expense	11 760 00	
Rent Expense	6 000 00	
Depreciation Expense, Dental Equipment	4 200 00	
Laboratory Expense	2 928 00	
Dental Supplies Expense	1 932 00	
Laundry and Cleaning Expense	1 512 00	
X-ray Supplies Expense	1 072 00	
Dental Instruments Expense	991 00	
Depreciation Expense, Office Furniture and Equipment	760 00	
Office Supplies Expense	556 00	
Repairs and Maintenance Expense	444 00	
Utilities Expense	389 00	
Insurance Expense	360 00	
Telephone Expense	206 00	
Miscellaneous Expense	312 00	
Total Expenses		33 422 00
Net Income		22 590 00

statement of owner's equity, always look into the capital account to see if indeed any additional was recorded.

J. A. Tanner, D.D.S.

Statement of Owner's Equity

For year ended December 31, 19—

J. A. Tanner, Capital, Jan. 1, 19—		26 279 00
Net Income for year	22 590 00	
Less: Withdrawals for year	16 640 00	
Increase in Capital		5 950 00
J. A. Tanner, Capital, Dec. 31, 19—		32 229 00

J. A. Tanner, D.D.S															
Balance Sheet															
December 31, 19—															

Assets															
Cash									3	8	9	3	00		
X-ray Supplies										3	0	9	00		
Dental Supplies										8	0	8	00		
Office Supplies											9	8	00		
Prepaid Insurance											6	4	00		
Dental Equipment	42	6	1	7	00										
Less Accumulated Depreciation	12	8	0	0	00	29	8	1	7	00					
Office Furniture and Equipment	3	9	0	0	00										
Less Accumulated Depreciation	2	8	6	0	00	1	0	4	0	00					
Total Assets						36	0	2	9	00					
Liabilities															
Notes Payable								3	8	0	0	00			
Owner's Equity															
J. A. Tanner, Capital						32	2	2	9	00					
Total Liabilities and Owner's Equity						36	0	2	9	00					

Adjusting and closing entries

Dr. Tanner (or his receptionist) records the adjusting and closing entries in the Sundry columns of the combined journal. These entries must be posted separately. For example, the adjusting entries are shown on page 166 in an abstract from the combined journal.

There are a number of aspects of the accounting for a professional enterprise which we have not yet dealt with:

1. Special funds, such as the change fund and the petty cash fund. (We shall discuss these in Chapter 8.)

2. Payroll deductions, such as withholdings for employees' income taxes, Social Security taxes, and other salary deductions. (We shall discuss these in Chapter 9.)

3. Payroll taxes levied on the employer, such as the matching for Social Security, and unemployment taxes. (We shall discuss these in Chapter 10.)

DATE		ACCOUNT NAME	POST REF.	SUNDRY		DENTAL SUPPLIES	
				DEBIT	CREDIT	DEBIT	
		Adjusting Entries					
19– Dec.	31	*Depr. Expense, Dental*					
		Equipment	520	4 2 0 0 00			
		Accum. Depr., Dental					
		Equipment	122		4 2 0 0 00		
	31	*Depr. Expense, Office*					
		Furniture and Equipment	521	7 6 0 00			
		Accum. Depr., Office					
		Furniture and Equipment	124		7 6 0 00		
	31	*X-ray Supplies Expense*	513	1 0 7 2 00			
		X-ray Supplies	112		1 0 7 2 00		
	31	*Dental Supplies Expense*	511	1 9 3 2 00			
		Dental Supplies	113		1 9 3 2 00		
	31	*Office Supplies Expense*	519	5 5 6 00			
		Office Supplies	114		5 5 6 00		
	31	*Insurance Expense*	518	3 6 0 00			
		Prepaid Insurance	115		3 6 0 00		
				8 8 8 0 00	8 8 8 0 00		

Accounting for other professional enterprises

Accounting records for other professional enterprises are similar to our dentist's records. Professional people use the modified cash basis, recording revenue when it is received in cash, and recording expenses when they are paid in cash. Adjusting entries are also made for supplies used, expired insurance, and depreciation on specialized equipment. Ledger cards for patients or clients are used, although they may be given special titles. For example, lawyers call the ledger cards of their clients Collection Dockets.

Lawyers have an additional asset account, Advances for Clients, representing amounts they have paid on behalf of their clients. Advances for Clients is consequently a receivable, similar to Accounts Receivable. Lawyers also have an additional liability account, Collections for Clients, representing amounts they receive on behalf of their clients. Collections for Clients is consequently a payable, similar to Accounts Payable. All in all, therefore, you can see that the same general accounting principles and procedures prevail in all professional enterprises.

Designing a combined journal

As we have said, the combined journal is widely used in professional offices and service-type business firms. It is interesting to look over the varieties of combined journals that are available at stores that sell office supplies. Some are bound journals, and others are loose-leaf-type books. The number of columns may vary from six to twenty, and they are available with or without column headings. Those which do have printed column headings represent a "canned" type of combined journal. In other words, these combined journals are all set up for a particular kind of business enterprise, with descriptions of how to channel routine transactions into the journal. For example, these journals are available for service stations, dry cleaners, doctors' offices, etc.

A person with even a limited knowledge of accounting can keep books as long as the transactions remain routine and fall into the established channels. However, in every business unusual or nonroutine transactions do seem to pop up from time to time, and therefore you need to have enough knowledge and background to be able to handle them. Understanding the entire accounting system is also essential if you are ever going to see *why* transactions are recorded as they are.

Combined journals with blank columns can be customized to meet specific requirements of a given business. Prior to labeling the columns, one first studies the operations of the business and makes up a chart of accounts. Next one chooses those accounts that are likely to be used frequently in recording typical transactions of the business. Naturally, if these accounts are used over and over again, one needs to set up special columns for them.

Illustration: combined journal used for a service-type enterprise

As an example of the combined journal for a service-type business, let us return to Neil's Cleaners, the business discussed in Chapters 1 through 6.

The person keeping the records first establishes the chart of accounts; then looks over the accounts to see how frequently each is used. She or he decides at the outset to use special columns for Cash debit and credit, Accounts Receivable debit and credit, Accounts Payable debit and credit, Wages Expense debit, and Income from Services credit. She or he then writes the transactions carried out during the first month of operations.

Observe the way each transaction is recorded in the combined journal shown on pages 168–169. One may use the combined journal in conjunction with either the accrual basis or the cash basis of accounting. You will recognize that the accrual basis is used by Neil's Cleaners.

June 1 Singleton invests $16,000 cash in his new business.

       2 Buys $9,000 worth of equipment, paying cash.

       2 Buys $2,000 worth of equipment on credit from Johnson Company.

       4 Pays $500 to Johnson Company to be applied against the firm's liability of $2,000.

       4 Buys cleaning fluids for $200 on credit from Acme Supply.

       7 Cash revenue received for the first week, $300.

       8 Pays $200 rent for the month.

    10 Pays wages to employees, $120, June 1 through June 10.

    10 Pays $160 for a 2-year liability insurance policy.

    14 Cash revenue received for second week, $380.

DATE	CHECK NO.	ACCOUNT NAME	POST REF.	SUNDRY DEBIT	SUNDRY CREDIT	ACCOUNTS DEBIT
19— June 1		Neil Singleton, Capital	311		16000 00	
2	1	Equipment	121	9000 00		
2		Equipment, Johnson				
		Co.	121	2000 00		
4	2	Johnson Company	—			
4		Supplies, Acme Supply	113	200 00		
7		Income from Services	—			
8	3	Rent Expense	512	200 00		
10	4	Wages Expense	—			
10	5	Prepaid Insurance	114	160 00		
14		Income from Services	—			
14		Advertising Expense,				
		Daily News	513	90 00		
15	6	Johnson Company	—			
15	7	Utilities Expense	514	110 00		
15	8	Daily News	—			
21		Income from Services	—			
23		Ace Rental	—			40 00
24	9	Wages Expense	—			
26		Equipment, Johnson				
		Co.	121	140 00		
30		Income from Services	—			
30		Ace Rental	—			
30	10	Neil Singleton,				
		Drawing	312	500 00		
				12400 00	16000 00	40 00
				(✓)	(✓)	(112)

June 14 Receives bill for newspaper advertising, $90, from the Daily News.

15 Pays $900 to Johnson Company as part payment on account.

15 Receives and pays bill for utilities, $110.

15 Pays $90 to Daily News for advertising. (This bill has been previously recorded.)

21 Cash revenue received for third week, $415.

23 Singleton enters into a contract with Ace Rental to clean their for-hire formal garments on a credit basis. Singleton sends bill to Ace Rental, $40, for services performed.

RECEIVABLE CREDIT	ACCOUNTS PAYABLE DEBIT	ACCOUNTS PAYABLE CREDIT	WAGES EXPENSE DEBIT	INCOME FROM SERVICES CREDIT	CASH DEBIT	CASH CREDIT	
					16 000 00		1
						900 00	2
							3
		2 000 00					4
	500 00					500 00	5
		200 00					6
				300 00	300 00		7
						200 00	8
			120 00			120 00	9
						160 00	10
				380 00	380 00		11
							12
		90 00					13
	900 00					900 00	14
						110 00	15
	90 00					90 00	16
				415 00	415 00		17
				40 00			18
			195 00			195 00	19
							20
		140 00					21
				480 00	480 00		22
30 00					30 00		23
							24
						500 00	25
30 00	1 490 00	2 430 00	315 00	1 615 00	1 760 5 00	1 177 5 00	26
(112)	(211)	(211)	(511)	(411)	(111)	(111)	27

June 24 Pays wages of employees, $195, June 11 through June 24.

26 Buys additional equipment on credit, $140, from Johnson Company.

30 Cash received for the remainder of the month, $480.

30 Receives $30 from Ace Rental to apply on amount previously billed.

30 Singleton withdraws $500 in cash for personal use.

The combined journal, as illustrated above, shows all these transactions at a glance; and it also has other advantages for firms where one person may be doing all the journalizing. Since it combines features of the general and special journals, it saves time and space and reduces posting errors.

Illustration: combined journal used for a service-type enterprise **169**

Summary

A person may keep accounting records for any business by the following methods: cash-receipts-and-disbursements basis, modified cash basis, or accrual basis. The most popular method for a professional enterprise is the modified cash basis, because it is practical and realistic. All three bases are acceptable for income tax purposes, but the business must consistently follow the chosen basis. Professional persons and service-type businesses most often use the combined journal.

Glossary

Accrual basis   An accounting method by which revenue is recorded when it is earned, regardless of when it is received. Expenses are recorded when they are incurred, regardless of when they are paid.

Cash-receipts-and-disbursements basis   An accounting method by which revenue is recorded only when it is received in cash, and expenses, consisting of all expenditures, are recorded only when they are paid in cash.

Modified cash basis   An accounting method by which revenue is recorded only when it is received in cash. Expenditures classified as expenses are recorded only when they are paid in cash. An exception is expenses paid in advance and affecting more than one fiscal period. For example, expenditures for supplies and insurance premiums are *prorated,* or apportioned over the fiscal periods covered. Expenditures for long-lived items are recorded as assets, and later depreciated or written off as an expense during their useful lives.

Questions

1. What is meant by the modified cash basis of accounting?

2. In regard to a combined journal, describe the procedure followed in posting amounts in the following columns: Cash Debit, Professional Fees Credit, Sundry Debit, Miscellaneous Expense Debit, Sundry Credit.

3. Where is a check mark ($\sqrt{}$) used in a combined journal, and what does it indicate?

4. What is the meaning of the numbers that appear in the Posting Reference column of the combined journal?

5. What is the purpose of the dashes that appear in the Posting Reference column of the combined journal?

6. Describe the process of proving the combined journal at the end of the month.

7. You have been asked to set up a combined journal for Dole's Appliance Repair. The business maintains charge accounts for customers, and it buys parts on account from creditors. The space occupied by the shop is rented on a monthly basis. C. A. Dole, the owner, makes withdrawals on a weekly basis. The firm subscribes to a telephone answering service on a monthly basis. There are no employees. List the money columns that you would suggest.

Exercises

Exercise 1 Using the straight-line method, calculate the depreciation for 1 year on the following assets of a dentist.

a. Dental equipment, life 8 years, cost $7,200; trade-in value at end of 8 years, zero.

b. Electric typewriter, life 5 years, cost $320; trade-in value at end of 5 years, $70.

Exercise 2 On the appointment record for the dentist, the total of the fees column is $936, and the total of the receipts column is $579. The dentist deposits $579 in the bank at the end of the day. Record the journal entry for the deposit.

Exercise 3 In the following T accounts, record the plus and minus signs and $696 depreciation for the fiscal period.

Depreciation Expense, Equipment   **Accumulated Depreciation, Equipment**

Exercise 4 Record the depreciation in Exercise 3 in a work sheet like the following.

ACCOUNT NAME	TRIAL BALANCE		ADJUSTMENTS	
	DEBIT	CREDIT	DEBIT	CREDIT
Equipment	18 0 0 0 00			
Accumulated Depreciation,				
Equipment		6 9 7 5 00		
	85 0 8 0 00	85 0 8 0 00		
Depreciation Expense , Equipment				

Exercise 5 Journalize the closing entries in the proper sequence for the following ledger accounts.

Professional Fees
56,460

Salary Expense
24,600

Rent Expense
7,200

Supplies Expense
540

Utilities Expense
490

Miscellaneous Expense
630

A. D. Roberts, Drawing
21,900

Depreciation Expense
4,470

Exercise 6 Using a form similar to the one shown below, record the proper account or classification of accounts in the blank spaces provided. Number 1 is given as an example.

1. Assets
2. Expenses
3. Revenue
4. Liabilities

5. Drawing
6. Accumulated Depreciation
7. Capital

Account Name	Trial Balance		Adjusted Trial Balance		Income Statement		Balance Sheet	
	Debit	Credit	Debit	Credit	Debit	Credit	Debit	Credit
	1		1				1	

Exercise 7 The Perleberg Insurance Agency uses a combined journal, which has the following columns.

Date
Account Name
Post. Ref.
Sundry debit
Sundry credit
Accounts Receivable debit
Accounts Receivable credit

Accounts Payable debit
Accounts Payable credit
Commissions Income credit
Salary Expense debit
Miscellaneous Expense debit
Cash debit
Cash credit

Answer the following.

a. Which money column totals are not posted?

b. How do you record an investment of additional cash in the business by B. L. Perleberg?

c. How do you determine the balance of Cash at any time during the month?

d. Which columns are used to record the payment of a month's rent?

Exercise 8 Arrange the steps in the accounting cycle in the appropriate sequence.

Journalizing adjusting entries
Preparing trial balance
Preparing financial statements
Journalizing transactions
Journalizing closing entries
Post-closing trial balance
Completing work sheet
Posting to ledger accounts
Formulating the data for the adjustments

Problems

Problem 7-1 B. L. Shreve, M.D., uses the following chart of accounts.

Assets

111 Cash
112 Medical Supplies
113 X-ray Supplies
114 Office Supplies
115 Medical Equipment
116 Accum. Dep., Medical Equipment
117 Office Furniture and Equipment
118 Accum. Dep., Office Furniture and Equipment
119 Automobile
120 Accum. Dep., Automobile

Liabilities

211 Notes Payable

Owner's Equity

311 B. L. Shreve, Capital
312 B. L. Shreve, Drawing
313 Income Summary

Revenue

411 Professional Fees

Expenses

511 Nurses' Salaries Expense
512 Office Salaries Expense
513 Rent Expense
514 Equipment Rental Expense
515 Medical Supplies Expense
516 X-ray Supplies Expense
517 Laboratory Expense
518 Laundry and Cleaning Expense
519 Office Supplies Expense
520 Dep. Exp., Medical Equipment
521 Dep. Exp., Office Furniture and Equipment
522 Dep. Exp., Automobile
523 Automobile Expense
524 Insurance Expense
525 Telephone Expense
526 Utilities Expense
527 Miscellaneous Expense

Dr. Shreve's records consist of an appointment record book, examination and charge reports, patients' ledger records, a combined journal, and a general ledger. The doctor fills out an examination and charge report each time a patient visits. The reports contain a description or listing of the treatments and tests administered and the amount of the charges. The charges are then recorded in the patient's ledger record. Monthly statements based on the patient's ledger record are mailed to the patient. Dr. Shreve's books are kept on the modified cash basis. These transactions took place during April.

April 1 Paid rent for the month, $1,350 to Simmonds and Skeen.

3 Bought medical supplies for cash from Joplin Surgical Supply, $390.

4 Paid office salaries, $780, for the month.

6 Received cash from patients during week, $6,240.

10 Paid telephone bill, $81.

12 Paid for laboratory expense to Quality Laboratories, $630.

13 Total cash received from patients during week, $4,398.

16 Bought x-ray supplies for cash from Thomas Supply Company, $183.

17 Dr. Shreve withdrew $780 for personal use.

19 Bought postage stamps, $39 (Miscellaneous Expense); paid cash.

April 20 Received cash from patients during week, $1,776.

   23 Paid for gas and oil to Bob's Service Station, $93.

   24 Paid Timely News Service for magazines, $61.50 (Miscellaneous Expense).

   27 Paid $72 for laundry service to Crystal Laundry.

   30 Paid nurses' salaries $1,890, for the month.

   30 Paid Johnson Janitorial Service, $123.

   30 Received cash from patients (April 21 through April 30), $1,371.50.

   30 Dr. Shreve withdrew $1,020 for personal use.

Instructions **1.** Journalize these transactions in the combined journal.

2. Prove the equality of the debit and credit totals on scratch paper.

Problem 7-2 Dr. C. J. Wiley owns and operates the Wiley Chiropractic Clinic. The trial balance section of the work sheet as of December 31, the end of the fiscal year, is presented below.

ACCOUNT NAME	TRIAL BALANCE DEBIT	TRIAL BALANCE CREDIT
Cash	9 2 4 0 00	
X-ray Supplies	1 8 9 3 00	
Office Supplies	6 4 0 50	
Prepaid Insurance	9 3 1 50	
Chiropractic Equipment	62 4 0 0 00	
Accumulated Depreciation, Chiropractic Equipment		25 0 8 0 00
Office Furniture and Equipment	5 8 0 5 00	
Accumulated Depreciation, Office Furniture and Equipment		4 2 1 5 00
Notes Payable		5 9 8 5 00
C. J. Wiley, Capital		37 9 5 6 00
C. J. Wiley, Drawing	21 7 5 0 00	
Professional Fees		46 0 7 4 00
Laundry and Cleaning Expense	1 2 6 0 00	
Office Salary Expense	8 4 0 0 00	
Rent Expense	5 1 0 0 00	
Telephone Expense	4 2 0 00	
Utilities Expense	5 5 8 00	
Repairs and Maintenance Expense	6 2 4 00	
Miscellaneous Expense	2 8 8 00	
	119 3 1 0 00	119 3 1 0 00

Data for the adjustments are as follows.

a. Additional depreciation of chiropractic equipment for the year, $3,600.

b. Additional depreciation of office furniture and equipment for the year, $930.

c. Inventory of x-ray supplies, $813.

d. Inventory of office supplies, $88.50.

e. Expired insurance, $816.

Instructions   Complete the work sheet.

Problem 7-3   The trial balance section of the work sheet for D. O. Sharp, architect, as of December 31, the end of the current year, is as follows.

ACCOUNT NAME	TRIAL BALANCE	
	DEBIT	CREDIT
Cash	5 9 9 2 00	
Supplies	1 9 9 6 40	
Office Equipment	33 1 8 0 00	
Accumulated Depreciation, Office		
Equipment		15 2 1 8 00
D. O. Sharp, Capital		17 5 5 7 40
D. O. Sharp, Drawing	22 6 8 0 00	
Professional Fees		70 9 5 2 00
Salary Expense	26 2 0 8 00	
Blueprint Expense	3 0 4 0 80	
Rent Expense	5 8 8 0 00	
Automobile Expense	1 2 8 8 00	
Travel Expense	2 0 7 2 00	
Entertainment Expense	7 8 9 60	
Miscellaneous Expense	6 0 0 60	
	103 7 2 7 40	103 7 2 7 40

Data for the adjustments are as follows.

a. Additional depreciation of office equipment, $4,774.

b. Inventory of supplies, $296.80.

Instructions   **1.** Complete the work sheet.

2. Prepare an income statement.

3. Prepare a statement of owner's equity.

4. Prepare a balance sheet.

5. Journalize the adjusting entries.

6. Journalize the closing entries.

Problem 7-4 Laura A. Harding, M.D., completed the following transactions during November of this year. Her chart of accounts is as follows.

Assets

111 Cash
112 Accounts Receivable
113 Supplies
114 Prepaid Insurance
121 Equipment
122 Accum. Dep., Equipment

Liabilities

211 Accounts Payable

Owner's Equity

311 Laura A. Harding, Capital
312 Laura A. Harding, Drawing
313 Income Summary

Revenue

411 Professional Fees

Expenses

511 Salary Expense
512 Rent Expense
513 Laboratory Expense
514 Utilities Expense
515 Dep. Exp., Equipment
516 Miscellaneous Expense

Nov. 2 Bought laboratory equipment on account from Central Surgical, $1,410. (Use two lines.)

2 Paid office rent for the month, $690.

2 Received cash on account from patients, $705: A. P. Lawrence, $240, Thomas Parker, $285; Anthony Anderson, $180. (Dr. Harding is on the accrual basis. Use three lines, recording individual amounts in both the Cash Debit column and the Accounts Receivable Credit column.)

4 Received cash for professional services rendered, $1,187.50.

6 Received and paid telephone bill for month, $36.

6 Received and paid electric bill, $127.50.

9 Recorded fees charged to patients on account for professional services rendered, $817.50: Steven C. Darling, $390; Hubert Hastings, $427.50. (Use two lines.)

16 Paid salary of nurse, $472.50.

19 Received cash for professional services, $465.

23 Returned part of equipment purchased on Nov. 2 and received a reduction on the bill, $90.

27 Billed patients on account for professional services rendered, $585: N. R. Russett, $135; Neil Suter, $240; Dale MacTavish, $210.

30 Paid salary of nurse, $472.50.

30 Paid salary of receptionist, $570, for the month.

30 Dr. Harding withdrew $1,260 cash for personal use.

Instructions

1. Record these transactions in a combined journal.

2. On scratch paper, prove the equality of the debit and credit totals.

3. Post to the accounts in the general ledger.

4. Prepare a trial balance.

Alternate problems

Problem 7-1A The following chart of accounts is used by S. L. Kneip, M.D.

Assets

111 Cash
112 Medical Supplies
113 X-ray Supplies
114 Office Supplies
115 Medical Equipment
116 Accum. Dep., Medical Equipment
117 Office Furniture and Equipment
118 Accum. Dep., Office Furniture and Equipment
119 Automobile
120 Accum. Dep., Automobile

Liabilities

211 Notes Payable

Owner's Equity

311 S. L. Kneip, Capital
312 S. L. Kneip, Drawing
313 Income Summary

Revenue

411 Professional Fees

Expenses

511 Salaries Expense
512 Rent Expense
513 Equipment Rental Expense
514 Medical Supplies Expense
515 X-ray Supplies Expense
516 Laboratory Expense
517 Laundry and Cleaning Expense
518 Office Supplies Expense
519 Dep. Exp., Medical Equipment
520 Dep. Exp., Office Furniture and Equipment
521 Dep. Exp., Automobile
522 Automobile Expense
523 Insurance Expense
524 Telephone Expense
525 Utilities Expense
526 Miscellaneous Expense

Dr. Kneip's records consist of an appointment record book, examination and charge reports, patients' ledger records, a combined journal, and a general ledger. The doctor fills out an examination and charge report each time a patient visits. The reports contain a description or listing of the treatments and tests administered and the amount of the charges. The charges are then recorded in the patient's ledger record. Monthly statements based on the patients' ledger records are mailed to patients. Dr. Kneip's books are kept on the modified cash basis.

The following transactions took place during September.

Sept. 1 Bought medical supplies for cash from McCoy Surgical Supply, $429.50.

1 Paid rent for the month, $1,275 to Mears Realty.

5 Paid office salaries, $885, for the month.

6 Received cash from patients during the week, $7,374.

7 Bought an examination table from McCoy Surgical Supply, costing $630, paying $180 in cash and agreeing by contract to pay the balance in three monthly installments of $150 each. (Credit Notes Payable.)

8 Paid telephone bill, $93.

9 Paid for laboratory expense to Fletcher Laboratories, $324.

13 Total cash received from patients during the week, $4,671.

16 Bought x-ray supplies for cash from Wilson Supply Company, $193.50.

Sept. 16 Dr. Kneip withdrew $925 for personal use.

20 Total cash received from patients during the week, $1,833.

23 Bought postage stamps, $90 (Miscellaneous Expense); paid cash.

25 Paid for gas and oil to Dick's Service Station, $98.25.

29 Paid $60 to United Building Maintenance for janitorial service.

30 Paid nurses' salaries, $2,013.

30 Dr. Kneip withdrew $1,380 for personal use.

30 Paid $92.10 to Economy Laundry for laundry service through September 30.

Instructions   **1.** Journalize these transactions in the combined journal.

2. Prove the equality of the debit and credit totals on scratch paper.

Problem 7-2A   Dr. Andrew C. Sinclair owns and operates the Sinclair Pet Clinic. The trial balance section of the work sheet as of December 31 of this year is as follows.

ACCOUNT NAME	TRIAL BALANCE	
	DEBIT	CREDIT
Cash	2 943 00	
X-ray Supplies	931 50	
Medical Supplies	1 828 50	
Prepaid Insurance	1 389 00	
Veterinary Equipment	56 580 00	
Accumulated Depreciation,		
Veterinary Equipment		22 365 00
Office Furniture and Equipment	2 526 00	
Accumulated Depreciation, Office		
Furniture and Equipment		1 830 00
Notes Payable		1 306 50
Andrew C. Sinclair, Capital		30 510 00
Andrew C. Sinclair, Drawing	23 400 00	
Professional Fees		57 778 50
Laundry and Cleaning Supplies		
Expense	1 452 00	
Wages Expense	13 090 50	
Rent Expense	7 800 00	
Utilities Expense	936 00	
Telephone Expense	216 00	
Repair Expense	493 50	
Miscellaneous Expense	204 00	
	113 790 00	113 790 00

The data for the adjustments are as follows.

a. Additional depreciation of veterinary equipment for the year, $4,290.

b. Additional depreciation of office furniture and equipment for year, $627.

c. Inventory of x-ray supplies, $193.50.

d. Inventory of medical supplies, $409.50.

e. Expired insurance, $1,291.50.

Instructions Complete the work sheet for the year.

Problem 7-3A The trial balance section of the work sheet for F. L. Logan, architect, as of December 31 (the end of the current year) is as follows.

ACCOUNT NAME	TRIAL BALANCE	
	DEBIT	CREDIT
Cash	4 4 5 0 60	
Supplies	3 0 4 0 80	
Office Equipment	44 4 0 5 20	
Accumulated Depreciation, Office Equipment		13 6 6 4 00
F. L. Logan, Capital		31 4 9 5 18
F. L. Logan, Drawing	22 0 9 2 00	
Professional Fees		65 4 6 1 20
Salary Expense	24 0 2 9 60	
Blueprint Expense	2 8 1 2 10	
Rent Expense	5 8 8 0 00	
Automobile Expense	1 2 4 0 66	
Travel Expense	1 8 0 8 80	
Entertainment Expense	5 8 3 14	
Miscellaneous Expense	2 7 7 48	
	110 6 2 0 38	110 6 2 0 38

The data for the adjustments are as follows.

a. Additional depreciation of office equipment, $4,174.80.

b. Inventory of supplies, $1,370.60.

Instructions
1. Complete the work sheet.
2. Prepare an income statement.
3. Prepare a statement of owner's equity.
4. Prepare a balance sheet.
5. Journalize the adjusting entries.
6. Journalize the closing entries.

Problem 7-4A Laura A. Harding, M.D., completed the transactions described below during November of this year. Her chart of accounts is as follows.

Assets

111 Cash
112 Accounts Receivable
113 Supplies
114 Prepaid Insurance
121 Equipment
122 Accum. Dep., Equipment

Liabilities

211 Accounts Payable

Owner's Equity

311 Laura A. Harding, Capital
312 Laura A. Harding, Drawing
313 Income Summary

Revenue

411 Professional Fees

Expenses

511 Salary Expense
512 Rent Expense
513 Laboratory Expense
514 Utilities Expense
515 Dep. Exp., Equipment
516 Miscellaneous Expense

Nov. 2 Bought laboratory equipment on account, $1,404 from Coast Medical Supplies. (Use two lines.)

2 Paid office rent for month, $690.

2 Received cash on account from patients, $705: M. C. Cummings, $127.50; Agnes Milton, $222; Frank Barber, $288; Simon Russett, $67.50. (Dr. Harding operates on the accrual basis. Use four lines, recording amounts in both the Cash Debit column and the Accounts Receivable Credit column.)

4 Received cash for professional services rendered, $1,213.

6 Received and paid telephone bill for month, $39.

8 Received and paid electric bill, $123.57.

9 Recorded fees charged to patients on account for professional services rendered, $703.50: D. Stevens, $373.50; M. Wendt, $330. (Use two lines.)

16 Paid salary of nurse, $502.50.

19 Received cash for professional services, $474.

23 Returned part of equipment purchased on May 2 and received a reduction on the bill, $63.

27 Billed patients on account for professional services rendered, $960: Emerson Schultz, $540; Mary MacIntyre, $217.50; David Allen, $202.50.

30 Paid salary of nurse, $502.50.

30 Paid salary of receptionist, $630.

30 Dr. Harding withdrew $1,477.50 cash for personal use.

Instructions **1.** Record these transactions in the combined journal.

2. On scratch paper, prove the equality of the debit and credit totals.

3. Post to the accounts in the general ledger.

4. Prepare a trial balance.

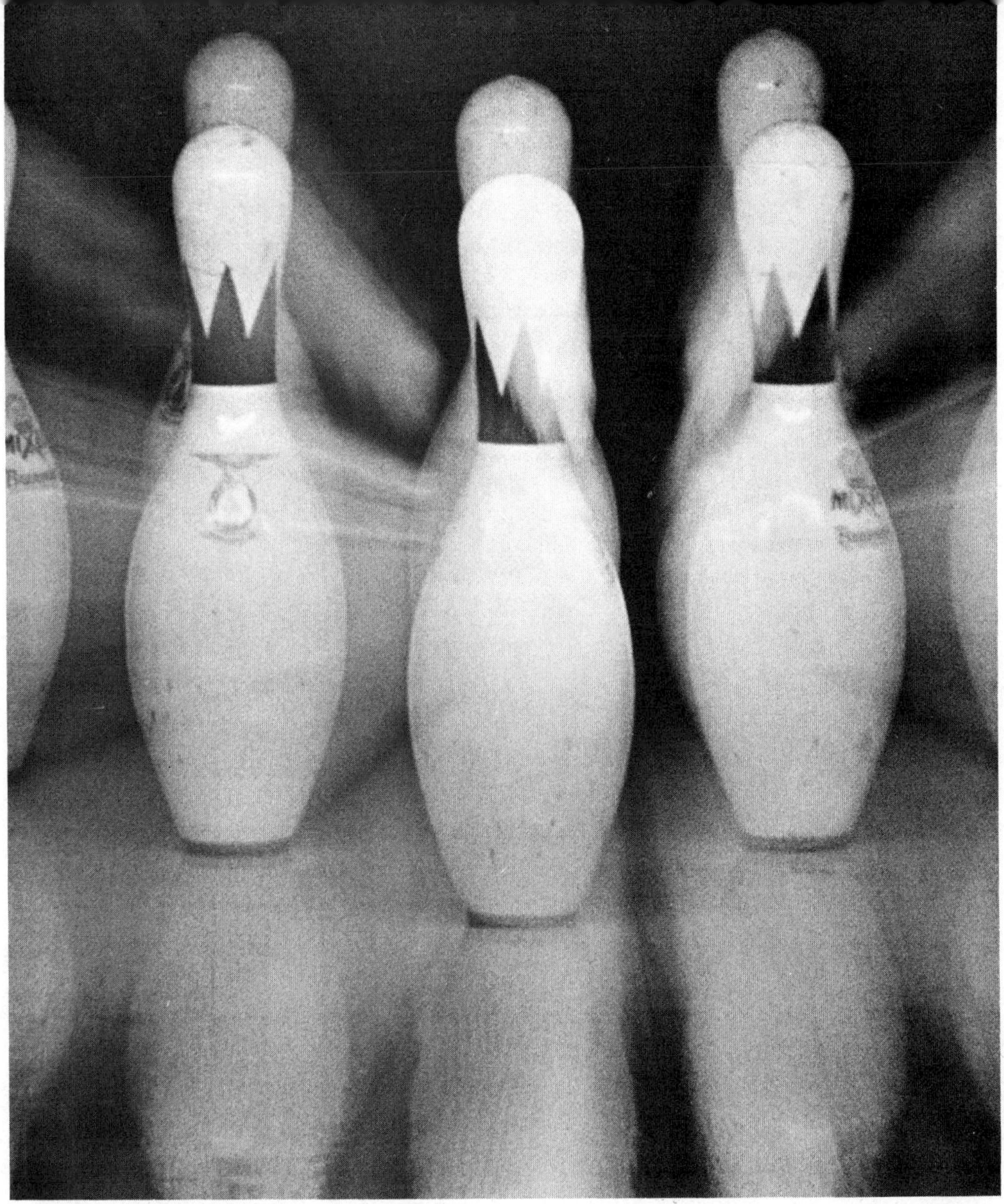

8 Bank accounts and cash funds

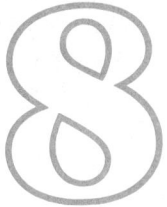

objectives

After you have completed this chapter, you will be able to do the following:
- Reconcile a bank statement.
- Journalize the requisite entries directly from the bank reconciliation.
- Journalize entries to establish and reimburse Petty Cash Fund.
- Complete petty cash vouchers and petty cash payments records.
- Journalize the entries to establish a Change Fund.
- Journalize transactions involving Cash Short and Over.

A VERY important aspect in any system of financial accounting, either for an individual or a business enterprise, is the efficient management of cash. For a business of any size, all cash received during a working day should be deposited at the end of the day, and all disbursements—with the exception of payments from Petty Cash—should be made by check. When we talk about cash, we mean currency, coins, checks, money orders, and bank drafts or bank cashier's checks. Personal checks are accepted on a conditional-payment status, that is, based on the condition that they're valid. In other words, we give checks the benefit of the doubt, and consider them to be good until they are proved to be no good.

In this chapter, we're also going to talk about cash funds—petty cash funds and change funds, which—in this sense—are separately held stores of cash.

Using a checking account

Although you may be familiar with the process of opening a checking account, making deposits, and writing checks, let's review these and other procedures associated with opening and maintaining a business checking account. We'll discuss here signature cards, deposit slips, night deposits, and ways of endorsing checks.

Signature card

When Donald N. Simpson founded West Lincoln Rental Equipment, he opened a checking account in the name of the business. When he made his first deposit, he filled out a *signature card* for the bank's files. Simpson gave his accountant the right to sign checks too, so the accountant also signed the card. This card gives the bank a copy of the official signatures of any persons authorized to sign checks. The bank can use it as a verification of any signatures on checks of West Lincoln Rental Equipment presented for payment. This, of course, helps the bank detect forgeries. An example of a signature card appears on the facing page.

Deposit slips

The bank provides deposit slips on which the customer records the amount of coins and currency he or she is depositing, and lists each individual check being deposited. A typical deposit slip is shown on page 184. For identification purposes, each check should be listed according to its American Bankers Association (ABA) transit number. The ABA number is the small fractional number located in the upper right corner of a check. The numerator indicates the city or state in which the bank is located and the specific bank in that area; the denominator indicates the Federal Reserve District in which the check is cleared and the routing number used by the Federal Reserve Bank. For example,

$$\frac{68\text{-}420}{1010}$$

The 68 identifies the city or state, and the 420 indicates the specific bank within that area. It would be enough just to list the top part only on the deposit slip. However, for your own information, in the denominator, the first 10 represents the Tenth Federal Reserve District, and the second 10 is the routing number used by the Federal Reserve Bank.

The depositor fills out the deposit slip in duplicate, giving one copy to the bank teller, and keeping the other copy. (This procedure occasionally varies from bank to bank.)

When the bank receives the deposited checks, it prints the amount of each check on the lower right side of the check in a very distinctive-looking script. The script is called "MICR," which stands for *magnetic ink character recognition.* The routing number used by the Federal Reserve Bank was previously printed on the lower left side of the blank check. The reason they use this MICR script is that electronic equipment used by banks to process the checks is able to read the script identifying the bank on which the check is drawn as well as the amount of the check. Of course, because this is done electronically, the process of handling checks is speeded up considerably.

Night deposits Most banks provide night depositories so that firms can make deposits after regular banking hours. Depositories are steel-lined chutes into which a firm's representative can drop a bag of cash, knowing that their day's receipts will be safe until the bank opens in the morning.

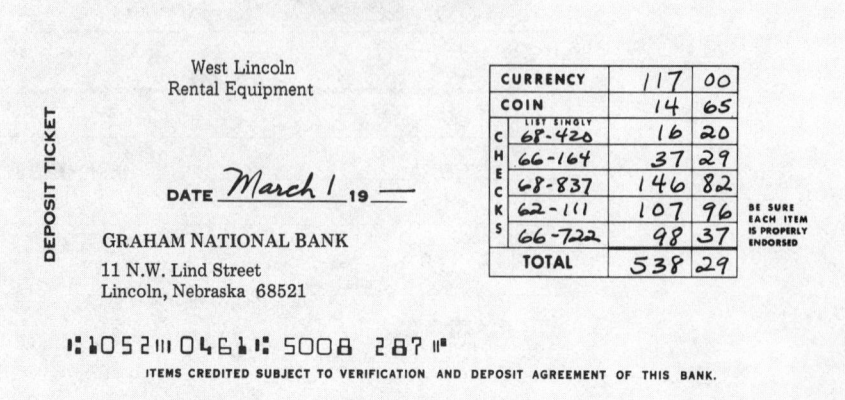

Endorsements The bank refuses to accept for deposit a check made out to a firm until someone from the firm has endorsed the check. The endorsement may be made by signature or by using a stamp. The endorsement (1) transfers title to the money, and (2) guarantees the payment of the check. In other words, if the check is not good, NSF (not sufficient funds), then the bank, in order to protect itself, is able to deduct the amount of the check from the depositor's account.

Note in the illustration on page 185 how an endorsement is written on the back of a check, on the left side. The endorsement should be written on the back on the left end of a check.

Our model company, West Lincoln Rental Equipment, endorses all incoming checks by putting its stamp on the back of the checks: "Pay to the Order of Graham National Bank, For Deposit Only, West Lincoln Rental Equipment."

This is called a *restrictive endorsement,* because it restricts or limits any further negotiation of the check; it forces the deposit of the check, since the endorsement is not valid for any other purpose.

Writing checks As you of course know, you have to use a check to withdraw money from a checking account. A check represents an order by the depositor, directing the bank to pay money to a designated person or firm: the *payee.*

The checks may be attached to check stubs. The stub has spaces to record the check number and amount, the date and payee, the purpose of the check, and the beginning and ending balances. *Note well:* The information recorded on the check stub is the basis for the journal entry. So check stubs are vitally important. A person in a hurry, or working under pressure, can sometimes neglect to fill in the check stubs; it is therefore best to record all the information on the check stub *before one makes out the check.*

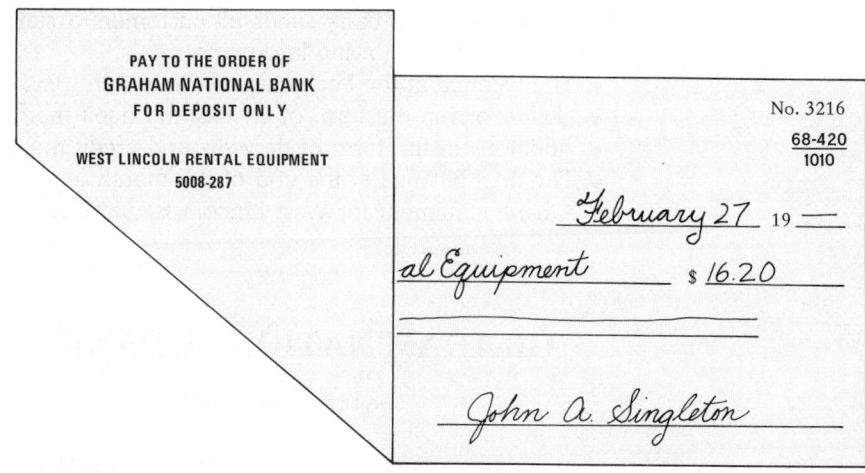

PAY TO THE ORDER OF
GRAHAM NATIONAL BANK
FOR DEPOSIT ONLY

WEST LINCOLN RENTAL EQUIPMENT
5008-287

No. 3216

68-420
1010

February 27 19 —

al Equipment $ *16.20*

John A. Singleton

It goes without saying that all checks should be written carefully, so that no dishonest person can successfully alter them. The payee's name goes on the first long line. Write the amount in figures close to the dollar sign, then write the amount in words at the extreme left of the line provided for this information. Write cents as a fraction of 100. For example, write $727.50 as "seven hundred twenty-seven and 50/100," or $69.00 as "sixty-nine and 00/100." From a legal standpoint, if there is a discrepancy between the amount in figures and the written amount, it is the written amount that prevails. However, as a general practice, the bank gets in touch with the depositor and asks what the correct amount should be.

Many firms use a *check writer,* which is a machine used to record, on the check itself, the amount in figures and in words. This neatly prevents anyone from altering the amount of the check.

Finally, the depositor's signature on the face of the check should match that of the signature card on file at the depositor's bank.

In the illustration we see a check with the accompanying stub, drawn on the account of West Lincoln Rental Equipment.

NO. *2023* $ *827.00*	West Lincoln Rental Equipment		No. 2023
DATE *Oct. 11* 19 —	3011 N.W. Clinton Street		68-461
TO *Paris Mfg. Co.*	Lincoln, Nebraska 68522		1052

	DOLLARS	CENTS
BAL. BRO'T. FOR'D.	6,952	95
AMT. DEPOSITED		
" "		
TOTAL		
AMT. THIS CHECK	827	00
BAL. CAR'D. FOR'D.	6,125	95

FOR *Merchandise*

October 11 19 —

PAY TO THE
ORDER OF *Paris Manufacturing Co.* $ *827.00*

Eight hundred twenty-seven and 00/100 ——— DOLLARS

GRAHAM NATIONAL BANK
11 N.W. Lind Street
Lincoln, Nebraska 68521

Donald N. Simpson

⑈1052⑈046⑈ 5008 287 ⑈

Bank statements

Once a month the bank sends all customers a statement of their accounts, giving them the following information.
- The balance at the beginning of the month
- Deductions in the form of checks and debit memos
- Additions in the form of deposits and credit memos
- The final balance at the end of the month

A bank statement for West Lincoln Rental Equipment is shown here.

GRAHAM NATIONAL BANK

11 N.W. Lind Street
Lincoln, Nebraska 68521

STATEMENT OF ACCOUNT

West Lincoln Rental Equipment
3011 N.W. Clinton Street
Lincoln, Nebraska 68522

ACCOUNT NO.
5008-287
STATEMENT DATE
October 31, 19

CHECKS AND OTHER DEBITS			DEPOSITS	DATE	BALANCE
		BALANCE BROUGHT FORWARD FROM LAST STATEMENT		Oct. 1, 19_	7,495.13
50.00	200.00	400.00	921.00	Oct. 1	7,766.13
46.00	174.23	671.74	1,476.22	Oct. 2	8,350.38
846.20	664.56		463.62	Oct. 3	7,303.24
719.00	61.68	591.84	789.43	Oct. 4	6,720.15
36.92	817.22	DM125.00	1,063.14	Oct. 7	6,804.15
523.00	786.40	374.00	1,211.96	Oct. 8	6,332.71
	943.64		CM606.00	Oct. 30	7,812.62
			873.19	Oct. 30	8,685.81
843.17	21.92	SC5.50	946.78	Oct. 31	8,762.00

CHECKING SUMMARY

BEGINNING BALANCE	TOTAL AMOUNT OF CHECKS & DEBITS		TOTAL AMOUNT OF DEPOSITS & CREDITS		SERVICE CHARGE AMOUNT	ENDING BALANCE
	NO.	AMOUNT	NO.	AMOUNT		
7,495.13	66	25,153.41	23	26,425.78	5.50	8,762.00

PLEASE EXAMINE THIS STATEMENT CAREFULLY. REPORT ANY POSSIBLE ERRORS IN 10 DAYS.

CODE SYMBOLS

CM Credit Memo
DM Debit Memo
EC Error Correction

OD Overdraft
SC Service Charge

CM Credit memo Increases or credits to the account, such as notes or accounts left with the bank for collection.

DM Debit memo Decreases or debits to the account, items returned such as NSF checks, special charges levied by the bank against the account.

EC Error correction Corrections of errors made by the bank, such as mistakes in transferring figures.

OD Overdraft An overwithdrawal, resulting in a negative balance in the account.

SC Service charge The amount charged by the bank for servicing the account, based on the number of items processed and the average balance of the account.

The bank statement is a valuable aid to efficiency, because it gives a double record of the Cash account. If a business entity deposits all cash receipts and makes all payments by check, then the bank is keeping an independent record of the firm's cash. Offhand, you might think that the two balances—the firm's and the bank's—should be equal, but this is most unlikely, because some transactions may have been recorded in the firm's account before being recorded in the bank's. Also there are often unavoidable delays (by either the firm or the bank) in recording transactions. There is generally a time lag of at least 2 days between the bank's cutoff date and the time it takes the post office to deliver the bank statement to the depositor. During this time, deposits made or checks written are recorded in the firm's checkbook, but are not yet recorded on the bank statement.

The bank usually mails statements to its depositors shortly after the end of the month. In the same envelope with the statement are the canceled checks (the firm's checks that have been cashed or cleared by the bank) and debit or credit memos. As we mentioned before, debit memos represent deductions and credit memos represent additions to a bank account. Each business entity keeps its accounts from its *own* point of view. Each customer's deposits, as far as the bank is concerned, are liabilities, in that the bank owes the customer the amount of the deposits. Using T accounts, it looks like this.

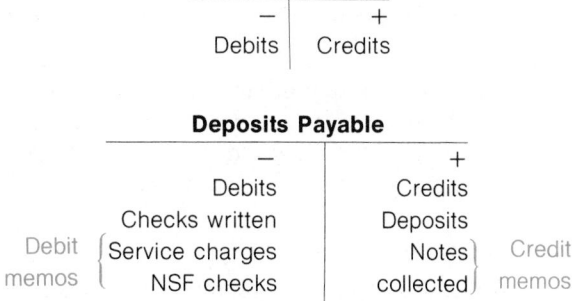

On the customer's books, of course, this comes under the account titled Cash, or Cash in Bank, or simply the name of the bank. Regardless of what title is used for the account, however, the balance of the account is referred to as the *book balance of Cash.*

Need for reconciling bank balance and book balance

The *book balance* is the balance of the Cash account in the general ledger. Since the bank statement balance and the book balance are not equal, a firm makes a *reconciliation* to discover the reasons for the difference between the two balances, and to correct any errors that may have been made by either the bank or the firm. This makes it possible to wind up with the same balance in each account, which is called the *adjusted balance,* or *true balance,* of the Cash account.

A variety of reasons or errors may cause the difference between the bank statement balance and the customer's cash balance. Some of the more usual ones are as follows.

Outstanding checks   Checks that have been written but which have not yet been received for payment by the time the bank sends out its statement. But the depositor, when writing out his or her checks, deducted the amounts from the Cash account in his/her books.

Late deposits   Deposits made after the bank statement was issued. Many accountants call these *deposits in transit.* The depositor has naturally already added them to the Cash account in his or her books, however.

Service charges   The bank charges for services rendered: for issuing checks, for collecting money, for receiving payment of notes turned over to it by the customer for collection, and for other such services. The bank notifies the depositor with a debit memorandum, and immediately deducts the fee from the balance of the bank account.

Collections   When the bank acts as a collection agent for its customers by accepting payments on promissory notes, installment accounts, and charge accounts, it adds the proceeds to the customer's bank account and sends a credit memorandum to notify the customer of the transaction.

NSF checks (not sufficient funds)   When a bank customer deposits a check, she or he counts it as cash. However, occasionally a check bounces, and then the bank sends the customer notice to that effect. The customer must then make a deduction from the Cash account.

Errors   In spite of internal control and systems designed to double-check against errors, sometimes either the customer or the bank may make a mistake. Often these errors do not become evident until the bank reconciliation is performed.

Follow these steps in reconciling a bank statement:

1. Canceled checks The bank stacks canceled checks returned to it in the order in which it paid them, and lists them in the same way on the bank statement. *While they are still stacked in this order,* compare each check with the bank statement, and note any discrepancies.

2. Deposits Look over the late deposits, or unrecorded deposits listed on the bank reconciliation of the previous month. Compare these with the deposits listed on this month's bank statement. These deposits should all be accounted for; note any discrepancy. Now compare the remaining deposits listed on the current bank statement with deposits written in the firm's accounting records. Consider any deposits not shown on the bank statement as late deposits, or deposits in transit.

3. Outstanding checks Next, arrange the canceled checks in the order of the check numbers. Look over the list of outstanding checks left over from the bank reconciliation of the previous month, and note the checks that have now been returned. Compare each canceled check with the entry in the journal. If the journal is not available, then compare the canceled checks with the check stubs. In either case, use a check mark (√) to indicate that the check has been paid and that the amount is correct. To further verify that money has been sent to the right payee, review the endorsements on the backs of the checks. Any payments that have *not* been checked off, including the outstanding checks from the previous bank reconciliation, are the present outstanding checks. In other words, they were not presented for payment by the time of the cutoff date of the bank statement.

4. Bank memorandums Trace the credit memos and the debit memos to the journal. If the memos have not been recorded, make separate journal entries for them.

As you can see, a bank can be an accountant's best friend. A large firm should require that the reconciliation be prepared by an employee who is not involved in recording business transactions.

As a more elementary illustration, let's take the case of J. P. Caldwell and Company, followed by the case of West Lincoln Rental Equipment.

J. P. Caldwell and Company The bank statement of J. P. Caldwell and Company indicates a balance of $2,119 as of March 31. The balance of the Cash account in their ledger as of that date is $1,552. Caldwell's accountant has taken the steps we've listed.

1. Verified that canceled checks were recorded correctly on the bank statement.

2. Noted that deposit made on March 31 was not recorded on the bank statement, $762.

3. Noted outstanding checks: No. 921, $626; No. 985, $69; No. 986, $438.

4. Noted credit memo: note collected by the bank, $200, not recorded in the journal. Noted debit memo: collection charge and service charge not recorded in the journal, $4.

The bank reconciliation may be made on a separate sheet of paper, or on the back of the bank statement, since some banks print the main headings on the form. Here are Caldwell's bank reconciliation and journal entries. The items in the reconciliation that require journal entries are highlighted in the illustration.

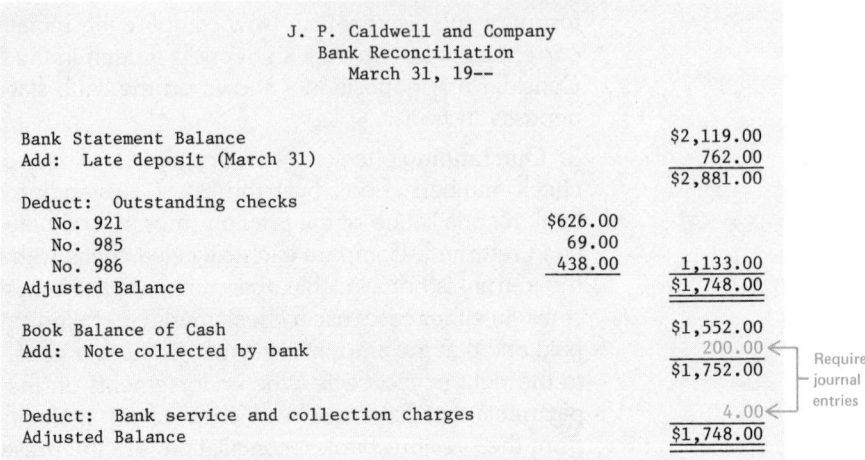

```
                        J. P. Caldwell and Company
                            Bank Reconciliation
                              March 31, 19--


Bank Statement Balance                                      $2,119.00
Add:  Late deposit (March 31)                                  762.00
                                                            $2,881.00
Deduct:  Outstanding checks
   No. 921                                    $626.00
   No. 985                                      69.00
   No. 986                                     438.00        1,133.00
Adjusted Balance                                            $1,748.00

Book Balance of Cash                                        $1,552.00
Add:  Note collected by bank                                   200.00 ←
                                                            $1,752.00      Require
                                                                          journal
                                                                          entries
Deduct:  Bank service and collection charges                    4.00 ←
Adjusted Balance                                            $1,748.00
```

Note that journal entries should be based on the bank reconciliation, since the true balance of Cash is $1,748, whereas the current balance on the firm's books is $1,552. You have undoubtedly seen that you can't change the balance of an account unless you first make a journal entry and then post the entry to the accounts involved. Consequently, you have to make journal entries only from the Book Balance of Cash section of the bank reconciliation. Debit additions to Cash and credit deductions from Cash. J. P. Caldwell and Company records the entries in their general journal.

	DATE		DESCRIPTION	POST REF.	DEBIT	CREDIT
1	19– Mar.	31	*Cash*		2 0 0 00		1
2			*Notes Receivable*			2 0 0 00	2
3			*Non-interest-bearing note signed by S. Alden*				3
4			*was collected by the bank.*				4
5							5
6		31	*Miscellaneous Expense*		4 00		6
7			*Cash*			4 00	7
8			*Service charge and collection charge levied*				8
9			*by the bank.*				9
10							10

Here service charges and collection charges are recorded in the same account, because the amounts are relatively small. However, some accountants may use separate expense accounts.

After posting the above entries, the T account for Cash looks like this:

Cash

Balance	1,552	Mar. 31	4
Mar. 31	200		
1,748	1,752		

Note that the balance in the T account is now equal to the adjusted balance on the bank reconciliation.

Form of bank reconciliation   Now that you have seen an illustration of a bank reconciliation, let's look at the standard form of a bank reconciliation for a hypothetical company.

Bank statement balance (last figure on the statement)		$4,000
Add		
Late deposits (already added to the Cash account)	$300	
Bank errors	20	320
		$4,320
Deduct		
Outstanding checks (they have already been deducted from the Cash account)	$960	
Bank errors	40	1,000
Adjusted balance (the true balance of Cash)		$3,320
Book balance of Cash (the latest balance of the Cash account if it has been posted up to date; otherwise take the beginning balance of Cash, plus cash receipts and minus cash payments)		$2,850
Add		
Credit memos (additions by the bank not recorded in the Cash account, such as collections of notes)	$500	
Book errors (that understate balance)	40	540
		$3,390
Deduct		
Debit memos (deductions by the bank not recorded in the Cash account, such as service charges or collection charges)	$ 20	
Book errors (that overstate balance)	50	70
Adjusted balance (the true balance of Cash)		$3,320

West Lincoln Rental Equipment The bank statement of West Lincoln Rental Equipment shows a final balance of $8,762 as of October 31. The present balance of the Cash account in the ledger, after West Lincoln's accountant has posted from the journal, is $7,806.50. The accountant took the following steps:

1. Verified that canceled checks were recorded correctly on the bank statement.

2. Discovered that a deposit of $1,003 made on October 31 was not recorded on the bank statement.

3. Noted outstanding checks: No. 1916, $461; No. 2022, $119; No. 2023, $827; No. 2024, $67.

4. Noted that a credit memo for a note collected by the bank from Ryan Plumbing and Heating, $600 principal plus $6 interest, was not recorded in the journal.

5. Found that Check No. 2001 for $523, payable to Mahon, Inc., on account was recorded in the journal as $532. (The correct amount is $523.)

6. Noted that a debit memo for a collection charge and service charge of $5.50 was not recorded in the journal.

7. Noted that debit memo for an NSF check for $125 from C. M. Lang Company was not recorded.

The accountant has to make the journal entries shown on page 193 in order to change the Cash account from the present balance of $7,806.50 to the true balance of $8,291. Again, those items that require journal entries are highlighted in the illustration.

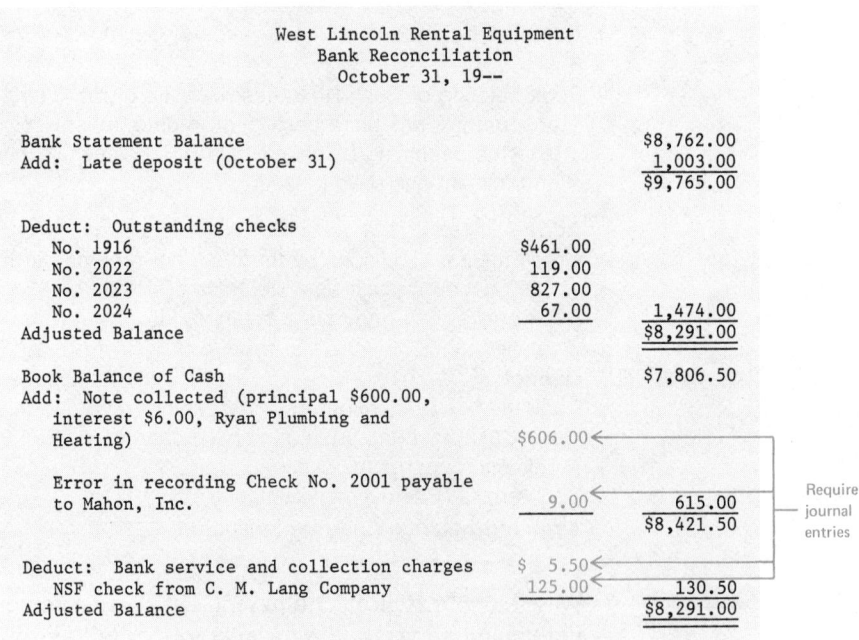

West Lincoln Rental Equipment
Bank Reconciliation
October 31, 19--

Bank Statement Balance		$8,762.00
Add: Late deposit (October 31)		1,003.00
		$9,765.00
Deduct: Outstanding checks		
No. 1916	$461.00	
No. 2022	119.00	
No. 2023	827.00	
No. 2024	67.00	1,474.00
Adjusted Balance		$8,291.00
Book Balance of Cash		$7,806.50
Add: Note collected (principal $600.00, interest $6.00, Ryan Plumbing and Heating)	$606.00	
Error in recording Check No. 2001 payable to Mahon, Inc.	9.00	615.00
		$8,421.50
Deduct: Bank service and collection charges	$ 5.50	
NSF check from C. M. Lang Company	125.00	130.50
Adjusted Balance		$8,291.00

Require journal entries

DATE		DESCRIPTION	POST REF.	DEBIT	CREDIT
19– Oct.	31	Cash		6 0 6 00	
		Notes Receivable			6 0 0 00
		Interest Income			6 00
		Bank collected note signed by Ryan Plumbing			
		and Heating.			
	31	Cash		9 00	
		Accounts Payable			9 00
		Error in recording Check No. 2001 payable to			
		Mahon, Inc.			
	31	Miscellaneous Expense		5 50	
		Cash			5 50
		Bank service charge and collection charge			
	31	Accounts Receivable		1 2 5 00	
		Cash			1 2 5 00
		NSF check received from C. M. Lang.			

The petty cash fund

Day after day, business firms are confronted with transactions involving small immediate payments, such as the cost of a telegram, delivery charges, postage due for mail, a new typewriter ribbon, etc. If the firm had to go through the usual procedure of making all payments by check, the time consumed would be frustrating, and the whole process unduly expensive. For many firms, just the cost of writing each check is more than $.50; this includes the cost of an employee's time in writing and reconciling the check. Suppose the mail carrier is at the door with a letter on which there is $.15 postage due. To write a check would be ridiculous. It only makes sense to pay in cash, out of the Petty Cash Fund. *Petty* means small; so the firm sets a maximum amount that can be paid out of the Petty Cash Fund. Payments larger than this maximum must be processed by regular check through the journal.

Establishing the petty cash fund

After the firm has decided on the maximum amount of a payment from petty cash, the next step is to estimate how much cash will be needed during a given period of time, such as a month. Small payments are made during the month from the Petty Cash Fund.

When keeping cash in the office, one also has to consider the element of security. If risk is great, the amount of the fund should be kept small, and the fund should be reimbursed at intervals of perhaps 1 week, or 2 weeks.

West Lincoln Rental Equipment decided to establish a Petty Cash Fund of $50 and put it under the control of the secretary. Accordingly, their accountant writes a check, cashes it at the bank, and records this in the journal as follows.

			COMBINED JOURNAL				PAGE_____

	DATE		ACCOUNT NAME	SUNDRY		CASH	
				DEBIT	CREDIT	DEBIT	CREDIT
1	19– Sep.	1	Petty Cash Fund	50 00			50 00	1
2								2
3								3
4								4
5								5
6								6
7								7
8								8
9								9
10								10

T accounts for this entry look like this:

Petty Cash Fund		Cash	
+	–	+	–
50			50

Because the Petty Cash Fund is an asset account, it is listed in the balance sheet immediately below Cash. Remember the following:

The Petty Cash Fund account is debited only once, and this happens when the fund is established initially.

The only exception would be a case in which the original amount was not large enough to handle the necessary transactions, and therefore the accountant had to make the Petty Cash Fund bigger—maybe change the $50 to $75. But, barring such a change in the size of the fund, Petty Cash is debited only once.

After the accountant cashes that original $50 check, he or she converts it into convenient denominations, such as quarters, dimes, etc., and puts the money in a locked drawer, in the secretary's desk, telling the secretary not to pay for anything larger than $5 out of Petty Cash.

Payments from the petty cash fund

The secretary now takes the responsibility for the Petty Cash Fund; he or she is designated as the only person who can make payments from it. In case of his or her illness, some other employee should be named as stand-in. There has to be a *petty cash voucher* to account for *every* payment from the fund, in other words, a receipt signed by the person who authorized the payment and by the person receiving payment. Even for these small payments of $5 or less, there would have to be collusion between the payee and the secretary in order for any theft to occur. The following illustration shows what a petty cash voucher looks like.

PETTY CASH VOUCHER

No. *1*   Date *September 2, 19—*

Paid to *Excell Delivery Service* $*2.00*

For *Delivery*

Account *Delivery Expense*

Approved by   Payment received by

R. Jason   *C. J. Comstock*

Reimbursement of the petty cash fund

At the end of the month, when the fund is nearly exhausted, the accountant reimburses the fund for expenditures made to bring the fund back up to the original amount. Consequently, it may be considered to be a revolving fund. If the amount initially put in the Petty Cash Fund is $50 and at the end of the month all that's left is $4, the accountant puts $46 in the fund as a reimbursement, thereby bringing it back up to $50 to start the new month.

For example, take Voucher no. 1 (shown in the illustration), in which $2 is charged to Delivery Expense. Let's say that, as the month goes by, $12 more is charged to Delivery Expense on other petty cash vouchers. Assume that the total amount spent from the fund during the month is $43. At the end of the month, the accountant makes a summarizing entry, debiting the accounts which have been recorded on the petty cash vouchers, and crediting Cash. For this month, she or he debits Delivery Expense for $14, debits other accounts for $29, and credits Cash for $43. By doing this, she or he officially journalizes the transactions so that they can be posted to the ledger accounts. The accountant writes a check payable to Cash, for $43, cashes it, and has the secretary put the money in the drawer, bringing the fund up to the original $50.

Some firms like a written record on one sheet of paper, so they keep a *petty cash payments record,* with columns in the Distribution of Accounts section labeled with the types of expenditures they make most often.

West Lincoln Rental Equipment made the following payments from its Petty Cash Fund during September.

Sept. 2 Paid $2 to Excell Delivery Service, Voucher no. 1.
       3 Bought pencils and pens, $3.20, Voucher no. 2.
       5 Paid local newspaper for advertising, $5, Voucher no. 3.
       7 Paid for mailing packages, $2.90, Voucher no. 4.

Sept. 10 Donald N. Simpson, the owner, withdrew $5 for personal use, Voucher no. 5.

14 Postage due on incoming mail, $.16, Voucher no. 6.

21 Bought typewriter ribbons, $4.10, Voucher no. 7.

22 Paid $3 to Excell Delivery Service, Voucher no. 8.

26 Paid for mailing packages, $3.80, Voucher no. 9.

27 Paid $3.50 to Fast Way Delivery, Voucher no. 10.

29 Bought memo pads, $4.40, Voucher no. 11.

29 Paid for collect telegram, $2.60, Voucher no. 12.

30 Paid $3.20 to Excell Delivery Service, Voucher no. 13.

30 Paid for having windows cleaned, $5, Voucher no. 14.

PETTY CASH PAY
Month of

	DATE	VOU. NO.	EXPLANATION		
1	Sep.	1		Established fund, Check No. 88, $50	
2		2	1	Excell Delivery Service	
3		3	2	Pencils and pens	
4		5	3	Local newspaper	
5		7	4	Postage for mailings	
6		10	5	Donald N. Simpson	
7					
8		14	6	Postage on incoming mail	
9		21	7	Typewriter ribbons	
10		22	8	Excell Delivery Service	
11		26	9	Postage for mailings	
12		27	10	Fastway Delivery	
13		29	11	Memo pads	
14		29	12	Collect telegram	
15		30	13	Excell Delivery Service	
16		30	14	Cleaning windows	
17		30		Totals	
18				Balance in Fund	$ 2.14
19				Reimbursed Ck. No. 136	47.86
20				Total	$50.00
21					
22					
23					
24					
25					
26					
27					

West Lincoln Rental Equipment uses a petty cash payments record to keep track of the payments according to purpose. This is only a supplementary record, *not* a journal. It is merely used as a basis for compiling the journal entry to reimburse the fund. West Lincoln's petty cash payments record is shown below.

Now the accountant makes the summarizing entry in order to officially journalize the transactions that have taken place. He or she takes the information directly from the petty cash payments record.

The T accounts and the journal entry are shown at the top of page 198.

Note that in the summarizing entry the accountant debits the accounts on whose behalf the payments were made, and credits the Cash account. *He or she leaves the Petty Cash Fund strictly alone.* Then she or he cashes a check for $47.86, and puts the cash in the secretary's desk drawer, thereby restoring the amount in the Petty Cash Fund to the original $50.

MENTS RECORD
September 19—

PAGE___1___

| PAYMENTS | DISTRIBUTION OF PAYMENTS | | | | |
	OFFICE SUPPLIES	DELIVERY EXPENSE	MISC. GEN. EXPENSE	SUNDRY ACCOUNT	AMOUNT
2 00		2 00			
3 20	3 20				
5 00				Advertising Expense	5 00
2 90		2 90			
5 00				D. N. Simpson, Drawing	5 00
16			16		
4 10	4 10				
3 00		3 00			
3 80		3 80			
3 50		3 50			
4 40	4 40				
2 60			2 60		
3 20		3 20			
5 00			5 00		
47 86	11 70	18 40	7 76		10 00

The petty cash fund **197**

	DATE		ACCOUNT NAME	SUNDRY DEBIT	SUNDRY CREDIT	CASH DEBIT	CASH CREDIT	
1	19– Sep.	30	Office Supplies	11 70			47 86	1
2			Delivery Expense	18 40				2
3			Micellaneous Expense	7 76				3
4			Advertising Expense	5 00				4
5			Donald N. Simpson,	5 00				5
6			Drawing					6

Office Supplies		Cash	
+	−	+	−
11.70			47.86

Delivery Expense	
+	−
18.40	

Miscellaneous Expense	
+	−
7.76	

Advertising Expense	
+	−
5.00	

Donald N. Simpson, Drawing	
+	−
5.00	

The change fund

Anyone who has ever tried to pay for a small item by handing the clerk a $20 bill knows that a firm which carries out numerous cash transactions needs a Change Fund.

Establishing the change fund

Before setting up a Change Fund, one has to decide on two things: (1) how much money needs to be in the fund, and (2) what denominations of bills and coins are needed. The Change Fund is like the Petty Cash Fund in that *it is debited only once: when it is established.* It is left at the initial figure unless the person in charge decides to make it larger. The Change Fund account, like the Petty Cash account, is also a current asset, and is recorded in the balance sheet immediately below Cash. If the Change Fund account is larger than the Petty Cash account, it precedes Petty Cash.

The owner of West Lincoln Rental Equipment, Mr. Simpson, decides to establish a Change Fund; he decides this at the same time he sets up his Petty Cash Fund. The entries for both transactions look like this.

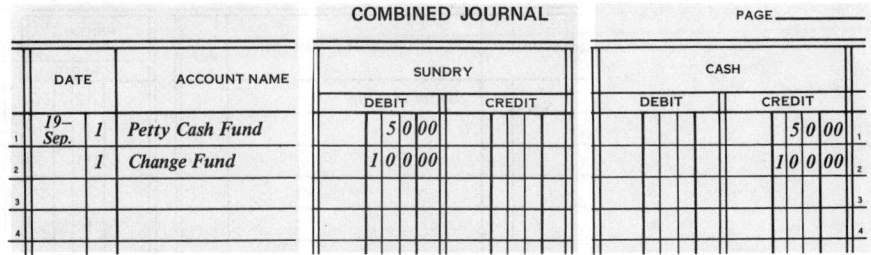

	DATE		ACCOUNT NAME	SUNDRY DEBIT	SUNDRY CREDIT	CASH DEBIT	CASH CREDIT	
1	19– Sep.	1	Petty Cash Fund	50 00			50 00	1
2		1	Change Fund	100 00			100 00	2
3								3
4								4

COMBINED JOURNAL — PAGE _____

The T accounts for establishing the change fund are as follows.

Change Fund		Cash	
+	−	+	−
100			100

So Simpson cashes a check for $100, gets the money in several denominations, and he's prepared to make change in any normal business transactions.

Depositing cash

At the end of each business day, Simpson deposits the cash taken in during the day, but he holds back the amount of the Change Fund, being sure that it's in convenient denominations. The *time* he makes up the Change Fund depends on what time his shop closes for the day, and what time the bank closes. Let's say that on September 1, West Lincoln Rental Equipment has $325 on hand at the end of the day. The T accounts look like this.

Cash		Rental Income	
+	−	−	+
225			225

Simpson records this in the combined journal as follows.

COMBINED JOURNAL — PAGE _____

	DATE		ACCOUNT NAME	POST REF.	RENTAL INCOME CREDIT	CASH DEBIT	CASH CREDIT	
1	19– Sep.	1	Rental Income		225 00	225 00		1
2								2
3								3

Now recall that the amount of the cash deposit is the total cash count less the amount of the Change Fund, so that's how the deposit happens to be $225. On another day the cash count is $327. So Simpson deposits $227 and the deposit is as shown below.

COMBINED JOURNAL							PAGE_____		
DATE	ACCOUNT NAME	POST REF.	RENTAL INCOME		CASH				
			CREDIT		DEBIT		CREDIT		
19– Sep 9	Rental Income		2 2 7 00		2 2 7 00				

Some business firms label the Cash account as *Cash in Bank,* and label the Change Fund as *Cash on Hand.*

Cash short and over

An inherent danger in making change is the human factor: Human beings make mistakes, especially when there are many customers to be waited on or when the business is temporarily short-handed. Ideally, mistakes should be eliminated. One reason that a business uses a cash register is to detect mistakes in the handling of cash. If, after removing the change fund, the day's receipts are less than the machine reading, then a cash shortage exists. Conversely, when the day's receipts are greater than the machine reading, a cash overage exists. However, because mistakes do happen, accounting records must be set up to cope with the situation. Both shortages and overages are recorded in the same account, which is called Cash Short and Over. (The Cash Short and Over account may also be used to handle shortages and overages in the Petty Cash Fund.) Shortages are considered to be an expense of operating a business and, therefore, are recorded on the debit side of the account. Overages are treated as another form of revenue and so are recorded on the credit side of the account.

For example, let's say that on September 14 West Lincoln Rental Equipment is faced with the following situation.

Cash Register Tape	Cash Count	Amount of the Change Fund
$281	$378	$100

After deducting the $100 in the Change Fund, Simpson will deposit $278. Note that this amount is less than the amount indicated by the cash register; therefore, a cash shortage exists. The following T accounts show how Simpson entered this transaction into the books.

Cash		Rental Income		Cash Short and Over
+	−	−	+	3
278			281	

The next day, September 15, the pendulum happens to swing in the other direction.

Cash Register Tape	Cash Count	Amount of the Change Fund
$356	$457	$100

The amount to be deposited is $357 ($457–$100). This figure is $1 greater than the $356 in rental income indicated by the cash register tape. Thus, there is a $1 cash overage on this occasion. The analysis of this transaction is shown below in T accounts.

Cash		Rental Income		Cash Short and Over
+	−	−	+	1
$357			$356	

Now let's summarize our discussion of the Cash Short and Over account by drawing these conclusions from the illustration.

1. At the close of the business day, the firm deposits the total day's receipts, holding back the Change Fund.

2. The firm records its rental income as being the amount shown on the cash register tape.

3. If the amount of cash actually received disagrees with the record of receipts, Cash Short and Over takes up the difference. In the first situation just described, there was a shortage of $3, so there was a debit to Cash Short and Over. In the second situation, there was an overage of $1, so there was a credit to Cash Short and Over. It is apparent that as a result of these transactions the account looks like this.

Cash Short and Over

Shortage 3	Overage 1

Because the Cash Short and Over account is used quite frequently, the accountant may provide for it in the combined journal. Many firms include a Cash Short and Over *debit* column for the shortages and a Cash Short and Over *credit* column for the overages. When recorded in the combined journal, West Lincoln Rental Equipment's revenue for September 14 and 15 looks as shown atop the following page.

DATE		ACCOUNT NAME	CASH SHORT AND OVER		PROFESSIONAL FEES	RENTAL INCOME	CASH	
			DEBIT	CREDIT	CREDIT	CREDIT	DEBIT	CREDIT
19—Sep.	14	Rental Income	3 00			2 8 1 00	2 7 8 00	
	15	Rental Income		1 00		3 5 6 00	3 5 7 00	

As far as errors are concerned, one would think that shortages would be offset by overages. However, customers are more likely to report shortages than overages. Consequently, to the firm shortages predominate. A firm may set a tolerance level for the cashiers. If the shortages consistently exceed the level of tolerance, either there is fraud involved or somebody is making entirely too many careless mistakes.

Throughout any fiscal period, the accountant continually has to record shortages and overages in the Cash Short and Over account. Let's say that West Lincoln's final balance is $21 on the debit side.

So West Lincoln winds up with a net shortage of $21. Therefore, *at the end of the fiscal period, if the account has a debit balance or net shortage, the accountant classifies it as an expense, and puts it in the income statement under Miscellaneous Expense.* The T account would look like this.

Cash Short and Over

Short	3	Over	1
	4		1
	3		2
	7		2
	5		1
	2		2
	3		1
	4		10
	21		31

Conversely, if the account has a credit balance or net overage, the accountant classifies it as a revenue account, and puts it in the income statement under Miscellaneous Income. This is an exception to the policy of recording accounts in financial statements under the name of their exact account title. Rather than attaching plus and minus signs to the Cash Short and Over account immediately, we wait until we find out its final balance.

Summary

A business firm has a valuable ally in its bank, because the bank maintains a record of cash which is independent of the firm's record of cash. That is, the bank does this if the business deposits all incoming cash in the bank, and makes all cash payments by check. The only exception to this—and it is a minor one—is the case of transactions involving Petty Cash.

The bank sends its statement accompanied by canceled checks, debit memos, and credit memos. Debit memos cover service and collection charges, as well as NSF checks. Credit memos cover the collection of notes or other items left for collection.

Each month the firm's accountant has to make a reconciliation between the bank account balance and the firm's Cash account balance because some transactions might not have been recorded by either the bank or the depositor, or errors might have been made by either.

In this chapter, we discussed two special funds: the Petty Cash Fund and the Change Fund. A fund, in every case, is a separate kitty of cash. When one establishes a fund, one makes a check payable to the particular fund, then cashes it, and converts it into convenient denominations. The original entry in each case is a debit to the fund account and a credit to Cash. The journal entry to reimburse Petty Cash is a debit to the accounts for which the money was expended (as shown by the petty cash payments record or a summary of the petty cash vouchers) and a credit to Cash. The Petty Cash Fund account is debited only at the time it is established, and remains at the same level, unless the firm decides to change the account's size. Whenever a firm makes a bank deposit, it holds back the amount of the Change Fund and converts it into the proper change.

The Cash Short and Over account takes care of errors in making change. A debit to Cash Short and Over denotes a shortage; a credit to Cash Short and Over denotes an overage.

Glossary

ABA number   The number assigned by the American Bankers Association to a given bank. The first part of the numerator denotes the city or state in which the bank is located; the second part denotes the bank on which the check is drawn. The denominator indicates the Federal Reserve District and the routing number used by the Federal Reserve Bank.

Bank reconciliation   A process by which an accountant determines whether there is a difference between the balance as shown on the bank statement and the balance of the Cash account in the firm's general ledger. The object is to determine the adjusted (or true) balance of the Cash account.

Bank statement   Periodic statement which a bank sends to the holder of a checking account listing deposits received and checks paid by the bank, as well as debit and credit memorandums.

Canceled checks Checks issued by the depositor that have been paid by the bank and listed on the bank statement. They are called canceled checks because they are canceled by a stamp or perforation, indicating that they have been paid.

Cash fund A sum of money set aside for a specific purpose.

Change Fund A cash fund used by a firm to make change for customers who pay cash for goods or services.

Deposit slip A printed form provided by a bank so that a customer can list in detail all the items being deposited; also known as a *deposit ticket*.

Endorsement The process by which the payee (party to whom the check is payable) transfers ownership of the check to a bank or another party. A check must be endorsed when deposited in a bank because the bank must have legal title to it in order to collect payment from the drawer of the check (the person or firm who wrote the check). In case the check cannot be collected, the endorser guarantees all subsequent holders (*Exception:* an endorsement "without recourse").

Late deposit Deposit not recorded on the bank statement because the deposit was made between the time of the bank's closing date for compiling items for its statement and the time the statement is received by the depositor; also known as a *deposit in transit*.

MICR Magnetic ink character recognition, the script the bank uses to print the number of the depositor's account and the bank's number at the bottom of checks and deposit slips. A number written in this script can be read by electronic equipment used by banks in clearing checks.

Monetary denominations Varieties of currency and coins, such as $5 bills, $1 bills, quarters, dimes, nickels, etc.

NSF check A check drawn against an account in which there are *Not Sufficient Funds;* this check is returned by the depositor's bank to the drawer's bank because of nonpayment; also known as a *dishonored check*.

Outstanding checks Checks which have been issued by the depositor and deducted on his/her records, but which have not reached the bank for payment and deduction by the time the bank issues its statement.

Petty Cash Fund A cash fund used to make small immediate cash payments.

Petty cash payments record A record indicating the amount of each petty cash voucher, and the accounts to which they are to be charged.

Petty cash voucher A form stating who got what from the Petty Cash fund, signed by (1) the person in charge of the fund, and (2) the person who received the cash.

Restrictive endorsement An endorsement, such as "Pay to the order of (name of bank), for deposit only," that limits further negotiation of a check. It forces the check's deposit, since the endorsement is not valid for anything else.

Service charge The fee the bank charges for handling checks, collections, and other items. It is in the form of a debit memorandum.

Signature card The form a depositor signs to give the bank a sample of his or her signature. The bank uses it to verify the depositor's signature on checks, on cash items that he or she may endorse for deposit, and on other business papers that he or she may present to the bank.

Questions

1. What is the purpose of a signature card?

2. What is the purpose of a bank reconciliation?

3. Indicate whether the following items in a bank reconciliation should be (a) added to the cash account balance, (b) deducted from the cash account balance, (c) added to the bank statement balance, (d) deducted from the bank statement balance.

(1) Deposit in transit

(2) NSF check

(3) Bank error charging the firm's account with another company's check

(4) Outstanding check

4. Describe in order the steps in reconciling a bank statement.

5. Explain the purpose served by a petty cash fund. Describe the entries to establish and reimburse the fund.

6. What is the purpose of a petty cash payments record?

7. What does a debit balance in Cash Short and Over represent? Where does it appear in the financial statements? What does a credit balance in Cash Short and Over represent? Where does it appear in the financial statements?

Exercises

Exercise 1 The Danville Hardware Company made the following bank reconciliation on April 30 of this year. Record the necessary entries in general journal form.

Bank Statement Balance		$2,598.00
Add: Deposit of April 30		203.00
		$2,801.00
Deduct: Outstanding checks		
No. 191	$280.00	
No. 192	210.00	490.00
Adjusted Balance		$2,311.00
Book Balance of Cash		$1,932.00
Add: Proceeds of note collected		420.00
		$2,352.00
Deduct: NSF check of Thomas Bacon	38.00	
Collection charge for note	3.00	41.00
Adjusted Balance		$2,311.00

Exercise 2 Pedro's Taco Shop deposits all receipts in the bank on the day received and makes all payments by check. On November 30, the Cash account showed a balance of $886 after all posting was completed. The bank statement received on November 30 had an ending balance of $602. Prepare a bank reconciliation using the following information, and record the necessary entries in general journal form.

a. The bank included with the November canceled checks a $4 debit memorandum for service charges.

b. Outstanding checks, $388.

c. The November 30 cash receipts, $632, were placed in the bank's night depository after banking hours on that date and were not listed on the bank statement.

d. Check No. 634, returned with the canceled checks, was correctly drawn for $62 in payment of the electric bill and was paid by the bank on November 16, but it was erroneously recorded in the check register and debited to the Utilities Expense account as though it were for $26.

Exercise 3 Stellingwerf Diner calls you in as an accountant. Prepare a bank reconciliation for them, given the following information about their bank account for March. Record the necessary entries in general journal form.

a. Balance of the Cash account in the general ledger, $2,817.66.

b. Last balance shown on bank statement, $2,555.34.

c. Service charge levied by bank appearing on debit memo, $8.32.

d. Deposit put in night depository on last day of the month, but not recorded on bank statement, $254.

Exercise 4 Frances B. Stranne's bank account for May of this year indicates a balance of $1,830.60 on May 31. Her bank balance according to her check stubs on that date is $1,186. A comparison of the bank statement, canceled checks, and the memorandums with the check stubs reveals the following. Prepare a bank reconciliation.

a. Checks outstanding $90.

b. A deposit of $272 had been recorded twice in her check record.

c. Stranne made a deposit of $832 on May 11, but forgot to record it in her check record.

d. The bank deducted $5.40 for service charges; Stranne had not recorded it in her check record.

Exercise 5 Make entries in general journal form to record the following.

a. Established a Petty Cash Fund. $75.

b. Reimbursed the Petty Cash fund for expenditures of $64; store supplies, $19; office supplies, $17; miscellaneous expense, $28.

Exercise 6 Make entries in general journal form to record the following.

a. Established a Change Fund, $220.

b. Record the cash sales for the day; the cash in the cash register is $843.

Exercise 7 The cash register tape for today indicates $982.16 as sales for the day. The cash count, including a $200 Change Fund, is $1,180.72. Make the entry to record how much cash you will deposit in the bank today.

Exercise 8 Describe the nature of the entries that have been posted to the following accounts after the Change Fund was established.

Change Fund		Sales		Cash	
200			948	946	
			940	941	
			1,036	1,032	

Cash Short and Over	
2	1
4	

Problems

Problem 8-1 The Richardson Company deposits all receipts in the bank each evening and makes all payments by check. On November 30, its Cash in Bank account has a balance of $2,083.45. The bank statement of November 30 shows a balance of $2,187.05. The following information pertains to reconciling the bank statement.

a. The reconciliation for October, the previous month, showed three checks outstanding on October 31: No. 1319 for $95, No. 1322 for $86.50, and No. 1323 for $116. Checks No. 1319 and 1323 were returned with the November bank statement; however, Check No. 1322 was not returned.

b. Checks No. 1386 for $49, No. 1389 for $31.60, No. 1390 for $121.50, and No. 1391 for $27 were written during November and have not been returned by the bank.

c. A deposit of $420 was placed in the night depository on November 30 and did not appear on the bank statement.

d. The canceled checks were compared with the entries in the check book, and it was observed that check No. 1387 for $89, was written correctly, payable to C. L. Farley, the owner, for personal use; however, the check was recorded in the check book as $98.

e. A bank debit memo for service charges, $3.

f. A bank credit memo for collection of a note signed by M. L. Rimpel, $202, including $200 principal and $2 interest.

Instructions **1.** Prepare a bank reconciliation.

2. Journalize the necessary entries in general journal form, assuming that the debit and credit memos have not been recorded.

Problem 8-2 On June 30, the Shotwell Company prepared its bank reconciliation with three outstanding checks: No. 1611 for $334, No. 1619 for $145, and No. 1620 for $274.40. The company, which deposits its receipts in the bank and makes all payments by check, receives the following statement from the Central National Bank. The debit memo for $74 is for an NSF check written by Thomas N. Kaiser. The debit memo for $6.20 is for a service charge.

CENTRAL NATIONAL BANK

Shotwell Company
7618 East Fenton Blvd.
Chicago, Illinois 60611

ACCOUNT NO.: 854-153-892

DATE: July 31, 19—

CHECKS AND OTHER DEBITS			DEPOSITS		DATE		BALANCE	
			BALANCE BROUGHT FORWARD		July	1	2,326	32
145	00	334 00	983	00		3	2,830	32
274	40					5	2,555	92
472	50	319 78	831	44		6	2,595	08
240	00					8	2,355	08
859	20		878	32		9	2,374	20
			756	40		11	3,130	60
74	80	76 98				12	2,978	82
			583	52		15	3,562	34
365	42	737 40				17	2,459	52
193	74		285	80		18	2,551	58
DM 74	00					22	2,477	58
38	40					25	2,439	18
DM 6	20		737	86		28	3,170	84

PLEASE EXAMINE THIS STATEMENT CAREFULLY. REPORT ANY POSSIBLE ERRORS IN 10 DAYS.

CODE SYMBOLS

CM Credit Memo
DM Debit Memo
EC Error Correction

OD Overdraft
SC Service Charge

A partial combined journal for the Shotwell Company is as follows.

COMBINED JOURNAL PAGE 9

	DATE	CHECK NO.	ACCOUNT NAME	LABORATORY EXPENSE DEBIT	MISC. EXPENSE DEBIT	CASH DEBIT	CASH CREDIT	
1	19— Jul. 1	1621					472 50	1
2	2	1622					319 78	2
3	3					983 00		3
4	5	1623					859 20	4
5	5	1624					240 00	5
6	6					831 44		6
7	7					878 32		7
8	9	1625					76 98	8
9	9	1626					74 80	9
10	12					756 40		10
11	14	1627					365 42	11
12	15					583 52		12
13	15	1628					737 40	13
14	16	1629					193 74	14
15	18					285 80		15
16	23	1630					38 40	16
17	28	1631					220 00	17
18	29					737 86		18
19	28	1632					142 38	19
20	29	1633					326 40	20
21	30					331 38		21
22	31					5387 72	4067 00	22
23								23
24								24
25								25
26								26

The Cash account in the general ledger is as follows.

GENERAL LEDGER

ACCOUNT Cash ACCOUNT NO. 111

DATE	ITEM	POST. REF.	DEBIT	CREDIT	BALANCE DEBIT	BALANCE CREDIT
19— Jun. 30	Balance	✓			1572 92	
Jul. 31		C9	5387 72		6960 64	
31		C9		4067 00	2893 64	

1. Prepare a bank reconciliation as of July 31.

2. Journalize the entries in general journal form, assuming that the debit memos have not been recorded.

Problem 8-3 On March 1 of this year, Hofer Burner Service Company established a Petty Cash Fund. The following petty cash transactions took place during the month.

Mar. 1 Cashed Check No. 956 for $80 to establish a Petty Cash Fund, and put the $80 in a locked drawer in the office.

3 Bought postage stamps $6, Voucher No. 1 (Office Supplies).

4 Issued Voucher No. 2 for taxi fare, $4 (Miscellaneous Expense).

6 Issued Voucher No. 3 for delivery charges on outgoing parts, $8.

9 B. W. Hofer withdrew $9.50 for personal use, Voucher No. 4.

13 Bought postage stamps, $7, Voucher No. 5.

19 Bought pens for office, $7.74, Voucher No. 6.

23 Paid $2 for trash removal, Voucher No. 7 (Miscellaneous Expense).

28 Paid $9 for window cleaning service, Voucher No. 8.

29 Paid $1.82 for pencils for office, Voucher No. 9.

31 Issued for cash Check No. 1098 for $55.06 to reimburse Petty Cash Fund.

Instructions **1.** Journalize the entry establishing the Petty Cash Fund in the general journal.

2. Record the disbursements of petty cash in the petty cash payments record.

3. Journalize the summarizing entry to reimburse the Petty Cash Fund.

Problem 8-4 During May of this year, the Mountainview Company has the following transactions involving its Change Fund, its Cash Short and Over, and its Income from Services account received in cash.

May 1 Established a Change Fund, $200.

6 Recorded cash revenue for the week: cash register tape, $1,372; cash count, $1,570.75.

13 Recorded cash revenue for the week: cash register tape, $1,621.20; cash count, $1,818.45.

20 Recorded cash revenue for the week: cash register tape, $1,548.35; cash count, $1,749.70.

31 Recorded cash revenue for the remainder of the month: cash register tape, $1,976.47; cash count, $2,172.85.

Instructions **1.** Record the entry establishing the Change Fund in the general journal.

2. Record the cash revenue in the general journal. In making bank deposits, the firm holds back the amount of the change fund.

3. Post the appropriate entries to the Cash Short and Over ledger account. Where will the balance of the account appear in the income statement?

Alternate problems

Problem 8-1A The Porterfield Company deposits all receipts in the bank and makes all payments by check. On September 30 its Cash in Bank account has a balance of $2,829.42. The bank statement on September 30 shows a balance of $2,999.21. You are given the following information with which to reconcile the bank statement.

a. The reconciliation for August, the previous month, showed three checks outstanding on August 31: No. 726 for $81.30, No. 729 for $127.40, and No. 730 for $38.46. Checks No. 726 and 729 were returned with the September bank statement; however, Check No. 730 was not returned.

b. A deposit of $274.23 was placed in the night depository on September 30 and did not appear on the bank statement.

c. Checks No. 741 for $31, No. 742 for $19.20, No. 743 for $106, and No. 744 for $14.56 were written during September, but were not returned by the bank.

d. A bank debit memo for service charges, $3.20.

e. A bank credit memo for collection of a note signed by Franklin L. Mason, $202, including $200 principal and $2 interest.

f. You compare the canceled checks with the entries in the check book and find that Check No. 737 for $48 was written correctly, payable to M. C. Summers, the owner, for her personal use. However, the check was recorded in the check register as $84.

Instructions   **1.** Prepare a bank reconciliation.

2. Journalize the necessary entries in general journal form, assuming that the debit and credit memos have not been recorded.

Problem 8-2A On July 31 Sisson's Carpet Cleaners prepared its bank reconciliation, with three outstanding checks: No. 912 for $344, No. 918 for $152, and No. 919 for $292. The company deposits its receipts in the bank and makes all payments by check. The Shannon National Bank sent Sisson's Carpet Cleaners the statement shown atop the next page. (The debit memo for $98 is for an NSF check written by A. C. Gibson. The debit memo for $4 is for a service charge.)

SHANNON NATIONAL BANK

Sisson's Carpet Cleaners
3152 N.E. Workman Ave.
Toledo, Ohio 44366

ACCOUNT NO.: 168-652-219

STATEMENT DATE: August 31, 19—

CHECKS AND OTHER DEBITS				DEPOSITS		DATE		BALANCE	
		BALANCE BROUGHT FORWARD				Aug.	1	1,944	00
				652	00		2	2,596	00
344	00	152	00				4	2,100	00
292	00			824	00		5	2,632	00
412	00	278	00				7	1,942	00
400	00						8	1,542	00
1,242	00			874	00		9	1,174	00
				736	00		14	1,910	00
74	00	28	00				17	1,808	00
				838	00		18	2,646	00
1,066	00						23	1,580	00
				796	00		24	2,376	00
188	00			582	00		28	2,770	00
DM 98	00	DM 4	00				31	2,668	00

PLEASE EXAMINE THIS STATEMENT CAREFULLY. REPORT ANY POSSIBLE ERRORS IN 10 DAYS.

CODE SYMBOLS

CM Credit Memo
DM Debit Memo
EC Error Correction

OD Overdraft
SC Service Charge

Sisson's Carpet Cleaners' partial combined journal is presented below.

COMBINED JOURNAL
PAGE 9

DATE		CHECK NO.	ACCOUNT NAME	DELIVERY EXPENSE DEBIT	MISC. EXPENSE DEBIT	CASH DEBIT	CASH CREDIT	
19— Aug.	2	920				652 00		1
	2						412 00	2
	3	921					278 00	3
	4	922					400 00	4
	5					824 00		5
	6	923					1242 00	6
	9					874 00		7
	12	924					74 00	8
	13	925					28 00	9
	14					736 00		10
	18					838 00		11
	19	926					1066 00	12
	24					796 00		13
	26	927					188 00	14
	27	928					238 00	15
	28					582 00		16
	30	929					486 00	17
	31					448 00		18
						5750 00	4412 00	19

Sisson's Carpet Cleaners' Cash account in the general ledger appears as follows.

GENERAL LEDGER
ACCOUNT _____ Cash _____ ACCOUNT NO. 111

DATE		ITEM	POST. REF.	DEBIT	CREDIT	BALANCE DEBIT	BALANCE CREDIT
19— Jul.	31	Balance	✓			1156 00	
19— Aug.	31		C9	5750 00		6906 00	
	31		C9		4412 00	2494 00	

Instructions
1. Prepare a bank reconciliation as of August 31.

2. Journalize the entries in general journal form, assuming that the debit memos have not been recorded.

Problem 8-3A On April 1 of this year, the Amberg Company established a Petty Cash Fund, and the following petty cash transactions took place during the month.

Apr. 1 Cashed Check No. 3168 for $70 to establish a Petty Cash Fund, and put the $70 in a locked drawer in the office.

4 Issued Voucher No. 1 for taxi fare, $4 (Miscellaneous Expense).

7 Issued Voucher No. 2 for typewriter ribbons, $6.20.

9 Paid $7.50 for an advertisement in college basketball program, Voucher No. 3.

16 Bought postage stamps, $6, Voucher No. 4 (Office Supplies).

20 Paid $8.50 to have snow removed from parking lot, Voucher No. 5 (Miscellaneous Expense).

25 Issued Voucher No. 6 for delivery charge, $4.45.

28 B. C. Amberg, the owner, withdrew $9 for personal use, Voucher No. 7.

29 Paid $1.72 for telegram, Voucher No. 8 (Miscellaneous Expense).

30 Paid $5.40 for delivery charge, Voucher No. 9.

30 Issued for cash Check No. 1311 for $52.77 to reimburse Petty Cash Fund.

Instructions **1.** Journalize the entry establishing the Petty Cash Fund in the general journal.

2. Record the disbursements of petty cash in the petty cash payments record.

3. Journalize the summarizing entry to reimburse the Petty Cash Fund.

Problem 8-4A The Vickers Company made the following transactions during July involving its Change Fund, its Cash Short and Over, and its Income from Services account received in cash.

July 1 Established a Change Fund, $300.

7 Recorded cash revenue for the week: cash register tape, $1,764; cash count, $2,062.25.

14 Recorded cash revenue for the week: cash register tape, $1,461.20; cash count, $1,759.

21 Recorded cash revenue for the week: cash register tape, $1,643; cash count, $1,944.85.

31 Recorded cash revenue for the week and the remainder of the month: cash register tape, $1,978; cash count, $2,274.50.

Instructions **1.** Record the entry establishing the Change Fund in the general journal.

2. Record the cash revenue in the general journal. In making bank deposits, the firm holds back the amount of the change fund.

3. Post the appropriate entries to the Cash Short and Over ledger account. Where will the balance of the account appear in the income statement?

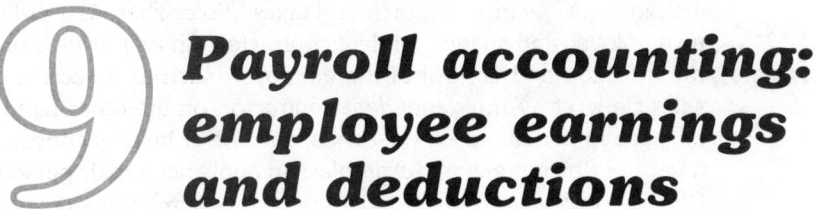

9 Payroll accounting: employee earnings and deductions

objectives

After you have completed this chapter, you will be able to do the following:
- Calculate total earnings based on an hourly, piece-rate, or commission basis.
- Determine deductions from tables of employees' income tax withholding.
- Complete a payroll register.
- Journalize the payroll entry from a payroll register.
- Maintain employees' individual earnings records.

UP TO NOW, we've been recording employees' wages as a debit to Salaries or Wages Expense and a credit to Cash, and we've really been talking only about gross pay. We haven't said a word about the various deductions that we all know are taken out of our gross pay before we get to the net amount, or take-home pay. In this chapter we'll be dealing with types and amounts of deductions and how to enter them in payroll records, as well as journal entries for recording the payroll and paying the employees.

Objectives of payroll records and accounting

There are two major reasons why we must maintain accurate payroll records. First, we must collect data in order to compute the compensation for each employee and for each payroll period.

Second, we must provide information needed to complete the various government reports—federal and state—that are required of all employers. Various laws require all business enterprises, both large and small, to withhold certain amounts from employees' pay for taxes, to make payments to government agencies by specified deadlines, and to submit reports on official forms. The governments impose penalties if the requirements are not met. So naturally employers are vitally concerned with payroll accounting, and anyone going into accounting, or involved with the management of any business, should be thoroughly acquainted with payroll accounting.

Employer/ employee relationships

Payroll accounting is concerned only with employees and their compensations, withholdings, records, reports, and taxes. *Note:* There is a distinction between an employee and an independent contractor. An *employee* is one who is under the direction and control of the employer, such as a secretary, bookkeeper, sales clerk, etc. An *independent contractor,* on the other hand, is one who is engaged for a definite job or service, and she or he may choose her or his own means of doing the work (*examples:* an appliance repair person, a plumber, a CPA firm). Payments made to independent contractors are in the form of fees or charges, and they are billed in one lump sum; consequently they are not subject to any withholding or payroll taxes.

Laws affecting compensation of employees

Both federal and state laws require that the employer act as a collecting agent, deducting specified amounts from employees' gross earnings and sending the withholdings to the appropriate government agencies, along with reports substantiating the figures. In addition, there are certain payroll taxes to be paid by the employer, based on the total wages paid to employees. Let's look at some of the more important laws that pertain to compensation of employees.

Federal income tax withholding

The withholding tax came into existence with the Current Tax Payment Act of 1943. The act requires not only that the employer withhold the tax and then pay it to the Internal Revenue Service, but also that employers keep records of the names and addresses of persons employed, their earnings and withholdings, and the amounts and dates of payment. The employer has to submit reports to the Internal Revenue Service on a quarterly basis (Form 941) and to the employee on an annual basis (W-2 form). With few exceptions, this requirement applies to employers of one or more persons. We'll discuss these reports and the related deposits in Chapter 10.

Federal Insurance Contributions Act (FICA)

This act, passed in 1935, provides for retirement pensions after a worker reaches age 62, disability benefits for any worker who becomes disabled (and for her or his dependents), and a health insurance program or Medicare after age 65. Both the employee and the employer have to pay FICA, or Social Security, taxes. The employer withholds FICA taxes from employees' wages and pays them to the Internal Revenue Service. The employer has to match the amount of FICA tax withheld from the employees' wages, and the employer's share is recorded under Payroll Tax Expense. We'll cover this in Chapter 10, as our concern here is with employees' deductions.

FICA tax rates apply to the gross earnings of an employee during the calendar year. After an employee has paid FICA tax on the maximum taxable earnings, the employer stops deducting FICA tax until the next calendar year begins. Congress has frequently changed the schedule of rates and taxable incomes. A rate of 6.5% applied to earnings up to $26,000, or a maximum of $1,690, will be assumed and used in this text for the illustrations and the problems.

The employer is required to keep records of the following information.

1. Personal data on employee: name, address, Social Security number, date of birth

2. Data on wage payments: dates and amounts of payments, and payroll periods

3. Amount of taxable wages paid: total amount earned so far during the year

4. Amount of tax withheld from each employee's earnings

Each quarter the employer has to submit reports to the Internal Revenue Service, recording the information on Form 941, the same form that is used to report the income tax withheld. The payment that the employer makes to the Internal Revenue Service consists of (1) the employee's share of the FICA tax, (2) the employer's matching portion of the FICA tax, and (3) the employee's income tax withheld. We'll talk about this in detail in Chapter 10.

Fair Labor Standards Act

The Fair Labor Standards Act, passed in 1938, specifies that employers engaged in interstate commerce must pay their employees overtime at the rate of $1\frac{1}{2}$ times the regular rate (time-and-a-half) for hours worked in excess of 40 per week. Frequently, union contracts stipulate additional overtime pay for work performed on Sundays and holidays. The act provides that certain management and supervisory employees are exempt from its regulations—these exempt employees are usually referred to as salaried personnel.

Federal Unemployment Tax Act (FUTA)

The purpose of the Federal Unemployment Tax Act is to provide financial support for the maintenance of employment offices throughout the country. This tax is paid by employers only.

The federal unemployment tax is based on the total earnings of each employee during the calendar year. Congress has frequently changed the rates and the amount of taxable income.

For the illustrations and the problems in this text, we will assume that employers will pay an effective federal unemployment tax rate of .7% (.007) of the first $8,000 of earnings of each employee during the calendar year (January 1 through December 31). In keeping with the procedure established by the act, the .7% tax rate is arrived at in a roundabout manner. Actually, the entire rate levied by the federal government is 3.4%; however, employers may deduct amounts they have paid in state unemployment taxes up to 2.7%. When an employer is entitled to make the full deduction, then the effective federal unemployment tax rate is .7% (3.4% − 2.7%). (Incidentally, all states levy a tax of at least 2.7%; therefore all employers can take the 2.7% deduction.)

Reports to the federal government must be submitted annually. The deadline is January 31 of the year following the preceding calendar year. We'll discuss these reports in Chapter 10.

State unemployment taxes

Each state is responsible for paying its own unemployment compensation benefits. The revenue provided by the state unemployment tax is used exclusively for this purpose. However, there is considerable variation among the states concerning the tax rates and the amounts of taxable income. The minimum tax rate levied by any state is 2.7% based on the taxable income stipulated in the Federal Unemployment Tax Act. States require employers to file reports on a quarterly or 3-month basis, listing employees' names, amount of wages paid to each employee, and a computation of the unemployment tax. We'll discuss these reports in Chapter 10.

Our illustration of payroll accounting is the firm of Sampson and Associates. This business is located in the state of Washington, which has an assumed unemployment tax rate of 3% on the first $9,600 of wages paid to each employee during the calendar year (Januaury 1 through December 31).

Workmen's compensation laws protect the employee and dependents against losses due to the employee's death or injury incurred on the job. Most states have laws requiring employers either to contribute to a state compensation insurance fund or to buy similar insurance from a private insurance company. The employer ordinarily pays the cost of the insurance premiums. The premium rates vary according to the degree of danger inherent in each job category. The employer has to keep records of job descriptions and classifications, as well as claims of insured persons.

Two-thirds of the states—besides requiring employers to deduct money from employees' earnings for federal income taxes—require employers to deduct money to pay state income taxes. A number of cities also require withholding for *city* income taxes. When these laws are in effect, the employer handles the reporting and payments in much the same manner as federal income taxes.

Employees may be paid a salary or wages, depending on the type of work and the period of time covered. Money paid to a person for managerial or administrative services is usually called a salary, and the time period covered is generally a month or a year. Money paid for either skilled or unskilled labor is usually called wages, and the time period covered is hours or weeks. Wages may also be paid on a piecework basis. In practice, the words *salaries* and *wages* are somewhat interchangeable. A company may supplement an employee's salary or wage by commissions, bonuses, cost-of-living adjustments, and profit-sharing plans. As a rule, an employee is paid in the form of a check or cash. However, he or she may also be compensated in the form of merchandise, lodging, meals, or other property. When the compensation is in these forms, one has to determine the fair value of property or service given in payment for the employee's labor.

When compensation is based on the passage of time, the accountant of course has to have a record of the number of hours worked by each employee. When there are only a few employees, this can be accomplished by means of a book record. When there are many employees, time clocks are the traditional method. Nowadays, for computer-operated time-keeping systems, employers use punched cards.

Let's take the case of Ronald R. Jones, who works for Sampson and Associates. His regular rate of pay is $6 per hour. The company pays time-and-a-half for hours worked in excess of 40. In addition, it pays him double time for any work he does on Sundays and holidays. Jones has a $\frac{1}{2}$-hour lunch break during an $8\frac{1}{2}$-hour day. He is not paid for the lunch break. His time card for the week looks something like this.

| \multicolumn{7}{c}{TIME CARD} |

Name Jones, Jorald L.

Week ending Nov. 7, 19—

Day	In	Out	In	Out	Hours Worked	
					Regular	Overtime
M	7⁵⁷	12⁰⁰	12³⁰	4³²	8	
T	7⁵⁶	12⁰⁶	12³⁶	4³⁷	8	
W	7⁵⁷	12⁰²	12³¹	4³¹	8	
T	8⁰⁰	12¹¹	12⁴⁰	6³²	8	2
F	8⁰⁰	12⁰³	12³³	5³³	8	1
S	7⁵⁹	1⁰²				5
S	7⁵⁵	12⁰⁴				4

Jones's gross wages are computed by one of two methods. The first method is as follows.

40 hours at straight time:	40 × $6 per hour =	$240
2 hours overtime on Thursday:	2 × $9 per hour =	18
1 hour overtime on Friday:	1 × $9 per hour =	9
5 hours overtime on Saturday:	5 × $9 per hour =	45
4 hours overtime on Sunday:	4 × 12 per hour =	48
Total gross wages		$360

The second method of calculating gross wages is often used when machine accounting is involved.

52 hours at straight time: 52 × $6 per hour = $312

Overtime premium

8 hours × $3 per hour premium = $24	
4 hours × $6 per hour premium = $24	
Total overtime premium	48
Total gross wages	$360

Salaries Employees who are paid on a regular salary basis may also be entitled to premium pay for overtime. Thus you have to figure out their regular hourly rate of pay before you determine their overtime rate. For example, let's consider the case of Donna Slocum, who gets a salary of $936 per month. She is entitled to overtime pay for all hours worked in excess of 40 during a week at the rate of $1\frac{1}{2}$ times her regular hourly rate. This past week she worked 44 hours, so we calculate her overtime pay as follows.

$936 per month × 12 months = $11,232 per year
$11,232 per year ÷ 52 weeks = $216 per week
$216 per week ÷ 40 hours = $5.40 per regular hour

Earnings for 44 hours

40 hours at straight time:	40 × $5.40 =	$216.00
4 hours overtime:	4 × $8.10 =	32.40
Total gross earnings		$248.40

Piece rate Workers under the piece-rate system are paid at the rate of so much per unit of production. For example, Peter Ryan, an apple picker, gets paid $8 for picking a bin of apples. If he picks 6 bins during the day, his total earnings are 6 × $8 = $48.

Commissions and bonuses Some salespersons are paid on a purely commission basis. However, a more common arrangement is a salary plus a commission or bonus. Assume that Rosie Perkins receives an annual salary of $9,600. Her employer agrees to pay her a 6% commission on all sales during the year in excess of $120,000. Her sales for the year total $210,000. Her bonus amounts to $90,000 × 6% = $5,400. Therefore her total earnings are $9,600 + $5,400 = $15,000.

Deductions from total earnings Anyone who has ever earned a paycheck has had experience with the many types of deductions that account for the shrinkage. The most usual deductions are due to the following.

1. Federal income tax withholding
2. State income tax withholding
3. FICA tax (Social Security), employee's share
4. Purchase of United States savings bonds
5. Union dues
6. Hospital and life insurance premiums
7. Contributions to a charitable organization
8. Repayment of personal loans from the company credit union
9. Savings through the company credit union

The amount of federal income tax withheld from an employee's wages depends on the amount of her or his total earnings and the number of exemptions claimed. An exemption is the amount of an individual's earnings that is exempt from income taxes (nontaxable). An employee is entitled to one personal exemption, plus an additional exemption if he or she is over 65 or blind, and an exemption for each dependent. Each employee has to fill out, for the employer, an Employee's Withholding Allowance Certificate (Form W-4).

Form **W-4** | Department of the Treasury—Internal Revenue Service
Employee's Withholding Allowance Certificate

Print your full name ▶ *Ronald R. Jones*   Your social security number ▶ *543 24 1680*

Address (including ZIP code) ▶ *1582 NORTH Pierce Street, Spokane, WA 99204*

Marital status: ☐ Single ☒ Married ☐ Married, but withhold at higher Single rate
Note: *If married, but legally separated, or spouse is a nonresident alien, check the single block.*

1 Total number of allowances you are claiming (from line F of the worksheet on page 2) *3*

2 Additional amount, if any, you want deducted from each pay (if your employer agrees) . . . . $

3 I claim exemption from withholding because (see instructions and check boxes below that apply):
   a ☐ Last year I did not owe any Federal income tax and had a right to a full refund of **ALL** income tax withheld, **AND**
   b ☐ This year I do not expect to owe any Federal income tax and expect to have a right to a full refund of **ALL** income tax withheld. If both

   a and b apply, enter "EXEMPT" here . . . . ▶
   c If you entered "EXEMPT" on line 3b, are you a full-time student? . . . .   ☐ Yes ☐ No

Under the penalties of perjury, I certify that I am entitled to the number of withholding allowances claimed on this certificate, or if claiming exemption from withholding, that I am entitled to claim the exempt status.

Employee's signature ▶ *Ronald R. Jones*   Date ▶ *February 1, 19—*

Employer's name and address (including ZIP code) (FOR EMPLOYER'S USE ONLY)   Employer identification number

---

The employer retains this form, as authorization to withhold money for the employee's federal income tax.

For convenience, most employers use the Wage Bracket Withholding tables contained in an Internal Revenue Service publication entitled *Circular E, Employer's Tax Guide* to determine the amount of federal tax to be withheld for each employee. These tables cover monthly, semimonthly, biweekly, weekly, and daily payroll periods, and are also subdivided on the basis of married and unmarried persons.

In order to determine the tax to be withheld from an employee's gross wages, first locate the wage bracket in the first two columns of the table. Next, find the column for the number of exemptions claimed, and read down this column until you get to the wage bracket line. A portion of the weekly federal income tax withholding table for married persons is on the facing page.

Assume that Ronald R. Jones, who claims three exemptions, had $360 gross wages for the week. His wage bracket is $360 to $370. Now, when we follow the three-exemption column, we see that the amount of income tax to be withheld from his wages is $48.10.

At first sight, it appears that $360 could fall in either the $350–$360 bracket or the $360–$370 bracket. However, note the headings of the bracket columns, "At least" and "But less than." A strict interpretation of the $350–$360 bracket really means $350–$359.99. Therefore, $360 must be included in the $360–$370 bracket.

WEEKLY Payroll Period — Employee MARRIED

And the wages are—		And the number of withholding allowances claimed is—										
At least	But less than	0	1	2	3	4	5	6	7	8	9	10 or more
		The amount of income tax to be withheld shall be—										
70	72	3.70	.80	0	0	0	0	0	0	0	0	0
72	74	4.00	1.10	0	0	0	0	0	0	0	0	0
74	76	4.30	1.40	0	0	0	0	0	0	0	0	0
76	78	4.60	1.70	0	0	0	0	0	0	0	0	0
78	80	4.90	2.00	0	0	0	0	0	0	0	0	0
80	82	5.20	2.30	0	0	0	0	0	0	0	0	0
82	84	5.50	2.60	0	0	0	0	0	0	0	0	0
84	86	5.80	2.90	.10	0	0	0	0	0	0	0	0
86	88	6.10	3.20	.40	0	0	0	0	0	0	0	0
88	90	6.40	3.50	.70	0	0	0	0	0	0	0	0
90	92	6.70	3.80	1.00	0	0	0	0	0	0	0	0
92	94	7.00	4.10	1.30	0	0	0	0	0	0	0	0
94	96	7.30	4.40	1.60	0	0	0	0	0	0	0	0
96	98	7.60	4.70	1.90	0	0	0	0	0	0	0	0
98	100	7.90	5.00	2.20	0	0	0	0	0	0	0	0
100	105	8.50	5.60	2.70	0	0	0	0	0	0	0	0
105	110	9.20	6.30	3.40	.50	0	0	0	0	0	0	0
110	115	10.00	7.10	4.20	1.30	0	0	0	0	0	0	0
115	120	10.70	7.80	4.90	2.00	0	0	0	0	0	0	0
120	125	11.50	8.60	5.70	2.80	0	0	0	0	0	0	0
125	130	12.20	9.30	6.40	3.50	.70	0	0	0	0	0	0
130	135	13.10	10.10	7.20	4.30	1.40	0	0	0	0	0	0
135	140	14.00	10.80	7.90	5.00	2.20	0	0	0	0	0	0
140	145	14.90	11.60	8.70	5.80	2.90	0	0	0	0	0	0
145	150	15.80	12.40	9.40	6.50	3.70	.80	0	0	0	0	0
150	160	17.20	13.70	10.60	7.70	4.80	1.90	0	0	0	0	0
160	170	19.00	15.50	12.10	9.20	6.30	3.40	.50	0	0	0	0
170	180	20.80	17.30	13.80	10.70	7.80	4.90	2.00	0	0	0	0
180	190	22.60	19.10	15.60	12.20	9.30	6.40	3.50	.60	0	0	0
190	200	24.40	20.90	17.40	14.00	10.80	7.90	5.00	2.10	0	0	0
200	210	26.20	22.70	19.20	15.80	12.30	9.40	6.50	3.60	.80	0	0
210	220	28.10	24.50	21.00	17.60	14.10	10.90	8.00	5.10	2.30	0	0
220	230	30.20	26.30	22.80	19.40	15.90	12.50	9.50	6.60	3.80	.90	0
230	240	32.30	28.30	24.60	21.20	17.70	14.30	11.00	8.10	5.30	2.40	0
240	250	34.40	30.40	26.40	23.00	19.50	16.10	12.60	9.60	6.80	3.90	1.00
250	260	36.50	32.50	28.50	24.80	21.30	17.90	14.40	11.10	8.30	5.40	2.50
260	270	38.60	34.60	30.60	26.60	23.10	19.70	16.20	12.70	9.80	6.90	4.00
270	280	40.70	36.70	32.70	28.60	24.90	21.50	18.00	14.50	11.30	8.40	5.50
280	290	42.80	38.80	34.80	30.70	26.70	23.30	19.80	16.30	12.90	9.90	7.00
290	300	45.10	40.90	36.90	32.80	28.80	25.10	21.60	18.10	14.70	11.40	8.50
$300	$310	$47.50	$43.00	$39.00	$34.90	$30.90	$26.90	$23.40	$19.90	$16.50	$13.00	$10.00
310	320	49.90	45.30	41.10	37.00	33.00	28.90	25.20	21.70	18.30	14.80	11.50
320	330	52.30	47.70	43.20	39.10	35.10	31.00	27.00	23.50	20.10	16.60	13.20
330	340	54.70	50.10	45.50	41.20	37.20	33.10	29.10	25.30	21.90	18.40	15.00
340	350	57.10	52.50	47.90	43.30	39.30	35.20	31.20	27.20	23.70	20.20	16.80
350	360	59.50	54.90	50.30	45.70	41.40	37.30	33.30	29.30	25.50	22.00	18.60
360	370	61.90	57.30	52.70	48.10	43.50	39.40	35.40	31.40	27.30	23.80	20.40
370	380	64.60	59.70	55.10	50.50	45.90	41.50	37.50	33.50	29.40	25.60	22.20
380	390	67.40	62.10	57.50	52.90	48.30	43.70	39.60	35.60	31.50	27.50	24.00
390	400	70.20	64.80	59.90	55.30	50.70	46.10	41.70	37.70	33.60	29.60	25.80
400	410	73.00	67.60	62.30	57.70	53.10	48.50	43.80	39.80	35.70	31.70	27.60
410	420	75.80	70.40	65.00	60.10	55.50	50.90	46.20	41.90	37.80	33.80	29.70
420	430	78.60	73.20	67.80	62.50	57.90	53.30	48.60	44.00	39.90	35.90	31.80
430	440	81.40	76.00	70.60	65.20	60.30	55.70	51.00	46.40	42.00	38.00	33.90
440	450	84.20	78.80	73.40	68.00	62.70	58.10	53.40	48.80	44.20	40.10	36.00
450	460	87.00	81.60	76.20	70.80	65.40	60.50	55.80	51.20	46.60	42.20	38.10
460	470	90.20	84.40	79.00	73.60	68.20	62.90	58.20	53.60	49.00	44.40	40.20
470	480	93.40	87.30	81.80	76.40	71.00	65.60	60.60	56.00	51.40	46.80	42.30
480	490	96.60	90.50	84.60	79.20	73.80	68.40	63.10	58.40	53.80	49.20	44.60
490	500	99.80	93.70	87.50	82.00	76.60	71.20	65.90	60.80	56.20	51.60	47.00

Many states that levy state income taxes also furnish employers with withholding tables. Other states use a fixed percentage of the federal income tax as the amount to be withheld for state taxes.

Employees' FICA tax withholding (Social Security)

To determine the FICA tax for each employee, simply multiply the FICA taxable wages by the FICA tax rate.

Let's get back to Ronald R. Jones, who had gross wages of $360 for the week ending November 7. Suppose that the total accumulated gross wages Jones earned prior to this payroll period were $12,658. His total gross wages including this payroll period are $13,018 ($12,658 + $360), which is well below the $26,000 assumed maximum taxable income. Therefore, multiply the FICA taxable wages (which are $360) by the FICA tax rate (6.5%): $360 × .065 = $23.40. Of course, if Jones's gross earnings prior to this payroll period had been greater than $26,000, then there would be no FICA tax deduction. (Tables for FICA tax withholding are also contained in the Internal Revenue Service publication entitled *Circular E, Employer's Tax Guide*.)

Payroll register

The payroll register is a form that summarizes the information about employees' wages and salaries for a given payroll period. In the illustration at the bottom of these pages, we see a payroll register that was prepared to show the data for each employee on a separate line. This would be suitable for a firm with a small number of employees, such as Sampson and Associates.

PAYROLL FOR

	NAME	TOTAL HOURS	EARNINGS REGULAR	EARNINGS OVERTIME	EARNINGS TOTAL	TAXABLE EARNINGS STATE UNEMPL.	TAXABLE EARNINGS FEDERAL UNEMPL.	FICA	FEDERAL INCOME TAX
1	Anderson, Dennis L.	45	200 00	37 50	237 50	120 00		237 50	32 30
2	Bowlen, Ralph P.	46	160 00	36 00	196 00	196 00	196 00	196 00	20 90
3	Daniels, John N.	49	200 00	67 50	267 50			267 50	34 60
4	Drew, Nancy R.	40	180 00		180 00	180 00	180 00	180 00	22 60
5	Farrell, Steven L.	40	192 00		192 00	192 00	192 00	192 00	20 90
6	Harwood, Lance C.	40	640 00		640 00			640 00	138 00
7	Jones, Ronald R.	52	240 00	120 00	360 00			360 00	48 10
8	Lyman, Mary C.	40	300 00		300 00			300 00	39 00
9	Miller, Robert M.	44	220 00	33 00	253 00			253 00	28 50
10	Olsen, Marvin C.	45	200 00	37 50	237 50	120 00		237 50	30 40
11	Stanfield, John D.	40	550 00		550 00			550 00	100 50
12	Tucker, Norma P.	52	240 00	108 00	348 00			348 00	52 50
13			3322 00	439 50	3761 50	808 00	568 00	3761 50	568 30
14									
15									
16									
17									
18									

9600   8000   26,000

The columns marked Taxable Earnings refer to the amount of pay that is subject to taxation; the employer has to pay a tax on this amount. The amount of the tax is found by multiplying the taxable income by the tax rate. (We'll take this up in Chapter 10.) However, for the present we are concerned with recording only the amount of taxable income. For example, Sampson and Associates operates in the state of Washington, which levies a state unemployment tax on the first $9,600 paid to each employee during the calendar year. After a given employee's earnings top $9,600 in one year, the employer doesn't have to pay any more state unemployment tax on that employee's pay. For example, take Dennis L. Anderson. His cumulative earnings prior to this payroll period were $9,480; as a result, only $120 of his current earnings are taxable for state unemployment. Therefore, we place $120 in the state unemployment taxable earnings column. A blank space in the state unemployment taxable column indicates that the employee has already earned more than $9,600 during this calendar year (prior to this payroll period).

As we said before, under the Federal Unemployment Tax Act the first $8,000 of compensation paid to each employee during the calendar year is taxable. After an employee has topped $8,000, the employer doesn't have to pay any more federal unemployment tax on that employee's pay. Look at Ralph P. Bowlen, Nancy R. Drew, and Steven L. Farrell. None of these people have earned more than $8,000 so far during the year from Sampson and Associates. Consequently, their entire earnings are taxable for both State and Federal unemployment taxes.

The FICA-taxable earnings pertain to both the employees' personal deductions for FICA and the employer's matching portion, based on the first $26,000

| | DEDUCTIONS | | | | | | PAYMENTS | | EXPENSE ACCOUNT DEBITED | |
FICA	U.S. BONDS	UNION DUES	HOSPITAL INSURANCE	OTHER CODE	AMOUNT	TOTAL	NET AMOUNT	CK. NO.	SALES SALARY EXPENSE	OFFICE SALARY EXPENSE
15 44	10 00	5 00	8 00	CC	2 00	72 74	164 76	273	237 50	
12 74		5 00	8 00			46 64	149 36	274	196 00	
17 39	16 00	5 00	10 00	CC	3 00	85 99	181 51	275		267 50
11 70		5 00	8 00			47 30	132 70	276		180 00
12 48		5 00	8 00			46 38	145 62	277	192 00	
41 60	20 00		10 00	CC	3 00	212 60	427 40	278	640 00	
23 40	5 00	5 00	10 00	CC	3 00	94 50	265 50	279	360 00	
19 50	5 00		10 00	CC	2 50	76 00	224 00	280	300 00	
16 44		5 00	8 00			57 94	195 06	281	253 00	
15 44		5 00	10 00	AR	20 00	80 84	156 66	282	237 50	
35 75			10 00	CC	3 00	149 25	400 75	283	550 00	
22 62		5 00	8 00	CC	2 00	90 12	257 88	284		348 00
244 50	56 00	45 00	108 00		38 50	1060 30	2701 20		2966 00	795 50

of earnings. The amounts in the FICA taxable earnings column therefore indicate that the employees have not earned $26,000 so far during the year.

The federal income tax withholding and the FICA (Social Security) deductions are required by law; the others are voluntary. One could set up special
columns for any frequently used deductions. Here, Community Chest and
Accounts Receivable are included as other deductions. The employee's deductions for FICA are determined by multiplying his or her FICA-taxable earnings
by the FICA tax rate. In the case of Dennis L. Anderson, his deduction for FICA
is $15.44 ($237.50 × .065).

The Net Amount column represents the employee's take-home pay. The last
columns are used for a distribution of the salary accounts to be debited. Sampson and Associates uses Sales Salary Expense and Office Salary Expense. The
sum of these two columns should equal the total earnings.

The payroll entry Because the payroll register summarizes the payroll data for the period, it
seems logical that it should be used as the basis for recording the payroll in the
ledger accounts. However, it does not have the status of a journal; consequently, a journal entry is necessary. Here is the entry in general journal form.

	DATE		DESCRIPTION	POST REF.	DEBIT	CREDIT	
1	19— Nov.	7	Sales Salary Expense		2 9 6 6 00		1
2			Office Salary Expense		7 9 5 50		2
3			Employees' Income Tax Payable			5 6 8 30	3
4			FICA Tax Payable			2 4 4 50	4
5			Employees' Bond Deductions Payable			5 6 00	5
6			Employees' Union Dues Payable			4 5 00	6
7			Employees' Hospitalization Insurance Payable			1 0 8 00	7
8			Employees' Community Chest Payable			1 8 50	8
9			Accounts Receivable, Marvin C. Olson			2 0 00	9
10			Salaries Payable			2 7 0 1 20	10
11			Payroll register, page 68, for week ended				11
12			Nov. 7.				12
13							13
14							14
15							15
16							16
17							17
18							18
19							19
20							20
21							21
22							22
23							23

GENERAL JOURNAL   PAGE __31__

Note that a firm records the total cost to the company for services of employees as debits to the salary expense accounts. To pay the employees, the firm now records the following journal entry.

	7	*Salaries Payable*		2 7 0 1 20	
		Cash			2 7 0 1 20
		Paid salaries for week ended Nov. 7. Issued			
		Check No. 667 payable to special payroll			
		bank account.			

In the two journal entries, the debit and credit to the Salaries Payable account cancel out each other. It would be possible to combine the two entries by making one credit to Cash. If a combined journal were in use, both of the above entries would be recorded in it, instead of in the general journal.

A firm having a large number of employees would likely open a special payroll account with its bank. One check is drawn on the regular bank account for the amount of the net pay for a payroll period. The bank then transfers funds from the regular checking account to the special payroll account. All payroll checks for the period are then drawn on the payroll account. Balances of Employees' Bond Deductions Payable, Employees' Union Dues Payable, and other employee deductions, are paid out of the regular bank account.

Paycheck All the data needed to make out a payroll check are available in the payroll register. Here is the paycheck for Ronald R. Jones.

EMPLOYEE	TOTAL HOURS	O.T. HOURS	REG. PAY RATE	REG. PAY	O.T. PREM. PAY	GROSS PAY	INC. TAX	FICA TAX	SAVINGS BONDS	UNION DUES	HOSP. INS.	OTHER	TOTAL DED.	NET PAY
Ronald R. Jones	52	12	6.00	240.00	120.00	360.00	48.10	23.40	5.00	5.00	10.00	CC 3.00	94.50	265.50

VALLEY NATIONAL BANK   98-461 / 1252

Payroll Account
SAMPSON AND ASSOCIATES
546 SOUTH FOSS STREET
SPOKANE, WASHINGTON 99203

Nov. 7 19——   No. 937

PAY TO THE
ORDER OF   Ronald R. Jones $ 265.50

Two hundred sixty-five and 50/100———————————————————————— DOLLARS

Robert C. Randall

⑊1252⑊0461⑊

NAME ___Jones, Ronald R.___

ADDRESS ___1582 North Pierce Street___

___Spokane, Washington 99204___

MALE ___X___   FEMALE ___

MARRIED ___X___   SINGLE ___

PHONE NO. ___663-2556___   DATE OF BIRTH ___9/19/39___

LINE NO.	PERIOD ENDED	DATE PAID	HOURS WORKED		EARNINGS			ACCUMULATED EARNINGS
			REG.	O.T.	REGULAR	OVERTIME	TOTAL	
40	10/3	10/4	40		240 00	72 00	312 00	11581 00
41	10/10	10/11	40	2	240 00	18 00	258 00	11839 00
42	10/17	10/18	40	2	240 00	18 00	258 00	12097 00
43	10/24	10/24	40	5	240 00	45 00	285 00	12382 00
44	10/30	11/1	40	4	240 00	36 00	276 00	12658 00
45	11/7	11/8	40	12	240 00	120 00	360 00	13018 00

Employees' individual earnings record

To comply with the government regulations described earlier, a firm has to keep current data on each employee's accumulated earnings, deductions, and net pay. The source of this information is the payroll register, and the information is transferred to the employee's individual earnings record each payday. A portion of the earnings record for Ronald R. Jones is shown above.

Summary

Payroll accounting is concerned with the following:

- Computing compensation for employees
- Taking out required and voluntary deductions
- Paying employees
- Paying various government agencies
- Submitting required reports to government agencies
- Paying private agencies for employees' deductions for insurance, etc.

In this chapter, we have discussed important provisions of federal and state laws pertaining to employment. In earlier chapters, we showed the entry recording compensation of employees as a debit to Salaries or Wages Expense and a credit to Cash. We have now made the transition from this simplified entry to the complete entry. The complete entry consists of debits to the salary expense accounts, credits to the various deductions payable, and finally a credit to Salaries Payable, or Cash, after Salaries Payable is canceled out.

First, we record the information for the payroll period in the payroll register. Next, using the payroll register as the source of information, we record payroll entries in the general journal or combined journal.

To comply with the employment laws, any business firm should maintain a payroll register and an employee's individual earnings record.

EARNINGS RECORD

EMPLOYEE NO. 5 DATE EMPLOYED 2/1/—

SOC. SEC. NO. 543-24-1680 NO. OF EXEMPTIONS 3

PAY RATE $6.00 PER HOUR X PER DAY

EQUIVALENT HOURLY RATE $6.00 PER WEEK PER MONTH

DATE TERMINATED

CLASSIFICATION FOR WORKMEN'S COMPENSATION INSURANCE Warehouse

		DEDUCTIONS						PAID	
INCOME TAX	FICA	BONDS	UNION DUES	HOSPITAL INSURANCE	OTHER CODE	OTHER AMOUNT	TOTAL	NET AMOUNT	CK. NO.
37 00	20 28	5 00	5 00	10 00	CC	3 00	80 28	231 72	887
24 80	16 77	5 00	5 00	10 00	CC	3 00	64 57	193 43	889
24 80	16 77	5 00	5 00	10 00	CC	3 00	64 57	193 43	901
30 70	18 53	5 00	5 00	10 00	CC	3 00	72 23	212 77	913
28 60	17 94	5 00	5 00	10 00	CC	3 00	69 54	206 46	925
48 10	23 40	5 00	5 00	10 00	CC	3 00	94 50	265 50	937

Glossary

Current Tax Payment Act Requires an employer to withhold employees' federal income tax as well as to pay and report the tax.

Employee One who works for compensation in the service of an employer.

Employee's individual earnings record A supplementary record showing personal payroll data and yearly cumulative earnings and deductions for each employee.

Employee's Withholding Exemption Certificate (Form W-4) This form specifies the number of exemptions claimed by each employee and gives the employer the authority to withhold money for an employee's income taxes and FICA taxes.

Exemption An amount of an employee's annual earnings not subject to income tax. The term is also called a withholding allowance.

Fair Labor Standards Act (Wages and Hours Law) An act requiring employers whose products are involved in interstate commerce to pay their employees time-and-a-half for all hours worked in excess of 40 per week.

FICA taxes Social security taxes paid by both employers and employees in equal amounts under the provisions of the Federal Insurance Contributions Act. The proceeds are used to pay old-age and disability pensions.

FUTA taxes Taxes paid by employers only under the provisions of the Federal Unemployment Tax Act. The proceeds are used to pay part of the costs of the federal-state unemployment programs.

Gross pay The total amount of an employee's pay before any deductions.

Net pay Gross pay minus deductions.

State unemployment taxes Taxes paid by employers only. The proceeds are used to pay unemployment benefits.

Workmen's compensation laws State laws guaranteeing employee benefits when the employee incurs an injury on the job.

1. Distinguish between an employee and an independent contractor.

2. List seven possible deductions from total earnings of an employee.

3. Explain the requirements of the Fair Labor Standards Act.

4. What are the main provisions of the Federal Insurance Contributions Act?

5. What is a wage-bracket withholding table?

6. Describe how a special payroll bank account is useful in paying the wages of employees.

7. What information is included in an employee's individual earnings record, and what is its function?

Exercises

Exercise 1 Using the tax table shown on page 223, and a form similar to the one below, determine the amount of federal income tax that an employer should withhold weekly for married employees who have the following wages and exemptions.

Total Wages	Total Exemptions	Tax Withheld
a. $150.92	1	?
b. $363.23	5	?
c. $435.72	6	?

Exercise 2 On January 31, Levy and Company's column totals of its payroll register showed its sales employees had earned $4,560, and its office employees had earned $940. FICA taxes were withheld at an assumed rate of 6.5%. Other deductions consisted of federal income tax, $501.60; bonds, $240; and hospital insurance, $320. Determine the amount of FICA taxes to be withheld and record the general journal entry for the payroll, crediting Salaries Payable for the net pay.

Exercise 3 Henry R. Knight works for the Eastern Mechanical Corporation, which must abide by the Fair Labor Standards Act, in that it must pay its employees time-and-a-half for all hours worked per week in excess of 40. Knight's pay rate is $6.90 per hour. His wages are subject to federal income tax and FICA deductions at the rate of 6.5%. He claims four income tax exemptions. Knight has a $\frac{1}{2}$-hour lunch during an $8\frac{1}{2}$-hour day. His time card is shown on the top of page 231.
   Complete the following.

a.	_____ hours at straight time × $6.90 per hour		$_____
b.	_____ hours overtime × $10.35 per hour		$_____
c.	Total gross wages		$_____
d.	Federal income tax withholding (from tax tables)	$_____	
e.	FICA withholding at 6.5%	$_____	
f.	Total withholding		$_____
g.	Net pay		$_____

TIME CARD

Name Knight, Henry

Week ending March 11, 19—

Day	In	Out	In	Out	Hours Worked Regular	Hours Worked Overtime
M	7⁵⁶	12⁰⁹	12³⁹	4³²	8	
T	7⁵²	12⁰⁵	12³⁵	5⁰⁴	8	1
W	7⁵⁹	12²⁰	12⁴⁰	5⁰³	8	1
T	8⁰⁰	12⁰⁸	12³⁸	4³⁴	8	
F	7⁵⁶	12⁰⁹	12³⁹	6³³	8	2
S	8⁰⁰	12⁰¹			4	
S						

Exercise 4 Neil Langdon, who works for Purity Dairy Products, worked 46 hours during the first week in March. His rate of pay is $6.20 per hour, and he receives time-and-a-half for all hours worked in excess of 40 per week. His wages are subject to the following deductions.

Federal income tax (from tax table)   Industrial accident insurance of 1%
FICA tax at 6.5%   Medical insurance, $15.40

He claims five exemptions for income tax purposes. Compute the following: regular wages, overtime wages, gross wages, and net pay.

Exercise 5 The following information was taken from the records of Hildebrand Fine Foods, Inc., a company that is subject to the Fair Labor Standards Act, for the first week of January.

NAME	HOURLY RATE	HOURS WORKED REG.	HOURS WORKED O.T.	TOTAL EARNINGS	HOSPITAL INSURANCE	FICA	SAVINGS BONDS	FEDERAL INCOME TAX	TOTAL	NET PAY
Jordan, A.	6.40	40	6				4 00	16 00		
Smith, B.	7.90	40	8				10 00	18 00		

Using the table shown on page 223, determine the income tax withheld. The FICA tax rate is 6.5%. Jordan and Smith claim two exemptions each. In general journal form, record the payroll entry, debiting Wages Expense for the amount of the total earnings and crediting Cash for the net pay.

Exercise 6 Tracy Deane works for Nationwide Water Softeners, Inc., a company engaged in interstate commerce, which is subject to the provisions of the Fair Labor Standards Act. Nationwide has just adopted a 4-day, 40-hour work week so that its employees will spend less time and gasoline commuting and will have longer weekends.

Deane's pay rate is $7.10 per hour. During the first week of the change to the 4-day week, her working hours were as follows: Monday, 12 hours; Tuesday, 10 hours; Wednesday, $11\frac{1}{2}$ hours; Thursday, $10\frac{1}{2}$ hours. Compute the amount of her gross earnings for the week.

Exercise 7 In the following summary of columnar totals of a payroll register, determine the amounts that have been omitted.

Earnings	
At regular rate	$6,741.57
At overtime rate	_____
Total earnings	_____
Deductions	
Income tax	1,019.60
FICA tax	426.74
Medical insurance	_____
Union dues	260.00
Total deductions	1,840.64
Net amount paid	5,638.93
Accounts Debited	
Sales Salary Expense	5,641.14
Office Salary Expense	936.70
Warehouse Salary Expense	_____

Exercise 8 From Exercise 7, the total earnings are $7,479.57; warehouse salaries are $901.73, and the amount of the deduction for medical insurance is $134.30. In general journal form, complete the payroll entry, crediting Salaries Payable for the net amount paid.

Problems

Problem 9-1 Thomas C. Pickett, an employee of Timely Products Company, worked 46 hours during the week of March 16 to 22. His rate of pay is $7.10 per hour, and he receives time-and-a-half for all work in excess of 40 hours per week. Pickett is married and claims two exemptions on his W-4 form. His wages are subject to the following deductions.

Federal income tax (from tax table)
FICA tax at 6.5%
Union dues, $4.60
Medical insurance, $18.30

Instructions Compute the following: his regular pay, his overtime pay, his gross pay, and his net pay.

Problem 9-2 The Travelers' Rest Motel has the following payroll information for the week ended March 18.

NAME	DAILY TIME							PAY RATE	FEDERAL INCOME TAX	UNION DUES	EARNINGS AT END OF PREVIOUS WEEK
	M	T	W	T	F	S	S				
Austin, C. T.	0	8	8	8	8	8	0	4 80	27 00	3 50	3 510 00
Brooks, K. W.	8	8	8	8	8	0	0	3 60	16 20		2 392 00
Edwards, N. L.	0	0	8	8	8	8	8	4 00	20 70	3 50	1 280 00
Milner, C. C.	0	4	8	8	8	8	8	3 60	18 60		1 686 00
Pierce, D. R.	8	8	8	8	8	4	0	4 50	27 00	3 50	3 430 00

The firm is subject to the Fair Labor Standards Act regarding minimum wages. However, being a motel, it is exempt from paying time-and-a-half for 44 hours of work or less. In other words, all hours are compensated at the regular rate. For each employee, taxable earnings for FICA are based on the first $26,000, and taxable earnings for unemployment insurance (state and federal) are based on the first $8,000. The amounts of employees' income tax withheld are given.

Instructions
1. Complete the payroll register, using 6.5% of earnings for calculating FICA tax withholding.

2. Prepare a general journal entry to record the payroll. The firm's general ledger contains a Wages Expense account and a Wages Payable account.

3. Assuming that the firm uses a special payroll bank account, make the entry in the general journal to record Check No. 53.

Problem 9-3 The Darrington Products Company is subject to the Fair Labor Standards Act, and accordingly pays time-and-a-half for all hours worked in excess of 40 per week. The following information is available from the time cards and employees' individual earnings records for the pay period ended March 16.

NAME	CLOCK CARD NO.	DAILY TIME							REGULAR RATE	INCOME TAX EXEMP.	UNION DUES	HOSPITAL INSURANCE	EARNINGS AT END OF PREVIOUS WEEK
		M	T	W	T	F	S	S					
Brown, M. R.	76	8	8	8	10	8	0	0	7 80	2	5 00	9 60	2,580 00
Cole, S. C.	77	8	8	8	8	8	0	0	8 55	2	5 00	9 60	1,815 00
Johnson, N. F.	78	8	8	8	8	8	4	4	7 50	4	5 00	10 50	3,255 00
Loomis, P. N.	79	8	8	9	9	8	6	0	7 80	3	5 00	10 00	3,345 00
Malloy, R. D.	80	8	8	8	8	8	0	0	9 00	4	5 00	10 50	3,480 00

For each employee, taxable earnings for FICA are based on the first $26,000, and taxable earnings for unemployment insurance (state and federal) are based on the first $8,000.

1. Complete the payroll register, using the wage bracket income tax withholding table. The FICA tax is 6.5%. Assume that all employees are married.

2. Prepare a general journal entry to record the payroll. The firm's general ledger contains a Wages Expense account and a Wages Payable account.

3. Assume that the firm uses a special payroll bank account and issues Check No. 113.

Problem 9-4 The Quinn Refrigeration Company is subject to the Fair Labor Standards Act, and accordingly pays its employees time-and-a-half for all hours worked in excess of 40 per week. The following information is available from Quinn's time book and the employee's individual earnings records for the payroll period ending December 8.

NAME	PAY RATE	HOURS WORKED	FEDERAL INCOME TAX	UNION DUES	HOSPITAL INSURANCE	EARNINGS AT END OF PREVIOUS WEEK
Burgess, B. L.	$7.10 per hour	46	47 90	6 00	14 00	16,950 00
Caswell, D. J.	$460.00 per week	40	73 60		16 00	22,540 00
Kirby, R. L.	$325.00 per week	40	52 30		12 00	15,925 00
Purcell, N. E.	$5.90 per hour	48	55 10	6 00	12 00	7,946 00

For each employee, taxable earnings for FICA are based on the first $26,000, and taxable earnings for unemployment are based on the first $8,000 (state and federal).

Instructions 1. Complete the payroll register, using a FICA tax of 6.5%.

2. Prepare a general journal entry to record the payroll. The firm's general ledger contains a Wages Expense account and a Wages Payable account.

3. Record the payment of the employees, assuming that the company issues individual checks to each employee out of its regular bank account beginning with Check No. 716.

Alternate problems

Problem 9-1A Ian C. Peters, an employee of Pacific Motor Freight, worked 47 hours during the week from February 15 to 21. His rate of pay is $7.40 per hour, and he gets time-and-a-half for work in excess of 40 hours per week. He is married and claims three exemptions on his W-4 form, and his wages are subject to the following deductions.

Federal income tax (from tax table)
FICA tax at 6.5%
Union dues, $5.65
Medical insurance, $15.80

Instructions Compute the following: his regular pay, overtime pay, gross pay, and net pay.

Problem 9-2A The Pender Motor Lodge has the following payroll information for the week ended March 6.

NAME	DAILY TIME							PAY RATE		FEDERAL INCOME TAX		UNION DUES		EARNINGS AT END OF PREVIOUS WEEK	
	M	T	W	T	F	S	S								
Bowen, N. B.	8	0	0	8	10	8	8	4	80	29	10	2	70	3,960	00
Buckley, A. C.	0	0	8	8	8	8	8	3	70	17	10	2	70	2,172	60
Kingman, M. E.	8	8	8	8	4	0	8	3	70	20	70			2,548	22
Nichols, P. A.	0	4	8	8	8	8	8	5	10	33	80	2	70	3,980	10
Stirling, T. J.	8	8	4	8	8	0	8	3	50	18	60			861	30

The firm is subject to the Fair Labor Standards Act regarding minimum wages. However, being a motel, it is exempt from paying time-and-a-half for 44 hours or less. In other words, all hours are compensated at the regular rate. For each employee, taxable earnings for FICA are based on the first $26,000, and taxable earnings for unemployment insurance (state and federal) are based on the first $8,000.

Instructions

1. Complete the payroll register, using 6.5% for calculating FICA tax withholding.

2. Prepare a general journal entry to record the payroll. The firm's general ledger contains a Wages Expense account and a Wages Payable account.

3. Assuming that the firm uses a special payroll bank account, make the entry in the general journal to record Check No. 53.

Problem 9-3A The Florida Products Company is subject to the Fair Labor Standards Act, and accordingly pays its employees time-and-a-half for all hours worked in excess of 40 per week. The following information is available from time cards and employee's individual earnings records for the pay period ended February 28.

NAME	CLOCK CARD NO.	DAILY TIME							REGULAR RATE		INCOME TAX EXEMP.	UNION DUES		HOSPITAL INSURANCE		EARNINGS AT END OF PREVIOUS WEEK	
		M	T	W	T	F	S	S									
Burnett, P. L.	69	8	8	8	10	9	0	0	7	20	1	6	00	13	60	2,298	00
Cheney, C.M.	70	8	8	8	8	8	5	0	7	20	3	6	00	15	00	2,388	00
Everett, W. N.	71	8	10	8	9	8	0	0	7	70	5	6	00	15	40	2,446	00
Price, N. O.	72	8	8	9	8	8	2	0	7	70	4	6	00	15	20	2,424	00
Pyle, W. E.	73	8	8	8	8	8	0	0	9	00	4	6	00	15	20	2,736	00

For each employee, taxable earnings for FICA are based on the first $26,000, and taxable earnings for unemployment insurance (state and federal) are based on the first $8,000.

Instructions

1. Complete the payroll register, using the wage-bracket income tax withholding tables. The FICA tax is 6.5%. Assume that all employees are married.

2. Prepare a general journal entry to record the payroll. The firm's general ledger contains a Wages Expense account and a Wages Payable account.

3. Assume that the firm uses a special payroll bank account and issues Check No. 113.

Problem 9-4A The Modern Trailer Company is subject to the Fair Labor Standards Act, and accordingly pays its employees time-and-a-half for all hours worked in excess of 40 per week. The following information is available from the time books and employee's individual earnings records for the pay period ended December 10.

NAME	PAY RATE	HOURS WORKED	FEDERAL INCOME TAX		UNION DUES		HOSPITAL INSURANCE		EARNINGS AT END OF PREVIOUS WEEK	
Fisher, S. O.	$7.20 per hour	41	52	10	8	00	13	00	14,600	00
Lindsay, L. E.	$400 per week	40	62	30			13	00	19,600	00
Moore, F. C.	$350 per week	40	45	70			14	00	17,150	00
Robinson, W. L.	$6.50 per hour	42	46	80	8	00	11	00	7,920	00

For each employee, taxable earnings for FICA are based on the first $26,000, and taxable earnings for unemployment insurance are based on the first $8,000 (state and federal).

Instructions **1.** Complete the payroll register, using a FICA tax of 6.5%.

2. Prepare a general journal entry to record the payroll. The firm's general ledger contains a Wages Expense account and a Wages Payable account.

3. Record the payment of the employees, assuming that the company issues individual checks to each employee out of its regular bank account beginning with Check Number 864.

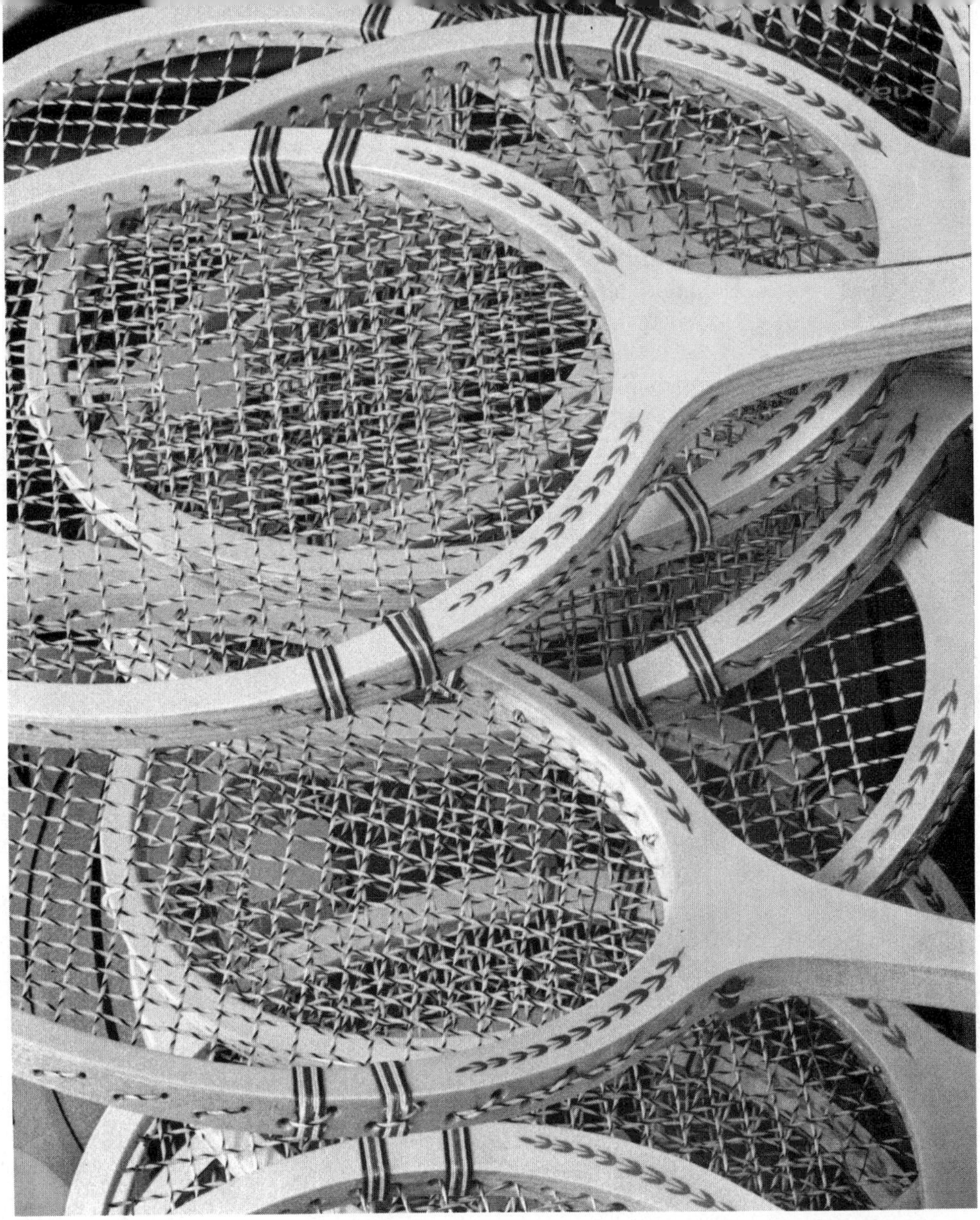

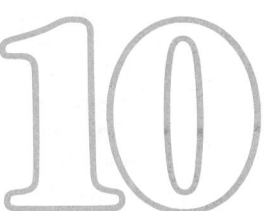

10 Payroll accounting: employer's taxes, payments, and reports

objectives

After you have completed this chapter, you will be able to do the following:
- Journalize entry to record payroll tax expense.
- Complete federal tax deposits and accompanying journal entries.
- Complete Employer's Quarterly Federal Tax Return, Form 941.
- Prepare wage and tax statements for employees, W-2 forms.
- Complete Transmittal of Income and Tax Statements, Form W-3.
- Prepare a quarterly report for state unemployment insurance and journalize related entry.
- Complete Employer's Annual Federal Unemployment Tax Return, Form 940.
- Calculate the premium for workmen's compensation insurance and journalize entry for payment in advance.
- Determine amount of adjustment for workmen's compensation insurance at end of year and record adjustment.
- Prepare a tax calendar for payments of employees' income and FICA taxes withheld and employer's payroll taxes.

IN CHAPTER 9, we talked about the computing and recording of payroll data such as gross pay, employees' income tax withheld, employees' FICA tax withheld, and various deductions requested by employees. Now we're going to get around to the payments of these withholdings, the taxes levied on the employer based on total payroll, and finally the official reports that you have to submit to government authorities.

Employer's identification number

As you know quite well, everyone who works has a Social Security number, a number which is a vital part of his or her federal income tax returns. For an employer, a counterpart to the Social Security number is the *employer identification number*. Each employer of one or more persons is required to have such a number, and it must be listed on all reports and payments of employees' federal income tax withholding and FICA taxes.

Employer's payroll taxes

An employer's payroll taxes are levied on the employer on the basis of the gross wages paid to the employees. Payroll taxes—like property taxes—are an expense of doing business. Sampson and Associates titles the account Payroll Tax Expense, and debits the account for its matching of FICA taxes as well as for state and federal unemployment taxes. Consequently, in T-account form, the Payroll Tax Expense account for Sampson and Associates would look like the example shown on the top of the facing page.

If an accountant subdivides operating expenses on the income statement, she or he classifies Payroll Tax Expense as a general expense account.

Payroll Tax Expense

+	−
FICA (employer's matching portion) Federal Unemployment Tax State Unemployment Tax	Closed at the end of the year along with all other expense accounts

Employer's matching portion of FICA tax

The FICA tax is imposed on both employer and employee. The firm's accountant deducts the employee's share from gross wages, and records it in the payroll entry under FICA Tax Payable, a liability account. He or she determines the employer's share by multiplying the same FICA tax rate (6.5% assumed) times the total FICA-taxable earnings [gross annual earnings (for the calendar year) for each employee up to an assumed $26,000]. The accountant gets the FICA-taxable earnings figure from the payroll register. In the following illustration we take another look at the Taxable Earnings columns from the payroll register for the week ended November 7, 19–, illustrated in Chapter 9 on pages 224–225.

Amount of employees' earnings based on no more than $8,000 per employee per year.

Amount of employees' earnings based on no more than $9,600 per employee per year. (Many states use $8,000 for each employee.)

Amount of employees' earnings based on no more than $26,000 per employee per year.

STATE UNEMPL.		FEDERAL UNEMPL.		FICA	
	TAXABLE EARNINGS				
1 2 0 00				2 3 7 50	
1 9 6 00		1 9 6 00		1 9 6 00	
				2 6 7 50	
1 8 0 00		1 8 0 00		1 8 0 00	
1 9 2 00		1 9 2 00		1 9 2 00	
				6 4 0 00	
				3 6 0 00	
				3 0 0 00	
				2 5 3 00	
1 2 0 00				2 3 7 50	
				5 5 0 00	
				3 4 8 00	
8 0 8 00		5 6 8 00		3 7 6 1 50	

Employer's FICA tax
$3,761.50 × .065 = $244.50

By T accounts, the entry to record the employer's portion of the FICA tax looks like this.

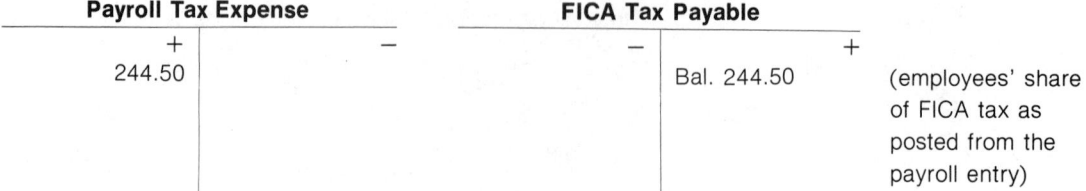

Payroll Tax Expense		FICA Tax Payable	
+	−	−	+
244.50			Bal. 244.50

(employees' share of FICA tax as posted from the payroll entry)

Note particularly that the FICA Tax Payable account is used for the tax liability of both the employer and the employee. This is logical because both FICA taxes are paid at the same time and the same place. There might be a discrepancy between the employer's and the employee's share of FICA taxes, due to the rounding-off process. The accountant calculates the employee's share by taking 6.5% of the taxable earnings of each worker, then adding these figures to find the total amount due for all employees. At the same time, she or he determines the employer's share by taking 6.5% of the taxable earnings of all the employees. The two figures may vary, but only by a few cents.

Employer's federal unemployment tax (FUTA)

The employer's federal unemployment tax is levied on the employer only. Congress may from time to time change the rate. But for now, let's assume that a rate of .7% (.007) of the first $8,000 earned by each employee during the year (3.4% federal unemployment tax less 2.7% credit for amounts paid to the state as state unemployment tax) applies. For the weekly payroll period for Sampson and Associates, the tax liability is $3.98 ($568 of unemployment-taxable earnings taken from the payroll register multiplied by .007). By T accounts, the entry is as follows.

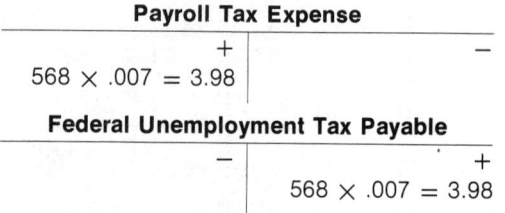

Payroll Tax Expense	
+	−
568 × .007 = 3.98	

Federal Unemployment Tax Payable	
−	+
	568 × .007 = 3.98

Employer's state unemployment tax

This tax, like the federal unemployment tax, is paid by the employer only. The rate of state unemployment tax varies considerably among the states. During recent years, with the trend toward higher unemployment benefits, many states have adopted a base of at least $8,000 and rates of 2.7% or higher. However, let us assume here that Sampson and Associates is subject to a rate of 3% of the first $9,600 of each employee's earnings. As shown in the portion of the payroll register illustrated on page 239, $808 of earnings are subject to the state unemployment tax. Accordingly, by T accounts, the state unemployment tax based on taxable earnings is as follows.

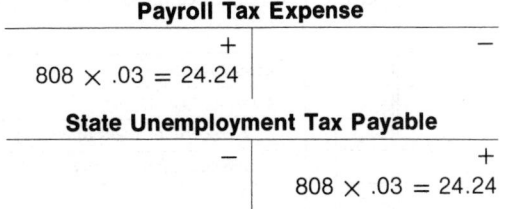

Payroll Tax Expense

+	−
808 × .03 = 24.24	

State Unemployment Tax Payable

−	+
	808 × .03 = 24.24

Journal entry for employer's payroll tax

In the foregoing, to make things clearer, figures for the three employer's payroll taxes have been presented separately. But now let's combine this information into one entry, which follows the regular payroll entry. Sampson and Associates pays its employees weekly, so it also makes its Payroll Tax Expense entry weekly.

GENERAL JOURNAL   PAGE_____

DATE	DESCRIPTION	POST REF.	DEBIT	CREDIT
	Payroll Tax Expense		272 72	
	FICA Tax Payable			244 50
	Federal Unemployment Tax Payable			3 98
	State Unemployment Tax Payable			24 24
	To record employer's share of FICA tax and			
	employer's federal and state unemployment			
	taxes.			

At this point let us restate in general journal form the entries that have been recorded, using the payroll register illustrated in Chapter 9 as the source of information. First, we record the payroll entry.

	DATE		DESCRIPTION	POST REF.	DEBIT	CREDIT	
1	19– Nov.	7	Sales Salary Expense		2966 00		1
2			Office Salary Expense		795 50		2
3			Employees' Income Tax Payable			568 30	3
4			FICA Tax Payable			244 50	4
5			Employees' Bond Deductions Payable			56 00	5
6			Employees' Union Dues Payable			45 00	6
7			Employees' Hospitalization Insurance Payable			108 00	7
8			Employees' Community Chest Payable			18 50	8
9			Accounts Receivable, Marvin C. Olson			20 00	9
10			Salaries Payable			2701 20	10
11			Payroll register, page 28, for week ended				11
12			Nov. 7.				12

Next, Sampson and Associates, on the basis of the previous entry, issues one check payable to a payroll bank account. To pay its employees, it will draw separate payroll checks on this payroll bank account.

	7	Salaries Payable		2 7 0 1 20	
		Cash			2 7 0 1 20
		To record payment of employees (by issuing			
		one check payable to payroll bank account).			

Finally the entry to record the employer's payroll taxes is journalized.

	7	Payroll Tax Expense		2 7 2 72	
		FICA Tax Payable			2 4 4 50
		Federal Unemployment Tax Payable			3 98
		State Unemployment Tax Payable			2 4 24
		To record employer's share of FICA tax and			
		employer's federal and state unemployment			
		taxes.			

Reports and payments of FICA taxes and employees' income tax withholding

After an employer has paid the employees, he or she has to make payments in the form of federal tax deposits for (1) employees' income taxes withheld, (2) employees' FICA taxes withheld, and (3) the employer's share of FICA taxes. These deposits, putting the employers on a pay-as-you-go basis, are made during the 3-month quarter. At the end of the quarter, the employer has to submit the Employer's Quarterly Federal Tax Return (Form 941) to the District Director of Internal Revenue, showing the amount of taxes due and listing the deposits.

For *large-sized* employers, if the combined total of undeposited employees' income taxes and FICA taxes levied on both employees and employer is greater than $2,000 for a *quarter-of-a-month period* (approximately 1 week), the employer has to make deposits within 3 banking days after the end of the period. These quarter-of-a-month periods end on the 7th, 15th, 22nd, and last day of any month. For example, assume an employer had $2,300 of undeposited taxes for a quarter-of-a-month period ending on Friday, September 7. Since the banks are closed on Saturday and Sunday, the employer would have to make the deposit by Wednesday, September 12.

For *medium-sized* employers, if the total undeposited income taxes and FICA taxes for any *month* is between $200 and $2,000, the employer has to make the deposit within 15 days after the end of the month.

But now suppose you're just a *small-sized* employer, and the total amount of your undeposited income taxes and FICA taxes at the end of the *quarter* is less than $200; you don't have to make a deposit until you submit your quarterly return, Form 941. Now remember that we're talking about a *quarter* (3 months). You keep records on the basis of a calendar year, with the first quarter ending March 31, the second quarter ending June 30, the third quarter ending September 30, and the fourth quarter ending December 31.

Sampson and Associates, for the week ended November 7, had the following taxes due to the government.

Employees' federal income tax withheld	$ 568.30
Employees' FICA taxes withheld	244.50
Employer's FICA tax	244.50
Total	$1,057.30

Because Sampson's tax liability is less than $2,000, it is not necessary to make a federal tax deposit at this time.

Assume that Sampson and Associates, for the week ended November 14, had the following taxes due to the government.

Employees' federal income tax withheld	$ 584.12
Employees' FICA taxes withheld	250.08
Employer's FICA tax	250.08
Total	$1,084.28

The total cumulative liability for the two-week period is now $2,141.58 ($1,057.30 + $1,084.28). Because the total cumulative liability is greater than $2,000, it is necessary for the firm to make a federal tax deposit at the end of the second week.

Sampson receives a federal tax deposit card (preprinted with the company's name and tax number) from the Internal Revenue Service. The accountant records the amount of the deposit and the name of the bank where the deposit is to be submitted (any authorized commercial bank or Federal Reserve bank). Commercial banks forward the deposits to the Federal Reserve banks, which are agents of the U.S. Treasury. The entry in general journal form to record the deposit of two weeks' taxes looks like this:

17	Employees' Federal Income Tax Payable	1 1 5 2 42		
	FICA Tax Payable	9 8 9 16		
	Cash		2 1 4 1 58	
	Issued check to record payment of federal			
	tax deposit.			

The T accounts are as follows.

Employees' Federal Income Tax Payable				FICA Tax Payable			
Nov. 17 1,152.42	Nov. 7	568.30		Nov. 17	989.16	Nov. 7	244.50
	Nov. 14	584.12				Nov. 7	244.50
						Nov. 14	250.08
						Nov. 14	250.08

Cash	
	Nov. 17 2,141.58

Employer's Quarterly Federal Tax Return (Form 941)

The return must be filed by the end of the month following the end of the quarter. After an employer has secured an identification number and has filed his or her first return, the Internal Revenue Service in the future sends forms directly to the employer. These forms will have the employer's name, address, and identification number filled in.

Sampson's sources of information for its Employer's Quarterly Federal Tax Return are the payroll registers and the general ledger accounts. Its Form 941 for the fourth quarter is shown on the facing page. Note that in the illustration the taxable FICA wages are multiplied by 13% (the 6.5% portion contributed by the employees plus the 6.5% matching portion contributed by the employer). Also, note the tax deposit section indicating the amount and date of each deposit.

Withholding statements for employees (W-2 forms)

The employer has to furnish W-2 forms to employees on or before the January 31 following the close of the preceding year, or within 30 days after an employee leaves service. The source of the information on the W-2 form is the employee's individual earnings record. The record for Ronald R. Jones, presented in Chapter 9, will be our source for this example. The accountant fills out Form W-2 in quadruplicate and gives copies B and C to the employee.

1 Control number		2 Employer's State number		For Official Use Only			
	222						
3 Employer's name, address, and ZIP code		4 Sub-total	Cor-rection	Void	Make No Entry Here See Note on the Back of Copy D		
Sampson and Associates 546 South Foss Street Spokane, WA 99203		☐	☐	☐			
		7 Employer's identification number					
		64-7218463					
10 Employee's social security number	11 Federal income tax withheld	12 Wages, tips, other compensation		13 FICA tax withheld		14 Total FICA wages	
543-24-1680	$1,584.09	$14,881.00		$967.27		$14,881.00	
15 Employee's name (first, middle, last)		16 Pension plan coverage? Yes/No		17 *		18 FICA tips	
Ronald R. Jones		No				0	
1582 North Pierce Street Spokane, WA 99204 19 Employee's address and ZIP code							
Wage and Tax Statement 19				Copy A For Social Security Administration *See Instructions for Forms W-2 and W-2P and back of Copy D			
Form W-2 ▼				Department of the Treasury—Internal Revenue Service			

Employer's Quarterly Federal Tax Return

			T	
			FF	
			FD	
			FP	
			I	
			T	

Your name, address, employer identification number, and calendar quarter of return. (If not correct, please change)

Name (as distinguished from trade name)
Ronald G. Sampson

Trade name, if any
Sampson and Associates

Address and ZIP code
546 South Foss Street
Spokane, WA 99203

Date quarter ended
December 31, 19--

Employer identification number
64-7218463

If address is different from prior return, check here ▶

1 Number of employees (except household) employed in the pay period that includes March 12th (complete for first quarter only)			
2 Total wages and tips subject to withholding, plus other compensation . . . . ➤		45,377	84
3 Total income tax withheld from wages, tips, annuities, gambling, etc.		6,891	76
4 Adjustment of withheld income tax for preceding quarters of calendar year		0	
5 Adjusted total of income tax withheld . . . . ➤		6,891	76
6 Taxable FICA wages paid . . . . $45,377.84 . . . multiplied by 13.0%=TAX . .		5,899	12
7 Taxable tips reported . . . . $................. multiplied by 6.5%=TAX . .		0	
8 Total FICA taxes (add lines 6 and 7) . . . . ➤		5,899	12
9 Adjustment of FICA taxes (see instructions)		0	
10 Adjusted total of FICA taxes . . . . ➤		5,899	12
11 Total taxes (add lines 5 and 10)		12,790	88
12 Advance earned income credit (EIC) payments, if any (see instructions)		0	
13 Net taxes (subtract line 12 from line 11)		12,790	88

Record of Federal Tax Deposits (See instructions on page 4)

Deposit period ending:		I. Tax liability for period	II. Date of deposit	III. Amount deposited
Overpayment from previous quarter				
First month of quarter	1st through 7th day	1,076.84		
	8th through 15th day	1,014.28	10/17/--	2,091.12
	16th through 22d day	1,122.30		
	23d through last day	1,106.41	11/2/--	2,228.71
A First month total . . . . **A**		4,319.83		4,319.83
Second month of quarter	1st through 7th day	1,063.66		
	8th through 15th day	1,084.28	11/17/--	2,141.58
	16th through 22d day	996.32		
	23d through last day	1,075.60	12/2/--	2,078.28
B Second month total . . . . **B**		4,219.86		4,219.86
Third month of quarter	1st through 7th day	1,112.76		
	8th through 15th day	1,114.18	12/17/--	2,226.94
	16th through 22d day	1,088.90		
	23d through last day	935.35	1/3/--	2,024.25
C Third month total . . . . **C**		4,251.19		4,251.19
D Total for quarter (add items A, B, and C) .		12,790.88		12,790.88
E Final deposit made for quarter. (Enter zero if the final deposit made for the quarter is included in item D)				

14 Total deposits for quarter (including final deposit made for quarter) and overpayment from previous quarter. (See instructions for deposit requirements on page 4.)		12,790	88

Note: *If undeposited taxes at the end of the quarter are $200 or more, deposit the full amount with an authorized financial institution or a Federal Reserve bank according to the instructions on the back of the Federal Tax Deposit Form 501. Enter this deposit in the Record of Federal Tax Deposits and include it on line 14.*

15 Undeposited taxes due (subtract line 14 from line 13—this should be less than $200). Pay to Internal Revenue Service and enter here . . . . ➤		0	

16 If line 14 is more than line 13, enter overpayment here ▶ $ _____ and check if to be: ☐ Applied to next return, or ☐ Refunded.

17 Number of Forms W-4 enclosed (see General Instructions and Specific Instructions for line 17) . . . . . .

18 If you are not liable for returns in the future, write "FINAL" (see instructions) ▶ _____ Date final wages paid ▶

Under penalties of perjury, I declare that I have examined this return, including accompanying schedules and statements, and to the best of my knowledge and belief it is true, correct, and complete.

Date ▶ January 29, 19--   Signature ▶ *Ronald G. Sampson*   Title ▶ Owner

Please file this form with your Internal Revenue Service Center (see instructions on "Where to File").   Form **941**

Sampson sends copy A of each employee's W-2 form to the District Director of Internal Revenue on or before January 31. The accountant attaches these to Form W-3, the Transmittal of Income and Tax Statements, shown here.

1 Control number			2 Employer's State number						
	33333		462-718						
Kind of Tax Statements Transmitted ▶	3 Official use ☐	4 Military ☐	5 Agriculture ☐	6 W-2 ☐	7 Original ☐	8 With TIN ☐			
	9 Railroad ☐	10 Household ☐	11 State or Local Gov. ☐	12 W-2P ☐	13 Corrected ☐	14 Without TIN ☐	15 Date of report 1/31/__		
16 State SSA number		17 Total advance EIC payment			18 Number of statements attached 12		19		
20 Total FICA tax withheld $11,373.44			21 Total Federal income tax withheld $27,680.11				22 Total FICA tips 0		
23 Total FICA wages $174,976.00			24 Total wages, tips, and other compensation $182,256.00				25 Gross annuities, pensions, retired pay, etc. 0		
26 Employer's identification number 64-7218463						27 Establishment number	28 Taxable annuities, pensions, retired pay, etc. 0		
29 Employer's name, address and ZIP code Ronald G. Sampson Sampson and Associates 546 South Foss Street Spokane, WA 99203					Internal Revenue Service—Department of the Treasury Form **W-3** Transmittal of Income and Tax Statements **19**				

Under penalties of perjury, I declare that I have examined this return, including accompanying documents, and to the best of my knowledge and belief, it is true, correct, and complete. In the case of documents without recipients' identifying numbers, I have complied with the requirements of the law by requesting such numbers from the recipients, but did not receive them.

Signature _Ronald G. Sampson_ Title Owner Date 1/31/___

To sum up: The employer must submit at the end of the calendar year, in one package, the following: (1) Employer's Quarterly Federal Tax Return for the fourth quarter, (2) copy A of all employees' W-2 forms, and (3) Form W-3. The employer keeps copy D of the W-2 forms.

On page 247 is the return for state unemployment insurance for Sampson and Associates for the first quarter, with the assumed state rate of 3% on the first $9,600 paid to each employee during the calendar year. The source for the wage report section is the employees' individual earnings records.

Various states differ with regard to both the rate and the taxable base for unemployment insurance. The state tax is usually due by the end of the month following the end of the calendar quarter; the due dates consequently coincide with the due dates of Form 941.

In general journal form, the entry is as follows.

19—Apr.	27	State Unemployment Tax Payable		1 3 6 7 54		
		Cash			1 3 6 7 54	
		To record payment of state unemployment				
		tax.				

EMS 5208-A

2. FEDERAL I.D. NO.	TAX OFFICE	EMP. CLASS	3. CALENDAR QUARTER ENDING DATE MO. / DAY / YR.	TAX RATE %	4. EMPLOYMENT SEC. NO. ACCOUNT	BR
64-721961	15	7	3 / 31 / --	3.0	462-718	810

STATE OF WASHINGTON
EMPLOYMENT SECURITY DEPARTMENT
OLYMPIA, WASHINGTON 98504

EMPLOYER'S QUARTERLY REPORT OF EMPLOYEE'S WAGES

ATTACH ADDITIONAL WAGE LISTING HERE

▶ READ INSTRUCTIONS ON BACK OF PAGE 3 BEFORE COMPLETING THIS FORM.

▶ IF ANY BUSINESS CHANGES HAVE OCCURRED, COMPLETE PAGE 3.

1. EMPLOYER'S NAME AND ADDRESS

Ronald G. Sampson
Sampson and Associates
546 South Foss Street
Spokane, WA 99203

LINE	5. EMPLOYEE'S SOCIAL SECURITY NUMBER			6. EMPLOYEE'S NAME LAST FIRST INITIAL	7. HOURS WORKED THIS QTR.	8. TOTAL WASHINGTON WAGES PAID THIS QUARTER	
L1	533	16	7285	Anderson, Dennis L.	582	3,215	00
L2	541	27	6982	Bowlen, Ralph P.	598	2,548	00
L3	539	87	1643	Daniels, John N.	572	2,990	00
L4	533	98	5379	Drew, Nancy R.	520	2,340	00
L5	526	71	8478	Farrell, Steven L.	520	2,496	00
L6	541	19	6143	Harwood, Lance C.	520	8,320	00
L7	543	24	1680	Jones, Ronald R.	520	3,588	00
L8	533	62	1745	Lyman, Mary C.	520	3,900	00
L9	541	38	9394	Miller, Robert M.	598	2,884	75
L10	540	29	7162	Olsen, Marvin C.	582	3,215	00
L11	539	12	2796	Stanfield, John D.	520	6,500	00
L12	529	92	8131	Tucker, Norma P.	572	3,588	00

	NO. OF PAGES	9. NO. OF EMPLOYEES	10. WAGES	
TOTALS FOR THIS PAGE	/////	12	45,584	75
GRAND TOTALS ALL PAGES	11. 1	12. 12	13. 45,584	75

PAGE 1 - ORIGINAL
EMPLOYMENT SECURITY DEPARTMENT COPY

— **DO NOT DETACH**

EMS 5208

▶ ATTACH CHECK HERE

25. EMPLOYER'S NAME AND ADDRESS

Ronald G. Sampson
Sampson and Associates
546 South Foss Street
Spokane, WA 99203

STATE OF WASHINGTON
EMPLOYMENT SECURITY DEPARTMENT
OLYMPIA, WASHINGTON 98504

EMPLOYER'S QUARTERLY TAX REPORT

▶ DO NOT MAKE ENTRIES IN THE SHADED AREAS.

DO NOT DETACH

COMPUTATION OF PAYMENT

		FOR DEPARTMENT USE		
14.	TOTAL WAGES (SAME AS ITEM 13)		45,584	75
15.	EXCESS WAGES		0	
16.	TAXABLE WAGES (ITEM 14 LESS ITEM 15)		45,584	75
17.	TAX DUE YOUR TAX RATE TIMES ITEM 16		1,367	54
18.	PENALTY - LATE PAYMENT (MINIMUM PENALTY - $2.00)		0	
19.	INTEREST		0	
20.	ADJUSTMENT (ATTACH STATEMENT OF ACCOUNT - FORM EMS 5229)		0	
21.	PENALTY - LATE REPORT ($10.00)		0	
22.	REMITTANCE (MAKE CHECKS PAYABLE TO: EMPLOYMENT SECURITY DEPARTMENT)		1,367	54

23. NUMBER OF COVERED EMPLOYEES	1ST MONTH 12	2ND MONTH 12	3RD MONTH 12

24. I CERTIFY THAT THE INFORMATION CONTAINED IN THIS REPORT IS TRUE AND CORRECT AND THAT NO PART OF THE TAX REPORTED WAS OR IS TO BE DEDUCTED FROM WORKERS WAGES.

SIGNATURE *Ronald G. Sampson*   TITLE Owner

DATE April 27, 19--   TELEPHONE NO. (509) 272-4414

26. ANNUAL TAXABLE WAGE BASE EACH EMPLOYEE	27. FEDERAL I.D. NO.	TAX OFFICE	EMP. CLASS	28. CALENDAR QUARTER ENDING DATE MO. DAY YR.	29. TAX RATE %	30. EMPLOYMENT SEC. NO. ACCOUNT	BR
$9,600	64-7218463	15	7	3 / 31 / --	3.0	462-718	810

PAGE 1 - ORIGINAL
EMPLOYMENT SECURITY DEPARTMENT COPY

Reports and payments of state unemployment insurance   **247**

Each employer who is subject to the Federal Unemployment Tax Act, as outlined in Chapter 9, must submit an Employer's Annual Federal Unemployment Tax Return, Form 940, not later than the January 31 following the close of the calendar year. This deadline may be extended until February 10, if the employer has made deposits paying the FUTA tax liability in full. The FUTA tax is calculated quarterly, during the month following the end of each calendar quarter. *If the accumulated tax liability is greater than $100, the tax is deposited in a commercial bank or Federal Reserve bank, accompanied by a preprinted federal tax deposit card,* like the form used to deposit employees' federal income tax withholding and FICA taxes. The due date for this deposit is the last day of the month following the end of the quarter, the same as the dates for the Employer's Quarterly Federal Tax Return and for state unemployment taxes.

The accountant computes the tax liability for the first quarter as follows.

Unemployment-taxable earnings times FUTA tax rate (.7%)
$45,584.75 × .007 = $319.09

The entry for the payment of the tax, in general journal form, is as follows.

19— Apr.	27	Federal Unemployment Tax Payable			3 1 9 09		
		Cash				3 1 9 09	
		To record payment of federal unemployment					
		tax.					

Unemployment-taxable earnings for the second quarter are $44,671.43, which means a tax liability of $312.70. Therefore the accountant makes a deposit. During the third quarter many employees passed the $8,000 mark for their total earnings for the calendar year, and the tax liability was accordingly reduced to $40.21.

Sampson does not have to make a deposit following the third quarter, because the total accumulated liability is less than $100. There is no tax liability for the fourth quarter; therefore, Sampson can pay the unpaid tax liability of $40.21 when it files the Employer's Annual Federal Unemployment Tax Return (Form 940).

The annual return (Form 940) for Sampson and Associates is shown on the opposite page.

The employer should complete the quarterly state unemployment tax return for the last quarter of the year before he or she tries to prepare the Employer's Annual Federal Unemployment Tax Return, because the data from the state returns are the source of information for the federal Form 940.

Form **940**		**Employer's Annual Federal**		**19**

Form **940**
Department of the Treasury
Internal Revenue Service

Employer's Annual Federal Unemployment Tax Return

		19

	T
	FF
	FD
	FP
	I
	T

If incorrect, make any necessary change ▶

Name (as distinguished from trade name)
Ronald G. Sampson

Trade name, if any
Sampson and Associates

Address and ZIP code
546 South Foss Street
Spokane, WA 99203

Calendar Year
19--

Employer identification number
64-7218463

Name of State 1	State reporting number as shown on employer's State contribution returns 2	Taxable payroll (as defined in State act) 3	Experience rate period 4 From—	To—	Experience rate 5	Contributions had rate been 2.7% (col. 3 × 2.7%) 6	Contributions payable at experience rate (col. 3 × col. 5) 7	Additional credit (col. 6 minus col. 7) 8	Contributions actually paid to State 9
Wash.	462-718	115,200.00	1/1	12/31	3.0	3,110.40	3,456.00		3,456.00
Totals ▶									3,456.00

10 Total tentative credit (column 8 plus column 9—see instructions on page 4)		3,456	00
11 Total remuneration (including exempt remuneration) **paid** during the calendar year for services of employees		182,256	00

Exempt Remuneration (See Instructions on Page 4)		(a) New jobs credit wages	(b) Amount paid
12 Exempt remuneration. (Explain each exemption shown, attaching additional sheet if necessary) ▶			
13 Remuneration in excess of the first $4,200 in column (a), and the first $6,000 in column (b), paid to individual employees exclusive of exempt amounts entered on line 12. Do not use State wage limitation			86,256.00
14 Total exempt remuneration (line 12 plus line 13)			86,256.00

15 a New jobs credit total wages (subtract line 12, column (a) from line 11) .			
b New jobs credit wages (subtract line 14, column (a) from line 11) . . .			
c Total taxable FUTA wages (subtract line 14, column (b) from line 11)		96,000	00
16 Gross Federal tax (multiply line 15c by .034)		3,264	00
17 Maximum credit (multiply line 15c by .027)	2,592.00		
18 Line 10 or line 17 whichever is smaller	2,592.00		
19 Amount, if any, of wages on line 15c attributable to Rhode Island $_____ × .003 . .			
20 Credit allowable (subtract line 19 from line 18)		2,592	00
21 Net Federal tax (subtract line 20 from line 16)		672	00

Record of Federal Tax Deposits for Unemployment Tax (Form 508)			
Quarter	Liability by period	Date of deposit	Amount of deposit
First	319.09	4/27	319.09
Second	312.70	7/12	312.70
Third			
Fourth			

22 Total Federal tax deposited		631	79
23 **Balance due** (subtract line 22 from line 21—this should not exceed $100). Pay to Internal Revenue Service . . . . ▶		40	21
24 Overpayment (subtract line 21 from line 22) . . . . ▶			
25 If no longer in business at end of year, write "Final" here . . . . ▶			

Under penalties of perjury, I declare that I have examined this return, including accompanying schedules and statements, and to the best of my knowledge and belief, it is true, correct and complete, and that no part of any payment made to a State unemployment fund claimed as a credit was or is to be deducted from the remuneration of employees.

Date ▶ 1/26/   Signature ▶   Title (Owner, etc.) ▶ Owner

Form **940**

As we said in Chapter 9, when we were describing the laws affecting employ-ment, most states require employers to provide workmen's compensation in-surance or industrial accident insurance, either through plans administered by the state or through private insurance companies authorized by the state. The employer usually has to pay all the premiums. The rate of the insurance pre-mium varies with the amount of risk the job entails. Handling molten steel ingots is a lot more dangerous than typing reports. So it is very important that employees be classified properly according to the insurance premium classifi-cations. For example, the rate for office work may be .15% of the payroll for office work, and the rate for industrial labor in heavy manufacturing may be 3.5% of the payroll for that category. These same figures may be expressed as $.15 per $100 of payroll and $3.50 per $100 of payroll.

Generally, the employer pays a premium in advance, based on his or her estimated payrolls for the year. After the year ends, the employer knows the exact amounts of the payrolls, so he or she can calculate the exact premium. At this time, depending on the difference between the estimated and the exact premium, the employer either pays an additional premium or gets a credit for overpayment.

At Sampson and Associates, there are two types of work classifications: office work and sales work. At the beginning of the year, its accountant com-puted the estimated annual premium, based on the predicted payrolls for the year, as follows.

Classification	Predicted Payroll	Rate	Estimated Premium
Office work	$ 38,000	.15%	$ 38,000 × .0015 = $ 57
Sales work	140,000	.5%	140,000 × .005 = 700
			Total estimated premium $757

Accordingly, as shown by T accounts, the accountant recorded the following entry.

Prepaid Insurance, Workmen's Compensation		Cash	
+	−	+	−
Jan. 10 757		Jan. 10 757	

Then, at the end of the calendar year, the accountant calculated the exact premium.

Classification	Exact payroll	Rate	Exact Premium
Office work	$ 39,000	.15%	$ 39,000 × .0015 = $ 58.50
Sales work	143,256	.5%	143,256 × .005 = 716.28
			Total exact premium $774.78

Therefore, the amount of the unpaid premium is

Total exact premium	$774.78
Less total estimated premium paid	757.00
Additional premium owed	$ 17.78

Now the accountant makes an adjusting entry, similar to the usual adjusting entry for expired insurance; this entry appears on the work sheet. Also he or she makes an additional adjusting entry for the extra premium owed. By T accounts, the entries are as follows.

Workmen's Compensation
Insurance Expense

+	−
Dec. 31 Adj. 757.00	
Dec. 31 Adj. 17.78	

Prepaid Insurance,
Workmen's Compensation

+	−
Jan. 10 Bal. 757	Dec. 31 Adj. 757

Workmen's Compensation
Insurance Payable

−	+
	Dec. 31 Adj. 17.78

Sampson and Associates will pay this amount of unpaid premium in January, together with the estimated premium for the next year.

Adjusting for accrued salaries and wages

Assume that $800 of salaries accrue for the time between the last payday and the end of the year. The adjusting entry is the same as introduced in Chapter 5.

Salary Expense		800 00	
Salaries Payable			800 00

Salaries Payable is a current liability account, and the employees' withholding taxes and deductions payable are also current liabilities. Actually, federal income taxes and FICA taxes levied on employees do not legally become effective until the employees are paid. Therefore, for the purpose of recording the adjusting entry, one should include the entire liability of the gross salaries and wages under Salaries Payable.

As we have seen, the following taxes come under the Payroll Tax Expense account: the employer's share of the FICA tax, the state unemployment tax, and the federal unemployment tax. The employer becomes liable for these taxes only when the employees are actually paid, rather than at the time the liability to the employees is incurred. From the standpoint of legal liability, there should be no adjusting entry for Payroll Tax Expense. From the standpoint of the income statement, however, doing without this entry would mean that this accrued expense for payroll taxes would not be included; thus the expenses would be understated and the net income would be overstated, although by a rather inconsequential amount. In other words, the legal element is not consistent with good accounting practice, but we have to abide by the law.

Tax calendar

Now let's put it all together: Assume that the employer's combined monthly totals of employees' FICA taxes, employer's FICA tax, and employees' income tax withheld are usually greater than $200 and less than $2,000. So the accountant, in order to keep up with the task of paying and reporting the various taxes, compiles a chronological list of the due dates. We are including only the payroll taxes here; however, sales taxes and property taxes should also be listed. When you think about the penalties for nonpayment of taxes by the due dates, this chronological list seems to be well worth the trouble.

Jan. 10 Pay estimated annual premium for workmen's compensation insurance. (This is an approximate date, as it varies among the states.)

31 Complete Employer's Quarterly Federal Tax Return, Form 941, for the fourth quarter, and pay employees' income tax withholding, employees' FICA tax withholding, and employer's FICA tax for wages paid during the month of December.

31 Issue copies B and C of Wage and Tax Statement, Form W-2, to employees.

31 Complete Transmittal of Income and Tax Statements, Form W-3, and attach copy A of W-2 forms for employees.

31 Pay state unemployment tax liability for the previous quarter and submit state return, employer's tax report.

31 Pay federal unemployment tax liability for previous year and submit Form 940, Employer's Annual Federal Unemployment Tax Return.

Feb. 15 Make federal tax deposit for employees' income tax withholding, employees' FICA tax withholding, and employer's FICA tax for wages paid during the month of January.

Mar. 15 Make federal tax deposit for employees' income tax withholding, employees' FICA tax withholding, and employer's FICA tax for wages paid during the month of February.

Apr. 30 Pay state unemployment tax liability for the previous quarter and submit state return, employer's tax report.

Apr. 30 Complete Employer's Quarterly Federal Tax Return, Form 941, for the first quarter, and pay employees' income tax withholding, employees' FICA tax withholding, and employer's FICA tax for wages paid during the month of March.

30 Make federal tax deposit for federal unemployment tax liability if it exceeds $100.

Summary

The assumed employer's taxes based on the payroll are as follows.

1. FICA tax, 6.5% of taxable income (the first $26,000 for each employee)

2. Federal unemployment tax, .7% of taxable income (the first $8,000 for each employee)

3. State unemployment tax, which varies from state to state, approximately 3% of taxable income (approximately the first $9,600 for each employee)

After recording each payroll entry from the payroll register, the accountant makes the following type of entry to record the employer's payroll taxes.

Payroll Tax Expense		2 7 2 72	
FICA Tax Payable			2 4 4 50
Federal Unemployment Tax Payable			3 98
State Unemployment Tax Payable			2 4 24
To record employer's share of FICA tax			
and employer's federal and state			
unemployment taxes.			

Payment of the tax liabilities and sample journal entries are as follows.

1. Payment of the combined amounts of employees' income tax withheld, employees' FICA tax withheld, and employer's FICA tax falls into three brackets:

a. If at the end of any quarter of a month (approximately 1 week) the cumulative amount of undeposited taxes so far for the calendar quarter (3 months) is $2,000 or more, deposit the taxes within 3 banking days after the end of the quarter-of-a-month period (7th, 15th, 22nd, and last day of month).

b. If at the end of any month (except the last month of a quarter) the cumulative amount of undeposited taxes for the quarter is at least $200 but less than $2,000, deposit the taxes within 15 days after the end of the month.

c. If at the end of a calendar quarter (3 months) the total amount of undeposited taxes is less than $200, no deposit is required, but make the payment at the time of submitting the Employer's Quarterly Federal Tax Return, Form 941.

1	19– Dec.	12	Employees' Federal Income Tax Payable			1	1	5	2	42							1
2			FICA Tax Payable				9	8	9	16							2
3			Cash								2	1	4	1	58		3
4			Issued check to record payment of federal														4
5			tax deposit.														5
6																	6
7																	7
8																	8
9																	9
10																	10

2. Payment of state unemployment tax on a quarterly basis accompanied by the quarterly return.

1	19– Apr.	27	State Unemployment Tax Payable			1	3	6	7	54							1
2			Cash								1	3	6	7	54		2
3			To record payment of state														3
4			unemployment tax.														4
5																	5
6																	6
7																	7
8																	8
9																	9

3. Payment of federal unemployment tax. If the amount of the accumulated tax liability exceeds $100 in a quarter, make a deposit, using the federal tax deposit form. Pay the remaining tax due by January 31 of the year following the close of the calendar year, using the Employer's Annual Federal Unemployment Tax Return, Form 940.

	27	Federal Unemployment Tax Payable			3	1	9	09							
		Cash							3	1	9	09			
		To record payment of federal													
		unemployment tax.													

4. Workmen's compensation insurance, based on a state plan or private insurance. At the beginning of the year, pay the premium in advance based on the estimated annual payroll. At the end of the year, when you know the actual payroll, adjust for the exact amount of the premium.

Glossary

Employer's identification number The number assigned each employer by the Internal Revenue Service for use in the submission of reports and payments for FICA taxes and federal income tax withheld.

Federal unemployment tax A tax levied on the employer only, amounting to .7% of the first $8,000 of total earnings paid to each employee during the calendar year. This tax is used to supplement state unemployment benefits.

Payroll Tax Expense A general expense account used for recording the employer's matching portion of the FICA tax, the federal unemployment tax, and the state unemployment tax.

Quarter A 3-month interval of the year, also referred to as a calendar quarter, as follows: first quarter, January, February, and March; second quarter, April, May, and June; third quarter, July, August, and September; fourth quarter, October, November, and December.

Quarter-of-a-month periods These are periods representing due dates for tax deposits designated by the Internal Revenue Service as follows: from the 1st to the 7th of the month (inclusive), from the 8th to the 15th of the month (inclusive), from the 16th to the 22nd of the month (inclusive), and from the 23rd to the last day of the month (inclusive).

State unemployment tax A tax levied on the employer only. Rates differ among the various states; however, they are generally 2.7% of the first $8,000 of total earnings paid to each employee during the calendar year, and are used to pay subsistence benefits to unemployed workers.

Workmen's compensation insurance This insurance, usually paid for by the employer, provides benefits for employees injured on the job. The rates vary according to the degree of risk inherent in the job. The plans may be sponsored by states or by private firms. The employer pays the premium in advance at the beginning of the year, based on the estimated payroll, and rates are adjusted after the exact payroll is known.

Questions

1. What payroll taxes are included under Payroll Tax Expense?

2. What information concerning the employee is included on a W-2 form?

3. How many copies of a W-2 form are prepared? To whom are the copies given?

4. What are Forms 940 and 941? How often are they prepared, and what are the due dates?

5. Explain the deposit requirement for federal unemployment insurance.

6. Generally, what is the time schedule for payment of premiums of workmen's compensation insurance?

7. Explain the advantage of establishing a tax calendar.

Exercises

Exercise 1 The payroll for the Ellis Company is as follows.

a. Gross earnings of employees	$200,000
b. Earnings subject to FICA tax	184,000
c. Earnings subject to federal unemployment tax	52,000
d. Earnings subject to state employment tax	52,000

Assuming that the payroll is subject to a FICA tax of 6.5% (.065), a state unemployment tax of 2.7% (.027), and a federal unemployment tax of .7% (.007), give the entry in general journal form to record the payroll tax expenses.

Exercise 2 The Adams Company had 100 employees throughout the year. The lowest-paid employee had gross earnings of $9,600. Assume that the Federal Unemployment Tax Act specifies a rate of 3.4% on the first $8,000 of gross earnings, and that the state unemployment tax is 2.7% of the same base. Adams Company, to conform with Form 940, is entitled to take credit against its federal tax by the amount paid to the state. (The effective federal unemployment tax is .7%.) Calculate the following.

a. The state unemployment tax for the year

b. The federal unemployment tax for the year

c. The total unemployment tax for the year

Exercise 3 The earnings for the calendar year for the employees of Duncan's Shoe Repair are as follows.

Employee	Cumulative Earnings
Gray, Betty C.	$ 9,800.00
Johnson, Martin D.	33,000.00
Lane, Doris S.	18,700.00
Mills, Ralph N.	2,500.00
	$64,000.00

The employees had to pay FICA tax during the year at the rate of 6.5% on the first $26,000 of their earnings; the employer had to pay a matching FICA tax. Unemployment insurance rates were 2.7% for the state and .7% for the federal government on the first $8,000 of an employee's earnings.

a. Determine the taxable earnings for FICA, state unemployment, and federal unemployment.

b. Determine the amount of taxes paid by the employees.

c. Determine the total of payroll taxes paid by the employer.

d. What percentage of the employer's total payroll of $64,000 was represented by payroll taxes?

Exercise 4 The salary expense of the Tyrell Company this year was $150,000, of which $10,000 was not subject to FICA tax and $70,000 was not subject to state and federal unemployment taxes. Calculate Tyrell's payroll tax expense for the year, using the following rates: FICA, 6.5% of first $26,000; state unemployment, 3.0% of first $8,000; federal unemployment, .7% of first $8,000.

Exercise 5 On January 13, at the end of the second weekly pay period during the year, the totals of United Transfer's payroll register showed that its driver employees had earned $4,600 and its office employees had earned $900. The employees were to have FICA taxes withheld at the rate of 6.5% of the first $26,000, plus $416 of federal income taxes, and $120 of union dues.

a. Calculate the amount of FICA taxes to be withheld, and write the general journal entry to record the payroll.

b. Write the general journal entry to record the employer's payroll taxes, assuming that the company has a state unemployment tax rate of 3.0% of the first $9,600 paid each employee, and that the federal unemployment tax is .7% of the first $8,000.

Exercise 6 The following information on earnings and deductions for the pay period ended December 14 is from M. E. Powers and Company's payroll records.

Name	Gross Pay	Earnings to End of Previous Week
Harris, C. E.	$380.00	$ 5,000.00
Larson, D. L.	640.00	32,000.00
Marsh, K. D.	400.00	20,000.00
Pruitt, N. C.	420.00	21,000.00

Prepare a general journal entry to record the employer's payroll taxes. The FICA tax is 6.5% of the first $26,000 of earnings for each employee. The state unemployment tax rate is 3.0% of the first $8,000 of earnings for each employee, and the federal unemployment tax is .7% (.007) of the same base.

Exercise 7 Suppose you are the accountant for a small business, and you get a premium notice for workmen's compensation insurance, stipulating the rates for the coming year. You have estimated that the year's premium will be as follows.

Classification	Estimated Wages and Salaries	Rate	Estimated Premium
Office work	$18,000	.1%	18.00
Sales work	90,000	.78%	$702.00
			$720.00

On January 29 the owner issued a check for $720. Record the entry in general journal form.

Exercise 8   At the end of the year, the accountant for the firm described in Exercise 7 discovers that the exact figures for the payroll are as follows:

Classification	Total Wages and Salaries	Rate	Exact Premium	
Office work	$18,000	.1 %		$ 18.00
Sales work	98,000	.78%		764.40
			Total exact premium	$782.40
			Less estimated premium paid	720.00
			Balance of premium due	$ 62.40

Record the adjusting entries for the insurance expired as well as for the additional premium due.

Problems

Problem 10-1   The column totals of the payroll register of the Patterson Chair Company for the week ended January 28 of this year show that the sales employees have earned $3,840 and the office employees $720. Patterson has deducted from the salaries of employees $592 for income taxes, $180 for medical insurance, $144 for union dues, and FICA tax at the rate of 6.5% (.065) on the first $26,000 of their earnings.

Instructions   Record the following entries in general journal form.

1. The payroll entry as of January 28.

2. The entry to record the payroll taxes as of January 28, assuming 2.7% (.027) for state unemployment insurance and .7% (.007) for federal unemployment insurance.

3. The payment of the employees as of January 31, assuming that Patterson issues one check payable to a payroll bank account.

Problem 10-2   The Oliver Clinical Laboratory had the following payroll for the week ended June 15.

Salaries		Deductions	
Technicians' salaries	$3,720.00	Income tax withheld	$574.00
Office salaries	780.00	FICA tax withheld	292.50
	$4,500.00	U. S. Savings Bonds	320.00
		Medical insurance	360.00

The assumed tax rates are as follows:

a. FICA 6.5% (.065) on the first $26,000 for each employee

b. State unemployment tax 2.7% (.027) on the first $8,000 for each employee

c. Federal unemployment tax .7% (.007) on the first $8,000 for each employee

Instructions Record the following in general journal form:

1. The payroll entry as of June 15.

2. The entry to record the employer's payroll taxes as of June 15, assuming that the total payroll is subject to the FICA tax, and that $2,800 is subject to unemployment taxes.

3. The payment of the employees as of June 18, assuming that Oliver Clinical Laboratory issued one check payable to a payroll bank account.

Problem 10-3 The Unique Products Company, of 3218 Julio Boulevard, Phoenix, Arizona 85002, received Form 941 from the Director of Internal Revenue. The identification number for Unique Products Company is 74-3949116. Its payroll for the quarter is as follows.

	NAME	TAXABLE EARNINGS			FICA WITHHELD	INCOME TAX WITHHELD
		TOTAL EARNINGS	UNEMPL. INSURANCE	FICA		
1	*Baileu, F. N.*	6,324.00		6,324.00	411.06	856.00
2	*Carpenter, M. A.*	4,768.00		4,768.00	309.92	632.00
3	*Cooke, H. E.*	3,832.00		3,832.00	249.08	506.00
4	*Elwell, H. A.*	4,340.00		4,340.00	282.10	588.00
5	*Gamble, D. O.*	2,952.00	2,096.00	2,952.00	191.88	398.00
6		22,216.00	2,096.00	22,216.00	1,444.04	2,980.00

The company has had five employees throughout the year. Assume that the employees have paid a FICA tax of 6.5% on the first $26,000 of their earnings and that the employer has paid a similar percentage on their earnings. F. R. Berni, the owner, has submitted the following federal tax deposits and written the accompanying checks.

On August 12, for the July Payroll		On September 13, for the August Payroll		On October 12, for the September Payroll	
Employees' income tax withheld	$ 942.00	Employees' income tax withheld	$ 988.00	Employees' income tax withheld	$1,050.00
Employees' FICA tax withheld	440.00	Employees' FICA tax withheld	471.11	Employees' FICA tax withheld	532.93
Employer's FICA tax	440.00	Employer's FICA tax	471.11	Employer's FICA tax	532.93
	$1,822.00		$1,930.22		$2,115.86

Instructions Complete Form 941 dated October 28.

Problem 10-4 The Keeler Company has the following balances in its general ledger as of March 1 of this year.

a. FICA tax payable (liability for February), $863.20

b. Employees' income tax payable (liability for February), $920.25

c. Federal unemployment tax payable (liability for January and February), $92.96

d. State unemployment tax payable (liability for January and February), $358.56

e. Medical insurance payable (liability for January and February), $1,140

The company completed the following transactions involving the payroll during March and April.

Mar. 12 Issued check for $1,783.45, payable to the Fidelity Bank and Trust, for the monthly deposit of February FICA taxes and employees' federal income tax withheld.

31 Recorded the payroll entry in the general journal from the payroll register for March. The payroll register has the following column totals.

Total earnings		$6,640.00
Employees' income tax deductions	$920.25	
Employees' FICA tax deductions	431.60	
Medical insurance deductions	356.00	
Total deductions		1,707.85
Net pay		$4,932.15
Sales salaries		5,610.00
Office salaries		1,030.00

31 Recorded payroll taxes in the general journal. Employees' FICA tax is 6.5%, employer's is also 6.5%, state unemployment insurance is 2.7%, and federal unemployment insurance is .7%.

Mar. 31 Issued check for $4,932.15 payable to a payroll bank account.

Apr. 14 Issued check for $1,496, payable to Noble Insurance Company in payment of employees' medical insurance for January, February, and March.

14 Issued check for $537.84, payable to the State Tax Commission, for state unemployment taxes for January, February, and March. The check was accompanied by the quarterly tax return.

14 Issued check for $1,783.45, payable to the Fidelity Bank and Trust, for the monthly deposit of March FICA taxes and employees' federal income tax withheld.

14 Issued check for $139.44, payable to the Fidelity Bank and Trust, for the deposit of federal unemployment insurance tax.

Instructions Record the transactions listed above in the general journal.

Alternate problems

Problem 10-1A The column totals of the payroll register of Raymond and Son for the week ended January 14 of this year show that the sales employees have earned $2,400 and the office employees $600. Raymond has deducted from the salaries of employees $392 for income taxes, $170 for medical insurance, $136 for union dues, and FICA tax at the rate of 6.5% (.065) on the first $26,000 of earnings.

Instructions Record the following in general journal form.

1. The payroll entry as of January 14.

2. The entry to record the employer's payroll taxes as of January 14, assuming 2.7% (.027) of the first $8,000 for state unemployment insurance and .7% (.007) of the first $8,000 for federal unemployment insurance.

3. The payment of the employees as of January 16, assuming that Raymond issues one check payable to a payroll bank account.

Problem 10-2A R. J. Madison and Company had the following payroll for the week ended June 24.

Salaries		Deductions	
Sales salaries	$3,280.00	Income tax withheld	$460.00
Office Salaries	560.00	FICA tax withheld	249.60
	$3,840.00	U. S. Savings Bonds	350.00
		Medical insurance	320.00

The assumed tax rates are as follows:

a. FICA tax, 6.5% (.065) on the first $26,000 for each employee

b. State unemployment tax, 2.7% (.027) on the first $8,000 for each employee

c. Federal unemployment tax, .7% (.007) on the first $8,000 for each employee

Instructions Record the following entries in general journal form:

1. The payroll entry as of June 24.

2. The entry to record the employer's payroll taxes as of June 24, assuming that the total payroll is subject to the FICA tax and that $2,810 is subject to unemployment taxes.

3. The payment of the employees as of June 27, assuming that R. J. Madison and Company issues one check payable to a payroll bank account.

Problem 10-3A For the third quarter of the year, Schmidt Company, 2116 Ramsey Street, Cincinnati, Ohio 45232, received Form 941 from the Director of Internal Revenue. The identification number of Schmidt Company is 66-7125964. Its payroll for the quarter is as follows.

	NAME	TOTAL EARNINGS	TAXABLE EARNINGS UNEMPL. INSURANCE	TAXABLE EARNINGS FICA	FICA WITHHELD	INCOME TAX WITHHELD
1	Mansen, M. C.	4560 00		4560 00	296 40	612 00
2	Lopez, A. L.	4320 00		4320 00	280 80	596 00
3	Meyers, F. C.	3740 00	520 00	3740 00	243 10	438 00
4	Moore, P. G.	3920 00	160 00	3920 00	254 80	462 00
5	West, A. R.	2400 00	2400 00	2400 00	156 00	292 00
6		18940 00	3080 00	18940 00	1231 10	2400 00

The company has had five employees throughout the year. Assume that the FICA tax payable by the employees is 6.5% of the first $26,000 of their earnings and that the FICA tax payable by the employer is 6.5% of the first $26,000 paid to the employees. J. P. Schmidt has submitted the following federal tax deposits and written the accompanying checks.

On August 14, for the July Payroll	On September 12, for the August Payroll	On October 14, for the September Payroll
Employees' income tax withheld $ 760.00	Employees' income tax withheld $ 840.00	Employees' income tax withheld $ 800.00
Employees' FICA tax withheld 391.18	Employees' FICA tax withheld 419.96	Employees' FICA tax withheld 419.96
Employer's FICA tax 391.18	Employer's FICA tax 419.96	Employer's FICA tax 419.96
$1,542.36	$1,679.92	$1,639.92

Instructions Complete Form 941 dated October 28.

Problem 10-4A The Zimmer Company has the following balances in its general ledger as of March 1 of this year.

a. FICA tax payable (liability for February), $884

b. Employees' income tax payable (liability for February), $1,020

c. Federal unemployment tax payable (liability for the months of January and February), $95.20

d. State unemployment tax payable (liability for the months of January and February), $367.20

e. Medical insurance payable (liability for January and February), $804

The company completed the following transactions involving the payroll during March and April.

Mar. 14 Issued check for $1,904, payable to Public Bank and Trust, for monthly deposit of February FICA taxes and employees' federal income tax withheld.

     31 Recorded the payroll entry in the general journal from the payroll register for March. The payroll register had the following column totals.

Total earnings		$6.800.00
Employees' income tax deductions	$1,020.00	
Employees' FICA tax deductions	442.00	
Medical insurance deduction	402.00	
Total deductions		1,864.00
Net pay		$4,936.00
Sales salaries		5,200.00
Office salaries		1,600.00

     31 Recorded payroll taxes in the general journal. Employees' FICA tax is 6.5%, employer's is also 6.5%, state unemployment insurance is 2.7%, and federal unemployment insurance is .7%.

     31 Issued check for $4,936 payable to a payroll bank account.

Apr. 6 Issued check for $1,206, payable to Unity Insurance Company, in payment of employees' medical insurance for January, February, and March.

     14 Issued check for $550.80, payable to the State Tax Commission, for state unemployment taxes for January, February, and March. The check was accompanied by the quarterly tax return.

     14 Issued check for $1,904, payable to Public Bank and Trust, for monthly deposit of March FICA taxes and employees' federal income tax withheld.

     14 Issued check for $142.80, payable to Public Bank and Trust, for deposit of federal unemployment insurance tax.

Instructions Record the transactions listed above in the general journal.

Review of T-account placement

The following sums up the placement of T accounts covered in Chapters 7 through 10 in relation to the fundamental accounting equation.

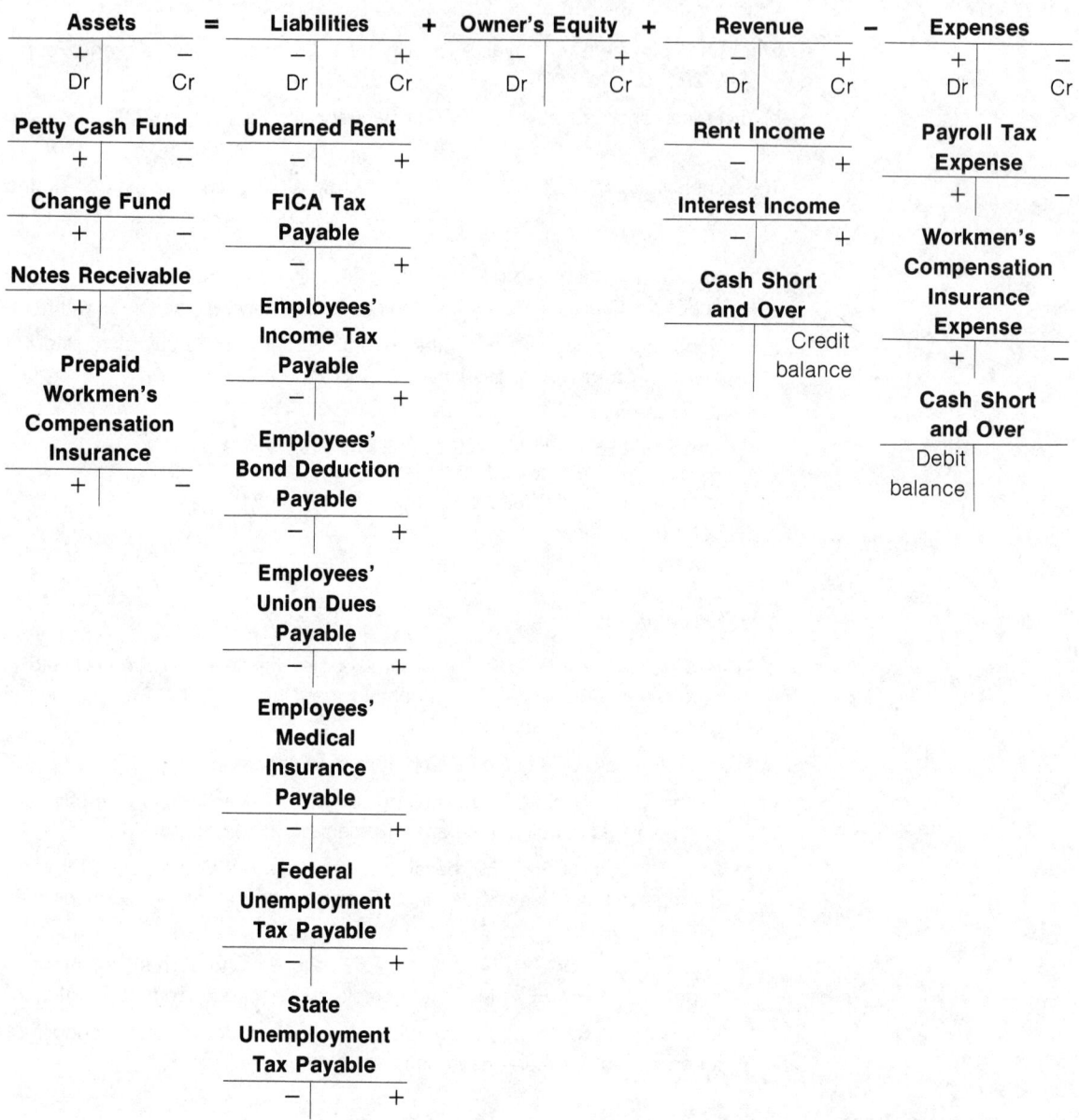

Assets	=	Liabilities	+	Owner's Equity	+	Revenue	−	Expenses
+ −		− +		− +		− +		+ −
Dr Cr		Dr Cr		Dr Cr		Dr Cr		Dr Cr

Petty Cash Fund
+ −

Change Fund
+ −

Notes Receivable
+ −

Prepaid Workmen's Compensation Insurance
+ −

Unearned Rent
− +

FICA Tax Payable
− +

Employees' Income Tax Payable
− +

Employees' Bond Deduction Payable
− +

Employees' Union Dues Payable
− +

Employees' Medical Insurance Payable
− +

Federal Unemployment Tax Payable
− +

State Unemployment Tax Payable
− +

Rent Income
− +

Interest Income
− +

Cash Short and Over
Credit balance

Payroll Tax Expense
+ −

Workmen's Compensation Insurance Expense
+ −

Cash Short and Over
Debit balance

The following summarizes the recording of transactions covered in Chapters 7 through 10, along with a classification of the accounts involved.

Transaction	Accounts Involved	Class.	Increase or Decrease	Therefore Debit or Credit
Established a Petty Cash Fund	Petty Cash Fund	A	I	Dr
	Cash	A	D	Cr
Reimbursed Petty Cash Fund	Expenses or Assets or Drawing	E, A, OE	I	Dr
	Cash	A	D	Cr
Established a Change Fund	Change Fund	A	I	Dr
	Cash	A	D	Cr
Recorded cash sales (amount on cash register tape was larger than cash count)	Cash	A	I	Dr
	Cash Short and Over	E		Dr
	Sales	R	I	Cr
Recorded cash sales (amount on cash register tape was less than cash count)	Cash	A	I	Dr
	Sales	R	I	Cr
	Cash Short and Over	R		Cr
Recorded service charges on bank account	Miscellaneous General Expense	E	I	Dr
	Cash	A	D	Cr
Recorded NSF check received from customer	Accounts Receivable	A	I	Dr
	Cash	A	D	Cr
Recorded interest-bearing note receivable collected by our bank	Cash	A	I	Dr
	Notes Receivable	A	D	Cr
	Interest Income	R	I	Cr
Recorded the payroll entry from the payroll register	Sales Salary Expense	E	I	Dr
	Office Salary Expense	E	I	Dr
	FICA Tax Payable	L	I	Cr
	Employees' Income Tax Payable	L	I	Cr
	Employees' Bond Deduction Payable	L	I	Cr
	Employees' Union Dues Payable	L	I	Cr
	Salaries Payable	L	I	Cr
Issued check payable to payroll bank account	Salaries Payable	L	D	Dr
	Cash	A	D	Cr

Transaction	Accounts Involved	Class.	Increase or Decrease	Therefore Debit or Credit
Recorded employer's payroll taxes	Payroll Tax Expense	E	I	Dr
	FICA Tax Payable	L	I	Cr
	State Unemployment Tax Payable	L	I	Cr
	Federal Unemployment Tax Payable	L	I	Cr
Recorded deposit of FICA taxes and employees' income tax withheld	Employees' Income Tax Payable	L	D	Dr
	FICA Tax Payable	L	D	. Dr
	Cash	A	D	Cr
Recorded deposit of federal unemployment tax	Federal Unemployment Tax Payable	L	D	Dr
	Cash	A	D	Cr
Paid state unemployment tax	State Unemployment Tax Payable	L	D	Dr
	Cash	A	D	Cr
Paid for workmen's compensation insurance in advance	Prepaid Workmen's Compensation Insurance	A	I	Dr
	Cash	A	D	Cr
Adjusting entry for workmen's compensation insurance, assuming an additional amount is owed	Workmen's Compensation Insurance Expense	E	I	Dr
	Prepaid Workmen's Compensation Insurance	A	D	Cr
	Workmen's Compensation Insurance Payable	L	I	Cr

11 Accounting for merchandise: sales

objectives

After you have completed this chapter, you will be able to do the following:
- Record transactions in sales journals.
- Post from sales journals to an accounts receivable ledger and a general ledger.
- Prepare a schedule of accounts receivable.
- Post directly from sales invoices to an accounts receivable ledger and a general ledger.

BY NOW you've had enough experience to complete the full accounting cycle for a service-type as well as a professional enterprise. To enlarge your accounting knowledge, let us now introduce accounting systems for merchandising enterprises. You will immediately realize that the same general principles of double-entry accounting prevail. This chapter describes specific accounts of merchandising firms; such a merchandising firm could be anything from a dress shop to a supermarket. The sales journal and the accounts receivable ledger are also presented. Just as we used Neil's Cleaners as a continuous illustration of a service-type business, we shall use North Central Plumbing Supply as an illustration of a merchandising business.

Special journals

In our previous descriptions of the accounting process, we have intentionally shown the entire procedure. In other words, we have taken the long way home, but there are certain shortcuts that you can use. Moreover, as far as understanding accounting is concerned, if you fully understand the long way, it's relatively easy to learn the shortcuts. The reverse is not true, in that you cannot readily understand the entire system if you are exposed to shortcuts only.

Any accounting system must be as efficient as possible. As a matter of fact, accounting is a means, or tool, by which to measure efficiency in a business. Consequently, one should take shortcuts wherever one can do so without sacrificing internal control (discussed in detail in Chapter 12).

As we shall see, using special journals is a form of shortcut. Using a two-column general journal for recording transactions which take place day after day is extremely time-consuming, because each individual debit and credit entry must be posted separately. The combined journal introduced in Chapter 7 improves the efficiency of the posting process. Special journals represent further improvement because they make possible the handling of specialized transactions and delegation of the work.

On the top of the next page is a list of the special journals that we shall introduce separately in the next few chapters.

When one uses any of these four journals, one must also use the general journal to record any *non*specialized transactions—in other words, any transactions that the special journals cannot handle. In this case the letter designation for the general journal is J.

Chapter	Special Journal	Letter Designation	Specialized Transaction
11	Sales journal	S	Sales of merchandise on account only
12	Purchases journal	P	Purchase of merchandise on account only
13	Cash receipts journal	CR	All cash received from any source
13	Cash payments journal	CP	All cash paid out for any purpose

Specific accounts for merchandising firms

A service or professional enterprise, such as the ones we have encountered, depends for its revenue on the rendering of services; for example, a service or professional enterprise uses such accounts as Income from Services or Professional Fees. A merchandising business, however, depends for its revenue on the sale of goods or merchandise, recording the amount of the sale under the account titled Sales.

Merchandise consists of a stock of goods that a firm buys and intends to resell, in the same physical condition, at a profit. Merchandise should be differentiated from other assets, such as equipment and supplies, which are acquired for use in the business and are not for resale.

Because the merchandising firm has to record transactions involving the purchase, handling, and sale of its merchandise, it also has to use some specific accounts and procedures that we have not yet discussed. As an introduction to these accounts, we now present the fundamental accounting equation with the new T accounts that are introduced in this chapter, as well as in Chapters 12 and 13.

Assets	=	Liabilities	+	Owner's Equity	+	Revenue	−	Expenses
+ −		− +		− +		− +		+ −
Dr Cr		Dr Cr		Dr Cr		Dr Cr		Dr Cr

Merchandise Inventory	Sales Tax Payable		Sales	and Purchases
+ −	− +		− +	+ −

Sales Returns and Allowances
+   −

Purchases Returns and Allowances
−   +

Sales Discount
+   −

Purchases Discount
−   +

The Sales account, as we have said, is a revenue account, and records the sale of merchandise.

The Purchases account records the cost of merchandise acquired for resale. Remember that the Purchases account is used strictly for the buying of merchandise. The plus and minus signs are the same as the signs for Merchandise Inventory. Purchases is placed under the heading of Expenses merely because the accountant closes it at the end of the fiscal period, along with the expense accounts.

The Sales Returns and Allowances account records the physical return of merchandise by customers, or a reduction in a bill due to the fact that merchandise was damaged. It is treated as a deduction from Sales.

The Purchases Returns and Allowances account records the firm's return of merchandise previously purchased, or a reduction in the bill due to damaged merchandise. It is treated as a deduction from Purchases.

The Sales Discount and Purchases Discount accounts record cash discounts granted for prompt payments, in accordance with the credit terms. We shall discuss these in connection with the cash journals.

The firm's accountant makes entries involving Merchandise Inventory only when the firm takes an actual physical count of the goods in stock; otherwise the accountant leaves this account strictly alone.

In the illustration, these accounts are shown in color to emphasize that we are treating them as deductions from the related accounts placed above them. The reason we list these accounts as deductions is that they appear as deductions in the financial statements. This is similar to the relationship between the Drawing account and the Capital account; remember that we deduct Drawing from Capital in the statement of owner's equity.

The type of transaction most frequently encountered in a merchandising business is the sale of merchandise. Some businesses sell on a cash-and-carry basis only; others sell on a credit basis only. Many firms offer both arrangements. The same general types of entries could pertain to both retail and wholesale enterprises. Here are some examples.

Sale of merchandise for cash, $100.

Cash			Sales	
+	–		–	+
100				100

Debit Cash and credit Sales; record this in the cash receipts journal.

Sale of merchandise on account, $200.

Accounts Receivable			Sales	
+	–		–	+
200				200

Debit Accounts Receivable and credit Sales; then record this in the sales journal.

All sales are recorded in response to an order received from a customer. The routines for processing orders and recording sales vary with the type and size of the business.

In a retail business, a salesperson usually prepares a sales ticket—either in duplicate or triplicate—for a sale on account. One copy is given to the customer, and another copy to the accounting department, where it will be used as the basis for an entry in the sales journal. A third copy may be used for a record of sales as, for example, when one is computing sales commissions or is involved in inventory control.

In a wholesale business, the company usually receives a written order from a customer, or from a salesperson who obtained the order from the customer. The order must then be approved by the credit department, after which it is sent to the billing department, where the sales invoice is prepared. As in the case of the sales ticket, the sales invoice may be made out either in duplicate or in triplicate.

For our illustration we shall use North Central Plumbing Supply, a wholesaler. One of their invoices follows.

North Central Plumbing Supply
1968 Arrow St., N.W.
Seattle, WA 98111

INVOICE

Sold To: T. L. Long Co.
18160 Federal St., S.W.
Seattle, WA 98110

DATE: August 1, 19—
Invoice No: 320
Order No: 5384
Shipped By: Their truck
Terms: 2/10, n/30

Quantity	Description	Unit Price	Total
100	3/4" galv. pipe, 10'	.235	235.00
50	1 1/2" cast-iron 90° reg. elbow	.90	45.00
40	1 1/2" cast-iron 90° street elbow	1.125	45.00
			325.00

As a basis for the introduction to the sales journal, we shall use three transactions as illustrations.

Aug. 1 Sold merchandise on account to T. L. Long Company, $325, Invoice No. 320.

3 Sold merchandise on account to Macon, Inc., $116, Invoice No. 321.

6 Sold merchandise on account to Acme Plumbing and Heating, $94, Invoice No. 322.

We can use T accounts to visualize these transactions.

Accounts Receivable		Sales	
+	−	−	+
325			325
116			116
94			94

If they were recorded in a general journal, they would appear as follows.

GENERAL JOURNAL PAGE __23__

		DESCRIPTION	POST REF.	DEBIT	CREDIT
19– Aug.	1	Accounts Receivable	113	325 00	
		Sales	411		325 00
		Invoice No. 320, T. L. Long Company.			
	3	Accounts Receivable	113	116 00	
		Sales	411		116 00
		Invoice No. 321, Macon, Inc.			
	6	Accounts Receivable	113	94 00	
		Sales	411		94 00
		Invoice No. 322, Acme Plumbing and			
		Heating.			

Next the journal entries would be posted to the accounts in the general ledger, as shown here.

GENERAL LEDGER

ACCOUNT _____ *Accounts Receivable* _____ ACCOUNT NO. __113__

DATE		ITEM	POST. REF.	DEBIT	CREDIT	BALANCE DEBIT	BALANCE CREDIT
19– Aug.	1		23	325 00		325 00	
	3		23	116 00		441 00	
	6		23	94 00		535 00	

ACCOUNT _____ *Sales* _____ ACCOUNT NO. __411__

DATE	ITEM	POST. REF.	DEBIT	CREDIT	BALANCE DEBIT	BALANCE CREDIT
19— Aug. 1		23		3 2 5 00		3 2 5 00
3		23		1 1 6 00		4 4 1 00
6		23		9 4 00		5 3 5 00

Obviously, there is a great deal of repetition in both journalizing and posting. The credit sales require three separate journal entries, three debit postings to Accounts Receivable, and three credit postings to Sales. Using a *sales journal* avoids all this repetition. We have presented all of this to show the advantages of the sales journal.

The sales journal

The sales journal records *sales of merchandise on account only*. This specialized type of transaction would result in debits to Accounts Receivable and credits to Sales. We shall now record the three transactions for North Central Plumbing Supply in the sales journal as a substitute for recording them in the general journal.

SALES JOURNAL PAGE __38__

DATE	INV. NO.	CUSTOMER'S NAME	POST. REF.	ACCTS. REC. DR. SALES CR.
19— Aug. 1	320	*T. L. Long Company*		3 2 5 00
3	321	*Macon, Inc.*		1 1 6 00
6	322	*Acme Plumbing and Heating*		9 4 00

Note that the one money column is headed *Accounts Receivable Debit* and *Sales Credit*. Each transaction requires only a single line. Repetition is avoided, and one can now find all entries for sales of merchandise on account in one place. Listing the invoice number is useful in case one should later want to make a further check on the details of a particular sale.

Posting from the sales journal

Using the sales journal also enables one to save time and space when one is posting to the ledger accounts. The transactions involving the sales of merchandise on account for the month of August are as shown at the top of the next page.

DATE	INV. NO.	CUSTOMER'S NAME	POST. REF.	ACCTS. REC. DR. SALES CR.	
19— Aug.	1	320	T. L. Long Company		3 2 5 00	1
	3	321	Macon, Inc.		1 1 6 00	2
	6	322	Acme Plumbing and Heating		9 4 00	3
	9	323	Manning Service Company		9 6 1 00	4
	11	324	Clark and Keller Hardware		8 6 00	5
	16	325	Home Hardware Company		2 1 5 00	6
	20	326	Henning's Plumbing		2 9 3 00	7
	23	327	Baker Building Supplies		5 6 0 00	8
	24	328	Clark and Keller Hardware		2 8 6 00	9
	28	329	Home Hardware Company		7 5 00	10
	30	330	Baker Building Supplies		3 8 7 00	11
	31	331	T. L. Long Company		5 6 00	12
	31	332	Robert D. Bishop, Inc.		8 7 1 00	13
					4 3 2 5 00	14
					(113)(411)	15
						16

Because all the entries are a debit to Accounts Receivable and a credit to Sales, one can now make a single posting to these accounts for the amount of the total as of the last day of the month. (In each of the following ledger accounts, assume there was no balance in the account prior to the transaction.)

GENERAL LEDGER

ACCOUNT ___Accounts Receivable___   ACCOUNT NO. ___113___

DATE	ITEM	POST. REF.	DEBIT	CREDIT	BALANCE	
					DEBIT	CREDIT
19— Aug.	31		S38	4 3 2 5 00		4 3 2 5 00	

ACCOUNT ___Sales___   ACCOUNT NO. ___411___

DATE	ITEM	POST. REF.	DEBIT	CREDIT	BALANCE	
					DEBIT	CREDIT
19— Aug.	31		S38		4 3 2 5 00		4 3 2 5 00

In the Posting Reference columns of the ledger accounts, the letter S designates the sales journal.

After posting to the Accounts Receivable account, go back to the sales journal and record the account number in parentheses directly below the total. The account number for the account being debited goes on the left. Repeat this process when posting to the sales account. Again, as a precaution, don't record these account numbers until you have completed the postings.

In most states there's a sales tax on retail sales of goods and services. The retailer collects the sales tax from customers and then later pays it to the tax authorities.

When goods or services are sold on a credit basis, the sales tax is charged to the customer and recorded at the time of the sale. The sales journal has to be redesigned to handle this type of transaction. For example, if a retail store sells an item for $100 and the sales tax is 4%, then, by T accounts, it would be recorded like this.

Accounts Receivable		Sales		Sales Tax Payable	
+	−	−	+	−	+
104			100		4

The accountant debits Sales Tax Payable and credits Cash when the sales tax is paid to the government.

Because we want to illustrate a sales journal for a retail merchandising firm operating in a state having a sales tax, we shall use a different illustration: Slovik and Sterns Fabrics. Its sales journal is presented below.

SALES JOURNAL   PAGE 96

DATE	INV. NO.	CUSTOMER'S NAME	ACCOUNTS RECEIVABLE DEBIT	SALES TAX PAYABLE CREDIT	SALES CREDIT
19– Apr. 1	9382	N. T. George	16 64	64	16 00
1	9383	Culver Apartments	22 88	88	22 00
1	9384	Richard Gladdon	52 00	2 00	50 00
2	9385	T. R. Sears	12 48	48	12 00
30	10121	Paul Murphy	124 80	4 80	120 00
30			2516 80	96 80	2420 00
			(113)	(214)	(411)

Each column is posted to the ledger accounts as a total at the end of the month. After posting the figures, the accountant records the account numbers in parentheses immediately below the total.

GENERAL LEDGER

ACCOUNT _____ *Accounts Receivable* _____ ACCOUNT NO. 113

DATE	ITEM	POST. REF.	DEBIT	CREDIT	BALANCE DEBIT	BALANCE CREDIT
19– Apr. 30		S96	2516 80		2516 80	

ACCOUNT _____ *Sales Tax Payable* _____ ACCOUNT NO. 214

DATE	ITEM	POST. REF.	DEBIT	CREDIT	BALANCE DEBIT	BALANCE CREDIT
19– Apr. 30		S96		96 80		96 80

ACCOUNT _____ *Sales* _____ ACCOUNT NO. _411_

DATE	ITEM	POST. REF.	DEBIT	CREDIT	BALANCE	
					DEBIT	CREDIT
19— Apr. 30		S96		2 4 2 0 00		2 4 2 0 00

The accounts receivable ledger

The Accounts Receivable account, as we have seen, represents the total amount owed to a business by its charge customers.

But there is a deficiency of information here, in that the business can't tell at a glance *how much* each individual charge customer owes. This handicaps the credit department. To correct this shortcoming, one must keep a separate account for each charge customer.

For a business having very few charge customers, it is possible to have a separate Accounts Receivable account in the general ledger for each charge customer. However, if there are many charge customers (which is the usual case), this would be too cumbersome. The trial balance, with each charge customer's account included, would be very long. Of course, the possibility for errors would also increase accordingly.

So it is more practical to have a separate book containing a list of all the charge customers and each one's respective balance. This is called the *accounts receivable ledger.* The Accounts Receivable account should still be maintained in the general ledger; when all the postings are up to date, the balance of this account should equal the total of all the individual balances of the charge customers. The Accounts Receivable account in the general ledger is called a *controlling account.* The accounts receivable *ledger,* containing the accounts or listing of all the charge customers, is really a special ledger, and it is called a *subsidiary ledger.* The interrelationship of these books is illustrated on the top of the facing page.

The accountant posts the individual amounts daily to the accounts receivable ledger, so that this ledger will have up-to-date information. At the end of the month, the accountant posts the total of the sales journal (in this case, $1,800) to the general ledger accounts as a debit to the Accounts Receivable (controlling) account and a credit to the Sales account. As indicated in the illustration on page 277, the balance of the Accounts Receivable (controlling) account at the end of the month must equal the total of the balances of the charge customer accounts in the accounts receivable ledger. The schedule of accounts receivable is merely a listing of the charge customers' individual balances.

After you post the amount from the sales journal to the charge customer's account in the accounts receivable ledger, put a check mark ($\checkmark$) in the Posting Reference column of the sales journal.

Let us now look at the sales journal of North Central Plumbing Supply for August with the daily postings that its accountant has made to the accounts receivable ledger, as well as the schedule of accounts receivable. These are shown at the bottom of page 277 and on pages 278–279.

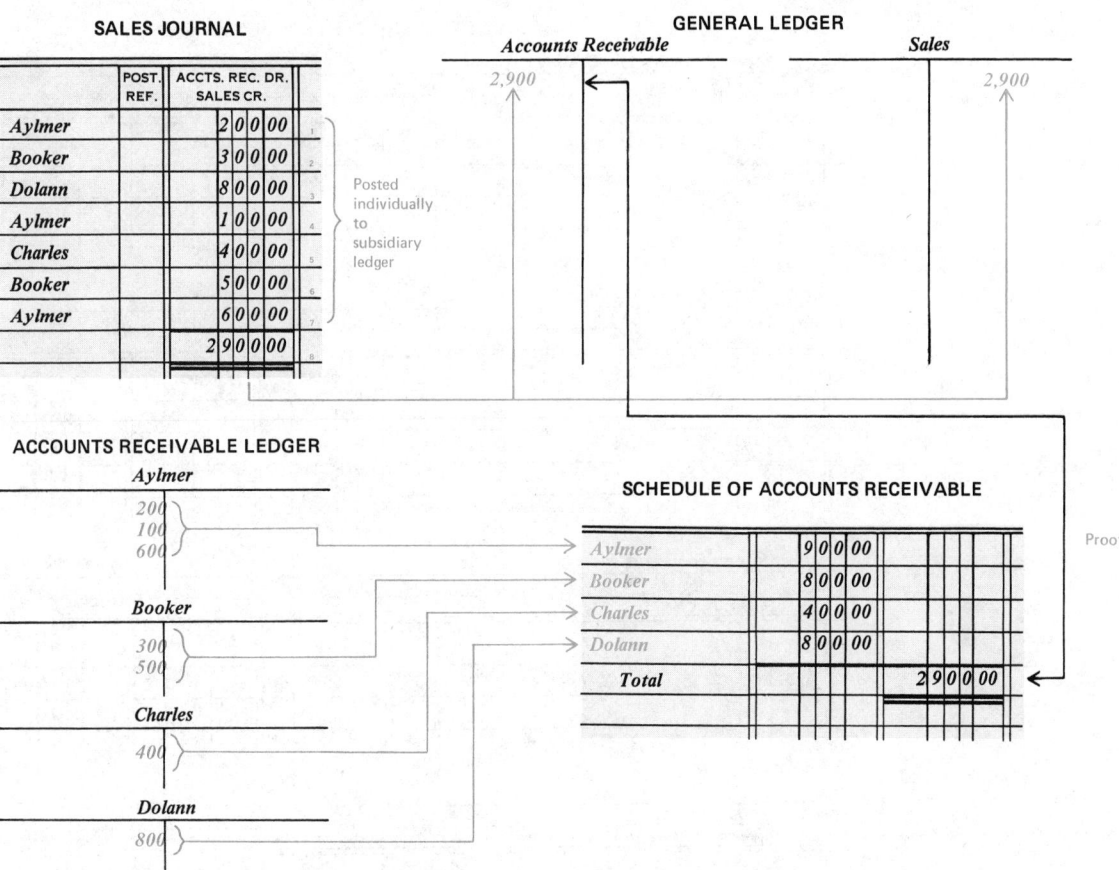

SALES JOURNAL
PAGE 38

	DATE	INV. NO.	CUSTOMER'S NAME	POST. REF.	ACCTS. REC. DR. SALES CR.	
1	19— Aug. 1	320	T. L. Long Company	✓	325 00	1
2	3	321	Macon, Inc.	✓	116 00	2
3	6	322	Acme Plumbing and Heating	✓	94 00	3
4	9	323	Manning Service Company	✓	961 00	4
5	11	324	Clark and Keller Hardware	✓	86 00	5
6	16	325	Home Hardware Company	✓	215 00	6
7	20	326	Henning's Plumbing	✓	293 00	7
8	23	327	Baker Building Supplies	✓	560 00	8
9	24	328	Clark and Keller Hardware	✓	286 00	9
10	28	329	Home Hardware Company	✓	75 00	10
11	30	330	Baker Building Supplies	✓	387 00	11
12	31	331	T. L. Long Company	✓	56 00	12
13	31	332	Robert D. Bishop, Inc.	✓	871 00	13
14	31				4325 00	14
15					(113)(411)	15

Name Acme Plumbing and Heating
Address 1015 Broadway, S.W.
Seattle, WA 98102

DATE		ITEM	POST. REF.	DEBIT	CREDIT	BALANCE
19—Aug.	6		S38	9 4 00		9 4 00

Name Baker Building Supplies
Address 17 No. Second St.
Renton, WA 98055

DATE		ITEM	POST. REF.	DEBIT	CREDIT	BALANCE
19—Aug.	23		S38	5 6 0 00		5 6 0 00
	30		S38	3 8 7 00		9 4 7 00

Name Robert D. Bishop, Inc.
Address 2168 Main St.
Kent, WA 98031

DATE		ITEM	POST. REF.	DEBIT	CREDIT	BALANCE
19—Aug.	31		S38	8 7 1 00		8 7 1 00

Name Clark and Keller Hardware
Address 2005 N. Powder St.
Everett, WA 98201

DATE		ITEM	POST. REF.	DEBIT	CREDIT	BALANCE
19—Aug.	11		S38	8 6 00		8 6 00
	24		S38	2 8 6 00		3 7 2 00

Name Henning's Plumbing
Address 21680 S.E. Twelfth Ave.
Portland, OR 97208

DATE		ITEM	POST. REF.	DEBIT	CREDIT	BALANCE
19—Aug.	20		S38	2 9 3 00		2 9 3 00

Name Home Hardware Company
Address 2810 Pender St. N.W.
Seattle, WA 98101

DATE		ITEM	POST. REF.	DEBIT	CREDIT	BALANCE
19—Aug.	16		S38	2 1 5 00		2 1 5 00
	28		S38	7 5 00		2 9 0 00

Name____ T. L. Long Company
Address____ 18160 Federal St., S.W.
_____ Seattle, WA 98110

	DATE	ITEM	POST. REF.	DEBIT	CREDIT	BALANCE
19– Aug.	1		S38	3 2 5 00		3 2 5 00
	31		S38	5 6 00		3 8 1 00

Name____ Macon, Inc.
Address____ 1720 Ninth St., N.W.
_____ Seattle, WA 98107

	DATE	ITEM	POST. REF.	DEBIT	CREDIT	BALANCE
19– Aug.	3		S38	1 1 6 00		1 1 6 00

Name____ Manning Service Company
Address____ 2720 N.W. 43rd Ave.
_____ Portland, OR 97210

	DATE	ITEM	POST. REF.	DEBIT	CREDIT	BALANCE
19– Aug.	9		S38	9 6 1 00		9 6 1 00

North Central Plumbing Supply

Schedule of Accounts Receivable

August 31, 19–

Acme Plumbing and Heating	9 4 00	
Baker Building Supplies	9 4 7 00	
Robert D. Bishop, Inc.	8 7 1 00	
Clark and Keller Hardware	3 7 2 00	
Henning's Plumbing	2 9 3 00	
Home Hardware Company	2 9 0 00	
T. L. Long Company	3 8 1 00	
Macon, Inc.	1 1 6 00	
Manning Service Company	9 6 1 00	
Total Accounts Receivable		4 3 2 5 00

In the accounts receivable ledger, the individual charge customer accounts are listed in alphabetical order. Most accountants prefer a loose-leaf binder so that they can insert accounts for new customers and remove other accounts; they do not use account numbers.

Assuming that these were the only transactions involving charge customers, the accountant prepares a schedule of accounts receivable, listing the balance of each charge customer.

Again we assume that there were no previous balances in the customer's accounts. So the Accounts Receivable (controlling) account in the general ledger will have the same balance, $4,325.

GENERAL LEDGER

ACCOUNT _____ *Accounts Receivable* _____ ACCOUNT NO. __113__

DATE	ITEM	POST. REF.	DEBIT	CREDIT	BALANCE DEBIT	BALANCE CREDIT
19— Aug. 31		S38	4 3 2 5 00		4 3 2 5 00	

Sales returns and allowances

This account handles two types of transactions having to do with merchandise that has previously been sold. A *return* means a physical return of the goods. An *allowance* means allowing a reduction from the original price due to the fact that the goods were defective or damaged. It may not be economically worthwhile to return the goods; each situation is a special case. In order to avoid writing a separate letter each time, one uses a special form which is called a *credit memorandum.* A typical one might look like this.

North Central Plumbing Supply
1968 Arrow St., N.W.
Seattle, WA 98111

CREDIT
MEMORANDUM
No. 69

Credit to:

Clark and Keller Hardware
2005 N. Powder St.
Everett, WA 98201

Date _August 25, 19—_

WE CREDIT YOUR ACCOUNT AS FOLLOWS:

1 pedestal sump pump (Randall) 1/3 h.p.,   45.00
  1 1/4" discharge tap

The Sales Returns and Allowances account is considered to be a deduction from Sales. In order to have a better record of the total returns and allowances, accountants use an account separate from Sales, and they deduct Sales Returns and Allowances from Sales in the income statement, as we shall see later. Let's consider this situation by using T accounts.

Transaction (a) On August 24, North Central sold merchandise on account to Clark and Keller Hardware, $286, and recorded this in the sales journal.

Transaction (b) On August 25, Clark and Keller Hardware returned $45 worth of the merchandise, and North Central issued a credit memorandum.

Assets		=	Liabilities		+	Owner's Equity		+	Revenue		−	Expenses	
+	−		−	+		−	+		−	+		+	−
Dr	Cr		Dr	Cr		Dr	Cr		Dr	Cr		Dr	Cr

Accounts Receivable

+	−
(a) 286	(b) 45

Sales

−	+
	(a) 286

Sales Returns and Allowances

+	−
(b) 45	

North Central's accountant debits Sales Returns and Allowances because North Central has greater returns and allowances than they did before, and credits Accounts Receivable because the charge customer (Clark and Keller) owes less than before.

One uses the word *credit* in "credit memorandum" because one credits Accounts Receivable. Suppose that during August, North Central Plumbing Supply issues two credit memorandums, and records the entries in the general journal as follows.

GENERAL JOURNAL PAGE 27

	DATE		DESCRIPTION	POST REF.	DEBIT	CREDIT	
1	19– Aug.	25	Sales Returns and Allowances		4 5 00		1
2			Accounts Receivable, Clark and Keller Hardware			4 5 00	2
3			Credit Memorandum No. 69.				3
4							4
5		31	Sales Returns and Allowances		1 1 6 00		5
6			Accounts Receivable, Home Hardware Company			1 1 6 00	6
7			Credit Memorandum No. 70.				7

Note that Accounts Receivable is not the only thing recorded in the general journal entry; it is followed by the name of the charge customer's account in the accounts receivable ledger. If the balance of the Accounts Receivable (controlling) account is to equal the total of the individual balances in the accounts receivable ledger, one must post to *both* the Accounts Receivable account in the general ledger *and* the account of Clark and Keller Hardware in the accounts receivable ledger. To take care of this double posting, one puts a slant line in the Posting Reference column. When the amount has been posted as a credit to this account, the accountant puts the account number of Accounts Receivable in the left part of the Posting Reference column. After the account of Clark and Keller Hardware has been posted as a credit, the accountant puts a check mark in the right portion of the Posting Reference column, then posts Sales Returns and Allowances in the usual manner. Here are the entries with posting completed. (No balance was recorded in the Accounts Receivable account because a credit balance would not be a normal balance for the account.)

GENERAL JOURNAL
PAGE __27__

	DATE		DESCRIPTION	POST. REF.	DEBIT	CREDIT	
1	19– Aug.	25	Sales Returns and Allowances	412	4 5 00		1
2			Accounts Receivable, Clark and Keller Hardware	113/✓		4 5 00	2
3			Credit Memorandum No. 69.				3
4							4
5		31	Sales Returns and Allowances	412	1 1 6 00		5
6			Accounts Receivable, Home Hardware Company	113/✓		1 1 6 00	6
7			Credit Memorandum, No. 70.				7
8							8
9							9

GENERAL LEDGER

ACCOUNT ___Accounts Receivable___ ACCOUNT NO. __113__

DATE		ITEM	POST. REF.	DEBIT	CREDIT	BALANCE DEBIT	BALANCE CREDIT
19– Aug.	25		J27		4 5 00		
	31		J27		1 1 6 00		

ACCOUNT ___Sales Returns and Allowances___ ACCOUNT NO. __412__

DATE		ITEM	POST. REF.	DEBIT	CREDIT	BALANCE DEBIT	BALANCE CREDIT
19– Aug.	25		J27	4 5 00		4 5 00	
	31		J27	1 1 6 00		1 6 1 00	

ACCOUNTS RECEIVABLE LEDGER

Name ___Clark and Keller Hardware___
Address ___2005 N. Powder St.___
___Everett, WA 98201___

DATE		ITEM	POST. REF.	DEBIT	CREDIT	BALANCE
19– Aug.	11		S38	8 6 00		8 6 00
	24		S38	2 8 6 00		3 7 2 00
	25		J27		4 5 00	3 2 7 00

Name   *Home Hardware Company*
Address *2810 Pender St. N.W.*
         Seattle, WA 98101

DATE		ITEM	POST. REF.	DEBIT	CREDIT	BALANCE
19— Aug.	16		S38	2 1 5 00		2 1 5 00
	28		S38	7 5 00		2 9 0 00
	31		J27		1 1 6 00	1 7 4 00

Sales returns and allowances involving sales taxes

If a customer returns merchandise to a retail store, and the customer was originally charged a sales tax, the sales tax must be returned to the customer. To illustrate, first, refer to the sales journal of Slovik and Sterns Fabrics on page 275 involving sales taxes. On April 3, assume that N. T. George returns the merchandise bought on April 1 for $16 plus $.64 sales tax. The general journal entry for the return is as follows.

GENERAL JOURNAL   PAGE _____

	DATE		DESCRIPTION	POST. REF.	DEBIT	CREDIT	
1	19— Apr.	3	*Sales Returns and Allowances*		1 6 00		1
2			*Sales Tax Payable*		64		2
3			*Accounts Receivable, N. T. George*			1 6 64	3
4			*Credit Memorandum No. 371.*				4

Posting directly from sales invoices

An accountant can take a further shortcut by posting directly from the sales invoices or sales slips. The accountant posts to the charge customer accounts in the accounts receivable ledger daily, directly from carbon copies of the sales invoices or sales slips. He or she writes the invoice number in the Posting Reference column in place of the journal page number. Then, at the end of the month, he or she brings the Accounts Receivable (controlling) account in the general ledger up to date by totaling all the sales invoices for the month, then making a general journal entry debiting Accounts Receivable and crediting Sales.

For a change, let us use a different firm as an illustration. The Mendozo Sports Equipment Company posts directly from its sales invoices; the total of its sales invoices for December is $17,296. Its accountant journalizes and posts the entry as follows.

GENERAL JOURNAL   PAGE __36__

	DATE		DESCRIPTION	POST. REF.	DEBIT	CREDIT	
1	19— Dec.	31	*Accounts Receivable*		17 2 9 6 00		1
2			*Sales*			17 2 9 6 00	2
3			*Summarizing entry for the total of the sales*				3
4			*invoices for the month.*				4

| ACCOUNT | | | | *Accounts Receivable* | | | | | | ACCOUNT NO. | *113* |

DATE		ITEM	POST. REF.	DEBIT	CREDIT	BALANCE	
						DEBIT	CREDIT
19— Dec.	31		J36	17 2 9 6 00		17 2 9 6 00	

| ACCOUNT | | | | *Sales* | | | | | | ACCOUNT NO. | *411* |

DATE		ITEM	POST. REF.	DEBIT	CREDIT	BALANCE	
						DEBIT	CREDIT
19— Dec.	31		J36		17 2 9 6 00		17 2 9 6 00

This is called a *summarizing entry* because it summarizes the credit sales for 1 month. Its accountant posts the entry to the accounts in the general ledger, which does away with the need for a sales journal, since the one summarizing entry in the general journal records the total sales for the month.

One invoice and the corresponding entry in the accounts receivable ledger might look like those shown here.

MENDOZO SPORTS EQUIPMENT COMPANY
1610 Alhambra Blvd.
San Diego, CA 92002

INVOICE

Sold To:
Reams and Son,
Sporting Goods
1600 S.W. Santa Clara Ave.
Portland, OR 97216

DATE: Dec. 4, 19—
Invoice No.: 6075
Order No.: 359
Shipped By: Express Collect
Terms: 2/10, n/30

Quantity	Description	Unit Price	Total
10	Molded unicellular foam ski/life vest (Davis) lg.	16.80	168.00

ACCOUNTS RECEIVABLE LEDGER

Name: *Reams and Son, Sporting Goods*
Address: *1600 S.W. Santa Clara Ave.*
Portland, OR 97216

DATE		ITEM	POST. REF.	DEBIT	CREDIT	BALANCE
19— Dec.	4		6075	1 6 8 00		1 6 8 00

The $168 figure would, of course, be posted to the general ledger as a part of the total comprising the summarizing entry.

Summary

Keeping special journals is a shortcut in the accounting process, which makes it possible to record a transaction on one line and to post column totals rather than individual figures. This chapter introduced three new kinds of accounts:

Sales is a revenue account like Income from Services; *Sales Returns and Allowances* is a deduction from Sales; and *Sales Tax Payable* is a liability account, since the company has to pay the balance to a state or local government.

The sales journal takes care of sales of merchandise on account only. The entries are posted *daily* to the accounts receivable ledger. At the end of the month the total is posted to the general ledger as a debit to the Accounts Receivable (controlling) account and a credit to the Sales account. When a customer returns merchandise that he or she has bought, or when his or her bill is reduced due to an allowance for defective or damaged merchandise, the Sales Returns and Allowances account is increased, and the Accounts Receivable account is decreased. The entry is recorded in the general journal and posted to both the general ledger and the accounts receivable ledger.

Another shortcut is using sales invoices or sales slips as a sales journal, thereby doing away with the sales journal. One posts to the charge customer accounts in the accounts receivable ledger directly from the sales invoices. At the end of the month, one adds all the sales invoices and makes a summarizing entry in the general journal for the amount of the total. This entry is a debit to Accounts Receivable and a credit to Sales.

Glossary

Controlling account An account in the general ledger which summarizes the balances of a subsidiary ledger.

Credit memorandum A written statement indicating a seller's willingness to reduce the amount of a buyer's debt. The seller records the amount of the credit memorandum under the Sales Returns and Allowances account.

Merchandise inventory A stock of goods that a firm buys with the intent of reselling in the same physical condition.

Sales discount A deduction from the original price, granted by the seller to the buyer for the prompt payment of an invoice.

Sales Returns and Allowances The account a seller uses to record the amount of a reduction granted to a customer either for the physical return of merchandise previously sold to the customer, or as compensation for merchandise that is damaged. This account is usually evidenced by a credit memorandum issued by the seller.

Sales tax A tax levied by a state or local government on the sale of goods. The tax is paid by the consumer, but collected by the merchant.

Special journal A book of original entry in which one records specialized types of transactions; each transaction is recorded on one line.

Subsidiary ledger A group of accounts representing individual subdivisions of a controlling account.

1. What information typically appears on a sales invoice?

2. What kind of ledger is an accounts receivable ledger? Are account numbers used? Why or why not?

3. Why is an accounts receivable ledger a necessity for a business having a large number of charge customers?

4. What is a schedule of accounts receivable?

5. What is the difference between a sales return and a sales allowance?

6. Why is it worthwhile to set up an account for sales returns and allowances when it would be possible to debit the sales account for any transaction involving a return or allowance?

7. Describe the method of posting directly from sales invoices.

Exercises

Exercise 1 Describe the transactions recorded in the following T accounts.

Cash		Accounts Receivable		Sales	
430		450	20		450
			430		

Sales Returns and Allowances	
20	

Exercise 2 Record the following transactions in general journal form.

a. Sold merchandise on account to L. B. Griffin, $240, Invoice No. 426.

b. Issued Credit Memorandum No. 36 to L. B. Griffin for merchandise returned, $40.

c. Received full payment from L. B. Griffin.

Exercise 3 Describe the transactions recorded in the following T accounts.

Cash		Accounts Receivable		Sales Tax Payable	
420		420	420		20

Sales	
	400

Exercise 4 Label the blanks as debit or credit.

			SALES JOURNAL			PAGE_____

DATE	SALES SLIP	CUSTOMER'S NAME	POST. REF.	ACCOUNTS RECEIVABLE ( )	SALES TAX PAYABLE ( )	SALES ( )

Exercise 5 Record the following transactions in general journal form.

a. Sold merchandise for cash to Axel Johnson, $260 plus 5% sales tax.

b. Johnson returned $40 of the merchandise. Issued Credit Memo No. 323 and paid Johnson $42 in cash, $40 for the amount of the returned merchandise plus $2 for the amount of the sales tax.

Exercise 6 A business firm uses carbon copies of its sales invoices to record sales of merchandise on account and carbon copies of its credit memorandums to record its sales returns and allowances. During September, the firm issued 214 invoices for $96,738.46 and 12 credit memorandums for $1,949.60. Present the summarizing entries, dated September 30, in general journal form, to record the sales and sales returns for the month.

Exercise 7 On Monday morning a sleepy accountant made the following errors in journalizing sales of merchandise on account in a single-column sales journal and posting to the general ledger and accounts receivable ledger. The errors were discovered at the end of the month before the closing entries were journalized and posted. Describe the means of correcting the errors.

a. The sales journal was footed correctly as $26,960, but it was posted as a debit and credit of $26,690.

b. A sale of $48 to T. R. Rosenkrans was posted to his account as $4.80.

c. A sale of $43 to A. C. Tuttle was entered in the sales journal correctly, but it was posted to Tuttle's account as $34.

Problems

Problem 11-1 Manning Wholesale Electric Company, which opened for business during October of this year, had the following sales of merchandise on account and sales returns and allowances during the month.

Oct. 5 Sold merchandise on account to Woodbury Electric, Invoice No. 1, $282.

9 Sold merchandise on account to C. L. Symmonds Company, Invoice No. 2, $312.

11 Sold merchandise on account to Rambo and Sehorn, Inc., Invoice No. 3, $760.

15 Sold merchandise on account to Pierson Hardware, Invoice No. 4, $684.

16 Issued Credit Memorandum No. 1, $84, to C. L. Symmonds Company for merchandise returned, Invoice No. 2.

21 Sold merchandise on account to Woodbury Electric, Invoice No. 5, $869.

22 Issued Credit Memorandum No. 2 to Rambo and Sehorn, Inc., for merchandise returned, $140, Invoice No. 3.

26 Sold merchandise on account to Pierson Hardware, Invoice No. 6, $348.

28 Sold merchandise on account to C. L. Symmonds Company, Invoice No. 7, $586.

Oct. 29 Sold merchandise on account to Woodbury Electric, Invoice No. 8, $141.

31 Issued Credit Memorandum No. 3, to Rambo and Sehorn, Inc., for damage done to merchandise during shipping, $42, Invoice No. 3.

Instructions **1.** Record the above sales of merchandise on account in the sales journal. Record the sales returns and allowances in the general journal.

2. Immediately after recording each transaction, post to the accounts receivable ledger.

3. At the end of the month, post the entries from the general journal and the sales journal to the general ledger. Post the sales journal amount as a total.

4. Prepare a schedule of accounts receivable.

5. Compare the balance of the Accounts Receivable control account with the total of the schedule of accounts receivable.

Problem 11-2 McCarver Brothers sells welding equipment on a wholesale basis. The following transactions took place during March of this year.

Mar. 1 Sold merchandise on account to Martin Construction Company, Invoice No. 761, $557.

5 Sold merchandise on account to T. H. Fleming Company, Invoice No. 762, $296.

6 Issued Credit Memorandum No. 50 to Martin Construction Company for merchandise returned, $43, Invoice No. 761.

11 Sold merchandise on account to Dick's Hardware, Invoice No. 763, $194.

13 Sold merchandise on account to Broderick and Herman, Invoice No. 764, $741.

18 Sold merchandise on account to Paisley School District No. 23, Invoice No. 765, $476.

22 Issued Credit Memorandum No. 51 to Broderick and Herman for merchandise returned, $69, Invoice No. 764.

24 Sold merchandise on account to Overman Farm Supply, Invoice No. 766, $483.

24 Sold merchandise on account to Dick's Hardware, Invoice No. 767, $762.

31 Issued Credit Memorandum No. 52 to Dick's Hardware for damage to merchandise, $92, Invoice No. 767.

Instructions **1.** Record these sales of merchandise on account in the sales journal. Record the sales returns and allowances in the general journal.

2. Immediately after recording each transaction, post to the accounts receivable ledger.

3. At the end of the month, post the entries from the general journal and the sales journal to the general ledger.

4. Prepare a schedule of accounts receivable.

Problem 11-3 Stewart Florists sells flowers on a retail basis. Most of the sales are for cash; however, a few steady customers have charge accounts. Stewart salespersons fill out sales slips for each sale. The state government levies a 5% retail sales tax, which is collected by the retailer. The following represent Stewart Florists' charge sales for November.

Nov. 4 Sold floral arrangement to O. L. Stafford, Sales Slip No. 243, $18, plus sales tax of $.90, total, $18.90.

6 Sold potted plant to Ruth Hurst, Sales Slip No. 268, $9, plus sales tax of $.45, total, $9.45.

11 Sold corsage to Florence Files, Sales Slip No. 271, $7, plus sales tax of $.35.

16 Sold wreath to American Legion for $34, plus sales tax, Sales Slip No. 276.

17 Knight Funeral Home bought several floral arrangements on account, Sales Slip No. 293, $120, plus sales tax.

20 Knight Funeral Home returned a flower spray, from Sales Slip No. 293. Delivery of the spray occurred after the funeral was over, so Stewart allowed full credit on the sale of $22 and the sales tax of $1.10.

21 First Federal Savings and Loan Association bought flower arrangements for their anniversary for $80, plus sales tax, Sales Slip No. 302.

22 Allowed First Federal Savings and Loan credit, $9, plus tax, because of withered blossoms in floral arrangements bought on Sales Slip No. 302.

Instructions
1. Record the transactions in either the sales journal or the general journal.

2. Immediately after recording each transaction, post to the accounts receivable ledger.

3. At the end of the month, post the entries from the general journal and the sales journal to the general ledger.

4. Prepare a schedule of accounts receivable.

Problem 11-4 Johannson Leather Goods Company uses carbon copies of its charge sales invoices as a sales journal and posts to the accounts receivable ledger directly from the sales invoices. At the end of the month, the accountant totals the invoices and makes an entry in the general journal summarizing the charge sales for the month. The charge sales invoices are as follows.

Mar. 4 L. C. Flemming Company, Invoice No. 3019, $450.

10 Southern Novelty Company, Invoice No. 3022, $679.

12 Harold T. Burnside, Invoice No. 3024, $213.

14 Burke and Schwab, Invoice No. 3027, $1,024.

18 Hamilton and Roy, Inc., Invoice No. 3028, $642.

20 Burgess and Weldon, Inc., Invoice No. 3030, $481.

26 Scott Specialty Company, Invoice No. 3031, $943.

Mar. 30 Robertson Amusement Company, Invoice No. 3042, $980.

    31 Southern Novelty Company, Invoice No. 3043, $1,318.

Instructions **1.** Post to the accounts receivable ledger directly from the sales invoices, listing the invoice number in the Posting Reference column.

2. Record the summarizing entry in the general journal for the total amount of the sales invoices.

3. Post the general journal entry to the appropriate accounts in the general ledger.

4. Prepare a schedule of accounts receivable.

Alternate problems

Problem 11-1A Manning Wholesale Electric, which opened for business during May of this year, had the following sales of merchandise on account and sales returns and allowances during the month.

May 2 Sold merchandise on account to Woodbury Electric, Invoice No. 1, $253.63.

    8 Sold merchandise on account to C. L. Symmonds Co., Invoice No. 2, $428.

   10 Sold merchandise on account to Rambo and Sehorn, Inc., Invoice No. 3, $858.60.

   15 Sold merchandise on account to Pierson Hardware, Invoice No. 4, $776.18.

   16 Issued Credit Memorandum No. 1, $62, to C. L. Symmonds Co. for merchandise returned, Invoice No. 2.

   21 Sold merchandise on account to Woodbury Electric, Invoice No. 5, $886.50.

   23 Issued Credit Memorandum No. 2, $117.40, to Rambo and Sehorn, Inc., for merchandise returned, Invoice No. 3.

   26 Sold merchandise on account to C. L. Symmonds Co., Invoice No. 6, $586.

   28 Sold merchandise on account to Pierson Hardware, Invoice No. 7, $328.48.

   29 Sold merchandise on account to Woodbury Electric, Invoice No. 8, $158.42.

   30 Issued Credit Memorandum No. 3, $62, to Rambo and Sehorn, Inc., for merchandise damaged in transit, Invoice No. 3.

Instructions **1.** Record these sales of merchandise on account in the sales journal. Record the sales returns and allowances in the general journal.

2. Immediately after recording each transaction, post to the accounts receivable ledger.

3. At the end of the month, post the entries from the general journal and the sales journal to the general ledger; post the sales journal amount as a total.

4. Prepare a schedule of accounts receivable.

5. Compare the balance of the Accounts Receivable control account with the total of the schedule of accounts receivable.

Problem 11-2A McCarver Brothers sells welding equipment on a wholesale basis. The following transactions took place during March of this year.

Mar. 2 Sold merchandise on account to Martin Construction Company, Invoice No. 822, $583.

6 Sold merchandise on account to T. H. Fleming Company, Invoice No. 823, $398.

7 Issued Credit Memorandum No. 61 to T. H. Fleming Company for merchandise returned, $64, Invoice No. 823.

12 Sold merchandise on account to Dick's Hardware, Invoice No. 824, $194.

14 Sold merchandise on account to Broderick and Herman, Invoice No. 825, $823.

20 Sold merchandise on account to Paisley School District no. 23, Invoice No. 826, $682.

23 Issued Credit Memorandum No. 62 to Broderick and Herman for merchandise returned, $79, Invoice No. 825.

25 Sold merchandise on account to Overman Farm Supply, Invoice No. 827, $586.

28 Sold merchandise on account to Dick's Hardware, Invoice No. 828, $741.

30 Issued Credit Memorandum No. 63 to Dick's Hardware for damage to merchandise, $44, Invoice No. 828.

Instructions **1.** Record these sales of merchandise on account in the sales journal. Record the sales returns and allowances in the general journal.

2. Immediately after recording each transaction, post to the accounts receivable ledger.

3. At the end of the month, post the entries from the general journal and the sales journal to the general ledger.

4. Prepare a schedule of accounts receivable.

Problem 11-3A Stewart Florists sells flowers on a retail basis. Most sales are for cash; however, a few steady customers have charge accounts. Stewart salespersons fill out sales slips for each sale. The state government levies a 5% retail tax, which is collected by the retailer. Stewart Florists' charge sales for November are as follows:

Nov. 4 Sold floral arrangement to O. L. Stafford, Sales Slip No. 236, $16, plus sales tax of $.80, total $16.80.

6 Sold potted plant to Ruth Hurst, Sales Slip No. 272, $9, plus sales tax of $.45, total $9.45.

11 Sold wreath to American Legion for $32, plus sales tax, Sales Slip No. 293.

17 Knight Funeral Home bought several floral arrangements on account, Sales Slip No. 298, $90, plus sales tax.

Nov. 20 Knight Funeral Home returned a flower spray, from Sales Slip No. 298. Delivery of the spray occurred after the funeral was over, so Stewart allowed full credit on the sale of $18, and the sales tax of $.90.

21 First Federal Savings and Loan Association bought flower arrangements for their anniversary for $118, plus sales tax, Sales Slip No. 309.

22 Allowed First Federal Savings and Loan Association credit, $10, plus tax, because of withered blossoms in floral arrangements bought on Sales Slip No. 309.

28 Sold corsage to Florence Files, Sales Slip No. 312, $8.40, plus sales tax.

Instructions **1.** Record the transactions in either the sales journal or the general journal.

2. Immediately after recording each transaction, post to the accounts receivable ledger.

3. At the end of the month, post the entries from the general journal and the sales journal to the general ledger.

4. Prepare a schedule of accounts receivable.

Problem 11-4A Johannson Leather Goods Company uses carbon copies of its charge sales invoices as a sales journal and posts to the accounts receivable ledger directly from the sales invoices. The invoices are totaled at the end of the month, and an entry is made in the general journal to summarize the charge sales for the month. The charge sales invoices for March are as follows.

Mar. 3 L. C. Flemming Company, Invoice No. 3016, $446.

8 Southern Novelty Company, Invoice No. 3040, $641.

10 Harold J. Burnside, Invoice No. 3052, $336.

12 Burke and Schwab, Invoice No. 3063, $745.

17 Hamilton and Roy, Inc., Invoice No. 3074, $264.

23 Burgess and Weldon, Inc., Invoice No. 3094, $395.

26 Scott Specialty Company, Invoice No. 3131, $563.

27 Robertson Amusement Company, Invoice No. 3133, $328.

30 Southern Novelty Company, Invoice No. 3140, $297.

Instructions **1.** Post to the accounts receivable ledger directly from the sales invoices, listing the invoice number in the Posting Reference column.

2. Record the summarizing entry in the general journal for the total amount of the sales invoices.

3. Post the general journal entry to the appropriate accounts in the general ledger.

4. Prepare a schedule of accounts receivable.

12 Accounting for merchandise: purchases

objectives

After you have completed this chapter, you will be able to do the following:
- Record transactions in a one-column purchases journal.
- Post from a one-column purchases journal to an accounts payable ledger and a general ledger.
- Prepare a schedule of accounts payable.
- Post directly from purchase invoices to an accounts payable ledger and a general ledger.
- Journalize transactions involving transportation charges on incoming goods.

WE'VE BEEN talking about the procedures, accounts, and special journals used to record the *selling* of merchandise. Now let's talk about those same elements as they apply to the *buying* of merchandise. This means that we'll be dealing with the Purchases account as well as Purchases Returns and Allowances. You'll see in this chapter that Accounts Payable is a controlling account, just as you saw in Chapter 11 that Accounts Receivable is a controlling account.

Purchasing procedures

When you think of the great variety in types and sizes of merchandising firms, it comes as no surprise to learn that there is also considerable variety in the procedures used to buy goods for resale. Some purchases may be for cash; however, in most cases, purchases are on a credit basis. In a small retail store, the owner may do the buying. In large retail and wholesale concerns, department heads or division managers do the buying, after which the purchasing department goes into action: placing purchase orders, following up the orders, receiving the goods, and seeing that deliveries are made to the right departments. The purchasing department also acts as a source of information on current prices, price trends, quality of goods, prospective suppliers, and reliability of suppliers.

The purchasing department as a rule requires that any buying orders be in writing, in the form of a purchase requisition. After the purchase requisition is approved, the purchasing department sends a *purchase order* to the supplier. A purchase order is the company's written offer to buy certain goods. The accountant does not make any entry at this point, because the supplier has not yet indicated acceptance of the order. A purchase order is made out in triplicate: One copy goes to the supplier, one stays in the purchasing department (as proof of what was ordered), and one goes to the department that sent out the requisition (this tells them that the goods they wanted have indeed been ordered.)

To continue with the illustration of North Central Plumbing Supply: The pipe department submits a purchase requisition to the purchasing department as shown at the top of the facing page.

North Central Plumbing Supply
1968 Arrow St., N.W.
Seattle, WA 98111

PURCHASE
REQUISITION

No. C-726

Department ___Pipe_____   Date of Request ___July 2, 19--___

Advise on delivery ___Mr. Holloway_____   Date Required ___Aug. 5, 19--___

Quantity	Description
1,000'	Flexible copper tubing 5/8", Type L, (50' roll)

Approved by _Steven Thompson_   Requested by _J. H. Holloway_

For Purchasing Dept. Use Only

Purchase Order No. ___7918_____   Issued to: Danton, Inc.

Date ___July 5, 19--_____   1616 Madlyn Ave.

                                                                          Los Angeles, CA 90026

The purchasing department completes the bottom part of the purchase requisition and sends out this purchase order.

North Central Plumbing Supply
1968 Arrow St., N.W.
Seattle, WA 98111

PURCHASE
ORDER

Sold To: Danton, Inc.
          1616 Madlyn Ave.
          Los Angeles, CA 90026

DATE: July 5, 19--
Order No: 7918
Shipped By: Freight Truck
Terms: 2/10, n/30

Quantity	Description	Unit Price	Total
1,000'	Flexible copper tubing 5/8", Type L (50' roll)	.285	285.00

Steven Thompson

The seller now sends an *invoice* to the buyer. This invoice should arrive in advance of the goods (or at least *with* the goods). From the seller's point of view, this is a sales invoice. If the sale is on credit, as we saw in Chapter 11, the seller's accountant makes an entry debiting Accounts Receivable and crediting Sales. To the buyer, this is a purchase invoice, so the buyer's accountant makes an entry debiting Purchases and crediting Accounts Payable. North Central Plumbing Supply receives from Danton, Inc. the following invoice.

DANTON, INC.
1616 Madlyn Ave.
Los Angeles, CA 90026

Invoice

DATE: July 31, 19--
SOLD TO North Central Plumbing Supply
1968 Arrow St., N.W.
Seattle, WA 98111

INVOICE NO.: 2706
ORDER NO.: 7918
SHIPPED BY: Western Freight Line
TERMS: 2/10, n/30

Quantity	Description	Unit Price	Total
1,000'	Flexible copper tubing 5/8", Type L (50' roll)	.285	285.00

Let us now extract from the fundamental accounting equation (recall Chapter 11) the T accounts involved in buying merchandise. Again, color is used to emphasize that these accounts are deductions from Purchases.

Assets		=	Liabilities		+	Owner's Equity		+	Revenue		−	Expenses	
+	−		−	+		−	+		−	+		+	−
Dr	Cr		Dr	Cr		Dr	Cr		Dr	Cr		Dr	Cr

and Purchases

+	−

Purchases Returns and Allowances

−	+

Purchases Discount

−	+

Bear in mind that the Purchases account is used exclusively for the buying of merchandise intended for resale. *If the firm buys anything else, the accountant records the amount under the appropriate asset or expense account.* At the end of the fiscal period, the balance in the Purchases account represents the total cost of merchandise bought during the period. As we said in Chapter 11, Purchases is classified as an expense only for the sake of convenience. This can be done because it is closed at the end of the fiscal period along with the expense accounts.

Purchases Returns and Allowances is a deduction from Purchases. So that we can keep track of the amount of the returns, we set up a separate account for them. In the income statement, we treat Purchases Returns and Allowances and Purchases Discount as deductions from Purchases; so, for consistency they are presented below Purchases in the fundamental accounting equation shown on the bottom of page 296. (We'll talk about Purchases Discount in Chapter 13.)

To get back to North Central Plumbing Supply: As we did in Chapter 11, we'll record three transactions in the general journal. Then—just to point up again the advantage of special journals as opposed to the general journal—we'll record the same three transactions in a special journal.

During the first week in August, the following transactions took place.

Aug. 2 Bought merchandise on account from Danton, Inc., $285, their Invoice No. 2706, dated July 31; terms 2/10, n/30.

3 Bought merchandise on account from Rogers and Simon Company, $760, their Invoice No. 982, dated August 2; terms net 30 days.

5 Bought merchandise on account from Argel Manufacturing Company, $692, their Invoice No. 10611, dated August 3; terms 2/10, n/30.

Regarding the credit terms of the transactions, the notation net 30 days means that the bill is due within 30 days after the date of the invoice. The notation 2/10, n/30 refers to the purchase or cash discount. It means that the seller offers a 2 percent discount if the bill is paid within 10 days after the date of the invoice, and that the whole bill must be paid within 30 days after the invoice date. We will be working with these credit terms in Chapter 13.

For the present, we are concerned with recording the purchases. Let's visualize these transactions in terms of T accounts.

Purchases			Accounts Payable	
+		−	−	+
285				285
760				760
692				692

If these transactions were recorded in the general journal, they would be as shown at the top of the next page.

	DATE		DESCRIPTION	POST. REF.	DEBIT	CREDIT	
1	19– Aug.	2	Purchases	511	2 8 5 00		1
2			Accounts Payable	211		2 8 5 00	2
3			Danton Inc., their Invoice No. 2706, terms				3
4			2/10, n/30, dated July 31.				4
5							5
6		3	Purchases	511	7 6 0 00		6
7			Accounts Payable	211		7 6 0 00	7
8			Rogers and Simon Company, their Invoice No.				8
9			982, terms net 30 days, dated Aug. 2.				9
10							10
11		5	Purchases	511	6 9 2 00		11
12			Accounts Payable	211		6 9 2 00	12
13			Argel Manufacturing Company, their Invoice				13
14			No. 10611, terms 2/10, n/30, dated Aug. 3.				14
15							15
16							16

Next the general journal entries would be posted to the general ledger.

GENERAL LEDGER

ACCOUNT _____ *Purchases* _____ ACCOUNT NO. _511_

DATE		ITEM	POST. REF.	DEBIT	CREDIT	BALANCE DEBIT	BALANCE CREDIT
19– Aug.	2		22	2 8 5 00		2 8 5 00	
	3		22	7 6 0 00		1 0 4 5 00	
	5		22	6 9 2 00		1 7 3 7 00	

ACCOUNT _____ *Accounts Payable* _____ ACCOUNT NO. _211_

DATE		ITEM	POST. REF.	DEBIT	CREDIT	BALANCE DEBIT	BALANCE CREDIT
19– Aug.	2		22		2 8 5 00		2 8 5 00
	3		22		7 6 0 00		1 0 4 5 00
	5		22		6 9 2 00		1 7 3 7 00

Purchases journal

The above repetition could have been avoided if the accountant had used a *purchases journal* instead of the general journal. The purchases journal is used for the *purchase of merchandise on account only*. In each case, with this special type of transaction, the accountant debits Purchases and credits Accounts Payable.

DATE		SUPPLIER'S NAME	INVOICE NO.	INVOICE DATE	TERMS	POST REF.	PURCH. DR. ACCTS. PAY. CR.
19–Aug.	2	Danton, Inc.	2706	7/31	2/10 n/30		285 00
	3	Rogers and Simon Company	982	8/2	n/30		760 00
	5	Argel Manufacturing Company	10611	8/3	2/10 n/30		692 00

Note that the one money column is headed Purchases Debit and Accounts Payable Credit. Each transaction can thus be recorded on one line.

Posting from the purchases journal

The accountant has now journalized the transactions involving the purchase of merchandise on account for August.

PURCHASES JOURNAL   PAGE 29

DATE		SUPPLIER'S NAME	INVOICE NO.	INVOICE DATE	TERMS	POST REF.	PURCH. DR. ACCTS. PAY. CR.
19–Aug.	2	Danton, Inc.	2706	7/31	2/10 n/30		285 00
	3	Rogers and Simon Company	982	8/2	n/30		760 00
	5	Argel Manufacturing Company	10611	8/3	2/10 n/30		692 00
	9	Sinclair Manufacturing Company	B643	8/6	1/10 n/30		165 00
	18	Tru-Fit Valve, Inc.	46812	8/17	n/60		228 00
	25	Donaldson and Farr	1024	8/23	2/10 n/30		376 00
	26	Danton, Inc.	2801	8/25	n/30		406 00
	31						2912 00
							(511)(211)

Since all the entries are debits to Purchases and credits to Accounts Payable, one can post these accounts as totals at the end of the month.

GENERAL LEDGER

ACCOUNT _____ Purchases _____ ACCOUNT NO. 511

DATE		ITEM	POST. REF.	DEBIT	CREDIT	BALANCE DEBIT	BALANCE CREDIT
19–Aug.	31		P29	2912 00		2912 00	

ACCOUNT _____ Accounts Payable _____ ACCOUNT NO. 211

DATE		ITEM	POST. REF.	DEBIT	CREDIT	BALANCE DEBIT	BALANCE CREDIT
19–Aug.	1	Balance	✓				356 00
	31		P29		2912 00		3268 00

In the Posting Reference column of the ledger accounts, P designates the purchases journal. After posting to the ledger accounts, the accountant goes back to the purchases journal and records the account numbers in parentheses directly below the total, placing the account number for the account being debited on the left. Transactions involving the buying of supplies or other assets should *not* be recorded in the purchases journal, because the purchases journal may be used only for the purchases of merchandise on account.

The accounts payable ledger

In Chapter 11 we called the Accounts Receivable account in the general ledger the *controlling* account, and explained that the accounts receivable ledger consisted of individual accounts for each charge customer, and that the accountant posts to the accounts receivable ledger every day.

Accounts Payable is a parallel case, because it is also a controlling account in the general ledger. The accounts payable ledger is also a subsidiary ledger, and consists of individual accounts for each creditor. Again, in the accounts payable ledger, posting is daily. After posting to the individual creditors' accounts, the accountant puts a check mark ($\sqrt{}$) in the Posting Reference column of the purchases journal. After he or she has finished all the posting to the controlling account and the accounts payable ledger, the total of the schedule of accounts payable should equal the balance of the Accounts Payable (controlling) account. Incidentally, one always uses the three-column form for the accounts payable ledger. Because the T account for Accounts Payable is

Accounts Payable

−	+

it follows that the three-column form is like this:

Accounts Payable Ledger

Debit	Credit	Balance
−	+	+

Now let's see the purchases journal and the postings to the ledger.

PURCHASES JOURNAL   PAGE 29

DATE		SUPPLIER'S NAME	INVOICE NO.	INVOICE DATE	TERMS	POST REF.	PURCH. DR. ACCTS. PAY. CR.
19— Aug.	2	Danton, Inc.	2706	7/31	2/10 n/30	✓	2 8 5 00
	3	Rogers and Simon Company	982	8/2	n/30	✓	7 6 0 00
	5	Argel Manufacturing Company	10611	8/3	2/10 n/30	✓	6 9 2 00
	9	Sinclair Manufacturing Co	B643	8/6	1/10 n/30	✓	1 6 5 00
	18	Tru-Fit Valve, Inc.	46812	8/17	n/60	✓	2 2 8 00
	25	Donaldson and Farr	1024	8/23	2/10 n/30	✓	3 7 6 00
	26	Danton, Inc.	2801	8/25	n/30	✓	4 0 6 00
	31						2 9 1 2 00
							(511)(211)

Name **Argel Manufacturing Company**
Address **2510 Madeira Ave.**
 San Francisco, CA 94130

DATE		ITEM	POST. REF.	DEBIT	CREDIT	BALANCE
19– Aug.	5		P29		692 00	692 00

Name **Danton, Inc.**
Address **1616 Madlyn Ave.**
 Los Angeles, CA 90026

DATE		ITEM	POST. REF.	DEBIT	CREDIT	BALANCE
19– Aug.	2		P29		285 00	285 00
	26		P29		406 00	691 00

Name **Donaldson and Farr**
Address **1600 S.W. Yelm St.**
 Portland, OR 97216

DATE		ITEM	POST. REF.	DEBIT	CREDIT	BALANCE
19– Aug.	25		P29		376 00	376 00

Name **Rogers and Simon Company**
Address **21325 186th Ave. No.**
 Seattle, WA 98101

DATE		ITEM	POST. REF.	DEBIT	CREDIT	BALANCE
19– July	27		P28		180 00	180 00
Aug.	3		P29		760 00	940 00

Name **Sinclair Manufacturing Company**
Address **1068 Casino Ave.**
 Los Angeles, CA 90023

DATE		ITEM	POST. REF.	DEBIT	CREDIT	BALANCE
19– Aug.	9		P29		165 00	165 00

Name **Tru-Fit Valve, Inc.**
Address **1620 Minard St.**
 San Francisco, CA 94130

DATE		ITEM	POST. REF.	DEBIT	CREDIT	BALANCE
19– July	29		P28		176 00	176 00
Aug.	18		P29		228 00	404 00

Note that in the accounts payable ledger—as in the accounts receivable ledger—the accounts of the individual creditors are listed in alphabetical order. In addition, one usually uses a loose-leaf binder, and there are no page numbers or account numbers.

Purchases returns and allowances

This account, as the title implies, handles either a return of merchandise previously purchased or an allowance made for merchandise that arrived in damaged condition. In both cases there is a reduction in the amount owed to the supplier. The buyer sends a letter or printed form to the supplier, who acknowledges the reduction by sending a *credit memorandum.* The buyer should wait for the notice of the agreed deduction before making the entry.

The Purchases Returns and Allowances account is considered to be a deduction from Purchases. In order to have a better record of the total returns and allowances, one uses a separate account. Purchases Returns and Allowances is deducted from the Purchases account in the income statement. (We'll get around to discussing this later.) For now, let's look at an illustration consisting of two entries on the books of North Central Plumbing Supply.

Transaction (a) On August 5, bought merchandise on account from Argel Manufacturing Co., $692, their Invoice No. 10611 of August 3, terms 2/10, n/30. Recorded this as a debit to Purchases and a credit to Accounts Payable. On August 6, returned $70 worth of the merchandise. Made no entry.

Transaction (b) On August 8, received Credit Memorandum No. 629 from Argel Manufacturing Company for $70. Recorded this as a debit to Accounts Payable and a credit to Purchases Returns and Allowances.

North Central credits Purchases Returns and Allowances because it has greater returns and allowances than before, and debits Accounts Payable because it owes the creditor less than before.

Suppose that North Central Plumbing Supply returned merchandise on two occasions during August, and received credit memorandums from the suppliers; the entries are recorded in the general journal.

	DATE		DESCRIPTION	POST REF.	DEBIT	CREDIT	
1	19— Aug.	8	Accounts Payable, Argel Manufacturing Company		70 00		1
2			Purchases Returns and Allowances			70 00	2
3			Credit Memo 629, Invoice No. 10611.				3
4							4
5		12	Accounts Payable, Sinclair Manufacturing Company		36 00		5
6			Purchases Returns and Allowances			36 00	6
7			Credit Memo 482, Invoice No. B643.				7
8							8
9							9

In this entry, Accounts Payable is followed by the name of the individual creditor's account. The accountant must post to both the Accounts Payable controlling account and the individual creditor's account in the accounts payable ledger. The journal entries are now repeated, and the posting is completed, as shown by the Posting Reference columns, in which the account numbers indicate postings to the accounts in the general ledger and the check marks indicate postings to the accounts in the accounts payable ledger.

	DATE		DESCRIPTION	POST REF.	DEBIT	CREDIT	
1	19— Aug.	8	Accounts Payable, Argel Manufacturing Company	211/√	70 00		1
2			Purchases Returns and Allowances	512		70 00	2
3			Credit Memo 629, Invoice No. 10611.				3
4							4
5		12	Accounts Payable, Sinclair Manufacturing Company	211/√	36 00		5
6			Purchases Returns and Allowances	512		36 00	6
7			Credit Memo 482, Invoice No. B643.				7
8							8
9							9

GENERAL LEDGER

ACCOUNT Accounts Payable ACCOUNT NO. 211

DATE		ITEM	POST. REF.	DEBIT	CREDIT	BALANCE DEBIT	BALANCE CREDIT
19— Aug.	1	Balance	√				356 00
	8		J27	70 00			286 00
	12		J27	36 00			250 00

DATE		ITEM	POST. REF.	DEBIT	CREDIT	BALANCE	
						DEBIT	CREDIT
19– Aug.	8		J27		70 00		70 00
	12		J27		36 00		1 06 00

ACCOUNTS PAYABLE LEDGER

Name ___ *Argel Manufacturing Company* ___
Address ___ *2150 Madeira Ave.* ___
San Francisco, CA 94130

DATE		ITEM	POST. REF.	DEBIT	CREDIT	BALANCE
19– Aug.	5		P29		6 92 00	6 92 00
	8		J27	70 00		6 22 00

Name ___ *Sinclair Manufacturing Company* ___
Address ___ *1068 Casino Ave.* ___
Los Angeles, CA 90023

DATE		ITEM	POST. REF.	DEBIT	CREDIT	BALANCE
19– Aug.	9		P29		1 65 00	1 65 00
	12		J27	36 00		1 29 00

Assuming that there were no other transactions involving Accounts Payable, the schedule of accounts payable would appear as follows. Note that the balances of the creditors' accounts, with the exception of the accounts for Argel Manufacturing Company and Sinclair Manufacturing Company, are taken from the accounts payable ledger shown on page 301.

North Central Plumbing Supply		
Schedule of Accounts Payable		
August 31, 19–		
Argel Manufacturing Company	6 22 00	
Danton, Inc.	6 91 00	
Donaldson and Farr	3 76 00	
Rogers and Simon Company	9 40 00	
Sinclair Manufacturing Company	1 29 00	
Tru-Fit Valve, Inc.	4 04 00	
Total Accounts Payable		3 1 62 00

The Accounts Payable controlling account in the general ledger is now posted up to date.

ACCOUNT _____ *Accounts Payable* _____ ACCOUNT NO. __211__

DATE		ITEM	POST. REF.	DEBIT	CREDIT	BALANCE DEBIT	BALANCE CREDIT
19– Aug.	1	Balance	✓				3 5 6 00
	8		J27	7 0 00			2 8 6 00
	12		J27	3 6 00			2 5 0 00
	31		P29		2 9 1 2 00		3 1 6 2 00

Transportation charges on incoming merchandise and other assets

When a firm buys merchandise, the total of the purchase invoice may include the transportation charges. If it does, this means that the supplier is selling on the basis of *FOB destination*. In other words, the supplier loads the goods *free on board* (FOB) the carrier and ships them to the customer without charge. The supplier is, of course, paying the freight charges, and naturally has to add these charges to the selling price of the goods.

For example, North Central Plumbing Supply (remember it's in Seattle) buys pipe fittings from a supplier in Chicago, with a note on the invoice that the terms are FOB Seattle. The total of the invoice is $1,200, and North Central knows that this figure includes the freight charges. We can show this by T accounts as follows.

Purchases		Accounts Payable	
+	–	–	+
1,200			1,200

What happens when the transportation charges are separate? In that case, there's a note on the invoice that the terms are FOB shipping point. This means that the supplier will load the goods free on board the carrier at the shipping point, but any freight charges from there on have to be paid by the buyer.

Suppose, for example, that North Central Plumbing Supply buys lavatories from a manufacturer in Detroit with terms FOB Detroit. Now the total of the invoice is $1,750, but in this case North Central Plumbing Supply has to pay the freight charges from Detroit to Seattle. The lavatories are shipped by rail, and North Central pays the railroad $125. In our minds we can picture the T accounts this way.

Purchases		Accounts Payable		Cash	
+	–	–	+	+	–
1,750			1,750		125
125					

Any merchandising concern must base its markups on the *delivered* cost of the merchandise. So, for this reason, the buyer debits any freight charges on incoming merchandise to Purchases. Thus the Purchases account represents both the *cost* of the merchandise and the *freight charges* the buyer has to pay for transporting the goods. In the case of FOB destination, the buyer has already paid the freight charges. So in the case of FOB shipping point, the buyer debits the Purchases account for the amount of the freight charges—which amounts to the same thing.

Any firm which sells on the basis of FOB destination must be able to cover all its costs, which of course include freight costs. Therefore the firm must include freight costs when it quotes the price for its goods. There is an interesting legal point here. Ordinarily, unless the title is expressly reserved, whoever pays the freight charges on the goods has title to the goods.

Some business firms, instead of debiting Purchases for freight charges on incoming merchandise, set up an expense account entitled Freight In or Transportation In. In the income statement, the accountant adds the balances of these accounts to the balance of the Purchases account in order to determine the *delivered* cost of the Purchases. However, here we shall follow the policy of debiting Purchases for freight charges on incoming merchandise.

Any shipping charges involved in the buying of any other assets, such as supplies or equipment, are debited to the account of the respective asset. For example, North Central Plumbing Supply bought display cases on account, at a cost of $2,700 plus freight charges of $90. As a convenience, the seller of the display cases paid the transportation costs for North Central Plumbing Supply and then added the $90 onto the invoice price of the cases. Let's visualize this by means of T accounts.

Store Equipment			Accounts Payable	
+	−		−	+
2,790				2,790

On the other hand, if North Central had paid the freight charges separately, the entry for the payment would be a debit to Store Equipment for $90 and a credit to Cash for $90.

Posting directly from purchase invoices

Posting from purchase invoices is just like posting from sales invoices (described in Chapter 11), in that it's also a shortcut. The accountant posts to the individual creditors' accounts daily, directly from the purchase invoices. The suppliers' invoice numbers are recorded in the Posting Reference column in place of the journal page number. The Accounts Payable controlling account in the general ledger is brought up to date at the end of the month by making a summarizing entry in the general journal, debiting Purchases and any asset accounts that may be involved, and crediting Accounts Payable.

Since posting directly from purchase invoices is a variation of the accounting system, we shall use a different illustration: Ron's Towing and Trailer Service.

This firm sorts out its invoices for the month, and finds that the totals are as follows: purchase of merchandise, $8,610; store supplies, $168; office supplies, $126; store equipment, $520. The accountant then makes a summarizing entry in the general journal, as follows.

GENERAL JOURNAL   PAGE __37__

	DATE		DESCRIPTION	POST. REF.	DEBIT	CREDIT	
1	19– Oct.	31	Purchases		8 6 1 0 00		1
2			Store Supplies		1 6 8 00		2
3			Office Supplies		1 2 6 00		3
4			Store Equipment		5 2 0 00		4
5			Accounts Payable			9 4 2 4 00	5
6			Summarizing entry for total purchase of				6
7			goods on account.				7
8							8
9							9
10							10
11							11

The accountant posts the above entry to the general ledger accounts.

GENERAL LEDGER

ACCOUNT _____ *Store Supplies* _____ ACCOUNT NO. __114__

DATE		ITEM	POST. REF.	DEBIT	CREDIT	BALANCE	
						DEBIT	CREDIT
19– Oct.	31		J37	1 6 8 00		1 6 8 00	

ACCOUNT _____ *Office Supplies* _____ ACCOUNT NO. __115__

DATE		ITEM	POST. REF.	DEBIT	CREDIT	BALANCE	
						DEBIT	CREDIT
19– Oct.	31		J37	1 2 6 00		1 2 6 00	

ACCOUNT _____ *Store Equipment* _____ ACCOUNT NO. __121__

DATE		ITEM	POST. REF.	DEBIT	CREDIT	BALANCE	
						DEBIT	CREDIT
19– Oct.	31		J37	5 2 0 00		5 2 0 00	

ACCOUNT _____ **Accounts Payable** _____ ACCOUNT NO. _211_

DATE		ITEM	POST. REF.	DEBIT	CREDIT	BALANCE	
						DEBIT	CREDIT
19— Oct.	31		J37		9 4 2 4 00		9 4 2 4 00

ACCOUNT _____ **Purchases** _____ ACCOUNT NO. _511_

DATE		ITEM	POST. REF.	DEBIT	CREDIT	BALANCE	
						DEBIT	CREDIT
19— Oct.	31		J37	8 6 1 0 00		8 6 1 0 00	

This procedure not only does away with the need for a purchases journal, but also includes the buying of any assets on account in the same summarizing entry. An example of an invoice follows.

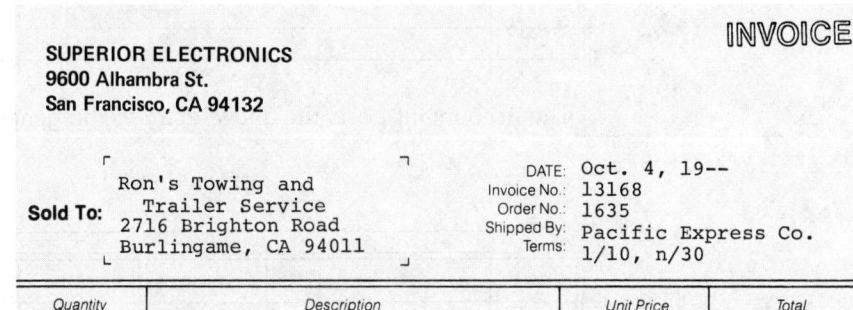

SUPERIOR ELECTRONICS
9600 Alhambra St.
San Francisco, CA 94132

INVOICE

Sold To: Ron's Towing and Trailer Service
2716 Brighton Road
Burlingame, CA 94011

DATE: Oct. 4, 19--
Invoice No.: 13168
Order No.: 1635
Shipped By: Pacific Express Co.
Terms: 1/10, n/30

Quantity	Description	Unit Price	Total
20	Mobile home antenna – TV	8.80	176.00

Ron's Towing and Trailer Service posts the amount of the invoice to the account of the supplier in the accounts payable ledger.

ACCOUNTS PAYABLE LEDGER

Name ___ *Superior Electronics*
Address ___ *9600 Alhambra St.*
San Francisco, CA 94132

DATE		ITEM	POST. REF.	DEBIT	CREDIT	BALANCE
19— Oct.	7		13168		1 7 6 00	1 7 6 00

Ron's Towing and Trailer Service will also include the $176 figure in the summarizing entry recorded in the general journal, debiting Purchases and crediting Accounts Payable. Note that the supplier's invoice number is recorded in the Posting Reference column in the account of Superior Electronics.

Internal control

We spoke briefly about the efficient management of cash in Chapter 11. We stated that all payments should be made either by check or from the petty cash fund, and all cash received should be deposited in the bank at the end of the day. The handling of cash in this manner is an illustration of internal control. When there is internal control, plans and procedures are injected into the accounting system in order to control operations. This is, of course, necessary when the owner or management must delegate authority. So the owner takes measures to (1) protect the assets against fraud and waste, (2) provide for accurate accounting data, (3) promote an efficient operation, and (4) encourage adherence to management policies. We'll be talking about the concept of internal control quite often throughout the text.

Internal control of purchases

Efficiency and security require that most companies work out careful procedures for buying and paying for goods. This is understandable, as large sums of money are usually involved. The control aspect generally involves the following measures.

1. Purchases are made only after proper authorization is given. Purchase requisitions and purchase orders are all prenumbered, so that each form may be accounted for.

2. The receiving department carefully checks and counts all goods upon receipt. Later the report of the receiving department is verified against the purchase order and the purchase invoice.

3. The person who authorizes the payment is someone other than the person doing the ordering, and other than the person actually writing the check. This person authorizes payment only after the verifications have been made.

4. The person who actually writes the check has not been involved in any of the foregoing purchasing procedures.

Summary

In this chapter, we introduced two new accounts: the Purchases account, which records the cost of merchandise acquired for resale, and the Purchases Returns and Allowances account, which is deducted from Purchases.

The purchases journal handles the purchase of merchandise *on account only,* and entries from it are posted daily to the accounts payable ledger. At the end of the month, the total is posted to the general ledger as a debit to the Purchases account and a credit to the Accounts Payable controlling account.

When merchandise is returned, the firm credits Purchases Returns and Allowances. If the customer had bought the goods on a charge-account basis, the firm debits Accounts Payable and records the entry in the general journal.

When a firm lists transportation charges on incoming goods separately, it debits them to the related accounts. For example, freight charges on merchandise bought are debited to Purchases, freight charges on office equipment bought are debited to Office Equipment, and so forth.

As a further shortcut, the firm may post to the accounts of the individual creditors in the accounts payable ledger directly from invoices of purchases of merchandise bought on credit. At the end of the month, the accountant makes a summarizing entry in the general journal, debiting Purchases and debiting any assets that were acquired, and crediting Accounts Payable for the total of the invoices.

Glossary

FOB Free on board; the goods are loaded on the carrier with no additional charge levied on the buyer.

FOB destination The seller pays the freight charges.

FOB shipping point The buyer pays the freight charges between the point of shipment and the destination.

Internal control Plans and procedures inherent in the accounting system with the following objectives: (1) to protect assets against fraud and waste, (2) to yield accurate accounting data, (3) to promote an efficient operation, and (4) to encourage adherence to management policies.

Purchase discount A cash discount allowed for prompt payment of an invoice; for example, 2 percent if the bill is paid within 10 days.

Purchase invoice A business form prepared by the seller that lists the items shipped, their cost, and the mode of shipment. The buyer considers it a purchase invoice; the seller considers it a sales invoice.

Purchase order A written order from the buyer of goods to the supplier, listing items wanted as well as terms of the transaction.

Purchase requisition A form used to request the purchasing department to buy something. This form is intended for internal use within a company.

Purchases Returns and Allowances The account used by the buyer to record a reduction granted by the supplier for either the return of merchandise or compensation for damage to the merchandise. The entry in the buyer's account is based on a credit memorandum received from the supplier.

Questions

1. How many copies of a purchase order are made, and who receives each copy?

2. What business paper authorizes the recording of a purchase transaction?

3. What does a check mark in the Posting Reference column of a purchases journal indicate?

4. How will an error in posting to an individual creditor's account generally be detected?

5. Why is it necessary for a business firm to account for transportation charges on incoming merchandise?

6. When an owner delegates authority, what measures must be taken to maintain control over the operations?

7. Describe the four procedures that most companies follow to effect internal control of purchases?

Exercises

Exercise 1 Describe the transactions in the following T accounts.

Cash		Purchases		Purchases Returns and Allowances		Accounts Payable	
	780	840			60	60	840
						780	

Exercise 2 Record the following transactions in general journal form.

a. Bought merchandise on account from Gilbert and Rogers, $720, Invoice No. C814.

b. Received Credit Memo No. 314 from Gilbert and Rogers for merchandise returned, $30.

c. Issued a check to Gilbert and Rogers in full payment of Invoice No. 814.

Exercise 3 Label the blanks as debit or credit.

	PURCHASES JOURNAL					PAGE____	
DATE	SUPPLIER'S NAME	INVOICE NO.	INVOICE DATE	TERMS	POST REF.	PURCH. ? ACCTS. PAY. ?	

Exercise 4 A business firm that posts directly from its purchases invoices sorts the invoices for the month and finds that the totals are as follows: purchases of merchandise, $7,846; store supplies, $132; office supplies, $86; office equipment, $143. Record the summarizing entry in general journal form.

Exercise 5 Record the following transactions in general journal form.

a. Bought merchandise on account from City Bindery, $543, Invoice No. 7197, FOB shipping point.

b. Paid Western Fast Freight for shipping charges on the above purchase, $38.

Exercise 6 On the above purchase, the Varsity Bookstore uses a markup of 20 percent of cost. Determine the selling price of the new merchandise.

Exercise 7 Record the following transactions in general journal form.

a. Bought a desk for use in the office from Modern Office Supply on account, Invoice No. E478, $362.

b. Paid Mountain States Freight Company for shipping the desk, $8.

Exercise 8 Post the following entry to general ledger and subsidiary ledger accounts similar to those shown below.

GENERAL JOURNAL   PAGE _44_

	DATE		DESCRIPTION	POST. REF.	DEBIT	CREDIT	
1	19— Jun.	15	Accounts Payable, L. B. Dixon Company		3 7 40		1
2			Purchases Returns and Allowances			3 7 40	2
3			Received Credit Memorandum No. 1087,				3
4			Invoice No. G729				4
5							5
6							6
7							7
8							8
9							9

GENERAL LEDGER

ACCOUNT _____ Accounts Payable _____ ACCOUNT NO. _212_

DATE		ITEM	POST. REF.	DEBIT	CREDIT	BALANCE DEBIT	BALANCE CREDIT
19— Jun.	1	Balance	✓				1 6 5 4 20

ACCOUNT _____ Purchases Returns and Allowances _____ ACCOUNT NO. _512_

DATE		ITEM	POST. REF.	DEBIT	CREDIT	BALANCE DEBIT	BALANCE CREDIT
19— Jun.	1	Balance	✓				8 4 20

ACCOUNTS PAYABLE LEDGER

Name _____ L. B. Dixon Company _____
Address _____

DATE		ITEM	POST. REF.	DEBIT	CREDIT	BALANCE
19— May	27		G729		1 2 8 00	1 2 8 00

Problems

Problem 12-1 The Adams Cycle and Toy Company uses a single-column purchases journal. On January 1 of this year, the balances of the ledger accounts are Accounts Payable, $563.87; Purchases, zero. In addition to a general ledger, Adams also uses an accounts payable ledger. Transactions for January related to the buying of merchandise are as follows.

Jan. 2 Bought forty 10-speed bicycles from Larkin Bicycle Company, Invoice No. 4816C, dated January 2; terms net 60 days; $2,376.

5 Bought locks from Security Lock Company, Invoice No. 19916, dated January 3; terms 2/10, n/30; $325.

7 Bought hand brakes from Ripley, Inc., Invoice No. 326BC, dated January 5; terms 1/10, n/30; $264.

10 Bought tires from Ultra Tire and Rubber, Invoice No. D7418, dated January 10; terms 2/10, n/30; $480.

14 Bought handle grips from Knighton Products Company, Invoice No. 3641, dated January 14; terms net 30 days, $98.

22 Bought twenty 5-speed bicycles from Larkin Bicycle Company, Invoice No. 5041C, dated January 21; terms net 60 days; $980.

28 Bought bicycle lights and reflectors from Knighton Products Company, Invoice No. 3678, dated January 28; terms net 30 days, $263.

29 Bought knapsacks from Hampton Manufacturing Company, Invoice No. 618BE dated January 28; terms 2/10, n/30; $286.

Instructions **1.** Open the following accounts in the accounts payable ledger and record the balances as of January 1: Hampton Manufacturing Company, $149.27; Knighton Products Company; Larkin Bicycle Company; Ripley, Inc., $231.80; Security Lock Company, $182.80; Ultra Tire and Rubber, zero (new account).

2. Record balance of $563.87 in the Accounts Payable controlling account as of January 1.

3. Record the transactions in the purchases journal beginning with page 81.

4. Post to the accounts payable ledger and the Accounts Payable controlling account.

5. Prepare a schedule of accounts payable.

6. Compare the balance of the Accounts Payable controlling account with the total of the schedule of accounts payable.

Problem 12-2 The Novel Gift Shop bought the following merchandise and supplies and had the following returns and allowances during May of this year.

May 3 Bought merchandise on account from Dorsett Pottery Company, Invoice No. 7416, dated May 2; terms 2/10, n/30; $740.

May 5 Bought merchandise on account from Novel Card Company, Invoice No. 21678, dated May 2; terms 1/10, n/30; $364.

7 Bought merchandise on account from Roe Supply Company, Invoice No. 19722, dated May 6; terms net 30 days; $614.

11 Bought office supplies on account from Moller and Son, Invoice No. 2995C, dated May 11; terms net 30 days; $216.

13 Received a credit memorandum from Novel Card Company for merchandise returned, $32, Credit Memo No. 618.

17 Bought merchandise on account from Axel Printing Company, Invoice No. 89912, dated May 16; terms 1/10, n/30; $540.

22 Bought office equipment on account from Reiman Equipment Company, Invoice No. 6166, dated May 19; terms net 30 days; $618.

27 Bought merchandise on account from Novel Card Company, Invoice No. 21714, dated May 24; terms 1/10, n/30; $828.

28 Received a credit memorandum from Roe Supply Company for merchandise returned, $82, Credit Memo No. 931.

29 Bought merchandise on account from Dorsett Pottery Company, Invoice No. 7528, dated May 28; terms 2/10, n/30, $1,486.

30 Bought store supplies on account from Ruble and Simpson, Invoice No. 86219, dated May 30; terms net 30 days; $40.

Instructions **1.** Open the following accounts in the general ledger and enter the balances as of May 1.

113	Store Supplies	$ 226
114	Office Supplies	114
121	Office Equipment	4,716
211	Accounts Payable	2,364
511	Purchases	7,496
512	Purchases Returns and Allowances	280

2. Open the following accounts in the accounts payable ledger and enter the balances in the Balance columns as of May 1: Axel Printing Company; Dorsett Pottery Company, $880; Moller and Son; Novel Card Company, $24; Reiman Equipment Company; Roe Supply Company, $1,460; Ruble and Simpson.

3. Record the transactions in either the general journal, page 27, or the purchases journal, page 6. Post the entries to the creditors' accounts in the accounts payable ledger immediately after you make each journal entry. Post the entries in the general journal immediately after you make each journal entry.

4. Post the total of the purchases journal at the end of the month to the Purchases account and the Accounts Payable controlling account.

5. Prepare a schedule of accounts payable.

6. Compare the balance of the Accounts Payable controlling account with the total of the schedule of accounts payable.

Problem 12-3 The Trailer Products Company records sales of merchandise daily, by posting directly from its sales invoices to the accounts receivable ledger. At the end of the month, a summarizing entry is made in the general journal. The purchase of goods on account is recorded in a similar manner, with the posting each day done directly from the invoices to the accounts payable ledger, and a summarizing entry is made in the general journal at the end of the month. Sales of merchandise and purchases of goods on account during September of this year were as follows.

Sales of merchandise

Sept.   4 Staley Store Corp., No. 2816, $2,460.

7 L. D. Morrison, No. 2817, $3,422.

11 M. A. Browne and Company, No. 2818, $1,718.

15 Bowers and Thielenk No. 2819, $2,542.

21 Franklin F. Breen, No. 2820, $1,523.

24 George A. Dearborn, No. 2821, $426.

25 Daniel B. Hull, No. 2822, $2,848.

26 Franklin and Flood, No. 2823, $673.

28 L. D. Morrison, No. 2824, $1,879.

30 Bowers and Thielen, No. 2825, $1,846.

30 Franklin and Flood, No. 2826, $3,186.

Purchases of goods on account

Sept.   3 Foster Corp., merchandise, No. 6814, $2,194.

7 Ramsey Wood Products, merchandise, No. 1829A, $1,920.

9 Sutton Manufacturing Company, merchandise, No. 28611, $4,726.

17 Templin and Flynn, store supplies, No. F8749, $218.

26 P. R. Fisher and Company, store supplies, No. 5165, $162.

29 Foster Corp., merchandise, No. 6927, $3,848.

30 Ramsey Wood Products, merchandise, No. 1847A, $4,325.

30 Fortner Equipment Company, store equipment, No. 67112, $394.

Instructions   **1.** Record the summarizing entry for sales of merchandise on account in the general journal.

2. Record the summarizing entry for the purchase of goods on account in the general journal.

Problem 12-4 The following transactions relate to the Keeler Supply Company during April of this year. Terms of sale are 2/10, n/30.

Apr.   1 Sold merchandise on account to Holland Hardware, Invoice No. 4432, $568.

5 Bought merchandise on account from Southern Manufacturing Company, Invoice No. D4119, $460; 1/10, n/30; dated April 5.

Apr. 9 Sold merchandise on account to Buckingham Department Store, Invoice No. 4433, $996.

11 Bought merchandise on account from Bushnell Products Company, Invoice No. 8911, $2,982.65; 2/10, n/30; dated April 11.

14 Received Credit Memo No. 83 for merchandise returned to Brunner and Son for $386, related to Invoice No. A4988.

17 Sold merchandise on account to Betty Ashby, Invoice No. 4434, $734.20.

18 Issued Credit Memo No. 42 to Buckingham Department Store for merchandise related to Invoice No. 4433, $84.

24 Bought merchandise on account from Atkinson Manufacturing Company, Invoice No. S1683, $1,562; 2/10, n/30; dated April 23.

28 Bought merchandise on account from Conklin and Eckberg Company, Invoice No. E71431, dated April 26, $56.20; 30 days net.

28 Sold merchandise on account to Garner Specialty Company, Invoice No. 4435, $3,198.

30 Issued Credit Memo No. 43 to Garner Specialty Company for merchandise related to Invoice No. 4435, $272.

Instructions **1.** Open the following accounts in the accounts receivable ledger: Ashby, Betty; Buckingham Department Store; Garner Specialty Company, $459; Holland Hardware.

2. Open the following accounts in the accounts payable ledger: Atkinson Manufacturing Company; Brunnel and Son, $990; Bushnell Products Company; Conklin and Eckberg; Southern Manufacturing Company.

3. Record the transactions in the sales, purchases, and general journals.

4. Post the entries to the accounts payable ledger daily.

5. Post the entries to the accounts receivable ledger daily.

Alternate problems

Problem 12-1A The Goodride Bicycle Shop uses a single-column purchases journal. On January 1 of this year the balances of the ledger accounts are Accounts Payable, $422.48; Purchases, zero. In addition to a general ledger, the shop also uses an accounts payable ledger. Transactions for January related to the purchase of merchandise are as follows.

Jan. 4 Bought sixty 10-speed bicycles from Suburban Bicycle Company, Invoice No. 26140, dated January 3; terms net 60 days; $5,920.

6 Bought tires from Amalgamated Tire Company, Invoice No. E9462, dated January 6; terms 2/10, n/30; $482.

7 Bought bicycle lights and reflectors from Everett Products Company, Invoice No. 18316, dated January 6; terms net 30 days; $268.

Jan. 10 Bought hand brakes from C. L. Burbank, Inc., Invoice No. 296FE, dated January 9; terms 1/10, n/30; $282.

18 Bought handle grips from Everett Products Company, Invoice No. 18426, dated January 18; terms net 30 days; $73.60.

23 Purchased thirty 5-speed bicycles from Suburban Bicycle Company, Invoice No. 26392, dated January 23; terms net 60 days; $1,326.

28 Bought knapsacks from Dormaier Manufacturing Company, Invoice No. 768AB, dated January 27; terms 2/10, n/30; $293.16.

30 Bought locks from Larson Lock Company, Invoice No. 48618, dated January 29; terms 2/10, n/30; $326.82.

Instructions **1.** Open the following accounts in the accounts payable ledger: Amalgamated Tire Company, $156; C. L. Burbank, Inc.; Dormaier Manufacturing Company, $82.28; Everett Products Company; Larson Lock Company, $184.20; Suburban Bicycle Company.

2. Record the balance of $422.48 in the Accounts Payable controlling account as of January 1.

3. Record the transactions in the purchases journal beginning with page 72.

4. Post to the accounts payable ledger and the Accounts Payable controlling account.

5. Prepare a schedule of accounts payable.

6. Compare the balance of Accounts Payable controlling account with the total of the schedule of accounts payable.

Problem 12-2A The Larchcliff Gift Shop had the following purchases of merchandise and supplies and related returns and allowances during March.

Mar. 4 Bought merchandise on account from Pittman Pottery Company, Invoice No. 7829, dated March 2; terms 2/10, n/30; $740.

5 Bought merchandise on account from Faulkner Supply Company, Invoice No. 12386D, dated March 3; terms net 30 days; $621.40.

8 Bought merchandise on account from Dewey and Son, Invoice No. 26880, dated March 8; terms net 30 days; $341.82.

12 Bought office supplies on account from Janssen Office Supply, Invoice No. 4389, dated March 12; terms net 30 days; $156.98.

14 Received a credit memorandum from Pittman Pottery Company for merchandise returned, $26, Credit Memo No. 872.

16 Bought merchandise on account from Vernon Card Company, Invoice No. 87127, dated March 16; terms 1/10, n/30; $848.40.

21 Bought office equipment from Kimball Equipment Company, Invoice No. 5682, dated March 19; terms net 30 days; $826.

Mar. 26 Bought merchandise on account from Vernon Card Company, Invoice No. 87429, dated March 26; terms 1/10, n/30; $890.40.

29 Received a credit memo from Faulkner Supply Company for merchandise returned, $79, Credit Memo No. A38.

30 Bought merchandise on account from Pittman Pottery Company, Invoice No. 7881, dated March 29; terms 2/10, n/30; $1,416.80.

30 Bought store supplies on account from Clements and Ross, Invoice No. 78166, dated March 30; terms net 30 days; $39.

31 Bought merchandise on account from Dewey and Son, Invoice No. 26919, dated March 30; terms net 30 days; $216.40.

31 Bought merchandise on account from Faulkner Supply Company, Invoice No. 12490D, dated March 29; terms net 30 days; $372.88.

Instructions **1.** Open the following accounts in the general ledger and enter the balances as of March 1.

113	Store Supplies	$ 386.16
114	Office Supplies	142.70
121	Office Equipment	4,864.40
211	Accounts Payable	2,990.14
511	Purchases	6,961.81
512	Purchases Returns and Allowances	274.18

2. Open the following accounts in the accounts payable ledger and enter the balances in the Balance columns as of March 1: Clements and Ross; Dewey and Son, $986.16; Faulkner Supply Company; Janssen Office Supply; Kimball Equipment Company; Pittman Pottery Company, $1,620; Vernon Card Company, $383.98.

3. Record the transactions either in the general journal, page 51, or the purchases journal, page 5. Post the entries to the creditors' accounts in the accounts payable ledger immediately after you record each journal entry. Post the entries to the general ledger after you record each general journal entry.

4. Post the total of the purchases journal at the end of the month to the Purchases account and the Accounts Payable controlling account.

5. Prepare a schedule of accounts payable.

6. Compare the balance of the Accounts Payable controlling account with the total of the schedule of accounts payable.

Problem 12-3A Goodfellow Products Company records sales of merchandise daily by posting directly from its sales invoices to the accounts receivable ledger. At the end of the month they make a summarizing entry in the general journal. They record purchases of goods on account the same way, daily, posting directly from the invoices to the accounts payable ledger and making a summarizing entry in the general journal at the end of the month. Sales of merchandise and purchases of goods on account during October of this year were as shown on the top of the next page.

Sales of merchandise

Oct. 5 Lancaster Specialty Shop, No. 4618, $418.47.

      8 L. D. Foland, No. 4619, $568.29.

    12 M. O. Kitterman and Company, No. 4620, $962.48.

    16 Kinzel and Savage, No. 4621, $1,492.70.

    23 Lane C. Rudolph, No. 4622, $926.75.

    25 Eldon B. Porter, No. 4623, $983.40.

    26 Ray C. Keeler, No. 4624, $1,011.

    29 Foley and Mason, No. 4625, $624.18.

    31 Kinzel and Savage, No. 4626, $391.

    31 L. D. Foland, No. 4627, $264.80.

Purchases of goods on account

Oct. 4 Massey and Blanchard, merchandise, No. D1194, $584.

      8 Moore Wood Products, merchandise, No. 26448, $1,720.

    10 Armstrong Manufacturing Company, merchandise, No. 84811, $3,940.

    11 Lancaster Supply Company, office supplies, No. AD484, $121.

    20 D. C. Hardy and Company, merchandise, No. C6411, $143.66.

    22 Harvey and Harvey, store supplies, No. N8642, $64.28.

    29 Moore Wood Products, merchandise, No. 26579, $2,942.

    31 Adkins Equipment Company, store equipment, No. 48121, $305.

Instructions **1.** Record the summarizing entry for the sale of merchandise on account in the general journal.

2. Record the summarizing entry for the purchase of goods on account in the general journal.

Problem 12-4A The following transactions relate to the Hobson Fixture Company during March of this year. Terms of sale are 2/10, n/30.

Mar. 2 Sold merchandise on account to Arthur Sloane, Invoice No. 11886, $960.

      4 Bought merchandise on account from Pierce Manufacturing Company, Invoice No. B2111, $474; 1/10, n/30; dated March 2.

    10 Sold merchandise on account to Peterson and Lee, Invoice No. 11887, $1,374.

    12 Bought merchandise on account from Vanderhoff and Associates, Invoice No. 8694, $4,440; 2/10, n/30; dated March 11.

    15 Received Credit Memo No. 78 for merchandise returned to N. D. Kimbrough Company, for $116, related to Invoice No. 6694.

    18 Sold merchandise on account to Milton Hale, Invoice No. 11888, $876.

Mar. 18 Issued Credit Memo No. 32 to Peterson and Lee, for merchandise returned, $84, related to Invoice No. 11887.

27 Bought merchandise on account from George L. Patterson and Son, Invoice No. 8449, $1,760; 2/10, EOM (within 10 days after the end of the month); dated March 26.

29 Bought office supplies on account from Thompson Stationery Company, Invoice No. S3284, dated March 28, $89, 30 days net.

30 Sold merchandise on account to Shaver and Tuttle, Invoice No. 11889, $2,840.

31 Issued Credit Memo No. 33 to Shaver and Tuttle for merchandise returned, $178, related to Invoice No. 11889.

Instructions
1. Open the following accounts in the accounts receivable ledger: Hale, Milton; Peterson and Lee, $417; Shaver and Tuttle, $983; Sloane, Arthur.

2. Open the following accounts in the accounts payable ledger: N. D. Kimbrough Company, $378; George L. Patterson and Son; Pierce Manufacturing Company; Thompson Stationery Company, Vanderhoff and Associates.

3. Record the transactions in the sales, purchases, and general journals.

4. Post entries to the accounts payable ledger daily.

5. Post entries to the accounts receivable ledger daily.

13

Cash receipts and cash payments

objectives

After you have completed this chapter, you will be able to do the following:
- Record transactions for a retail merchandising business in a cash receipts journal.
- Record transactions for a wholesale merchandising business in a cash receipts journal.
- Post from a cash receipts journal to a general ledger and an accounts receivable ledger.
- Determine cash discount according to credit terms, and record cash receipts from charge customers who are entitled to deduct the cash discount.
- Record transactions in a cash payments journal for a service enterprise.
- Record transactions in a cash payments journal for a merchandising enterprise.
- Record transactions in a check register.
- Post from a cash payments journal and a check register to a general ledger and an accounts payable ledger.
- Record transactions involving trade discounts.

WE HAVE SEEN that using the sales journal and the purchases journal enables an accountant to carry out the journalizing and posting processes much more efficiently. These special journals make it possible to record an entry on one line, and to post column totals rather than individual figures. This can also make possible a division of labor, because the journalizing functions can be delegated to different persons. The *cash receipts journal* and *cash payments journal* carry these advantages further.

Cash receipts journal

The cash receipts journal records all transactions in which cash comes in, or increases. When the cash receipts journal is used, all transactions in which cash is debited *must* be recorded in it. It may be used for a service as well as a merchandising business. To get acquainted with the cash receipts journal, let's list some typical transactions of a retail merchandising business which result in an increase in cash. So that you'll see the transactions at a glance, let's record them immediately in T accounts.

May 3: Sold merchandise for cash, $100, plus $4 sales tax.

Cash		Sales		Sales Tax Payable	
+	−	−	+	−	+
104			100		4

May 4: Sold merchandise, $100 plus $4 sales tax; but the customer used a bank charge card. The firm deposits the bank credit card receipts, and the bank *deducts a discount* and credits the firm's account with cash. This discount is often 2% of the total of sales plus sales tax. The firm therefore records the

amount of the discount under Credit Card Expense. (From the amount that would ordinarily be debited to Cash, deduct the bank charge, consisting of 2% of the total of sales plus sales tax, and debit this amount to Credit Card Expense instead of to Cash: $104 \times .02 = \$2.08$, therefore $\$100 + \$4 - \$2.08 = \$101.92$.)

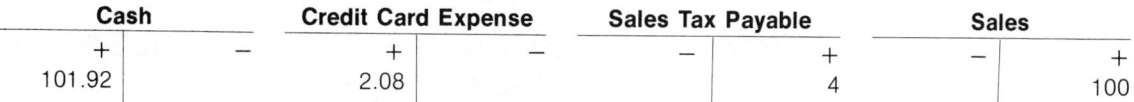

Cash		Credit Card Expense		Sales Tax Payable		Sales	
+	−	+	−	−	+	−	+
101.92		2.08			4		100

May 5: Collected $208 cash on account from John Oatey, a charge customer.

Cash		Accounts Receivable	
+	−	+	−
208			208

May 7: The owner, Eric Adams, invested cash in the business, $3,000.

Cash		Eric Adams, Capital	
+	−	−	+
3,000			3,000

May 8: Sold equipment for cash at cost, $150.

Cash		Equipment	
+	−	+	−
150			150

Now let's appraise these five transactions: The first three would be frequent; the last two could conceivably take place, but they would be rather infrequent. If one were designing a cash receipts journal, it would be logical to include a Cash debit column because all the transactions involve an increase in cash. If a business regularly collects cash from charge customers, there should be an Accounts Receivable credit column. If a firm often sells merchandise for cash and collects a sales tax, there should be a Sales credit column and a Sales Tax Payable credit column. If the business honors bank charge cards, there should be a Credit Card Expense debit column to take care of the amount deducted by the bank.

However, the credit to Eric Adams, Capital, and the credit to Equipment occur very seldom, so it wouldn't be practical to set up special columns for them, as they can be handled adequately by a Sundry credit column, which can be used for credits to all other accounts that have no special column.

Now let's record the same transactions in a cash receipts journal. First we repeat the transactions on the top of the next page.

May 3 Sold merchandise for cash, $100, plus $4 sales tax.

4 Sold merchandise, $100 plus $4 sales tax, and the customer used a bank charge card. Discount charged by the bank is 2% of the amount of the total of sales plus sales tax.

5 Collected cash from John Oatey, a charge customer, on account, $208.

7 The owner, Eric Adams, invested cash in the business, $3,000.

8 Sold equipment for cash, at cost, $150.

At the end of the month we can post the special columns in the cash receipts journal as totals to the general ledger accounts. These include Accounts Receivable credit, Sales credit, Sales Tax Payable credit, Credit Card Expense debit, and Cash debit. We post the items in the Sundry Accounts credit column individually, and post the figures in the Accounts Receivable credit column separately to the accounts in the accounts receivable ledger. The posting letter designation for the cash receipts journal is CR.

CASH RECEIPTS JOURNAL PAGE 41

DATE	ACCOUNT CREDITED	POST REF.	SUNDRY ACCOUNTS CREDIT	ACCOUNTS RECEIVABLE CREDIT	SALES CREDIT	SALES TAX PAYABLE CREDIT	CREDIT CARD EXPENSE DEBIT	CASH DEBIT
19— May 3	Sales				100 00	4 00		104 00
4	Sales				100 00	4 00	2 08	101 92
5	John Oatey			208 00				208 00
7	E. Adams, Capital		3000 00					3000 00
8	Equipment		150 00					150 00

Here are some other transactions made during the month that involve increases in cash. (Remember that these transactions are for a retail business.)

May 11 Borrowed $300 from the bank, receiving cash and giving the bank a promissory note.

16 Sold merchandise for cash, $200, plus $8 sales tax.

21 Sold merchandise for cash, $50, plus $2 sales tax; customer used a bank charge card.

26 Collected cash from Kenneth Ralston, a charge customer, on account, $62.40.

28 Sold merchandise for cash, $40, plus $1.60 sales tax.

31 Sold merchandise for cash, $150, plus $6 sales tax; customer used a bank charge card.

31 Collected cash from Donald Madden, a charge customer, on account, $26.

Let us assume that all the month's transactions involving debits to Cash have now been recorded in the cash receipts journal. The cash receipts journal and charts below illustrate the postings to the general ledger and the accounts receivable ledger.

CASH RECEIPTS JOURNAL PAGE 41

DATE	ACCOUNT CREDITED	POST REF.	SUNDRY ACCOUNTS CREDIT	ACCOUNTS RECEIVABLE CREDIT	SALES CREDIT	SALES TAX PAYABLE CREDIT	CREDIT CARD EXPENSE DEBIT	CASH DEBIT
19— May 3	Sales	—			100 00	4 00		104 00
4	Sales	—			100 00	4 00	2 08	101 92
5	John Oatey	✓		208 00				208 00
7	E. Adams, Capital	311	3000 00					3000 00
8	Equipment	121	150 00					150 00
11	Notes Payable	211	300 00					300 00
16	Sales	—			200 00	8 00		208 00
21	Sales	—			50 00	2 00	1 04	50 96
26	K. Ralston	✓		62 40				62 40
28	Sales	—			40 00	1 60		41 60
31	Sales	—			150 00	6 00	3 12	152 88
31	D. Madden	✓		26 00				26 00
31			3450 00	296 40	640 00	25 60	6 24	4405 76
			(✓)	(113)	(411)	(213)	(513)	(111)

Individual amounts in the Accounts Receivable credit column are posted daily.

Individual amounts in the Sundry credit column are posted daily.

Totals are posted at the end of the month.

Accounts Receivable Ledger

Donald Madden

	May 31	26

Johnny Oatey

	May 5	208

Kenneth Ralston

	May 26	62.40

General Ledger

Eric Adams, Capital

−	+	
	May 7	3,000

Equipment

+	−	
	May 8	150

Notes Payable

−	+	
	May 11	300

Cash

+	−
May 31 4,405.76	

Credit Card Expense

+	−
May 31 6.24	

Sales Tax Payable

−	+	
	May 31	25.60

Sales

−	+	
	May 31	640

Accounts Receivable

+	−	
	May 31	296.40

In the Posting Reference column, the Check marks ($\checkmark$) stand for the fact that one has posted the amounts in the Accounts Receivable credit column to the individual charge customers' accounts as credits. The account numbers indicate that one has posted the amounts in the Sundry Accounts credit column separately to the accounts described in the Account Credited column. One also puts a check mark ($\checkmark$) under the total of the Sundry column. This means "do not post," as the figures are posted separately, as described above. A check mark in accounting thus has two meanings: (1) *that the individual account has been posted in the subsidiary ledger,* as in the Accounts Receivable credit column; and (2) *that the total is not to be posted,* as in the case of the Sundry column.

A dash in the Posting Reference column indicates that an individual amount is being posted as a part of a column total. For example, on May 3 the $100 credit to Sales will be posted as a part of the $640 total.

Let's say it's the end of the month. We total the columns, then check the accuracy of the footings by proving that the sum of the debit totals equals the sum of the credit totals.

	Debit totals
Cash	$4,405.76
Credit Card Expense	6.24
	$4,412.00

	Credit totals
Sundry Accounts	$3,450.00
Accounts Receivable	296.40
Sales	640.00
Sales Tax Payable	25.60
	$4,412.00

Credit terms

The seller always stipulates credit terms: How much credit can be allowed to a customer? And how much time should the customer be given to pay the full amount? The *credit period* is the time the seller allows the buyer before full payment has to be made. Retailers generally allow 1 month.

Wholesalers and manufacturers often have a *cash discount* specified in their credit terms. A cash discount is the amount a customer can deduct if she or he pays the bill within a short time. Naturally this discount acts as an incentive for charge customers to pay their bills promptly.

For example, say that a wholesaler offers customers credit terms of 2/10, n/30. This means that the customer gets a 2% discount if he or she pays the bill within 10 days after the invoice date. If the customer can't pay the bill within the 10 days, then he or she has to pay the entire amount within 30 days after the invoice date. Other cash discounts that may be used are the following.

1/15, n/60 The seller offers a 1% discount if the bill is paid within 15 days after the invoice date, and the whole bill must be paid within 60 days after the invoice date.

2/10, EOM, n/60 The seller offers a 2% discount if the bill is paid within 10 days after the end of the month, and the whole bill must be paid within 60 days after the invoice date.

A wholesaler or manufacturer offering a cash discount adopts one cash discount as a credit policy, and makes this available to all its customers.

The seller considers cash discounts to be sales discounts; the buyer, on the other hand, considers cash discounts as purchases discounts. In this section we are concerned with the sales discount. The Sales Discount account, like Sales Returns and Allowances, is a deduction from Sales.

To illustrate, we return to North Central Plumbing Supply. The following transactions take place, and we'll record them in T accounts so we can see them at a glance.

Transaction (a) August 1: Sold merchandise on account to T. L. Long Company, Invoice No. 320, $325, terms 2/10, n/30.

Transaction (b) August 10: Received check from T. L. Long Company for $318.50 in payment of Invoice No. 322, less cash discount ($325.00 − $6.50 = $318.50).

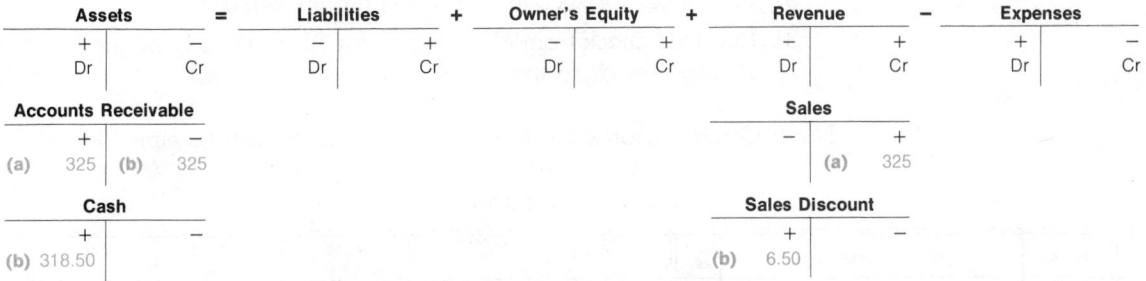

Since North Central Plumbing Supply offers this cash discount to all customers, and since charge customers often pay their bills within the discount period, North Central sets up a Sales Discount debit column in the cash receipts journal.

CASH RECEIPTS JOURNAL   PAGE _18_

	DATE	ACCOUNT CREDITED	POST. REF.	SUNDRY ACCOUNTS CR.	ACCOUNTS REC. CR.	SALES CR.	SALES DISCOUNT DR.	CASH DR.	
1	19— Aug. 10	T. L. Long Company			325 00		6 50	318 50	1
2									2
3									3

On the next page are some more transactions of North Central Plumbing Supply involving increases in cash during August of this year. Remember that the standard credit terms for all charge customers are 2/10, n/30.

Aug. 15 Cash sales for first half of the month, $460.

16 Received check from Acme Plumbing and Heating for $92.12 in payment of Invoice No. 322, less cash discount ($94.00 − $1.88 = $92.12).

17 Received payment on a promissory note given by John R. Stokes, $300 principal, plus $3 interest. (The amount of the interest is recorded in the Interest Income account.)

21 Received check from Clark and Keller Hardware for $84.28 in payment of Invoice No. 324, less cash discount ($86.00 − $1.72 = $84.28).

23 Sold store equipment for cash at cost, $126.

26 Robert C. Randall, the owner, invested an additional $4,000 cash in the business.

26 Received check from Home Hardware Company for $97.02 in payment of Invoice No. 325, less the amount of Credit Memorandum No. 70, $99, less cash discount ($99 − $1.98 = $97.02).

30 Received check from Henning's Plumbing for $287.14 in payment of Invoice No. 326, less cash discount ($293 − $5.86 = $287.14).

31 Cash sales for second half of the month, $620.

31 Received check from Macon, Inc., for $116. (This is longer than the 10-day period, so they missed the cash discount.)

North Central records these transactions in their cash receipts journal.

CASH RECEIPTS JOURNAL PAGE 18

	DATE		ACCOUNT CREDITED	POST. REF.	SUNDRY ACCOUNTS CR.	ACCOUNTS REC. CR.	SALES CR.	SALES DISCOUNT DR.	CASH DR.	
1	19– Aug.	10	T. L. Long Company			325 00		6 50	318 50	1
2		15	Sales				460 00		460 00	2
3		16	Acme Plumbing and Heating			94 00		1 88	92 12	3
4		17	Notes Receivable		300 00					4
5			Interest Income		3 00				303 00	5
6		21	Clark and Keller Hardware			86 00		1 72	84 28	6
7		23	Store Equipment		126 00				126 00	7
8		26	Robert C. Randall, Capital		4000 00				4000 00	8
9		26	Home Hardware Company			99 00		1 98	97 02	9
10		30	Henning's Plumbing			293 00		5 86	287 14	10
11		31	Sales				620 00		620 00	11
12		31	Macon, Inc.			116 00			116 00	12
13		31			4429 00	1013 00	1080 00	17 94	6504 06	13
14										14
15										15
16										16
17										17

North Central's accountant proves the equality of debits and credits:

	Debit totals
Cash debit	$6,504.06
Sales Discount debit	17.94
	$6,522.00

	Credit totals
Sundry Accounts credit	$4,429.00
Accounts Receivable credit	1,013.00
Sales credit	1,080.00
	$6,522.00

Cash payments journal: service enterprise

The cash payments journal, as the name implies, records all transactions in which cash goes out, or decreases. When the cash payments journal is used, all transactions in which cash is credited *must* be recorded in it. It may be used for a service as well as a merchandising business.

To get acquainted with the cash payments journal, let's list some typical transactions of a service firm (such as a dry cleaner or a bowling alley) or of a professional enterprise which result in a decrease in cash. So that you'll see the transactions at a glance, let's record them directly in T accounts.

May 2: Paid Henry Moore Company, a creditor, on account, Check No. 63, $220.

Accounts Payable		**Cash**	
−	+	+	−
220			220

May 4: Bought supplies for cash, $90, Check No. 64.

Supplies		**Cash**	
+	−	+	−
90			90

May 5: Paid wages for 2 weeks, Check No. 65, $1,216 (previously recorded in the payroll entry).

Wages Payable		**Cash**	
−	+	+	−
1,216			1,216

May 6: Paid rent for the month, $350, Check No. 66.

Rent Expense		**Cash**	
+	−	+	−
350			350

Now let's appraise these four transactions. The first one would occur very often, as payments to creditors would be made several times a month. Of the last three transactions, the debit to Wages Payable might occur twice a month, the debit to Rent Expense once a month, and the debit to Supplies every now and then.

If one were designing a cash payments journal, it would be logical to include a Cash credit column because all the transactions involve a decrease in cash. Since payments are made to creditors often, there should be an Accounts Payable debit column. One could set up any other column if it were used often enough to warrant it. Otherwise, a Sundry debit column would take care of all the other transactions.

Now let's record these same transactions in a cash payments journal, and include a column entitled Check Number. If you think a moment, you'll see that this is consistent with good management of cash, in that all expenditures should be paid for by check, except for Petty Cash. First let's repeat the transactions.

May 2 Paid Henry Moore Company, a creditor, on account, $220, Check No. 63.

4 Bought supplies for cash, $90, Check No. 64.

5 Paid wages for the first 2 weeks, $1,216, Check No. 65 (previously recorded in the payroll entry).

6 Paid rent for the month, $350, Check No. 66.

CASH PAYMENTS JOURNAL   PAGE 62

DATE		CK. NO.	ACCOUNT DEBITED	POST. REF.	SUNDRY ACCOUNTS DR.	ACCOUNTS PAYABLE DR.	CASH CR.
19— May	2	63	Henry Moore Company			220 00	220 00
	4	64	Supplies		90 00		90 00
	5	65	Wages Payable		1216 00		1216 00
	6	66	Rent Expense		350 00		350 00

Note that you list all checks in consecutive order, even those checks which must be voided. In this way, every check is accounted for, which is necessary for internal control.

At the end of the month, post the special columns as totals to the general ledger accounts, but not the total of the Sundry Accounts debit column. Post the figures in this column individually, after which you place the account number in the Posting Reference column. Post the figures in the Accounts Payable debit column separately to the individual accounts in the accounts payable ledger, and after posting, put a check mark ($\sqrt{}$) in the Posting Reference column. The posting letter designation for the cash payments journal is CP. Other transactions involving decreases in cash during May are as follows.

May 7 Paid $360 for a 3-year premium for fire insurance, Check No. 67.

9 Paid Treadwell, Inc., a creditor, on account, $418, Check No. 68.

11 Issued Check No. 69 in payment of delivery expense, $62.

14 Paid Johnson and Son, a creditor, on account, $110, Check No. 70.

16 Issued Check No. 71 to the Melton State Bank, for Note Payable, $660, $600 on the principal and $60 interest.

19 Voided Check No. 72.

19 Bought equipment for $800, paying $200 down. Issued Check No. 73. The rest of this entry is recorded in the general journal as explained on page 332.

20 Paid wages for 2 weeks, Check No. 74, $1,340 (previously recorded in the payroll entry).

22 Issued Check No. 75 to Peter R. Morton Advertising Agency for advertising, $94.

26 Paid telephone bill, $26, Check No. 76.

31 Issued check for freight bill on equipment purchased on May 19, $28, Check No. 77.

31 Paid Teller and Noble, a creditor, on account, $160, Check No. 78.

The transactions listed above are recorded in the Cash Payments journal as illustrated below.

CASH PAYMENTS JOURNAL PAGE 62

	DATE	CK. NO.	ACCOUNT DEBITED	POST. REF.	SUNDRY ACCOUNTS DR.	ACCOUNTS PAYABLE DR.	CASH CR.	
1	19— May 2	63	Henry Moore Company	✓		2 20 00	2 20 00	1
2	4	64	Supplies	113	90 00		90 00	2
3	5	65	Wages Payable	411	1 2 16 00		1 2 16 00	3
4	6	66	Rent Expense	412	3 50 00		3 50 00	4
5	7	67	Prepaid Insurance	114	3 60 00		3 60 00	5
6	9	68	Treadwell, Inc.	✓		4 18 00	4 18 00	6
7	11	69	Delivery Expense	413	62 00		62 00	7
8	14	70	Johnson and Son	✓		1 10 00	1 10 00	8
9	16	71	Notes Payable	211	6 00 00			9
10			Interest Expense	414	60 00		6 60 00	10
11	19	72	Void	✓				11
12	19	73	Equipment	✓	2 00 00		2 00 00	12
13	20	74	Wages Payable	411	1 3 40 00		1 3 40 00	13
14	22	75	Advertising Expense	415	94 00		94 00	14
15	26	76	Telephone Expense	416	26 00		26 00	15
16	31	77	Equipment	121	28 00		28 00	16
17	31	78	Teller and Noble	✓		1 60 00	1 60 00	17
18	31				4 4 26 00	9 08 00	5 3 34 00	18
19					(✓)	(2 1 2)	(1 1 1)	19

In the purchase of an asset involving a cash down payment with the remainder on account, it would be necessary to record the transactions in two journals. For example, this transaction: Bought equipment for $800 from Burns Company, paying $200 down with the remainder to be paid in 30 days. In the general journal, debit Equipment for $800, credit Accounts Payable, Burns Company for $600, and credit Cash for $200. In the Posting Reference column of this entry, place a check mark on the line with Cash. Record the second entry in the cash payments journal, debiting Equipment for $200 in the Sundry Accounts Debit column and crediting Cash for $200 in the Cash Credit column. In the Posting Reference column of this entry, place a check mark so that the $200 debit to Equipment will not be posted. The net result is that Equipment is debited for the full amount of $800, Cash is credited for $200, and Accounts Payable is credited for $600. The general journal entry would appear as follows:

GENERAL JOURNAL   PAGE _____

	DATE		DESCRIPTION	POST REF.	DEBIT	CREDIT	
1	May	19	Equipment		800 00		1
2			Accounts Payable, Burns Company			600 00	2
3			Cash	✓		200 00	3
4			Payment is due in 30 days.				4
5							5
6							6
7							7
8							8
9							9
10							10
11							11
12							12
13							13
14							14
15							15
16							16
17							17
18							18
19							19
20							20
21							21
22							22
23							23
24							24
25							25
26							26
27							27

Individual amounts in the Accounts Payable debit column are posted daily.

Individual amounts in the Sundry debit column are posted daily.

Totals are posted at the end of the month.

Accounts Payable Ledger

Johnson and Son

May 14	110	

Henry Moore and Company

May 2	220	

Teller and Noble

May 31	160	

Treadwell, Inc.

May 9	418	

Burns Company

	May 19	600

General Ledger

Supplies

	+	−
May 4	90	

Wages Payable

	−	+
May 5	1,216	
20	1,340	

Rent Expense

	+	−
May 6	350	

Prepaid Insurance

	+	−
May 7	360	

Delivery Expense

	+	−
May 11	62	

Notes Payable

	−	+
May 16	600	

Interest Expense

	+	−
May 16	60	

Equipment

	+	−
May 19	800	
31	28	

Advertising Expense

	+	−
May 22	94	

Telephone Expense

	+	−
May 26	26	

Cash

	+	−
		May 31	5,334

Accounts Payable

	−	+
May 31	908	May 19	600

At the end of the month, after totaling the columns, check the accuracy of the footings by proving that the sum of the debit totals equals the sum of the credit totals. Since you have posted the individual amounts in the Sundry debit column to the general ledger, the posting that remains to be done consists of the credit to the Cash account for $5,334 and the debit to the Accounts Payable (controlling) account for $908.

	Debit totals
Sundry debit	$4,426.00
Accounts Payable debit	908.00
	$5,334.00

	Credit totals
Cash credit	$5,334.00

Cash payments journal: merchandising enterprise

There is one slight difference between the cash payments journal for a merchandising enterprise and that for a service enterprise. This difference has to do with the cash discounts that are available to a merchandising business. Recall that cash discounts are the amount that the buyer may deduct from the bill; this acts as an incentive to make the buyer pay the bill promptly. The buyer considers the cash discount to be a Purchases Discount, because it relates to his or her purchase of merchandise. The Purchases Discount account, like Purchases Returns and Allowances, is a deduction from Purchases, so the buyer, in his or her income statement, treats it as such.

Let us return to North Central Plumbing Supply, and assume that the following transactions take place. To demonstrate the debits and credits, let's show some typical transactions in the form of T accounts.

Transaction (a) August 2: Bought merchandise on account from Danton, Inc., their invoice no. 2706, $285; terms 2/10, n/30; dated July 31.

Transaction (b) August 8: Issued check no. 76, $279.30, to Danton, Inc., in payment of invoice no. 2706, less the cash discount, $5.70.

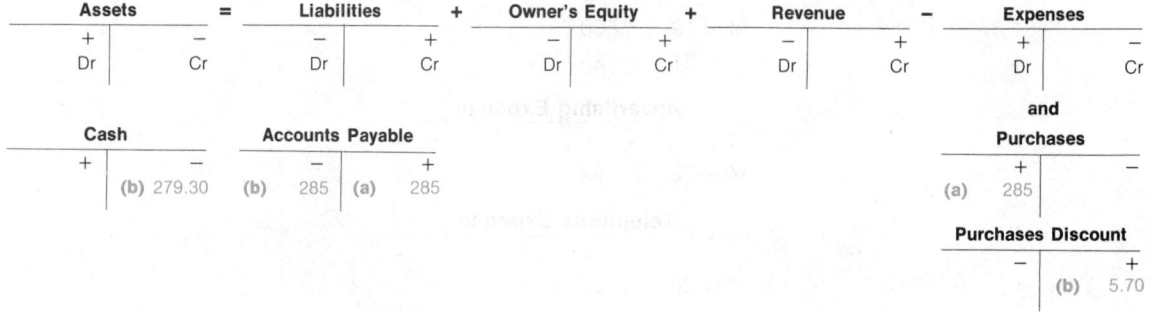

Any well-managed business takes advantage of a purchases discount whenever possible. So if a discount is available to the business, it is worthwhile to set up a special Purchases Discount credit column in the cash payments journal.

CASH PAYMENTS JOURNAL

	DATE		CK. NO.	ACCOUNT NAME	POST. REF.	SUNDRY ACCOUNTS DR.	ACCOUNTS PAYABLE DR.	PURCHASES DISCOUNT CR.	CASH CR.	
1	19– Aug.	8	76	Danton, Inc.			2 8 5 00	5 70	2 7 9 30	1
2										2
3										3
4										4
5										5
6										6
7										7
8										8
9										9
10										10
11										11

Here are some other transactions of North Central Plumbing Supply involving decreases in cash during August. Note that credit terms vary among the different creditors.

Aug. 10 Paid wages for two-week period; Check No. 77, $1,680 (previously recorded in the payroll entry).

11 Issued Check No. 78, $609.56, to Argel Manufacturing Company, in payment of Invoice No. 10611, less return, $622, less cash discount, 2/10, n/30 ($622 × .02 = $12.44; $622 − $12.44 = $609.56).

12 Bought supplies for cash, $70; issued Check No. 79 payable to Davenport Office Supplies.

15 Issued Check No. 80 to Sinclair Manufacturing Company in payment of their Invoice No. B643, less return, $127.71, less cash discount, $1.29 ($129 − $1.29 = $127.71).

16 Bought merchandise for cash, $200; Check No. 81, payable to Jones Sheet and Tube.

19 Issued Check No. 82 to Reliable Express Company for freight cost on merchandise purchased, $60.

23 Voided Check No. 83.

23 Issued Check No. 84 to American Fire Insurance Company for insurance premium for 1 year, $120.

25 Paid wages for 2-week period; $1,750, Check No. 85 (previously recorded in the payroll entry).

27 Paid F. R. Waller $46 for merchandise he returned on a cash sale, Check No. 86.

31 Issued Check No. 87, $760, to Rogers and Simon Company in payment of invoice no. 982 (net 30 days).

Let us now record these transactions in the cash payments journal.

CASH PAYMENTS JOURNAL   PAGE __26__

	DATE	CK. NO.	ACCOUNT NAME	POST. REF.	SUNDRY ACCOUNTS DR.	ACCOUNTS PAYABLE DR.	PURCHASES DISCOUNT CR.	CASH CR.	
1	19— Aug. 8	76	Danton, Inc.			285 00	5 70	279 30	1
2	10	77	Wages Payable		1680 00			1680 00	2
3	11	78	Argel Manufacturing Company			622 00	12 44	609 56	3
4	12	79	Supplies		70 00			70 00	4
5	15	80	Sinclair Manufacturing Company			129 00	1 29	127 71	5
6	16	81	Purchases		200 00			200 00	6
7	19	82	Purchases		60 00			60 00	7
8	23	83	Void						8
9	23	84	Prepaid Insurance		120 00			120 00	9
10	25	85	Wages Payable		1750 00			1750 00	10
11	27	86	Sales Returns and Allowances		46 00			46 00	11
12	31	87	Rogers and Simon Company			760 00		760 00	12
13	31				3926 00	1796 00	19 43	5702 57	13
14									14
15									15
16									16
17									17
18									18
19									19
20									20
21									21
22									22
23									23
24									24
25									25

Check register   Instead of using a cash payments journal as a book of original entry, one can use a check register. The check register is merely a large checkbook with perforations so that it is easy to tear out the checks. The page opposite the checks has columns which may be labeled for special accounts, such as bank credit (in place of Cash), Accounts Payable debit, etc. The checks are prenumbered, and one records each check issued on the columnar sheet. This is common practice for a small business in which the owner writes the checks himself or herself. One posts directly from the check register.

Suppose North Central Plumbing Supply had used a check register instead of the cash payments journal. Its August transactions would appear as shown on the facing page.

	DATE		CK. NO.	PAYEE	ACCOUNT DEBITED	POST. REF	SUNDRY ACCTS. DEBIT				ACCTS. PAY. DEBIT			PURCH. DISC. CREDIT			VALLEY BANK CREDIT				
1	19– Aug.	8	76	Danton, Inc.	Danton, Inc.						2	85	00		5	70	2	79	30		1
2		10	77	Payroll	Wages Payable		1	680	00								1	680	00		2
3		11	78	Argel Mfg.	Argel Mfg.						6	22	00		12	44	6	09	56		3
4		12	79	Davenport	Supplies			70	00									70	00		4
5		15	80	Sinclair Mfg.	Sinclair Mfg.						1	29	00		1	29	1	27	71		5
6		16	81	Jones Sheet	Purchases		2	00	00								2	00	00		6
7		19	82	Reliable Exp.	Purchases			60	00									60	00		7
8		23	83	Void																	8
9		23	84	American Fire	Prepaid Ins.			120	00									120	00		9
10		25	85	Payroll	Wages Payable		1	750	00								1	750	00		10
11		27	86	F. R. Waller	Sales Ret. and Allow.			46	00									46	00		11
12		31	87	Rogers & Simon Co.	Rogers & Simon Co.						7	60	00				7	60	00		12
13		31					3	926	00		17	96	00		19	43	57	02	57		13

You can see for yourself that the difference between the cash payments journal and the check register is minor. Recall that one substitutes the bank credit column for the Cash credit column. The check register lists the payee of the check. The Accounts Payable debit column and the Purchases Discount credit column are included to handle payments to creditors.

Two additional columns, Deposits and Bank Balance, could be added, to give a current balance of the Valley National Bank or Cash account. The posting process for each book of original entry would be the same.

In a small business, the owner or manager usually signs all the checks. However, if the owner delegates the authority to sign checks to some other person, that person should *not* have access to the accounting records. Why? Well, this helps to prevent fraud, because a dishonest employee could conceal a cash disbursement in the accounting records. In other words, for a medium-to large-size business, it's worth a manager's while to keep a separate book, which in this case is the cash payments journal. One person writes the checks, and another person records the checks in the cash payments journal. This means that one person acts as a check on the other, and there would have to be collusion between the two people for embezzlement to take place. Again, this precaution is consistent with a good system of internal control.

Check register   **337**

Manufacturers and wholesalers of many lines of products publish annual catalogs listing their products at retail prices. These concerns offer their customers substantial reductions (often as much as 40%) from the list or catalog prices. The reductions from the list prices are called *trade discounts*. Firms grant sales discounts and purchases discounts for prompt payment of invoices, but trade discounts are not related to cash payments. Manufacturers and wholesalers use trade discounts to avoid reprinting catalogs when selling prices change. They simply change the selling prices in the catalogs by issuing a new list of trade discounts to be applied to the catalog prices.

Firms may quote trade discounts as a single percentage. Example: A distributor of furnaces grants a single discount of 40% off the listed catalog price of $8,000. In this case, the selling price is calculated as follows.

List or catalog price	$8,000
Less: Trade discount of 40% ($8,000 × .4)	3,200
Selling price	$4,800

Neither the seller nor the buyer records trade discounts in the accounts; they enter only the selling price. By T accounts, the furnace distributor records the sale as:

Accounts Receivable		**Sales**	
+	−	−	+
4,800			4,800

The buyer records the purchase as:

Purchases		**Accounts Payable**	
+	−	−	+
4,800			4,800

Firms may also quote trade discounts as a chain or series of percentages. For example, a distributor of automobile parts grants discounts of 30%, 10%, and 10% off the listed catalog price of $900. In this case, the selling price is calculated as follows.

List or catalog price	$900.00
Less: First trade discount of 30% ($900 × .3)	270.00
Remainder after first discount	$630.00
Less: Second trade discount of 10% ($630 × .1)	63.00
Remainder after second discount	$567.00
Less: Third discount of 10% ($567 × .1)	56.70
Selling price	$510.30

By T accounts, the automobile parts distributor records the sale as shown on the top of the next page.

Accounts Receivable		Sales	
+	−	−	+
510.30			510.30

The buyer records the purchase as shown here:

Purchases		Accounts Payable	
+	−	−	+
510.30			510.30

In the situation involving a chain of discounts, the additional discounts are granted for large-volume transactions, either in dollar amounts or in sizes of shipments, such as carload lots.

Cash discounts could also apply in situations involving trade discounts. Example: Suppose that the credit terms of the above sale included a cash discount of 2/10, n/30, and that the buyer pays the invoice within 10 days. The seller applies the cash discount to the selling price. By T accounts, the seller records the transaction as:

Cash		Sales Discount		Accounts Receivable	
+	−	+	−	+	−
500.09		10.21			510.30

The buyer records the transaction as:

Cash		Purchase Discount		Accounts Payable	
+	−	−	+	−	+
	500.09		10.21	510.30	

Summary

When a business entity uses a cash receipts journal, it *must* record every transaction which results in a debit to cash in this journal. The person handling the books sets up special columns in the journal to take care of debits or credits to accounts that are used frequently. In accounting, *Sundry* means miscellaneous, so one records entries in the Sundry column when there is no appropriate special column. The accountant posts daily from the Accounts Receivable credit column to the individual charge customers' accounts in the accounts receivable ledger. After posting, he or she puts a check mark (✓) in the Posting Reference column. The accountant also posts the amounts in the Sundry credit column daily. After these entries are posted, the account numbers are recorded in the Posting Reference column. The special columns are posted as totals at the end of the month. After posting, the accountant writes the account numbers in parentheses under the totals.

When a business entity uses a cash payments journal, it *must* record every transaction which results in a credit to cash in this journal. This enables the accountant to determine quickly the balance of the Cash account. It follows that if all incoming cash is recorded in the cash receipts journal, and if all outgoing cash is recorded in the cash payments journal, then one can readily determine the current balance of cash at any time during the month by adding the receipts to the beginning balance of cash and deducting the outgoing payments.

Smaller firms often use a check register as a substitute for the cash payments journal. Either book of original entry may be used by service as well as merchandising enterprises. The posting procedure for both a cash payments journal and a check register is similar to the posting procedure for a cash receipts journal.

In transactions involving trade discounts, one deducts the trade discounts from the list prices to arrive at the selling prices. Both sellers and buyers record the transactions at the selling prices.

Glossary

Bank charge card A bank credit card, like the credit cards used by millions of private citizens. The card holder pays what she or he owes directly to the issuing bank. The business firm deposits the credit card receipts; the amount of the deposit equals the total of the receipts, less a discount deducted by the bank.

Trade discount A substantial reduction from the list or catalog prices of goods, granted by the seller.

Questions

1. Describe the posting procedure for a cash receipts journal with a Sundry Accounts Credit column and several special columns including an Accounts Receivable Credit column.

2. When a cash receipts journal and a cash payments journal are in use, how does one determine the exact balance of cash on a specific date during the month?

3. What does 1/10, n/30 mean?

4. Is the normal balance of Sales Discount a debit or a credit?

5. In a cash receipts journal, both the Accounts Receivable Credit column and the Cash Debit column were erroneously under added by $100. How will this error be discovered?

6. Explain the difference between the handling of delivery costs on merchandise sold and the handling of freight costs on merchandise purchased.

7. What is the difference between a cash discount and a trade discount?

Exercises

Exercise 1 Describe the transactions recorded in the following T accounts.

Cash		Sales Tax Payable		Accounts Receivable		Sales	
416			16	416	416		400

Exercise 2 Record the transactions listed below in general journal form.

Aug. 2 Sold merchandise on account to C. Peters, $900, 2/10, n/30.

4 Issued Credit Memo No. 295 to C. Peters for damaged merchandise, $40.

12 Received a check from Peters in full payment of bill.

Exercise 3 Describe the transactions recorded in the following T accounts.

Cash	Sales Tax Payable	Sales
205.80	10	200

Credit Card Expense
4.20

Exercise 4 Label the blanks as debit or credit.

		CASH RECEIPTS JOURNAL						PAGE _____	
DATE	ACCOUNT CREDITED	POST. REF.	SUNDRY ACCOUNTS	ACCOUNTS REC.	SALES	SALES DISCOUNT	CASH		
1									1
2									2
3									3
4									4
5									5
6									6
7									7
8									8
9									9
10									10
11									11

Exercise 5 Describe the transaction recorded in the following T accounts.

Cash	Accounts Payable			Purchases Discount
784	800	Bal.	800	16

Exercise 6 Record the transactions listed here in general journal form.

Mar. 9 Bought merchandise on account from Packwood Electrical Supply, $1,700, 2/10, n/30.

21 Received a credit memo for $200 for defective goods returned.

Apr. 8 Paid Packwood Electrical Supply in full.

Exercise 7 Label the blanks as debit or credit.

CASH PAYMENTS JOURNAL   PAGE _____

	DATE	CK. NO.	ACCOUNT NAME	POST. REF.	SUNDRY ACCOUNTS	ACCOUNTS PAYABLE	PURCHASES DISCOUNT	CASH	
1									1
2									2
3									3
4									4
5									5
6									6
7									7
8									8
9									9
10									10
11									11
12									12
13									13
14									14
15									15

Exercise 8 Describe the transactions recorded in the following T accounts.

Cash		Accounts Payable		Purchases	
	1,568	200	1,800	1,800	

Purchases Returns and Allowances		Purchases Discount	
	200		32

Problems

Problem 13-1 The Jorgenson Luggage Company, a retail concern, sells on these bases: (1) cash, (2) charge accounts, and (3) bank credit cards. The following transactions involved cash receipts for the firm during April of this year. The state imposes a 4% sales tax on retail sales.

Apr. 6 Total cash sales for the week, $850, plus $34 sales tax.

6 Total sales for the week paid for by bank credit cards, $950, plus $38 sales tax. The bank charges 2% on the total of the actual sales ($988 × .02 = $19.76).

7 B. L. Gault, the owner, invested an additional $3,400.

Apr. 10 Collected cash from Nathan Carey, a charge customer, $54.60.

11 Sold store equipment for cash, at cost, $240.

13 Total cash sales for the week, $1,200, plus $48 sales tax.

13 Total sales for the week paid for by bank credit cards, $750, plus $30 sales tax.

17 Borrowed $5,400 from the bank, receiving cash and giving the bank a promissory note.

19 Collected cash from Ted Boyce, a charge customer, $52.

20 Total sales for the week paid for by bank credit cards, $600, plus $24 sales tax.

20 Total cash sales for the week, $1,600, plus $64 sales tax.

22 Received cash as refund for return of merchandise bought, $82.

24 Collected cash from C. M. Reems, a charge customer, $162.

29 Total sales for the week paid for by bank credit cards, $244, plus $9.76 sales tax.

29 Collected cash from Robert Reynolds, a charge customer, $93.66.

29 Total cash sales for the week, $1,650, plus $66 sales tax.

Instructions
1. Record the transactions in the cash receipts journal.
2. Total and rule the cash receipts journal.
3. Prove the equality of debit and credit totals.

Problem 13-2 Reynolds Company sells candy wholesale, primarily to vending-machine operators. Terms of sales on account are 2/10, n/30, FOB shipping point. The following transactions involving cash receipts and sales of merchandise took place in May of this year.

May 1 Received $980 cash from L. Sparks in payment of April 22 invoice of $1,000, less cash discount.

4 Received $792 cash in payment of a $720 note receivable and interest of $72.

7 Received $686 cash from K. L. Valdez in payment of April 29 invoice of $700, less cash discount.

8 Sold merchandise on account to D. Brady, Invoice No. 272, $486.

16 Cash sales for first half of May, $3,284.

17 Received cash from D. Brady in payment of Invoice No. 272, less cash discount.

20 Received $321 cash from Ralph Riley in payment of April 16 invoice; no discount.

21 Sold merchandise on account to R. O. Eastwood, Invoice No. 285, $836.

May 24 Received $318 cash refund for return of defective equipment bought in April for cash.

    27 Sold merchandise on account to E. A. Kielmeyer, Invoice No. 292, $540.

    31 Cash sales for second half of May, $3,462.

Instructions **1.** Journalize the transactions for May in the cash receipts journal and the sales journal.

2. Total and rule the journals.

Problem 13-3 The Murphy Bookshop uses a check register to keep track of expenditures. The following transactions occurred during February of this year.

Feb. 3 Issued Check No. 4312, $705.60, to Kirkpatrick Publishers for the amount of their Invoice No. 68172 for $720, less 2% cash discount (previously recorded).

    4 Paid freight bill to Keller Express Company, $48, for books purchased, issuing Check No. 4313.

    6 Paid rent for the month, $320; Check No. 4314, to Moore Land Company.

   11 Paid for advertising in Campus News, $58, Check No. 4315.

   11 Paid New England Book Company $930.60, Check No. 4316, for their Invoice No. A3322 for $940 less 1% cash discount (previously recorded).

   17 Paid wages for first half of February, $480; Check No. 4317 (previously recorded).

   21 C. N. Murphy, the owner, withdrew $300 for personal use; Check No. 4318.

   26 Made payment on bank loan, $550; Check No. 4319, consisting of $500 on the principal and $50 interest, Coast National Bank.

   27 Paid Garrett Publishing Company $926, Check No. 4320, for their Invoice No. 7768 (no discount, previously recorded).

   28 Voided Check No. 4321.

   28 Paid wages expense for second half of February, $480; Check No. 4322 (previously recorded).

Instructions **1.** Record the transactions in the check register.

2. Total and rule the check register.

3. Prove the equality of the debit and credit totals.

Problem 13-4 The following transactions were completed by Arrow Electronics Supply during January, which is the first month of this fiscal year. Terms of sale are 2/10, n/30.

Jan. 2 Paid rent for the month, $600; Check No. 6981.

Jan. 2 J. M. Troutman, the owner, invested an additional $2,200 in the business.

4 Bought merchandise on account from Vance and Company, $2,840; their Invoice No. A691, 2/10, n/30, dated January 2.

4 Received check from Vernon Appliance for $980 in payment of $1,000 invoice, less discount.

4 Sold merchandise on account, to F. R. Palmer, $750, Invoice No. 6483.

6 Received check from Patrick and Randall for $637 in payment of $650 invoice less discount.

7 Issued Check No. 6982, $490, to Finley and Lynch, in payment of their Invoice No. C1272 for $500 less discount.

7 Bought supplies on account from Dunlap Office Supply, $98, their Invoice No. 1906B.

7 Sold merchandise on account to Ellison and Clark, $890, Invoice No. 6484.

9 Issued Credit Memo No. 43 to F. R. Palmer, $50, for merchandise returned.

11 Cash sales for January 1 to 10, $4,514.

11 Paid Vance and Company $2,783.20; Check No. 6983, in payment of $2,840 invoice, less discount.

14 Sold merchandise on account to Vernon Appliance, $1,950, Invoice No. 6485.

18 Bought merchandise on account from Cascade Products, $4,930; their Invoice No. 7281D, 2/10, n/60, dated January 16.

21 Issued Check No. 6984, $282, for advertising.

21 Cash sales for January 11 to 20, $3,990.

23 Paid Cook Fast Freight, Check No. 6985, $86, for transportation of merchandise purchased.

23 Received Credit Memo No. 163, $425, from Cascade Products for merchandise returned.

29 Sold merchandise on account to Burns Supply, $1,940, Invoice No. 6486.

31 Cash sales, January 21 to 31, $4,428.

31 Issued Check No. 6986 for $49, for miscellaneous expenses.

31 Recorded payroll entry from the payroll register: total salaries, $6,100; employees' income tax withheld, $854; FICA tax withheld, $366.

31 Recorded the payroll taxes: FICA, $366; state unemployment tax, $244; federal unemployment tax, $30.

31 Issued Check No. 6987, $4,880, for salaries for the month.

31 J. M. Troutman, the owner, withdrew $950 for personal use, Check No. 6988.

Instructions **1.** Record the transactions for January, using a sales journal, page 73; a purchases journal, page 56; a cash receipts journal, page 38; a cash payments journal, page 45; a general journal, page 100. The chart of accounts is shown on the next page.

111 Cash
113 Accounts Receivable
114 Merchandise Inventory
115 Supplies
116 Prepaid Insurance
121 Equipment

211 Accounts Payable
215 Salaries Payable
216 Employees' Income Tax Payable
217 FICA Tax Payable
218 State Unemployment Tax Payable
219 Federal Unemployment Tax Payable

311 J. M. Troutman, Capital
312 J. M. Troutman, Drawing

411 Sales
412 Sales Returns and Allowances
413 Sales Discount

511 Purchases
512 Purchases Discount
513 Purchases Returns and Allowances
521 Salaries Expense
522 Payroll Tax Expense
527 Rent Expense
531 Miscellaneous Expense

2. Post daily those entries involving the Sundry columns and the general journal to the accounts receivable ledger, the accounts payable ledger, and the general ledger; also post daily the entries in the Sundry columns of the special journals.

3. Add the columns of the special journals, and prove the equality of debit totals and credit totals on scratch paper.

4. Post the appropriate totals of the special journals to the general ledger.

5. Prepare a trial balance.

6. Prepare a schedule of accounts receivable and a schedule of accounts payable. Do the totals equal the balances of the related controlling accounts?

Alternate problems

Problem 13-1A The Kellogg Luggage Company, a retail store, sells on these bases: (1) cash, (2) charge accounts, and (3) bank credit cards. The following transactions involve cash receipts for the firm for March of this year. The state imposes a 4% sales tax on retail sales. (Kellogg Luggage uses a tax table to determine the amount of sales tax for cash sales, so the sales tax they collect does not exactly equal 4% of taxable sales.)

Mar. 7 Total cash sales for the week, $950, plus $38 sales tax.

7 Total sales from bank credit cards for the week, $850, plus $34 sales tax. The bank charges 2% on the total of the actual sale ($884 × .02 = $17.68).

11 D. S. Fowler, the owner, invested an additional $3,126.

12 Sold office equipment for cash, at cost, $246.

12 Collected cash from Nathan Conner, a charge customer, $54.29.

Mar. 14 Total cash sales for the week, $1,388.62, plus $55.54 sales tax.

14 Total sales for the week on the basis of bank credit cards, $840, plus $33.60 sales tax.

18 Collected cash from Douglas Cook, a charge customer, $88.25.

19 Borrowed $4,960 from the bank, receiving cash and giving the bank a promissory note.

21 Total cash sales for the week, $1,738, plus $69.52 sales tax.

21 Total sales from bank credit cards for the week, $832, plus $33.28 sales tax.

22 Collected cash from S. G. Farley, a charge customer, $193.75.

24 Kellogg Luggage received cash as a refund for the return of merchandise they purchased, $248.

27 Collected cash from Norbert Gorton, a charge customer, $92.48.

30 Total sales from bank credit cards for the week, $244.60, plus $9.78 sales tax.

30 Total cash sales for the week, $1,997.24, plus $79.83 sales tax.

Instructions   **1.** Record the transactions in the cash receipts journal.

2. Total and rule the cash receipts journal.

3. Prove the equality of debit and credit totals.

Problem 13-2A The J. E. Johnson Company sells candy wholesale, primarily to vending-machine operators. Terms of sales on account are 2/10, n/30, FOB shipping point. The following transactions involving cash receipts and sales of merchandise took place in May of this year.

May 2 Received $686 cash from N. Lewis in payment of April 23 invoice of $700, less cash discount.

5 Received $990 cash in payment of $900 note receivable and interest of $90.

8 Sold merchandise on account to G. Lindsay, Invoice No. 862, $420.

9 Received $784 in cash from Steven Dole in payment of April 30 invoice of $800, less cash discount.

15 Received cash from G. Lindsay in payment of Invoice No. 862, less discount.

16 Cash sales for first half of May, $3,447.

19 Received $253 in cash from Randy Hunt in payment of April 14 invoice, no discount.

22 Sold merchandise on account to T. B. Anderson, Invoice No. 887, $585.

25 Received $326 cash refund for return of defective equipment bought in April for cash.

28 Sold merchandise on account to M. E. Alvarez, Invoice No. 910, $728.

31 Cash sales for the second half of May, $3,394.

Instructions **1.** Journalize the transactions for May in the cash receipts journal and the sales journal.

2. Total and rule the journals.

Problem 13-3A The Thompson Bookstore uses a check register to keep track of expenditures. The following transactions occurred during February of the year.

Feb. 1 Issued Check No. 4311 to Brewster Book Company for their Invoice No. 3113E; $640 less cash discount of $12.80, $627.20 (previously recorded).

    2 Paid freight bill to Brender Express Company, $53, for merchandise purchased, issuing Check No. 4312.

    4 Paid rent for month of February, $345; Check No. 4313, to Stanford Realty.

    9 Paid for advertising in Campus News, $48, Check No. 4314.

    10 Paid National Publishing Company $990, Check No. 4315, for their Invoice No. D642 in the amount of $1,000 less 1% cash discount (previously recorded).

    15 Paid wages for first half of month, $538; Check No. 4316 (previously recorded).

    19 R. Dearborn, the owner, withdrew $500 for personal use; Check No. 4317.

    25 Made payment on bank loan, $930; Check No. 4318, consisting of $900 on principal and $30 interest, Fenway National Bank.

    27 Issued to Piedmont Publishing Company, Check No. 4319, $429, for their Invoice No. 6317 (no discount, previously recorded).

    28 Voided Check No. 4320.

    28 Paid wages for second half of month, $538; Check No. 4321 (previously recorded).

    28 Received and paid telephone bill, $56; Check No. 4322, payable to Southeast Telephone Company.

Instructions **1.** Record the transactions in the check register.

2. Total and rule the check register.

3. Prove the equality of the debit and credit totals.

Problem 13-4A The following transactions were completed by Arrow Electronics Supply during January, the first month of this fiscal year. Terms of sale are 2/10, n/30.

Jan. 2 Paid rent for month, $550; Check No. 6981.

    2 J. M. Troutman, the owner, invested an additional $2,240 in the business.

    4 Bought merchandise on account from Vance and Company, $2,710; their Invoice No. A691, 2/10, n/30, dated January 2.

Jan. 4 Received check from Vernon Appliance for $980 in payment of invoice for $1,000, less discount.

4 Sold merchandise on account to F. R. Palmer, $650, Invoice No. 6483.

6 Received check from Patrick and Randall for $637 in payment of $650 invoice, less discount.

7 Issued Check No. 6982, $588, to Finley and Lynch, in payment of their Invoice No. C1271, for $600, less discount.

7 Bought supplies on account from Dunlap Office Supply, $84.80, their Invoice No. 1906B.

7 Sold merchandise on account to Ellison and Clark, $850, Invoice No. 6484.

9 Issued Credit Memo No. 43 to F. R. Palmer, $30, for merchandise returned.

11 Cash sales for January 1 to 10, $4,442.60.

11 Paid Vance and Company $2,655.80; Check No. 6983, in payment of their $2,710 invoice, less discount.

14 Sold merchandise on account to Vernon Appliance, $1,900, Invoice No. 6485.

14 Received check from F. R. Palmer, $607.60, in payment of $650 invoice, less return of $30 and less discount.

18 Bought merchandise on account from Cascade Products, $3,740; their Invoice No. 7281D, 2/10, n/60, dated January 16.

21 Issued Check No. 6984, $265, for advertising.

21 Cash sales for January 11 to 20, $3,565.

23 Received Credit Memo No. 163, $96, from Cascade Products for merchandise returned.

23 Paid Cook Fast Freight, Check No. 6985, $78, for transportation of merchandise purchased.

29 Sold merchandise on account to Burns Supply, $1,864; Invoice No. 6486.

31 Cash sales for January 21 to 31, $3,987.

31 Issued Check No. 6986, $45, for miscellaneous expenses.

31 Recorded payroll entry from the payroll register: total salaries, $5,800; employees' income tax withheld, $812; FICA tax withheld, $348.

31 Recorded the payroll taxes: FICA, $348; state unemployment tax, $232; federal unemployment tax, $29.

31 Issued Check No. 6987, $4,640, for salaries for the month.

31 J. M. Troutman, the owner, withdrew $970 for personal use, Check No. 6988.

Instructions **1.** Record the transactions for January, using a sales journal, page 91; a purchases journal, page 74; a cash receipts journal, page 56; a cash payments journal, page 63; a general journal, page 119. The chart of accounts is shown on the next page.

111 Cash
113 Accounts Receivable
114 Merchandise Inventory
115 Supplies
116 Prepaid Insurance
121 Equipment

211 Accounts Payable
215 Salaries Payable
216 Employees' Income Tax Payable
217 FICA Tax Payable
218 State Unemployment Tax Payable
219 Federal Unemployment Tax Payable

311 J. M. Troutman, Capital
312 J. M. Troutman, Drawing

411 Sales
412 Sales Returns and Allowances
413 Sales Discount

511 Purchases
512 Purchases Discount
513 Purchases Returns and Allowances
521 Salaries Expense
522 Payroll Tax Expense
527 Rent Expense
531 Miscellaneous Expense

2. Post daily those entries involving the Sundry columns and the general journal to the accounts receivable ledger, the accounts payable ledger, and the general ledger; also post daily the entries in the Sundry columns of the special journals.

3. Add the columns of the special journals, and prove the equality of debit totals and credit totals on scratch paper.

4. Post the appropriate totals of the special journals to the general ledger.

5. Prepare a trial balance.

6. Prepare a schedule of accounts receivable and a schedule of accounts payable. Do the totals equal the balances of the related controlling accounts?

14

Work sheet and adjusting entries for a merchandising business

objectives

After you have completed this chapter, you will be able to do the following:
- Complete a work sheet for a merchandising business involving adjustments for merchandise inventory, depreciation, expired insurance, supplies used, accrued wages or salaries, and unearned revenue.
- Journalize the adjusting entries for a merchandising business.

FOR QUITE some time we've been talking about the way to keep special journals and accounts when one is dealing with a merchandising enterprise. Now let's take another step forward in the accounting cycle for a merchandising business: *adjustments* and *work sheets*.

The columnar classifications and procedures for completing the work sheet are basically the same as those described in Chapter 5. A merchandising business—like a service business—requires adjustments for supplies used, expired insurance, depreciation, and accrued wages. However, there is an additional adjustment that applies exclusively to a merchandising enterprise: the adjustment for merchandise inventory. Still another adjustment, which could apply to either a merchandising or a service business, is the adjustment for unearned revenue. Note that doing away with the Adjusted Trial Balance columns reduces the size of the work sheet. This chapter will also discuss the work sheet with respect to the handling of the specialized accounts of a merchandising business.

Adjustment for merchandise inventory

In Chapter 11, when we introduced the Merchandise Inventory account, we put it under the heading of assets, and said that the balance of the account should be changed only when a physical inventory has been taken. This is consistent with a system of periodic inventories in which one records purchase of merchandise as a debit to Purchases, for the amount of the cost, and sale of merchandise as a credit to Sales, for the amount of the selling price.

Consider this example: A firm has a balance of Merchandise Inventory of $18,000, which represents the value of the inventory at the beginning of the fiscal period. Then at the end of the fiscal period, the firm takes an actual count of the stock on hand, and determines the value of the ending inventory to be $22,000. Naturally, in any business, goods are constantly being bought, sold, and replaced. Evidently the reason why the value of the ending inventory is larger than that of the beginning inventory is that the firm bought a greater amount than it sold. When we adjust the Merchandise Inventory account, we want to install the new figure of $22,000 in the account. We do this by a two-step process.

Step 1 Eliminate or close the Merchandise Inventory account into Income Summary by the amount of the beginning inventory.

Let's look at this entry in the form of T accounts.

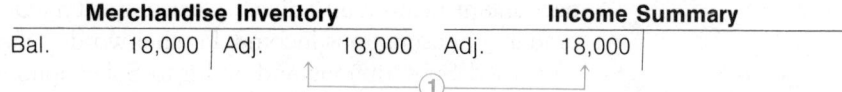

Merchandise Inventory				Income Summary	
Bal.	18,000	Adj.	18,000	Adj.	18,000

We handle this the same way we handle the closing of any other account, by balancing off the account, or making the balance equal to zero. This is why we enter it as a credit to Merchandise Inventory. Now we do the opposite to Income Summary, which is a debit to this account.

Step 2 Enter the ending Merchandise Inventory, because one must record on the books the cost of the asset remaining on hand.

Let's repeat the T accounts and Step 1.

Merchandise Inventory				Income Summary			
Bal.	18,000	Adj.	18,000	Adj.	18,000	Adj.	22,000
Adj.	22,000						

Here we debit Merchandise Inventory because this is the plus side of the account, and we do the opposite to Income Summary, which is, of course, a credit.

The reason we adjust the Merchandise Inventory account in these two steps is that both the beginning and the ending figures appear separately in the income statement, which is prepared directly from the Income Statement columns of the work sheet. Adjusting the inventory this way is considered to be more meaningful than taking a shortcut and adjusting for the difference between the beginning and the ending inventory values, since the amount of the difference does not appear as a distinct figure in the income statement.

Adjustment for unearned revenue

Let us now introduce another adjusting entry: unearned revenue. As we said, this entry could pertain to a service as well as to a merchandising business. Occasionally, cash is received in advance for services to be performed in the future. For example, a dormitory receives a semester's rent in advance, a dining hall sells meal tickets in advance, a concert association sells season tickets in advance, a magazine receives subscriptions in advance, or an insurance company receives premiums in advance. If the amounts received by each of these types of organizations will be earned during the present fiscal period, the amounts should be credited to revenue accounts. On the other hand, if the amounts received will *not* be earned during the present fiscal period, the amounts should be credited to unearned revenue accounts. An unearned revenue account is classified as a liability, because an organization is liable for the amount received in advance until it is earned.

To illustrate, assume that Mark Publishing Company receives $60,000 in cash for subscriptions covering two years and records them originally as debits to Cash and credits to Unearned Subscriptions. At the end of the year, Mark finds that $44,000 of the subscriptions have been earned. Accordingly, Mark's accountant records an adjusting entry, debiting Unearned Subscriptions and crediting Subscriptions Income. In other words, take the earned portion out of Unearned Subscriptions and add it to Subscriptions Income. By T accounts, the situation looks like this.

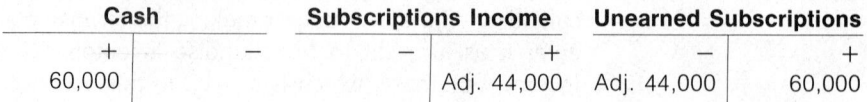

Cash		Subscriptions Income		Unearned Subscriptions	
+	−	−	+	−	+
60,000			Adj. 44,000	Adj. 44,000	60,000

As another example, suppose that North Central Plumbing Supply rents desk space to a manufacturer's representative for $150 per month. On November 1, he pays North Central $450 for 3 months' rent in advance. Because North Central's present fiscal period ends on December 31, the 3 months' rent received in advance will not be earned during this fiscal period. So North Central's accountant records the transaction as a debit to Cash of $450 and a credit to Unearned Rent of $450. On December 31, because 2 months' rent has now been earned, their accountant must make an adjusting entry to transfer $300 from Unearned Rent to Rent Income. By T accounts the situation looks like this:

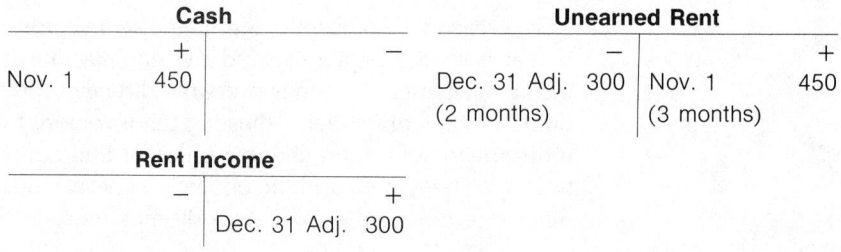

Cash		Unearned Rent	
+	−	−	+
Nov. 1 450		Dec. 31 Adj. 300	Nov. 1 450
		(2 months)	(3 months)

Rent Income	
−	+
	Dec. 31 Adj. 300

To review the accounts of North Central Plumbing Supply, the chart of accounts is presented below. The account-number arrangement will be discussed in Chapter 15.

Assets (100–199)

111 Cash
112 Notes Receivable
113 Accounts Receivable
114 Merchandise Inventory
115 Supplies
116 Prepaid Insurance
121 Equipment
122 Accumulated Depreciation, Equipment
125 Building
126 Accumulated Depreciation, Building
127 Land

Liabilities (200–299)

211 Notes Payable
212 Accounts Payable
213 Wages Payable
217 Unearned Rent
221 Mortgage Payable

Owner's Equity (300–399)

311 Robert C. Randall, Capital
312 Robert C. Randall, Drawing
313 Income Summary

Revenue (400–499)	Expenses (500–599)
411 Sales	511 Purchases
412 Sales Discount	512 Purchases Discount
413 Sales Returns and Allowances	513 Purchases Returns and Allowances
421 Rent Income	521 Wages Expense
422 Interest Income	522 Depreciation Expense, Equipment
	523 Supplies Expense
	531 Depreciation Expense, Building
	532 Taxes Expense
	533 Insurance Expense

Let's demonstrate the adjustments by first looking at the trial balance section of North Central Plumbing Supply's work sheet.

ACCOUNT NAME	TRIAL BALANCE		ADJUSTMENTS	
	DEBIT	CREDIT	DEBIT	CREDIT
Cash	10 9 6 1 00			
Notes Receivable	2 0 0 0 00			
Accounts Receivable	14 6 8 0 00			
Merchandise Inventory	31 5 0 0 00			
Supplies	7 2 0 00			
Prepaid Insurance	4 8 0 00			
Equipment	16 8 0 0 00			
Accum. Depr., Equipment		8 2 0 0 00		
Building	50 0 0 0 00			
Accum. Depr., Building		16 0 0 0 00		
Land	6 0 0 0 00			
Notes Payable		1 5 0 0 00		
Accounts Payable		18 2 0 0 00		
Unearned Revenue		4 5 0 00		
Mortgage Payable		4 0 0 0 00		
Robert C. Randall, Capital		73 2 8 7 00		
Robert C. Randall, Drawing	9 6 0 0 00			
Sales		88 0 9 0 00		
Sales Discount	9 4 0 00			
Sales Returns and Allowances	4 2 0 00			
Interest Income		6 0 00		
Purchases	42 8 0 0 00			
Purchases Discount		6 2 4 00		
Purchases Returns and Allowances		4 1 6 00		
Wages Expense	22 9 0 0 00			
Taxes Expense	9 8 0 00			
Interest Expense	4 6 00			
	210 8 2 7 00	210 8 2 7 00		

Data for the adjustments

The data that will be used for adjustments is as follows:

a.–b. Ending merchandise inventory, $29,400

c. Rent earned, $300

d. Ending supplies inventory, $206

e. Insurance expired, $160

f. Additional year's depreciation of equipment, $2,400

g. Additional year's depreciation of building, $2,000

h. Additional wages owed to employees but not paid at end of year, $610

At first glance, listing the adjustment data appears to be a relatively minor task. However, in a business situation, as we said before, one must take actual physical counts of the inventories, and match them up with the costs. One has to check insurance policies to determine the amount of insurance that has expired. Finally, one has to write off or depreciate, in a systematic manner, the cost of equipment and building. Incidentally, for income tax purposes, land cannot be depreciated. Even if the building and the lot were bought as one package for one price, one must separate the value of the building from the value of the land. For real estate taxes, the county assessor appraises the building and the land separately. If there is no other qualified appraisal available, one can use the assessor's ratio or percentage as a basis for separating building value and land value.

Now let's look at the data for these adjustments in the form of T accounts.

Merchandise Inventory				Income Summary			
	+		–	**(a)**	31,500	**(b)**	29,400
Bal.	31,500	**(a)**	31,500				
(b)	29,400						

Unearned Rent				Rent Income			
	–		+		–		+
(c)	300	Bal.	450			**(c)**	300

Supplies				Supplies Expense			
	+		–		+		–
Bal.	720	**(d)**	514	**(d)**	514		

Prepaid Insurance				Insurance Expense			
	+		–		+		–
Bal.	480	**(e)**	160	**(e)**	160		

Accumulated Depreciation, Equipment				Depreciation Expense, Equipment			
	–		+		+		–
		Bal.	8,200	**(f)**	2,400		
		(f)	2,400				

Accumulated Depreciation, Building

−	+	
	Bal.	16,000
	(g)	2,000

Depreciation Expense, Building

+		−
(g)	2,000	

Wages Expense

+		−
Bal.	22,900	
(h)	610	

Wages Payable

−	+	
	(h)	610

We now record these in the Adjustments column of the work sheet, using the same letters in identifying the adjustments, as follows.

ACCOUNT NAME	TRIAL BALANCE DEBIT	TRIAL BALANCE CREDIT	ADJUSTMENTS DEBIT	ADJUSTMENTS CREDIT
Cash	10 961 00			
Notes Receivable	2 000 00			
Accounts Receivable	14 680 00			
Merchandise Inventory	31 500 00		(b)29 400 00	(a)31 500 00
Supplies	720 00			(d) 514 00
Prepaid Insurance	480 00			(e) 160 00
Equipment	16 800 00			
Accum. Depr., Equipment		8 200 00		(f) 2 400 00
Building	50 000 00			
Accum. Depr., Building		16 000 00		(g) 2 000 00
Land	6 000 00			
Notes Payable		1 500 00		
Accounts Payable		18 200 00		
Unearned Rent		450 00	(c) 300 00	
Mortgage Payable		4 000 00		
Robert C. Randall, Capital		73 287 00		
Robert C. Randall, Drawing	9 600 00			
Sales		88 090 00		
Sales Discount	940 00			
Sales Returns and Allowances	420 00			
Interest Income		60 00		
Purchases	42 800 00			
Purchases Discount		624 00		
Purchases Returns and Allowances		416 00		
Wages Expense	22 900 00		(h) 610 00	
Taxes Expense	980 00			
Interest Expense	46 00			
	210 827 00	210 827 00		

Account	Adjustments Debit	Adjustments Credit
Income Summary	(a) 31 5 00 00	(b) 29 4 00 00
Rent Income		(c) 3 00 00
Supplies Expense	(d) 5 1 4 00	
Insurance Expense	(e) 1 6 0 00	
Depreciation Expense, Equipment	(f) 2 4 00 00	
Depreciation Expense, Building	(g) 2 0 00 00	
Wages Payable		(h) 6 1 0 00
	66 8 8 4 00	66 8 8 4 00

Completion of the work sheet

Now we carry the account balances from the Trial Balance and Adjustments columns directly to the Income Statement and Balance Sheet columns. In the interest of efficiency, we do away with the Adjusted Trial Balance columns. It was worth our while to include these columns in the earlier presentation because they acted as a teaching device, and as an intermediate checkpoint to prove that the accounts were in balance before we carried them forward to the Income Statement and Balance Sheet columns. However, obviously the Adjusted Trial Balance columns are not necessary in order for one to complete the work sheet. Business practice requires that accounting be done by the most efficient and economical means, and therefore one eliminates the Adjusted Trial Balance columns.

Observe in particular the way we carry forward the figures for Merchandise Inventory and Income Summary. *Income Summary is the only account in which we don't combine the debit and credit figures;* instead we carry them into the Income Statement columns as *two distinct figures.* As we said, the reason is that both figures appear in the income statement itself. We'll talk about this more in Chapter 15.

When you are developing the work sheet, complete one stage at a time, as in the following illustration:

1. Record the trial balance, and make sure that the total of the Debit column equals the total of the Credit column.

2. Record the adjustments in the Adjustments columns, and make sure that the totals are equal.

3. Complete the Income Statement and Balance Sheet columns by recording the adjusted balance of each account, as indicated by the following classification of accounts.

Income Statement		Balance Sheet	
Debit	**Credit**	**Debit**	**Credit**
		A	L
		+	+
E	R	Drawing	Cap.
			+
			Accum.
			Deprec.

The completed work sheet would look like the one illustrated on pages 360–361. Study the illustration, noting especially the way we treat these special accounts for a merchandising business:

	Location in Work Sheet			
	Income Statement		Balance Sheet	
Account Name	**Debit**	**Credit**	**Debit**	**Credit**
Merchandise Inventory			29,400	
Sales		88,090		
Sales Discount	940			
Sales Returns and Allowances	420			
Purchases	42,800			
Purchases Discount		624		
Purchases Returns and Allowances		416		
Income Summary	31,500	29,400		

ACCOUNT NAME	TRIAL BALANCE DEBIT	TRIAL BALANCE CREDIT	ADJUSTMENTS DEBIT	ADJUSTMENTS CREDIT
Cash	10 9 6 1 00			
Notes Receivable	2 0 0 0 00			
Accounts Receivable	14 6 8 0 00			
Merchandise Inventory	31 5 0 0 00		(b) 29 4 0 0 00	(a) 31 5 0 0 00
Supplies	7 2 0 00			(d) 5 1 4 00
Prepaid Insurance	4 8 0 00			(e) 1 6 0 00
Equipment	16 8 0 0 00			
Accum. Depr., Equipment		8 2 0 0 00		(f) 2 4 0 0 00
Building	50 0 0 0 00			
Accum. Depr., Building		16 0 0 0 00		(g) 2 0 0 0 00
Land	6 0 0 0 00			
Notes Payable		1 5 0 0 00		
Accounts Payable		18 2 0 0 00		
Unearned Rent		4 5 0 00	(c) 3 0 0 00	
Mortgage Payable		4 0 0 0 00		
Robert C. Randall, Capital		73 2 8 7 00		
Robert C. Randall, Drawing	9 6 0 0 00			
Sales		88 0 9 0 00		
Sales Discount	9 4 0 00			
Sales Returns and Allowances	4 2 0 00			
Interest Income		6 0 00		
Purchases	42 8 0 0 00			
Purchases Discount		6 2 4 00		
Purchases Returns and Allowances		4 1 6 00		
Wages Expense	22 9 0 0 00		(h) 6 1 0 00	
Taxes Expense	9 8 0 00			
Interest Expense	4 6 00			
	210 8 2 7 00	210 8 2 7 00		
Income Summary			(a) 31 5 0 0 00	(b) 29 4 0 0 00
Rent Income				(c) 3 0 0 00
Supplies Expense			(d) 5 1 4 00	
Insurance Expense			(e) 1 6 0 00	
Depreciation, Expense, Equipment			(f) 2 4 0 0 00	
Depreciation Expense, Building			(g) 2 0 0 0 00	
Wages Payable				(h) 6 1 0 00
			66 8 8 4 00	66 8 8 4 00
Net Income				

INCOME STATEMENT		BALANCE SHEET	
DEBIT	CREDIT	DEBIT	CREDIT
		10 961 00	
		2 000 00	
		14 680 00	
		29 400 00	
		206 00	
		320 00	
		16 800 00	
			10 600 00
		50 000 00	
			18 000 00
		6 000 00	
			1 500 00
			18 200 00
			4 000 00
			73 287 00
		9 600 00	
	88 090 00		
940 00			
420 00			
	60 00		
42 800 00			
	624 00		
	416 00		
23 510 00			
980 00			
46 00			
3 150 00	2 940 00		
	300 00		150 00
514 00			
160 00			
240 00			
200 00			
			610 00
105 270 00	118 890 00	139 967 00	126 347 00
13 620 00			13 620 00
118 890 00	118 890 00	139 967 00	139 967 00

Here's the way the adjusting entries look, as taken from the Adjustments column of the work sheet.

GENERAL JOURNAL   PAGE 96

	DATE		DESCRIPTION	POST REF.	DEBIT	CREDIT	
1			*Adjusting Entries*				1
2	19– Dec.	31	Income Summary		31 5 0 0 00		2
3			Merchandise Inventory			31 5 0 0 00	3
4							4
5		31	Merchandise Inventory		29 4 0 0 00		5
6			Income Summary			29 4 0 0 00	6
7							7
8		31	Unearned Rent		3 0 0 00		8
9			Rent Income			3 0 0 00	9
10							10
11		31	Supplies Expense		5 1 4 00		11
12			Supplies			5 1 4 00	12
13							13
14		31	Insurance Expense		1 6 0 00		14
15			Prepaid Insurance			1 6 0 00	15
16							16
17		31	Depreciation Expense, Equipment		2 4 0 0 00		17
18			Accumulated Depreciation, Equipment			2 4 0 0 00	18
19							19
20		31	Depreciation Expense, Building		2 0 0 0 00		20
21			Accumulated Depreciation, Building			2 0 0 0 00	21
22							22
23		31	Wages Expense		6 1 0 00		23
24			Wages Payable			6 1 0 00	24
25							25

Summary

The work sheet is a device accountants use to organize the account balances so that they can prepare the income statement and the balance sheet. Typical adjustments that affect both service and merchandising firms are the recording of supplies used, insurance expired, depreciation of equipment and buildings, accrued wages, and unearned revenue. Merchandising firms have an additional adjustment for Merchandise Inventory. The companion account in this adjusting entry is Income Summary. Adjusting the Merchandise Inventory account is a two-step process. First, eliminate or close the beginning inventory. Second, restate, or add on, the ending inventory, in order to record the current balance of the account. In the work sheet, carry the

Income Summary account as two separate figures from the Adjustments columns into the Income Statement columns.

Glossary

Physical inventory An actual count of the stock of goods on hand; also referred to as a *periodic inventory*.

Unearned revenue Revenue received in advance for services to be performed later; considered to be a liability until the revenue is earned.

Questions

1. Explain the two-step process for adjusting merchandise inventory.

2. What is the difference between merchandise inventory and supplies?

3. What is a physical, or periodic, inventory?

4. For a firm using a system of periodic inventories, which inventory (beginning merchandise or ending merchandise) appears in the firm's trial balance at the end of the fiscal period?

5. On the income summary line of a work sheet, $31,500 appears in the Income Statement Debit column and $29,400 appears in the Income Statement Credit column. Which figure represents the beginning merchandise inventory?

6. In which column of the work sheet is Sales Discount recorded?

7. When a dormitory received a semester's rent in advance, an entry was made debiting Cash and crediting Unearned Rent. At the end of the year, a large portion of the rent has been earned. What adjusting entry would you suggest?

Exercises

Exercise 1 The beginning inventory of a merchandising business was $54,000, and the ending inventory is $80,000. What entries are needed at the end of the fiscal period to adjust Merchandise Inventory?

Exercise 2 List the following in all the columns in which they appear in the work sheet (with the exception of the Adjustments column): Expenses, Accumulated Depreciation, Liabilities, Drawing, Assets, Net Income (*Example:* Capital).

Trial Balance		Adjustments		Income Statement		Balance Sheet	
Debit	**Credit**	**Debit**	**Credit**	**Debit**	**Credit**	**Debit**	**Credit**
	Capital						Capital

Exercise 3 From the ledger account for Supplies shown on page 364, journalize the complete entries from which each of the items identified by journal reference was posted.

ACCOUNT _____ *Supplies* _____ ACCOUNT NO. _126_

DATE		ITEM	POST. REF.	DEBIT	CREDIT	BALANCE DEBIT	BALANCE CREDIT
19– Jan.	1	Balance	✓			1 4 0 0 00	
Apr.	20		CP41	4 0 0 00		1 8 0 0 00	
Sep.	28		CP63	2 0 0 00		2 0 0 0 00	
Dec.	31	Adjusting	J91		7 0 0 00	1 3 0 0 00	

Exercise 4 Determine the annual amount of depreciation on each of the following:

a. A building costing $75,000, expected life of 25 years, no salvage value at the end of 25 years; use the straight-line method.

b. Office equipment costing $6,000, expected life of 5 years, trade-in value of $500 at the end of 5 years; use the straight-line method.

Exercise 5 Determine the amount of expired insurance for the fiscal year, January 1 through December 31, from the following account.

ACCOUNT _____ *Prepaid Insurance* _____ ACCOUNT NO. _118_

DATE		ITEM	POST. REF.	DEBIT	CREDIT	BALANCE DEBIT	BALANCE CREDIT
19– Jan.	1	Balance (4 mo.)	✓			4 8 0 00	
May	1	(12 months)	CP59	1 6 8 0 00		2 1 6 0 00	

Exercise 6 In the Income Statement columns of the work sheet, we record the Income Summary account as $70,000 in the debit column and $76,000 in the credit column. Identify the beginning and ending merchandise inventory.

Exercise 7 From the ledger account for Wages Expense, journalize the complete entry from which each of the items identified by number was posted.

ACCOUNT _____ *Wages Expense* _____ ACCOUNT NO. _514_

DATE		ITEM	POST. REF.	DEBIT	CREDIT	BALANCE DEBIT	BALANCE CREDIT
19– Dec.	28	(1)	CP39	2 6 0 0 00		92 5 0 0 00	
	31	(2)	J42	8 0 0 00		93 3 0 0 00	
	31	(3)	J43		93 3 0 0 00	— — — —	— — — —

Problems

Problem 14-1 The trial balance of Parkside Variety as of December 31, the end of their current fiscal year, is as follows.

Parkside Variety		
Trial Balance		
December 31, 19–		
Cash	9 563 92	
Merchandise Inventory	63 522 84	
Store Supplies	1 441 12	
Prepaid Insurance	960 00	
Store Equipment	37 480 00	
Accumulated Depreciation, Store Equipment		24 320 00
Accounts Payable		14 578 80
Sales Tax Payable		243 36
M. L. Severson, Capital		55 630 00
M. L. Severson, Drawing	29 440 00	
Sales		179 036 74
Sales Returns and Allowances	1 443 04	
Purchases	81 243 46	
Purchases Discount		1 497 90
Purchases Returns and Allowances		1 878 94
Salary Expense	36 658 80	
Rent Expense	14 400 00	
Miscellaneous Expense	1 032 56	
	277 185 74	277 185 74

Here are the data for the adjustments.

a.–b. Merchandise Inventory at December 31, $66,832.56.

c. Supplies inventory, $396.40.

d. Insurance expired, $360.

e. Salaries accrued, $563.

f. Depreciation of store equipment, $3,880.

Instructions Complete the work sheet.

Problem 14-2 The balances of the ledger accounts of Osborn Sporting Goods as of December 31, the end of their fiscal year, are as follows.

Cash	$ 11,592
Accounts Receivable	42,962
Merchandise Inventory	121,838
Supplies	1,570
Prepaid Insurance	1,628
Store Equipment	36,924
Accumulated Depreciation, Store Equipment	29,420
Office Equipment	9,436
Accumulated Depreciation, Office Equipment	1,720
Notes Payable	4,000
Accounts Payable	30,822
Wages Payable	—
Unearned Rent	3,200
J. L. Osborn, Capital	120,532
J. L. Osborn, Drawing	28,000
Income Summary	—
Sales	952,000
Sales Returns and Allowances	9,748
Rent Income	—
Purchases	543,098
Purchases Discount	7,634
Purchases Returns and Allowances	13,440
Wages Expense	55,200
Depreciation Expense, Store Equipment	—
Depreciation Expense, Office Equipment	—
Supplies Expense	—
Insurance Expense	—
Interest Expense	772

Data for the adjustments are as follows.

a.–b. Merchandise Inventory at December 31, $101,676.

c. Wages accrued at December 31, $1,956.

d. Supplies inventory at December 31, $744.

e. Depreciation of store equipment, $5,868.

f. Depreciation of office equipment, $1,732.

g. Insurance expired during the year, $632.

h. Rent earned, $2,400.

Instructions   1. Complete the work sheet.

2. Journalize the adjusting entries.

Problem 14-3 A portion of the work sheet of Gordon Ott and Company for the year ending December 31 is as follows.

ACCOUNT NAME	INCOME STATEMENT DEBIT	INCOME STATEMENT CREDIT	BALANCE SHEET DEBIT	BALANCE SHEET CREDIT
Cash			9 3 4 0 00	
Merchandise Inventory			76 9 4 0 00	
Supplies			2 5 6 00	
Prepaid Insurance			2 4 0 00	
Store Equipment			39 2 8 0 00	
Accum. Depr., Store Equipment				26 2 2 0 00
Accounts Payable				14 6 0 0 00
Gordon Ott, Capital				68 9 4 0 00
Gordon Ott, Drawing			27 6 0 0 00	
Sales		173 4 2 0 00		
Sales Returns and Allowances	1 5 2 0 00			
Purchases	84 2 6 0 00			
Purchases Discount		1 6 0 0 00		
Purchases Returns and Allowances		9 4 0 00		
Salary Expense	37 5 6 0 00			
Rent Expense	14 8 0 0 00			
Income Summary	65 6 8 0 00	76 9 4 0 00		
Depr. Expense, Store Equipment	4 0 4 0 00			
Insurance Expense	7 6 0 00			
Supplies Expense	9 4 4 00			
Salaries Payable				5 6 0 00
	209 5 6 4 00	252 9 0 0 00	153 6 5 6 00	110 3 2 0 00

Instructions
1. Determine the entries that appeared in the Adjustments columns and present them in general journal form.

2. Determine the net income for the year and the amount of the owner's capital at the end of the year.

Problem 14-4 The accounts in the ledger of Swenson Variety, with the balances as of December 31, the end of their fiscal year, are as follows.

Cash	$ 12,600
Accounts Receivable	2,040
Merchandise Inventory	120,600
Store Supplies	1,620
Prepaid Insurance	2,940
Store Equipment	56,100
Accumulated Depreciation, Store Equipment	12,600
Building	90,000
Accumulated Depreciation, Building	36,600
Land	18,000
Notes Payable	10,800
Accounts Payable	19,260
Sales Tax Payable	5,940
Salaries Payable	
C. E. Swenson, Capital	171,000
C. E. Swenson, Drawing	54,000
Income Summary	—
Sales	468,000
Sales Returns and Allowances	8,700
Purchases	303,000
Purchases Discount	4,800
Purchases Returns and Allowances	6,900
Salaries Expense	52,500
Advertising Expense	6,150
Depreciation Expense, Store Equipment	—
Depreciation Expense, Building	—
Store Supplies Expense	—
Insurance Expense	—
Utilities Expense	5,610
Sales Tax Expense	270
Miscellaneous Expense	990
Interest Expense	780

Data for the adjustments are as follows.

a.–b. Merchandise Inventory at December 31, $124,800.

c. Store supplies inventory at December 31, $540.

d. Depreciation of store equipment, $3,600.

e. Depreciation of building, $4,200.

f. Salaries accrued at December 31, $1,650.

g. Insurance expired during the year, $2,280.

Instructions 1. Complete the work sheet.

2. Journalize the adjusting entries.

Alternate problems

Problem 14-1A The trial balance of Martin Variety as of December 31, the end of their current fiscal year, is as follows.

Martin Variety										
Trial Balance										
December 31, 19–										
Cash	9 1 3 6 54							
Merchandise Inventory	62 8 5 4 82							
Store Supplies	1 4 6 6 84							
Prepaid Insurance	1 0 2 0 00							
Store Equipment	37 3 4 0 00							
Accumulated Depreciation, Store Equipment		24 8 3 6 00
Accounts Payable		14 2 8 6 96
Sales Tax Payable		2 4 6 98
C. S. Martin, Capital		55 0 5 9 84
C. S. Martin, Drawing	29 0 0 0 00	
Sales		177 9 6 6 34
Sales Returns and Allowances	1 4 9 3 84	
Purchases	81 4 3 7 84	
Purchases Discount		1 5 0 3 64
Purchases Returns and Allowances		1 8 5 7 82
Salary Expense	36 5 6 8 86	
Rent Expense	14 4 0 0 00	
Miscellaneous Expense	1 0 3 8 84	
	275 7 5 7 58	275 7 5 7 58

Here are the data for the adjustments.

a.–b. Merchandise Inventory at December 31, $65,749.80.

c. Supplies inventory, $404.32.

d. Insurance expired, $736.

e. Salaries accrued, $586.80.

f. Depreciation of store equipment, $3,920.

Instructions Complete the work sheet.

Problem 14-2A The balances of the ledger accounts of Hillier Office Supplies as of June 30, the end of their fiscal year, are as follows.

Cash	$ 14,775
Accounts Receivable	51,300
Merchandise Inventory	72,900
Supplies	1,470
Prepaid Insurance	1,080
Store Equipment	26,790
Accumulated Depreciation, Store Equipment	16,200
Office Equipment	9,600
Accumulated Depreciation, Office Equipment	4,815
Notes Payable	3,600
Accounts Payable	42,900
Salaries Payable	—
Unearned Rent	2,700
L. E. Hillier, Capital	95,340
L. E. Hillier, Drawing	24,000
Income Summary	—
Sales	466,500
Sales Returns and Allowances	3,210
Rent Income	—
Purchases	391,500
Purchases Discount	2,280
Purchases Returns and Allowances	7,170
Salaries Expense	44,250
Depreciation Expense, Store Equipment	—
Depreciation Expense, Office Equipment	—
Insurance Expense	—
Supplies Expense	—
Interest Expense	630

Here are the data for the adjustments.

a.–b. Merchandise Inventory at June 30, $114,600.

c. Salaries accrued at June 30, $1,440.

d. Insurance expired during the year, $900.

e. Supplies inventory at June 30, $285.

f. Depreciation of store equipment, $3,750.

g. Depreciation of office equipment, $1,950.

h. Rent earned $2,250.

Instructions
1. Complete the work sheet.
2. Journalize the adjusting entries.

ACCOUNT NAME	INCOME STATEMENT DEBIT	INCOME STATEMENT CREDIT	BALANCE SHEET DEBIT	BALANCE SHEET CREDIT
Cash			7 736 00	
Merchandise Inventory			74 298 00	
Supplies			298 00	
Prepaid Insurance			250 00	
Store Equipment			37 960 00	
Accum. Depr., Store Equipment				29 440 00
Accounts Payable				13 760 00
Randall Hawley, Capital				75 142 00
Randall Hawley, Drawing			30 800 00	
Sales		171 816 00		
Sales Returns and Allowances	1 434 00			
Purchases	88 592 00			
Purchases Discount		1 636 00		
Purchases Returns and Allowances		964 00		
Salary Expense	37 852 00			
Rent Expense	14 400 00			
Income Summary	68 228 00	74 298 00		
Depr. Expense, Store Equipment	4 360 00			
Insurance Expense	552 00			
Supplies Expense	884 00			
Salaries Payable				588 00
	216 302 00	248 714 00	151 342 00	118 930 00

Instructions **1.** Determine the entries that appeared in the Adjustments columns and present them in general journal form.

2. Determine the net income for the year and the amount of the owner's Capital at the end of the year.

Problem 14-4A Here are the accounts in the ledger of Bryant's Health Food Store, with the balances as of December 31, the end of their fiscal year.

Cash	$ 11,280
Accounts Receivable	1,554
Merchandise Inventory	116,100
Store Supplies	1,284
Prepaid Insurance	2,286
Store Equipment	77,490
Accumulated Depreciation, Store Equipment	17,160
Building	78,000
Accumulated Depreciation, Building	29,340
Land	15,000
Accounts Payable	14,070
Sales Tax Payable	2,784
Salaries Payable	—
Mortgage Payable	43,860
C. C. Bryant, Capital	151,830
C. C. Bryant, Drawing	46,500
Income Summary	—
Sales	379,254
Sales Returns and Allowances	3,888
Purchases	262,968
Purchases Discount	4,410
Purchases Returns and Allowances	3,261
Salaries Expense	23,400
Advertising Expense	1,962
Depreciation Expense, Store Equipment	—
Depreciation Expense, Building	—
Store Supplies Expense	—
Insurance Expense	—
Utilities Expense	1,158
Sales Tax Expense	162
Miscellaneous Expense	813
Interest Expense	2,160

Here are the data for the adjustments.

a.–b. Merchandise Inventory at December 31, $113,070.

c. Insurance expired during the year, $1,254.

d. Depreciation of store equipment, $8,580.

e. Depreciation of building, $4,200.

f. Salaries accrued at December 31, $420.

g. Store supplies inventory at December 31, $318.

Instructions
1. Complete the work sheet.
2. Journalize the adjusting entries.

15

Financial statements and closing entries for a merchandising firm

objectives

After you have completed this chapter, you will be able to do the following:
* Prepare a classified income statement for a merchandising firm.
* Prepare a classified balance sheet for any type of business.
* Compute working capital and current ratio.
* Journalize the closing entries for a merchandising firm.
* Determine which adjusting entries should be reversed.

CHAPTERS 5 and 7 discussed at length the income statements for a service and a professional enterprise, respectively. Then, in Chapters 11 and 14, we discussed the specialized accounts and journals for merchandising enterprises; in Chapter 14 we also explained the work sheet.

This chapter will formulate financial statements directly from work sheets. We will also explain the functions of closing entries and reversing entries as means of completing the accounting cycle. On page 375 we'll reproduce part of the work sheet for North Central Plumbing Supply that we presented in Chapter 14. First we look at the financial statements in their entirety, and then we'll explain their various subdivisions.

The income statement

As you know, each of the figures that appears in the Income Statement columns of the work sheet will be used in the income statement. Incidentally, this is why we kept the figures for the beginning and ending Merchandise Inventory separate; each now appears on the Income Summary line. On page 376 we show the entire income statement. Pause for a while and look it over; then we'll break it down into its component parts.

The outline of the income statement follows a logical pattern, and it is pretty much the same for any type of merchandising business. Being able to use the income statement and extract parts from it is very useful when one is assembling information in order to make decisions. But, to be able to realize the full use of an income statement, you need to know the skeleton outline of an income statement backward and forward, so that you can visualize it at a moment's notice. So, let's look at the statement piece by piece.

Net Sales	$86,730
− Cost of Merchandise Sold	43,860
= Gross Profit	$42,870
− Operating Expenses	29,564
= Net Income from Operations	$13,306

To hammer home the concepts of *gross* and *net,* let's take a simple case of a transaction that takes place many thousands of times a day, all over the world: selling a house.

ACCOUNT NAME	TRIAL BALANCE DEBIT	TRIAL BALANCE CREDIT	INCOME STATEMENT DEBIT	INCOME STATEMENT CREDIT
Cash	10 961 00			
Notes Receivable	2 000 00			
Accounts Receivable	14 680 00			
Merchandise Inventory	31 500 00			
Supplies	720 00			
Prepaid Insurance	480 00			
Equipment	16 800 00			
Accum. Depr., Equipment		8 200 00		
Building	50 000 00			
Accum. Depr., Building		16 000 00		
Land	6 000 00			
Notes Payable		1 500 00		
Accounts Payable		18 200 00		
Unearned Rent		450 00		
Mortgage Payable		4 000 00		
Robert C. Randall, Capital		73 287 00		
Robert C. Randall, Drawing	9 600 00			
Sales		88 090 00		88 090 00
Sales Discount	940 00		940 00	
Sales Returns and Allowances	420 00		420 00	
Interest Income		60 00		60 00
Purchases	42 800 00		42 800 00	
Purchases Discount		624 00		624 00
Purchases Returns and Allowances		416 00		416 00
Wages Expense	22 900 00		23 510 00	
Taxes Expense	980 00		980 00	
Interest Expense	46 00		46 00	
	210 827 00	210 827 00		
Income Summary			31 500 00	29 400 00
Rent Income				300 00
Supplies Expense			514 00	
Insurance Expense			160 00	
Depreciation, Expense, Equipment			2 400 00	
Depreciation Expense, Building			2 000 00	
Wages Payable				
			105 270 00	118 890 00
Net Income			13 620 00	
			118 890 00	118 890 00

North Central Plumbing Supply

Income Statement

For year ended December 31, 19—

Revenue from Sales:				
Sales			88090 00	
Less: Sales Returns and Allowances		940 00		
Sales Discount		420 00	1360 00	
Net Sales				86730 00
Cost of Merchandise Sold:				
Merchandise Inventory, Jan. 1, 19—			31500 00	
Purchases	42800 00			
Less: Purchases Returns and Allowances $624.00				
Purchases Discount 416.00	1040 00			
Net Purchases			41760 00	
Merchandise Available for Sale			73260 00	
Less: Merchandise Inventory, Dec. 31, 19—			29400 00	
Cost of Merchandise Sold				43860 00
Gross Profit				42870 00
Operating Expenses:				
Wages Expense			23510 00	
Depreciation Expense, Equipment			2400 00	
Depreciation Expense, Building			2000 00	
Taxes Expense			980 00	
Supplies Expense			514 00	
Insurance Expense			160 00	
Total Operating Expenses				29564 00
Net Income from Operations				13306 00
Other Income:				
Rent Income			300 00	
Interest Income			60 00	
Total Other Income			360 00	
Other Expenses:				
Interest Expense			46 00	314 00
Net Income				13620 00

Cynthia Jones, a few years back, bought a house and a lot for $32,000. Last week she sold the house and lot for $60,000. The real estate agent who did the actual selling gets a sales commission of 7%. How much did Jones make as clear profit?

Sale price of property	$60,000
− Cost of property sold	32,000
= Gross Profit (or Gross Margin)	$28,000
− Agent's commission expense	4,200
= Net Income or Net Profit (gain on the sale)	$23,800

Gross profit is the profit on the sale of the property before any expense has been deducted; it may also be called *gross margin*. *Net income* or *net profit* is the final or clear profit after all the *expenses* have been deducted. On a single-sale situation such as this, we refer to the final outcome as the net profit. But for a business having a number of sales and expenses, most accountants use the term *net income*. However, regardless of whether one uses the word *profit* or the word *income, net* refers to clear profit.

Revenue from sales

All right, now let's look at the Revenue from Sales section in the accounts of North Central Plumbing Supply.

Revenue from Sales:			
Sales		88 0 9 0 00	
Less: Sales Returns and Allowances	9 4 0 00		
Sales Discount	4 2 0 00	1 3 6 0 00	
Net Sales			86 7 3 0 00

When we introduced Sales Returns and Allowances and Sales Discounts, we treated them as deductions from Sales. You can see that we needed to do this because this is the way they are treated in the income statement.

Cost of merchandise sold

The section of the income statement that requires the greatest amount of concentration is the Cost of Merchandise Sold. Let us therefore repeat it in its entirety.

Cost of Merchandise Sold:			
Merchandise Inventory, Jan. 1, 19—		31 5 0 0 00	
Purchases	42 8 0 0 00		
Less: Purchases Returns and Allowances $624.00			
Purchases Discount 416.00	1 0 4 0 00		
Net Purchases		41 7 6 0 00	
Merchandise Available for Sale		73 2 6 0 00	
Less: Merchandise Inventory, Dec. 31, 19—		29 4 0 0 00	
Cost of Merchandise Sold			43 8 6 0 00

First let's look closely at the Purchases section.

Purchases		42 8 0 0 00		
Less: Purchases Returns and Allowances $624.00				
Purchases Discount 416.00		1 0 4 0 00		
Net Purchases			41 7 6 0 00	

Note a parallel here to the Sales section, in that, in order to arrive at Net Purchases, we deduct both Purchases Returns and Allowances and Purchases Discount from Purchases.

Now let's take in the full Cost of Merchandise Sold section. Does this seem like a reasonable summing up of the situation?

Amount we started with (beginning inventory)	$31,500
+ Net amount we purchased	41,760
= Total amount that could have been sold (available)	$73,260
− Amount left over (ending inventory)	29,400
= Cost of the merchandise that was actually sold	$43,860

Or

Merchandise Inventory, Jan. 1, 19—	$31,500
Net Purchases	41,760
Merchandise Available for Sale	$73,260
Less Merchandise Inventory, Dec. 31, 19—	29,400
Cost of Merchandise Sold	$43,860

Remember that *net purchases* means total Purchases less both Purchases Returns and Allowances and Purchases Discount.

Operating expenses

Operating expenses, as the name implies, are the regular expenses of doing business. They may be listed in descending order, with the largest amount first. If one has a Miscellaneous Expense account, one always places it last, regardless of its amount. We shall follow this order in this text. There's another way of handling it, though; many accountants list the accounts and their respective balances in the order that the accounts appear in the ledger.

Many firms may use subclassifications of operating expenses, such as the following.

Selling expenses Any expenses directly connected with the selling activity, such as these:

- Sales Salaries Expense
- Sales Commissions Expense
- Advertising Expense
- Store Supplies Expense
- Delivery Expense
- Depreciation Expense, Store Equipment

General expenses Any expenses related to the office or the administration, or any expense that cannot be directly connected with a selling activity:

- Office Salaries Expense
- Taxes Expense
- Depreciation Expense, Office Equipment
- Rent Expense
- Insurance Expense
- Office Supplies Expense

If the Cash Short and Over account has a debit balance (net shortage), the balance is added to and reported as Miscellaneous General Expense. Conversely, if the Cash Short and Over account has a credit balance (net overage), the balance is added to and reported as Miscellaneous Income.

In preparing the income statement, classifying expense accounts as selling expenses or general expenses is a matter of judgment. The only reason we're not using this breakdown here is that we're trying to keep the number of accounts to a minimum. In other words, we don't want you to get bogged down in a large number of accounts, making it more difficult to understand the main concepts. We don't want you to lose sight of the forest on account of the trees.

Net income from operations Now let's repeat the skeleton outline.

```
  Sales
− Cost of Merchandise Sold
= Gross Profit
− Operating Expenses
= Net Income from Operations
```

If the Operating Expenses are the sort that are regular, recurring types of expenses of doing business, then Net Income from Operations should be the regular or recurring net income. When you are comparing the results of operations over a number of years, the net income from operations is a most significant figure to use each year as a basis for comparison.

Other income

The Other Income classification, as the name implies, records any revenue account other than revenue from Sales. What we are trying to do is to isolate Sales at the top of the income statement as the major revenue account, so that the gross profit figure represents the profit made on the sale of merchandise *only*. Additional accounts that may appear under the heading of Other Income are: Rent Income (the firm is subletting part of its premises); Interest Income (the firm is the holder of an interest-bearing note or contract); Gain on Disposal of Plant and Equipment (the firm makes a profit on the sale of plant and equipment); Miscellaneous Income (the firm has an overage recorded in the Cash Short and Over account).

Other expenses

The classification of Other Expenses records any nonrecurring expenses, such as Interest Expense and Loss on Disposal of Plant and Equipment.

The balance sheet

On page 381, we now present a partial work sheet for North Central Plumbing Supply (again, based on the one used in Chapter 14).

Now here again we find that each figure that appears in the Balance Sheet columns of the work sheet will be used in the statement of owner's equity and the balance sheet. These two statements appear below and on page 382.

North Central Plumbing Supply				
Statement of Owner's Equity				
For year ended December 31, 19—				
Robert C. Randall, Capital, January 1, 19—			69 2 8 7 00	
Additional Investment, August 26, 19—			4 0 0 0 00	
Total			73 2 8 7 00	
Add: Net Income for the Year	13 6 2 0 00			
Less: Withdrawals for the Year	9 6 0 0 00			
Increase in Capital			4 0 2 0 00	
Robert C. Randall, Capital, December 31, 19—			77 3 0 7 00	

ACCOUNT NAME	TRIAL BALANCE DEBIT	TRIAL BALANCE CREDIT	BALANCE SHEET DEBIT	BALANCE SHEET CREDIT
Cash	10 961 00		10 961 00	
Notes Receivable	2 000 00		2 000 00	
Accounts Receivable	14 680 00		14 680 00	
Merchandise Inventory	31 500 00		29 400 00	
Supplies	720 00		206 00	
Prepaid Insurance	480 00		320 00	
Equipment	16 800 00		16 800 00	
Accum. Depr., Equipment		8 200 00		10 600 00
Building	50 000 00		50 000 00	
Accum. Depr., Building		16 000 00		18 000 00
Land	6 000 00		6 000 00	
Notes Payable		1 500 00		1 500 00
Accounts Payable		18 200 00		18 200 00
Unearned Rent		450 00		150 00
Mortgage Payable		4 000 00		4 000 00
Robert C. Randall, Capital		73 287 00		73 287 00
Robert C. Randall, Drawing	9 600 00		9 600 00	
Sales		88 090 00		
Sales Discount	940 00			
Sales Returns and Allowances	420 00			
Interest Income		60 00		
Purchases	42 800 00			
Purchases Discount		624 00		
Purchases Returns and Allowances		416 00		
Wages Expense	22 900 00			
Taxes Expense	980 00			
Interest Expense	46 00			
	210 827 00	210 827 00		
Income Summary				
Rent Income				
Supplies Expense				
Insurance Expense				
Depreciation, Expense, Equipment				
Depreciation Expense, Building				
Wages Payable				610 00
			139 967 00	126 347 00
Net Income				13 620 00
			139 967 00	139 967 00

North Central Plumbing Supply

Balance Sheet

December 31, 19—

Assets			
Current Assets:			
Cash		10 961 00	
Notes Receivable		2 000 00	
Accounts Receivable		14 680 00	
Merchandise Inventory		29 400 00	
Supplies		206 00	
Prepaid Insurance		320 00	
Total Current Assets			57 567 00
Plant and Equipment:			
Equipment	16 800 00		
Less Accumulated Depreciation	10 600 00	6 200 00	
Building	50 000 00		
Less Accumulated Depreciation	18 000 00	32 000 00	
Land		6 000 00	
Total Plant and Equipment			44 200 00
Total Assets			101 767 00
Liabilities			
Current Liabilities:			
Notes Payable		1 500 00	
Mortgage Payable (current portion)		1 000 00	
Accounts Payable		18 200 00	
Wages Payable		610 00	
Unearned Rent		150 00	
Total Current Liabilities			21 460 00
Long-term Liabilities:			
Mortgage Payable			3 000 00
Total Liabilities			24 460 00
Owner's Equity			
Robert C. Randall, Capital			77 307 00
Total Liabilities and Owner's Equity			101 767 00

We have already discussed the statement of owner's equity. North Central Plumbing Supply's statement of owner's equity shows why the balance of the Capital account has changed from the beginning of the fiscal period to the end of it, and also includes the feature of an additional investment made during the period. Data relating to additional investments are available from an analysis of the Capital account, not from the work sheet. After one has added the additional investment to the beginning capital, the remainder of the statement is the same as our previous illustrations. If there is no additional investment, then one can just go ahead and record the net income, less withdrawals, and the resulting increase or decrease in capital.

This is the first time that a classified balance sheet has been presented. Classifications in accounting are generally uniform for all types of business enterprises. You are strongly urged to take the time to learn the following definitions of the classifications and the order of accounts within them. If you do, you will forever after have a standard routine for compiling the balance sheet, and this will save you a lot of grief and time.

Current assets

Current Assets consist of cash and any other assets or resources which are expected to be realized in cash, or to be sold or consumed during the normal operating cycle of the business.

Accountants list Current Assets in the order of their convertibility into cash, or in other words, their *liquidity*. (If you've got an asset such as a car or a diamond, and you sell it quickly and turn it into cash, you are said to be turning it into a *liquid* state.) If the first four accounts under Current Assets (see North Central Plumbing Supply's balance sheet) are present, always record them in the same order: (1) Cash, (2) Notes Receivable, (3) Accounts Receivable, and (4) Merchandise Inventory.

Notes Receivable are promissory notes held by the firm, or promise-to-pay notes. (*Example:* Suppose you are the owner of a lumber yard, and you sell lumber to a builder who does not have enough cash to pay for it, but has a ready buyer for the finished house. The builder therefore gives you a *promissory note,* stating that you will be paid within 90 days.) Notes Receivable is placed ahead of Accounts Receivable, because promissory notes are considered to be more liquid than Accounts Receivable. (Reason: The holder of the note can raise more cash by borrowing from a bank, pledging the notes as security for the loan.) Supplies and Prepaid Insurance are considered to be prepaid items that will be used up or expire eventually over time; that's why they appear at the bottom of the Current Assets section. (There is no particular reason to list Supplies before Prepaid Insurance. Prepaid Insurance could just as easily have preceded Supplies.)

Plant and equipment

Plant and equipment are relatively long-lived assets that one holds for use in the production or sale of other assets or services; some accountants refer to them as *fixed assets.* The three types of accounts that usually appear in this category are equipment, buildings, and land (refer to the balance sheet for North Central Plumbing Supply once again). Note that the Equipment and Building accounts are followed by their respective Accumulated Depreciation accounts. (Remember how we spoke of Accumulated Depreciations as being deductions from assets?) Plant and equipment are listed in the order of their length of life, with the shortest-lived asset (equipment) recorded first. A firm which has some delivery equipment, for example, lists it first, because of its relatively short life. In other words, Plant and Equipment go in order from the least fixed to the most fixed; Land is placed last in this category.

Current liabilities

Current liabilities are debts that will become due within a short period, usually within 1 year, and will normally be paid, when due, from current assets. List current liabilities in the order of their urgency of payment, putting the most pressing obligation first. Notes Payable precedes Accounts Payable, just as Notes Receivable precedes Accounts Receivable. The Mortgage Payable (current portion), which also may precede Accounts Payable, is the payment one makes to reduce the principal of the mortgage in a given year. Wages Payable follows the other three current liabilities; this is true of any accrued liabilities such as Commissions Payable. Any unearned revenue accounts fall at the bottom of the list of current liabilities.

Long-term liabilities

Long-term liabilities are debts that are payable over a comparatively long period, usually more than 1 year. Ordinarily the only account that would be in this category for a sole-proprietorship (or one-owner) type of business is Mortgage Payable. One single amount in a category can be recorded in the column on the extreme right.

Working capital and current ratio

Both the management and the short-term creditors of a firm are vitally interested in two questions.

1. Does the firm have a sufficient amount of capital to operate?
2. Does the firm have the ability to pay its debts?

Two measures that are used to answers these questions are a firm's working capital and its current ratio, and the necessary data is taken from a classified balance sheet.

Working capital is determined by subtracting current liabilities from current assets, thus

$$\text{Working capital} = \text{current assets} - \text{current liabilities}$$

The normal operating cycle for most firms is one year. Because current assets equal cash—or items that can be converted into cash within one year—and current liabilities equal the total amount that the company must pay out within one year, "working capital" is appropriately named. It is the amount of capital the company has available to use or work with. The working capital for North Central Plumbing Supply is as follows.

$$\text{Working capital} = \$57,567 - \$21,460 = \$36,107$$

A firm's ability to pay its debts is revealed by the firm's current ratio. The current ratio is determined by dividing current assets by current liabilities.

$$\text{Current ratio} = \frac{\text{current assets (amount coming in within one year)}}{\text{current liabilities (amount going out within one year)}}$$

The current ratio for North Central Plumbing Supply is calculated like this:

$$\text{Current ratio} = \frac{\$57,567}{\$21,460} = 2.68:1$$

$$21,460\overline{)57,567} \quad \begin{array}{c} 2.68 \\ \end{array}$$

In the case of North Central Plumbing Supply, there is $2.68 coming in within one year for every dollar going out within one year.

When banks are considering granting loans to merchandising firms, a minimum current ratio of $2:1$ is generally required.

Chart of accounts

In Chapter 4, when we introduced the chart of accounts and the account-number arrangement, we said that the first digit represents the classification of the accounts:

Assets	1 _ _
Liabilities	2 _ _
Owner's Equity	3 _ _
Revenue	4 _ _
Expenses	5 _ _

The second digit stands for the *sub*classification.

Assets	1 _ _
Current Assets	11 _
Plant and Equipment	12 _
Liabilities	2 _ _
Current Liabilities	21 _
Long-term Liabilities	22 _
Owner's Equity	3 _ _
Capital	31 _
Revenue	4 _ _
Revenue from Sales	41 _
Other Income	42 _
Expenses	5 _ _
Cost of Merchandise Sold	51 _
Selling Expenses	52 _
General Expenses	53 _
Other Expenses	54 _

The third digit indicates the placement of the account within the subclassification.

Closing entries

In Chapter 6 we discussed closing entries for a service business; now let's discuss closing entries for a merchandising business. The same methods apply to both types of business. That is, you want to balance off the revenue, expense, and Drawing accounts. So you go through the same four steps as in a service business. At the end of this fiscal period, close the revenue and expense accounts in order to start the next fiscal period with a clean slate. Also close the Drawing account, because it too applies to one fiscal period only. These accounts are called *temporary equity* accounts.

When you're working out your closing entries, you can take a shortcut by balancing off each figure in the Income Statement columns of the work sheet. For example, if the entries in the Income Statement columns look like this:

Account Name	Income Statement Column	
	Debit	Credit
Sales		60,000
Purchases	40,000	
Salary Expense	10,000	
Miscellaneous Expense	5,000	
	55,000	60,000
Net Income	5,000	
	60,000	60,000

In the first entry to close off the revenue account, debit Sales for $60,000 and credit Income Summary for $60,000. In the second entry to close off the Purchases, Salary Expense, and Miscellaneous Expense accounts, credit Purchases for $40,000, credit Salary Expense for $10,000, credit Miscellaneous Expense for $5,000, and debit Income Summary for $55,000.

The work sheet on the next page shows the Income Statement columns. After you have looked them over, let's take up those four steps and see how we came out.

Four steps in the closing procedure

To repeat, these are the four steps that should be followed when closing:

1. Close the revenue accounts as well as the other accounts appearing in the income statement and having credit balances. (Debit the figures that are credited in the Income Statement column of the work sheet, except the figures on the Income Summary line.) See journal atop page 388.

ACCOUNT NAME	TRIAL BALANCE		INCOME STATEMENT	
	DEBIT	CREDIT	DEBIT	CREDIT
Cash	10 961 00			
Notes Receivable	2 000 00			
Accounts Receivable	14 680 00			
Merchandise Inventory	31 500 00			
Supplies	720 00			
Prepaid Insurance	480 00			
Equipment	16 800 00			
Accum. Depr., Equipment		8 200 00		
Building	50 000 00			
Accum. Depr., Building		16 000 00		
Land	6 000 00			
Notes Payable		1 500 00		
Accounts Payable		18 200 00		
Unearned Rent		450 00		
Mortgage Payable		40 000 00		
Robert C. Randall, Capital		73 287 00		
Robert C. Randall, Drawing	9 600 00			
Sales		88 090 00		88 090 00
Sales Discount	940 00		940 00	
Sales Returns and Allowances	420 00		420 00	
Interest Income		60 00		60 00
Purchases	42 800 00		42 800 00	
Purchases Discount		624 00		624 00
Purchases Returns and Allowances		416 00		416 00
Wages Expense	22 900 00		23 510 00	
Taxes Expense	980 00		980 00	
Interest Expense	46 00		46 00	
	210 827 00	210 827 00		
Income Summary			31 500 00	29 400 00
Rent Income				300 00
Supplies Expense			514 00	
Insurance Expense			160 00	
Depreciation, Expense, Equipment			2 400 00	
Depreciation Expense, Building			2 000 00	
Wages Payable				
			105 270 00	118 890 00
Net Income			13 620 00	
			118 890 00	118 890 00

	DATE		DESCRIPTION	POST REF.	DEBIT	CREDIT	
1			*Closing Entries*				1
2	19– Dec.	31	Sales		88 0 9 0 00		2
3			Rent Income		3 0 0 00		3
4			Interest Income		6 0 00		4
5			Purchases Discount		6 2 4 00		5
6			Purchases Returns and Allowances		4 1 6 00		6
7			Income Summary			89 4 9 0 00	7
8							8

2. Close the expense accounts as well as the other accounts appearing in the income statement and having debit balances. (Credit the figures that are debited in the Income Statement column of the work sheet, except the figure on the Income Summary line.)

	DATE		DESCRIPTION	POST REF.	DEBIT	CREDIT	
1	Dec.	31	Income Summary		73 7 7 0 00		1
2			Sales Discount			9 4 0 00	2
3			Sales Returns and Allowances			4 2 0 00	3
4			Purchases			42 8 0 0 00	4
5			Wages Expense			23 5 1 0 00	5
6			Taxes Expense			9 8 0 00	6
7			Interest Expense			4 6 00	7
8			Supplies Expense			5 1 4 00	8
9			Insurance Expense			1 6 0 00	9
10			Depreciation Expense, Equipment			2 4 0 0 00	10
11			Depreciation Expense, Building			2 0 0 0 00	11
12							12

3. Close the Income Summary account into Robert C. Randall, Capital (by the amount of the Net Income).

	DATE		DESCRIPTION	POST REF.	DEBIT	CREDIT	
1	Dec.	31	Income Summary		13 6 2 0 00		1
2			Robert C. Randall, Capital			13 6 2 0 00	2
3							3

Income Summary

Adjusting	31,500	Adjusting	29,400
(Beginning		(Ending	
Merchandise		Merchandise	
Inventory)		Inventory)	
(Expenses)	73,770	(Revenue)	89,490
Clos. (Net Inc.)	13,620		

Robert C. Randall, Capital

−	+	
	Balance	73,287
	(Net Inc.)	13,620

4. Close the Drawing account into the Capital account.

		GENERAL JOURNAL			PAGE _____	
DATE		DESCRIPTION	POST REF.	DEBIT	CREDIT	
Dec.	31	Robert C. Randall, Capital		9 6 0 0 00		1
		Robert C. Randall, Drawing			9 6 0 0 00	2
						3
						4
						5
						6
						7
						8
						9
						10

Robert C. Randall, Drawing

	+		−
Balance	9,600	Closing	9,600

Robert C. Randall, Capital

−		+	
(Drawing)	9,600	Balance	73,287
		(Net Inc.)	13,620

Note that you close Purchases Discount and Purchases Returns and Allowances in Step 1 along with the revenue accounts. Note also that, in Step 2, you close Sales Discount and Sales Returns and Allowances along with the expense accounts. Finally, bear in mind that the Income Summary account previously contains adjusting entries for merchandise inventory.

Reversing entries

Reversing entries are general journal entries which are the exact reverse of certain adjusting entries. A reversing entry enables the accountant to record routine transactions in the usual manner, *even though* an adjusting entry affecting one of the accounts involved in the transaction has intervened. We can see this concept best by looking at an example.

Suppose there's an adjusting entry for accrued wages owed to employees at the end of the fiscal year. (Recall that we talked about this in Chapter 5.) Assume that the employees of a certain firm are paid altogether $200 per day for a 5-day week, and that payday occurs every Friday throughout the year. When the employees get their checks at 5:00 P.M. on Friday, the checks include their wages for that day as well as the preceding 4 days. And say that one year the last day of the fiscal period happens to fall on Wednesday, December 31. A diagram of this situation would look like this:

							End of Fiscal Year			
				Dec. 26	Dec. 29	Dec. 30	Dec. 31		Jan. 2	
Mon	Tue	Wed	Thur	Fri	Mon	Tue	Wed	Thur	Fri	
200	200	200	200	200	200	200	200	200	200	
←————Payroll period————				→	←————Payroll period————					→
				Payday $1,000			Accrued $600		Payday $1,000	

Each Friday during the year, the payroll has been debited to the Wages Expense account and credited to the Cash account. As a result, Wages Expense has a debit balance of $51,400. Here is the adjusting entry in T account form.

Wages Expense		Wages Payable	
+	−	−	+
Bal. 51,400			Dec. 31 Adj. 600
Dec. 31 Adj. 600			

After the accountant completes the closing process, he or she clears the Wages Expense account, which yields a zero balance. However, the Wages Payable account continues to have a credit balance. In this case, the only way out is to record the $1,000 payroll on January 2 as a debit of $600 to Wages Payable, a debit of $400 to Wages Expense, and a credit of $1,000 to Cash. This means that the employee who records the payroll not only has to record this particular payroll differently from all other weekly payrolls for the year, but also has to refer back to the adjusting entry to determine the portion of the $1,000 to be debited to Wages Payable and Wages Expense, respectively. But in the company's delegation of responsibility, the employee who records the payroll may not have access to the adjusting entries.

One can avoid the necessity of referring to the earlier entry and of dividing the debit total between the two accounts by *recording a reversing entry as of the first day of the following fiscal period.* One makes an entry which is the exact reverse of the adjusting entry, as follows.

	DATE		DESCRIPTION	POST REF.	DEBIT	CREDIT	
			GENERAL JOURNAL PAGE *118*				
1			*Reversing Entries*				1
2	19– Jan.	1	Wages Payable		6 0 0 00		2
3			Wages Expense			6 0 0 00	3
4							4
5							5
6							6
7							7
8							8
9							9
10							10
11							11
12							12
13							13
14							14

Let us now bring the T accounts up to date.

Wages Expense

	+		−
Bal.	51,400	Dec. 31 Clos.	52,000
Dec. 31 Adj.	600		
		Jan. 1 Rev.	600

Wages Payable

	−		+
Jan. 1 Rev.	600	Dec. 31 Adj.	600

The reversing entry has the effect of transferring the $600 liability from Wages Payable to the credit side of Wages Expense. Wages Expense will temporarily have a credit balance until the next payroll is recorded in the routine manner. In the above illustration, this occurs on January 2, for $1,000. Here are the T accounts for this.

Wages Expense

	+		−
Bal.	51,400	Dec. 31 Clos.	52,000
Dec. 31 Adj.	600		
Jan. 2	1,000	Jan. 1 Rev.	600

Wages Payable

	−		+
Jan. 1 Rev.	600	Dec. 31 Adj.	600

There is now a *net debit balance* of $400 in Wages Expense. To see this, look at the ledger accounts atop the following page.

ACCOUNT _____ *Wages Expense* _____ ACCOUNT NO. _514_

DATE		ITEM	POST. REF.	DEBIT	CREDIT	BALANCE DEBIT	BALANCE CREDIT
19– Dec.	26		CP16	1000 00		51400 00	
	31	Adjusting	J116	600 00		52000 00	
	31	Closing	J117		52000 00	— — — —	— — — —
19– Jan.	1	Reversing	J118		600 00		600 00
	2		CP17	1000 00		400 00	

ACCOUNT _____ *Wages Payable* _____ ACCOUNT NO. _213_

DATE		ITEM	POST. REF.	DEBIT	CREDIT	BALANCE DEBIT	BALANCE CREDIT
19– Dec.	31	Adjusting	J116		600 00		600 00
19– Jan.	1	Reversing	J118	600 00		— — —	— — —

The reversing entry for accrued salaries or wages applies to service companies as well as to merchandising ones. You can see that a reversing entry consists of simply switching around an adjusting entry. The question is, Which adjusting entries should be reversed? Here's a handy rule of thumb that will help you decide.

If an adjusting entry increases an asset account or liability account which does not have a previous balance, then reverse the adjusting entry.

With the exception of the first year of operations, Merchandise Inventory and contra accounts—such as Accumulated Depreciation—will always have previous balances. Consequently, adjusting entries involving these accounts should never be reversed.

Let's apply this rule to the adjusting entries for North Central Plumbing Supply.

Income Summary	
Adj. 31,500	

Merchandise Inventory		
+		−
Bal. 31,500		Adj. 31,500

(Do not reverse; Merchandise Inventory is an asset, but it has a previous balance.)

Merchandise Inventory		
+		−
Bal. 31,500		Adj. 31,500
Adj. 29,400		

Income Summary	
Adj. 31,500	Adj. 29,400

(Do not reverse; Merchandise Inventory is an asset, but it has a previous balance.)

Rent Income	
−	+
	Adj. 300

Unearned Rent	
−	+
Adj. 300	Bal. 450

(Do not reverse; Unearned Rent is a liability, but it was decreased. Also, it had a previous balance.)

Supplies Expense	
+	−
Adj. 514	

Supplies	
+	−
Bal. 720	Adj. 514

(Do not reverse; Supplies is an asset account, but it was decreased. Also, it had a previous balance.)

Insurance Expense	
+	−
Adj. 160	

Prepaid Insurance	
+	−
Bal. 480	Adj. 160

(Do not reverse; Prepaid Insurance is an asset account, but it was decreased. Also, it had a previous balance.)

Depreciation Expense, Equipment	
+	−
Adj. 2,400	

Accumulated Depreciation, Equipment	
−	+
	Bal. 8,200
	Adj. 2,400

(Do not reverse; Accumulated Depreciation is an asset, but it has a previous balance, with the exception of the first year.)

Depreciation Expense, Building	
+	−
Adj. 2,000	

Accumulated Depreciation, Building	
−	+
	Bal. 16,000
	Adj. 2,000

(Do not reverse; Accumulated Depreciation is an asset, but it has a previous balance, with the exception of the first year.)

Wages Expense	
+	−
Bal. 22,900	
Adj. 610	

Wages Payable	
−	+
	Adj. 610

(Reverse; Wages Payable is a *liability* account, and it was *increased*. Also, it has no previous balance.)

Whenever we introduce additional adjusting entries, we'll make it a point to state whether these adjusting entries should be reversed.

The skeleton outline of the income statement is as follows.

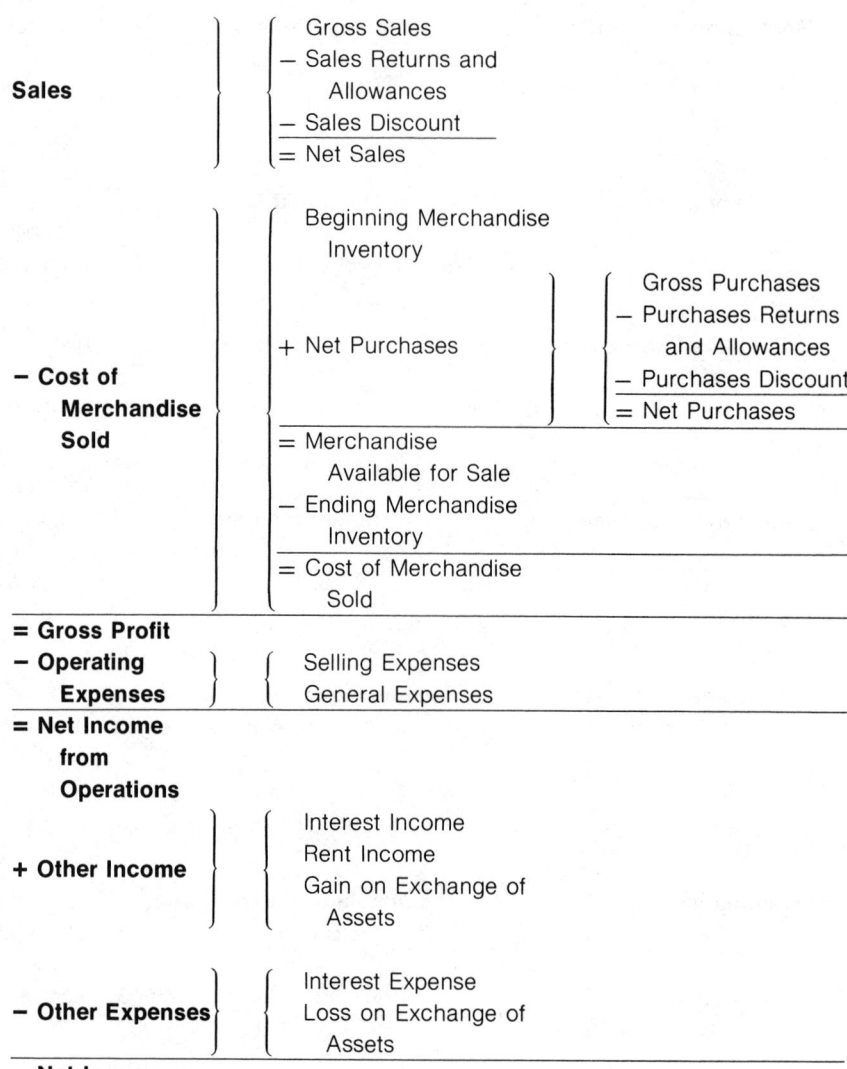

The skeleton outline of the balance sheet looks like this.

Assets

Current Assets (Listed in the order of their convertibility into cash.)
1. Cash
2. Notes Receivable
3. Accounts Receivable

4. Prepaid items (Supplies; Prepaid Insurance)

Plant and Equipment (Listed in the order of their length of life; the asset with the shortest life is placed first. Land is placed last.)

1. Equipment

2. Buildings

3. Land

Liabilities

Current Liabilities (Listed in the order of their urgency of payment, the most pressing obligation is placed first.)

1. Notes Payable

2. Mortgage Payable or Contracts Payable (current portion)

3. Accounts Payable

4. Accrued liabilities (Wages Payable; Commissions Payable)

5. Unearned revenue

Long-term Liabilities (Contracts Payable; Mortgage Payable)

Owner's Equity

Capital balance at end of the fiscal year

$$\text{Working capital} = \text{current assets} - \text{current liabilities}$$

$$\text{Current ratio} = \frac{\text{current assets}}{\text{current liabilities}}$$

There are four steps in making closing entries for a merchandising business.

Step 1 Close all revenue accounts, Purchases Discount, and Purchases Returns and Allowances into Income Summary.

Step 2 Close all expense accounts, Sales Discount, and Sales Returns and Allowances into Income Summary.

Step 3 Close Income Summary into Capital.

Step 4 Close Drawing into Capital.

When you make reversing entries, record them as of the first day of the period following the adjusting entries.

Glossary

Cost of merchandise sold Merchandise Inventory at beginning of fiscal period, plus net purchases, minus Merchandise Inventory at end of fiscal period. Terms often used to describe the same thing are *cost of goods sold* and *cost of sales*.

	Merchandise Inventory (beginning)
+	Net Purchases
=	Merchandise Available for Sale
−	Merchandise Inventory (ending)
=	Cost of Merchandise Sold

Current assets Cash and any other assets or resources which are expected to be realized in cash or sold or consumed during the normal operating cycle of the business.

Current liabilities Debts that are due within a short period, usually 1 year, and which are normally paid from current assets.

Current ratio A firm's current assets divided by its current liabilities. Portrays a firm's short-term-debt-paying ability.

General expenses Expenses incurred in the administration or operation of a business, including office expenses and any expenses that are not wholly classified as Selling Expenses or Other Expenses.

Gross profit Net sales minus Cost of Merchandise Sold, or profit before deducting expenses. Gross profit may also be called *gross margin*.

$$\begin{array}{l} \text{Net Sales} \\ \underline{- \text{ Cost of Merchandise Sold}} \\ = \text{Gross Profit} \end{array}$$

Liquidity The ability of an asset to be quickly turned into cash, either by selling it or by putting it up as security for a loan.

Long-term liabilities Debts that you don't have to pay right away, but can pay over a comparatively long period, usually more than 1 year.

Net income The final figure on an income statement after all expenses have been deducted from revenues.

Net purchases Total purchases, minus Purchases Returns and Allowances and minus Purchases Discount.

$$\begin{array}{l} \text{Purchases} \\ - \text{ Purchases Returns and Allowances} \\ \underline{- \text{ Purchases Discount}} \\ = \text{Net Purchases} \end{array}$$

Net sales Total sales, minus Sales Returns and Allowances and minus Sales Discount.

$$\begin{array}{l} \text{Sales} \\ - \text{ Sales Returns and Allowances} \\ \underline{- \text{ Sales Discount}} \\ = \text{Net Sales} \end{array}$$

Notes receivable Written promises to pay received from customers and due in a period of less than 1 year.

Plant and equipment Long-lived assets that are held for use in the production or sale of other assets or services. They may also be called *fixed assets*.

Reversing entry The reverse of certain adjusting entries, recorded as of the first day of the following fiscal year.

Selling expenses Expenses directly related to the sale of merchandise, such as salaries of sales staff, expenses for advertising, and expenses for delivery.

Temporary equity Accounts whose balances apply to one fiscal period only, such as revenues, expenses, and the Drawing account. Temporary-equity accounts are also called nominal accounts.

Working capital   the excess of a firm's current assets over its current liabilities. Portrays the amount of capital a firm has to work with during a normal operating cycle.

Questions

1. In the closing procedure, what happens to Purchases Discount?

2. What is the difference between current liabilities and long-term liabilities? Give an example of each.

3. In this chapter, the Adjusted Trial Balance columns of a work sheet have been omitted. Does this affect the use of the work sheet?

4. Describe how to calculate the cost of merchandise sold.

5. What is the order of listing accounts in the current assets section of the balance sheet?

6. What is the order of listing accounts in the plant and equipment section of a balance sheet?

7. What is the rule used to recognize whether or not an adjusting entry should be reversed?

Exercises

Exercise 1   M. C. Turnbull bought a house for $26,000. Nine years later, after spending $7,000 on permanent improvements, he sold it for $58,000. The real estate agent who sold the house charged a 6% commission. What is Turnbull's net profit?

Exercise 2   Arrange the following accounts as they would appear in the Current Assets section of the balance sheet.

Supplies	$ 615
Accounts Receivable	27,000
Merchandise Inventory	54,000
Cash	10,350
Prepaid Insurance	540
Notes Receivable	3,600
Prepaid Advertising	330

Exercise 3   The Meredith Music Company, at the beginning of the year, held merchandise valued at $58,000. Their net purchases during the year amounted to $252,000. The merchandise inventory at the end of the year is $51,900. Determine (1) merchandise available for sale, and (2) cost of merchandise sold.

Exercise 4   Calculate the missing items in the following.

	Sales	Sales Returns	Net Sales	Beginning Inventory	Net Purchases	Merch. Available	Ending Inventory	Cost of Merch. Sold	Gross Profit
a.	$93,000	$2,250	—	$55,500	$63,750	$119,250	$51,000	$68,250	—
b.	$114,000	—	$111,000	$54,000	$97,500	—	$73,500	$78,000	—
c.	—	$4,500	$235,500	$31,500	—	$186,000	$34,500	—	$84,000

Exercise 5 During the year just past, Trotter and Company had net sales of $294,000 and net purchases of $244,500. Their ending merchandise inventory was $48,000, and their beginning merchandise inventory was $43,500. How much is their gross profit?

Exercise 6 From the following T accounts, record the closing entries.

Sales	
	150,000

Salary Expense	
24,000	

Sales Returns and Allowances	
3,000	

Rent Expense	
9,000	

Purchases	
90,000	

Miscellaneous Expense	
9,450	

Purchases Returns and Allowances	
	2,250

D. Neel, Drawing	
24,000	

Purchases Discount	
	2,700

D. Neel, Capital	
	130,500

Income Summary	
33,000	39,000

Exercise 7 The following items appeared in the Income Statement columns of a work sheet prepared for Noland Sales and Service. W. O. Noland withdrew $15,300 from the business during the fiscal period. Prepare entries to close the revenue and expense accounts, Income Summary, and W. O. Noland, Drawing.

Nolan Sales and Service
Work Sheet
For the year ended June 30, 19—

ACCOUNT NAME	INCOME STATEMENT	
	DEBIT	CREDIT
Sales		150 000 00
Sales Returns and Allowances	4 500 00	
Purchases	90 000 00	
Purchases Discount		1 800 00
Purchases Returns and Allowances		1 200 00
Salaries Expense	14 400 00	
Commissions Expense	9 600 00	
Rent Expense	5 400 00	
Miscellaneous Expense	900 00	
Income Summary	27 000 00	39 000 00
	151 800 00	192 000 00
Net Income	40 200 00	
	192 000 00	192 000 00

Exercise 8 From the following information, present a statement of owner's equity.

L. O. Merrill, Capital		
24,750	Bal.	90,000
		27,000

Income Summary			
Adj.	72,000	Adj.	76,500
	157,500		180,000
Closing	27,000		

L. O. Merrill, Drawing		
24,750	Closing	24,750

Problems

Problem 15-1 A partial work sheet for Miller Electrical Supply is presented below. The merchandise inventory at the beginning of the fiscal period is $53,200. C. L. Miller is the owner; he withdrew $25,000 during the year.

Miller Electrical Supply

Work Sheet

For year ended December 31, 19—

ACCOUNT NAME	INCOME STATEMENT	
	DEBIT	CREDIT
Sales		328 000 00
Sales Discount	3 708 00	
Sales Returns and Allowances	4 480 00	
Interest Income		1 840 00
Purchases	212 240 00	
Purchases Returns and Allowances		2 980 00
Wages Expense	43 200 00	
Rent Expense	9 600 00	
Commissions Expense	10 320 00	
Interest Expense	964 00	
Income Summary	53 200 00	44 360 00
Supplies Expense	832 00	
Insurance Expense	1 040 00	
Depreciation Expense, Equipment	3 600 00	
Depreciation Expense, Building	4 800 00	
	347 984 00	377 180 00
Net Income	29 196 00	
	377 180 00	377 180 00

Instructions 1. Prepare an income statement.

2. Journalize the closing entries.

Problem 15-2 The partial work sheet for Hunter Electronics is presented below.

Hunter Electronics

Work Sheet

For year ended December 31, 19—

ACCOUNT NAME	BALANCE SHEET	
	DEBIT	CREDIT
Cash	12 9 1 5 00	
Notes Receivable	6 3 0 0 00	
Accounts Receivable	33 2 7 0 00	
Merchandise Inventory	55 3 4 4 00	
Supplies	4 2 0 00	
Prepaid Taxes	6 3 0 00	
Prepaid Insurance	5 4 0 00	
Delivery Equipment	5 4 0 0 00	
Accum. Depr., Delivery Equipment		4 4 7 0 00
Testing Equipment	7 2 3 0 00	
Accum. Depr., Testing Equipment		5 4 2 4 00
Store Equipment	4 3 9 2 00	
Accum. Depr., Store Equipment		1 6 7 4 00
Building	60 0 0 0 00	
Accumulated Depreciation, Building		18 9 0 0 00
Land	7 8 0 0 00	
Notes Payable		4 2 1 5 00
Accounts Payable		28 1 4 0 00
Mortgage Payable (current portion)		1 8 0 0 00
Mortgage Payable		55 2 0 0 00
S. T. Hunter, Capital		67 3 1 4 00
S. T. Hunter, Drawing	22 4 4 0 00	
Wages Payable		9 8 4 00
	216 6 8 1 00	188 1 2 1 00
		28 5 6 0 00
	216 6 8 1 00	216 6 8 1 00

Instructions 1. Prepare a statement of owner's equity (no additional investment).

2. Prepare a balance sheet.

3. Determine the amount of the working capital.

4. Determine the amount of the current ratio (carry to one decimal point).

Problem 15-3 The following accounts appear in the ledger of the Huntsinger Company on December 31, the end of this fiscal year.

Cash	$ 5,400
Accounts Receivable	14,100
Merchandise Inventory	55,500
Store Supplies	690
Prepaid Insurance	1,080
Store Equipment	27,900
Accumulated Depreciation, Store Equipment	2,700
Accounts Payable	10,800
Wages Payable	—
J. N. Huntsinger, Capital	73,620
J. N. Huntsinger, Drawing	36,000
Income Summary	—
Sales	234,000
Sales Returns and Allowances	3,000
Purchases	147,000
Purchases Discount	2,400
Purchases Returns and Allowances	3,450
Wages Expense	24,000
Advertising Expense	3,900
Depreciation Expense, Store Equipment	—
Store Supplies Expense	—
Rent Expense	8,400
Insurance Expense	—

The data needed for adjustments on December 31 are as follows.

a.–b. Merchandise Inventory, December 31 $53,400

   c. Store Supplies Inventory, December 31   390

   d. Insurance expired   615

   e. Depreciation for the year   1,395

   f. Accrued wages on December 31   270

Instructions   **1.** Prepare a work sheet for the fiscal year ended December 31.

  2. Prepare an income statement.

  3. Prepare a statement of owner's equity.

  4. Prepare a balance sheet.

  5. Journalize the adjusting entries.

  6. Journalize the closing entries.

  7. Journalize the reversing entry.

Problem 15-4 The partial work sheet for Harwood and Company for the year ending June 30 is as shown on the next page.

Harwood and Company
Work Sheet
For year ended June 30, 19—

ACCOUNT NAME	INCOME STATEMENT DEBIT	INCOME STATEMENT CREDIT	BALANCE SHEET DEBIT	BALANCE SHEET CREDIT
Cash			28 2 0 0 00	
Accounts Receivable			92 0 0 0 00	
Merchandise Inventory			112 4 0 0 00	
Supplies			8 4 0 00	
Prepaid Insurance			1 2 2 0 00	
Delivery Equipment			12 4 0 0 00	
Accum. Depr., Delivery Equipment				5 8 0 0 00
Store Equipment			33 4 0 0 00	
Accum. Depr., Store Equipment				9 6 0 0 00
Accounts Payable				60 2 0 0 00
Salaries Payable				1 2 4 0 00
B. R. Harwood, Capital				167 8 2 0 00
B. R. Harwood, Drawing			28 0 0 0 00	
Income Summary	109 2 0 0 00	112 4 0 0 00		
Sales		520 0 0 0 00		
Purchases	404 0 0 0 00			
Purchases Discount		4 8 0 0 00		
Purchases Returns and Allowances		7 6 0 0 00		
Salaries Expense	48 0 0 0 00			
Truck Expense	8 6 0 0 00			
Supplies Expense	2 2 0 0 00			
Depr. Expense, Delivery Equipment	2 4 0 0 00			
Depr. Expense, Store Equipment	2 8 0 0 00			
Insurance Expense	1 8 4 0 00			
Miscellaneous Expense	1 9 6 0 00			
	581 0 0 0 00	644 8 0 0 00	308 4 60 00	244 6 60 00
Net Income	63 8 0 0 00			63 8 0 0 00
	644 8 0 0 00	644 8 0 0 00	308 4 60 00	308 4 60 00

Instructions

1. Journalize the seven adjusting entries.
2. Journalize the closing entries.
3. Journalize the reversing entry.

Alternate problems

Problem 15-1A The partial work sheet for the Grant Cycle and Toy Company is presented below. The merchandise inventory at the beginning of the fiscal period is $49,584. D. J. Grant is the owner; he withdrew $30,000 during the year.

Grant Cycle and Toy Company

Work Sheet

For year ended December 31, 19—

ACCOUNT NAME	INCOME STATEMENT DEBIT	INCOME STATEMENT CREDIT
Sales		326 592 80
Sales Discount	1 908 00	
Sales Returns and Allowances	5 229 20	
Interest Income		324 98
Purchases	209 456 00	
Purchases Returns and Allowances		1 656 00
Wages Expense	39 524 00	
Rent Expense	9 360 00	
Commissions Expense	9 440 00	
Interest Expense	656 32	
Income Summary	49 584 00	43 972 00
Supplies Expense	637 20	
Insurance Expense	936 00	
Depreciation Expense, Equipment	3 340 00	
Depreciation Expense, Building	4 800 00	
	334 870 72	372 545 78
Net Income	37 675 06	
	372 545 78	372 545 78

Instructions

1. Prepare an income statement.
2. Journalize the closing entries.

Problem 15-2A The following partial work sheet is for the Ellen Novelty Company.

Ellen Novelty Company

Work Sheet

For year ended December 31, 19—

ACCOUNT NAME	BALANCE SHEET	
	DEBIT	CREDIT
Cash	9 723 00	
Notes Receivable	3 600 00	
Accounts Receivable	42 879 60	
Merchandise Inventory	56 697 00	
Supplies	474 00	
Prepaid Taxes	613 50	
Prepaid Insurance	630 00	
Delivery Equipment	5 565 00	
Accum. Depr., Delivery Equipment		4 305 00
Store Equipment	6 570 00	
Accum. Depr., Store Equipment		4 995 00
Office Equipment	5 424 00	
Accum. Depr., Office Equipment		4 170 00
Building	63 000 00	
Accum. Depr., Building		21 600 00
Land	8 400 00	
Notes Payable		5 430 00
Accounts Payable		29 591 70
Mortgage Payable (current portion)		2 700 00
Mortgage Payable		55 713 00
M. C. Ellen, Capital		65 058 90
M. C. Ellen, Drawing	25 194 00	
Wages Payable		1 278 00
	228 770 10	194 841 60
Net Income		33 928 50
	228 770 10	228 770 10

Instructions
1. Prepare a statement of owner's equity (no additional investment).
2. Prepare a balance sheet.

3. Determine the amount of the working capital.

4. Determine the amount of the current ratio (carry to one decimal point).

Problem 15-3A The following accounts appear in the ledger of the Crandall Company as of December 31, the end of this fiscal year.

Cash	$ 4,350
Accounts Receivable	14,910
Merchandise Inventory	51,480
Store Supplies	735
Prepaid Insurance	975
Store Equipment	29,640
Accumulated Depreciation, Store Equipment	2,880
Accounts Payable	10,485
Wages Payable	—
P. H. Crandall, Capital	72,195
P. H. Crandall, Drawing	28,260
Income Summary	—
Sales	222,630
Sales Returns and Allowances	2,640
Purchases	146,310
Purchases Discount	2,565
Purchases Returns and Allowances	4,395
Wages Expense	23,100
Advertising Expense	3,150
Depreciation Expense, Store Equipment	—
Store Supplies Expense	—
Rent Expense	9,600
Insurance Expense	—

The data needed for adjustments on December 31 are as follows.

a.–b.	Merchandise Inventory, December 31	$48,240
c.	Store Supplies Inventory, December 31	270
d.	Insurance expired for the year	630
e.	Depreciation for the year	1,290
f.	Accrued wages on December 31	165

Instructions
1. Prepare a work sheet for the fiscal year ended December 31.
2. Prepare an income statement.
3. Prepare a statement of owner's equity.
4. Prepare a balance sheet.
5. Journalize the adjusting entries.

6. Journalize the closing entries.

7. Journalize the reversing entry.

Problem 15-4A The following partial work sheet covers the affairs of Davenport and Company for the year ending June 30.

Davenport Company

Work Sheet

For year ended June 30, 19—

ACCOUNT NAME	INCOME STATEMENT		BALANCE SHEET	
	DEBIT	CREDIT	DEBIT	CREDIT
Cash			32 3 84 34	
Accounts Receivable			104 6 34 54	
Merchandise Inventory			123 4 57 44	
Supplies			1 0 32 00	
Prepaid Insurance			1 3 20 00	
Delivery Equipment			12 9 20 00	
Accum. Depr., Delivery Equipment				6 4 80 00
Store Equipment			36 5 00 00	
Accum. Depr., Store Equipment				10 3 60 00
Accounts Payable				67 4 37 34
Salaries Payable				8 5 2 00
T. N. Davenport, Capital				199 9 22 58
T. N. Davenport, Drawing			37 4 40 00	
Income Summary	115 2 26 00	119 4 56 00		
Sales		536 3 52 40		
Purchases	417 2 80 00			
Purchases Discount		5 7 46 00		
Purchases Returns and Allowances		7 8 28 00		
Salaries Expense	51 4 00 00			
Truck Expense	9 3 42 00			
Supplies Expense	2 5 64 00			
Depr. Expense, Delivery Equipment	2 7 00 00			
Depr. Expense, Store Equipment	2 8 96 00			
Insurance Expense	1 9 20 00			
Miscellaneous Expense	1 4 18 00			
	604 7 46 00	669 3 82 40	349 6 88 32	285 0 51 92
Net Income	64 6 36 40			64 6 36 40
	669 3 82 40	669 3 82 40	349 6 88 32	349 6 88 32

Instructions **1.** Journalize the adjusting entries.

2. Journalize the closing entries.

3. Journalize the reversing entry.

Review of T-account placement

The following sums up the placement of T accounts covered in Chapters 11 through 15 in relation to the fundamental accounting equation. Color indicates those accounts that are treated as deductions from the related accounts above them.

Assets		=	Liabilities		+	Owner's Equity		+	Revenue		−	Expenses	
+	−		−	+		−	+		−	+		+	−
Dr	Cr		Dr	Cr		Dr	Cr		Dr	Cr		Dr	Cr

Merchandise Inventory

+	−

Sales

−	+

and Purchases

+	−

Sales Returns and Allowances

+	−

Purchases Returns and Allowances

−	+

Sales Discount

+	−

Purchases Discount

−	+

Credit Card Expense

+	−

Review of representative transactions

The following summarizes the recording of transactions covered in Chapters 11 through 15, along with a classification of the accounts involved.

Transaction	Accounts Involved	Class.	Increase or Decrease	Therefore debit or credit
Sold merchandise on account	Accounts Receivable	A	I	Dr
	Sales	R	I	Cr
Sold merchandise on account involving sales tax	Accounts Receivable	A	I	Dr
	Sales	R	I	Cr
	Sales Tax Payable	L	I	Cr
Issued credit memo to customer for merchandise returned	Sales Returns and Allowances	R	I	Dr
	Accounts Receivable	A	D	Cr

Transaction	Accounts Involved	Class.	Increase or Decrease	Therefore debit or credit
Summarizing entry for the total of sales invoices for sales on account for the month	Accounts Receivable	A	I	Dr
	Sales	R	I	Cr
Bought merchandise on account	Purchases	Purchases	I	Dr
	Accounts Payable	L	I	Cr
Received credit memo from supplier for merchandise returned	Accounts Payable	L	D	Dr
	Purchases Returns and Allowances	Purchases	I	Cr
Summarizing entry for the total of purchases of all types of goods on account	Purchases	Purchases	I	Dr
	Store Supplies	A	I	Dr
	Office Supplies	A	I	Dr
	Store Equipment	A	I	Dr
	Accounts Payable	L	I	Cr
Paid for transportation charges on incoming merchandise	Purchases	Purchases	I	Dr
	Cash	A	D	Cr
Sold merchandise, involving sales tax, for cash	Cash	A	I	Dr
	Sales	R	I	Cr
	Sales Tax Payable	L	I	Cr
Sold merchandise involving a sales tax and the customer used a bank charge card	Cash	A	I	Dr
	Credit Card Expense	E	I	Dr
	Sales	R	I	Cr
	Sales Tax Payable	L	I	Cr
Charge customer paid bill within the discount period	Cash	A	I	Dr
	Sales Discount	R	I	Dr
	Accounts Receivable	A	D	Cr
Paid invoice for the purchase of merchandise within the discount period	Accounts Payable	L	D	Dr
	Cash	A	D	Cr
	Purchases Discount	Purchases	I	Cr
First adjusting entry for merchandise inventory	Income Summary	OE	—	Dr
	Merchandise Inventory	A	D	Cr
Second adjusting entry for merchandise inventory	Merchandise Inventory	A	I	Dr
	Income Summary	OE	—	Cr
Adjusting entry for unearned revenue (Rent Income)	Unearned Rent	L	I	Cr
	Rent Income	R	D	Dr
Reversing entry for adjustment for accrued wages	Wages Payable	L	D	Dr
	Wages Expense	E	D	Cr

16 Accounting for notes payable

objectives

After you have completed this chapter, you will be able to do the following:
- Recognize a promissory note.
- Calculate the interest on promissory notes.
- Determine the due dates of promissory notes.
- Record journal entries pertaining to the following:

Note given to secure an extension of time on an open account.

Payment of an interest-bearing note at maturity.

Note given in exchange for merchandise or other property purchased.

Note given to secure a cash loan, when the borrower receives full face value of the note.

Note given to secure a cash loan, when the bank discounts the note.

Renewal of a note at maturity.

Adjustment for accrued interest on notes payable.

Adjustment for prepaid interest on notes payable.

CREDIT PLAYS an extremely important role in the operation of most business enterprises. We have seen that credit may be extended on a charge-account basis, with payment due generally in 30 days. This type of credit involves the Accounts Payable and Accounts Receivable accounts. Credit may also be granted on the basis of giving or receiving notes for specific transactions. This sort of credit involves the Notes Payable and Notes Receivable accounts. The notes represent formal instruments of credit and are known as *promissory notes*. They are customarily used as evidence of credit transactions for periods longer than 60 days. For example, promissory notes may be used in sales of equipment on the installment plan, and for transactions involving large amounts of money.

Promissory notes are also used to grant extensions of credit beyond the regular credit terms. For example, suppose that the Jones Company buys merchandise from Casper Brothers on the basis of 2/10, n/30. The Jones Company finds that it can't pay its bill within the 30-day period. To preserve its credit standing, the Jones Company offers a note. The advantages to Casper Brothers are as follows: (1) they now have specific evidence of the transaction, (2) the note may carry interest, and (3) they can borrow from the bank by pledging the note as security for a loan. Business concerns may also borrow from banks on the basis of issuing their own promissory notes.

In general, then, most companies at one time or another become involved with notes, either by issuing notes to creditors, receiving notes from customers, or issuing notes to banks incidental to borrowing money. Consequently, an accountant must be acquainted with the procedures for the handling of promissory notes.

In this chapter we shall discuss transactions involving notes payable. Chapter 17 will describe transactions involving notes receivable.

Promissory notes

A *promissory note*—usually referred to simply as a *note*—is a written promise to pay a certain sum at a fixed or determinable future time. As in the case of a check, it must be payable to the order of a particular person or firm, known as the *payee*. It must also be signed by the person or firm making the promise, known as the *maker*. In the following illustration, Argel Manufacturing Company is the payee, and North Central Plumbing Supply is the maker.

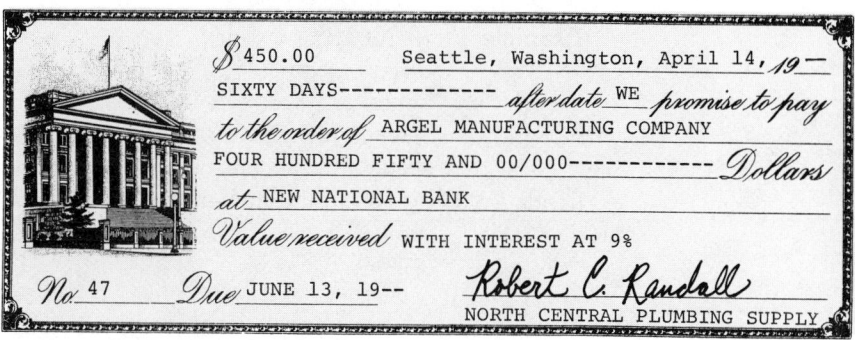

$450.00   Seattle, Washington, April 14, *19—*

SIXTY DAYS------------ *after date* WE *promise to pay to the order of* ARGEL MANUFACTURING COMPANY

FOUR HUNDRED FIFTY AND 00/000------------ *Dollars*

at NEW NATIONAL BANK

Value received WITH INTEREST AT 9%

No. 47   *Due* JUNE 13, 19--   *Robert C. Randall*

NORTH CENTRAL PLUMBING SUPPLY

Calculating interest

Interest is a charge made for the use of money. To the maker of the note, interest is an expense. The amount of interest a maker pays is expressed as a certain percentage of the principal of the note for a period of 1 year (or less). The formula for calculating interest is as follows:

Interest (in dollars)	=	**Principal** of note (in dollars)	×	**Rate** of interest (as a percentage of the principal)	×	**Time** of note (expressed as a year or fraction of a year)

The *principal* is the face amount of the note. The *rate of interest* is a percentage of the principal, such as 6% or 7%. Since 1% equals $\frac{1}{100}$ or .01, then 6% equals $\frac{6}{100}$ or .06.

Time, or the length of life of the note, is expressed in terms of days or months. It is the period between the date of issue of the note (starting date) and the date of maturity of the note (due date or interest payment date). It is stated in terms of a year or fraction of a year, such as:

$$1 \text{ year } = 1 \qquad 90 \text{ days } = \frac{90}{360}$$

$$6 \text{ months } = \frac{6}{12} \qquad 24 \text{ days } = \frac{24}{360}$$

$$3 \text{ months } = \frac{3}{12}$$

The usual commercial practice is to use a 360-day year, thus making the denominator of the fraction 360. However, agencies of the federal government use the actual number of days in the year.

Cancelation is a handy method of simplifying calculations. Since there is a multiplication sign between each element in the interest formula, one can cancel by dividing any one element of the numerator and any one element of the denominator by the same number. It is very important that you be able to calculate interest correctly; therefore please follow through each step of the following examples.

Example 1 $2,000, 8%, 1 year

$$\text{Interest} = \text{Principal} \times \text{Rate} \times \text{Time}$$

$$\text{Interest} = 2{,}000 \times \frac{8}{100} \times 1$$

Divide 2,000 by 100 in the numerator and 100 by 100 in the denominator.

$$\text{Interest} = \overset{20}{2{,}000} \times \frac{8}{\underset{1}{100}} \times 1 = \frac{20 \times 8 \times 1}{1} = \$160$$

Example 2 $4,000, 9%, 3 months.

$$\text{Interest} = \text{Principal} \times \text{Rate} \times \text{Time}$$

$$\text{Interest} = 4{,}000 \times \frac{9}{100} \times \frac{3}{12}$$

Divide 4,000 by 100 in the numerator and 100 by 100 in the denominator.

$$\text{Interest} = \overset{40}{4{,}000} \times \frac{9}{\underset{1}{100}} \times \frac{3}{12}$$

Next, divide 3 by 3 in the numerator and 12 by 3 in the denominator.

$$\text{Interest} = \overset{40}{4{,}000} \times \frac{9}{\underset{1}{100}} \times \frac{\overset{1}{3}}{\underset{4}{12}}$$

Then, divide 40 by 4 in the numerator and 4 by 4 in the denominator.

$$\text{Interest} = \overset{\overset{10}{40}}{4{,}000} \times \frac{9}{\underset{1}{100}} \times \frac{\overset{1}{3}}{\underset{\underset{1}{4}}{12}} = \frac{10 \times 9 \times 1}{1 \times 1} = \$90$$

Example 3 $6,000, 6%, 60 days.

$$\text{Interest} = \text{Principal} \times \text{Rate} \times \text{Time}$$

$$\text{Interest} = 6{,}000 \times \frac{6}{100} \times \frac{60}{360}$$

Divide 6,000 by 100 in the numerator and 100 by 100 in the denominator.

$$\text{Interest} = \overset{60}{\cancel{6,000}} \times \frac{6}{\underset{1}{\cancel{100}}} \times \frac{60}{360}$$

Next, divide 6 by 6 in the numerator and 360 by 6 in the denominator.

$$\text{Interest} = \overset{60}{\cancel{6,000}} \times \frac{\overset{1}{\cancel{6}}}{\underset{1}{\cancel{100}}} \times \frac{60}{\underset{60}{\cancel{360}}}$$

Then, divide 60 by 60 in the numerator and 60 by 60 in the denominator.

$$\text{Interest} = \overset{60}{\cancel{6,000}} \times \frac{\overset{1}{\cancel{6}}}{\underset{1}{\cancel{100}}} \times \frac{\overset{1}{\cancel{60}}}{\underset{\underset{1}{\cancel{60}}}{\cancel{360}}} = \$60$$

Example 4   \$3,640, 6%, 45 days.

$$\text{Interest} = \text{Principal} \times \text{Rate} \times \text{Time}$$

$$\text{Interest} = 3,640 \times \frac{6}{100} \times \frac{45}{360}$$

Divide 3,640 by 100 in the numerator and 100 by 100 in the denominator. (Dividing by 100 is the same as moving the decimal point two places to the left.)

$$\text{Interest} = \overset{36.4}{\cancel{3,640}} \times \frac{6}{\underset{1}{\cancel{100}}} \times \frac{45}{360}$$

Next, divide 6 by 6 in the numerator and 360 by 6 in the denominator.

$$\text{Interest} = \overset{36.4}{\cancel{3,640}} \times \frac{\overset{1}{\cancel{6}}}{\underset{1}{\cancel{100}}} \times \frac{45}{\underset{60}{\cancel{360}}}$$

Next, divide 45 by 5 in the numerator and 60 by 5 in the denominator.

$$\text{Interest} = \overset{36.4}{\cancel{3,640}} \times \frac{\overset{1}{\cancel{6}}}{\underset{1}{\cancel{100}}} \times \frac{\overset{9}{\cancel{45}}}{\underset{\underset{12}{\cancel{60}}}{\cancel{360}}}$$

Next, divide 9 by 3 in the numerator and 12 by 3 in the denominator.

$$\text{Interest} = \overset{36.4}{\cancel{3,640}} \times \frac{\overset{1}{\cancel{6}}}{\underset{1}{\cancel{100}}} \times \frac{\overset{\overset{3}{\cancel{9}}}{\cancel{45}}}{\underset{\underset{\underset{4}{\cancel{12}}}{\cancel{60}}}{\cancel{360}}}$$

Then, divide 36.4 by 4 in the numerator and 4 by 4 in the denominator.

$$\text{Interest} = \overset{\overset{9.1}{\cancel{36.4}}}{\cancel{3,640}} \times \frac{\overset{1}{\cancel{6}}}{\underset{1}{\cancel{100}}} \times \frac{\overset{\overset{3}{\cancel{9}}}{\cancel{45}}}{\underset{\underset{\underset{1}{\cancel{4}}}{\cancel{12}}}{\cancel{360}}} = \frac{9.1 \times 1 \times 3}{1 \times 1} = 9.1 \times 3 = \$27.30$$

Example 5 $5,684, 8%, 23 days.

$$\text{Interest} = \text{Principal} \times \text{Rate} \times \text{Time}$$

$$\text{Interest} = 5,684 \times \frac{8}{100} \times \frac{23}{360}$$

Divide 5,684 by 100 in the numerator and 100 by 100 in the denominator.

$$\text{Interest} = \overset{56.84}{\cancel{5,684}} \times \frac{8}{\underset{1}{\cancel{100}}} \times \frac{23}{360}$$

Next, divide 8 by 4 in the numerator and 360 by 4 in the denominator.

$$\text{Interest} = \overset{56.84}{\cancel{5,684}} \times \frac{\overset{2}{\cancel{8}}}{\underset{1}{\cancel{100}}} \times \frac{23}{\underset{90}{\cancel{360}}}$$

One could divide 2 by 2 in the numerator and 90 by 2 in the denominator, but it is apparent that the cancelation process is coming to an end, and it would be more convenient to divide later by 90 or 9 rather than by 45. Therefore, divide 23 by 10 in the numerator and 90 by 10 in the denominator. (Dividing by 10 is the same as moving the decimal point one place to the left.)

$$\text{Interest} = \overset{56.84}{\cancel{5,684}} \times \frac{\overset{2}{\cancel{8}}}{\underset{1}{\cancel{100}}} \times \frac{\overset{2.3}{\cancel{23}}}{\underset{\underset{9}{\cancel{90}}}{\cancel{360}}} = \frac{56.84 \times 2 \times 2.3}{1 \times 9}$$

$$\begin{array}{ccc}
\text{Interest} = & \begin{array}{r} 56.84 \\ \underline{\times 2.3} \\ 17052 \\ \underline{11368} \\ 130.732 \end{array} & \begin{array}{r} 130.732 \\ \underline{\times 2} \\ 261.464 \end{array} \quad \begin{array}{r} 29.052 \\ 9\overline{)261.464} \\ \underline{18} \\ 81 \\ \underline{81} \\ 4 \\ \underline{0} \\ 46 \\ \underline{45} \\ 14 \end{array}
\end{array}$$

$$\text{Interest} = \$29.05$$

Example 6 60-day, 6% (shortcut). An examination of the third example, $6,000 at 6% for 60 days, shows the following.

$$\text{Interest} = \text{Principal} \times \text{Rate} \times \text{Time}$$

$$\text{Interest} = \cancel{6{,}000} \times \frac{\overset{1}{\cancel{6}}}{\underset{1}{\cancel{100}}} \times \frac{\overset{1}{\cancel{60}}}{\underset{1}{\cancel{360}}} = 60$$

$60 is 1% of $6,000, or .01 of $6,000.

As in this case, the interest on any note that runs exactly 60 days and earns interest at exactly 6% is always *1% of the principal* of the note.

Therefore, to compute the interest on any given principal for exactly 60 days at exactly 6%, one has only to multiply the principal by 1%, or .01, or move the decimal point two places to the left: $6,000 \times .01 = 6,0.00 = 60$. The rule also applies to fractions of 60 days, as along as the 6% element is held constant. For example,

> 60 days at 6% interest = 1% of principal
> 30 days at 6% interest = $\frac{1}{2}$% of principal
> 45 days at 6% interest = $\frac{3}{4}$% of principal
> 90 days at 6% interest = $1\frac{1}{2}$% of principal

Take the case of $8,000 at 6% for 90 days.

> 1% of $8,000 = $ 80.00 (move decimal point two places to the left)
> + $\frac{1}{2}$% of $8,000 = $ 40.00 ($\frac{1}{2}$ of 80)
> _____
> $1\frac{1}{2}$% of $8,000 = $120.00

The rule also applies to fractions of 6%, as long as the 60-day element is held constant. For example,

> 60 days at 6% interest   = 1% of principal
> 60 days at 9% interest   = $1\frac{1}{2}$% of principal
> 60 days at 4% interest   = $\frac{2}{3}$% of principal
> 60 days at $7\frac{1}{2}$% interest = $1\frac{1}{4}$% of principal

Take the case of $12,000 at $7\frac{1}{2}$% for 60 days.

> 1% of $12,000 = $120.00 (move decimal point two places to the left)
> + $\frac{1}{4}$% of $12,000 = $ 30.00 ($\frac{1}{4}$ of 120)
> _____
> $1\frac{1}{4}$% of $12,000 = $150.00

The rule is also useful in estimating the interest, as in the following example. Suppose we have $9,000 at 6% for 32 days. 32 days at 6% interest is approximately equal to $\frac{1}{2}$% of the principal.

> 1% of $9,000 = $90.00 (move decimal point two places to the left)
> $\frac{1}{2}$% of $9,000 = $45.00 ($\frac{1}{2}$ of 90)

Obviously the answer should be in the neighborhood of $45. If you work out the problem by the long method, and if the answer varies greatly from $45, then it must surely be incorrect.

Determining due dates

As we have said, the period of time a note has to run may be expressed in either days or months. If the time of the note is expressed in months, the maturity date is the corresponding day in the month after the specified number of months have elapsed. For example, a note dated March 12 with a time period of 3 months has a due date of June 12. In those cases in which there is no date in the month of maturity that corresponds to the issuance date, the due date becomes the last day of the month. For example, a 3-month note dated January 31 would be due on April 30.

But suppose that the period of time a note has to run is expressed in days. In counting the number of days, begin counting with the day after the date the note was issued, since the note states "after date." The last day, however, is counted. Let us say that a promissory note has a due date which is specified as 60 days after April 14. The calendar shows the due date as being June 13:

April						
S	M	T	W	T	F	S
		1	2	3	4	5
6	7	8	9	10	11	12
13	14	15	16	17	18	19
20	21	22	23	24	25	26
27	28	29	30			

16 days
14th to the 30th
30 − 14 = 16 days left

May						
S	M	T	W	T	F	S
				1	2	3
4	5	6	7	8	9	10
11	12	13	14	15	16	17
18	19	20	21	22	23	24
25	26	27	28	29	30	31

+ 31 days

June						
S	M	T	W	T	F	S
1	2	3	4	5	6	7
8	9	10	11	12	13	14
15	16	17	18	19	20	21
22	23	24	25	26	27	28
29	30					

= 47 days have passed
60 − 47 = 13
June 13 due date

In summary, the due date is determined by the following steps.

1. Determine the number of days remaining in the month of issue by subtracting the date of the note from the number of days in the month in which it is dated.

2. Add as many full months as possible without exceeding the number of days in the note, counting the full number of days in these months.

3. Determine the number of days remaining in the month in which the note matures by subtracting the total days counted so far from the number of days in the note, as shown here.

April (30–14)	= 16 days left in April
May	= 31 days
Total days so far	= 47 days
June (60–47)	= 13th day of June (due date)

Here is an additional illustration. Suppose you have a 120-day note dated May 27.

May (31–27)	= 4 days left in May
June	= 30 days
July	= 31 days
August	= 31 days
Total days so far	= 96 days
September (120–96)	= 24th day of September (due date)

Transactions involving notes payable

The following types of transactions involve the issuance and payment of notes payable:

1. Note given to a supplier in return for an extension of time for payment of an open account (charge account)

2. Note given in exchange for merchandise or other property purchased

3. Note given as evidence of a loan

4. Note renewed at maturity

The accounts particularly involved are Notes Payable (classified as a current liability on the balance sheet) and Interest Expense (classified as Other Expense on the income statement).

Note given to secure an extension of time on an open account

When a firm wishes to obtain an extension of time for the payment of an account, the firm may ask a supplier to accept a note for all or part of the amount due. For example, let's say that North Central Plumbing Supply prefers to not pay their open account with Argel Manufacturing Company when it becomes due. Argel agrees to accept a 60-day, 9%, $450 note from North Central in settlement of the charge account. The entry that caused the account to be put on Argel's books in the first place came about when North Central bought merchandise on account on March 15, with terms 2/10, n/30. North Central recorded the transaction as a debit to Purchases for $450 and a credit to Accounts Payable. Argel Manufacturing Company, for $450. Now North Central records the issuance of the note in their general journal with the entry shown here.

	19– Apr.	14	Accounts Payable, Argel Manufacturing Company			4 5 0 00			
			Notes Payable				4 5 0 00		
			Gave a 60-day, 9% note in settlement of our						
			open account						

By T accounts, the transactions look like this:

Purchases		Accounts Payable				Notes Payable		
+		−		−	+	−		+
March 15 450		April 14 450	March 15 450				April 14 450

Observe that the above entry cancels out the Accounts Payable, Argel Manufacturing Company, account and substitutes Notes Payable. The note does not *pay* the debt, but merely changes the account from Accounts Payable to Notes Payable. Argel prefers the note to the open account because, in the case of default and a subsequent lawsuit to collect, the possession of the note improves Argel's legal position, since the note is written evidence of the debt and the amount owed. In addition, Argel is entitled to 9% interest.

Payment of an interest-bearing note at maturity

When a note payable falls due, payment may be made directly to the holder, or it may be made to a bank in which the note was left for collection. The maker of course knows the identity of the original payee, but he or she may not know who the holder of the note is at maturity, because the payee may have transferred the note by endorsement to another party, or may have left it with a bank for collection. When a note is left with a bank for collection, the bank usually mails the maker a *notice of maturity* specifying the details of the note. For example, Argel Manufacturing Company turned the note over to its bank, the New National Bank, for collection. Accordingly, the bank sent North Central a notice of maturity of note.

North Central Plumbing Supply pays the note on June 13. In general journal form, the entry is as follows.

	19– Jun.	13	Notes Payable			4 5 0 00		
			Interest Expense			6 75		
			Cash				4 5 6 75	
			Paid note to Argel Manufacturing Company.					

Because Interest = Principal × Rate × Time, we have these calculations.

$$\text{Interest} = \overset{4.5}{\cancel{450}} \times \frac{\overset{3}{\cancel{9}}}{\underset{1}{\cancel{100}}} \times \frac{\overset{1}{\cancel{60}}}{\underset{\underset{2}{\cancel{6}}}{\cancel{360}}} = \frac{4.5 \times 3}{2} = \frac{13.5}{2} = \$6.75$$

Or: 60 days at 9% = $1\frac{1}{2}$% of Principal. So Interest = $1\frac{1}{2}$% of Principal:

1% of Principal = 450 × .01	= $4.50
+ $\frac{1}{2}$% of Principal = ($\frac{1}{2}$ × 4.50) =	2.25
$1\frac{1}{2}$% of Principal =	$6.75

The organization for the entry is shown by T accounts.

Cash		Notes Payable		Interest Expense	
+	−	−	+	+	−
	456.75	450.00		6.75	

In practice, the accountant would record the foregoing transactions directly in the cash payments journal rather than in the general journal. However, to simplify the discussion of the entries, all the illustrated transactions will be presented here in general journal form. In the summary, the same transactions are repeated, and they are recorded in the appropriate special journal. As stated in Chapter 15, Notes Payable is listed in the current liabilities section of a balance sheet. Interest Expense is listed in the other expense section of an income statement.

Note given in exchange for assets purchased

Occasionally, when the price of an item is high or the credit period is long, a buyer gives a note instead of buying the item on account. For example, North Central Plumbing Supply issues a 60-day, 8% interest-bearing note for $2,400 to the Elwood Equipment Company in exchange for equipment purchased May 3, and records the transaction in their general journal as follows.

	19–				
1	May	3	Store Equipment	2 4 0 0 00	
2			Notes Payable		2 4 0 0 00
3			*Acquired shelves and counters from Elwood*		
4			*Equipment Company, 60 days, 8%.*		
5					
6					

By T accounts, it looks like this.

Store Equipment		Notes Payable	
+	−	−	+
2,400			2,400

When North Central pays the note at maturity, the entry in their books is the same as the entry they would make for the payment of any interest-bearing note. In general journal form, it looks like this.

	19–				
1	Jul.	2	Notes Payable	2 4 0 0 00	
2			Interest Expense	3 2 00	
3			Cash		2 4 3 2 00
4			*Paid note to Elwood Equipment Company.*		
5					
6					

May (31–3) = 28 days left in May
June = 30 days

Total days so far = 58 days
July (60–58) = 2nd day of July (due date)

And since Interest = Principal × Rate × Time,

$$\text{Interest} = \cancel{2400}^{24} \times \frac{\overset{4}{\cancel{8}}}{\cancel{100}_{1}} \times \frac{\overset{1}{\cancel{60}}}{\cancel{360}_{\underset{1}{\cancel{60}}}} = 4 \times 8 = \$32$$

Or: 8% for 60 days = $1\frac{1}{3}$% of Principal, so Interest = $1\frac{1}{3}$% of Principal:

$$
\begin{array}{rl}
1\% \text{ of Principal} = & \$24 \\
+ \ \frac{1}{3}\% \text{ of Principal} = & 8 \\
\hline
1\frac{1}{3}\% \text{ of Principal} = & \$32
\end{array}
$$

Note given to secure a cash loan

There are often periods in which firms need to stock up on merchandise in large amounts in order to meet seasonal demands. Sometimes their usual receipts from customers aren't enough to cover the sudden great volume of purchases. During such periods, business firms customarily borrow money from banks, through the medium of short-term notes, in order to finance their operations.

Borrowing from a bank when borrower receives full face value of note

In one type of bank loan, a business firm signs an interest-bearing note and receives the full face value of the note. The borrower repays the principal plus interest. For example, on May 11 North Central Plumbing Supply borrows $1,200 from Valley National Bank for 120 days with interest of 7% payable at maturity. The entry to record the transaction is as follows.

	19– May	11	Cash		1 2 0 0 00		
2			Notes Payable			1 2 0 0 00	2
3			Gave Valley National Bank a 120-day, 7%				3
4			note.				4
5							5

May (31–11) = 20 days left in May
June = 30 days
July = 31 days
August = 31 days

Total days so far = 112 days
September (120–112) = 8th day of September (due date)

Note paid to
the bank at
maturity

After North Central has paid the note and interest, their accountant makes the
following entry on their books.

	19–Sep.	8	Notes Payable			1 2 0 0 00				1
2			Interest Expense			2 8 00				2
3			Cash					1 2 2 8 00		3
4			Paid note to Valley National Bank.							4
5										5
6										6
7										7
8										8
9										9
10										10

$$\text{Interest} = \text{Principal} \times \text{Rate} \times \text{Time}$$

$$\text{Interest} = \overset{4}{\cancel{1,200}} \times \frac{7}{\cancel{100}} \times \frac{\overset{1}{\cancel{120}}}{\underset{1}{\cancel{360}}} = 4 \times 7 = \$28$$

Borrowing
from a bank
when bank
discounts note
(deducts
interest in
advance)

In another type of bank loan, the bank deducts the interest in advance. For
example, on May 19 North Central Plumbing Supply borrows $6,000 for 60
days from Northwest National Bank; the bank requires North Central to sign a
non-interest-bearing note. From the face value of the note, the bank deducts
9% interest for 60 days, so North Central actually gets only $5,910. This inter-
est deducted in advance by a bank is called the *discount*. The principal of the
loan left after the discount has been subtracted is called the *proceeds*, which is
the amount the borrower has available to use. The calculations are as follows.

$$\text{Interest} = \text{Principal} \times \text{Rate} \times \text{Time}$$

$$\text{Interest} = \cancel{6,000} \times \frac{9}{\cancel{100}} \times \frac{\overset{1}{\cancel{60}}}{\underset{1}{\cancel{360}}} = \$90$$

Or: Interest = $1\frac{1}{2}$% of Principal = 6,000 × .015 = $90.

As we said, the bank deducts the discount from the face amount of the note,
before making the money available to the borrower.

Principal	$6,000
Less discount	90
Proceeds	$5,910

Entry when note discounted at bank matures before end of fiscal period

As long as a note begins and matures during the same fiscal period, the borrower may debit all the interest (or discount) to Interest Expense. The note that North Central Plumbing Supply submits to the bank is dated May 19 and therefore matures July 18. Since North Central's fiscal period is from January 1 to December 31, North Central can include the entire amount of interest in Interest Expense. Accordingly, North Central records the transaction as follows.

19– May	19	Cash	5 9 1 0 00		1
		Interest Expense	9 0 00		2
		Notes Payable		6 0 0 0 00	3
		Discounted our 60-day non-interest-bearing			4
		note at the Northwest National Bank, discount			5
		rate 9%.			6

Note paid to the bank at maturity

When the note becomes due, North Central pays the bank just the *face value of the note,* and records the transaction as follows.

19– Jul.	18	Notes Payable	6 0 0 0 00		1
		Cash		6 0 0 0 00	2
		Paid Northwest National Bank on our note			3
		payable discounted.			4

May (31 − 19) = 12 days left in May
June   = 30 days

Total days so far = 42 days
July (60 − 42) = 18th day of July (due date)

Entry when note discounted at bank matures after end of fiscal period

Now suppose that the time period of the note overlaps into the next fiscal period. North Central must then initially record the amount of the discount as a debit to Prepaid Interest, since the interest the bank collects in advance does not apply altogether to the present fiscal period; part of the interest applies to the next fiscal period. Recall our discussion about the payment in advance of premiums on insurance policies, in which we said that one debits Prepaid Insurance for the amount of the insurance premiums paid in advance. The same policy applies here. Let's say that on December 1 North Central borrows $1,800 from a bank for 120 days. The bank deducts 8% interest (in advance) for 120 days and gives North Central $1,752. North Central's fiscal period is from January 1 to December 31, so their accountant's entry in the general journal is as at the top of the next page. (Some accountants prefer to record the interest deducted in advance as Interest Expense. This method necessitates an adjusting entry debiting Prepaid Interest and crediting Interest Expense. A reversing entry is also required.)

As in the case of Prepaid Insurance, the accountant has to make an adjusting entry at the end of the year to record the amount of the expense. We shall explain this procedure later in this chapter.

	19– Dec.	1	Cash			1 7 5 2 00		
			Prepaid Interest			4 8 00		
			Notes Payable				1 8 0 0 00	
			Discounted our 120-day non-interest-bearing					
			note at the bank, discount rate 8%.					

In a discounted-note transaction, since all the interest is deducted at the time the loan is made, the note must state that only the face amount is to be paid at maturity. The note, for example, may read: "90 days after date we promise to pay $1,800 with no interest," and that is why this is referred to as a *noninterest-bearing* note. Of course this is a misnomer, since the bank has actually already collected $48 in return for letting the borrower use $1,752. However, since the interest or discount is deducted in advance at the time the transaction occurs, the note must state that no additional interest is to be collected at maturity.

Renewal of note at maturity

What if the maker (or borrower) is unable to pay a note in full at maturity? Then he or she may arrange to renew all or part of the note. At this time, he or she usually pays the interest on the old note. For example, assume that on May 27 North Central Plumbing Supply issues a 60-day note to Danton, Inc., for $1,500, with interest at 8%. The original entry in general journal form is as follows.

	19– May	27	Accounts Payable, Danton, Inc.			1 5 0 0 00		
			Notes Payable				1 5 0 0 00	
			Issued a 60-day, 8% note.					

Renewal of note with payment of interest

When a firm renews an interest-bearing note, their accountant first makes an entry to pay the interest on the existing note, up to the present date. This entry occurs on July 26, the maturity date of the note.

	19– Jul.	26	Interest Expense			2 0 00		
			Cash				2 0 00	
			Interest payment on note to Danton, Inc.					

$$\text{May } (31 - 27) \quad = \quad 4 \text{ days left in May}$$
$$\underline{\text{June} \qquad\qquad = 30 \text{ days}}$$
$$\text{Total days so far} = 34 \text{ days}$$
$$\text{July } (60 - 34) \quad = 26\text{th day of July (due date)}$$

$$\text{Interest} = \text{Principal} \times \text{Rate} \times \text{Time}$$

$$\text{Interest} = \overset{\overset{5}{\cancel{15}}}{\cancel{1{,}500}} \times \frac{\overset{4}{\cancel{8}}}{\underset{1}{\cancel{100}}} \times \frac{\overset{1}{\cancel{60}}}{\underset{\underset{\underset{1}{2}}{6}}{\cancel{360}}} = 5 \times 4 = \$20$$

The accountant then makes a separate entry for the issuance of the new note, to run for 30 days at 9% (the interest rate has been increased) as follows.

26	Notes Payable		1 5 0 0 00		
	Notes Payable			1 5 0 0 00	
	Canceled note to Danton, Inc., by issuing note				
	30 days, 9%.				

Renewal of note with payment of interest and part payment of principal

Now, what if the maker decides she or he can pay *part* of a note at maturity? Let us assume that, instead of taking the above course of action, North Central pays $500 on the principal of the note which is due (the old note), and also pays the entire interest on it. In other words, the maker pays the interest up to the present date for the old note, plus $500 to reduce the principal from $1,500 to $1,000, and issues a *new* note for $1,000.

26	Notes Payable		5 0 0 00		
	Interest Expense		2 0 00		
	Cash			5 2 0 00	
	Interest payment on note to Danton, Inc.,				
	and part payment on the principal.				
26	Notes Payable		1 0 0 0 00		
	Notes Payable			1 0 0 0 00	
	Canceled note to Danton, Inc., by issuing				
	note, 30 days, 9%.				

In the case of notes that start in one fiscal period and mature in the next, adjusting entries must be made both for accrued interest and for discounts on notes payable. Otherwise, neither the expenses incurred by the business firm during a fiscal period nor its liabilities at the end of the fiscal period would be correctly stated.

Accrued interest on notes payable

On all interest-bearing notes, interest expense *accrues*, or *accumulates*, daily. Consequently, if any notes payable are outstanding at the end of a fiscal period, their accrued interest should be calculated and recorded. For example, assume that a firm has two notes payable outstanding as of December 31, the end of the current fiscal period.

$2,000, 90 days, 9%, dated December 5
$3,600, 60 days, 7%, dated December 16

We can diagram the period of each note like this.

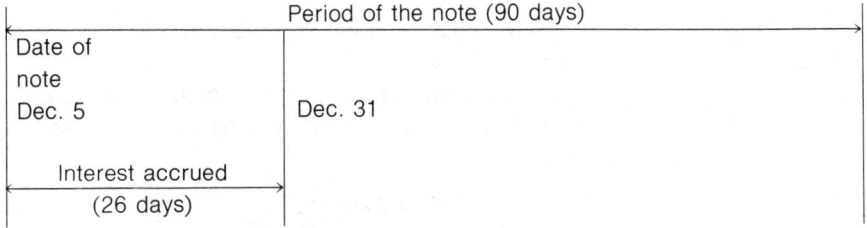

	Period of the note (90 days)
Date of note Dec. 5	Dec. 31
Interest accrued (26 days)	

Interest = Principal × Rate × Time

$$Interest = 2,000 \times \frac{9}{100} \times \frac{26}{360} = \$13$$

	Period of the note (60 days)
Date of note Dec. 16	Dec. 31
Interest accrued (15 days)	

Interest = Principal × Rate × Time

$$Interest = 3,600 \times \frac{7}{100} \times \frac{15}{360} = \$10.50$$

Obviously both notes overlap into the next fiscal period; if they didn't, there would be no need for an adjustment. When one is paying interest on notes— except for notes discounted at a bank—one usually pays the principal and interest together, on the day the note matures, or falls due. But since *these* notes have not matured, naturally the interest expense has been neither paid nor recorded. Therefore the firm has to make an adjustment, since the accountant tries to portray the firm's expenses and liabilities for the current fiscal period as accurately as possible. In general journal form, the adjusting entry for the interest expense accrued on the two notes is as follows.

	19– Dec.	31	Adjusting Entry									
1												1
2			Interest Expense					2 3 50				2
3			Interest Payable							2 3 50		3
4												4

Like all other adjustments, this one would be first recorded in the Adjustments columns of the work sheet. By T accounts, it looks like this.

Interest Expense				Interest Payable			
+		−		−		+	
Dec. 31 Bal.	724.00					Dec. 31 Adj.	23.50
Dec. 31 Adj.	23.50						

On the balance sheet, Interest Payable is classified as a current-liability account.

This situation parallels that of the adjustment for accrued salaries, in which the objective is to record the extra amount of salaries owed at the end of the year.

Salary Expense				Salaries Payable			
+		−		−		+	
Dec. 31 Adj	xxx					Dec. 31 Adj.	xxx

There is another similarity between this adjustment for accrued interest and the adjustment for accrued salaries: Both require reversing entries. The rule for reversing entries (recall Chapter 15) is: If an adjusting entry increases an asset or liability account which does not have a previous balance, then reverse the adjusting entry. Entries involving contra accounts are never reversed. The credits to Interest Payable and Salaries Payable both represent increases to liability accounts. The reversing entry enables one to record the routine entry for the payment of an interest-bearing note at maturity as a debit to Notes Payable, a debit to Interest Expense, and a credit to Cash.

Discount on notes payable

Recall that when a note payable is discounted at a bank, the bank deducts the interest (based on the principal of the note) in advance. Furthermore, if the note overlaps into the next fiscal period, the maker records the interest as Prepaid Interest. We remarked that this is just like the recording of Prepaid Insurance at the end of the year. Now let us carry this comparison a bit further. Gradually, with the passage of time, Prepaid Insurance becomes an expense, so one has to make an adjusting entry to record it. Assuming that $360 was paid in advance, and that the expense (expired insurance) now amounts to $120, here is what the T accounts look like.

	Insurance Expense				Prepaid Insurance		
	+		−		+		−
Dec. 31 Adj.	120			Bal.	360	Dec. 31 Adj.	120

Similarly, with the passage of time, Prepaid Interest gradually becomes an expense, and one has to make an adjusting entry to record it. Here is what the T accounts look like, assuming that $48 was deducted by the bank and that the expense (expired interest) now amounts to $12.

	Interest Expense				Prepaid Interest		
	+		−		+		−
Dec. 31 Adj.	12			Bal.	48	Dec. 31 Adj.	12

Now let us refer back to our example (page 423) of the original entry made on December 1, in which the firm discounted its own noninterest-bearing note at a bank. The note is to run for 120 days, and the bank discounts it at 8%. North Central's fiscal period, remember, is from January 1 to December 31.

$$\text{Interest} = \text{Principal} \times \text{Rate} \times \text{Time}$$

$$\text{Interest} = 1,800 \times \frac{8}{100} \times \frac{30}{360} = \$12$$

Since 30 days elapse between December 1 and December 31, North Central's accountant has to make an adjusting entry to record the Interest Expense.

	19– Dec.	31		Adjusting Entry									
				Interest Expense				1 2 00					
				Prepaid Interest						1 2 00			

ⁿ T accounts, it looks this way.

	Interest Expense				Prepaid Interest		
	+		−		+		−
Dec. 31 Adj.	12			Dec. 1	48	Dec. 31 Adj.	12

In addition to recording Interest Expense, the adjusting entry also serves to reduce the balance of Prepaid Interest to its correct amount.

Both accounts now reflect true balances for the end of the fiscal year, and the Interest Expense account is closed along with all the other expense accounts.

Now let us proceed one step further, and make the entries for the final payment of the note to the bank. These may be separated into two entries; the first is like the payment of any noninterest-bearing note.

	19– Mar.	31	Notes Payable		1 8 0 0 00		
			Cash			1 8 0 0 00	
			Paid the bank the 120-day non-interest-				
			bearing note, dated Dec. 1, and discounted				
			at 8%.				

The Prepaid Interest that was on the books has now become entirely an expense, so it is converted into Interest Expense.

		31	Interest Expense		3 6 00		
			Prepaid Interest			3 6 00	
			The discount for the current year for the				
			120-day non-interest-bearing note, dated				
			Dec. 1, and discounted at 8%.				

By T accounts, it looks like this.

Interest Expense				Prepaid Interest			
+		−		+		−	
Dec. 31 Adj.	12	Dec. 31 Clos.	12	Dec. 1	48	Dec. 31 Adj.	12
Mar. 31	36					Mar. 31	36

Summary

A business can obtain credit by means of an open account or charge account, or by writing a promissory note providing for payment of the principal either in one sum or in installments.

The formula for calculating interest is: Interest = Principal × Rate × Time. The principal is the face amount of the note. The rate is a percentage of the principal. The time is a year or fraction of a year. Normally, in determining the maturity date, one uses the exact number of days in each month.

Illustrations of transactions involving notes payable are given on pages 429–432. Each is first recorded in general journal form, just as in previous cases. (To conserve space, we omit the explanations here.) However, if the Cash account is involved, the entry is journalized in the form of either a cash receipts journal or a cash payments journal.

April 14: Issued a 60-day, 9% note, for $450, payable to Argel Manufacturing Company, in place of the open-book account.

			Accounts Payable, Argel Manufacturing Co.			4 5 0 00				
			Notes Payable					4 5 0 00	

June 13: Paid the note given to Argel Manufacturing Company at maturity.

			Notes Payable			4 5 0 00				
			Interest Expense			6 75				
			Cash					4 5 6 75	

The same entry in a cash payments journal looks like this.

CASH PAYMENTS JOURNAL   PAGE _____

DATE	CK. NO.	ACCOUNT NAME	POST. REF.	SUNDRY ACCOUNTS DR.	ACCOUNTS PAYABLE DR.	PURCHASES DISCOUNT CR.	CASH CR.
19– Jun.	13	Notes Payable		4 5 0 00			4 5 6 75
		Interest Expense		6 75			

May 3: Issued a 60-day, 8% note, for $2,400, payable to the Elwood Equipment Company, for equipment.

			Store Equipment			2 4 0 0 00				
			Notes Payable					2 4 0 0 00	

July 2: Paid note given to Elwood Equipment Company at maturity.

			Notes Payable			2 4 0 0 00				
			Interest Expense			3 2 00				
			Cash					2 4 3 2 00	

The same entry in a cash payments journal looks like this.

CASH PAYMENTS JOURNAL   PAGE _____

DATE	CK. NO.	ACCOUNT NAME	POST. REF.	SUNDRY ACCOUNTS DR.	ACCOUNTS PAYABLE DR.	PURCHASES DISCOUNT CR.	CASH CR.
19– Jul.	2	Notes Payable		2 4 0 0 00			2 4 3 2 00
		Interest Expense		3 2 00			

May 11: Borrowed $1,200 from the Valley National Bank, giving them a 120-day, 7% note (received full face amount).

1		*Cash*			1 2 0 0 00			1
2		*Notes Payable*					1 2 0 0 00	2
3								3

The same entry in a cash receipts journal looks like this.

CASH RECEIPTS JOURNAL   PAGE _____

	DATE	ACCOUNT CREDITED	POST. REF.	SUNDRY ACCOUNTS CR.	ACCOUNTS REC. CR.	SALES CR.	CASH DR.	
1	19– May 11	Notes Payable		1 2 0 0 00			1 2 0 0 00	1
2								2

September 8: Paid loan in full, at maturity, to the Valley National Bank.

1		*Notes Payable*			1 2 0 0 00			1
2		*Interest Expense*			2 8 00			2
3		*Cash*					1 2 2 8 00	3
4								4

The same entry in a cash payments journal looks like this.

CASH PAYMENTS JOURNAL   PAGE _____

	DATE	CK. NO.	ACCOUNT NAME	POST. REF.	SUNDRY ACCOUNTS DR.	ACCOUNTS PAYABLE DR.	PURCHASES DISCOUNT CR.	CASH CR.	
1	19– Sep.	8	Notes Payable		1 2 0 0 00			1 2 2 8 00	1
2			Interest Expense		2 8 00				2
3									3

May 19: Borrowed $6,000 from Northwest National Bank for 90 days; discount rate is 6%; issued a noninterest-bearing note for $6,000.

1		*Cash*			5 9 1 0 00			1
2		*Interest Expense*			9 0 00			2
3		*Notes Payable*					6 0 0 0 00	3
4								4
5								5

The same entry in a cash receipts journal appears atop the facing page.

DATE		ACCOUNT CREDITED	POST. REF.	SUNDRY ACCOUNTS		SALES CR.	CASH DR.
				DEBIT	CREDIT		
19— May	19	*Interest Expense*		9 0 00			5 9 1 0 00
		Notes Payable			6 0 0 0 00		

July 18: Paid bank when loan matured.

		Notes Payable			6 0 0 0 00		
		Cash					6 0 0 0 00

The same entry in a cash payments journal looks like this.

DATE		CK. NO.	ACCOUNT NAME	POST. REF.	SUNDRY ACCOUNTS DR.	ACCOUNTS PAYABLE DR.	PURCHASES DISCOUNT CR.	CASH CR.
19— Jul.	18		*Notes Payable*		6 0 0 0 00			6 0 0 0 00

May 27: Issued a 60-day note payable to Danton, Inc., for $1,500, with interest at 8%, in place of open-book account.

		Accounts Payable, Danton, Inc.		1 5 0 0 00			
		Notes Payable			1 5 0 0 00		

July 26: Paid interest up to the present date on note given to Danton, Inc., and issued a new 30-day note for $1,500 with interest at 9%.

		Interest Expense		2 0 00			
		Cash					2 0 00

The entry involving Cash, recorded in a cash payments journal, looks like this.

DATE		CK. NO.	ACCOUNT NAME	POST. REF.	SUNDRY ACCOUNTS DR.	ACCOUNTS PAYABLE DR.	PURCHASES DISCOUNT CR.	CASH CR.
19— Jul.	26		*Interest Expense*		2 0 00			2 0 00

Also we would have:

1		Notes Payable		1 5 0 0 00	
2		Notes Payable			1 5 0 0 00
3					

We discussed two kinds of end-of-year adjustments:

a. Accrued interest on notes payable. Suppose the figure is $23.50. The entry is like the adjusting entry for accrued salaries.

b. Prepaid interest expired on notes payable. Suppose the figure is $12. The entry is like the adjusting entry for expired insurance.

ACCOUNT NAME	TRIAL BALANCE		ADJUSTMENTS		INCOME STATEMENT		BALANCE SHEET	
	DEBIT	CREDIT	DEBIT	CREDIT	DEBIT	CREDIT	DEBIT	CREDIT
Prepaid Interest	4 8 00			(b) 1 2 00			3 6 00	
Interest Expense	7 2 4 00		(a) 2 3 50		7 5 9 50			
			(b) 1 2 00					
Interest Payable				(a) 2 3 50				2 3 50

Glossary

Accrued interest on notes payable   For notes payable beginning in one fiscal period and maturing in the following fiscal period, accrued interest is the interest expense from the date of issue of the note until the last day of the fiscal period.

Discounting a note payable   The procedure by which a bank collects interest in advance when it loans money.

Maker   An individual or firm which signs a promissory note.

Maturity date   The due date of a promissory note.

Payee   The party receiving payment.

Principal   The face amount of a note.

Proceeds   The principal of a loan less the discount.

Promissory note   A written promise to pay a certain sum at a fixed and determinable future time.

Questions

1. What are three characteristics of a promissory note?

2. Define the two parties to a promissory note.

3. What is the basic formula for the calculation of interest?

4. Describe the 60 day, 6% method of calculating interest.

5. Explain the situation whereby a firm discounts its own noninterest-bearing note at a bank.

6. Regarding a case where a business has borrowed from a bank, and the bank discounts the business' note, why is the effective rate of interest higher than the discount rate charged by the bank?

7. Explain why it is necessary to make an adjusting entry for accrued interest on an interest-bearing note payable. Should the entry be reversed?

Exercises

Exercise 1 Determine the interest on the following notes.

	Principal	Number of Days	Interest Rate
a.	$1,200	60	6%
b.	900	60	8%
c.	1,600	90	9%
d.	1,550	63	7½%
e.	780	45	7%

Exercise 2 Determine the maturity dates on the following notes.

	Date of Issue	Time Period
a.	March 28	60 days
b.	October 18	90 days
c.	June 26	30 days
d.	December 12	3 months
e.	July 1	120 days

Exercise 3 On March 16, G. D. Radach Company gives a 90-day, 6% note for $2,000 to Lyon Company on account.

a. What is the due date of the note?

b. How much interest is to be paid on the note at maturity?

c. On Radach's books, show entries, in general journal form, to record the following: (1) issuance of the note by the maker, (2) payment of the note at maturity.

Exercise 4 As the result of a loan from the Hobbs State Bank, the Gilbert Company signed a 90-day, noninterest-bearing note for $28,000, which the bank discounted at 7%. Present the entries for the maker in general journal form to record the following, assuming that the note is paid in the same fiscal period.

a. Issuance of the note.

b. Payment of the note at maturity.

Exercise 5 In arranging for a 60-day loan from a bank, Harbor Machinery Company has the option of giving either a $72,000, 7% interest-bearing note that will be accepted at face value, or a $72,000 noninterest-bearing note discounted at 7%.

a. What is the amount of interest in each case?

b. What is the amount Harbor Machinery Company actually receives in each case?

c. Which of the two alternatives is more favorable to Harbor Machinery Company?

Exercise 6 On August 1, Flagel Shake Shop bought the land and building that it was formerly renting. The terms of sale are land, $9,000; building, $42,000; cash downpayment, $15,000; and the balance in the form of an 8% note, secured by a 10-year mortgage on the property. The terms of the note provide for 120 monthly payments of $260 each on the principal plus interest on the unpaid balance. Give entries in general journal form to record the following.

a. The transaction on August 1.

b. The payment of the first installment on September 1.

c. The payment of the second installment on October 1.

Exercise 7 On October 9, Mountain View Sales issued a 90-day, 8% note to Norton Supply Company, a creditor, for $7,200. Present the entries in general journal form to record the following.

a. Issuance of the note on October 9.

b. Adjusting entry for accrued interest on December 31, the end of the fiscal year.

Exercise 8 On December 4, Mountain View Sales borrowed $9,600 from Central National Bank for 60 days, with a discount rate of 8%. Accordingly, Mountain View Sales signed a noninterest-bearing note for $9,600. The end of the fiscal year is December 31. Give entries in general journal form to record the following.

a. Issuance of the note on December 4.

b. Adjusting entry on December 31.

c. Payment of the note at maturity (two entries) on February 2.

Problems

Problem 16-1 The following were among the transactions of the Salmon Company.

Jan. 12 Bought merchandise on account from S. T. Fritz Company, $1,800.

Feb. 15 Bought merchandise on account from Stevens and Company, $2,400.

Mar. 17 Gave a 30-day, 6% note for $2,400 to Stevens and Company to apply on account.

Apr. 16 Paid Stevens and Company the amount owed on the note of March 17.

May 24 Borrowed $6,000 from Pioneer National Bank, giving a 60-day, 7% note for that amount (received full face value).

July 23 Paid Pioneer National Bank the amount due on the note of May 24.

Instructions Record these transactions in general journal form.

Problem 16-2 The following were among the transactions of Woodworth and Company during this year.

Jan. 26 Bought merchandise on account from Neilson and Frisk, $2,700.

Feb. 27 Gave a 30-day, 8% note for $2,700 to Neilson and Frisk to apply on account.

Mar. 29 Paid Neilson and Frisk the amount owed on the note of February 27.

Apr. 3 Bought merchandise on account from Gavin Hardware Company, $6,300.

May 4 Gave a 30-day, 6% note for $6,300 to Gavin Hardware Company to apply on account.

June 3 Paid Gavin Hardware Company the interest due on the note of May 4, and renewed the obligation by issuing a new 60-day, 8% note for $6,300.

Aug. 2 Paid Gavin Hardware Company the amount owed on the note of June 3.

18 Borrowed $7,500 from Spencer National Bank for 90 days; discount rate is 8%. Accordingly, signed a noninterest-bearing note for $7,500.

Nov. 16 Paid Spencer National Bank at maturity of loan.

Instructions Record these transactions in general journal form.

Problem 16-3 The following were among the transactions of Witten and Company during this year.

Jan. 29 Bought merchandise on account from Rowe and Saunders, $3,900, 2/10, n/30.

Feb. 28 Gave a 30-day, 7% note to Rowe and Saunders, dated February 28, to apply on account, covering purchase of January 29.

Mar. 30 Paid $900 as part payment on principal as well as the full interest on note given to Rowe and Saunders; issued a new note for $3,000, 60 days, 8%, dated March 30.

May 29 Paid amount owed on note dated March 30.

July 20 Borrowed $4,500 from Atlanta Trust Bank for 90 days, discount rate is 7%. Accordingly, signed a noninterest-bearing note for $4,500.

Oct. 18 Paid amount owed on note given to Atlanta Trust Bank, dated July 20.

Nov. 16 Bought a cash register and display shelves for $3,300 from Foster Supply Company. Issued a note, 90 days, 8%, dated Nov. 16.

Dec. 31 Recorded the adjusting entry for accrued interest on the note given to Foster Supply Company.

Instructions Using the cash receipts journal, the cash payments journal, and the general journal, record these transactions in the appropriate journal.

Problem 16-4 The following were among the transactions of Walker Industrial Tool Company during the year ending December 31.

June   6 Gave a note to Lange Construction Company, $25,200, for an addition to the showroom, 60 days, 8%, dated June 6.

      28 Borrowed $8,400 from Tri-County Mutual Bank signing a 3-month, 8%, note for that amount, dated June 28 (received full face value).

July 18 Gave a note to Johnson Equipment Company for data processing equipment, $14,460, at 9% for 90 days, dated July 18. The invoice was not previously recorded.

Aug.   5 Paid the amount owed on the note given to Lange Construction Company.

Sept. 28 Paid interest on note given to Tri-County Mutual Bank; renewed loan by issuing note for 60 days at 8%, dated September 28.

Oct. 16 Paid amount owed on note given to Johnson Equipment Company.

      27 Gave two notes to Francis Machine Company in settlement of their September 26 invoice for merchandise, as follows: $4,500, 30 days, 8%, dated October 27; $4,500, 60 days, 8%, dated October 27. The invoice was not previously recorded.

Nov. 26 Paid amount owed on 30-day note given to Francis Machine Company.

      27 Paid note given to Tri-County Mutual Bank.

Dec. 11 Issued note payable to Story and Rule Company in settlement of November 11 bill for merchandise, $6,900, at 7% for 60 days, dated December 11. The invoice was previously recorded.

      16 Borrowed $11,250 from Adams National Bank for 60 days; discount rate is 7%; issued a noninterest-bearing note for $11,250 (debit Prepaid Interest, as the note extends into the next fiscal period).

      26 Paid amount owed on the 60-day note given to Francis Machine Company.

Instructions   **1.** Record these transactions in a general journal.

2. Record the adjusting entries for the notes issued to Story and Rule Company and Adams National Bank.

Alternate problems

Problem 16-1A The following were among the transactions of the F. J. Fowler Company during this year.

Jan. 14 Bought merchandise on account from J. C. Nelson Company $2,400.

      22 Paid J. C. Nelson Company for the invoice of January 14, less 2% discount.

Feb. 18 Bought merchandise on account from Gallaher and Company, $2,850.

Mar. 20 Gave a 60-day, 6% note for $2,850 to Gallaher and Company to apply on account.

May 19 Paid Gallaher and Company the amount owed on the note of March 20.

June 3 Borrowed $5,700 from Midwest National Bank, giving a 90-day, 7% note for that amount (received full face value).

Sept. 1 Paid Midwest National Bank the amount due on the note of June 3.

Instructions   Record these transactions in general journal form.

Problem 16-2A   The following were among the transactions of Hanson Motors and Machine during this year.

Feb. 12 Bought merchandise on account from John T. Coe Company, $2,640.

Mar. 13 Gave a 30-day, 7% note for $2,640 to John T. Coe Company to apply on account.

Apr. 12 Paid John T. Coe Company amount owed on note of March 13.

May 2 Bought merchandise on account from Harris Tool Company, $6,900.

June 3 Gave a 30-day, 8% note for $6,900 to Harris Tool Company to apply on account.

July 3 Paid Harris Tool Company interest due on note of June 3 and renewed obligation by issuing a new 60-day, 9%, note for $6,900.

Sept. 1 Paid Harris Tool Company amount owed on note of July 3.

24 Borrowed $9,000 from Conrad National Bank for 90 days; discount rate is 7%. Accordingly, signed a noninterest-bearing note for $9,000.

Dec. 23 Paid Conrad National Bank at maturity of loan.

Instructions   Record these transactions in general journal form.

Problem 16-3A   The following were among the transactions of Brady Appliances during this year.

Jan. 16 Bought merchandise on account from P. J. Smith Company, $4,800.

Feb. 15 Gave a 30-day, 7%, note to P. J. Smith Company, dated Feb. 15, to apply on account, covering purchase of January 16.

Mar. 17 Paid $1,200 as part payment of principal as well as full interest on the note given to P. J. Smith Company; issued new note for $3,600, 60 days, 8%, dated March 17.

May 12 Borrowed $6,600 from the Florida National Bank for 90 days; discount rate is 7%. Accordingly, signed a noninterest-bearing note for $6,600.

16 Paid amount owed on the note issued to P. J. Smith Company, dated March 17.

Aug. 10 Paid amount owed on the note issued to the Florida National Bank, dated May 12.

Nov. 25 Bought two calculators for $8,400 from Sperry Office Supply; issued a note, 60 days, 8%.

Dec. 31 Recorded the adjusting entry for accrued interest on the note given to Sperry Office Supply.

Instructions   Using the cash receipts journal, the cash payments journal, and the general journal, record these transactions in the appropriate journal.

Problem 16-4A   The following were among the transactions of the Modern Restaurant Supply Company during the year ending December 31.

May   29 Gave note to Grissom and Son, $27,000, for an addition to the building, 60 days at 8%, dated May 29.

June 26 Borrowed $9,600 from New York Exchange Bank, signing a 3-month, 8% note for that amount, dated June 26 (received full face value).

July   20 Gave note to Hadley Office Equipment for data processing equipment, $13,350, at 9% for 90 days, dated July 20. The invoice was not previously recorded.

28 Paid amount on note given to Grissom and Son.

Sept. 26 Paid interest on note issued to New York Exchange Bank; renewed loan by issuing new note for 60 days at 8%, dated September 26.

Oct.   18 Paid amount owed on the note given to Hadley Office Equipment.

29 Gave two notes to Jones Manufacturing Company in settlement of October 29 invoice for merchandise, as follows: $5,400 note for 30 days at 8%, dated October 29; $5,400 note for 60 days at 8%, dated October 29. The invoice was not previously recorded.

Nov. 25 Paid note given to New York Exchange Bank.

28 Paid amount owed on the 30-day note given to Jones Manufacturing Company.

Dec.   11 Issued note to Buchanan and Foss Company in settlement of November 21 invoice for merchandise, $6,750, at 9% for 60 days, dated December 11. The invoice was previously recorded.

21 Borrowed $12,600 from Fisher National Bank for 60 days; discount rate is 7%; signed a noninterest-bearing note for $12,600 (debit Prepaid Interest, since note extends into next fiscal period).

28 Paid amount owed on 60-day note given to Jones Manufacturing Company.

Instructions   **1.** Record these transactions in a general journal.

2. Record the adjusting entries for notes issued to Buchanan and Foss Company and Fisher National Bank.

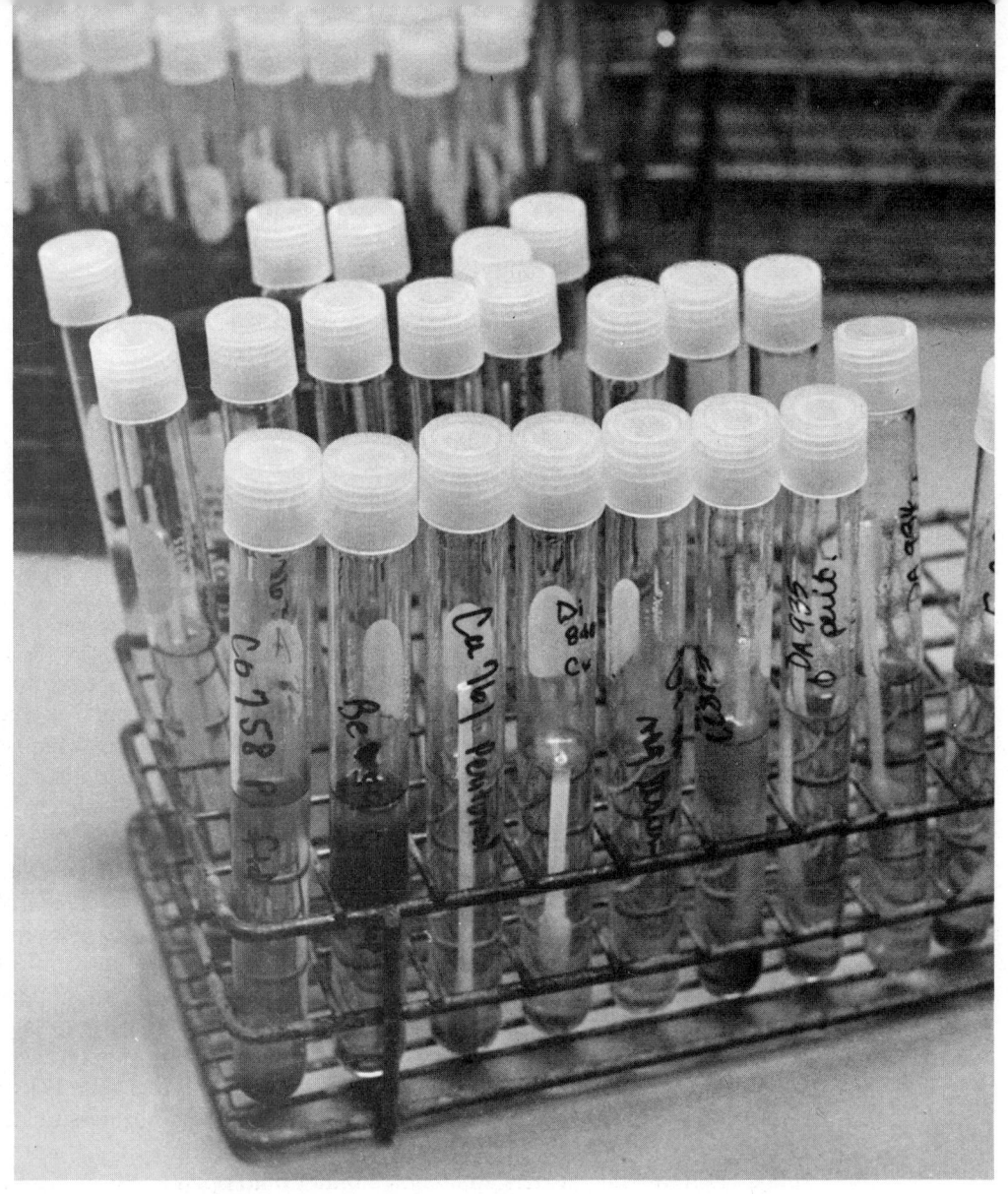

17 *Accounting for notes receivable*

objectives

After you have completed this chapter, you will be able to record journal entries pertaining to these transactions:
- Receipt of a note from a charge customer.
- Receipt of payment of an interest-bearing note at maturity.
- Receipt of a note as a result of granting a personal loan.
- Receipt of a note in exchange for merchandise or other property.
- Renewal of a note at maturity.
- Dishonored notes receivable.
- Collection on a note receivable formerly dishonored.
- Discounting an interest-bearing note.
- Dishonoring of a discounted note receivable.
- Adjustment for accrued interest on notes receivable.

BUSINESS FIRMS receive promissory notes for a variety of reasons, either regularly or occasionally. Sometimes a business firm accepts a promissory note from a customer at the time of sale. But companies frequently also accept promissory notes from their charge-account customers who may request an extension of time to settle past-due accounts. In this way they in effect substitute notes receivable for open accounts. The net result is that the charge customer gets an extension of time for the payment of a debt.

Obviously, this is not as good as having the cash in hand. However, it is advantageous to the company in that (1) the note represents proof of the original transaction, (2) the note may bear interest, and (3) the note may be pledged as security for a loan from a bank. In this last situation, banks loan a higher proportion of the total of notes (Notes Receivable), as compared to open accounts (Accounts Receivable). For example, a loan may be granted for 100% of the face value of notes versus 60% of the face value of open accounts.

Notes receivable may also come into being when a company grants loans to employees or preferred customers or suppliers. In some business fields, the credit period is often longer than the normal 30-day period; here, the transactions are frequently evidenced by notes rather than open accounts. Examples are sales of farm machinery, construction equipment, trucks, etc.

Let us now have a look at the way to journalize transactions involving notes receivable. The accounts particularly involved are Notes Receivable (classified as a current asset on the balance sheet) and Interest Income (classified as Other Income on the income statement).

Transactions for notes receivable

First, let us say that all notes received are recorded in a single account, *Notes Receivable*. Second, throughout this chapter we are going to use North Central Plumbing Supply to illustrate such transactions. Now let's begin with a simple example.

On March 6, North Central Plumbing Supply sold $480 worth of merchandise to Henning's Plumbing, with their customary terms of 2/10, n/30, and recorded the original entry in their sales journal. On April 6, Henning's sent North Central a note for $480, payable within 30 days, at 8% interest; the note, dated April 6, was in settlement of the transaction of March 6. North Central Plumbing Supply recorded this new development in their general journal as follows.

	GENERAL JOURNAL		PAGE _____	

	DATE		DESCRIPTION	POST REF.	DEBIT	CREDIT	
1	19– Apr.	6	Notes Receivable		480 00		1
2			Accounts Receivable, Henning's Plumbing			480 00	2
3			Received a 30-day, 8% note, dated Apr. 6,				3
4			in settlement of open account.				4
5							5

By T accounts, the transactions look like this.

Accounts Receivable		Sales		Notes Receivable	
+	–	–	+	+	–
Mar. 6 480	Apr. 6 480		Mar. 6 480	Apr. 6 480	

Receipt of
payment of an
interest-bearing
note at maturity

On May 6 Henning's paid North Central in full: principal plus interest. North Central recorded the transaction in their general journal as follows.

	DATE		DESCRIPTION	POST REF.	DEBIT	CREDIT	
1	19– May	6	Cash		483 20		1
2			Notes Receivable			480 00	2
3			Interest Income			3 20	3
4			Received full payment of Henning's note.				4
5							5

Let's look at the T accounts for this entry.

Cash		Notes Receivable		Interest Income	
+	–	+	–	–	+
483.20			480.00		3.20

In practice, this transaction would be recorded directly in the cash receipts journal rather than in the general journal. But, for the sake of simplicity and clarity, we'll use the general journal format to illustrate entries throughout this chapter. In the summary, we'll repeat the transactions and record them in the appropriate journals.

Notes received as a result of granting personal loans

Sometimes employees, preferred customers, or suppliers may want to borrow cash from the business, and in that case the business often accepts a note receivable. Let's say that Roger Fennell, an employee of North Central Plumbing Supply, borrows $336 from his employer, for 3 months at 6%. His note is dated April 8. In general journal form, the entry is as shown below.

	19– Apr.	8	Notes Receivable		3 3 6 00		1
			Cash			3 3 6 00	2
			Granted a loan to Roger Fennell, 3 months,				3
			6%, dated Apr. 8.				4

When the loan reaches maturity, Fennell pays the principal plus interest.

	19– Jul.	8	Cash		3 4 1 04		1
			Notes Receivable			3 3 6 00	2
			Interest Income			5 04	3
			Roger Fennell's note, dated Apr. 8.				4

Note received in exchange for merchandise or other property

Recall that we said that some business firms who sell high-priced durable goods in which the credit period is longer than the normal 30 days may fairly regularly accept notes from their customers. (This does not include installment sales; they are discussed separately in Appendix C.)

On April 9, North Central Plumbing Supply sold merchandise to Maxwell Heating and Air Conditioning for $900. Maxwell gave North Central a promissory note, promising to pay the full amount within 60 days; the note specified 7% interest. When this type of transaction occurs occasionally, the transaction is recorded in the general journal as follows.

	19– Apr.	9	Notes Receivable		9 0 0 00		1
			Sales			9 0 0 00	2
			Maxwell Heating and Air Conditioning,				3
			60-day, 7% note, dated Apr. 9.				4

However, if this type of transaction were to occur frequently, North Central would have a Notes Receivable debit column in the sales journal, just to record such transactions.

Renewal of note at maturity and payment of interest

If the maker of a note is unable to pay the entire principal at maturity, he or she may be allowed to renew all or a part of the note.

Now suppose that Maxwell Heating and Air Conditioning was not able to pay the note at maturity, and offered to pay the interest on the current note and issue a new note, for 30 days at 8%. North Central records the entries in general journal form, as follows.

	19— Jun.	8	Cash			1 0 50			
			Interest Income				1 0 50		
			Maxwell Heating and Air Conditioning note,						
			dated Apr. 9.						
		8	Notes Receivable			9 0 0 00			
			Notes Receivable				9 0 0 00		
			Maxwell Heating and Air Conditioning						
			renewal of note, dated Apr. 9, new note						
			is dated June 8, 30 days, 8%.						

Note that, in actuality, there is only one Notes Receivable ledger account. When a firm renews a note, it is customary for the debtor or maker to pay the interest on the old note and issue a new one.

Renewal of note with payment of interest and partial payment of principal

Sometimes the maker of a note cancels the original note by paying the interest, plus part of the principal, and issuing a new one. Suppose that as a substitute for the $900 note described above, Maxwell gives North Central $300 toward the principal and a new note for $600, in addition to the interest on the old note.

North Central would record the transactions in the general journal as shown at the top of the next page.

	19– Jun.	8	Cash			3 1 0 50		1
2			Interest Income				1 0 50	2
3			Notes Receivable				3 0 0 00	3
4			Maxwell Heating and Air Conditioning note,					4
5			dated Apr. 9, and partial payment of the					5
6			principal.					6
7								7
8		8	Notes Receivable			6 0 0 00		8
9			Notes Receivable				6 0 0 00	9
10			Maxwell Heating and Air Conditioning partial					10
11			payment and renewal of note, dated Apr. 9;					11
12			the new note is dated June 8, 30 days, 8%.					12
13								13
14								14

Dishonored notes receivable

When the maker of a note fails to pay the principal amount or to renew the note at maturity, the note is said to be *dishonored*. The maker of the note is still obligated to pay the principal plus interest, and the creditor should take legal steps to collect the debt. However, the balance of the Notes Receivable account should show only the principals of notes that have not yet matured. Therefore a note that is past due, or dishonored, should be removed from the Notes Receivable account and returned to the Accounts Receivable account; the amount listed should be the principal plus interest.

For example, North Central Plumbing Supply holds an $800, 7%, 60-day note, dated April 20, from Baker Building Supplies, who fails to pay by the due date. Thus the note is dishonored at maturity. Accordingly, North Central makes the following entry in its general journal to remove the dishonored note from the Notes Receivable account.

	19– Jun.	19	Accounts Receivable, Baker Building Supplies			8 0 9 33		1
2			Notes Receivable				8 0 0 00	2
3			Interest Income				9 33	3
4			Baker Building Supplies dishonored their					4
5			$800, 7%, 60-day note, dated Apr. 20.					5
6								6

Baker Building Supplies owes both the principal and the interest, and the account should reflect the full amount owed. Note particularly that North Central credits the Interest Income account, even though Baker didn't pay the interest. This is consistent with the accrual basis of accounting, in which revenue is recorded when it is *earned*, rather than when it is received. If Baker Building Supplies should ever ask North Central to act as a credit reference, or if Baker ever asks for credit in the future, their account will show all past dealings, including the dishonored note.

Collection of a dishonored note

Now suppose that 30 days after their note has been dishonored, Baker Building Supplies pays up the balance of its account, plus an additional 30 days' interest at 7% on the amount owed. The entry in North Central's general journal is as follows.

	DATE		DESCRIPTION	POST REF.	DEBIT	CREDIT
1	19– Jul.	19	Cash		8 1 4 05		1
2			Accounts Receivable, Baker Building Supplies			8 0 9 33	2
3			Interest Income			4 72	3
4			Baker Building Supplies paid the dishonored				4
5			note, plus interest for 30 days at 7%.				5
6							6

So North Central gets its money in the long run anyway, and it can now consider the matter closed.

Discounting notes receivable

One advantage a business firm gets from accepting notes receivable is that they can use the notes to help them borrow money from a bank by pledging the notes as security for a loan. This is known as *discounting notes receivable*.

We said in Chapter 16 that in discounting notes, the bank merely deducts its interest charge in advance. Furthermore, the deduction or discount is figured on the value of the note at its maturity, consisting of the principal plus the interest, as indicated on the note. Therefore, when the firm borrows from a bank, it endorses the note and delivers it to the bank in exchange for cash. The bank holds the note until it becomes due, and collects the maturity value from the maker of the note. The time period of the loan is the time remaining on the customer's note.

A discounted note: illustration 1 North Central Plumbing Supply, to grant an extension on an open account, accepted an 8%, 60-day note for $540, dated April 20, from Clark and Keller Hardware. To raise cash to buy additional merchandise, on May 5 North Central borrowed from Valley National Bank, giving Clark and Keller's note as security for the loan; the bank charged a discount rate of 7%. A diagram of the situation looks like this.

Period of the note (60 days)	
Date of note Apr. 20	Date borrowed May 5
North Central holds note	Bank holds note (discount period)

Now remember that North Central is borrowing money from the bank on the basis of the maturity value of the note pledged as security for the loan. The time period of the loan consists of the interval between the date the note is given to the bank and the maturity date of the note. This is referred to as the *discount period*. Now we ask: How many days are there in the discount period? For emphasis, let us repeat the diagram in abbreviated form.

	Period of the note (60 days)	
Apr. 20	May 5	
├──15 days──┤	Discount period	
	(60 − 15 = 45 days)	

Next we determine the value of the note at its maturity, and deduct the amount of the bank's discount from it, using the following listing or formula.

Principal ($540)
+ Interest to maturity date (8%, 60 days)
= Value at maturity
− Discount (7%, 45 days)
= Proceeds

After we set up the problem, we can complete the calculation.

Principal	$540.00
+ Interest (8%, 60 days)	7.20
= Value at maturity	$547.20
− Discount (7%, 45 days)	4.79
= Proceeds	$542.41

Interest = Principal × Rate × Time

$$\text{Interest} = 540 \times \frac{8}{100} \times \frac{60}{360} = \$7.20$$

Interest = Principal × Rate × Time

$$\text{Interest} = 547.20 \times \frac{7}{100} \times \frac{45}{360} = \$4.788$$

Note that in our calculations we figure the discount on the value of the note at maturity ($547.20, 7%, 45 days). The *proceeds* are the amount that North Central Plumbing Supply receives from the bank; this amount is therefore debited to Cash. If the amount of the proceeds is greater than the amount of the principal, the difference represents Interest Income, since North Central Plumbing Supply made money on the deal. In general journal form, the entry looks like that shown at the top of the facing page.

In keeping with what we said above, if the amount of the proceeds is larger than the principal, the extra amount represents Interest Income. Conversely, if the amount of the proceeds is less than the principal, the deficiency represents Interest Expense.

	19– May	5	Cash				5 4 2 41					1
2			Notes Receivable					5 4 0 00			2
3			Interest Income					2 41			3
4			Discounted at the bank Clark and Heller								4
5			Hardware's note, dated Apr. 20. The bank								5
6			discount rate is 7%.								6
7											7
8											8
9											9
10											10
11											11

Contingent
liability

At the time North Central Plumbing Supply discounted Clark and Keller's note at the bank, North Central had to endorse the note. By this endorsement, North Central was agreeing to pay the note when it became due, if it were not paid by the maker. Therefore the endorser is contingently liable for payment of the note. If the note is dishonored by the maker, the endorser is liable. In other words, the liability of the endorser is contingent on the possible dishonoring of the note by the maker. It follows that if the credit rating of the endorser of the note is good, a bank is usually willing to accept and discount a note. The endorser, by virtue of his or her endorsement or guarantee, agrees to pay the note at maturity *if* it is not paid by the maker. The amount of the contingent liability should be shown on the endorser's balance sheet as a footnote.

Payment of a
discounted
note by the
maker

The bank collects the principal plus the interest on a discounted note directly from the maker. When the maker pays the bank, the endorser no longer has any contingent liability, and so at the same time the footnote to the endorser's balance sheet can be eliminated. A journal entry is not required.

A discounted note: illustration 2 On April 25 North Central Plumbing Supply received a 6%, 90-day, $600 note, dated April 24, from Manning Service Company. On May 4 North Central discounted the note at the bank. The discount rate charged by the bank is 7%. In handling discounted notes receivable, you should by all means follow a definite step-by-step procedure.

1. Diagram the situation.

```
                           Period of the note (90 days)
|                                                                            |
| Date of | Date                                                            |
| note    | discounted                                                      |
| Apr. 24 | May 4                                                           |
|                                                                            |
|                                    Discount period                         |
|←10 days→|                         (90 − 10 = 80 days)                     |
```

2. Determine the discount period. Endorser holds the note, April 24 through May 4.

$$
\begin{array}{ll}
\text{April } (30 - 24) = 6 \text{ days left in April} \\
\text{May} \qquad\qquad = 4 \text{ days} \\
\hline
\text{Days held} \qquad = 10 \text{ days}
\end{array}
$$

Discount period (bank holds note)
90 days − 10 days = 80 days

3. Record the formula.

$$
\begin{array}{l}
\text{Principal (\$600)} \\
+ \text{ Interest (6\%, 90 days)} \\
\hline
= \text{ Value at maturity} \\
- \text{ Discount (7\%, 80 days)} \\
\hline
= \text{ Proceeds}
\end{array}
$$

4. Complete the formula.

Principal	$600.00
+ Interest (6%, 90 days)	9.00
= Value at maturity	$609.00
− Discount (7%, 80 days)	9.47
= Proceeds	$599.53

Interest = Principal × Rate × Time

$$\text{Interest} = 600 \times \frac{6}{100} \times \frac{90}{360} = \$9.00$$

Interest = Principal × Rate × Time

$$\text{Interest} = 609 \times \frac{7}{100} \times \frac{80}{360} = \$9.473$$

5. Record the entry, recognizing that the amount of the proceeds is a debit to Cash. If the amount of the proceeds is less than the principal, debit Interest Expense for the difference.

19– May	4	Cash			5 9 9 53			
		Interest Expense				47		
		Notes Receivable					6 0 0 00	
		Discounted at the bank Manning Service						
		Company's note, dated Apr. 24. The bank						
		discount rate is 7%.						

Suppose that the bank cannot get the maker of the note to pay the principal plus the interest on a pledged note. The bank immediately notifies the firm which endorsed and discounted the note. To take legal advantage of the contingent-liability relationship of the endorser, the bank must formally protest the note. It does so by preparing and mailing to each endorser a Notice of Dishonor and Protest. This is a statement, signed by a notary public, identifying the note and affirming that the note was duly presented to the maker for payment and that payment was refused. The fee levied by the bank, known as a *protest fee,* is charged initially to the endorser, who passes this fee along to the maker. In essence, any amount that the endorser must pay on behalf of the maker is charged to the maker.

For example, let's say that Manning Service Company dishonors its notes that was discounted at the bank by North Central Plumbing Supply. The bank issues a formal Notice of Dishonor and Protest and charges a protest fee of $3. As a consequence, the bank deducts $612 from the account of North Central Plumbing Supply ($600 principal + $9 interest + $3 protest fee). North Central Plumbing Supply records the entry in its general journal as follows.

	19– Jul.	23	Accounts Receivable, Manning Service Company		6 1 2 00		
			Cash			6 1 2 00	
			Dishonor of Manning Service Company's				
			note, dated Apr. 24, 90 days, 6%, principal				
			$600, interest $9 and protest fee $3.				

It's only fair that the protest fee be charged against the maker, and as a result the maker's account at North Central is increased by this amount. *There is no account called "Protest Fee."*

Now say that Manning Service Company finally comes through, and on July 31 they pay the note, dated April 24 and dishonored on July 23, plus 7% interest from July 23 until July 31. In North Central's general journal, the entry looks like this.

	19– Jul.	31	Cash		6 1 2 95		
			Accounts Receivable, Manning Service Company			6 1 2 00	
			Interest Income			95	
			Received payment on the Manning Service				
			Company note, dated Apr. 24, discounted at				
			the bank on May 4, dishonored on July 23;				
			received additional interest at 7% for period				
			July 23 through 31.				

A discounted note: illustration 3 On May 10 McCready and Son gave North Central Plumbing Supply an 8%, 60-day, $2,640 note, dated May 9. On June 2 North Central Plumbing Supply discounted the note at the bank. The bank charges a discount rate of $7\frac{1}{2}\%$.

1. Diagram the situation.

	Period of the note (60 days)	
Date of note May 9	Date discounted June 2	
←————24 days————→		Discount period (60 − 24 = 36 days)

2. Determine the discount period. Endorser holds note through June 2.

$$
\begin{aligned}
\text{May } (31-9) &= 22 \text{ days left in May} \\
\text{June} &= \ \ 2 \text{ days} \\
\hline
\text{Days held} &= 24 \text{ days}
\end{aligned}
$$

Discount period (bank holds note)
60 days − 24 days = 36 days

3. Record the formula.

Principal ($2,640)
+ Interest (8%, 60 days)
= Value at maturity
− Discount ($7\frac{1}{2}\%$, 36 days)
= Proceeds

4. Complete the formula.

Principal	$2,640.00
+ Interest (8%, 60 days)	35.20
= Value at maturity	$2,675.20
− Discount ($7\frac{1}{2}\%$, 36 days)	20.06
= Proceeds	$2,655.14

Interest = Principal × Rate × Time

$$\text{Interest} = 2{,}640 \times \frac{8}{100} \times \frac{60}{360} = \$35.20$$

Interest = Principal × Rate × Time

$$\text{Interest} = 2{,}675.20 \times \frac{7\frac{1}{2}}{100} \times \frac{36}{360} = \$20.064$$

5. Record the entry as shown atop page 451. If the amount of the proceeds is greater than the principal, credit Interest Income for the difference.

	19— Jun.	2	Cash			2 6 5 5 14						
			Notes Receivable					2 6 4 0 00				
			Interest Income					1 5 14				
			Discounted at bank the note received from									
			McCready and Son dated May 9. The bank									
			discount rate is 7½%.									

End-of-fiscal-period adjustments: accrued interest on notes receivable

Accrued interest income on notes receivable is a situation that is parallel to accrued interest expense on notes payable (Chapter 16). Whenever a firm receives or issues an interest-bearing note, the interest accrues or accumulates daily. As a result, any interest-bearing notes having time periods extending into the next fiscal period require adjusting entries in order for the financial statements to present a true picture of the firm's net income and financial condition.

For example, let's say that a firm has two notes receivable on December 31, the end of the fiscal period.

$4,000, 90 days, 8%, dated November 28
$5,200, 60 days, 7%, dated December 20

We can show the situation by a diagram.

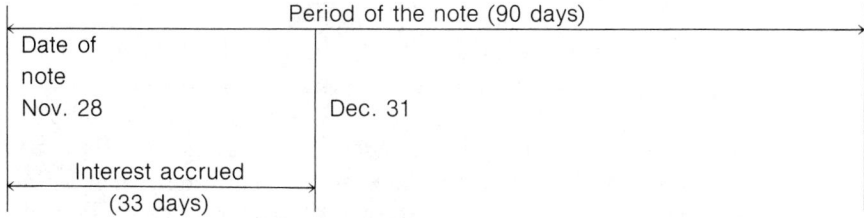

Interest = Principal × Rate × Time

$$\text{Interest} = 4{,}000 \times \frac{8}{100} \times \frac{33}{360} = \$29.33$$

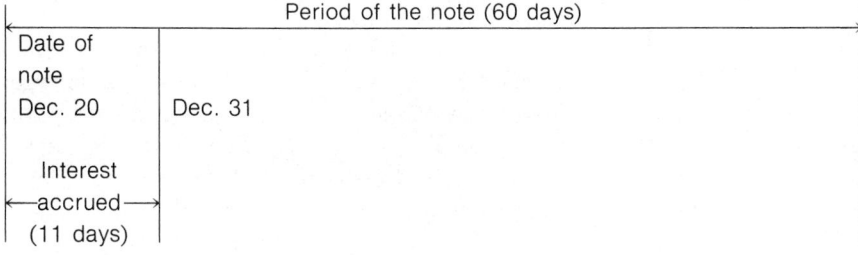

Interest = Principal × Rate × Time

$$\text{Interest} = 5{,}200 \times \frac{7}{100} \times \frac{11}{360} = \$11.12$$

End-of-fiscal-period adjustments: accrued interest on notes receivable   **451**

By custom, the maker doesn't pay the interest until the note becomes due. Since these notes have not matured, the interest income has been neither paid nor recorded.

In the firm's general journal, the adjusting entry for the interest income accrued on the two notes looks like this.

	19–Dec.	31	Adjusting Entry				
1			Adjusting Entry				1
2			Interest Receivable		40 45		2
3			Interest Income			40 45	3
4							4

Like all other adjustments, the above should first be recorded in the Adjustments columns of the work sheet. Here is a T-account picture of the situation.

Interest Receivable				Interest Income		
	+		−	−		+
Dec. 31 Adj.	40.45				Dec. 31 Bal.	619.70
					Dec. 31 Adj.	40.45

Remember that the type of interest accompanying notes receivable is Interest Income. On the balance sheet, Interest Receivable is classified as a current-asset account.

The accountant would reverse this adjusting entry as of the first day of the next fiscal period, because it results in an increase in a balance sheet account, Interest Receivable. When the note matures, the reversing entry makes it possible for the accountant to record the routine entry for the receipt of payment of an interest-bearing note, which is a debit to Cash, a credit to Notes Receivable, and a credit to Interest Income. In other words, the Interest Income account does not have to be subdivided any further. This procedure is most convenient, especially when a significant number of notes are involved.

Summary

A firm may grant credit on the basis of an open account or charge account, or on the basis of a promissory note.

Here we repeat the illustrations of transactions involving notes receivable. Each transaction is first recorded in general journal form, as we explained previously. However, if the Cash account is involved, the entry is also journalized in the cash receipts journal. (To conserve space, we omit explanations here.)

April 6: Received a note for $480 from Henning's Plumbing Company, in settlement of the sale of March 6, 30 days, 8%.

		Notes Receivable		480 00		
1		Notes Receivable		480 00		1
2		Accounts Receivable, Henning's Plumbing			480 00	2
3						3

May 6: Received payment of principal plus interest on the Henning's Plumbing Company's note at maturity.

1		Cash		4 8 3 20		
2		Notes Receivable			4 8 0 00	
3		Interest Income			3 20	
4						

The same entry in a cash receipts journal looks like this.

CASH RECEIPTS JOURNAL   PAGE_____

	DATE	ACCOUNT CREDITED	POST. REF.	SUNDRY ACCOUNTS CR.	ACCOUNTS REC. CR.	SALES CR.	CASH DR.
1	19— May 6	Notes Receivable		4 8 0 00			4 8 3 20
2		Interest Income		3 20			
3							
4							

April 8: Granted a loan to Roger Fennell, an employee, $336, for 3 months, 6%, dated April 8.

1		Notes Receivable		3 3 6 00		
2		Cash			3 3 6 00	
3						
4						

The same entry in a cash payments journal looks like this.

CASH PAYMENTS JOURNAL   PAGE_____

	DATE	CK. NO.	ACCOUNT DEBITED	POST. REF.	SUNDRY ACCOUNTS DR.	ACCOUNTS PAYABLE DR.	CASH CR.
1	19— Apr.	8	Notes Receivable		3 36 00		3 36 00
2							
3							

July 8: Received payment from Roger Fennell of principal plus interest on the 3-month, 6% loan granted him on April 8.

1		Cash		3 4 1 04		
2		Notes Receivable			3 3 6 00	
3		Interest Income			5 04	
4						

The same entry in a cash receipts journal looks like this.

CASH RECEIPTS JOURNAL   PAGE_____

	DATE		ACCOUNT CREDITED	POST. REF.	SUNDRY ACCOUNTS CR.	ACCOUNTS REC. CR.	SALES CR.	CASH DR.	
1	19— Jul.	8	Notes Receivable		3 3 6 00			3 4 1 04	1
2			Interest Income		5 04				2
3									3

April 9: Received a note for $900 from Maxwell Heating and Air Conditioning for merchandise, 60 days, 7%, dated April 9.

	DATE	DESCRIPTION	POST REF.	DEBIT	CREDIT	
1		Notes Receivable		9 0 0 00		1
2		Sales			9 0 0 00	2
3						3

June 8: Maxwell Heating and Air Conditioning paid the interest on its note of April 9, then renewed note by issuance of a new note, 30 days, 8%, dated June 8.

	DATE	DESCRIPTION	POST REF.	DEBIT	CREDIT	
1		Cash		1 0 50		1
2		Interest Income			1 0 50	2
3						3
4		Notes Receivable		9 0 0 00		4
5		Notes Receivable			9 0 0 00	5
6						6

The first entry, as recorded in the cash receipts journal, looks like this.

CASH RECEIPTS JOURNAL   PAGE_____

	DATE		ACCOUNT CREDITED	POST. REF.	SUNDRY ACCOUNTS CR.	ACCOUNTS REC. CR.	SALES CR.	CASH DR.	
1	19— Jun.	8	Interest Income		1 0 50			1 0 50	1
2									2
3									3

June 19: Baker Building Supplies dishonored its note of April 20 for $800, at 7%, for 60 days.

	DATE	DESCRIPTION	POST REF.	DEBIT	CREDIT	
1		Accounts Receivable, Baker Building Supplies		8 0 9 33		1
2		Notes Receivable			8 0 0 00	2
3		Interest Income			9 33	3
4						4

July 19: Baker Building Supplies paid its dishonored note, plus additional interest for 30 days at 7%.

	DATE	DESCRIPTION	POST. REF.	DEBIT	CREDIT	
1		*Cash*		8 1 4 05		1
2		*Accounts Receivable, Baker Building Supplies*			8 0 9 33	2
3		*Interest Income*			4 72	3
4						4

The same entry in the cash receipts journal looks like this.

CASH RECEIPTS JOURNAL   PAGE _____

	DATE	ACCOUNT CREDITED	POST. REF.	SUNDRY ACCOUNTS CR.	ACCOUNTS REC. CR.	SALES CR.	CASH DR.	
1	19– Jul. 19	*Accounts Receivable, Baker Building Supplies*		8 0 9 33			8 1 4 05	1
2		*Interest Income*		4 72				2
3								3
4								4

May 5: Discounted at Valley National Bank the note received from Clark and Keller Hardware, dated April 20, $540, 8%, 60 days. The discount rate is 7%.

	DATE	DESCRIPTION	POST. REF.	DEBIT	CREDIT	
1		*Cash*		5 4 2 41		1
2		*Notes Receivable*			5 4 0 00	2
3		*Interest Income*			2 41	3
4						4

The same entry, as recorded in the cash receipts journal, looks like this.

CASH RECEIPTS JOURNAL   PAGE _____

	DATE	ACCOUNT CREDITED	POST. REF.	SUNDRY ACCOUNTS CR.	ACCOUNTS REC. CR.	SALES CR.	CASH DR.	
1	19– May 5	*Notes Receivable*		5 4 0 00			5 4 2 41	1
2		*Interest Income*		2 41				2
3								3
4								4

May 4: Discounted at Valley National Bank the note received from Manning Service Company, dated April 24, $600, 6%, 90 days. The discount rate is 7%.

	DATE	DESCRIPTION	POST. REF.	DEBIT	CREDIT	
1		*Cash*		5 9 9 53		1
2		*Interest Expense*		47		2
3		*Notes Receivable*			6 0 0 00	3
4						4

The same entry, recorded in the cash receipts journal, looks like this.

CASH RECEIPTS JOURNAL   PAGE_____

	DATE		ACCOUNT CREDITED	POST. REF.	SUNDRY ACCOUNTS DEBIT	SUNDRY ACCOUNTS CREDIT	SALES CR.	CASH DR.	
1	19— May	4	Notes Receivable			6 0 0 00		5 9 9 53	1
2			Interest Expense		47				2
3									3
4									4
5									5
6									6

July 23: Notified by Valley National Bank that Manning Service Company dishonored their note previously discounted on May 4. Paid bank the principal, $600, plus interest, $9, plus protest fee, $3.

1		Accounts Receivable, Manning Service Company		6 1 2 00			1
2		Cash				6 1 2 00	2
3							3
4							4
5							5

The same entry in the cash payments journal looks like the following.

CASH PAYMENTS JOURNAL   PAGE_____

	DATE	CK. NO.	ACCOUNT DEBITED	POST. REF.	SUNDRY ACCOUNTS DR.	ACCOUNTS PAYABLE DR.	CASH CR.	
1	19— Jul.	23	Accounts Receivable, Manning					1
2			Service Company		6 1 2 00		6 1 2 00	2
3								3
4								4
5								5
6								6

July 31: Manning Service Company paid the note dated April 24, previously discounted at the bank and dishonored, plus $.95 interest from July 23 through 31.

1		Cash		6 1 2 95			1
2		Accounts Receivable, Manning Service Company				6 1 2 00	2
3		Interest Income				95	3
4							4
5							5
6							6

The same entry, recorded in a cash receipts journal, looks like this.

CASH RECEIPTS JOURNAL PAGE_____

	DATE		ACCOUNT CREDITED	POST. REF.	SUNDRY ACCOUNTS CR.	ACCOUNTS REC. CR.	SALES CR.	CASH DR.	
1	19– Jul.	31	*Accounts Receivable, Manning Service Company*		6 1 2 00			6 1 2 95	1
2			*Interest Income*		95				2
3									3
4									4
5									5
6									6

June 2: Discounted at Valley National Bank the note received from McCready and Son, dated May 9, $2,640, 8%, 60 days. The discount rate is 7½%.

1		*Cash*		2 6 5 5 14			1
2		*Notes Receivable*			2 6 4 0 00		2
3		*Interest Income*			1 5 14		3
4							4
5							5
6							6

The same entry, recorded in the cash receipts journal, looks like this.

CASH RECEIPTS JOURNAL PAGE_____

	DATE		ACCOUNT CREDITED	POST. REF.	SUNDRY ACCOUNTS CR.	CASH DR.	
1	19– Jun.	2	Notes Receivable		2 6 4 0 00	2 6 5 5 14	1
2			Interest Income		1 5 14		2
3							3
4							4
5							5
6							6
7							7

The notes receivable register is an auxiliary record in which a firm records pertinent details of notes. A firm which receives a significant number of notes finds such a register very useful.

When a firm has interest-bearing notes that extend from one fiscal period into the next, an adjusting entry is required. Since the interest is not collected until the note becomes due, it is necessary to record the interest income for the first fiscal period. The adjusting entry is this: debit Interest Receivable and credit Interest Income. In the work sheet, the entry appears as shown atop pages 458 and 459.

ACCOUNT NAME	TRIAL BALANCE	
	DEBIT	CREDIT
Interest Income		6 1 9 70
Interest Receivable		

The adjusting entry is reversed, because Interest Receivable is an asset account with no previous balance, and it was increased.

Glossary

Accrued interest on notes receivable When a note receivable begins in one fiscal period and matures in the following one, accrued interest represents interest income from the date of the note until the last day of the fiscal period.

Contingent liability A potential liability that may develop as a result of endorsing a note when a note receivable is discounted at a bank.

Discounting a note receivable Borrowing from a bank by pledging a note receivable as security for the loan. The amount of the loan equals the maturity value of the note, and the bank deducts the interest or discount in advance (at the time it grants the loan).

Discount period The time between the date a note receivable is discounted and the date it matures.

Dishonored note receivable When the maker of a note fails to pay the principal and interest at the maturity date, the maker is said to be dishonoring the note.

Maturity value The principal (face value) of a note plus interest from date of note until due date.

Proceeds The amount of cash which the holder of a note receivable receives when he or she discounts that note at a bank.

Protest fee In the case of a note receivable which has been discounted by a bank, if the maker of the note dishonors it (fails to pay the bank by the due date), the bank charges a protest fee for compiling and mailing a Notice of Dishonor and Protest.

Questions

1. Why is a note receivable considered to be superior to an account receivable?

2. Describe possible situations in which notes receivable may come into existence.

3. What is meant by dishonoring a note receivable, and what happens to a dishonored note receivable?

4. What is the formula for discounting an interest-bearing note receivable?

5. Explain the contingent liability relationship of an endorser of a note.

ADJUSTED TRIAL BALANCE		INCOME STATEMENT		BALANCE SHEET	
DEBIT	CREDIT	DEBIT	CREDIT	DEBIT	CREDIT
	(a) 40 45		660 15		
(a) 40 45				40 45	

6. Regarding classified financial statements, in which classifications are Notes Receivable and Interest Income placed?

7. Explain why it is necessary to make an adjusting entry for accrued interest on an interest-bearing note receivable. Should the adjusting entry be reversed?

Exercises

Exercise 1 The Robert Woodbury Company received a 90-day, 8% note for $1,200, dated March 9, from Norman C. Hobson, a charge customer.

a. What is the due date of the note?

b. What is the amount of interest to be received at maturity?

Exercise 2 Given the data in Exercise 1, write entries in general journal form on the books of the Robert Woodbury Company to record the following.

a. Receipt of the note from Hobson.

b. Receipt of the principal and interest at maturity.

Exercise 3 Given the data in Exercise 1, write entries in general journal form on Norman C. Hobson's books to record the following.

a. Issuance of the note by Hobson.

b. Payment of the note at maturity.

Exercise 4 On May 6 the Stella Whiteaker Company received a 90-day, 9% note for $1,000, dated May 6, for merchandise sold to the Timmin Company. Whiteaker Company endorsed the note in favor of its bank on May 28. The bank discounted the note at 8%, paying Whiteaker $1,007.05. Determine the following facts.

a. Number of days the Stella Whiteaker Company held the note

b. Number of days in the discount period

c. Face value

d. Maturity value

e. Proceeds

f. Interest income or expense recorded by the payee (the Stella Whiteaker Company)

Exercise 5 Prepare entries in general journal form to record the following.

June 8 Sold merchandise on account to Howard Williams, $1,260, terms 2/10, n/30.

June 8 Received $360 in cash from Howard Williams, and a note for $900, 60 days, 6%, dated July 8.

Aug. 13 Discounted note at the bank at 8%.

Exercise 6 A discounted notes receivable is dishonored by the maker, the Reister Company. The endorser pays the bank the face value of the note, $400, the interest $6, plus a protest fee of $3. In general journal form journalize the entry to record the payment by the endorser.

Exercise 7 Prepare entries in general journal form to record the following transactions for the Holt Company.

Mar. 3 The Holt Company received from Amalgamated Stores at $6,000, 90-day, 6% note, dated March 3, as an extension of a charge account.

13 Discounted note at the bank at 9%.

June 1 Amalgamated Stores dishonored the note; Holt paid the bank the amount due on the note, plus a protest fee of $3.

July 1 Holt received from Amalgamated Stores the amount due on the dishonored note, plus interest for 30 days at 6% on the total amount owed.

Problems

Problem 17-1 Here are selected transactions carried out by Norton and Company this year.

Jan. 14 Sold merchandise on account to T. R. Winton Company, $2,400, 2/10, n/30.

24 Received check from T. R. Winton Company for the sale of January 14.

Feb. 18 Sold merchandise on account to Pierce and Sikes, $2,850, 2/10, n/30.

Mar. 19 Received a 30-day, 6% note for $2,850 from Pierce and Sikes on account.

Apr. 18 Received check from Pierce and Sikes for the amount owed on the note of March 19.

June 2 Sold merchandise to Wilson Refrigeration, $3,600, receiving their 90-day, 7% note. (The sale was not previously recorded.)

Aug. 31 Received payment from Wilson Refrigeration for the amount owed on its note of June 2.

Instructions Record the above transactions in a general journal.

Problem 17-2 Here are some of the transactions carried out by Robinson and Company this year.

Jan. 9 Sold merchandise on account to Todd Electrical Supply, $2,640, 2/10, n/30.

Feb. 8 Received a 30-day, 7% note for $2,640 from Todd Electrical Supply on account.

Mar. 10 Todd Electrical Supply paid the amount due on its note of February 8.

Apr. 27 Sold merchandise on account to Peebles Electric, $3,300, 2/10, n/30.

May 27 Received a 45-day, 6% note for $3,300 from Peebles Electric on account.

July 11 Peebles Electric paid the interest on their note of May 27, and renewed the obligation by issuing a new 60-day, 7% note for $3,300.

Sept. 9 Received check from Peebles Electric for the amount owed on its note of July 11.

     12 Sold merchandise to Neely Service Company, $4,200, receiving its 30-day, 7% note. (The sale was not previously recorded.)

     22 Discounted the note received from Neely Service Company at the Southern State Bank; discount rate, 6%.

Instructions Record these transactions in a general journal.

Problem 17-3 Selected transactions of the Romano Restaurant Supply Company carried out this year are as follows.

Jan. 8 Sold merchandise on account to J. Wilson, $7,260, 2/10, n/30.

Feb. 7 Received a 30-day, 7% note from J. Wilson, $7,260, dated February 7.

Mar. 9 Received $3,302.35 from J. Wilson as part payment on the note dated February 7, $3,260 as part-payment on the principal and $42.35 as interest on $7,260 for 30 days at 7%. Received a new note for $4,000, 30 days, 8%, dated March 9.

Apr. 2 Sold merchandise to Tony's Pizza, $3,600, receiving their 90-day, 7% note dated April 2. (The sale was not previously recorded.)

      8 Received a check from J. Wilson for the amount owed on the note dated March 9.

     10 Discounted the note received from Tony's Pizza at the Rocky Mountain National Bank; discount rate, 6%.

May   6 Sold merchandise on account to Keith's Steak House, $1,920, 2/10, n/30.

June 5 Received a $1,920 note from Keith's Steak House, 45 days, 6%, dated June 5.

July 20 Keith's Steak House dishonored its note dated June 5.

Instructions Using a sales journal, a cash receipts journal, and a general journal, record the above transactions in the appropriate journal.

Problem 17-4 Here are some selected transactions of Snyder Logging Supply carried out during the year ending December 31.

June   3 Received a note for $2,625 from Southeast Pine Company for merchandise, 60 days, 8%. (The sale was not previously recorded.)

14 Received a $3,300 note from Woodward and Flowers, a charge customer, 30 days, 8%.

July   1 Received a $4,200 note from Clayton Equipment Company, a charge customer, 90 days, 7%.

14 Received a check from Woodward and Flowers in payment of principal plus interest on their note.

Aug.   2 Received payment of interest from Southeast Pine Company for their note of June 3, and also received a new note for $2,625, 30 days, 8%.

15 Received a note from Erickson Lumber Company, a charge customer, $2,400, 60 days, 8%.

Sept.   1 Southeast Pine Company paid its note dated August 2, principal plus interest.

4 Discounted the note received from Erickson Lumber Company, dated August 15, at the Piedmont State Bank, discount rate 8%.

29 Clayton Equipment Company dishonored its note.

Dec.   4 Received a note from Huling Machinery Company, a charge customer, $2,385, 60 days, 8%.

Instructions   **1.** Record the transactions in the general journal.

2. Record the adjusting entry for Huling Machinery Company's note.

Alternate problems

Problem 17-1A The Stanley Paint Company carried out the following transactions this year.

Jan. 19 Sold merchandise on account to L. C. Graham Company, $2,700, 2/10, n/30.

29 Received check from L. C. Graham Company for the sale of January 19.

Feb. 23 Sold merchandise on account to George Construction Company, $3,150, 2/10, n/30.

Mar. 24 Received a 60-day, 6% note for $3,150 from George Construction Company on account.

May 23 Received a check from George Construction Company for the amount owed on the note of March 24.

June   8 Sold merchandise on account to Hewitt and Son for $3,900, receiving its 90-day, 7% note. (The sale was not previously recorded.)

Sept. 6 Received payment from Hewitt and Son for the amount owed on its note of June 8.

Instructions   Record the above transactions in a general journal.

Problem 17-2A   The Taft Distributing Company carried out the following selected transactions this year.

Jan. 14 Sold merchandise on account to Henry Service Company, $2,880, 1/10, n/30.

Feb. 13 Received a 30-day, 7% note for $2,880 from Henry Service Company on account.

Mar. 15 Henry Service paid the amount due on their note of February 13.

Apr. 29 Sold merchandise on account to Keller Arcade, $3,600, 1/10, n/30.

May 29 Received a 60-day, 7% note for $3,600 from Keller Arcade on account.

July 28 Keller Arcade paid the interest on its note of May 29, and renewed the obligation by issuing a new 60-day, 8% note for $3,600.

Sept. 26 Received check from Keller Arcade for the amount owed on its note of July 28.

Oct.   2 Sold merchandise to B. A. Gilbert Company for $5,400, receiving their 30-day, 7% note. (The sale was not previously recorded.)

      22 Discounted the note received from B. A. Gilbert Company at the Randolph State Bank; discount rate 6%.

Instructions   Record these transactions listed in a general journal.

Problem 17-3A   Here are some selected transactions carried out by the Wolfe Hotel Supply Company this year.

Jan. 11 Sold merchandise on account to Cape Lawson Motor Lodge, $5,960, 2/10, n/30.

Feb. 10 Received a 30-day, 6% note from Cape Lawson Motor Lodge for $5,960, dated February 10.

Mar. 12 Received $2,989.80 from Cape Lawson Motor Lodge as payment on their note dated February 10: $2,960 as part payment on the principal, and $29.80 as interest on $5,960 for 30 days at 6%. Received a new note for $3,000 for 30 days at 7%, dated March 12.

Apr. 11 Sold merchandise to Harry's Motel, receiving its 60-day, 6% note, dated April 11, in the amount of $4,000. (The sale was not previously recorded.)

      11 Received a check from Cape Lawson Motor Lodge for the amount owed on the note of March 12.

May 21 Discounted the note received from Harry's Motel at the Mountain State Bank, discount rate 8%.

27 Sold merchandise on account to Sixth Avenue Motor Inn for $3,180, 2/10, n/30.

June 26 Received a $3,180 note from Sixth Avenue Motor Inn for 90 days at 6%, dated June 26.

Sept. 24 Sixth Avenue Motor Inn dishonored its note dated June 26.

Instructions Use a sales journal, a cash receipts journal, and a general journal to record the above transactions. Record each transaction in the appropriate journal.

Problem 17-4A The Wilson Machinery Company completed the following transactions during the year ending December 31.

June 8 Received a note for $2,700 from Gonzales Building Maintenance Company for the sale of merchandise, 90 days, 7%. (The sale was not previously recorded.)

21 Received a $4,050 note from Keene and Keene, a charge customer, 30 days, 7%.

July 6 Received a $4,500 note from Gilmore Tool Company, a charge customer, 90 days, 8%.

21 Received a check from Keene and Keene in payment of principal and interest on their note.

Aug. 7 Received payment of interest from Gonzales Building Maintenance Company for their note of June 8 and also received a new note for $2,700, 30 days, 8%.

22 Received a $2,250 note from Midwest Equipment Company, a charge customer, 60 days, 7%.

Sept. 6 Gonzales Building Maintenance Company paid their note dated August 7, principal plus interest.

11 Discounted the note received from Midwest Equipment dated August 22, at the Rivers State Bank; discount rate 8%.

Oct. 4 Gilmore Tool Company dishonored its note.

Dec. 16 Received a $6,750 note from Nelson Machine Tool Company, a charge customer, 60 days, 7%.

Instructions **1.** Record the above transactions in a general journal.

2. Record the adjusting entry for the note received on December 16 from Nelson Machine Tool Company.

18 Accounting for valuation of receivables

objectives

After you have completed this chapter, you will be able to do the following:
- Record the adjusting entry for estimated bad-debt losses by using the allowance method of handling bad debts.
- Determine the amount of the adjusting entry by aging Accounts Receivable or by using a percentage of Accounts Receivable.
- Calculate the amount of the adjusting entry by using a percentage of sales or net sales.
- Journalize the entries to write off Accounts Receivable as being uncollectible under both the allowance method and the direct write-off method of accounting for bad-debt losses.
- Journalize entries to reinstate Accounts Receivable previously written off.

THE USE of credit for both buying and selling goods and services has become standard practice for business firms of all types and levels: retailers, wholesalers, and manufacturers.

Up to this time, you have learned to record sales of merchandise on account as a debit to Accounts Receivable and a credit to Sales. Next, when the account is collected, you learned to record the transaction as a debit to Cash and a credit to Accounts Receivable. However, business firms which sell goods or services on credit inevitably find that all the Accounts Receivable will not be fully collected. Consequently, the unpaid account must be eventually written off as uncollectible, or a bad debt. In other words, a firm which grants credit "can't win 'em all," so the firm is obliged to provide for the anticipated losses. In this chapter we'll discuss ways to provide for losses as well as to write off charge accounts that are no longer collectible.

We shall examine two methods of accounting for uncollectible accounts; both are acceptable to the federal income tax authorities. The allowance-for-bad-debts method is the more popular one, because it enables the firm to match up sales of one year with bad-debt losses of the same year, and thereby most accurately portray revenue and expense. Large firms, or firms selling primarily on a credit basis, use this method; we shall place our main emphasis on this method because of its relative importance. Small firms, or firms selling primarily on a cash basis, use the direct write-off method, and we shall talk about this in the last part of the chapter.

The credit department

The credit department, because it governs the extension of credit to charge customers, has to keep a watchful eye on present customers, as well as evaluate the debt-paying ability of prospective customers and determine the maximum amount of credit to be extended to each. Retail stores selling to individuals rely on reports from local retail credit bureaus. Wholesalers and manufacturers, when they grant credit to customers, utilize reports of national credit-rating institutions such as Dun and Bradstreet, wholesale credit bureaus, and the financial statements of prospective customers. Business firms that make many sales on credit find it worthwhile to subscribe to credit bureaus or credit-rating agencies. These credit-reporting organizations maintain files of current financial information on charge customers, establish credit ratings for each charge customer, and on request conduct special investigations.

It's always bad, of course, if a business firm has high credit losses, since any firm needs to be paid for its sales on account. If a firm has no credit losses, this is also bad, since this indicates that the firm must be turning down applications for credit, even though most applicants would indeed pay their bills. In this last situation, the firm not only loses many immediate sales, but also reaps considerable ill will, because it turns down so many prospective customers. Therefore a sound credit policy should provide for a limited amount of credit losses; it is the function of the credit department to keep the losses within the tolerance limits.

Matching bad-debt losses with sales

A basic principle of the accrual basis of accounting is that revenue for a fiscal period must be matched by the expenses incurred in earning that revenue during that same period. This principle is consistent with our earlier presentation of adjusting entries. For example, in adjusting for depreciation, we debit Depreciation Expense, Equipment and credit Accumulated Depreciation, Equipment. As you recall, depreciation represents the loss in usefulness of the equipment for a particular year. In making the adjustment, we are allocating this expense to the one year of operations. By the same token, when the firm sells merchandise on account to a customer who may eventually default on his or her obligation, the firm has a bad-debt loss potential that must be provided for in the year in which the sale is made. Consequently, the firm should anticipate this bad-debt loss or expense in the year in which the sale is made.

At the time of making the sale, the firm does not *know* that it has incurred a loss, because it anticipates that the customer will pay his/her obligation. In other words, the firm making the credit sale has increased its revenue account, but it does not know at the time of the sale that the revenue will not be received. As a matter of fact, the firm will not be certain of the loss until it has repeatedly failed in attempts to collect the bill. So the final recognition of the loss will probably occur many months after the sale. In order to match up the bad-debt losses of the year with the sales of the same year, the firm must make an estimate of the losses as a means of providing for them in advance. The use of the allowance method of accounting for bad debts provides the means of matching bad debt losses with the applicable sales.

The allowance method of accounting for bad debts

Most business firms use the allowance method of accounting for bad debts. This involves an adjusting entry that is recorded first in the Adjustment columns of the work sheet in a manner similar to that for the adjustment for accrued salaries, which was described in greater detail earlier during the discussion of payroll accounting in Chapter 10. In general journal and T-account form, the adjusting entry for the estimated bad-debt losses is as shown in the illustrations at the top of the following page.

		Adjusting Entry						
19– Dec.	31	Bad Debts Expense		7 0 0 00				
		Allowance for Doubtful Accounts				7 0 0 00	

Bad Debts Expense		**Allowance for Doubtful Accounts**	
+	−	−	+
Adj. 700			Bal. 1,100
			Adj. 700

The purpose of the adjusting entry is to increase Bad Debts Expense by the amount of the estimated loss, and also to show a realistic figure for the book value of Accounts Receivable. Allowance for Doubtful Accounts is classified as a deduction from Accounts Receivable. As such, it is a contra account, similar to Accumulated Depreciation as being a contra account. Because a firm cannot know with certainty which accounts it won't be able to collect fully, the accountant can't credit Accounts Receivable directly. You could compare this concept to a life insurance company which insures 1,000 newborn infants. The insurance company doesn't *know* who will be alive at age 21, but on the basis of experience, it can *estimate* how many will be alive at age 21.

Similarly, on the basis of its experience, a business firm is able to estimate what this year's bad-debt losses will be. The firm bases its estimate on this year's sales, but it can't designate with certainty *which* credit sales will not be paid. Prior to the adjustments, *the Bad Debts Expense account has no previous balance, as the account is not used during the fiscal period, only at the end.* The firm's accountant increases it by the adjusting entry and subsequently closes it, along with all the expense accounts. On the contrary, Allowance for Doubtful Accounts has a balance that is carried over from previous years. Accounts Receivable, being an asset account, is not closed, and the same treatment is accorded to Allowance for Doubtful Accounts, which accompanies Accounts Receivable. The placement of these accounts is illustrated by a partial work sheet, shown at the bottom of this and the following page.

	TRIAL BALANCE	
ACCOUNT NAME	DEBIT	CREDIT
Accounts Receivable	60 0 0 0 00	
Allowance for Doubtful Accounts		1 1 0 0 00
Bad Debts Expense		

Note that Allowance for Doubtful Accounts, as a deduction from Accounts Receivable, is recorded in the credit columns opposite Accounts Receivable. The $700 adjustment is added to the previous credit balance of $1,100, resulting in $1,800 being recorded in the Balance Sheet credit column. Also, note that Allowance for Doubtful Accounts is handled in a manner similar to that of Accumulated Depreciation. Both are recorded as credits in the Adjustments and Balance Sheet columns of the work sheet; also, the adjustments never need to be reversed, because both accounts will have previous balances after the first year of operations.

Bad debts expense and allowance for doubtful accounts on financial statements

The Bad Debts Expense account appears on the income statement as an operating expense. Some firms further subdivide operating expenses into selling expenses and general expenses, in which case they list Bad Debts Expense in the category of general expenses. (*Reason:* The decision to grant credit is usually a function of the administrative rather than the sales staff.)

Allowance for Doubtful Accounts is listed immediately below Accounts Receivable in the Current Assets section of the balance sheet, like this.

J. J. Walters and Company		
Balance Sheet		
December 31, 19—		
Assets		
Current Assets:		
Cash		12 0 0 0 00
Notes Receivable		8 0 0 0 00
Accounts Receivable	60 0 0 0 00	
Less Allowance for Doubtful Accounts	1 8 0 0 00	58 2 0 0 00

The $58,200 represents the anticipated net realizable value of Accounts Receivable; this is also known as the *book value*. Again, one classifies Allowance for Doubtful Accounts as a *valuation or contra account,* since it is a deduction from an asset. Sometimes accountants use other names for this account, such as Allowance for Bad Debts, Allowance for Uncollectible Accounts, and Estimated Uncollectible Accounts.

ADJUSTMENTS		INCOME STATEMENT		BALANCE SHEET	
DEBIT	CREDIT	DEBIT	CREDIT	DEBIT	CREDIT
				60 0 0 0 00	
	(a) 7 0 0 00				1 8 0 0 00
(a) 7 0 0 00		7 0 0 00			

Management—on the basis of its judgment and past experience—has to make a reasonable estimate of the amount of its uncollectible accounts. Of course, it stands to reason that any such estimate is modified by the trend of business conditions. In a period of prosperity and high employment, one can expect fewer losses due to uncollectible accounts than in a period of recession.

The two alternative approaches commonly used in estimating the amount of the adjustment for Bad Debts Expense are (1) base the estimate on an analysis or aging of Accounts Receivable, and (2) base the estimate on a percentage of the current year's sales.

Estimating bad debts on the basis of an analysis of Accounts Receivable In this method, an examination is made of each charge customer's account to estimate the proportion of the total amount of Accounts Receivable that are likely to be uncollectible. Since this figure should be the new balance of Allowance for Doubtful Accounts, *one makes an adjusting entry large enough to increase the present balance of the Allowance for Doubtful Accounts up to the estimated uncollectible amount.*

For example, let's look at the Winston Stanley Company, whose present credit balance in the Allowance for Doubtful Accounts is $410; they estimate that $3,580 of Accounts Receivable are uncollectible. We make the adjusting entry for $3,170 ($3,580 − $410). This is illustrated by T accounts as follows.

Bad Debts Expense		Allowance for Doubtful Accounts	
+	−	−	+
Adj. 3,170			Bal. 410
			Adj. 3,170
			3,580

The new balance of Allowance for Doubtful Accounts is now $3,580, the amount of receivables that the firm estimates to be uncollectible.

Aging the Accounts Receivable The most common technique for analyzing Accounts Receivable in order to estimate the total uncollectible amount is to *age* each charge customer's account, by (1) determining the number of days old each account is, and (2) determining the number of days past due. One then makes out a working paper, dividing the ages of the accounts into categories or age groups, as shown in the portion below. One can then think of this as an *aging schedule,* and here the result is an estimate of $3,580 as uncollectible.

ANALYSIS OF ACCOUNTS RECEIVABLE BY AGE

CUSTOMER'S NAME	BALANCE	NOT YET DUE	DAYS PAST DUE					
			1–30	31–60	61–90	91–180	181–365	OVER 365
A. B. Allen	$722.00	$ 722.00			$			
B. N. Baker	464.00				464.00			
C. L. Chase	136.90			136.90				
D. R. Dalton	914.00	914.00						
E. V. Early	593.10			593.10				
Total		$78,200.00	$4,030.00	$3,280.00	$1,975.00	$1,260.00	$834.00	$421.00

All the accounts in the accounts receivable ledger are listed by both name and amount. As an account grows older, the likelihood increases that it will prove to be uncollectible. Next, on the basis of its past experience, a firm estimates that a given percentage of each age group of accounts is uncollectible. The firm then multiplies the total amount for each age group by the percentage considered to be uncollectible for that group. The resultant figure is the amount that is estimated to be uncollectible for that age group. Here is an example.

Age Interval	Amount	Estimated Percentage Uncollectible	Allowance for Doubtful Accounts
Not yet due	$78,200	2%	$78,200 × .02 = $1,564.00
1 to 30 days past due	4,030	4%	4,030 × .04 = 161.20
31 to 60 days past due	3,280	10%	3,280 × .1 = 328.00
61 to 90 days past due	1,975	20%	1,975 × .2 = 395.00
91 to 180 days past due	1,260	30%	1,260 × .3 = 378.00
181 to 365 days past due	834	50%	834 × .5 = 417.00
More than 365 days past due	421	80%	421 × .8 = 336.80
	$90,000		$3,580.00

To sum up: The firm estimates that $3,580 of Accounts Receivable is uncollectible. So it now has to bring the balance of Allowance for Doubtful Accounts up to the desired figure of $3,580. Allowance for Doubtful Accounts has a present credit balance of $410, so the firm adjusts for the difference, $3,170. After the accountant posts the adjusting entry, the footing of Allowances for Doubtful Accounts indicates the desired balance, as determined by the aging procedure. The adjusting data and its effect on the accounts are illustrated in the work sheet shown atop pages 472 and 473.

Bad Debts Expense ($3,170) will appear in the income statement in the general-expense portion of Operating Expenses. Like all expenses, it will be closed at the end of the year into Income Summary. For emphasis, let's repeat the placement of the accounts in the balance sheet.

Assets			
Current Assets:			
Accounts Receivable	90 0 0 0 00		
Less Allowance for Doubtful Accounts	3 5 8 0 00	86 4 2 0 00	

ACCOUNT NAME	TRIAL BALANCE	
	DEBIT	CREDIT
Accounts Receivable	90 0 0 0 00	
Allowance for Doubtful Accounts		4 1 0 00
Bad Debts Expense		

Estimating bad debts on the basis of a percentage of Accounts Receivable
Some business firms feel that the aging procedure is too time-consuming; they prefer a quicker but less efficient method for estimating the amount of uncollectible Accounts Receivable. These firms take an average of the actual bad-debt losses of the previous year as a percentage of Accounts Receivable. For example, the William Carr Company calculated the amount of the adjustment for bad debts as follows.

End of Year	Balance of Accounts Receivable	Total Actual Losses from Accounts Receivable (Accounts Receivable written off)
1981	$22,000	$ 770
1982	28,000	764
1983	24,000	686
	$74,000	$2,220

Their average loss over 3 consecutive years was 3%:

$$\frac{2,220}{74,000} = .03 = 3\%$$

Assume that at the end of 1984, their balance of Accounts Receivable was $29,200, and the credit balance of Allowance for Doubtful Accounts was $172. The amount of Accounts Receivable they estimated to be uncollectible was $876 ($29,200 × .03 = $876). Since $876 was the desired figure, the amount of the adjustment was $704 ($876 − $172 = $704). When you are figuring the adjustment for bad debts on the basis of a percentage of Accounts Receivable, you again (as in the case of aging Accounts Receivable) *make an adjusting entry to bring the balance of Allowance for Doubtful Accounts up to the desired figure.* By T accounts, the adjusting entry looks as shown on the next page.

Stanley Company
Sheet
December 31, 19—

	ADJUSTED TRIAL BALANCE		INCOME STATEMENT		BALANCE SHEET	
	DEBIT	CREDIT	DEBIT	CREDIT	DEBIT	CREDIT
1					90 0 0 0 00	
2,3		(a) 3 1 7 0 00				3 5 8 0 00
4,5	(a) 3 1 7 0 00		3 1 7 0 00			

	Bad Debts Expense			**Allowance for Doubtful Accounts**	
	+	−	−		+
Adj.	704			Bal.	172
				Adj.	704
					876

You would then record the adjustment in the work sheet as shown in the illustration across the top of pages 474 and 475.

Let's examine a portion of the balance sheet derived from the work sheet.

William Carr Company
Balance Sheet
December 31, 1984

Assets			
Current Assets:			
Cash			16 8 9 1 00
Notes Receivable			1 6 0 0 00
Accounts Receivable	29 2 0 0 00		
Less Allowance for Doubtful Accounts	8 7 6 00	28 3 2 4 00	

This shows that the book value of Accounts Receivable was $28,324.

As we said in Chapter 17, when we were dealing with notes receivable, business firms that sell heavy machinery frequently sell on the basis of notes receivable. When notes receivable arise specifically from the sale of merchandise, the adjustment for estimated bad debts should be based on the combined uncollectible portions of Accounts Receivable and Notes Receivable. The partial balance sheet for the Ender Machinery Company on page 474 portrays this situation (with an extra line added for Trade Receivables).

ACCOUNT NAME	TRIAL BALANCE	
	DEBIT	CREDIT
Cash	16 8 9 1 00	
Notes Receivable	1 6 0 0 00	
Accounts Receivable	29 2 0 0 00	
Allowance for Doubtful Accounts		1 7 2 00
Bad Debts Expense		

Ender Machinery Company

Balance Sheet

December 31, 19—

Assets		
Current Assets:		
Cash		76 1 7 0 00
Notes Receivable	86 7 0 0 00	
Accounts Receivable	94 3 2 0 00	
Total Trade Receivables	181 0 2 0 00	
Less Allowance for Doubtful Accounts	5 9 6 0 00	175 0 6 0 00

Estimating bad debts on the basis of a percentage of sales Some business firms prefer a simplified alternative method for determining the amount of the adjustment for Bad Debts Expense: multiplying the current year's sales by a set percentage rate, and then recording the adjusting entry for the exact amount.

For example, the actual losses from sales on account for the J. P. Duncan Company have averaged approximately 1% of net sales (Sales less Sales Returns and Allowances and less Sales Discount). They make virtually all sales on a credit basis. On the basis of this information, the company computes the amount of the adjustment as 1% of net sales.

Here is the figure for net sales, as shown in the income statement.

Sales		640 0 0 0 00
Less: Sales Returns and Allowances	26 0 0 0 00	
Sales Discount	1 2 0 0 00	27 2 0 0 00
Net Sales		612 8 0 0 00

ADJUSTMENTS		INCOME STATEMENT		BALANCE SHEET		
DEBIT	CREDIT	DEBIT	CREDIT	DEBIT	CREDIT	
				16 8 9 1 00		1
				1 6 0 0 00		2
				29 2 0 0 00		3
	(a) 7 0 4 00				8 7 6 00	4
(a) 7 0 4 00		7 0 4 00				5
						6

Now 1% of net sales is $6,128 ($612,800 × .01), *so the firm uses this amount directly for the adjusting entry,* adding it to both accounts, as shown below.

Bad Debts Expense		**Allowance for Doubtful Accounts**	
+	−	−	+
Adj. 6,128			Bal. 216
			Adj. 6,128
			6,344

The adjustment would be recorded in the work sheet as shown in the illustration across the top of pages 476 and 477.

A portion of the balance sheet is shown below.

J. P. Duncan Company

Balance Sheet

June 30, 19—

Assets			
Current Assets:			
Accounts Receivable	48 0 0 0 00		
Less Allowance for Doubtful Accounts	6 3 4 4 00	41 6 5 6 00	

Many companies which sell on both a cash and a charge-account basis compute the amount of their adjustment for bad debts on net credit sales. For example, assume that the Fenwick Company sells merchandise on both a cash and a charge-account basis. Charge sales, recorded in a sales journal, total $490,000. Sales Returns and Allowances and Sales Discounts relating to credit sales are $18,000 and $2,900, respectively. The Fenwick Company records the adjustment for bad debts at $\frac{3}{4}$% of net credit sales. The adjustment is illustrated on page 476 with the calculation following it.

ACCOUNT NAME	TRIAL BALANCE	
	DEBIT	CREDIT
Accounts Receivable	48 0 0 0 00	
Allowance for Doubtful Accounts		2 1 6 00
Sales		640 0 0 0 00
Sales Returns and Allowances	26 0 0 0 00	
Sales Discount	1 2 0 0 00	
Bad Debts Expense		

Charge Sales		490 0 0 0 00
Less: Sales Returns and Allowances	18 0 0 0 00	
Sales Discount	2 9 0 0 00	20 9 0 0 00
Net Credit Sales		469 1 0 0 00

$$\begin{array}{r} 469{,}100 \\ \times\,.0075 \\ \hline 3{,}518.25 \end{array}$$

By T accounts, the adjustment looks like this.

Bad Debts Expense			Allowance for Doubtful Accounts	
+		−	−	+
Adj. 3,518.25				Bal. 220.32
				Adj. 3,518.25
				3,738.57

Note that a firm using this simplified method multiplies net sales or net sales on credit by the given percentage in order to determine the amount of the adjustment. The present balance of Allowance for Doubtful Accounts is *not* involved in the calculation. However, if the given percentage does not adequately provide for the firm's losses (that is, if it yields either too little or too much), the firm can simply change the percentage.

Writing off uncollectible accounts
Up to now, we have seen that the firm's accountant first records the adjusting entry for bad debts in the appropriate columns of the work sheet. For the sake of additional clarification, the relevant accounts are also illustrated in T-account form on the facing page.

Company

Sheet

June 30, 19—

	ADJUSTMENTS		INCOME STATEMENT		BALANCE SHEET	
	DEBIT	CREDIT	DEBIT	CREDIT	DEBIT	CREDIT
					48 00 00 00	
		(a) 6 1 2 8 00				6 3 4 4 00
				640 00 00 00		
			26 00 00 00			
			1 2 0 0 00			
	(a)6 1 2 8 00		6 1 2 8 00			

Bad Debts Expense		**Allowance for Doubtful Accounts**	
+	−	−	+
Adj. 3,518.25			Bal. 220.32
			Adj. 3,518.25
			3,738.57

Next the firm's accountant closes Bad Debts Expense, along with all expenses, into the Income Summary account. The company did not use the Bad Debts Expense account during the year, so the only entries recorded in it are the adjusting entry and the closing entry. This represents the beginning and the end of Bad Debts Expense for the fiscal period. After the closing entry has been posted, the accounts look like this.

Bad Debts Expense		**Allowance for Doubtful Accounts**	
+	−	−	+
Adj. 3,518.25	Clos. 3,518.25		Bal. 220.32
			Adj. 3,518.25

Allowance for doubtful accounts

It is apparent that Allowance for Doubtful Accounts remains open. Rather than having the balance continually increased through successive adjustments recorded on the credit side of the account, the accountant uses the debit side of the account for writing off charge accounts that are considered to be definitely uncollectible.

We can consider Allowance for Doubtful Accounts as a reservoir: We fill it up at the end of the year through the medium of the adjusting entry by crediting the account. Next, during the following year, we drain off the reservoir through the medium of write-offs by debiting the account. To avoid the possibility of the reservoir's "running dry," the accountant should make the amount of the adjusting entry large enough to provide for all possible write-offs, and still have a balance left over with which to begin the next year.

Entry to write off a charge account in full

Suppose that a firm decides, after all attempts to collect a customer's debt have failed, that the account is definitely uncollectible. In such a case, the firm should write off the amount due. Assume that on March 12, the J. P. Duncan Company decides that the account of a customer, Ronald D. Oakes, is uncollectible. Their accountant records the write-off by making the following entry.

		GENERAL JOURNAL			PAGE _116_
	DATE	DESCRIPTION	POST REF.	DEBIT	CREDIT
1	19– Mar. 12	Allowance for Doubtful Accounts		71 40		1
2		Accounts Receivable, Ronald D. Oakes			71 40	2
3		Wrote off the account as uncollectible				3
4						4

By T accounts, the entry looks like this:

Accounts Receivable				Allowance for Doubtful Accounts			
+		–		–		+	
Bal.	48,000.00	Mar. 12	71.40	Mar. 12	71.40	Bal.	6,344.00
				(Oakes write-off)			

The accountant also posts the entry to the account of Ronald D. Oakes in the accounts receivable ledger.

DATE		ITEM	POST. REF.	DEBIT	CREDIT	BALANCE
19– Mar.	1	Balance	✓			71 40
	12		J116		71 40	– – –

Note that the above entry does not change the net realizable value or book value of the Accounts Receivable.

Account Name	Balances before Write-offs	Balances after Write-offs
Accounts Receivable	$48,000.00	$47,928.60
Less Allowance for Doubtful Accounts	6,344.00	6,272.60
Book value (net realizable value)	$41,656.00	$41,656.00

Also note that *the entry to write off an account does not involve an expense account* because the expense is provided for by a previous adjusting entry, which was made long in advance. This points up the fact that the estimated expense was recorded during the year in which the sale was made, even though the account was written off during a later year.

Compound
entry to write
off a number
of accounts as
uncollectible

Rather than writing off each uncollectible account separately during the year, at the end of the year a firm may write off a number of accounts in the form of a compound entry. For example, assume that on December 31 the McNair Company writes off the following accounts of charge customers as being uncollectible: C. D. Davis, $72,00; M. R. Franklin, $29.00; O. C. Hillier, $18.00; and M. A. Tilden, $93.00. Their accountant records the write-offs by making the following entry.

	19– Dec.															
1		Allowance for Doubtful Accounts				2 1 2 00									1
2		Accounts Receivable, C. D. Davis							7 2 00		2
3		Accounts Receivable, M. R. Franklin							2 9 00		3
4		Accounts Receivable, O. C. Hillier							1 8 00		4
5		Accounts Receivable, M. A. Tilden							9 3 00		5
6		Wrote off the accounts as uncollectible									6
7											7

Entry to write
off a charge
account paid in
part

Sometimes there is a part payment involved in a write-off of an account. When this happens, it is usually due to a bankruptcy settlement. The federal laws governing bankruptcy legally excuse a debtor from paying off all his or her obligations. For example, on April 21 the J. P. Duncan Company received 10 cents on the dollar in settlement of a $364 account owed by their customer, M. A. Smythe, a bankrupt. In general journal form, the entry is as follows.

	19– Apr.	21	Cash				3 6 40									
1							3 6 40						1
2			Allowance for Doubtful Accounts				3 2 7 60						2
3			Accounts Receivable, M. A. Smythe							3 6 4 00		3
4			Settlement in bankruptcy, wrote off account									4
5			balance as uncollectible									5
6											6
7											7

The total amount of Accounts Receivable written off during a given year does not ordinarily agree with the estimates of uncollectible accounts previously debited to Bad Debts Expense and credited to Allowance for Doubtful Accounts. In the usual situation, the amounts written off as uncollectible turn out to be less than the estimated amount; this means that at the end of a given year there is a credit balance in Allowance for Doubtful Accounts. However, if (as sometimes happens) the amounts written off are greater than the estimated amounts, Allowance for Doubtful Accounts temporarily has a debit balance. The debit balance will be eliminated by the adjusting entry at the end of the year, which results in a credit to, or increase in Allowance for Doubtful Accounts.

Collection of accounts previously written off

Every now and then the sunshine comes along when you least expect it, and an account previously written off as uncollectible may later be recovered, either in part or in full. In such cases, the firm's accountant restores the account to the books, or reinstates it by an entry which is the exact opposite of the write-off entry.

As an example, the J. P. Duncan Company sells merchandise on account to Cecil E. Dowell for $405, on May 5. Here is the entry in general journal form.

19— May	5	Accounts Receivable, Cecil E. Dowell		4 0 5 00			
		Sales			4 0 5 00		
		Sold merchandise on account, 2/10, n/30					

The Duncan Company makes many futile attempts to collect, and the statute of limitations finally expires. Since the statute of limitations is set at 3 years in many states, let's say that the Duncan Company has not been able to collect any money at all from Dowell during a 3-year period, and that Dowell has remained within the jurisdiction of the court. All right, this means that the debt is outlawed by the statute of limitations. In other words, the firm cannot use the courts to force the debtor to pay up. Accordingly, three years later, the accountant for the J. P. Duncan Company writes off the account of Cecil E. Dowell as uncollectible.

19— Jun.	10	Allowance for Doubtful Accounts		4 0 5 00			
		Accounts Receivable, Cecil E. Dowell			4 0 5 00		
		Wrote off the account as uncollectible					

But on September 15, Cecil E. Dowell suddenly pays his account in full! The entry to reinstate the account is the reverse of the entry used to write off the account.

19— Sep.	15	Accounts Receivable, Cecil E. Dowell		4 0 5 00			
		Allowance for Doubtful Accounts			4 0 5 00		
		Reinstated the account					

The way is now clear to record the collection of the account.

1	*19–* *Sep.*	15	Cash							4	0	5	00							1
2			Accounts Receivable, Cecil E. Dowell												4	0	5	00		2
3			Collection in full of account																	3
4																				4

Now suppose that Cecil E. Dowell had gone into bankruptcy, and settled his account with the J. P. Duncan Company by paying them 5 cents on the dollar. The Duncan Company would realize that there was no hope of collecting any more, so their accountant would reinstate the account only for the amount collected, like this.

1	Accounts Receivable, Cecil E. Dowell							2	0	25							1
2	Allowance for Doubtful Accounts											2	0	25			2
3	Settlement in bankruptcy, 5% of $405;																3
4	reinstated the account to the extent of the																4
5	settlement																5
6																	6

The subsequent entry to record the cash payment would be as follows.

1	Cash							2	0	25							1
2	Accounts Receivable, Cecil E. Dowell											2	0	25			2
3	Settlement in bankruptcy, 5% of $405																3
4																	4
5																	5

Direct write-off of bad debts

Direct write-off is a simpler system for writing off charge accounts determined to be uncollectible. An adjusting entry is not recorded, since there is no attempt to provide for bad-debt losses in advance, or to match revenue with related expenses. Instead, when a firm decides that a charge account is never going to be paid, the accountant makes an entry in the general journal debiting Bad Debts Expense and crediting Accounts Receivable. As we said before, this method is used primarily for a small business or a professional enterprise.

For example, on April 16, the Sloan Company sold merchandise on account to C. T. Slocum for $44.20, with the following entry in the general journal.

1	*19–* *Apr.*	16	Accounts Receivable, C. T. Slocum							4	4	20								1
2			Sales												4	4	20			2
3			Sale of merchandise on account, n/30																	3
4																				4
5																				5

Slocum never pays his bill. Finally, three years later, on September 1, the acccount is written off as follows.

	19– Sep.	1	Bad Debts Expense			4 4 20			
			Accounts Receivable, C. T. Slocum				4 4 20	
			To write off an uncollectible account					

By T accounts, the entries look like this.

Accounts Receivable				Sales				Bad Debts Expense		
+		–		–		+		+		–
Apr. 16 44.20		Sept. 1 44.20		Dec. 31 Closed		Apr. 16 44.20		Sept. 1 44.20		

You can see that revenue does not match expenses for a particular year. The Slocum Company counted the original sale of $44.20, thereby overstating true revenue for that year. It counted Bad Debts Expenses three years later, thereby overstating expenses for that year. Note that the Slocum Company did not use the account titled Allowance for Doubtful Accounts. In other words, if you wait until you consider an account to be a bad debt and then write it off, with no provision for realistically estimating the doubtful accounts in advance, you are in a rather hand-to-mouth situation. In the balance sheet, Accounts Receivable is stated at the gross amount only; there is no book value or net realizable value. The entry to reinstate an account previously written off is a debit to Accounts Receivable and a credit to Bad Debts Expense.

Summary

A firm may account for bad debts by two different methods: *the allowance method* and *the direct write-off method*. The allowance method is the most effective, and is used extensively. A great advantage is that it enables a firm to match the bad-debt losses of one period with the revenue of the same period. The allowance method requires an adjusting entry at the end of the year debiting Bad Debts Expense and crediting Allowance for Doubtful Accounts for the estimated amount of bad-debt losses for the period. A firm does not use the Bad Debts Expense account during the year, but only at the end of the year, to make an adjusting entry. The accountant then closes Bad Debts Expense immediately, along with the expense accounts. Bad Debts Expense appears in the income statement under the general-expense section of Operating Expenses. Allowance for Doubtful Accounts is a contra account, since it is a deduction from Accounts Receivable. It appears immediately below Accounts Receivable in the Current Assets section of the balance sheet. To write off a charge account as being uncollectible, an accountant debits Allowance for Doubtful accounts and credits Accounts Receivable. To reinstate an account previously written off, the accountant makes an entry which is the opposite of this entry.

A firm which uses the allowance method of accounting for bad debts determines the amount of the allowance by (1) aging the Accounts Receivable or (2) taking a given percentage of Accounts Receivable. *When the adjusting entry is based on an analysis of Accounts Receivable, the accountant brings the Allowance for Doubtful Accounts up to the desired figure.* The present balance of the Allowance for Doubtful Accounts account must be used in the calculation.

An alternative method of determining the amount of the adjusting entry is to use a percentage of sales or net sales. *When a firm bases the estimate on any type of sales figure, the accountant simply finds the percentage amount and uses that amount in the adjusting entry.*

The direct write-off method of accounting for bad debts is used primarily by small business firms and professional enterprises. When using this simplified method, the accountant does not make any adjusting entry, and so does not use any Allowance for Doubtful Accounts account. When a firm deems an account to be uncollectible, the entry the firm makes during the year is a debit to Bad Debts Expense and a credit to Accounts Receivable.

Glossary

Aging Accounts Receivable A means of analyzing the uncollectible portion of Accounts Receivable by allocating the outstanding balance of each charge customer's account according to the length of time it has been due; one then multiplies the totals for each time period by a percentage deemed to be uncollectible.

Allowance method of accounting for bad-debt losses This requires an adjusting entry debiting Bad Debts Expense and crediting Allowance for Doubtful Accounts. Write-offs of uncollectible accounts are debited to Allowance for Doubtful Accounts and credited to Accounts Receivable.

Bankruptcy A federal law legally excusing a debtor from obligations incurred.

Book value of Accounts Receivable The balance of Accounts Receivable after one has deducted the balance of Allowance for Doubtful Accounts; also called the net realizable value of Accounts Receivable.

Direct write-off method of accounting for bad-debt losses With this method, used by small business firms, no adjusting entry is needed. The accountant debits write-offs of uncollectible accounts to Bad Debts Expense and credits them to Accounts Receivable.

Statute of limitations Laws which limit the period of time of a debt during which the courts may be used to force the debtor to pay; usually 3 years for charge accounts.

Questions

1. Regarding classified financial statements, in which classification are Allowance for Doubtful Accounts and Bad Debts Expense placed?

2. Explain the nature of Allowance for Doubtful Accounts, how it comes into existence, and what happens to it.

3. Explain the process of aging accounts receivable.

4. In what situation would Allowance for Doubtful Accounts have a debit balance?

5. How is the book value of Accounts Receivable figured?

6. When an account is written off under the allowance method of accounting for bad debts, why doesn't the book value of Accounts Receivable decrease?

7. Why is the allowance method of handling bad debts considered to be more effective than the direct write-off method?

Exercises

Exercise 1 The Shafer Company analyzed its Accounts Receivable balances on December 31 and determined the following aged balances.

Age Interval	Balance	Estimated Percentage Uncollectible
Not yet due	$60,000	1%
30 to 60 days past due	14,000	2%
61 to 120 days past due	6,000	5%
121 to 365 days past due	2,000	30%
More than 1 year past due	1,000	60%
	$83,000	

On December 31, before any adjustments, the credit balance of Allowance for Doubtful Accounts is $1,100. What is the adjusting entry for estimated credit losses on December 31?

Exercise 2 The Sinclair Company uses the allowance method of handling losses due to bad debts. They consider estimated losses to be 3% of Accounts Receivable. On December 31 the Accounts Receivable balance was $90,000, and Allowance for Doubtful Accounts had a credit balance of $100. Journalize the adjusting entry to record the estimated bad-debt losses.

Exercise 3 The Dean Owens Company uses the allowance method of handling losses due to bad debts. On December 31, before any adjustments have been recorded, the ledger contains the following balances.

Sales	$220,000
Sales Returns and Allowances	20,000

The Dean Owens Company estimates that bad-debt losses will be $\frac{1}{2}$% of net sales. Journalize the adjusting entry to record the estimated bad-debt losses. The present balance of Allowance for Doubtful Accounts is $150.00.

Exercise 4 The Lattimer Paint Company had the following transactions this year. Assuming that the Lattimer Paint Company uses the allowance method of accounting for bad-debt losses, record the three transactions in general journal form. The present balance of Allowance for Doubtful Accounts is $350.

a. Wrote off the account of A. Almond as uncollectible, $170.

b. Reinstated the account of B. Bates that had been written off during the preceding year, $64; received $64 cash in full payment.

c. Estimated bad-debt losses to be 1% of credit sales of $50,000.

Exercise 5 With reference to Exercise 4, assume that the Barnes Company uses the direct write-off method of accounting for bad-debt losses. Record transactions **a** and **b** in general journal form.

Exercise 6 At the end of this year, the Martin Company's Accounts Receivable account has a balance of $60,000. Net sales for the year total $900,000. Determine the amount of the adjusting entry to record the estimated bad-debt losses under each of the following conditions. Assume that Allowance for Doubtful Accounts had a credit balance of $520.

a. Analysis of the charge accounts in the accounts receivable ledger indicates doubtful accounts of $5,240.

b. Bad-debt losses are estimated at ½% of net sales.

Exercise 7 With reference to Exercise 6, determine the amount of the Martin Company's entry to record the estimated bad-debt losses under each of the following conditions.

a. Analysis of the charge accounts in the accounts receivable ledger indicates doubtful accounts of $6,920.

b. Bad-debt losses are estimated at ¾% of net sales.

Exercise 8 Record the following transactions in general journal form for the Baker Company; these transactions occurred during this fiscal year.

Jan. 11 Sold merchandise to Maxine Byrd on account, $4,500.

     19 Received a check from Maxine Byrd in settlement of her account.

Mar. 20 Sold merchandise to Norman Granger on account, $6,000.

Apr. 20 Received a 6%, 90-day note from Norman Granger in settlement of his account, $6,000.

May 20 Discounted Granger's note at the bank; the bank levied a discount rate of 9%.

July 19 Granger dishonored his note previously discounted. The Baker Company paid the bank the principal, plus interest, plus a protest fee of $4.

Dec. 30 Wrote off the account of Norman Granger as worthless.

Problems _____

Problem 18-1 The Gibson Company, which uses the aging process for Accounts Receivable, classifies its charge accounts by age intervals. The amounts and estimated percentage of uncollectible accounts are listed in the table at the top of the next page.

Age Interval	Balance	Estimated Percentage Uncollectible
Not yet due	$124,320	2%
1 to 30 days past due	6,340	5%
31 to 60 days past due	5,752	10%
61 to 90 days past due	3,280	20%
91 to 180 days past due	1,920	25%
181 to 365 days past due	432	40%
More than 1 year past due	284	70%
	$142,328	

Gibson's Allowance for Doubtful Accounts has a credit balance of $612.26.

Instructions **1.** Complete the table.

2. Record the adjusting entry in general journal form.

Problem 18-2 The balance sheet prepared by Donovan Associates for December 31 of last year included $192,000 in Accounts Receivable and $11,960 in Allowance for Doubtful Accounts. The following transactions occurred during January of this year.

a. Sales of merchandise on account, $171,000.

b. Sales returns and allowances related to sales of merchandise on account, $4,677.

c. Cash payments by charge customers (no cash discounts), $162,939.

d. Accounts Receivable from T. C. Webster Company written off as uncollectible, $1,113.

e. By the aging process, at January 31 it was decided that Allowance for Doubtful Accounts should be adjusted to a balance of $18,204.

f. Closed Bad Debts Expense account.

Instructions **1.** Record the entries in general journal form. Record the letter in the Date column.

2. Post the appropriate journal entries to the accounts for Allowance for Doubtful Accounts and Bad Debts Expense.

Problem 18-3 On January 1 of this year, the Roth Company's Allowance for Doubtful Accounts account had a $1,922 credit balance. During the year Roth completed the following selected transactions.

Feb. 11 Wrote off the $654 account of North Side Company; the company had gone out of business leaving no assets.

May 6 Wrote off the account of John Graham, $348.32, as uncollectible.

19 Received $182 unexpectedly from Stella Wells. The account had been written off two years earlier. Reinstated the account for $182, and recorded the collection of $182.

Aug. 3 Collected 10% of the $252 owed by Douglas Myers, a bankrupt. Wrote off the remainder as uncollectible.

Sept. 21 Received $180 from John Graham as part payment of the account written off on May 6. Graham stated in a letter that he expects to pay the balance in the near future. Accordingly, reinstated the account for the amount of the original obligation, $348.32.

Dec. 29 Journalized a compound entry to write off the following accounts: Nathan Ainsworth, $352.40; Rachel Valdez, $248.72; Todd Dowler, $228.

31 Recorded the adjusting entry for estimated bad-debt losses at $\frac{1}{2}$% of charge sales of $296,000.

31 Closed the Bad Debts Expense account.

Instructions **1.** Record the balance in the ledger account of Allowance for Doubtful Accounts.

2. Record the entries in general journal form.

3. Post the entries to ledger accounts for Allowance for Doubtful Accounts and Bad Debts Expense.

Problem 18-4 The following are among the transactions completed by Eastside Pool Supply this year.

Jan. 8 Sold merchandise on account to Webber Motel, $1,840.

Feb. 6 Wrote off the account of Donald Vaughn, Inc., $1,372. The company went out of business, leaving no assets to attach.

7 Received a note from Webber Motel, $1,480, 6%, 60 days, in settlement of the sale of January 8. The note is dated February 7.

Mar. 12 Reinstated the account of Newberry Apartments that had been written off in the preceding year; received $316 in full payment.

Apr. 8 Webber Motel dishonored their note due today. Charged principal plus interest to Accounts Receivable.

Aug. 17 Received $138 unexpectedly from Ruth Becker. The account had been written off last year in the amount of $138. Reinstated the account and recorded the collection of $138.

Sept. 28 Received 10% of the $1,494.80 balance owed by Webber Motel from the referee in bankruptcy and wrote off the remainder as worthless.

Oct. 15 Reinstated the account of Dillon Manor that had been written off two years earlier and received $652 in full payment.

Dec. 29 Journalized a compound entry to write off the following accounts as uncollectible: Anderson Lodge, $328; Norman Watkins, $152.28; Alexander Construction Company, $1,968; Bannister Terrace, $1,586.40.

31 On the basis of an analysis of Accounts Receivable, which amounted to $86,402.54, estimated that $4,592 will be uncollectible. Recorded the adjusting entry.

31 Recorded the entry to close the appropriate account to Income Summary.

1. Open the following accounts, recording the credit balance as of January of this fiscal year.

114	Allowance for Doubtful Accounts	$6,352.00
313	Income Summary	_____
627	Bad Debts Expense	_____

2. Journalize in general journal form the transactions as well as the adjusting and closing entries described above. After each entry, post to the three selected ledger accounts.

3. Prepare the Current Assets section of the balance sheet. Other pertinent accounts are: Cash, $13,640.32; Supplies, $1,942; Merchandise Inventory, $98,652; Prepaid Insurance, $720.

Alternate problems

Problem 18-1A The accountant for Jason's Shoe Store uses the process of aging Accounts Receivable to classify their charge accounts. The amounts and the accountant's estimated percentage of accounts that are uncollectible are presented below.

Age Interval	Balance	Estimated Percentage Uncollectible
Not yet due	$153,836	2%
1 to 30 days past due	7,888	4%
31 to 60 days past due	4,638	10%
61 to 90 days past due	1,496	20%
91 to 180 days past due	248	30%
181 to 365 days past due	348	50%
More than 1 year past due	282	70%
	$168,736	

Jason's Shoe Store's Allowance for Doubtful Accounts has a present credit balance of $1,096.48.

Instructions **1.** Complete the table.

2. Record the adjusting entry in general journal form.

Problem 18-2A On December 31 of last year, the accountant for Morton and Son prepared a balance sheet which included $192,000 in Accounts Receivable and $11,960 in Allowance for Doubtful Accounts. Selected transactions **a** through **f** at the top of the next page occurred during January of this year.

a. Sales of merchandise on account, $174,000.

b. Sales Returns and Allowances related to sales of merchandise on account, $4,684.50.

c. Cash payments by charge customers (no cash discounts), $164,671.50.

d. Accounts Receivable from Davies Company written off as uncollectible, $1,129.50.

e. By the process of aging Accounts Receivable, on January 31, the accountant for Morton and Son decided that Allowance for Doubtful Accounts should be adjusted to a balance of $19,114.50.

f. The accountant closed Bad Debts Expense.

Instructions **1.** Record the entries in general journal form.

2. Post the appropriate entries to the accounts for Allowance for Doubtful Accounts and Bad Debts Expense.

Problem 18-3A On January 1 of this year Jacobs' Wholesale Grocery had a credit balance of $4,340 in Allowance for Doubtful Accounts. During the year Jacobs completed the following selected transactions.

Feb.   7 Wrote off as uncollectible a $432 account of Farmer Grocery, which had gone out of business, leaving no assets.

May   4 Wrote off the account of Martin and Riley as uncollectible, $250.80.

        17 Collected 5% of the $1,444 owed by Sharon Carson, a bankrupt. Wrote off the remainder as worthless.

Aug.   2 Received $428.40 unexpectedly from the Ronald Gilmore Company, whose account had been written off 2 years earlier. Reinstated the account for $428.40 and recorded the collection.

Sept. 11 Received $150 from Martin Riley as part of the account written off on May 4. Riley wrote a letter saying that he expects to pay the balance soon. Accordingly, reinstated the account for the amount of the original obligation, $250.80.

Dec. 30 Journalized a compound entry to write off the following accounts as uncollectible: Thomas Farley, $384.32; Freeway Restaurant, $272.82; Southside Drive-In, $566.30.

        31 Recorded adjusting entry for estimated bad-debt losses at $\frac{1}{2}$% of charge sales of $536,000.

        31 Closed the Bad Debts Expense account.

Instructions **1.** Record the balance in the ledger account of Allowance for Doubtful Accounts.

2. Record entries in general journal form.

3. Post entries to the ledger accounts for Allowance for Doubtful Accounts and Bad Debts Expense.

Problem 18-4A The following transactions were among those completed by Bryant Restaurant Supply this year.

Jan. 6 Sold merchandise on account to Barclay Cafe, $1,640.

Feb. 15 Wrote off as uncollectible the account of Sandra's Drive-In, $1,384.30. This company had gone out of business, leaving no assets to attach.

      17 Received a note dated February 17 from Barclay Cafe for $1,640, 6%, 60 days, in settlement of the sale of January 6.

Mar. 15 Reinstated the account of Grant's Drive-In that had been written off in the preceding year; received $386.32 in full payment.

Apr. 18 Barclay Cafe dishonored their note due today. Charged principal plus interest to Accounts Receivable.

Aug. 3 Received $148 unexpectedly from Thomas Bowers, whose account had been written off last year in the amount of $148. Reinstated the account and recorded the collection of $148.

Sept. 17 Received 10% of the $1,656.40 balance owed by Barclay Cafe from the referee in bankruptcy and wrote the remainder off as worthless.

Oct. 14 Reinstated the account of Granger's Fine Foods that had been written off 2 years earlier, and received $582 in full payment.

Dec. 29 Journalized a compound entry to write off as uncollectible the following accounts: Barrett Motel, $318; Roger Brewster, $237.20; Bellamy Coffee Shop, $945; Parkway Drive-In, $1,486.32

      31 On the basis of an analysis of Accounts Receivable of $183,022.36, estimated that $5,490 will be uncollectible. Record the adjusting entry.

      31 Recorded the entry to close the appropriate account to Income Summary.

Instructions **1.** Open the following accounts, recording the credit balance as of January 1 of this fiscal year.

114	Allowance for Doubtful Accounts	$5,058.00
313	Income Summary	_____
627	Bad Debts Expense	_____

2. Record in general journal form the transactions as well as the adjusting and closing entries described above. After each entry, post to the three selected ledger accounts.

3. Prepare the Current Asset section of the balance sheet. Other pertinent accounts are: Cash, $11,383.74; Supplies, $1,795.52; Merchandise Inventory, $96,768; Prepaid Insurance, $686.

19 Accounting for valuation of inventories

objectives

After you have completed this chapter, you will be able to do the following:
- Determine unit cost, the value of the ending inventory, and the cost of merchandise sold by the following methods: (1) specific identification, (2) weighted average cost, (3) first-in, first-out, and (4) last-in, first-out.
- Journalize transactions relating to perpetual inventories.
- Complete a perpetual inventory record card.

ONE OF the most important aspects of the operation of any merchandising business is the accounting for, and evaluation of, the merchandise in stock. Let us look back briefly at what we've said so far about this. We defined *merchandise inventory* as goods purchased by the company and held for resale to customers in the ordinary course of business. By T accounts, we have pictured Merchandise Inventory and related accounts as follows.

Assets		Revenue		Expenses	
+	−	−	+	+	−
Merchandise Inventory		**Sales**		**Purchases**	
Only when a physical inventory has been taken			Selling of merchandise, recorded at selling price	Buying of merchandise, recorded at cost, including transportation costs	
		Sales Returns and Allowances		**Purchases Returns and Allowances**	
		Return of merchandise previously sold, recorded at selling price			Return of merchandise previously purchased, recorded at cost
		Sales Discount		**Purchases Discount**	
		Cash discounts offered to customers			Cash discounts on buying merchandise

We have assumed that firms operate on the basis of periodically taking a physical inventory, and include the most up-to-date figure in the Adjustments columns of the work sheet. We have also assumed that firms make two adjustments:

a. They close off or "reverse out" the beginning merchandise inventory.

b. They add the ending merchandise inventory.

As an illustration, assume that a firm has a beginning merchandise inventory amounting to $84,000. The cost of the ending merchandise inventory is $92,000. The adjustment was first described by T accounts as follows.

Merchandise Inventory				Income Summary			
+		−		**(a)**	84,000	**(b)**	92,000
Bal. 84,000	**(a)**	84,000					
(b) 92,000							

The same adjustments appear in the work sheet.

In this example, the ending inventory figure of $92,000 is given. However, in a practical business situation, the cost of the ending inventory must be determined. Counting the goods on hand is a relatively easy but time consuming procedure compared to the more difficult task of assigning a dollar amount to them in a time of changing prices. We'll talk mainly about the Merchandise Inventory account because of its relative importance. However, the same principle applies to other assets, such as supplies for a service business, or raw materials for a manufacturing concern.

We're going to tackle the evaluation of inventories in two ways: First, some merchandising firms (like the above) take a physical inventory of merchandise on hand and then attach a value to it. This is known as *periodic inventory*. Second, some merchandising firms keep running records of inventories by recording all transactions, so that at any given time they know what they have on hand, and the current cost of each item. This is known as *perpetual inventory*.

The importance of inventory valuation

Merchandise Inventory is the only account that appears on both major financial statements. On the balance sheet, it appears under Current Assets. On the income statement, it is listed under Cost of Merchandise Sold. The reason that the valuation of merchandise inventory is so important is that in many business firms it is the asset with the largest dollar amount. Likewise, as a part of Cost of Merchandise Sold, it vitally affects the net income, because the Cost of Merchandise Sold is the largest deduction from Sales. As a result, inventory determination plays an important role in matching costs with revenue for a given period.

Differing costs of ending merchandise inventory have a dramatic effect on net income. We can see this in the income statements shown on the following two pages.

Sales (net)		203 0 0 0 00
Cost of Merchandise Sold		
Merchandise Inventory (beginning)	84 0 0 0 00	
Purchases (net)	160 0 0 0 00	
Merchandise Available for Sale	244 0 0 0 00	
Less Merchandise Inventory (ending)	92 0 0 0 00	
Cost of Merchandise Sold		152 0 0 0 00
Gross Profit		51 0 0 0 00
Expenses		30 0 0 0 00
Net Income		21 0 0 0 00

Now assume that instead of setting $92,000 as the value for ending merchandise inventory, one could quite legally set its value at $82,000. The result would be a net income of only $11,000 (see below), instead of $21,000. Of course, this would mean less income tax as well.

Sales (net)		203 0 0 0 00
Cost of Merchandise Sold		
Merchandise Inventory (beginning)	84 0 0 0 00	
Purchases (net)	160 0 0 0 00	
Merchandise Available for Sale	244 0 0 0 00	
Less Merchandise Inventory (ending)	82 0 0 0 00	
Cost of Merchandise Sold		162 0 0 0 00
Gross Profit		41 0 0 0 00
Expenses		30 0 0 0 00
Net Income		11 0 0 0 00

From this we can see that if the ending merchandise inventory is overstated (too much) by $10,000, the net income will be overstated (too much) by $10,000, because the two are directly proportional to each other. Similarly, *if the ending mechandise inventory is understated (too little), net income will be understated (too little)*.

But there's something else you have to take into account. Since the *ending* inventory of one year becomes the *beginning* inventory of the following year, the net income of the following year is also affected, but in an opposite manner. To see this, let's continue our illustration into year 2. The $92,000 *ending* inventory of year 1 becomes the *beginning* inventory of year 2.

Sales (net)		236 0 0 0 00
Cost of Merchandise Sold		
Merchandise Inventory (beginning)	92 0 0 0 00	
Purchases (net)	184 0 0 0 00	
Merchandise Available for Sale	276 0 0 0 00	
Less Merchandise Inventory (ending)	100 0 0 0 00	
Cost of Merchandise Sold		176 0 0 0 00
Gross Profit		60 0 0 0 00
Expenses		35 0 0 0 00
Net Income		25 0 0 0 00

Now what happens when the $82,000 ending inventory of year 1 becomes the beginning inventory of year 2?

Sales (net)		236 0 0 0 00
Cost of Merchandise Sold		
Merchandise Inventory (beginning)	82 0 0 0 00	
Purchases (net)	184 0 0 0 00	
Merchandise Available for Sale	266 0 0 0 00	
Less Merchandise Inventory (ending)	100 0 0 0 00	
Cost of Merchandise Sold		166 0 0 0 00
Gross Profit		70 0 0 0 00
Expenses		35 0 0 0 00
Net Income		35 0 0 0 00

From this we can see that if the beginning merchandise inventory is overstated by $10,000, the net income will be understated by $10,000, because the two are indirectly proportional to each other. Similarly, *if the beginning merchandise inventory is understated, net income will be overstated.*

In other words, over a two-year period, the net income will be correct, since the overstatement of one year is canceled out by the understatement of the following year, and vice versa. We can summarize all this as shown in the table on the next page.

Year	Ending Inventory of $92,000		Ending Inventory of $82,000	
		Net Income		Net Income
1		$21,000		$11,000
2		25,000		35,000
	Total	$46,000	Total	$46,000

If the *ending* inventory is	Net income for the period will be
Overstated	Overstated
Understated	Understated
If the *beginning* inventory is	**Net income for the period will be**
Overstated	Understated
Understated	Overstated

The need for inventories

Firms that want to satisfy their customers have to maintain large and varied inventories, because naturally all of us would rather shop in stores that give us a wide selection. This, of course, implies that the firm does not run out of goods at the end of the year. The successful firm has to buy enough merchandise in advance to satisfy the demands of its customers. Efficient purchasing also dictates that the firm take advantage of quantity discounts as well as special buys of seasonal or distressed goods. So, well-run business firms keep fairly large stocks of merchandise on hand at all times.

Taking a physical inventory

Many merchandising firms, at a given moment in time, possess no record that shows the exact quantity and cost of merchandise on hand. They do make spot checks from time to time as part of inventory control, but they can determine *exact* amounts only by physically counting the goods on hand. Think about grocery stores and variety stores, and what a job it would be for them to keep track of every item they have on hand and what it cost! Indeed, some stores that carry a particularly wide array of merchandise in large amounts wait until their stock is reasonably low. Many department stores, for example, choose to take a physical inventory of their stock toward the end of January, after the holiday rush and the post-holiday special sales.

Firms use various procedures and internal checks when they take inventory, to be certain that they don't miss any items or include any items more than once. Usually employees work in pairs, with one person counting the items and the other recording the information on inventory tickets or schedules. Some firms use an electronic recorder. As part of internal control, people from the management level may make spot checks on the inventory counts. Most firms take inventory after regular business hours, and record data on inventory sheets, such as the one shown on the facing page for North Central Plumbing Supply.

INVENTORY

DATE _January 2, 19—_   SHEET NO. _326_

CALLED BY _Jack Lyon_   COSTED BY _H. H. C._

ENTERED BY _Tom Peterson_   METHOD OF COSTING _LIFO_

DEPARTMENT _Copper Tubing and Fittings_   EXTENDED BY _J. C._

LOCATION _Store & Warehouse_   EXAMINED BY _M. R._

DESCRIPTION	QUANTITY	UNIT	UNIT COST	EXTENSIONS
90° street elbow (copper to fitting)				
1/2"	273	ea.	67 @ .19 206 @ .23	$ 60.11
3/4"	319	ea.	146 @ .32 173 @ .38	112.46
90° drop ear elbow (copper to inside thread)				
1/2" to 3/8"	194	ea.	194 @ .42	81.48
1/2" to 1/2"	222	ea.	222 @ .46	102.12
45° elbow (copper to copper)				
1/2"	976	ea.	200 @ .14 400 @ .16 376 @ .17	155.92
3/4"	818	ea.	600 @ .31 218 @ .32	255.76
1"	149	ea.	149 @ .59	87.91
Tee (copper to copper inside thread)				
3/8"	733	ea.	140 @ .33 593 @ .37	265.61
				$3,682.71

When people take inventory, they must be careful to count only those goods which belong to the firm. They must exclude goods that have been sold and are awaiting shipment, as well as goods held on a consignment basis. Merchandise sold on the basis of FOB destination should be included in the ending inventory of the seller, since the seller is paying the freight charges and thus still has title. Sometimes a firm must also count goods that it does not have on hand. This situation occurs when the supplier has turned the goods over to a transportation company, and the goods are shipped FOB shipping point. Remember, this means that the buyer is paying the freight charges and as a result normally has title to the goods.

Methods of assigning costs to ending inventory

After the items are described and counted, the unit costs are inserted in the inventory sheet and the total costs are extended. How does one determine unit cost? You might think that this would be rather elementary. Indeed, it would be—if all the purchases of a given article had been made at the same price per unit. To determine the total unit cost, you'd only need to look up one invoice, check the unit price, then multiply it by the number of items present. Simple! But nothing is ever that simple, unfortunately. Usually a firm buys a number of batches of a given item during the year, and—especially these days—the unit cost varies. A can of shoe polish that cost 50 cents in January may cost 60 cents in October. So which unit cost should one assign to the goods on hand?

There are four main methods of assigning costs to goods in the ending inventory: (1) specific identification, (2) weighted average cost, (3) first in, first out, and (4) last in, first out.

Inventory evaluation: illustration 1   For example, North Central Plumbing Supply keeps an inventory of electric water heaters (1,400-watt, 52-gallon capacity) purchased from Argel Manufacturing Company. This year North Central sells 80 of these heaters, and has 26 remaining in stock. North Central started out the year with 22 in stock, and bought more as the year went by, as follows.

Jan. 1	Beginning inventory	22 units @ $57 = $1,254
Mar. 16	Purchase	30 units @ 62 = 1,860
July 29	Purchase	36 units @ 65 = 2,340
Nov. 18	Purchase	18 units @ 68 = 1,224
	Total available	106 units $6,678

Now let's compute the cost of merchandise sold (80 water heaters) and the value of the ending inventory (26 water heaters). We'll use four different methods.

Specific identification

When a firm sells "big-ticket" items (examples: cars, appliances, furniture, etc.), it can keep track of the purchase price of each individual article, and consequently determine the exact cost of the merchandise sold. Because the water heaters have separate serial numbers, North Central can identify each heater with a separate purchase invoice listing the unit cost. Along comes the end of the year, and when they take inventory, North Central finds that they have left in stock 26 water heaters; 12 of these they had bought in November, 10 they had bought in July, and 4 they had bought back in March. They assign the costs to the ending inventory as follows.

12 units @ $68 =	$ 816
10 units @ 65 =	650
4 units @ 62 =	248
26 units	$1,714

North Central determines the cost of merchandise sold by subtracting the value of the ending inventory from the total available for sale.

Total water heaters available (106 units)	$6,678
Less ending inventory (26 units)	1,714
Cost of Merchandise Sold (80 units)	$4,964

Weighted average cost

An alternative to keeping track of the cost of each item purchased is to find the weighted average cost per unit of all like articles available for sale during the period. First, North Central has to find the total cost of the water heaters it had on hand during the year by multiplying the number of units by their respective purchase costs, just as they did before.

22 units @ $57 = $1,254
30 units @ 62 = 1,860
36 units @ 65 = 2,340
18 units @ 68 = 1,224
106 units $6,678

Next North Central finds the average cost per heater.

$6,678 ÷ 106 units = $63 weighted average cost per unit
Value of ending inventory = 26 units × $63   each = $1,638
Cost of Merchandise Sold = 80 units × $63   each = $5,040

According to this method, the beginning inventory is *weighted* (that is, multiplied by the number of units), and consequently each purchase is weighted by the number of units involved in that purchase. In other words, the more you buy at a time, the more influence that purchase has on the average cost.

First-in, first-out (FIFO) method

The first-in, first-out (FIFO) method is based on the flow-of-cost assumption that merchandise sold should be charged against revenue in the order in which the costs were incurred. To determine the cost of merchandise sold, the accountant records the first (oldest) cost first, then the next-oldest cost, and so on. First-in, first-out is a logical way for a firm to rotate its stock of merchandise. As an example, think of a grocery store selling milk. Because milk will sour, the oldest milk is moved up to the front of the shelf. As a result, the ending inventory consists of the freshest milk.

Again, let us return to the illustration of North Central's water heaters. To repeat, 106 water heaters were available for sale during the year.

22 units @ $57 = $1,254
30 units @ 62 = 1,860
36 units @ 65 = 2,340
18 units @ 68 = 1,224
106 units $6,678

North Central sold 80 units. Their accountant calculates the total cost of the heaters on a first-in, first-out (FIFO) basis, like this.

$$
\begin{array}{lll}
\text{22 units @ \$57} & = & \text{\$1,254} \\
\text{30 units @ \ \ 62} & = & \text{1,860} \\
\text{28 units @ \ \ 65} & = & \text{1,820} \\
\hline
\text{80 units} & & \text{\$4,934}
\end{array}
$$

North Central has 26 units on hand in the ending inventory. Their accountant records the ending inventory at the most recent costs, like this.

$$
\begin{array}{lll}
\text{18 units @ \$68} & = & \text{\$1,224} \\
\text{\ 8 units @ \ 65} & = & \text{520} \\
\hline
\text{26 units} & & \text{\$1,744}
\end{array}
$$

The accountant now verifies the total cost of the 80 units sold.

Total available − Ending Inventory = Cost of Merchandise Sold

$6,678 − $1,744 = $4,934

Last-in, first-out (LIFO) method

The last-in, first-out (LIFO) method is based on the flow-of-cost assumption that merchandise sold should be charged against revenue in the order in which the last or latest cost is listed first, followed by the next latest, and so on. As the name implies, last in, first out means that the most recently purchased articles are sold first, and the articles remaining in the ending inventory are the oldest items. As an example, think of a coal yard selling coal. When the coal yard buys coal from its supplier, the new coal is added to the top of the pile. When the coal yard sells coal to its customers, coal is taken off the top of the pile. Consequently, the ending inventory consists of those first few tons at the bottom of the pile. And unless the pile is exhausted, they will never be sold.

Meanwhile, back at North Central, the firm sold 80 units. Their accountant calculates the cost of the heaters on a last-in, first-out (LIFO) basis, like this.

$$
\begin{array}{lll}
\text{18 units @ \$68} & = & \text{\$1,224} \\
\text{36 units @ \ \ 65} & = & \text{2,340} \\
\text{26 units @ \ \ 62} & = & \text{1,612} \\
\hline
\text{80 units} & & \text{\$5,176}
\end{array}
$$

North Central has 26 units on hand in the ending inventory. Their accountant records the ending inventory at the earliest costs, like this.

$$
\begin{array}{lll}
\text{22 units @ \$57} & = & \text{\$1,254} \\
\text{\ 4 units @ \ 62} & = & \text{248} \\
\hline
\text{26 units} & & \text{\$1,502}
\end{array}
$$

The accountant now verifies the total cost of the 80 units sold.

Total available − Ending inventory = Cost of Merchandise Sold

$6,678 − $1,502 = $5,176

Comparison of methods

If prices don't change very much, all inventory methods give just about the same results. However, in a dynamic market in which prices are constantly rising and falling, each method may yield different amounts. Here is a comparison of the results of the sale of the water heaters using the above four methods.

Method	Cost of Merchandise Sold (80 units)	Ending Inventory (26 units)
Specific identification	$4,964	$1,714
Weighted average cost	5,040	1,638
First in, first out	4,934	1,744
Last in, first out	5,176	1,502

Assume that North Central sells the 80 water heaters for $90 apiece. The four methods yield the following gross profits.

	Specific Identification	Weighted Average Cost	First In, First Out	Last In, First Out
Sales	$7,200	$7,200	$7,200	$7,200
Cost of Merchandise Sold	4,964	5,040	4,934	5,176
Gross Profit	$2,236	$2,160	$2,266	$2,024

So we can see from all this that the effects of the methods are as follows:

1. Specific identification matches costs exactly with revenues.

2. Weighted average cost is a compromise between LIFO and FIFO, both for the amount of the ending inventory and the cost of merchandise sold.

3. FIFO portrays the most realistic figure for ending merchandise inventory in the Current Assets section of the balance sheet. The ending inventory is evaluated at the most recent costs.

4. LIFO portrays the most realistic figure for Cost of Merchandise Sold because the items that have been sold will have to be replaced, and at the most recent costs.

Tax effect of LIFO

From the above we can conclude that LIFO yields the smallest gross profit and hence the smallest income tax. This is true because LIFO reflects rising prices, and the most recent costs are assigned to the Cost of Merchandise Sold. For the past 30 years, since prices have just kept going up, there has been a built-in tax advantage for users of LIFO. If prices were ever to start falling, LIFO would become a disadvantage from the standpoint of taxes.

Consistency

We have seen that a firm can increase or decrease its gross profit, and likewise its net income and income tax, by changing the flow-of-cost assumption from one method to another, such as a change from FIFO to LIFO. Although a firm may change its method of assigning inventory costs, it may not change back and forth repeatedly. Consistency in the method of determining cost of merchandise sold and the related cost of the ending inventory is necessary because of income tax considerations (that is, a firm can't switch back and forth in order to evade some of its income tax). The firm also has to stick to the same method of reporting in financial statements to the owners and creditors of a firm. Consistency is a fundamental principle of accounting!

Lower-of-cost-or-market rule

All the above methods for determining the cost of the ending inventory are based on the cost per unit. We used examples in which prices were mostly rising. However, sometimes the replacement cost of items in stock is *less* than the original market cost. The word *market* refers to the current price charged in the market. It is the price at which, *at the time of taking the inventory,* the items could be bought, through the usual channels and in the usual quantities. The current prices may be quoted in catalogs or reflect contract quotations.

If the replacement cost is lower than the original market cost, the inventory may be valued at the lowest cost. For example, the inventory of a store consists of 20 ski coats purchased originally for $22 each (total, $440). At the time of taking the inventory, the same type of ski coats may be purchased (replaced) for $18 each (total, $360). Under the lower-of-cost-or-market rule, the inventory may be valued at $360. In this example, the original cost of $22 may have been determined by either the specific-identification method, the weighted-average-cost method, or the FIFO method. Under the tax law, the cost may *not* be determined by the LIFO method, because this method already offers tax advantages.

Perpetual inventories

Business firms such as equipment or appliance dealers which sell a limited variety of products of relatively high value maintain book records of their inventories on hand. They record additions to or deductions from their inventories *directly* in Merchandise Inventory accounts. This is known as the perpetual-inventory system, because the firms perpetually (or continually) *know* the *amount* of goods on hand. This system involves the following accounts, as illustrated by T accounts.

Merchandise Inventory		Cost of Merchandise Sold		Sales	
+	−	+	−	−	+
Buying Merch. recorded at cost	Selling Merch. recorded at cost	Cost of merch. sold			Amt. rec'd for merch. sold

The only entries that a firm using the periodic system makes in Merchandise Inventory are the adjusting entries made at the end of the year. But a firm using the perpetual-inventory system makes entries directly in the Merchandise Inventory account constantly throughout the year. One virtue of this is that it enables the firm to do away with the Purchases and Purchases Returns and Allowances accounts. A firm using the perpetual-inventory system may record transactions as either the gross or the net amount.

To illustrate the perpetual-inventory system, let's look at a series of entries in general journal form, with transactions recorded at the gross amount.

Bought merchandise on account, $800, 2/10, n/30.

1	Merchandise Inventory		8 0 0 00	
2	Accounts Payable			8 0 0 00
3				

Paid the invoice within the discount period.

1	Accounts Payable		8 0 0 00	
2	Cash			7 8 4 00
3	Purchases Discount			1 6 00
4				
5				

Sold the merchandise on account for $900.
(Two entries are required
to record a sale under a perpetual-inventory system.)

1	Accounts Receivable		9 0 0 00	
2	Sales			9 0 0 00
3				
4	Cost of Merchandise Sold		8 0 0 00	
5	Merchandise Inventory			8 0 0 00
6				
7				

For a firm using the perpetual-inventory system, one can compare the Cost of Merchandise Sold account to an expense account, in that both are increased by debits, and both are closed at the end of the year.

Firms may take physical inventories both during and at the end of the year to verify the book balance of the perpetual inventory, and adjust any discrepancy between the book balance and the amount of the physical count by debiting the Cost of Merchandise Sold account. Suppose the book figure for Merchandise Inventory is $16,250, and the physical count shows $16,140 of merchandise on hand. The adjusting entry is shown on the following page.

1	Cost of Merchandise Sold		1 1 0 00	
2	Merchandise Inventory			1 1 0 00
3				
4				
5				
6				

When a firm uses the perpetual-inventory system, Merchandise Inventory is a controlling account. The firm maintains individual cards in the subsidiary ledger for each kind of product, recording the number of units received as "units received," the number of units sold as "units sold," and recording the remaining balance after each receipt or sale. Companies may keep perpetual inventories by any of the four methods we talked about. For example, assume that North Central Plumbing Supply maintains a perpetual inventory on pumps, on a LIFO basis, as follows.

INVENTORY RECORD CARD

ITEM __Self-priming centrifugal pump (1/2 hp)__   LOCATION __Warehouse Pump Section__

MAXIMUM __40__   MINIMUM __8__   METHOD __LIFO__

	RECEIVED			SOLD			BALANCE		
DATE	UNITS	COST	TOTAL	UNITS	COST	TOTAL	UNITS	COST	TOTAL
1/2							14	$72	$1,008
2/6				4	$72	$288	10	72	720
2/22	30	$75	$2,250				10	72	720
							30	75	2,250
3/14				6	75	450	10	72	720
							24	75	1,800
3/29				8	75	600	10	72	720
							16	75	1,200
Total	30	—	$2,250	18	—	$1,338	—	—	$1,200

The ending balance of 26 units amounts to $1,920 ($720 + $1,200). The gross profit would amount to $822, as follows:

Sales (from sales journal)	$2,160
Less Cost of Merchandise Sold	1,338
Gross Profit	$ 822

The weighted-average-cost flow can be used with a perpetual-inventory system. Rather than computing the average price for each inventory item at the end of a period, a new average is calculated each time a purchase is made. This average method is called a *moving average*. When goods are sold, their cost is determined by multiplying the number of units sold by the average cost existing at that time.

Perpetual-inventory records in electronic data processing accounting systems

When we introduced the subject of perpetual-inventory systems, we said that they are most appropriate for firms selling a limited variety of products of relatively high value. This is indeed true for hand-operated techniques. However, electronic computers—which have large data storage capacities and can retrieve an item of stored information in fractions of a second—have enabled business firms to maintain perpetual inventories involving a wide variety of products, and with a large volume of transactions. Let's take as an example an automobile parts distribution center.

Each item of stock in the inventory is assigned a code number. Whenever the amounts of the items change, information concerning the changes is fed into the computer by means of an on-line data entry terminal. The computer performs the arithmetic operations and determines the new balance in accordance with the inventory method in use: LIFO, FIFO, or moving average. Thus the firm can determine the current status of any given item instantaneously. Whenever desired, the computer can list the balances of all the items in the inventory, in terms of both units and dollars. Some firms which have their own computers or employ an independent data processing concern get such a listing or printout daily.

Our discussion of perpetual inventories has been geared to merchandising firms. However, manufacturing concerns use perpetual inventories almost exclusively. A lumber mill, for example, uses the balances of daily inventories as a basis for deciding which sizes of lumber to cut: $2'' \times 8'$, $1'' \times 6'$, etc.

Summary

The value of the merchandise inventory appears in the Cost of Merchandise Sold section of the income statement.

If the ending inventory is	Net income will be
Overstated	Overstated
Understated	Understated
If the beginning inventory is	**Net income will be**
Overstated	Understated
Understated	Overstated

The value of the ending merchandise inventory also appears in the Current Assets section of the balance sheet.

There are four methods of determining the cost of the ending inventory.

1. Specific invoice prices: Used for items of high value when a firm can identify each item on hand and its respective price.

2. Weighted average cost: Number of units × Unit price = Total cost. Total cost ÷ Total number of units = Average cost per unit. Number of units in inventory × Average cost per unit = Value of ending inventory.

3. First-in, first-out: Costs are charged against revenue in the order in which they were incurred. This method portrays the most realistic figure for the Current Assets section of the balance sheet.

4. Last-in, first-out: Costs that are charged against revenue are the most recent costs. Emphasis is placed on the income statement. This method portrays the most realistic figure for the Cost of Merchandise Sold section of the income statement.

In an era of rising prices, the LIFO method yields the smallest net income. Firms must be consistent in their use of inventory methods.

Perpetual inventories are book records of what a firm has in stock. The Merchandise Inventory account is a controlling account. Merchandise Inventory is debited when goods are bought and credited when goods are sold. Cost of Merchandise sold is a specific account, handled much like an expense account.

Glossary

First-in, first-out Process of assigning costs to merchandise sold, based on the flow-of-cost assumption that units are sold in the order in which they were acquired. Unsold units on hand at date of inventory are assumed to be valued at the most recent costs.

Last-in, first-out Process of assigning costs to merchandise sold, based on the flow-of-cost assumption that units sold are recorded at the costs of the most recently acquired units. Unsold units on hand at date of inventory are assumed to be valued at the earliest costs.

Lower-of-cost-or-market rule When there is a difference between the cost price and the market price of goods, the lower price is used for determining the value of the ending inventory. The term *market price* means current replacement price.

Moving average A modification of the weighted-average-cost method, used for computing the average cost of a perpetual inventory. The firm determines the average unit price each time it buys more units.

Periodic-inventory system Determining the amount of goods on hand by periodically taking a physical count.

Perpetual inventory A book record of the ending inventory showing the unit costs of the items received and the items sold. This gives the firm a running balance of the inventory on hand.

Specific-identification method Counting the actual cost of each individual item in the ending inventory.

Weighted-average-cost method Determining the cost of the ending inventory by multiplying the average cost per unit by the number of remaining units.

Questions

1. List the four methods of assigning costs to ending inventory.

2. What is an advantage and a disadvantage of LIFO?

3. During periods of inflation, which inventory method will result in the lowest reported profits?

4. Due to an error, merchandise costing $2,000 was omitted from the ending inventory. What effect does the omission have on the company's gross profit?

5. What is the difference between the periodic (physical) system and the perpetual system of accounting for inventories?

6. When a perpetual inventory system is in use, what are the necessary journal entries for buying merchandise on account and selling merchandise on account?

7. In a perpetual inventory system, what happens to the Cost of Merchandise Sold account at the end of the fiscal period?

Exercises

Exercise 1 Renfro Equipment Company's beginning inventory for May consisted of 3,400 units at $3 each. Purchases and sales during May were as follows.

May   3   Sold 1,200 units

        9   Purchased 1,600 units @ $3.00

      14   Sold 2,200 units

      21   Purchased 1,900 units @ $3.10

      30   Sold 800 units

Calculate the cost of the ending inventory under each of the following pricing methods: weighted average cost; first-in, first-out; last-in, first-out.

Exercise 2 In the income statement for Shaw Company, the ending inventory was recorded as $106,000, and gross profit was recorded as $42,000. According to a recount of the ending inventory, the correct amount is $110,000. What should be the amount of the gross profit?

Exercise 3 The accounts of the Crimson Gift Shop, which uses the periodic-inventory method, contain the following balances at the end of the first month of this fiscal year.

Merchandise Inventory	$ 92,000
Purchases	126,000
Purchases Discount	5,000
Purchases Returns and Allowances	11,000
Sales	169,000
Sales Discounts	4,500
Sales Returns and Allowances	11,500

Assuming that the ending inventory, determined by physical count, is $81,000, determine the cost of merchandise sold and the gross profit, using an income statement outline.

Exercise 4 The records of Thrifty Auto Parts show the data listed at the top of page 508 as of June 30, the end of the fiscal year. Determine the value of the ending merchandise inventory.

a. Cost of merchandise on hand, based on a physical count, $128,000.

b. Cost of defective merchandise (to be thrown away) included in **a** above, $340.

c. Merchandise purchased June 27, FOB shipping point, delivered to the transportation company on June 28, $660.

d. Merchandise sold to a customer on June 29, which is paid for in full and awaiting shipping instructions, $720; not included in **a** above.

e. Merchandise shipped out FOB destination on June 28, with an expected delivery date of approximately 4 days, $900; not included in **a** above.

Exercise 5 An abbreviated income statement for the Robert Shaver Company for this fiscal year is shown below.

Sales (net)		190 0 0 0 00
Cost of Merchandise Sold:		
Merchandise Inventory, January 1	67 0 0 0 00	
Purchases (net)	158 0 0 0 00	
Merchandise Available for Sale	225 0 0 0 00	
Merchandise Inventory, December 31	72 0 0 0 00	
Cost of Merchandise Sold		153 0 0 0 00
Gross Profit		37 0 0 0 00
Expenses		17 0 0 0 00
Net Income		20 0 0 0 00

An accountant discovers that the ending inventory is overstated by $8,000. What effect does this have on cost of merchandise sold, gross profit, and net income?

Exercise 6 Powell Wholesale Jewelers keeps perpetual inventories on ring mountings, using the first-in, first-out method. Determine the cost of merchandise sold in each sale and the inventory balance after each sale for the following purchases and sales of ring mounting #93.

Jan. 1 Inventory of 30 units @ $75 each

20 Sold 16 units

Feb. 4 Purchased 20 units @ $78 each

17 Sold 17 units

Mar. 4 Sold 10 units

20 Purchased 16 units @ $80 each

Exercise 7 Casper Refrigeration maintains an inventory of compressors, #652. The beginning inventory of #652 and the purchases of them during the year were as listed at the top of the facing page.

Jan. 1 Inventory of 22 units @ $92 each

Mar. 12 Purchased 32 units @ $92 each

Aug. 16 Purchased 18 units @ $96 each

Oct. 27 Purchased 12 units @ $98 each

By physical count, the ending inventory is 26 units. Determine the value of the ending inventory and the cost of the merchandise sold by the following methods: weighted average cost; first-in, first-out; last-in, first-out.

Exercise 8 The J. C. Barnett Company's fiscal year is from January 1 through December 31. The following figures are available.

Inventory, January 1	$146,000 (by physical count)
Inventory, December 31	162,000 (by physical count)

a. Record the adjusting entries, assuming that the company uses the periodic-inventory system.

b. Record the adjusting entry, assuming that the company uses the perpetual-inventory system, and that the book balance of the ending inventory is $161,000.

Problems

Problem 19-1 Ellis Chemical's inventory of Product 9 on January 1 of one year was 16,000 gallons, which was bought at a cost of $.50 per gallon. In addition to the beginning inventory, the firm bought more Product 9 during the next 6 months, as shown in the following table.

Date	Quantity (gallons)	Cost per Gallon	Total Cost
Jan. 1 inventory	16,000	$.50	$8,000
23	10,000	.51	5,100
Feb. 5	12,000	.52	6,240
22	9,000	.52	4,680
Mar. 6	11,000	.51	5,610
29	8,000	.54	4,320
Apr. 17	9,000	.54	4,860
May 19	6,000	.54	3,240
June 18	4,000	.56	2,240

Ellis Chemical's inventory on June 30 was 9,000 gallons. During this six-month period, they sold all their Product 9 at $.60 per gallon. Assume there was no loss through evaporation or leakage.

Instructions **1.** Find the cost of the ending inventory by the following methods:

a. Weighted average cost

b. First-in, first-out

c. Last-in, first-out

2. Determine the cost of merchandise sold according to the three methods of taking inventory.

3. Determine the amount of the gross profit according to the three methods of taking inventory.

4. In your opinion, which inventory method seems to reflect the most realistic gross profit? Why? If a balance sheet was prepared, which inventory method seems to reflect the most current value of the asset, Merchandise Inventory? Why?

Problem 19-2 Barnes Radio and TV uses the periodic-inventory system. Data pertaining to the inventory on January 1, the beginning of the fiscal year, as well as purchases during the year and the inventory count on December 31, are as follows.

	Model		
	CL311	**DE243**	**6X16**
Inventory, Jan.	11 @ $432	3 @ $786	21 @ $318
First purchase	17 @ 444	7 @ 782	28 @ 322
Second purchase	22 @ 452	9 @ 788	30 @ 322
Third purchase	16 @ 452	6 @ 796	32 @ 330
Fourth purchase	12 @ 458		26 @ 332
Inventory, Dec. 31	14	8	32

Instructions   **1.** Determine the cost of the inventory on December 31 by the first-in, first-out method.

2. Determine the cost of the inventory on December 31, by the last-in, first-out method.

3. Determine the cost of the inventory on December 31 by the weighted-average-cost method.

Problem 19-3 The Allen Company's beginning inventory of item 982B and dates of purchases and sales for a three-month period are as follows.

Date	Number of Units		Purchase Price per Unit	Selling Price per Unit
Jan. 1	Inventory	160	$44.00	
16	Purchase	220	44.20	
18	Sale	70		$52.00
29	Sale	140		52.00
Feb. 4	Purchase	180	46.00	
9	Sale	120		53.00
16	Purchase	200	48.00	
27	Sale	170		56.00
Mar. 11	Sale	90		56.00
19	Purchase	120	48.60	
23	Sale	75		56.00
29	Sale	80		56.40

Allen Company maintains a perpetual-inventory record using the first-in, first-out method. Data for the month of January are recorded in your book of accounting stationery.

Instructions **1.** Record the data for purchases of item 982B and for cost of merchandise sold in a perpetual-inventory record using the first-in, first-out method for the months of February and March.

2. Determine the total cost of merchandise sold during the 3-month period.

3. Determine the total sales for the 3-month period.

4. Determine the gross profit from sales of item 982B for this period.

Problem 19-4 The Fuller Equipment Company made the following transactions during the month.

Jan. 3 Bought merchandise on account from Robertson Manufacturing Company, $9,000, terms 2/10, n/30.

6 Received Credit Memo No. 1723 from Robertson Manufacturing Company for the return of merchandise bought on January 3, $600.

12 Issued Check No. 4336, $8,232, payable to Robertson Manufacturing Company in payment of invoice dated January 3.

15 Sold merchandise on account to Franklin and Alvarez, $4,050; the cost of the merchandise was $3,663.

30 Sold merchandise on account to Barnhart and Son, $5,496; the cost of the merchandise was $4,569.

31 Recorded the adjusting entry for ending merchandise inventory determined by physical count, $121,389. The beginning inventory was $121,575. The balance in the inventory account under the perpetual-inventory system is $121,743.

Instructions **1.** Record the above transactions in general journal form, assuming that the Fuller Equipment Company uses the perpetual-inventory system and records purchases at the gross amount.

2. Record the above transactions in general journal form, assuming that the Fuller Equipment Company uses the periodic-inventory system and records purchases at the gross amount.

Alternate problems

Problem 19-1A On January 1 of this year, Roe Company had an inventory of Liquid 19 of 1,200 gallons, which cost $.42 per gallon. In addition to the beginning inventory, purchases during the next 6 months were as shown at the top of page 512.

Date	Quantity (gallons)	Cost per Gallon	Total Cost
Jan. 1 inventory	1,200	$.42	$ 504
21	9,000	.44	3,960
Feb. 17	8,000	.46	3,680
Mar. 8	6,000	.46⅔	2,800
Apr. 16	11,000	.46	5,060
May 2	8,000	.44	3,520
June 1	9,000	.47	4,230
28	7,000	.48	3,360

The inventory on June 30 was 15,000 gallons. During this six-month period, Roe Company sold Liquid 19 for $.54 per gallon. Assume there was no loss through evaporation or leakage.

Instructions 1. Find the value of the ending inventory by the three following methods.
   a. Weighted average cost
   b. First-in, first-out
   c. Last-in, first-out

2. Determine the cost of merchandise sold according to the three methods of taking inventory.

3. Determine the gross profit according to the three methods of taking inventory.

4. In your opinion, which inventory method seems to reflect the most realistic gross profit? Why? If a balance sheet were prepared, which inventory method seems to reflect the most current value of the asset, Merchandise Inventory? Why?

Problem 19-2A Northland Electronics uses the periodic-inventory system. Data for their inventories on January 1, the beginning of their fiscal year, as well as purchases during the year and the inventory count at December 31 are shown below.

	Model		
	CL311	DE243	6X16
Inventory, Jan. 1	6 @ $436	4 @ $692	17 @ $336
First purchase	9 @ 450	7 @ 722	21 @ 344
Second purchase	11 @ 460	8 @ 722	33 @ 344
Third purchase	8 @ 460	6 @ 736	14 @ 348
Fourth purchase	7 @ 466		
Inventory, Dec. 31	8	7	23

Instructions 1. Determine the cost of the inventory on December 31 by the first-in, first-out method.

2. Determine the cost of the inventory on December 31 by the last-in, first-out method.

3. Determine the cost of the inventory on December 31 by the weighted-average-cost method.

Problem 19-3A The Allen Company's beginning inventory of item 982B and dates of purchases and sales for a three-month period are as follows.

Date		Number of Units		Purchase Price per Unit	Selling Price per Unit
Jan.	1	Inventory	160	$44.00	
	16	Purchase	220	44.20	
	18	Sale	70		$52.00
	29	Sale	140		52.00
Feb.	6	Purchase	240	45.60	
	8	Sale	130		53.00
	19	Sale	190		53.00
	26	Purchase	220	46.20	
Mar.	3	Sale	70		54.00
	15	Purchase	150	48.00	
	21	Sale	80		54.00
	30	Sale	145		56.00

Allen Company maintains a perpetual inventory record using the first-in, first-out method. Data for the month of January are recorded in your accounting stationery.

Instructions **1.** Record the data for purchases of item 982B and for cost of merchandise sold in a perpetual-inventory record using the first-in, first-out method for the months of February and March.

2. Determine the total cost of merchandise sold during the 3-month period.

3. Determine the total sales for the 3-month period.

4. Determine the gross profit from sales of item 982B for the period.

Problem 19-4A The Jefferson Sporting Goods Company carried out the following transactions during the year.

Jan. 2 Bought merchandise on account from Ingraham Machine Products, $12,600, terms 2/10, n/30.

5 Received Credit Memo No. 2116 from Ingraham Machine Products for the return of merchandise bought on January 2, $900.

11 Issued Check No. 9411, $11,466; payable to Ingraham Machine Products, in payment of the invoice dated January 2.

22 Sold merchandise on account to Aldrich School District, $8,640; the cost of the merchandise was $7,038.

30 Sold merchandise on account to Keep-fit Health Spa, $5,472; the cost of the merchandise was $4,428.

31 Recorded the adjusting entry for the ending merchandise inventory determined by physical count, $289,152. The beginning inventory was $288,987. The balance in the inventory account under the perpetual-inventory system is $289,221.

Instructions   **1.** Assuming that Jefferson uses the perpetual-inventory system, record the transactions in general journal form, with purchases recorded at the gross amount.

2. Assuming that Jefferson uses the periodic-inventory system, record the transactions in general journal form, with purchases recorded at the gross amount.

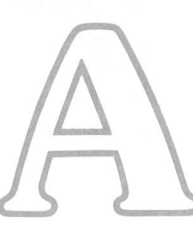

Appendix A: Methods of estimating the value of inventories

IN CHAPTER 1, we characterized accounting as the eyes and ears of management. Management sees and hears through the medium of financial reports summarizing the results of business operations. Management, in order to function efficiently, must have interim income statements and balance sheets prepared monthly. One reason why management needs a physical inventory at the end of the year is that inventory balance figures are an integral element of financial statements. However, because the taking of physical inventories is both time-consuming and expensive, it is more expedient to estimate, each month, the value of the ending inventories, and to use these estimates on the monthly financial statements. Let us therefore take a look at the two most frequently used methods of estimating the value of inventories—the retail method and the gross-profit method.

Retail method of estimating the value of inventories

As the name implies, this method is widely used by retail concerns, particularly department stores. The retailer buys merchandise at cost, then adds the normal markup, and prices the goods at the retail level. The *normal markup*— which is the normal amount, or percentage, that you add to the cost of an item to arrive at its selling price—covers operating expenses and profit. When a firm uses the retail method of estimating inventories, it must record the Purchases-related accounts at both cost and retail values. The firm's accountant records retail values in supplementary records, and also records the physical inventory taken at the end of the previous year at both cost and retail values.

Illustration 1 Sampson Sporting Goods takes a physical inventory at the end of each year, and estimates the value of the ending inventory at the end of each month for its monthly financial statements.

The accountant for Sampson Sporting Goods needs to work out the following information to estimate the value of the ending merchandise inventory at cost.

• Cost value and retail value of merchandise on hand at the beginning of the month. (The inventory at the beginning of a given month is the same as the inventory at the end of the preceding month.)

	AT COST	AT RETAIL
Merchandise Inventory (beginning)	41 2 0 0 00	68 6 0 0 00

• Net purchases of merchandise during the month, both cost value and retail value. To obtain the retail figures, the accountant adds the normal markup to the cost figures, as shown on the top of the next page.

	AT COST		AT RETAIL
Purchases		83 000 00	138 410 00
Less: Purch. Ret. and Allow.	3 200 00		
Purchases Discounts	1 000 00	4 200 00	7 010 00
Net Purchases		78 800 00	131 400 00

• Net sales for the month. All sales are recorded at retail price levels, as listed on sales slips and cash register tapes.

	AT RETAIL	
Sales		151 650 00
Less: Sales Returns and Allowances	7 000 00	
Sales Discounts	2 650 00	9 650 00
Net Sales		142 000 00

The accountant can determine this information by following these four steps:

1. Determine the dollar value of merchandise available for sale, at cost and at retail. The cost figures are the same as the Merchandise Available for Sale figure that is part of the Cost of Mechandise Sold section of the income statement.

	At cost	At retail
Beginning Inventory	$ 41,200	$ 68,600
+ Net Purchasees	78,800	131,400
= Merchandise Available for Sale	$120,000	$200,000

2. Find the ratio of the cost value of merchandise available to the retail value of merchandise available.

$$\frac{\text{Cost value of merchandise available for sale}}{\text{Retail value of merchandise available for sale}} = \frac{\$120,000}{\$200,000} = 60\%$$

3. Retail value of ending inventory.

Retail value of merchandise available	$200,000
− Net Sales	142,000
= Retail value of ending inventory	$ 58,000

Think of the retail value of the ending inventory this way: If the firm had $200,000 of merchandise available for sale, and $142,000 was actually sold, then the amount left over should be $58,000.

4. Convert the retail value of the ending inventory into the cost value of the ending inventory by using this formula.

$$\$58,000 \times 60\% = \$58,000 \times .6 = \$34,800$$

Therefore, on its income statement for the month, Sampson Sporting Goods records the value of the ending inventory as $34,800. If the retail value is $58,000 and 40% of this figure represents markup, the remaining 60% must be the cost.

Illustration 2 C. T. Skinner Company had the following account balances, as shown by T accounts.

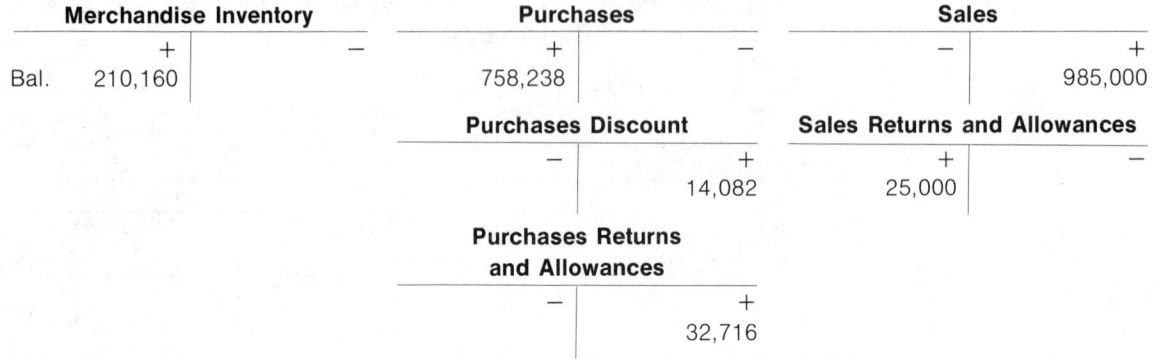

Retail value of beginning inventory, $296,000 (the accountant picks up this figure from a report dated the end of the preceding month).

Net Purchases = Purchases − Purchases Returns and Allowances − Purchases Discount
  = $758,238 − $32,716 − $14,082
  = $711,440

Retail value of net purchases, $984,000 (the normal markup is added to the cost figure).

Net Sales = Sales − Sales Returns and Allowances
  = $985,000 − $25,000
  = $960,000

Again, the information is obtained by following the four steps:

1. Determine the dollar value of merchandise available for sale, at cost and at retail.

	At cost	At retail
Beginning Inventory	$210,160	$ 296,000
+ Net Purchases	711,440	984,000
= Merchandise Available for Sale	$921,600	$1,280,000

2. Find the ratio of the cost value of merchandise available to the retail value of merchandise available.

$$\frac{\text{Cost value of merchandise available for sale}}{\text{Retail value of merchandise available for sale}} = \frac{\$921,600}{\$1,280,000} = 72\%$$

3. Retail value of ending inventory, as on the top of page 519.

Retail value of merchandise available	$1,280,000
− Net Sales	960,000
= Retail value of ending inventory	$ 320,000

4. Convert retail value of ending inventory into cost value of ending inventory by using this formula.

$$\$320,000 \times 72\% = \$320,000 \times .72 = \$230,400$$

In the above illustrations, there is a built-in assumption that the retailer will maintain the normal markup. In other words, we are assuming that the composition or mix of the items in the ending inventory, in terms of the ratio of cost price to retail price, will remain the same for the entire stock of merchandise available for sale.

Markups and markdowns

In the above illustrations, the retailers used normal markups, but there are stores which use additional markups and markdowns. Retailers impose additional markups on top of normal markups when the merchandise involved is in great demand. Because of the highly desirable nature of the goods (for example, up-to-the-minute fashions in clothes), a store may feel that it can get higher-than-normal prices for the goods. Conversely, for slow-moving merchandise, when there is a clearance sale, a store uses markdowns.

When a store using the retail inventory method imposes additional markups and markdowns, it must keep track of them, so that it can calculate the ratio of the cost value of merchandise available to the retail value of merchandise available. For an example of how a store keeps track of markups and markdowns, look at the following illustration.

Step 1 Merchandise available for sale, at cost and at retail.

	At cost	At retail
Beginning Inventory	$ 60,000	$ 90,000
+ Net Purchases	110,000	165,000
+ Additional markups		4,000
= Merchandise Available for Sale	$170,000	$259,000

Step 2 Ratio of cost value of merchandise available to retail value of merchandise available is as follows.

$$\frac{\text{Cost value of merchandise available for sale}}{\text{Retail value of merchandise available for sale}} = \frac{\$170,000}{\$259,000} = 66\%$$

Step 3 Retail value of ending inventory.

Retail value of merchandise available for sale	$259,000
− Net Sales	200,000
− Markdowns	3,000
= Retail value of ending inventory	$ 56,000

Step 4 Convert retail value of ending inventory into cost value of ending inventory.

$$\$56,000 \times .66 = \$36,960$$

The accountant adds any additional markups in the retail column of his working paper, because such markups result in an increase in the retail value of the merchandise available for sale. For example, let's say that the price of a popular item is $40, so a store seizes the opportunity and marks it up to $49; this is a $9 increase in the retail value of the merchandise available for sale. On the other hand, when a store marks down the price of an item, the accountant deducts the amount of the markdown from the retail value of the merchandise available for sale (step 3) to obtain the retail value of the merchandise inventory at the end of a given month. For example, say that the price tag of an item is $389, but nobody's buying. So the store marks it down to $359. This means that there has been a $30 decrease in the retail value of this merchandise available for sale.

End-of-year procedure

As we have said, it is very important to take a physical inventory at the end of the year. Physical inventories may also be taken periodically during the year to spot-check the estimated inventories. Most retail stores record items in stock on the inventory sheets at retail prices (in other words, they take the total of all the price tags). This makes it necessary to convert the total of the retail values into the total of the cost values, as in step 4. For example, suppose that the total retail value of the merchandise on all the inventory sheets is $96,000, and the ratio of cost value to retail value is

$$\frac{\text{Cost value of merchandise available}}{\text{Retail value of merchandise available}} = 70\%$$

Thus the cost value of the merchandise is $96,000 \times .7 = \$67,200$. The only difference between the steps taken to prepare the end-of-the-year statement and the steps taken to prepare the interim or monthly statements is that, at the end of the year, there is a physical count of the merchandise, and consequently one can just begin with step 4.

However, to find out the magnitude of shoplifting, or to verify the accuracy of the evaluation of the physical inventory, some firms go through the full procedure of estimating the value of the inventory at the end of the year, then taking a physical count of the goods on hand, and comparing this value with the value of the estimated inventory.

Gross-profit method of estimating the value of inventories

Sometimes a firm may find that the total of the retail prices of the beginning inventory and purchases isn't readily available; in such cases, the firm naturally can't use the retail method of estimating the value of the ending inventory. The *gross-profit method* is an alternative procedure that achieves the same objective. As the name implies, the key element in this method of estimating the value of inventories is the percentage of gross profit the firm makes over a given period of time.

The term *gross profit,* as used on income statements, represents Net Sales less Cost of Merchandise Sold.

Net Sales	$60,000
− Cost of Merchandise Sold	45,000
= Gross Profit	15,000

You arrive at the figure for the percentage of gross profit by dividing the gross profit by the net sales, like this.

$$\text{Percentage of gross profit} = \frac{\text{Gross Profit}}{\text{Net Sales}} = \frac{\$15,000}{\$60,000} = 25\%$$

A 25% gross-profit rate means that there is 25¢ of gross profit for every $1 of net sales. *Gross profit* is the profit earned on the sale of merchandise *before* expenses are deducted. You can compute the gross-profit rate or percentage by using figures from a recent income statement. Alternatively, you may compute the percentage of gross profit from income statements from past years, using averages of figures. The variation from year to year is usually relatively minor, unless marked changes have taken place in the buying and selling policies of the firm.

You need the following information for the current year.

- Sales (balance of account to date)
- Sales Returns and Allowances (balance of account to date)
- Sales Discounts (balance of account to date, if any)
- Beginning Merchandise Inventory (ending inventory of the previous period)
- Purchases (balance of account to date)
- Purchases Returns and Allowances (balance of account to date)
- Purchases Discount (balance of account to date)

Illustration 1 On the night of April 29, the Midtown Hardware Store was destroyed by fire. However, a heroic sales clerk ran into the building and rescued the company's books and records of transactions. For insurance purposes, the owner must estimate the value of the inventory by the gross-profit method. The owner knows that the average gross-profit percentage for the past 5 years is 32%. By journalizing and posting the transactions of the current month, the company's accounts can be brought up to date from these sources.

- Sales (from sales journal, cash receipts journal, and invoices for April 29)
- Sales Returns and Allowances (from cash receipts and general journals)
- Merchandise Inventory, December 31 (ending inventory of last fiscal period)
- Purchases (from purchases journal and invoices for April 29)
- Purchases Returns and Allowances (from general journal)
- Purchases Discount (from cash payments journal)

The owner of Midtown Hardware arranges these figures in the customary income statement format, extending from Sales to Gross Profit.

```
                          Midtown Hardware Store
                             Income Statement
                  For period January 1, through April 29, 19--

Revenue from Sales:
  Sales                                                              $217,000.00
  Less: Sales Returns and Allowances                                   17,000.00
  Net Sales                                                          $200,000.00
Cost of Merchandise Sold:
  Merchandise Inventory, Jan. 1, 19--                   $ 72,000.00
  Purchases                               $143,400.00
  Less: Purchases Returns and Allowances  $14,000.00
        Purchases Discount                  2,400.00    16,400.00
  Net Purchases                                          127,000.00
  Merchandise Available for Sale                        $199,000.00
  Less: Merchandise Inventory, Apr. 29, 19--
  Cost of Merchandise Sold
Gross Profit                                                       $
```

$$\text{Percentage of gross profit} = \frac{\text{Gross Profit}}{\text{Net Sales}} = \frac{\text{Gross Profit}}{\$200,000} = 32\%$$

$$\text{Gross Profit} = .32 \times \$200,000 = \$64,000$$

Now we fill in the Gross Profit blank in the income statement.

```
                          Midtown Hardware Store
                             Income Statement
                  For period January 1, through April 29, 19--

Revenue from Sales:
  Sales                                                              $217,000.00
  Less: Sales Returns and Allowances                                   17,000.00
  Net Sales                                                          $200,000.00
Cost of Merchandise Sold:
  Merchandise Inventory, Jan. 1, 19--                   $ 72,000.00
  Purchases                               $143,400.00
  Less: Purchases Returns and Allowances  $14,000.00
        Purchases Discount                  2,400.00    16,400.00
  Net Purchases                                          127,000.00
  Merchandise Available for Sale                        $199,000.00
  Less: Merchandise Inventory, Apr. 29, 19--
  Cost of Merchandise Sold
Gross Profit                                                        $ 64,000.00
```

Obviously, in order to find the value of the merchandise at the end (April 29), we should work backward. The cost of merchandise sold is the difference between net sales and gross profit, or $136,000 ($200,000 − $64,000). The equation is as shown here.

$$\text{Cost of Merchandise Sold} = \text{Net sales} - \text{Gross Profit}$$
$$= \$200{,}000 - \$64{,}000$$
$$= \$136{,}000$$

Now that we have filled in the figures for Gross Profit and Cost of Merchandise Sold, the partial income statement (from Merchandise Available for Sale through Gross Profit) looks like this.

```
Merchandise Available for Sale                          $199,000.00
Less: Merchandise Inventory, Apr. 29, 19--
  Cost of Merchandise Sold                                136,000.00
Gross Profit                                            $ 64,000.00
```

The value of the merchandise inventory on April 29 is the difference between the value of the merchandise available for sale and the cost of merchandise sold, or $63,000 ($199,000 − $136,000). The equation is as follows.

$$\text{Value of ending inventory} = \text{Value of merchandise available for sale} - \text{Cost of merchandise sold}$$
$$= \$199{,}000 - \$136{,}000$$
$$= \$63{,}000$$

```
Merchandise Available for Sale                          $199,000.00
Less: Merchandise Inventory, Apr. 29, 19--                63,000.00
  Cost of Merchandise Sold                                136,000.00
Gross Profit                                            $ 64,000.00
```

The income statement is a very useful device in the box of tools that you have been accumulating. That is why we suggested earlier that you memorize the form initially in order to implant it firmly in your mind; then it will always be at your fingertips when you need it to do a specific job.

Illustration 2 Hillsdale Orchard Supply has an average gross-profit rate of 34%. Their account balances on May 31 of this year are shown by the T accounts and partial income statement illustrated on page 524.

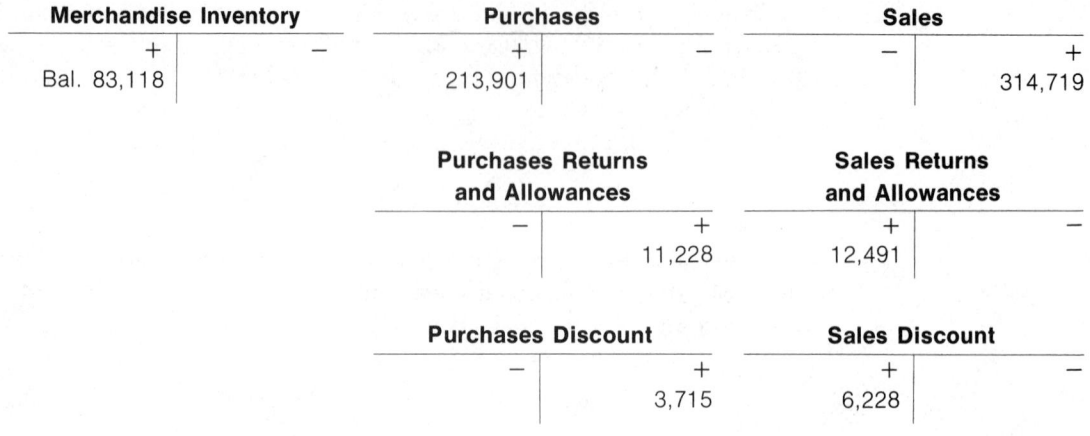

Merchandise Inventory		Purchases		Sales	
+	−	+	−	−	+
Bal. 83,118		213,901			314,719

Purchases Returns and Allowances		Sales Returns and Allowances	
−	+	+	−
	11,228	12,491	

Purchases Discount		Sales Discount	
−	+	+	−
	3,715	6,228	

```
                         Hillsdale Orchard Supply
                              Income Statement
                    For period January 1 through May 31, 19--

Revenue from Sales:
  Sales                                                                    $314,719.00
  Less: Sales Returns and Allowances                      $ 12,491.00
        Sales Discount                                       6,228.00       18,719.00
  Net Sales                                                                $296,000.00
Cost of Merchandise Sold:
  Merchandise Inventory, Jan. 1, 19--                      $ 83,118.00
  Purchases                                   $213,901.00
  Less: Purchases Returns and Allowances      $11,228.00
        Purchases Discount                      3,715.00    14,943.00
Net Purchases                                               198,958.00
Merchandise Available for Sale                             $282,076.00
Less: Merchandise Inventory, May 31, 19--                  (86,716.00)
  Cost of Merchandise Sold                                                 (195,360.00)
Gross Profit                                                               $100,640.00
```

$$\text{Percentage of gross profit} = \frac{\text{Gross Profit}}{\text{Net Sales}} = \frac{\text{Gross Profit}}{\$296,000} = 34\%$$

$$\text{Gross Profit} = .34 \times \$296,000 = \$100,640$$

The cost of merchandise sold is equal to net sales minus gross profit, or $195,360 ($296,000 − $100,640). The ending merchandise inventory is the value of the merchandise available for sale minus the cost of merchandise sold, or $86,716 ($282,076 − $195,360).

Problems

Problem A-1 You are given the following information for the Surfside Gift Shop at the end of their fiscal year, September 30.

	At cost	At retail
Sales		$176,526
Sales Returns and Allowances		7,106
Purchases	$107,232	176,752
Purchases Returns and Allowances	4,684	5,496
Merchandise Inventory, August 31	39,448	65,416

Instructions   **1.** Determine the cost value of the ending merchandise inventory as of September 30, presenting details of your computations.

2. At the end of the year, the Surfside Gift Shop takes a physical inventory at market selling prices and finds that the retail stock totals $65,968. There is a possibility that the difference between the estimated ending inventory and the actual physical inventory is due to shoplifting. Convert the value of the physical inventory at retail into its value at cost, and determine the amount of the loss.

Problem A-2 On May 12 of this year, a fire destroyed the entire stock of merchandise of the Fisher Camera Store. Most of the accounting records were destroyed also. However, from assorted statements and documents, the firm's accountant was able to piece together the following balances of several accounts. Over the past 3 years, the percentage of gross profit averaged 40%.

Merchandise Inventory, Jan. 1 (beginning of fiscal year)	$ 83,458
Account balances of May 12	
Purchases	114,584
Purchases Returns and Allowances	656
Sales	142,280
Sales Returns and Allowances	440

Instructions   Determine the cost value of the ending merchandise inventory as of May 12, giving details of your computations.

Problem A-3 On the morning of July 21, the owner of Bell's Men's Store, when he opened his store, discovered that a robbery had taken place over the weekend and that a large part of the stock had been stolen. However, the information on page 526 for the period January 1 through July 21 was available. Each year during the past 4 years, the store had earned an average 34% gross profit on sales.

Merchandise Inventory, Jan. 1	$126,838
(beginning of fiscal year)	
Account balances, as of July 27	
Purchases	288,930
Purchases Returns and Allowances	7,324
Purchases Discounts	5,496
Sales	397,492
Sales Returns and Allowances	4,292

Instructions **1.** Determine the cost value of the ending merchandise inventory as of July 21, giving details of your computations.

2. By physical count, the cost value of the remaining inventory on hand is $53,960. What is the amount of the loss to be claimed for insurance purposes?

20 Accounting for valuation of plant and equipment

objectives

After you have completed this chapter, you will be able to do the following:
- Allocate costs to Land, Land Improvements, and Buildings accounts.
- Calculate depreciation by the straight-line method, units-of-production method, double-declining-balance method, and sum-of-years'-digits method.
- Differentiate between capital expenditures and revenue expenditures.
- Differentiate between expenditures for ordinary and for extraordinary repairs.
- Determine the book value of assets.
- Record journal entries pertaining to discarding of assets fully depreciated, discarding of assets not fully depreciated, sale of assets involving a loss, sale of assets involving a gain, exchange of assets involving a loss on the trade, exchange of assets involving a gain on the trade, maintaining a plant and equipment subsidiary ledger.

WE DESCRIBED Plant and Equipment as an account classification in Chapter 15, in connection with the classified balance sheet. Assets in this category have a useful life longer than one year, and so are often referred to as long-lived or fixed assets. Another identifying feature is that such assets were originally bought for use in the business, as opposed to merchandise, which was bought for the purpose of resale. Items most frequently included under Plant and Equipment are equipment, furniture, machinery, tools, buildings, land improvements, and land.

Initial costs of plant and equipment

The original cost of plant and equipment includes all normal expenditures necessary to acquire and install them. For example, the cost of a cash register includes not only its invoice price (less any discount for paying cash), but sales tax, freight charges, insurance costs while it is being transported, and costs of unpacking and assembling. Assuming that the buyer of the cash register pays these additional charges in cash, the accountant for the buyer debits Store Equipment and credits Cash. Suppose the firm bought a second-hand cash register and had to have it repaired before it could be used. The cost of the repairs would be debited to the relevant asset account, in this case Store Equipment.

The accountant should debit only normal and necessary costs to the asset accounts. So this rules out expenditures that result from carelessness, vandalism, or other abnormal causes. For example, suppose that an employee who was unpacking the cash register dropped it. The cost of the repair is not considered to be a part of the cost of the cash register, but is charged to an expense account, such as Repair Expense or Miscellaneous Expense. This cost is charged as an expense and not as an asset because the repair does not *add* to the usefulness of the cash register—it simply restores its usefulness.

Differentiating costs of land, land improvements, and buildings

There is no legal recognition for the depreciation of land. Yet a buyer usually buys a package including the land, land improvements, and the building. In other words, the buyer pays one price for one package. So the question is: How should the price be allocated among the three elements?

When there is no qualified appraisal available, then one accepts the ratio established by the county assessor. For example, suppose that someone buys some real property, including land and a building, for $500,000. The assessor evaluated this property for tax purposes at $300,000, valuing the land at $60,000 and the building at $240,000. The percentage the assessor allocated to the land is $60,000/$300,000 = 20%. The percentage the assessor allocated to the building is $240,000/$300,000 = 80%. Therefore, the amount of value which the buyer should allocate to land is $500,000 × .2 = $100,000; to building, $500,000 × .8 = $400,000. For bookkeeping purposes, one also has to separate land improvements from buildings because of the different lengths of life involved.

Land

Suppose that someone buys a piece of land—just land, no building. The cost of the land includes the amount paid for the land plus incidental charges connected with the sale: real estate agents' commissions, escrow and legal fees, delinquent taxes paid by the buyer, plus any costs of surveying, clearing, draining, or grading the land. In addition, the city or county—either at the time of purchase or later—may assess the buyer for such improvements as the installation of paved streets, curbs, sidewalks, and sewers. The buyer debits these items to the Land account, since they are considered to be as permanent as the land. If a business entity buys land for a building site and the land happens to have old buildings standing on it, the firm debits the cost of the structures as well as the costs of demolishing them to the Land account.

Land improvements

An accountant uses the category Land Improvements to record expenditures for improvements that are (1) not as permanent as the land, or (2) not directly associated with a building. Examples are driveways, parking lots, trees and shrubs, fences, and outdoor lighting systems.

Buildings

The cost of a building includes not only money spent for labor and materials, but architectural and engineering fees, money spent for insurance premiums during construction, and all other necessary and normal expenditures applicable to the project.

The nature and recording of depreciation

The usefulness of assets declines due to such causes as physical wear and exhaustion, inadequacy, and obsolescence. As we said in Chapter 5, depreciation represents a systematic procedure for allocating the cost of plant and equipment to the periods in which the firm receives services from the assets. An item of supplies may be bought and used up in one fiscal period; if it is used, its cost is charged to the same fiscal period. On the other hand, a plant asset will be used over several fiscal periods. To be consistent with the matching principle, the cost of the plant asset must be spread out over the several periods.

The firm treats depreciation as a debit to Depreciation Expense and a credit to Accumulated Depreciation. It treats Accumulated Depreciation as a deduction from the respective asset account. This means that depreciation is a contra account. We referred to this entry earlier as an internal transaction, in the sense that no outsider is involved. One can record depreciation as an adjusting entry at the end of each month, or postpone recording it until the end of the fiscal year. *Exception:* When there is a change in the assets, such as a sale or a trade-in, one first records depreciation of the asset from the beginning of the fiscal year until the date of the change *before* making any other accounting entries.

Determining the amount of depreciation

Determining the depreciation of a long-lived asset requires taking into account three elements.

1. The depreciation base: cost less trade-in or salvage value

2. The length of the useful life of the asset

3. The method of depreciation chosen to allocate the depreciation base over the useful life of the asset

Depreciation base

When a business entity first puts an asset into service, it's hard to predict the amount of the trade-in or salvage value, especially when such a trade-in must be imagined as happening many years in the future. Many firms make estimates based on their own experience, or on data supplied by trade associations or government agencies. If the firm expects the salvage value to be insignificant in comparison with the cost of the asset, the accountant often assumes the salvage value to be zero.

Useful life

The length of an asset's useful life is affected not only by physical wear and exhaustion but also by technological change and innovation. For accounting purposes, the useful life of an asset is based on the expected use of the asset, in keeping with the company's replacement policy. An average car, for example, may have a useful life of five years. However, for reasons of competition, a car rental company may replace its cars every year, in order to offer customers the latest models. And a company operating a fleet of cars for its sales force may replace the cars every three years.

Calculating depreciation

The objective of recording depreciation is to spread out systematically the cost of a long-lived asset over the length of the asset's useful life. However, a firm doesn't need to use the same method of depreciation for all its assets.

The four most common methods of computing depreciation are (1) the straight-line method, (2) the units-of-production method, (3) the double-declining-balance method, and (4) the sum-of-the-years'-digits method. All are permitted by the Internal Revenue Code.

Straight-line method A firm that uses the straight-line method of calculating depreciation charges an equal amount of depreciation for each year of service anticipated. The accountant computes the amount that can be written off annually as depreciation by dividing the depreciation base by the number of years of useful life predicted for the asset. This is the type we illustrated in Chapter 5. The percentage rate of depreciation per year is determined by dividing the number of years of useful life into 1. For instance, take an asset with a life of eight years:

$$\frac{1}{8 \text{ years}} = .125 = 12\frac{1}{2}\%$$

One always applies the depreciation rate against the depreciation base (cost less trade-in value).

$$\text{Depreciation per year} = \frac{\text{Cost} - \text{Trade-in value}}{\text{Useful life (in years)}}$$

Now let's look at two examples.

Example 1   A truck costs $9,000 and has a useful life of 6 years. The estimated trade-in value at end of 6 years is $1,200.

$$\text{Depreciation per year} = \frac{\$9,000 - \$1,200}{6} = \frac{\$7,800}{6} = \$1,300$$

$$\text{Depreciation rate per year} = \frac{1}{6 \text{ years}} = .16\frac{2}{3} = 16\frac{2}{3}\%$$

Example 2   A neon sign costs $1,600 and has a useful life of 8 years. The estimated trade-in value at end of 8 years is zero.

$$\text{Depreciation per year} = \frac{\$1,600 - 0}{8} = \frac{\$1,600}{8} = \$200$$

$$\text{Depreciation rate per year} = \frac{1}{8 \text{ years}} = .125 = 12\frac{1}{2}\%$$

Units-of-production method The units-of-production method enables one to allow for an asset which is used a great deal more in one year than in another. You can obtain the depreciation charge per unit of production by dividing the depreciation base by the total estimated units of production.

$$\text{Depreciation per unit of production} = \frac{\text{Cost} - \text{Trade-in value}}{\text{Estimated units of production}}$$

Example 1 A salesperson's car costs $5,400 and has a useful life of 60,000 miles. Estimated trade-in value at end of 60,000 miles is $1,200. The car is driven 18,000 miles this year.

$$\text{Depreciation per mile} = \frac{\$5,400 - \$1,200}{60,000 \text{ miles}} = \frac{\$4,200}{60,000 \text{ miles}}$$

$$= \$.07 \text{ per mile } (7\cent)$$

Depreciation for 18,000 miles = 18,000 miles × $.07 per mile = $1,260

Example 2 A bulldozer costs $35,000 and has a useful life of 4,000 hours. Estimated salvage value after 4,000 hours is $3,000. The firm uses the bulldozer for 380 hours this year.

$$\text{Depreciation per hour} = \frac{\$35,000 - \$3,000}{4,000 \text{ hours}} = \frac{\$32,000}{4,000 \text{ hours}}$$

$$= \$8 \text{ per hour}$$

Depreciation for 380 hours = 380 hours × $8 hour = $3,040

Double-declining-balance method

The double-declining-balance method is popular because it allows larger amounts for depreciation during the early life of the asset. This results in lower income tax during the early years of the asset's life as compared to that when the straight-line method is used. Hence, the tax bill is less, and the cash savings can be used elsewhere. Some accountants reason that the amount charged to depreciation of an asset should be higher during the early years of owning the asset in order to offset the higher repair and maintenance expenses of the asset's later years. In this way, the total annual expense would then tend to be equalized over the entire life of the asset.

For an asset that has a life of three years or more, under the double-declining-balance method, a firm may calculate depreciation by multiplying the book value (cost less accumulated depreciation) at the beginning of the year by *twice* the straight-line method; this applies only to new equipment and certain residential buildings. (For used equipment and nonresidential buildings, the maximum allowable rate is $1\frac{1}{2}$ times the straight-line rate. This method is called the *declining-balance method*.)

To compute depreciation by the double-declining-balance method, follow these steps:

1. Calculate the straight-line depreciation rate.

2. Multiply the straight-line rate by 2.

3. Multiply the book value of the asset at the beginning of the year by double the straight-line rate.

Example 1 A firm's word processing equipment costs $20,000 and has a useful life of five years. Estimated trade-in value at end of five years is zero.

1. Straight-line depreciation rate = $\dfrac{1}{5 \text{ years}}$ = .2 = 20%.

2. Twice the straight-line rate = $.2 \times 2 = .4$.

3. Depreciation per year = Book value at beginning of year $\times$ .4.

Year	Book Value at Beginning of Year	Depreciation Expense	Book Value at End of Year
1	$20,000.00	$20,000 × .4 = $8,000.00	$20,000 − $8,000.00 = $12,000.00
2	12,000.00	12,000 × .4 = 4,800.00	12,000 − 4,800.00 = 7,200.00
3	7,200.00	7,200 × .4 = 2,880.00	7,200 − 2,880.00 = 4,320.00
4	4,320.00	4,320 × .4 = 1,728.00	4,320 − 1,728.00 = 2,592.00
5	2,592.00	2,592 × .4 = 1,036.80	2,592 − 1,036.80 = 1,555.20

Under the double-declining-balance method, the book value never reaches zero.

Example 2 A delivery truck costs $6,000 and has a useful life of 6 years. Estimated trade-in value at end of 6 years is $1,000.

1. Straight-line depreciation rate $= \dfrac{1}{6 \text{ years}} = .1667 = \dfrac{1}{6}$. Since the decimal equivalent of $\frac{1}{6}$ has a remainder (.1667), it is more accurate to use the fraction.

2. Twice the straight-line rate $= \frac{1}{6} \times 2 = \frac{2}{6} = \frac{1}{3}$.

3. Depreciation per year = Book value at beginning of year $\times \frac{1}{3}$.

Year	Book Value at Beginning of Year	Depreciation Expense	Book Value at End of Year
1	$6,000.00	$6,000.00 × ⅓ = $2,000.00	$6,000.00 − $2,000.00 = $4,000.00
2	4,000.00	4,000.00 × ⅓ = 1,333.33	4,000.00 − 1,333.33 = 2,666.67
3	2,666.67	2,666.67 × ⅓ = 888.89	2,666.67 − 888.89 = 1,777.78
4	1,777.78	1,777.78 × ⅓ = 592.59	1,777.78 − 592.59 = 1,185.19
5	1,185.19	1,185.19 − 1,000 = 185.19	1,185.19 − 185.19 = 1,000.00
6	1,000.00	0	1,000.00 − 0 = 1,000.00
		Total $5,000.00	

Observe carefully that the trade-in or salvage value is not counted until the last year.

Note: When one uses the double-declining-balance method and there is a trade-in value involved, the book value gradually declines until it reaches the amount of the trade-in value. This is the end of the depreciation schedule; no further depreciation is allowable. For example, take the delivery truck. During the fifth year, if one has been taking the depreciation in the usual manner as being one-third of the book value at the beginning of the year, one would determine the amount of the depreciation for the year and the ending book value as follows.

$$\$1,185.19 \times \tfrac{1}{3} = \$395.06 = \text{Depreciation expense}$$
$$\$1,185.19 - 395.06 = \$790.13 = \text{Book value at end of year}$$

Obviously the book value of the truck had now dipped below the amount of its established trade-in value. Consequently one must make an adjustment during this year so that the truck's ending book value will be the same as its trade-in value. Even though its useful life was set at 6 years, in actuality the truck is depreciated to the limit in 5 years. Incidentally, the double-declining-balance method is the only method by which one figures in the trade-in value at the end of the depreciation schedule.

Sum-of-the-years'-digits method

The sum-of-the-years'-digits method yields a large proportion of depreciation during the early years of an asset's life. It does this on a reducing-fraction basis. To compute depreciate by this method, follow these steps:

1. Decide how many years the asset is likely to last. Then find the sum of the years' digits. For example, suppose the asset has an expected life of 3 years. Then add to find the sum of year 1, year 2, and year 3.

$$1 + 2 + 3 = 6$$

One can also determine the sum of the years by the following formula.

$$\frac{Life^2 + Life}{2}$$

For example, a life of 3 years would be

$$\frac{3^2 + 3}{2} = \frac{9 + 3}{2} = \frac{12}{2} = 6$$

2. Record the years in reverse (or descending) order as the numerator of the fraction, and the sum of the years' digits as the denominator of the fraction:

$$\tfrac{3}{6} + \tfrac{2}{6} + \tfrac{1}{6} = \tfrac{6}{6}$$

3. Multiply the decreasing fractions by the depreciation base (cost less trade-in value).

Example 1 A printing press costs $11,200 and has a useful life of 5 years. Estimated salvage value at end of 5 years is $400. The depreciation base is $10,800 ($11,200 − $400).

Step 1	Step 2		Year	Depreciation Expense
1	5	$\tfrac{5}{15}$	1	$\tfrac{5}{15} \times \$10,800 = \$\ 3,600$
2	4	$\tfrac{4}{15}$	2	$\tfrac{4}{15} \times\ \ 10,800 =\ \ \ \ 2,880$
3	3 and	$\tfrac{3}{15}$	3	$\tfrac{3}{15} \times\ \ 10,800 =\ \ \ \ 2,160$
4	2	$\tfrac{2}{15}$	4	$\tfrac{2}{15} \times\ \ 10,800 =\ \ \ \ 1,440$
5	1	$\tfrac{1}{15}$	5	$\tfrac{1}{15} \times\ \ 10,800 =\ \ \ \ \ \ 720$
15		$\tfrac{15}{15}$		$\$10,800$

Example 2 A fork-lift truck costs $4,500 and has a useful life of 6 years. Estimated salvage value at end of 6 years is $300.

Step 1	Step 2		Year	Depreciation Expense
1	6	$\frac{6}{21}$	1	$\frac{6}{21} \times \$4{,}200 = \$1{,}200$
2	5	$\frac{5}{21}$	2	$\frac{5}{21} \times 4{,}200 = 1{,}000$
3	4	$\frac{4}{21}$	3	$\frac{4}{21} \times 4{,}200 = 800$
4	3 and	$\frac{3}{21}$	4	$\frac{3}{21} \times 4{,}200 = 600$
5	2	$\frac{2}{21}$	5	$\frac{2}{21} \times 4{,}200 = 400$
6	1	$\frac{1}{21}$	6	$\frac{1}{21} \times 4{,}200 = 200$
21		$\frac{21}{21}$		$\$4{,}200$

Comparison of the three methods You can see in the following charts that the double-declining-balance method and the sum-of-the-years'-digits method yield relatively large amounts of depreciation during the early years of use of an asset. For this reason they are examples of *accelerated depreciation*. In the example shown, assume that a hoist costs $6,000 and has a useful life of 4 years. Estimated value at the end of 4 years is $400.

Straight-line Method

Year	Depreciation per Year	Accumulated Depreciation	Book Value at End of Year
1	$\dfrac{\$6{,}000 - \$400}{4 \text{ years}} = \dfrac{\$5{,}600}{4} = \$1{,}400$	$\$1{,}400$	$\$6{,}000 - \$1{,}400 = \$4{,}600$
2	1,400	$\$1{,}400 + \$1{,}400 = 2{,}800$	$6{,}000 - 2{,}800 = 3{,}200$
3	1,400	$2{,}800 + 1{,}400 = 4{,}200$	$6{,}000 - 4{,}200 = 1{,}800$
4	1,400	$4{,}200 + 1{,}400 = 5{,}600$	$6{,}000 - 5{,}600 = 400$
	Total $\$5{,}600$		

Double-declining-balance Method (based on twice the straight-line rate)

Year	Beginning Book Value	Depreciation per Year	Accumulated Depreciation	Book Value at End of Year
1	$6,000	$\$6{,}000 \times .5 = \$3{,}000$	$\$3{,}000$	$\$6{,}000 - \$3{,}000 = \$3{,}000$
2	3,000	$3{,}000 \times .5 = 1{,}500$	$\$3{,}000 + \$1{,}500 = 4{,}500$	$6{,}000 - 4{,}500 = 1{,}500$
3	1,500	$1{,}500 \times .5 = 750$	$4{,}500 + 750 = 5{,}250$	$6{,}000 - 5{,}250 = 750$
4	750	$750 - 400 = 350$	$5{,}250 + 350 = 5{,}600$	$6{,}000 - 5{,}600 = 400$
		Total $\$5{,}600$		

Sum-of-the-years'-digits Method

Year	Depreciation per Year	Accumulated Depreciation	Book Value at End of Year
1	$\frac{4}{10} \times \$5{,}600 = \$2{,}240$	$\$2{,}240$	$\$6{,}000 - \$2{,}240 = \$3{,}760$
2	$\frac{3}{10} \times 5{,}600 = 1{,}680$	$\$2{,}240 + \$1{,}680 = 3{,}920$	$6{,}000 - 3{,}920 = 2{,}080$
3	$\frac{2}{10} \times 5{,}600 = 1{,}120$	$3{,}920 + 1{,}120 = 5{,}040$	$6{,}000 - 5{,}040 = 960$
4	$\frac{1}{10} \times 5{,}600 = 560$	$5{,}040 + 560 = 5{,}600$	$6{,}000 - 5{,}600 = 400$
10	$\frac{10}{10}$ $\$5{,}600$		

The firm may calculate its regular depreciation by either the straight-line, double-declining-balance, or sum-of-the-years'-digits methods.

Depreciation for periods of less than a year

Suppose that a business entity acquires a depreciable asset sometime during the year. In that case, the accountant usually figures depreciation to the nearest whole month. If the firm held the asset for *less* than half a given month, the accountant doesn't count that month. But if the firm has held it for *more* than half of a given month, the accountant counts it as a whole month.

For example, suppose a firm buys an asset on June 11; depreciation would be computed from June 1, counting the entire month. But if it bought that asset on June 17, no depreciation would be computed for the month of June.

Here are other examples (assume that the fiscal year ends on December 31).

Date Acquired	Cost	Trade-in Value	Method	Useful Life	Depreciation for First Year
April 12	$9,000	$1,000	Straight line	5 years	$\dfrac{\$9,000 - \$1,000}{5 \text{ years}} = \$1,600$ per year $\$1,600 \times \frac{9}{12} = \$1,200$ for 9 months
October 19	6,000	200	Double declining balance	8 years	$\$6,000 \times \frac{1}{4} = \$1,500$ per year $\$1,500 \times \frac{2}{12} = \$250$ for 2 months
August 8	6,800	500	Sum of the years' digits	6 years	$\$6,300 \times \frac{6}{21} = \$1,800$ per year $\$1,800 \times \frac{5}{12} = \$750$ for 5 months

Capital and revenue expenditures

An *expenditure* refers to spending, either by paying cash now or by promising to pay in the future for services received or assets purchased. In addition to paying the initial price for an asset, one often has to pay out more, either to maintain the asset's operating efficiency or to increase its capacity. So there are two classifications of expenditures: capital and revenue.

Capital expenditures include the initial costs of plant and equipment; they also include any costs of increasing the capacity or prolonging the life of assets. You reap the benefits of capital expenditures during more than one accounting period. Examples are expenditures for buying a building, air-conditioning it, enlarging it, replacing a stairway with an elevator, etc. All these expenditures result in debits to an asset account.

Revenue expenditures include the costs of maintaining the operation of an asset, such as the expense of making normal repairs. Examples are expenditures for painting, plumbing repairs, fuel, property taxes, etc. Thus these expenditures benefit you only during the current accounting period, and are recorded as debits to expense accounts.

Extraordinary-repairs expenditures

Extraordinary repairs, in accounting, means a major overhaul or reconditioning that will extend the useful life of an asset beyond its original estimated life. An accountant records expenditures for extraordinary repairs as debits to Accumulated Depreciation and credits to Cash or Accounts Payable.

For example, a firm buys a company car for $6,000; the car's estimated useful life is 4 years, and its trade-in value is $1,600; straight-line annual depreciation expense is $1,100. After three years the firm puts in a new engine and has other major repairs done, for which it spends $1,400 in cash. The entry in general journal form is as follows.

1		*Accumulated Depreciation, Automobile*		1 4 0 0 00		1
2		*Cash*			1 4 0 0 00	2
3		*New engine installed in company car.*				3
4						4

This extraordinary repair extends the life of the car from the present 1 additional year to 3 additional years. Here are relevant balances, together with the posting of the entry for the $1,400 payment as shown by T accounts.

Automobile

+	−
Jan. 3, 1980 6,000	

Accumulated Depreciation, Automobile

−	+
Jan. 6, 1983 1,400	Dec. 31, 1980 1,100
	Dec. 31, 1981 1,100
	Dec. 31, 1982 1,000

The car's book value before the extraordinary repair was $2,700 ($6,000–$3,300). The reason the accountant debited the Accumulated Depreciation account (rather than the asset account) is that the original cost figure is preserved in the asset account. In this example, the car that the firm bought cost $6,000, not $7,400. We can see this in the balance sheet as follows.

Plant and Equipment			
Automobile		6 0 0 0 00	
Less Accumulated Depreciation		1 9 0 0 00	4 1 0 0 00

When it comes to recording the remaining depreciation of the asset, the accountant now has a new cost base, which he or she uses to determine the new depreciation base. Assume that the trade-in value is still $1,600.

New book value	$4,100
Less trade-in value	1,600
New depreciation base	$2,500

$2,500 ÷ 3 years = $833.33

Disposition of plant and equipment

Sooner or later a business entity disposes of its long-lived assets by (1) discarding or retiring them, (2) selling them, or (3) trading them in for other assets. If the assets are not fully depreciated, the accountant has to make an entry first, to bring the depreciation up to date. Let's look at some examples. (Ordinarily entries involving Cash would be recorded in the cash journals; however, for simplification and clarity, we shall present all the following entries in general journal form.)

Discarding or retiring plant and equipment

When long-lived assets are no longer useful to the business and have no market value, a firm discards them.

Discarding of fully depreciated assets A display case which cost $1,400 and has previously been fully depreciated is now given away as junk. The present status of the accounts is as follows.

Store Equipment		Accumulated Depreciation, Store Equipment	
+	−	−	+
Bal. 1,400		Bal. 1,400	

The journal entry to record the disposal of the asset looks like this.

1		Accumulated Depreciation, Store Equipment		1 4 0 0 00	
2		Store Equipment			1 4 0 0 00
3		Discarded a fully depreciated display case.			

Note: Fully depreciated assets are retained on the books as long as they are still in use, but the firm may not take any additional depreciation on them.

Discarding an asset not fully depreciated A firm has a time clock which cost them $1,600 and discards it with no salvage value realized. Accumulated Depreciation up to the end of the previous year is $1,450; depreciation for the current year is $90. The present balances of the accounts are as follows.

Office Equipment		Accumulated Depreciation, Office Equipment	
+	−	−	+
Bal. 1,600		Bal. 1,450	

Record the entry to depreciate the asset up to date.

		Depreciation Expense, Office Equipment		9 0 00	
		Accumulated Depreciation, Office Equipment			9 0 00
		Depreciation on time clock for the partial			
		year.			

The T accounts look like this.

Depreciation Expense, Office Equipment		Accumulated Depreciation, Office Equipment	
+	−	−	+
90			Bal.　1,450
			90

The journal entry to record the disposal of the asset is as follows.

1		Accumulated Depreciation, Office Equipment	1 5 4 0 00		1
2		Loss on Disposal of Plant and Equipment	6 0 00		2
3		Office Equipment		1 6 0 0 00	3
4		Discarded a time clock.			4

The T accounts look like this.

Accumulated Depreciation, Office Equipment		Loss on Disposal of Plant and Equipment		Office Equipment	
−	+	+	−	+	−
1,540	Bal.　1,450	60		Bal.　1,600	1,600
	90				

The book value of the asset is $60 ($1,600 − $1,540). Because the firm realized nothing from the disposal of the asset; consequently, the loss is the same as the amount of the book value.

The account, Loss on Disposal of Plant and Equipment, is an expense account which appears under Other Expense in the income statement.

Selling of plant and equipment　Naturally it's very hard to estimate the exact trade-in or salvage value of a long-lived asset. So it's quite likely that when a firm sells or trades in such an asset, the amount realized from the asset may differ from the estimated amount.

Sale of an asset at a loss　Suppose that a firm sells a drill press for $135. This drill press originally cost $1,900; accumulated depreciation up to the end of the previous year was $1,560. Yearly depreciation is $180. The drill press is sold on August 21.

The present balances of the accounts are as follows:

Factory Equipment		Accumulated Depreciation, Factory Equipment	
+	−	−	+
Bal.　1,900			Bal.　1,560

We record the depreciation of the asset to the present date.

	Depreciation Expense, Factory Equipment		1 2 0 00					
	Accumulated Depreciation, Factory Equipment				1 2 0 00			
	Depreciation on drill press for 8 months							
	($180 × 8/12 = $120)							

By T accounts, the situation looks like this.

Depreciation Expense, Factory Equipment		Accumulated Depreciation, Factory Equipment	
+	−	−	+
120		Bal.	1,560
			120

The entry, in general journal form, to record the sale of the drill press is as follows.

1		Cash		1 3 5 00					1
2		Accumulated Depreciation, Factory Equipment		1 6 8 0 00					2
3		Loss on Disposal of Plant and Equipment		8 5 00					3
4		Factory Equipment				1 9 0 0 00			4
5		Sold a drill press for $135, having an original							5
6		cost of $1,900 and accumulated depreciation							6
7		of $1,680.							7
8									8
9									9
10									10
11									11

For purposes of illustration, let us record the above entry in the T accounts as follows.

Cash		Accumulated Depreciation, Factory Equipment	
+	−	−	+
135		1,680	Bal. 1,560
			120

Loss on Disposal of Plant and Equipment		Factory Equipment	
+	−	+	−
85	Bal. 1,900		1,900

Note that the book value of the drill press is $220 ($1,900 − $1,680). When the firm sells it for $135, the loss is $85.

Sale of an asset at a gain   Suppose that a firm sells a printing press for $310. The firm had originally paid $4,200; accumulated depreciation up to the end of the previous year was $3,960. Yearly depreciation is $120. the printing press is sold on October 18. The present balances of the accounts are as follows.

	Printing Equipment			Accumulated Depreciation, Printing Equipment	
	+	−	−	+	
Bal.	4,200			Bal.	3,960

We record the depreciation of the asset to the present date.

	Depreciation Expense, Printing Equipment	1 0 0 00	
	Accumulated Depreciation, Printing Equipment		1 0 0 00
	Recorded depreciation through October 18.		
	Depreciation for 10 months is $100		
	($120 × 10/12 = $100).		

By T accounts, the situation looks like this.

Depreciation Expense, Printing Equipment		Accumulated Depreciation, Printing Equipment	
+	−	−	+
100		Bal.	3,960
			100

The entry, in general journal form, to record the sale of the printing press is as follows.

	Cash	3 1 0 00	
	Accumulated Depreciation, Printing Equipment	4 0 6 0 00	
	Printing Equipment		4 2 0 0 00
	Gain on Disposal of Plant and Equipment		1 7 0 00
	Sold a printing press for $310, having an		
	original cost of $4,200 and accumulated		
	depreciation of $4,060.		

By T accounts, the situation looks like this.

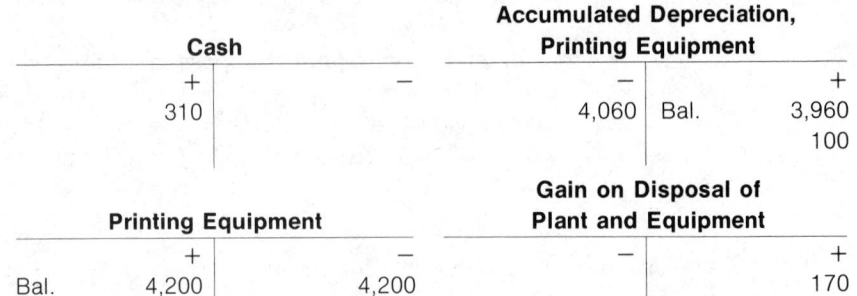

The account, Gain on Disposal of Plant and Equipment, is a revenue account, which appears under Other Income in the income statement.

The book value of the printing press is $140 ($4,200 − $4,060). Since the firm sells it for $310, the firm's gain is $170.

Exchange of long-lived assets for other assets Often a business trades in one asset for another, using the old item as part payment for the new one. The trade-in allowance may differ from the book value of the asset. If the trade-in allowance is greater than the book value, the firm has a gain; if less than the book value, it has a loss. However, federal income tax laws state that when assets held for productive use are exchanged for other assets acquired for similar use, *no gain or loss is recognized.* In effect, the gain or loss is absorbed into the recorded cost of the new asset.

Exchange when trade-in value is less than book value Suppose that a firm bought a delivery truck for $4,900. Four years later, the truck has an Accumulated Depreciation of $4,200. The firm buys a new truck, with a list price of $5,600, trading in the old one, for which they are allowed only $400, and paying the difference in cash. Assume that the depreciation for the year is already up to date. The present status of the accounts is as follows.

Delivery Equipment		Accumulated Depreciation, Delivery Equipment	
+	−	−	+
Bal. 4,900			Bal. 4,200

The firm's accountant records the transaction by the following steps.

1. Credit cash, $5,200 (quoted price of new truck, $5,600, minus $400, which is the trade-in allowance on old truck).

2. Close or clear the account of the old asset: credit Delivery Equipment, $4,900.

3. Close or clear the account of the Accumulated Depreciation of the old asset: debit Accumulated Depreciation, $4,200.

4. Debit the account of the new asset for the difference between total debits and total credits, $5,900 ($5,200 + $4,900 − $4,200 = $5,900). You can recognize this as being the book value of the old asset plus the amount of cash or notes given.

Here is how one records these entries in general journal form.

(4) *Delivery Equipment*		5 9 0 0 00	
(3) *Accumulated Depreciation, Delivery Equipment*		4 2 0 0 00	
(1) *Cash*			5 2 0 0 00
(2) *Delivery Equipment*			4 9 0 0 00
Bought a new delivery truck having a list			
price of $5,600. Received a trade-in			
allowance of $400 on old delivery truck,			
having an original cost of $4,900 and			
accumulated depreciation of $4,200.			

You can see from this that when you use the income tax method of accounting, the loss is absorbed in the cost of the new equipment. In this case the accountant added the loss of $300 to the price of the new equipment, as follows.

Cost of old equipment	$4,900
− Accumulated depreciation	4,200
Book value	$ 700
− Trade-in allowance	400
Loss	$ 300
Quoted price of new equipment	$5,600
+ Loss absorbed in recorded cost of new equipment	300
Recorded cost of new equipment	$5,900

You can also use this technique to verify the cost recorded for the new equipment. For income tax purposes, the firm cannot count the $300 loss at this time; however, the firm does have an additional $300 that it can count as depreciation in the future.

Exchange when trade-in value is greater than book value A business bought an automated file for $2,600. After some years it decides to trade it in on a new model. The old one has an accumulated depreciation of $2,480 *on the date* of the trade-in, leaving a net book value of $120. The new file has a list price of $3,350; however, the salesperson gives the firm a generous trade-in allowance of $310 on the old equipment, and the firm pays the difference in cash. The present status of the accounts is as shown atop the following page.

	Office Equipment			Accumulated Depreciation, Office Equipment	
	+		−	−	+
Bal.	2,600			Bal.	2,480

The firm's accountant records the transaction by the following steps.

1. Credit Cash, $3,040 (quoted price of new file, $3,350, minus $310, which is the trade-in allowance on old model).

2. Close or clear the account of the old asset: credit Office Equipment, $2,600.

3. Close or clear the account of the Accumulated Depreciation on the old asset: debit Accumulated Depreciation, $2,480.

4. Debit the account of the new asset for the difference between the total debits and credits, $3,160 ($3,040 + $2,600 − $2,480 = $3,160). You can recognize this as being the book value of the old asset plus the amount of cash or notes given.

Here's how one records the entries in general journal form.

(4)	*Office Equipment*	3 1 6 0 00	
(3)	*Accumulated Depreciation, Office Equipment*	2 4 8 0 00	
(1)	Cash		3 0 4 0 00
(2)	*Office Equipment*		2 6 0 0 00
	Bought a new automated file having a list		
	price of $3,350. Received a trade-in		
	allowance of $310 on old file, which had		
	an original cost of $2,600 and an accumu-		
	lated depreciation of $2,480.		

When the accountant records the new equipment as costing less than the list price, this indicates that a gain is involved, a gain which has been absorbed in the price of the new equipment.

Cost of old equipment	$2,600
− Accumulated depreciation	2,480
Book value	$ 120
− Trade-in allowance	310
Gain	$ 190

Quoted price of new equipment	$3,350
− Gain absorbed in recorded cost	
of new equipment	190
Recorded cost of new equipment	$3,160

For income tax purposes, the firm does not count the gain at this time. However, the amount that the firm can count as depreciation in the future has been reduced by $190.

Plant and equipment records

We have seen that depreciation is regarded as an expense. Thus depreciation vitally affects the net income of any business. Because net income is affected, the amount of income tax is likewise affected. And not only Depreciation Expense, but also Loss (or Gain) on Disposal can affect net income. For income tax purposes, the business must be able to justify the amount of depreciation taken, as well as the gain or loss on disposal of assets.

We have discussed Plant and Equipment as a category on a classified balance sheet. Now let's look at an example.

Plant and Equipment			
Delivery Equipment	20 0 0 0 00		
Less Accumulated Depreciation	12 0 0 0 00	8 0 0 0 00	
Store Equipment	18 0 0 0 00		
Less Accumulated Depreciation	14 0 0 0 00	4 0 0 0 00	
Office Equipment	6 0 0 0 00		
Less Accumulated Depreciation	4 5 0 0 00	1 5 0 0 00	
Building	40 0 0 0 00		
Less Accumulated Depreciation	28 0 0 0 00	12 0 0 0 00	
Land Improvements	3 0 0 0 00		
Less Accumulated Depreciation	2 3 0 0 00	7 0 0 00	
Land		6 0 0 0 00	
Total Plant and Equipment			32 2 0 0 00

The asset accounts represent functional groups. When you are listing asset accounts, as we have said before, list them so that the asset which has the shortest life comes first, then the next shortest, and so on. Immediately after you list an asset account which is subject to depreciation, write its respective Accumulated Depreciation account.

An example of an asset representing a functional group is the Store Equipment account. Store Equipment includes all types of equipment used in the operation of a store, such as display cases, cash registers, counters, storage shelves, etc. To account for the depreciation of each item of store equipment, maintain a separate record card for each item in the plant and equipment ledger. Store Equipment now becomes a controlling account, and the plant and equipment ledger becomes a subsidiary ledger. This relationship is similar to that of Accounts Receivable as a controlling account and the accounts receivable ledger as a subsidiary ledger, with an account for each individual charge customer. An illustration of an account in the plant and equipment ledger is shown atop the following page.

PLANT AND EQUIPMENT RECORD

ITEM _____ *Cash Register* _____ ACCOUNT NO. _____ *122-1* _____

SERIAL NO. _____ *ND37-4163* _____ MAKER _____ *Security, Inc.* ___

FROM WHOM PURCHASED _____ *Rogers Equipment Company* _____ EST. SALVAGE

ESTIMATED LIFE ___ *5* ___ VALUE _____ *$50* _____

DEPRECIATION METHOD ___ *Straight line* ___ DEPRECIATION PER YEAR ___ *$150.00* ___ DEPRECIATION PER MONTH ___ *$12.50* ___ RATE OF DEPRECIATION ___ *20%* ___

| DATE | EXPLANATION | ASSET | | | ACCUMULATED DEPRECIATION | | | BOOK VALUE |
		DEBIT	CREDIT	BALANCE	DEBIT	CREDIT	BALANCE	
7/3/82		800		800				800
12/31/82						75	75	725
12/31/83						150	225	575
12/31/84						150	375	425

Account 122 is the number of the general ledger account for Store Equipment. Account 122-1 is the first piece of equipment classified under Store Equipment. One finds the amount of the adjusting entry for Depreciation Expense, Store Equipment by adding the current depreciation for each piece of equipment within the classification.

The plant and equipment record enables the accountant to determine the amount of the adjusting entry for depreciation as well as to keep a record of the accumulated depreciation and book value. Plant and equipment records are also invaluable to an accountant who has to prepare insurance claims in the event of insured losses.

Summary

The figures listed for original costs of plant and equipment comprise all necessary and normal expenditures, including transportation and installation costs of an asset. An accountant may use the tax assessor's ratio to separate the value of land from the value of buildings when the two have been purchased as one package. Land improvements are depreciable; these improvements include the costs of driveways, parking lots, trees and shrubs, and outdoor lighting systems.

Depreciation represents the decline in usefulness of an asset due to such causes as physical wear and exhaustion, inadequacy, and obsolescence.

Depreciation is recorded as a debit to the Depreciation Expense of the asset and a credit to the Accumulated Depreciation of the asset. The depreciation base is the cost of the asset less the trade-in or salvage value. We introduced four methods of determining depreciation.

$$\text{Straight-line method} = \frac{\text{Cost} - \text{Trade-in value}}{\text{Useful life (in years)}}$$

$$\text{Units-of-production method} = \frac{\text{Cost} - \text{Trade-in value}}{\text{Estimated units of production}}$$

Double-declining-balance method = Book value at beginning of year × Twice the straight-line rate
(The trade-in value is counted at the end of the schedule of depreciation.)

Sum-of-the-years'-digits method = Reducing fraction × (Cost − Trade-in value)

For the sum-of-the-years'-digits method, the numerator of the fraction is the years of the asset's life placed in reverse order. The denominator of the fraction is the sum of the years of the asset's life.

Capital expenditures, which are debited to the asset accounts, are costs incurred to buy or increase the capacity of assets. Extraordinary-repairs expenditures, which significantly prolong the life of an asset, are recorded as debits to the Accumulated Depreciation account of the asset.

When a firm changes its Plant and Equipment accounts, as a result of selling, exchanging, or discarding its assets, the accountant must close or clear the asset accounts along with their respective Accumulated Depreciation accounts. When a firm discards, sells, or trades in an asset which has not yet been fully depreciated, the accountant must first depreciate the asset up to the present date. When the amount received for the old asset is less than the asset's book value, the accountant debits Loss on Disposal of Plant and Equipment.

When a firm trades in one asset for another which has a similar function, the accountant's entry must include the four steps on pages 542 and 543.

Plant and equipment records should consist of a controlling account and a subsidiary ledger. The subsidiary ledger should contain a card for each piece of equipment, listing the date acquired, cost, and depreciation taken to date. For income tax purposes, a subsidiary ledger is a must.

Glossary

Accelerated depreciation   Relatively large amounts of depreciation recorded during the early years of an asset's use; decreasing in later years.

Capital expenditures   Costs incurred for the purchase of plant and equipment, as well as the cost of increasing the capacity of assets; the firm receives services or benefits from this plant and equipment for more than one accounting period.

Depreciation base   Cost of plant and equipment less trade-in or salvage value.

Extraordinary-repair expenditures   Costs incurred for major overhauls or reconditioning of assets; repairs which significantly prolong the life of the asset.

Gain on disposal   When a firm sells or trades in an asset and receives an amount in excess of the book value for that asset, this advantage is called a Gain on Disposal.

Income tax method for exchange of assets   When a firm exchanges assets held for productive use for other assets acquired for similar use, no gain or loss is recognized; the gain or loss is absorbed in the recorded cost of the new assets.

Land improvements   An asset account covering the cost of driveways, parking lots, trees and shrubs, fences, and outdoor lighting systems.

Loss on disposal   When a firm sells or trades in an asset and receives an amount less than the book value for that asset, this disadvantage is called Loss on Disposal.

Revenue expenditures Costs incurred to maintain the operation of assets, such as normal repair expenses and fuel expenses.

Questions

1. How does the accountant's meaning of the term *depreciation* differ from the nonaccountant's meaning of the term?

2. List four things that an accountant must know about an asset, classified as plant and equipment, in order to calculate its depreciation expense.

3. Which methods of depreciation are classified as accelerated depreciation?

4. Distinguish between capital expenditures and revenue expenditures.

5. When an old truck is traded in on a new truck, how is the cost basis of the new truck calculated for income tax purposes?

6. Distinguish between expenditures for ordinary repairs and expenditures for extraordinary repairs.

7. Describe the use and operation of a plant and equipment ledger. What items are listed on each card in a plant and equipment ledger?

Exercises

Exercise 1 At the beginning of the fiscal year, Herman's Pancake House bought cooking equipment for $6,720, with an estimated salvage value of $420 and an estimated useful life of six years. Determine the amount of the depreciation for the first year by the following methods.

a. Straight-line method

b. Double-declining-balance method at twice the straight-line rate

c. Sum-of-the-years'-digits method

Exercise 2 A bulldozer cost a contractor $30,000, has an estimated trade-in value of $3,200 and is expected to have a useful life of 10,000 hours. During April the contractor operated the bulldozer for 180 hours. Determine the amount of depreciation for the month.

Exercise 3 Jacobson Plywood bought a dry kiln for $72,000, terms 2/10, n/30, FOB factory. Jacobson paid the invoice within the discount period, along with $760 transportation charges. Jacobson also paid installation costs of $990 and power connection costs of $832. How much should Jacobson debit to its Plant and Equipment account?

Exercise 4 On April 4, Town Cab Company sold a taxicab for cash, $460. The following details are from the subsidiary ledger: Cost, $5,850; Accumulated Depreciation as of the previous December 31, $4,240; Monthly Depreciation, $85. Make entries in general journal form to record the depreciation up to the present date and the sale of the asset.

Exercise 5 On May 13 of this year, Milly's Separates Shop discarded a display case; there was no salvage value. The following details are from the subsidiary ledger: Cost, $494; Accumulated Depreciation as of December 31, the end of last year, was $494. Journalize the necessary entry.

Exercise 6 On August 18, Baker Real Estate discarded a carpet (Office Equipment) with no salvage value. The following details are from the subsidiary ledger: Cost, $860, Accumulated Depreciation as of the previous December 31, $512; Monthly Depreciation, $9. Journalize entries to record the depreciation of the carpet up to date and to record the disposal of the carpet.

Exercise 7 On October 19, Tony's Pizza Palace traded in the old delivery truck on a new one which cost $5,440. Tony's got a trade-in allowance of $720 on the old truck and paid the difference in cash. The subsidiary account shows the following: Cost (of old truck), $3,990; Accumulated Depreciation as of last December 31, $3,418; Monthly Depreciation, $52. Using the income tax method, make entries in general journal form to record the depreciation of the old truck up to date and to record the exchange of assets.

Exercise 8 On May 13, Cordova and Son, a machine shop, trades in a lathe (Machinery) on a new one priced at $5,116, receiving a trade-in allowance of $710 on the old lathe. Cordova makes a down payment of $800 in cash and issues a 60-day, 8% note for the remainder. The subsidiary account shows the following: Cost, $2,989; Accumulated Depreciation as of last December 31, $2,474; Monthly Depreciation, $38. Using the income tax method, make entries in general journal form to record the depreciation of the lathe up to date, and to record the exchange of assets.

Problems

Problem 20-1 At the beginning of a fiscal year, the Kramer Products Company buys a machine for $30,000. The machine has an estimated life of five years and an estimated trade-in value of $3,000.

Instructions Determine the annual depreciation of the machine for each of the expected five years of its life, the accumulated depreciation at the end of each year, and the book value of the machine at the end of each year by each of the following methods, using the columns provided:

a. Straight-line method

b. Double-declining-balance method at twice the straight-line rate

c. Sum-of-the-years'-digits method

Problem 20-2 During a three-year period, Johnson Auto Parts completed the transactions pertaining to its delivery truck shown atop the following page.

Year 1

Jan.   8 Bought a used pick-up truck for $2,680, paying cash.

Nov. 16 Paid garage $238 for maintenance repairs to truck.

Dec. 31 Recorded the adjusting entry for depreciation for the fiscal year, using the straight-line method of depreciation. The estimated life of the truck is four years, and it has a trade-in value of $1,080.

Dec. 31 Closed the appropriate accounts to the Income Summary account.

Year 2

Apr.   3 Paid garage $86 for tune-up and minor repairs.

July 16 Bought two new tires, $82.

Dec. 31 Recorded the adjusting entry for depreciation.

      31 Closed the appropriate accounts to the Income Summary account.

Year 3

May 19 Paid garage for maintenance repairs to truck, $428.

June 19 Traded in the used truck on a new one, priced at $4,840, receiving a trade-in allowance of $1,720; paid difference in cash. Recorded the entry to depreciate the old truck up to date. Recorded entry for the exchange, using the income tax method.

Dec. 31 Recorded adjusting entry for depreciation of the new truck for the fiscal year, using the straight-line method of depreciation. The estimated life of the new truck is 6 years, with a trade-in value of $600.

      31 Closed the appropriate accounts to the Income Summary account.

Instructions   **1.** Record all these transactions in the general journal.

2. After journalizing each entry, post to the following ledger accounts: Delivery Equipment; Accumulated Depreciation, Delivery Equipment; Truck Repair Expense; Depreciation Expense, Delivery Equipment.

Problem 20-3   During a three-year period, the Mitchell Electric Company completed the following transactions connected with its electronic computer.

Year 1

June 30 Bought an electronic computer, $90,300, paying $30,300 in cash, and issuing a series of four notes for $15,000 each, to come due at six-month intervals, payments to include principal plus 6% interest to maturity on each note.

July   1 Paid installation charges for the computer, $2,700.

Dec. 31 Paid the principal, $15,000, plus interest of $450 on the first note.

      31 Recorded adjusting entry for depreciation on the computer for the fiscal year, using the double-declining-balance method at twice the straight-line

rate ($18,600; verify this figure). The estimated life of the computer is five years, with a trade-in value of $8,700.

Dec. 31 Closed the appropriate accounts to the Income Summary account.

Year 2

Mar. 16 Paid for maintenance repairs to the computer, $4,377.

June 30 Paid the principal, $15,000, plus interest of $900 on the second note.

Dec. 31 Paid the principal, $15,000, plus interest of $1,350 on the third note.

     31 Recorded the adjusting entry for depreciation for the fiscal year ($74,400 × $\frac{2}{5}$ = $29,760; verify this figure).

     31 Closed the appropriate account to the Income Summary account.

Year 3

June 21 Paid for maintenance repairs to the computer, $2,544.

     30 Paid the principal, $15,000, plus interest of $1,800 on the fourth note.

Sept. 26 Mitchell Electric Company decides to get rid of its computer and use the services of a data processing firm in the future. Sold the computer for $18,000, receiving cash. Recorded entry to depreciate the computer up to date ($13,392; but verify this figure). Recorded the entry accounting for the sale of the machine.

Dec. 31 Closed the appropriate accounts to the Income Summary account.

Instructions   **1.** Record the transactions in general journal form.

2. Post to the following ledger accounts after recording each journal entry: Equipment; Accumulated Depreciation, Equipment; Depreciation Expense, Equipment; Equipment Maintenance Expense; Interest Expense; Loss on Disposal of Plant and Equipment.

Problem 20-4   The general ledger of the Morrison Insurance Agency includes controlling accounts for Office Equipment and for Accumulated Depreciation, Office Equipment. Morrison's accountant also records the details of each item of office equipment in a subsidiary ledger. The following transactions affecting office equipment occurred during a three-year period.

Year 1

Jan. 11 Bought the following items from Norris Office Supplies, for cash:
Executive desk, $1,080, Account No. 122-1, estimated life ten years, trade-in value zero.
Executive chair, $380, Account No. 122-2, estimated life ten years, trade-in value zero.
Filing cabinet, $240, Account No. 122-3, estimated life fifteen years, metal, trade-in value zero.
(The above assets are depreciated on the basis of the straight-line method.)

Jan. 12 Paid Ross Cabinet Shop $1,440 for a custom-made counter, Account No. 122-4, estimated life ten years, trade-in value zero; depreciation by straight-line method.

14 Purchased a Smart and Turner electric typewriter from Nothern Equipment Company, $760, Serial No. TL-18619, Account No. 122-5, estimated life five years, estimated trade-in value, $100; depreciated by sum-of-years'-digits method.

Dec. 31 Recorded the adjusting entry for depreciation of Office Equipment for the fiscal year (total depreciation, $526; but verify this figure).

31 Closed the Depreciation Expense, Office Equipment account into the Income Summary account.

Year 2

June 29 Bought a rug from Warrington Furniture on account, $960, Account No. 122-6; estimated life eight years, trade-in value zero; depreciation by double-declining-balance method at twice the straight-line rate.

Dec. 31 Recorded the adjusting entry for depreciation of office equipment for the fiscal year (depreciation for 6 months on the rug; total depreciation, $602; but verify this figure).

31 Closed the Depreciation Expense, Office Equipment account into the Income Summary account.

Year 3

June 21 Traded in the executive desk for a new one, which cost $1,360, from Walters Stationery and Supply, Account No. 122-7, receiving a trade-in allowance of $640 on the old desk and paying the balance in cash. Expected life of the new desk is eight years, with zero trade-in value. Use straight-line method of depreciation. Recorded the entry to depreciate the old desk up to date. Recorded the entry for exchange of assets using the income-tax method.

Dec. 31 Recorded the adjusting entry for depreciation of office equipment for the fiscal year (depreciation for 6 months on the desk; total depreciation, $635.63; but verify this figure).

31 Closed the Depreciation Expense, Office Equipment account into the Income Summary account.

Instructions **1.** Record the transactions in the general journal.

2. With the purchase of each new asset, open an account in the subsidiary ledger.

3. After each entry, post to the two controlling accounts and to the subsidiary ledger.

4. Make a list of balances in the subsidiary ledger accounts and compare the totals with the balances of the two controlling accounts.

Alternate problems

Problem 20-1A At the beginning of a fiscal year, the Birke Wood Products Company buys a truck for $18,000. The truck's estimated life is five years, and its estimated trade-in value is $1,800.

Instructions Determine the annual depreciation for each of the estimated five years of life, the accumulated depreciation at the end of each year, and the book value of the truck at the end of each year by the following methods, using the columns provided:

a. Straight-line method

b. Double-declining-balance method at twice the straight-line rate

c. Sum-of-the-years'-digits method

Problem 20-2A During a three-year period the Jordan Oil Company completed the following transactions related to its oil delivery truck.

Year 1

Jan.   6 Bought a used tanker truck for $24,800, paying cash.

Oct. 21 Paid garage $252 for maintenance repairs to the truck.

Dec. 31 Recorded the adjusting entry for depreciation for the fiscal year. The estimated life of the truck is four years, and it has a trade-in value of $5,200. Jordan uses the straight-line method of depreciation.

    31 Closed the appropriate accounts to the Income Summary account.

Year 2

Mar.   9 Paid garage $104 for tune-up of truck.

Aug. 27 Paid for tire recaps, $480.

Dec. 31 Recorded the adjusting entry for depreciation for the fiscal year.

    31 Closed the appropriate accounts to the Income Summary account.

Year 3

Apr. 21 Paid garage for maintenance repairs to truck, $632.

June 27 Traded in the used truck on a new truck, which costs $39,200, receiving a trade-in allowance of $15,600 and paying the difference in cash. Recorded the entry to depreciate the truck up to date. Recorded the entry for the exchange, using the income tax method.

Dec. 31 Recorded the adjusting entry for depreciation of the new truck for the fiscal year. The estimated life of the truck is six years, and it has a trade-in value of $2,550. Jordan uses the straight-line method of depreciation.

    31 Closed the appropriate accounts to the Income Summary account.

Instructions **1.** Record the transactions in the general journal.

2. After journalizing each entry, post to the following ledger accounts: Delivery Equipment; Accumulated Depreciation, Delivery Equipment; Truck Repair Expense; Depreciation Expense, Delivery Equipment.

Problem 20-3A During a three-year period, Suburban Shopping News completed the following transactions pertaining to its printing press.

Year 1

June 30 Bought a printing press, $30,600, paying $6,600 in cash and issuing a series of four notes for $6,000 each, to come due at six-month intervals; payments to include principal plus interest of 6% to maturity on each note.

July   3 Paid transportation charges for the press, $420.

     8 Paid installation charges for the press, $1,380.

Dec. 31 Paid the principal, $6,000, plus interest of $180 on the first note.

     31 Recorded the adjusting entry for depreciation for the fiscal year. The estimated life of the press is four years; it has a salvage value of $3,000. Suburban's accountant uses the double-declining-balance method, at twice the straight-line rate ($8,100; but verify this figure).

     31 Closed the appropriate accounts to the Income Summary account.

Year 2

May   4 Paid for normal mechanical repairs, $936.

June 30 Paid the principal, $6,000, plus interest of $360 on the second note.

Dec. 31 Paid the principal, $6,000, plus interest of $540 on the third note.

     31 Recorded the adjusting entry for the fiscal year ($12,150; but verify this figure).

     31 Closed the appropriate accounts to the Income Summary account.

Year 3

May 11 Paid for normal mechanical repairs, $1,078.50.

June 30 Paid the principal, $6,000, plus interest of $720 on the fourth note.

Sept. 21 Suburban Shopping News decides to get rid of its press and use the services of a commercial printer in the future. Sold the press for $6,300. Recorded entry to depreciate the press up to date ($4,556.25). Recorded entry to account for the sale of the press.

Dec. 31 Closed the appropriate accounts to the Income Summary account.

Instructions **1.** Record the transactions in the general journal.

2. After recording each journal entry, post to the following ledger accounts: Equipment; Accumulated Depreciation, Equipment; Depreciation Expense, Equipment; Equipment Maintenance Expense; Interest Expense; Loss on Disposal of Plant and Equipment.

Problem 20-4A The general ledger of the Wonner Travel Agency includes controlling accounts for Office Equipment and Accumulated Depreciation, Office Equipment. Wonner's accountant also records the details of each item of office equipment in a subsidiary ledger. During a three-year period the following transactions affecting office equipment took place.

Year 1

Jan. 8 Bought the following items from Union Office Furniture Company for cash.
Filing cabinet, $240, Account No. 122-1, expected life fifteen years, trade-in value zero.
Executive desk, $960, Account No. 122-2, expected life twelve years, trade-in value zero.
Executive chair, $360, Account No. 122-3, expected life twelve years, trade-in value zero.
(The above assets are depreciated on the basis of the straight-line method.)

9 Paid Excell Cabinet Shop $1,280 for a custom-made counter, Account No. 122-4; expected life ten years, trade-in value zero; straight-line method.

11 Bought a Larsen typewriter, Serial No. FA-16218, Account No. 122-5, from Warren Equipment Company for $720; estimated life five years, estimated trade-in value $120; sum-of-the-years'-digits method.

Dec. 31 Recorded the adjusting entry for depreciation of office equipment for the fiscal year (total depreciation, $454; but verify this figure).

31 Closed the Depreciation Expense, Office Equipment account into the Income Summary account.

Year 2

June 24 Bought a rug from Farley Carpet Company on account, Account No. 122-6, price $1,280, estimated life eight years, trade-in value zero; double-declining-balance method at twice the straight-line rate.

Dec. 31 Recorded the adjusting entry for depreciation of office equipment for the fiscal year (depreciation for six months on the rug; total depreciation, $574; verify this figure).

31 Closed the Depreciation Expense, Office Equipment account into the Income Summary account.

Year 3

June 29 Traded in the executive chair for a new one from Hildebrand Office Supplies, Account No. 122-7. The new chair cost $520, has an estimated life of eight years, and a zero trade-in value. Wonner received a trade-in allowance of $230 on the old chair, and paid the balance in cash (straight-line method of depreciation). Recorded the entry to depreciate the old chair up to date. Recorded the entry for the exchange of assets, using the income tax method.

Dec. 31 Recorded the adjusting entry for depreciation of office equipment for the fiscal year (depreciation for six months on the chair; total depreciation, $659.94; but verify this figure).

31 Close the Depreciation Expense, Office Equipment account into the Income Summary account.

Instructions

1. Record the transactions in the general journal.

2. Each time Wonner buys a new asset, open an account in the subsidiary ledger.

3. After each entry, post to the two controlling accounts and to the subsidiary ledger.

4. Make a list of the balances in the subsidiary ledger accounts, and compare the totals with the balances of the two controlling accounts.

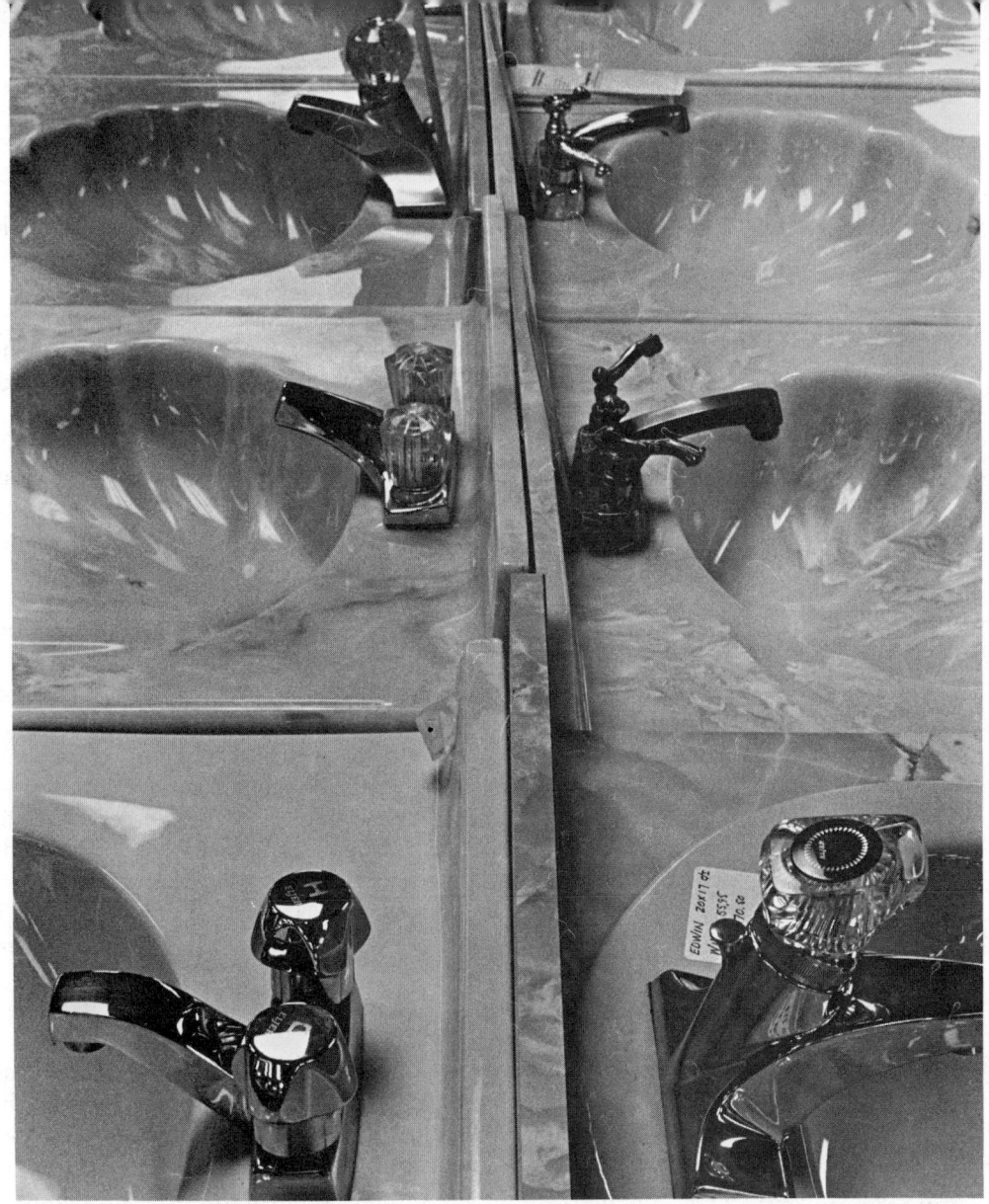

21

The voucher system of accounting

objectives

After you have completed this chapter, you will be able to do the following:

- Prepare vouchers.
- Record vouchers in a voucher register.
- Record payment of vouchers in a check register.
- Record transactions involving canceling or altering an original voucher due to (1) return of a purchase after the original voucher has been recorded, (2) a note payable issued after the original voucher has been recorded, (3) an arrangement for installment payments after the original voucher has been recorded, or (4) a correction of an amount after the original voucher has been recorded.
- Record the receipt and payment of invoices by the net amount method.

WE HAVE often used the term *internal control* in connection with cash receipts and payments. The objectives of internal control are (1) to prevent errors, (2) to prevent the stealing of cash or other assets by employees and customers, and (3) to provide for the efficient management of the owner's investment. To meet these objectives, business transactions should be recorded in an arrangement where one person acts as a check or verification on another person. In other words, no one person is "out on a limb" by himself or herself. As the size of the economic unit increases, the owner becomes less directly involved in the transactions. Consequently, internal control becomes more important. The voucher system has been devised as a means of achieving internal control and enabling the owner or manager to maintain contact with day-by-day transactions.

Objectives of the voucher system

The objective of the voucher system is to *control the incurring of all liabilities and the making of all expenditures*—in other words, to control the purchase of (1) merchandise or materials, (2) other assets, and (3) services. An owner or chief executive who uses the voucher system is thereby able to delegate authority. At the same time, he or she can maintain control over these transactions through the medium of signatures. An executive who signs a voucher has presumably read it, and by signing it signifies approval of the incurring of an obligation or the making of a payment. That is why the voucher system provides for the efficient management of the owner's investment. This is of vital importance, especially when large sums of money are involved.

The following four steps all involve the efficient management of resources. They aren't, of course, exclusive to the voucher system. However, when a firm is using the voucher system, these four steps are implied.

1. All expenditures must be backed up by purchase orders or other authorizations.

2. Goods and services received must be inspected and approved.

3. Invoices from suppliers must be checked against respective purchase orders and verified as to accuracy of the computations of the amounts listed, shipping costs, and credit terms. Computation of amounts listed on the invoices, such as unit prices multiplied by the number of units purchased, are called *price extensions.*

4. All payments must be made by check, except for payments made from petty cash.

The voucher system focuses on these four steps listed and includes the following component parts, each of which we shall describe in detail.

- Vouchers
- Voucher register
- Check register
- Unpaid Voucher file
- Paid Voucher file
- General journal

At the outset, bear in mind that the voucher system is appropriate only for a business that is medium- to large-sized. In other words, one that has a volume of transactions big enough to make the extra paperwork economically feasible, and one that customarily pays its bills when they are due instead of making part payments or installment payments. Also bear in mind that the voucher system has fixed channels in which to record routine types of transactions. Transactions that are *not* of a routine nature do not fit into these channels and therefore require special treatment by means of special entries in the general journal.

Vouchers

The dictionary defines a *voucher* as a piece of paper that serves as proof of a transaction. Recall that we used the word in Chapter 8 in connection with petty cash. The petty cash voucher not only describes the transaction, but also provides for signatures of the employee in charge of the fund and of the person receiving payment.

When a business is using the voucher system, one has to fill out a voucher for *every* invoice or bill received, *whether it is to be paid immediately or in the future.* The voucher describes the terms of the transaction, and the invoice or bill is attached (usually stapled) to the voucher. If one is buying merchandise, the voucher lists the name and address of the supplier, the date of the invoice, the amount, and the credit terms. Then there are always blanks for the necessary signatures, signifying approval of amounts, terms, and so forth.

Characteristics of vouchers

Just as there is variation in the form of *invoices* from one company to another, there is also variation in the form of *vouchers* from one company to another. Some enterprises use a voucher that is in the form of a jacket which has a pocket or envelope, so that the invoice can be included with the voucher.

Although vouchers for different business firms or government units do vary a bit from one to another, the following characteristics are usually present.

- Vouchers must be prepared for every incoming bill, and are numbered consecutively.
- Name and address of payee or creditor appear on vouchers.
- Amount and credit terms of invoice appear on vouchers.
- Vouchers state due dates so that firms can take advantage of possible cash discounts.
- For internal control, vouchers require signatures (1) approving payment, and (2) showing that payment has been recorded in the account books.
- Vouchers record payment: date paid and check number.

A completed voucher, with the invoice or bill stapled to it, describes an entire transaction, as well as the procedure for processing the voucher.

Preparation Each voucher bears an identification number, which appears both inside and *and approval* outside the voucher. To cite a familiar example, let us assume that North Cen- *of vouchers* tral Plumbing Supply has now achieved such a volume of business that it is using a voucher system, and that it has received from its supplier, Danton, Inc., the invoice shown here.

DANTON, INC.
1616 Madlyn Ave.
Los Angeles, CA 90026

Invoice

DATE:	October 1, 19--
SOLD North Central Plumbing Supply	**INVOICE NO.:** 3394
TO 1968 Arrow Street, N.W.	**ORDER NO.:** 9764
Seattle, WA 98111	**SHIPPED BY:** Western Freight Line
	TERMS: 2/10, n/30

Quantity	Description	Unit Price	Total
2,600'	Galv. steel pipe (10' lengths) 3/4"	.275	715.00

North Central's accountant, using the invoice as the source of information, fills out the voucher shown on the facing page. The inside or face of the voucher lists the particulars of the transaction.

The accountant staples the invoice to the voucher and circulates the two for the required approval signatures. When the voucher and the attached invoice get back to the accounting department, the accountant fills in the following required information on the outside of the voucher: the accounts to be debited and credited, the due date, the name and address of the payee, and the payment information (see the illustration on page 562).

The Account Distribution section is used to record the account titles and amounts to be debited, the total amount to be credited to Vouchers Payable, and the initials of the person authorized to determine the distribution. The accounts to be debited are, of course, selected on the basis of the types of goods and services purchased.

The *due date* represents the last day on which one can take advantage of the cash discount (taking into consideration the time required for mail delivery). For example, the invoice of Danton, Inc., was dated October 1, with terms of 2/10, n/30. The discount period ends on October 11. However, if 3 days are necessary for mail delivery, the due date is moved back from October 11 to October 8, so that the cash will be in the hands of the creditor by October 11.

```
ACCOUNT DISTRIBUTION                              VOUCHER NO.  117

  ACCOUNT DEBITED        AMOUNT      Due Date   10/8
                                     Pay To
Purchases                715.00                 Danton, Inc.
Supplies                                        1616 Madlyn Ave.
Wages Expense                                   Los Angeles, CA 90026
Miscellaneous Expense




                                     SUMMARY OF CHARGES

                                       Amount of invoice      $715.00
                                       Less cash discount       14.30
                                       Net amount             $700.70










                                     RECORD OF PAYMENT

                                       Paid by check no.      390
                                       Date of check          10/8
Total Vouchers Payable Cr.  715.00     Amount of check       700.70


ACCOUNT DISTRIBUTION by  R.R.H      ENTERED IN VOUCHER REG. by  mcl.
```

The Vouchers Payable account

When you use a voucher system, you substitute the Vouchers Payable account for Accounts Payable. For example, as we saw before, when a firm buys merchandise on account, the accountant enters it as a debit to Purchases and a credit to Vouchers Payable. Similarly, when a firm buys store equipment on account, the accountant records it as a debit to Store Equipment and a credit to Vouchers Payable. The voucher now represents the amount of the invoice or bill. When the obligation is paid, the payment is recorded as a debit to Vouchers Payable and a credit to Cash.

The voucher system and expenses

We have stressed the fact that when you're using a voucher system, you have to write out a voucher *every time you incur a liability,* and this includes liabilities incurred for expenses as well as those incurred for acquiring assets. For example, suppose that when the telephone bill comes in, you notice some long-distance toll charges. First verify that these were business calls, then make out a voucher, and attach the telephone bill to the inside of it. In the column headed Account Distribution, record the bill as a debit to Telephone Expense and a credit to Vouchers Payable. When a check is issued in payment of the voucher, record the entry in the check register as a debit to Vouchers Payable and a credit to Cash. Again let us emphasize that *all* liabilities are recorded in the Vouchers Payable account.

The voucher register

The *voucher register* has the status of a journal, and accordingly is a book of original entry. All vouchers must be recorded in it, in numerical order. Think of it as being an expanded purchases journal. The voucher register has only one credit column, Vouchers Payable credit, but a number of debit columns. Headings for the credit columns are selected on the basis of their frequency of use. A merchandising business, for example, would always have a Purchases debit column because a merchant naturally buys a great volume of merchandise on account. The voucher register may vary widely, of course, depending on the size of the business and the number of accounts. In addition to the money columns, the voucher register also has space for recording the voucher number, name of creditor, date of payment, and check number. The voucher register for North Central Plumbing Supply is on the top of pages 564–565.

When you first record the voucher, leave the Payment Date and Check Number columns blank, and then after you've recorded the payment in the check register, go back to the voucher register and enter the date of payment and the number of the check. In the illustration just seen, Vouchers No. 123 and 149 have not been paid yet; Voucher No. 126 was "paid" by issuing a note (this transaction will be discussed later in this chapter); Voucher No. 122 was issued payable to a payroll account. (It is assumed that this payroll entry was previously recorded in the general journal, crediting Wages Payable.)

Posting from the voucher register

The entries in the Sundry Accounts columns are posted *daily* to the general ledger, just as the Sundry Accounts columns of the other special journals are posted daily. The check mark ($\sqrt{}$) under the column total means "do not post." At the end of the month, total all the columns, and prove the equality of the debit and credit entries by comparing the combined total of the debit columns with the total of the Vouchers Payable credit column. After you have proved the voucher register to be in balance, post the special-column totals to the general ledger. To give evidence of the posting of each total, write the account number in parentheses immediately below the column total. In the ledger accounts, write the letters VR and the page number to show that the posting came from the voucher register.

The check register

Any economic unit using a voucher system uses the check register (see Chapter 13 for a discussion of it) as a book of original entry, in conjunction with the voucher register. It works this way: Since checks are issued only in

DATE	VOU. NO.	CREDITOR	PAYMENT		VOUCHERS PAYABLE CREDIT	PURCHASES DEBIT	SUPPLIES DEBIT
			DATE	CK. NO.			
19– Oct. 1	117	Danton, Inc.	10	8	390	7 1 5 00	7 1 5 00	
1	118	Reliable Express Co.	10	1	383	4 2 00	4 2 00	
3	119	Davenport Of. Sup.	10	3	384	4 8 72		4 8 72
5	120	Rockland Insurance Company	10	5	387	7 4 00		
9	121	Rogers & Simon Co.	10	18	404	3 2 8 00	3 2 8 00	
10	122	Payroll Bank Acc.	10	10	393	1 6 9 0 00		
12	123	Northwest Journal				7 6 00		
12	124	Elwood Equip. Co.	10	12	395	1 1 6 00		
15	125	Robert C. Randall	10	15	399	5 0 0 00		
15	126	True-Fit Valve, Inc.	10	18	By note	4 2 1 00	4 2 1 00	
29	149	Argel Mfg. Co.				7 1 4 00	7 1 4 00	
30	150	Safety National Bank	10	30	412	1 5 0 7 50		
31						10 6 9 8 68	4 5 5 3 20	1 2 1 79
						(212)	(511)	(115)

payment of approved and recorded vouchers, the entry in the check register is always a debit to Vouchers Payable and a credit to Cash. A Vouchers Payable debit column in the check register offsets the Vouchers Payable credit column in the voucher register. Recall that after you record the entry in the check register, you enter the notation of the payment on the appropriate line in the voucher register and on the outside of the voucher in the Record of Payment section. First prove the column totals of the check register to see that the debits equal the credits, and then post the amounts as totals, as shown here.

CHECK REGISTER PAGE _11_

DATE	CK. NO.	PAYEE	VOU. NO.	VOU. PAYABLE DEBIT	PURCH. DISC. CREDIT	CASH CREDIT
19– Oct. 1	383	Reliable Express Company	118	4 2 00		4 2 00
3	384	Davenport Office Supplies	119	4 8 72		4 8 72
3	385	Sinclair Manufacturing Company	114	2 0 6 00	2 06	2 0 3 94
4	386	Argel Manufacturing Company	115	5 4 0 00	1 0 80	5 2 9 20
5	387	Rockland Insurance Company	120	7 4 00		7 4 00
6	388	Void				
6	389	Rogers and Simon Company	116	4 6 4 00	9 28	4 5 4 72
8	390	Danton, Inc.	117	7 1 5 00	1 4 30	7 0 0 70
30	412	Safety National Bank	150	1 5 0 7 50		1 5 0 7 50
31				6 4 0 4 98	7 5 84	6 3 2 9 14
				(212)	(512)	(111)

WAGES PAYABLE DEBIT	ADV. EXPENSE DEBIT	MISC. EXP. DEBIT	SUNDRY ACCOUNTS DR.		
			ACCOUNT	POST. REF	AMOUNT
			Prepaid Insurance	116	74 00
1690 00					
	76 00				
			Sales Returns and Allowances	412	116 00
			Robert C. Randall, Drawing	312	500 00
			Notes Payable	211	1500 00
			Interest Expense	521	7 50
3314 00	112 00	83 69			2514 00
(213)	(518)	(519)			(✓)

Filing unpaid vouchers

Business firms usually prepare vouchers in duplicate. In the system used by North Central Plumbing Supply, invoices are attached to the original copy of the voucher and it is circulated within the company for the necessary signatures of approval. After a voucher is recorded in the voucher register, it is filed under the name of the creditor. (Other companies prepare only one voucher and file it only under the date on which it is supposed to be paid.) At North Central, the Unpaid Voucher file also contains any other outstanding vouchers or credit memos. This file, listed by names of creditors, now comprises a subsidiary ledger. In fact, at North Central this file is used as a substitute for the accounts payable ledger.

The *second* copy of the voucher goes to the treasurer, who files it chronologically according to due date. This Unpaid Voucher file helps the treasurer to forecast how much cash is needed to pay outstanding bills, and ensures that the firm will pay its bills promptly, in order to take advantage of cash discounts.

Filing paid vouchers

Now let's assume that the firm has paid its bill. The vouchers with their attached invoices are first removed from the Unpaid Voucher files, and the payment is recorded in the check register and in the Payment column of the voucher register. Then the two vouchers are combined, marked paid, and filed in numerical order in a Paid Vouchers file. Many firms staple a copy of the check to the paid voucher, which means that the Paid Vouchers file contains a complete set of documents for every payment of cash.

At the end of the month, the accountant lists all the vouchers payable, taking the information directly from the Unpaid Voucher file, and writing the amount owed, as well as the name of each creditor, just as in the schedule of accounts payable.

		North Central Plumbing Supply					
		Schedule of Unpaid Vouchers					
		October 31, 19–					
VOU. NO.		NAME OF CREDITOR					
123	*Northwest Journal*			7 6 00			
149	*Argel Manufacturing Company*			7 1 4 00			
	Total Vouchers Payable					7 9 0 00	

Situations
requiring
special
treatment

When a firm is using the voucher system, inevitably it runs into an occasional nonroutine type of transaction which does not fit into the fixed channels of the voucher system, and therefore requires special treatment in the form of an entry in the general journal. One can consider these types of treatment as adjustments to the voucher system. Let us now look at four such types of transactions.

Return of a
purchase
before original
voucher has
been recorded

Normally a firm with an efficient purchasing department, if it's going to return any merchandise, returns it before the vouchers are recorded in the voucher register. The accountant records the deduction right on the invoice, and records the invoice in the voucher register for the net amount. For example, North Central Plumbing Supply buys $1,200 worth of merchandise on account. Before their accountant records the invoice, North Central returns $100 worth of the merchandise to the supplier, and receives a credit memorandum. The accountant staples the credit memorandum to the invoice, deducts $100 from the face amount, and records the invoice in the voucher register as a debit to Purchases for $1,100 and a credit to Vouchers Payable for $1,100.

Return of a
purchase after
original
voucher has
been recorded

Now what happens when a firm returns an item after the accountant has recorded the voucher listing its purchase in the voucher register?

On September 29, North Central Plumbing Supply bought $566 worth of merchandise from Argel Manufacturing Company. North Central's accountant recorded the transaction in the voucher register as a debit to Purchases for $566 and a credit to Vouchers Payable for $566, as shown on the top of the next page.

DATE		VOU. NO.	CREDITOR	PAYMENT		VOUCHERS PAYABLE CREDIT	PURCHASES DEBIT
				DATE	CK. NO.		
Sep.	29	115	Argel Mfg. Co.			566 00	566 00

A few days later, North Central returned $26 worth of defective merchandise to Argel and got a credit memorandum from Argel. North Central's accountant recorded this in the general journal as follows.

GENERAL JOURNAL   PAGE __37__

DATE		DESCRIPTION	POST REF.	DEBIT	CREDIT
19— Oct.	1	Vouchers Payable		26 00	
		Purchases Returns and Allowances			26 00
		Returned defective merchandise to Argel			
		Manufacturing Company, receiving their			
		Credit Memo No. 4611, Voucher No. 115			

You will recognize that this entry is like the usual entries anyone makes for returns of merchandise, except that here one uses Vouchers Payable instead of Accounts Payable and doesn't have to post anything to the accounts payable ledger. North Central's accountant deducts the amount of the return ($26) on Voucher No. 115, and staples Argel's credit memorandum to it; then the accountant makes a notation in the Payment column of the voucher register, on the upper half of the line used to record the original voucher. North Central pays the invoice on October 4, and their accountant records the issuance of Check No. 386 in the check register as a debit to Vouchers Payable for $540, a credit to Purchases Discount for $10.80, and a credit to Cash for $529.20. The notations in the Payment column of the voucher register look like this:

DATE		VOU. NO.	CREDITOR	PAYMENT		VOUCHERS PAYABLE CREDIT	PURCHASES DEBIT
				DATE	CK. NO.		
Sep.	29	115	Argel Mfg. Co.	10 1	Ret.	566 00	566 00
				10 4	386		

By T accounts, the entries look like this:

Purchases		
+		−
Sept. 29 VR2	566	

Vouchers Payable			
−		+	
Oct. 1 J37	26	Sept. 29 VR2	566
Oct. 4 CkR11	540		

Purchases Returns and Allowances		
−		+
	Oct. 1 J37	26

Cash in Bank		
+		−
	Oct. 4 CkR11	529.20

Purchases Discount		
−		+
	Oct. 4 CkR11	10.80

Issuing a "notes payable" after original voucher has been recorded

Suppose that someone in the firm issues a note canceling a voucher; then an entry should be made in the general journal debiting Vouchers Payable and crediting Notes Payable. For example, let's say that on October 15 North Central Plumbing Supply bought $421 worth of merchandise from True-Fit Valve, Inc., and issued Voucher No. 126, which was recorded in the voucher register. On October 18, North Central issued a note for $421, 30 days, 8%, canceling the original voucher. North Central's general journal entry is as follows:

GENERAL JOURNAL				PAGE 37	
DATE	DESCRIPTION	POST REF.	DEBIT	CREDIT	
Oct. 18	Vouchers Payable		421 00		
	Notes Payable			421 00	
	Canceled Voucher No. 126, payable to				
	True-Fit Valve, Inc., and issued a 30-day, 8%				
	note, dated Oct. 18				

In the Payment columns of the voucher register, on the line on which Voucher No. 126 is recorded, the accountant writes "10/18" in the Date column and "By note" in the Check Number column.

VOUCHER REGISTER									Page 3
DATE	VOU. NO.	CREDITOR	PAYMENT		VOUCHERS PAYABLE CREDIT	PURCHASES DEBIT	SUPPLIES DEBIT		
			DATE	CK. NO.					
Oct. 15	126	True-Fit Valve, Inc.	10 18	By note	421 00	421 00			

She or he also makes a notation on the voucher indicating that it has been canceled by the issuance of a note, then transfers the voucher from the Unpaid Voucher file and puts it into the Paid Voucher file.

On November 17, when the note comes due, North Central prepares a new voucher and records it in the voucher register as a debit to Notes Payable for $421 in the Sundry Accounts debit column, a debit to Interest Expense for $2.81 in the Sundry Accounts debit column ($421, 8%, 30 days), and a credit to Vouchers Payable for $423.81 in the Vouchers Payable credit column. Next, the voucher is paid; North Central's accountant records the payment in the check register as part of the usual routine as a debit to Vouchers Payable for $423.81 and a credit to Cash for $423.81. By T accounts, the entries appear as follows.

Purchases				Vouchers Payable			
+		−		−		+	
Oct. 15 VR3	421.00			Oct. 18 J37	421.00	Oct. 15 VR3	421.00
				Nov. 17 CkR17	423.81	Nov. 17 VR4	423.81

Interest Expense				Notes Payable			
+		−		−		+	
Nov. 17 VR4	2.81			Nov. 17 VR4	421.00	Oct. 18 J37	421.00

Cash			
+		−	
		Nov. 17 CkR17	423.81

Installment payments planned at time of original purchase

In a voucher system, invoices generally are paid in full. Sometimes, however, management prefers to pay for an item in installments. When this happens, the company's accountant prepares a separate voucher and records it in the voucher register for each installment. As an illustration, assume that on November 2 North Central bought an office safe for $750 from Newell Office Equipment Company, with a down payment of $250, and two installments of $250 each, payable on November 17 and December 2. North Central's accountant prepares three vouchers and records them in the voucher register.

VOUCHER REGISTER   PAGE 4

DATE	VOU. NO.	CREDITOR	VOUCHERS PAYABLE CREDIT	SUNDRY ACCOUNTS DR.		
				ACCOUNT	POST. REF	AMOUNT
Nov. 2	154	Newell Office Equipment Co.	250 00	Office Equipment		750 00
2	155	Newell Office Equipment Co.	250 00			
2	156	Newell Office Equipment Co.	250 00			

Each voucher has a due date that corresponds to the date the installment is to be paid. Voucher No. 154 is paid immediately. Voucher No. 155 is filed according to its due date, November 17. Voucher No. 156 is filed according to its due date, December 2.

Installment payments planned after original voucher has been recorded

However, suppose that the buyer records the entire amount of the invoice on one voucher, and *later* decides to pay the invoice in installments. The accountant must now cancel the original voucher by means of a general journal entry, and then issue new vouchers for each installment.

For example, suppose that North Central buys merchandise from Donaldson and Farr, and records the transaction in the voucher register as follows.

			VOUCHER REGISTER					Page 2
DATE	VOU. NO.	CREDITOR	PAYMENT		VOUCHERS PAYABLE CREDIT	PURCHASES DEBIT	SUPPLIES DEBIT	
			DATE	CK. NO.				
Sep. 21	103	Donaldson and Farr	10 16	V127	900 00	900 00		
				V128				
				V129				

When North Central's accountant originally records the transaction, he or she leaves the Payment column blank. On October 16, North Central arranges to pay the $900 debt in three installments of $300 each, with due dates of October 21, November 5, and November 21. Accordingly, the accountant makes an entry in the general journal as follows.

Oct. 19	Vouchers Payable			900 00	
	Purchases				900 00
	Canceled Voucher No. 103 payable to				
	Donaldson and Farr, the amount to be paid				
	in three equal installments, due Oct. 21,				
	Nov. 5, and Nov. 21.				

The accountant then notes "10/16" and the voucher numbers for the installments in the Payment column of the voucher register and makes entries in the voucher register for three new vouchers, as on the top of page 571.

DATE	VOU. NO.	CREDITOR	PAYMENT		VOUCHERS PAYABLE CREDIT	PURCHASES DEBIT	SUPPLIES DEBIT
			DATE	CK. NO.			
Oct. 16	127	Donaldson and Farr			300 00	300 00	
16	128	Donaldson and Farr			300 00	300 00	
16	129	Donaldson and Farr			300 00	300 00	

North Central then puts Voucher No. 103—the original voucher that was canceled—in the Paid Voucher file, and puts Vouchers No. 127, 128. and 129 in the Unpaid Voucher file, in the usual manner.

Correcting an amount after original voucher has been recorded

The procedure of required approvals and verifications of the records used in the voucher system will not entirely eliminate errors. However, it should reduce them to a minimum. If an error is discovered *after* a voucher has been recorded in the voucher register, the accountant may correct it by means of a general journal entry. The purpose of the entry is to cancel the original voucher by reversing the original entry. Since this has the effect of clearing the accounts, it paves the way for the issuance of a new voucher for the correct amount. For example, North Central Plumbing Supply bought merchandise from Argel Manufacturing Company for $546 and issued Voucher No. 102, as follows.

DATE	VOU. NO.	CREDITOR	PAYMENT		VOUCHERS PAYABLE CREDIT	PURCHASES DEBIT	SUPPLIES DEBIT
			DATE	CK. NO.			
Sep. 20	102	Argel Mfg. Co.	10 19	V130	546 00	546 00	

When North Central's accountant recorded the voucher, he or she left the Payment columns of the voucher register blank. On October 19 someone discovered an error in the price extensions; the correct amount of the invoice should have been $518. The entry necessary to correct the situation is as follows.

Oct. 19	Vouchers Payable			546 00	
	Purchases				546 00
	Canceled Voucher No. 102 payable to Argel				
	Manufacturing Company, due to error in				
	amount of invoice.				

The last entry makes possible the issuance of a new voucher for the correct amount, as follows.

| | | | | | PAYMENT | | VOUCHERS | PURCHASES | SUPPLIES |
DATE		VOU. NO.	CREDITOR		DATE	CK. NO.	PAYABLE CREDIT	DEBIT	DEBIT
Oct.	19	130	Argel Mfg. Co.				518 00	518 00	

VOUCHER REGISTER — *Page 3*

The accountant makes a notation in the Payment columns of the voucher register that Voucher No. 102 has been canceled by writing "10/19" and the new voucher number, "130." He or she makes a similar notation on Voucher No. 102 itself, then places it in the Paid Voucher file. If he or she discovers the error during the same month that the voucher was issued, he or she can handle the correction the same way, or make the correction directly on the original voucher and in the voucher register by drawing a line through the incorrect amount and inserting the correct one. The accountant can do this because the transaction has not yet been posted.

The voucher system as a management tool

The voucher system illustrates how well the accounting procedure implements internal control, and also how the voucher system helps firms manage financial resources efficiently. In this respect, it has the following advantages.

1. Vouchers supply up-to-date information on due dates and amounts owed. The financial manager is more interested in knowing *when* payment is due than in knowing to whom the amount is payable; she or he needs to plan for cash requirements. The information is provided in the *tickler file* (unpaid vouchers filed by due dates).

2. Vouchers systematize the taking of cash discounts. A firm that takes cash discounts saves a lot of money. The tickler file helps to ensure that it will save this money, by informing the firm about the last day to take advantage of cash discounts.

3. Payments cover specific invoices. Each check issued covers a specific invoice, which eliminates confusion about amounts owed to creditors.

4. Authority may be delegated and responsibility fixed. This advantage stems from the system of required approval signatures. Because the approval is given when the goods arrive or the service is received, if something is not satisfactory, it is given immediate attention.

Recording purchases at the net amount

Until now, even when we were discussing the voucher system, we have always assumed that the firm's accountant records purchases as costing the gross amount. For example, at the beginning of this chapter on page 560, we saw an invoice from Danton, Inc., for $715, terms 2/10, n/30, which North Central's accountant recorded as a debit of $715 to Purchases and a credit of $715 to Vouchers Payable. (If North Central had not been using the voucher system, the Accounts Payable account would have been credited.) As an alternative, some firms which like to take advantage of all cash discounts may record purchases at the net amount, which would be $700.70 ($715 less 2% cash discount of $14.30).

The recording of purchases at the net amount refers to the recording of the gross amount of a purchase after the cash discount has been deducted.

A company that records purchases at the net amount does not necessarily have to use a voucher system. However, since firms that use voucher systems are usually medium- to large-sized business operations which take advantage of cash discounts whenever possible, many of these concerns do record purchases at the net amount.

To compare gross-amount procedure versus net-amount procedure, let's look at some sample transactions in general journal form, using both methods.

Transaction (a) Bought merchandise on account from Skinner and Roe, $6,000, terms 2/10, n/30. Issued Voucher No. 2811.

Transaction (b) Issued Check No. 3748 in payment of Voucher No. 2811, less the cash discount.

Gross-amount procedure

(a) In voucher register:

Purchases	6,000	
Vouchers Payable		6,000

(b) In check register:

Vouchers Payable	6,000	
Purchases Discount		120
Cash		5,880

Net-amount procedure

(a) In voucher register:

Purchases	5,880	
Vouchers Payable		5,880

(b) In check register:

Vouchers Payable	5,880	
Cash		5,880

Using the net-amount procedure to record purchases eliminates the Purchases Discount account. But both methods yield the same net purchase that appears in the Cost of Merchandise Sold section of the income statement, because when you use the Purchases Discount account, you deduct it from Gross Purchases in order to arrive at Net Purchases.

Enterprises using the net-amount system naturally take advantage of all cash discounts available to them. However, sometimes, because of carelessness or oversight, one may miss out on the cash discount. In this case, one uses the account Purchases Discounts Lost, as illustrated here.

Transaction (c) Bought merchandise on account from J. H. Thomas Company, $3,200, terms 2/10, n/30. Issued Voucher No. 3092, May 17.

Transaction (d) Issued Check No. 4167 in payment of Voucher No. 3092, $3,200, June 17.

Gross-amount procedure

(c) In voucher register:

Purchases	3,200	
Vouchers Payable		3,200

(d) In check register:

Vouchers Payable	3,200	
Cash		3,200

Net-amount procedure

(c) In voucher register:

Purchases	3,136	
Vouchers Payable		3,136

(d) In check register:

Vouchers Payable	3,136	
Purchases Discounts Lost	64	
Cash		3,200

When one uses the net-amount procedure in conjunction with a voucher system, one puts a notation in the Payment column of the voucher register, indicating the discount lost, as shown here.

DATE		PAYMENT CHECK NO.	
Jan.	17	*Discounts lost 4167*	

One also adds a Purchases Discounts Lost debit column to the check register. Purchases Discounts Lost is classified as an expense account:

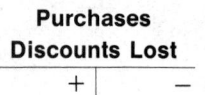

**Purchases
Discounts Lost**

This is closed into Income Summary along with all the expense accounts in the one large compound entry. On the income statement, Purchases Discounts Lost is classified as an Other Expense account. Additional accounts in this classification are Interest Expense and Loss on Disposal of Plant and Equipment (recall Chapter 15). For internal control, the prime advantage of using the net-amount procedure is that if a firm fails to take discounts, this fact becomes known to the management, since it stands out as an exception. If this was due to someone's carelessness, the management can take steps to see that this kind of oversight doesn't recur. As an alternative, some accountants put the balance of Purchases Discounts Lost in the Cost of Merchandise Sold section of the income statement.

Summary

The voucher system is a procedure for recording and paying all liabilities incurred by a firm. The firm prepares a voucher in duplicate for each invoice (or bill) received, whether the obligation is to be paid immediately or in the future. The documents, consisting of the purchase invoice, or bill, and the purchase order, are attached to the first copy of the voucher, which is circulated to the appropriate people so that they can add their official approval signatures. Next the accountant records the voucher in the voucher register, and files both copies of the vouchers in separate Unpaid Voucher files. He or she files the original voucher, with documents attached, in the Unpaid Voucher file which is arranged alphabetically by names of creditors, and the second copy in the Unpaid Voucher file which is arranged chronologically by due dates (the tickler file). He or she uses the alphabetical file to prepare the schedule of vouchers payable. When a firm is using the voucher system, it often substitutes the Vouchers Payable account for Accounts Payable.

Firms that use a voucher system use a check register. The Vouchers Payable debit column in the check register offsets the Vouchers Payable credit column in the voucher register. Both the check register and voucher register are books of original entry.

The voucher system promotes internal control and the efficient management of financial resources. However, it is rigid, in that it establishes fixed channels for handling routine transactions. Nonroutine transactions that do not fit into fixed channels require special treatment in the form of special entries in the general journal. Nonroutine transactions involve the following: *After the original voucher has been recorded,* the firm either (1) returns part (or all) of the merchandise, or (2) issues a Notes Payable, or (3) makes part payments in the form of installments, or (4) makes a correction on a bill or invoice.

When a firm uses the net amount procedure, it records purchase invoices at the net figure (gross amount less cash discount). Normally, when the invoice is paid, the transaction is listed as a debit to Vouchers Payable and a credit to Cash. If the invoice is not paid within the discount period, at the time of payment the firm has to record the transaction as a debit to Vouchers Payable, a debit to Purchases Discounts Lost, and a credit to Cash. Or, if the firm is not using the voucher system, it substitutes Accounts Payable for Vouchers Payable. Under both systems, the Purchases Discounts Lost account is generally classified as an Other Expense account.

Glossary

Net-amount procedure Recording of incoming invoices at net amount (gross amount less cash discount).

Price extensions Computations of amounts listed on an invoice, unit prices multiplied by the number of units purchased.

Tickler file A file of unpaid vouchers arranged chronologically according to due dates.

Voucher A paper or document summarizing the terms of a transaction. It includes signatures or initials which vouch for its correctness, authorize its entry in the books, and approve its payment at the appropriate time.

Voucher register A book of original entry in which all vouchers are recorded as credits to Vouchers Payable and debits to other accounts.

Voucher system A procedure for the recording and payment of all liabilities incurred through the issuance of vouchers. It involves a voucher register and check register, Unpaid Voucher files, and Paid Voucher files.

Questions

1. When a business is using a voucher system, what types of transactions require the filling out of a voucher?

2. Describe each of the two unpaid voucher files.

3. Regarding the purchase of merchandise, what must be done when a credit memo is received after the original voucher has been recorded?

4. When a voucher system is in use, is it necessary to have an accounts payable ledger?

5. Explain briefly how the voucher system serves as a management tool.

6. Regarding the purchase of merchandise, what must be done when installment payments are planned after the original voucher has been recorded?

7. Describe the net-amount procedure for recording purchases.

Exercises

Exercise 1 Record the following transactions in general journal form, indicating above the entry the title of the book of original entry in which each should be recorded. Assume that a voucher register and a check register are being used.

May 1 Prepared Voucher No. 616 for $930, in favor of Lewis Real Estate, for rent for the month.

  3 Prepared Voucher No. 617 for $3,900, in favor of Turnbull Company, for merchandise purchased; terms 2/10, n/30.

  4 Issued Check No. 738 in payment of Voucher No. 616.

  14 Issued Check No. 739 in payment of Voucher No. 617.

May 14 Prepared Voucher No. 618 in favor of Tuttle Office Supply for typewriter ribbons and carbon paper purchased, $95.58.

14 Issued Check No. 740 in payment of Voucher No. 618.

Exercise 2 In general journal form, make entries to record the following.

a. Prepared Voucher No. 939 to establish a change fund, $150.

b. Issued Check No. 1113 in payment of Voucher No. 939.

Exercise 3 Using the gross-amount procedure, record in general journal form the following related transactions.

Apr. 6 Bought merchandise on account from Norman Larson Company, $9,600, terms 2/10, n/30. Issued Voucher No. 3842.

9 Received Credit Memo No. A 326 from Norman Larson Company for return of defective merchandise purchased April 6, $420.

15 Issued Check No. 4868 in payment of Voucher No. 3842 less the return and less the discount.

Exercise 4 Enter the following in general journal form.

a. Issued Voucher No. 683 to establish a Petty Cash Fund, $135.

b. Prepared Check No. 712 in payment of Voucher No. 683.

c. The present balance in the Petty Cash Fund is $16.77. Petty cash receipts indicate the following expenditures.

Store Supplies	$32.40
Office Supplies	29.76
Miscellaneous General Expense	56.07

Issued Voucher No. 741 to reimburse the Petty Cash Fund, $118.23.

d. Issued Check No. 856 in payment of Voucher No. 741.

Exercise 5 Assuming that invoices are recorded by the net-amount procedure, prepare general journal entries to record the following transactions.

Oct. 2 Received from Webster and Son a $9,300 invoice for merchandise dated October 1, terms, 2/10, n/30. Issued Voucher No. 7662 authorizing payment and filed voucher for payment on last day of discount period.

14 Discovered that Voucher No. 7662 had been filed in error for payment on this date. Refiled it for payment on last day of credit period, November 1.

Nov. 1 Issued Check No. 8592, in payment of Voucher No. 7662.

Exercise 6 Using the gross-amount procedure, record the related transactions on the top of page 578 in general journal form.

Jan. 6 Bought merchandise on account from A. L. Welch Company, $5,580, terms 1/10, n/30. Issued Voucher No. 7934.

9 Gave a sixty-day, 8% note to A. L. Welch Company, dated January 9; canceled Voucher No. 7934.

Mar. 7 Issued Voucher No. 9961, $5,654.40, in favor of A. L. Welch Company for our note: principal $5,580, interest $74.40.

7 Prepared Check No. 1172 in payment of Voucher No. 9961.

Exercise 7 The following column totals appear in a voucher register at the end of June.

Purchases		$15,638.80
Supplies		736.38
Wages Expense		9,648.20
Vouchers Payable		29,450.00
Miscellaneous Expense		258.62
Sundry Accounts		
Notes Payable	$2,000.00	
Interest Expense	120.00	
Store Equipment	1,048.00	

In general journal form, make the entry summarizing the voucher transactions for the month.

Problems _____

Problem 21-1 The Waterbury Company, which uses a voucher system, issued the following vouchers during February that were unpaid on March 1.

VOU. NO.	COMPANY	FOR	DATE OF VOUCHER	AMOUNT
716	Turner and Company	Merchandise	Feb. 24	2 3 2 5 00
719	Lindsay and Watson	Merchandise	Feb. 28	3 6 0 0 00
				5 9 2 5 00

The Company made the following transactions during March.

Mar. 1 Issued Voucher No. 721 in favor of Lindemeier Realty Company for March rent, $1,110.

1 Issued Check No. 926 in payment of Voucher No. 721, $1,110.

2 Bought merchandise on account from Miller Manufacturing Company, $2,850, terms 2/10, n/30. Issued Voucher No. 722. (Invoices are recorded for the gross amount.)

3 Issued Check No. 927 in payment of Voucher No. 716, $2,301.75 ($2,325 less 1% cash discount).

Mar. 7 Issued Voucher No. 723 in favor of Regional Telephone Company for telephone bill, $108.

7 Issued Check No. 928 in payment of Voucher No. 723.

9 Issued Check No. 929 in payment of Voucher No. 719, $3,528 ($3,600 less 2% cash discount.)

11 Issued Check No. 930 in payment of Voucher No. 722, less the cash discount.

14 Bought merchandise on account from Great Lakes Products Company, $5,130, terms 2/10, EOM. Issued Voucher No. 724.

23 Issued Voucher No. 725 for note payable previously recorded in the general journal: principal, $3,000, plus interest of $36. The note is payable to the First National Bank.

23 Paid Voucher No. 725 by issuing Check No. 931.

23 Issued Check No. 932 in payment of Voucher No. 724, less the cash discount.

31 Issued Voucher No. 726 for Wages Payable, $2,925, in favor of the payroll bank account. (Assume that the payroll entry was previously recorded in the general journal.)

31 Paid Voucher No. 726 by issuing Check No. 933.

Instructions **1.** Under the date of the original purchase, enter the unpaid invoices in the voucher register, beginning with Voucher No. 716. Then draw double lines across all columns to separate the vouchers of February from those of March.

2. Record the transactions for March in the voucher register at the gross amount. Also record the appropriate transactions in the check register.

3. Total and rule the voucher register and the check register.

4. On scratch paper, prove the equality of the debits and credits in the voucher register and the check register.

Problem 21-2 The R. J. Guthrie Company, which uses a voucher system, has the following unpaid vouchers on April 30.

VOU. NO.	COMPANY	FOR	DATE OF INVOICE	AMOUNT
7219	Huber and Ramsey	Merchandise	Apr. 22	11 6 8 0 00
7222	Hopkins Supply Company	Store Equipment	Apr. 24	4 5 4 5 00
7223	Schultz and Company	Merchandise	Apr. 27	6 4 0 0 00
				22 6 2 5 00

The R. J. Guthrie Company made the following transactions during May.

May 1 Issued Voucher No. 7226 in favor of Fidelity Insurance Company as a one-year premium on fire insurance policy, $432.

May 1 Paid Voucher No. 7219 by issuing Check No. 9626, $11,446.40 ($11,680 less 2% cash discount).

3 Issued Check No. 9627 in payment of Voucher No. 7226.

5 Issued Voucher No. 7227 in favor of Green Motor Freight for transportation charges on merchandise purchases, $84.

5 Paid Voucher No. 7227 by issuing Check No. 9628.

6 Issued Check No. 9629 in payment of Voucher No. 7223, $6,272 ($6,400 less 2% cash discount).

10 Established a Petty Cash Fund of $240. Issued Voucher No. 7228.

10 Paid Voucher No. 7228 by issuing Check No. 9630.

12 Issued Voucher No. 7229 in favor of Reynolds and Howard for the purchase of merchandise, $10,240, terms 2/10, n/30.

14 Bought office stationery from Holland Envelope Company, $1,240, terms n/30. Issued Voucher No. 7230.

16 Received credit memorandum for $1,040 from Reynolds and Howard for merchandise returned to them, Credit Memorandum No. 769.

19 Issued Voucher No. 7231 in favor of Hughes County for 6 months' property taxes, $1,800.

19 Paid Voucher No. 7231 by issuing Check No. 9631.

21 Issued Check No. 9632 in payment of Voucher No. 7229, $9,016 ($10,240 less $1,040 return, less cash discount).

24 Bought merchandise on account from Gross and Rogers, $9,632, terms 2/10, n/30. Issued Voucher No. 7232.

24 Paid Voucher No. 7222 by issuing Check No. 9633.

27 Received credit memorandum for $944 from Gross and Rogers for damaged merchandise, Credit Memorandum No. 1211.

31 Issued Voucher No. 7233 to reimburse Petty Cash Fund. The charges were:

Store Supplies	$84.00
Office Supplies	74.92
R. J. Guthrie, Drawing	40.00
Miscellaneous Expense	24.30

31 Issued Check No. 9634 in payment of Voucher No. 7233.

31 Issued Voucher No. 7234 for Wages Payable, $7,720, in favor of payroll bank account. (Assume that the payroll entry was previously recorded in the general journal.)

31 Paid Voucher No. 7234 by issuing Check No. 9635, payable to payroll bank account.

Instructions **1.** Under the date of the original purchase, enter the unpaid invoices in the voucher register, beginning with Voucher No. 7219. Then draw double lines across all columns to separate the vouchers of April from those of May.

2. Enter the transactions for May in the voucher register at the gross amount. Also record the appropriate transactions in the check register and general journal.

3. Total and rule the voucher register and check register for the transactions recorded in May.

Problem 21-3 The Huffman Company uses a voucher system to record invoices at the gross amount. During August of this year it completed the following transactions affecting Vouchers Payable.

Aug. 1 Issued Voucher No. 1079 in favor of Holliday Company for the purchase of merchandise having an invoice price of $3,900, terms 30 days.

4 Prepared Voucher No. 1080 for $975, Voucher No. 1081 for $975, and Voucher No. 1082 for $975. The Huffman Company incurred this debt because it bought an electronic calculator from Hale Office Supply, with terms of $975 cash on delivery, $975 in 30 days and $975 in 60 days. (Use three lines.)

4 Issued Check No. 1426 in payment of voucher 1080.

7 Issued Voucher No. 1083 in favor of Griffith Supply Company for store supplies, $243, terms n/30.

9 Prepared Voucher No. 1084 in favor of Townsend Products Company for the purchase of merchandise having an invoice price of $6,000 with a 25% trade discount (record voucher for $4,500), terms 2/10, n/30.

11 Prepared Voucher No. 1085 in favor of Burroughs Real Estate for rent for the month, $1,425.

11 Issued Check No. 1427 in payment of Voucher No. 1085.

14 Issued Voucher No. 1086 in favor of Hull Transportation Company for freight charges on merchandise purchased, $84.

14 Prepared Check No. 1428 in payment of Voucher No. 1086.

15 Canceled Voucher No. 1079 because the invoice is to be paid in two installments, as follows: Voucher No. 1087 for $1,950, payable September 1; Voucher No. 1088, payable September 15, $1,950. Issued Voucher No. 1087 and 1088.

16 Received a credit memorandum from Townsend Products Company for merchandise returned, $180, Credit Memo No. 211.

17 Issued Check No. 1429 in payment of Voucher No. 1084, $4,233.60 ($4,500, less $180 return, less cash discount).

22 Issued Voucher No. 1089 in favor of National Telephone Company for telephone bill, $107.13.

22 Prepared Check No. 1430 in payment of Voucher No. 1089.

31 Prepared Voucher No. 1090 for Wages Payable, $2,940, in favor of a payroll bank account. (Assume that the payroll entry was recorded previously in the general journal.)

Aug. 31 Issued Check No. 1431 in payment of Voucher No. 1090.

31 Issued Voucher No. 1091 in favor of L. C. Huffman, the owner, for a personal withdrawal, $1,470.

31 Prepared Check No. 1432 in payment of Voucher No. 1091.

Instructions **1.** Record the transactions for August in the voucher register, the check register, and the general journal.

2. Total and rule the voucher register and the check register.

3. Post the amounts from the registers and the general journal to the Vouchers Payable account.

4. Prepare a schedule of unpaid vouchers. Compare this total with the balance of the Vouchers Payable account.

Problem 21-4 The C. R. Cunningham Company, which uses a voucher system, has the following unpaid vouchers on August 31. The firm follows the practice of recording invoices at the net amount.

VOU. NO.	COMPANY	FOR	DATE OF INVOICE	AMOUNT
4993	Robbins and White	Store Equipment	Aug. 26	6 7 5 0 00
4998	Riggs Equipment Company	Office Equipment	Aug. 28	7 9 0 5 00
				14 6 5 5 00

The company made the following transactions during September.

Sept. 1 Issued Voucher No. 5003 in favor of Consolidated Power and Light for electric bill, $174.

1 Paid Voucher No. 5003 by issuing Check No. 6815.

3 Canceled Voucher No. 4993 because the invoice is to be paid in three installments, as follows: Voucher No. 5004, payable September 15, $2,250; Voucher No. 5005, payable October 1, $2,250; and Voucher No. 5006, payable October 15, $2,250.

4 Bought merchandise on account from Thompson Products Company for $8,100, terms 2/10, n/30. Issued Voucher No. 5007 (record invoice at $7,938, using the net amount).

7 C. R. Cunningham, the owner, withdrew $960 for personal use. Issued Voucher No. 5008.

8 Prepared Check No. 6816 in payment of Voucher No. 5008.

9 Riggs Equipment Company agrees to accept sixty-day, 8% note, dated September 9. Accordingly, canceled Voucher No. 4998.

13 Issued Check No. 6817 in payment of Voucher No. 5007.

15 Prepared Check No. 6818 in payment of Voucher No. 5004.

Sept. 15 Prepared Voucher No. 5009 for $735 for sales commissions.

15 Issued Check No. 6819 in payment of Voucher No. 5009.

20 Bought merchandise on account from D. R. Tucker Company, $9,600, terms 1/10, EOM. Issued Voucher No. 5010 (record the invoice as $9,504).

22 Issued Voucher No. 5011 in favor of Eastern Express Company for freight bill on the purchase from D. R. Tucker Company, $84.

24 Discovered an error in the computations on the invoice from D. R. Tucker Company, reducing the amount by $360. Canceled Voucher No. 5010; issued Voucher No. 5012 for $9,147.60.

27 Prepared Voucher No. 5013, $561, in favor of Security Savings and Loan for mortgage payment: principal, $270; interest, $291.

28 Issued Check No. 6820 in payment of Voucher No. 5013.

30 Prepared Voucher No. 5014 for Wages Payable, $3,123, in favor of a payroll bank account. (Assume that the payroll entry was previously recorded in the general journal.)

30 Paid Voucher No. 5014 by issuing Check No. 6821.

Instructions **1.** Under the date of the original purchase, enter the unpaid invoices in the voucher register, beginning with Voucher No. 4993. Then draw double lines to separate the vouchers of August from those of September. Record the total of the two vouchers as a balance in the Vouchers Payable account.

2. Record the transactions for September in the voucher register, the check register, and the general journal.

3. Total and rule the voucher register and the check register.

4. Post the amounts from the registers and the general journal to the Vouchers Payable account.

5. Prepare a schedule of unpaid vouchers. Compare the total with the balance of the Vouchers Payable account.

Alternate problems

Problem 21-1A   Buchanan and Sons, which uses a voucher system, has the following vouchers that were issued during June and that were unpaid on July 1.

VOU. NO.	COMPANY	FOR	DATE OF VOUCHER	AMOUNT
933	Leonard and Company	Merchandise	Jun. 25	2 1 3 9 00
936	Brunner and Mitchell	Merchandise	Jun. 26	3 5 7 0 00
				5 7 0 9 00

The following transactions were completed during July.

July 1 Issued Voucher No. 938 in favor of Burgess Land Company for July rent, $1,230.

2 Issued Check No. 1116 in payment of Voucher No. 938, $1,230.

5 Bought merchandise on account from Mills Manufacturing Company, $7,440, terms 2/10, n/30. Issued Voucher No. 939. (Invoices are recorded at the gross amount.)

5 Issued Check No. 1117 in payment of Voucher No. 933, $2,117.61 ($2,139 less 1% cash discount).

8 Issued Voucher No. 940 in favor of United Telephone Company for telephone bill, $126.

8 Issued Check No. 1118 in payment of Voucher No. 940.

8 Issued Check No. 1119 in payment of Voucher No. 936, $3,498.60 ($3,570 less 2% cash discount).

13 Issued Check No. 1120 in payment of Voucher No. 939, less the cash discount.

16 Bought merchandise on account from Faulkner Products Company, $5,925, terms 2/10, EOM. Issued Voucher No. 941.

24 Issued Voucher No. 942 for a note payable, previously recorded in the general journal: principal $6,750, plus interest of $78. The note is payable to the Citizens State Bank.

24 Paid Voucher No. 942 by issuing Check No. 1121.

25 Issued Check No. 1122 in payment of Voucher No. 941, less the cash discount.

31 Issued Voucher No. 943 for Wages Payable, $4,041, in favor of the payroll bank account. (Assume that the payroll entry was previously recorded in the general journal.)

31 Paid Voucher No. 943 by issuing Check No. 1123.

Instructions **1.** Under the date of the original purchase, enter the unpaid invoices in the voucher register, beginning with Voucher No. 933. Then draw double lines across all columns to separate the vouchers of June from those of July.

2. Enter the transactions for July in the voucher register at the gross amount. Also record the appropriate transactions in the check register.

3. Total and rule the voucher register and the check register.

4. On scratch paper, prove the equality of the debits and credits in the voucher register and the check register.

Problem 21-2A The T. R. Trevino Company, which uses a voucher system, has the following unpaid vouchers on April 30.

VOU. NO.	COMPANY	FOR	DATE OF INVOICE	AMOUNT
3618	Griffith Supply Company	Store Equipment	Apr. 15	3 8 8 5 00
3634	Burns and Lehman	Merchandise	Apr. 28	7 4 6 0 00
3636	R. L. Meyers and Company	Merchandise	Apr. 29	9 6 0 0 00
				20 9 4 5 00

The company made the following transactions during May.

May 1 Issued Voucher No. 3649 in favor of Columbia Insurance Company for three-year premium on fire insurance policy, $780.

1 Paid Voucher No. 3618 by issuing Check No. 7118, $3,885.

2 Issued Check No. 7119 in payment of Voucher No. 3649.

4 Issued Voucher No. 3650 in favor of Bryant Fast Freight for transportation charges on merchandise purchases, $112.

5 Paid Voucher No. 3650 by issuing Check No. 7120.

7 Issued Check No. 7121 in payment of Voucher No. 3634, $7,385.40 ($7,460 less 1% cash discount).

8 Issued Check No. 7122 in payment of Voucher No. 3636, $9,504 ($9,600 less 1% cash discount).

11 Established a Petty Cash Fund of $250. Issued Voucher No. 3651.

11 Paid Voucher No. 3651 by issuing Check No. 7123.

13 Issued Voucher No. 3652 in favor of Burke and Henderson for merchandise, $13,880, terms 2/10, n/30.

16 Bought advertising space for 2 weeks in the Daily Times. Issued Voucher No. 3653 in the amount of $300.

17 Received a credit memorandum for $652 from Burke and Henderson for merchandise returned to them, Credit Memorandum No. 333.

19 Issued Voucher No. 3654 in favor of Chase County for six months' property taxes, $2,160.

20 Paid Voucher No. 3654 by issuing Check No. 7124.

21 Issued Check No. 7125 in payment of Voucher No. 3652, $12,963.44 ($13,880 less $652 return, less cash discount).

23 Bought merchandise on account from Henry and Griffin, $5,928, terms 1/10, n/30. Issued Voucher No. 3655.

28 Received a credit memorandum for $1,032 from Henry and Griffin for damaged merchandise, Credit Memorandum No. 753D.

31 Issued Voucher No. 3656 to reimburse Petty Cash Fund. The charges were:

Store Supplies	$81.00
Office supplies	30.32
T. R. Trevino, Drawing	48.00
Miscellaneous Expense	28.56

May 31 Issued Check No. 7126 in payment of Voucher No. 3656.

    31 Issued Voucher No. 3657 for Wages Payable, $5,940, in favor of payroll bank account. (Assume that the payroll entry was previously recorded in the general journal.)

    31 Paid Voucher No. 3657 by issuing Check No. 7127, payable to payroll bank account.

Instructions **1.** Under the date of the original purchase, enter the unpaid invoices in the voucher register, beginning with Voucher No. 3618. Then draw double lines across all columns to separate the vouchers of April from those of May.

2. Enter the transactions for May in the voucher register at the gross amount. Also record the appropriate transactions in the check register and general journal.

3. Total and rule the voucher register and check register for the transactions recorded for May.

Problem 21-3A Gregory Sales Company uses a voucher system in which it records invoices at the gross amount. During July it completed the following transactions affecting Vouchers Payable.

July 1 Prepared Voucher No. 1481 in favor of Richards and Reed for the purchase of merchandise having an invoice price of $4,800; terms 30 days.

    3 Prepared Voucher No. 1482 for $1,080, Voucher No. 1483 for $1,080, and Voucher No. 1484 for $1,080. The debt arose because Gregory Sales bought an electronic calculator from Griffith Office Supply. The terms are $1,080 cash or delivery, $1,080 in 30 days, and $1,080 in 60 days. (Use three lines.)

    5 Issued Check No. 1614 in payment of Voucher No. 1482.

    8 Issued Voucher No. 1485 in favor of Severson Supply Company for the purchase of store supplies, $259.50, terms n/30.

    9 Prepared Voucher No. 1486 in favor of Trotter Realty for rent for the month, $1,290.

    9 Issued Check No. 1615 in payment of Voucher No. 1486.

    14 Prepared Voucher No. 1487 in favor of Thomas Motor Freight for freight charges on merchandise purchased, $69.

    14 Issued Check No. 1616 in payment of Voucher No. 1487.

    15 Prepared Voucher No. 1488 in favor of Gustafson Products Company for the purchase of merchandise having an invoice price of $5,400 with a 25% trade discount (record voucher for $4,050, terms 2/10, n/30.

    16 Canceled Voucher No. 1481 because the invoice will be paid in two installments as follows: Voucher No. 1489, payable August 1, $2,400; Voucher No. 1490, payable August 15, $2,400. Prepared Vouchers No. 1489 and 1490.

    18 Received a credit memorandum from Gustafson Products Company for merchandise returned, $240, Credit Memo No. 714.

July 21 Prepared Voucher No. 1491 in favor of Amalgamated Telephone Company for telephone bill, $126.24.

21 Issued Check No. 1617 in payment of Voucher No. 1491.

23 Issued Check No. 1618 in payment of Voucher No. 1488, $3,733.80 ($4,050 less $240 return, less cash discount).

31 Prepared Voucher No. 1492 for Wages Payable, $2,763, in favor of payroll bank account. (Assume that the payroll entry was recorded previously in the general journal.)

31 Issued Check No. 1619 in payment of Voucher No. 1492.

31 Prepared Voucher No. 1493 in favor of T. R. Gregory, the owner, for a personal withdrawal, $1,590.

31 Issued Check No. 1620 for the payment of Voucher No. 1493.

Instructions **1.** Record the transactions for July in the voucher register, the check register, and the general journal.

2. Total and rule the voucher register and the check register.

3. Post the amounts from the registers and the general journal to the Vouchers Payable account.

4. Prepare a schedule of unpaid vouchers. Compare the total with the balance of the Vouchers Payable account.

Problem 21-4A The Murdock Sales Company uses a voucher system by which it records invoices at the net amount. It has the following unpaid vouchers on October 31.

VOU. NO.	COMPANY	FOR	DATE OF INVOICE	AMOUNT			
5139	*Howard Supply Company*	*Store Equipment*	*Oct. 25*	9	6	00	00
5145	*Trotter Equipment Company*	*Office Equipment*	*Oct. 27*	10	7	00	00
				20	3	00	00

The company made the following transactions during November.

Nov. 1 Prepared Voucher No. 5151 in favor of Universal Power and Light for electric bill, $218.

1 Paid Voucher No. 5151 by issuing Check No. 6872.

2 Bought merchandise on account from Stewart Manufacturing Company, $11,700, terms 2/10, n/30. Prepared Voucher No. 5152 (record invoice for $11,466, using the net amount).

3 Canceled Voucher No. 5139 because the invoice is to be paid in three installments, as follows: Voucher No. 5153, due November 15, $3,200; Voucher No. 5154, due December 1, $3,200; and Voucher No. 5155, due December 15, $3,200.

Nov. 6 Romella Murdock, the owner, withdrew $1,180 for personal use. Issued Voucher No. 5156.

    7 Issued Check No. 6873 in payment of Voucher No. 5156.

    8 Trotter Equipment Company agreed to accept sixty-day, 8% note, dated November 8. Accordingly, canceled Voucher No. 5145.

    12 Issued Check No. 6874 in payment of Voucher No. 5152.

    14 Issued Check No. 6875 in payment of Voucher No. 5153.

    15 Prepared Voucher No. 5157 for $1,028 for sales commissions expense, in favor of salespersons. The expense was not previously recorded.

    15 Issued Check No. 6876 in payment of Voucher No. 5157, payable to salespeople.

    21 Bought merchandise on account from T. S. Richards Company, $13,440, terms 1/10, EOM. Issued Voucher No. 5158 (record the invoice for $13,305.60).

    23 Prepared Voucher No. 5159 in favor of Powers Freight Company for freight bill on the purchase from T. S. Richards Company, $118.

    23 Issued Check No. 6877 in payment of Voucher No. 5159.

    25 Discovered an error in the computations on the invoice from T. S. Richards, reducing amount due by $440. Canceled Voucher No. 5158 and issued Voucher No. 5160, $12,870.

    28 Prepared Voucher No. 5161, $718, in favor of Tucker Savings and Loan, for mortgage payment: principal, $352; interest, $366.

    28 Issued Check No. 6878 in payment of Voucher No. 5161.

    30 Prepared Voucher No. 5162 for Wages Payable, $4,138, in favor of payroll bank account. (Assume that the payroll entry was previously recorded in the general journal.)

    30 Paid Voucher No. 5162 by issuing Check No. 6879.

Instructions

1. Under the date of the original purchases, enter the unpaid invoices in the voucher register, beginning with Voucher No. 5139. Then draw double lines to separate the vouchers of October from those of November. Record the total of the two vouchers as a balance in the Vouchers Payable account.

2. Record the transactions for November in the voucher register, the check register, and the general journal.

3. Total and rule the voucher register and the check register.

4. Post the amounts from the registers and the general journal to the Vouchers Payable account.

5. Prepare a schedule of unpaid vouchers. Compare this total with the balance of the Vouchers Payable account.

22

Accounting for partnerships

objectives

After you have completed this chapter, you will be able to do the following:
- Prepare a section of an income statement relating to division of net income for a partnership involving division of income on the basis of fractional shares, on the basis of ratio of capital investments, and on the basis of salary and interest allowances.
- Journalize the closing entries for a partnership.
- Prepare a statement of partners' capital.
- Journalize entries involving the sale of a partnership interest or withdrawal of a partner.
- Journalize entries pertaining to the liquidation of a partnership involving the immediate sale of the assets for cash.

UP TO this time, we have been dealing entirely with sole proprietorships. In this chapter and the ones that follow, we shall deal with the other two forms of business organizations: partnerships and corporations. In the professions and in firms that stress personal service, partnerships are widely used. Each professional practitioner can maintain her or his own clientele, yet share with colleagues the expenses of operating an office or clinic. Partnerships are also popular in manufacturing and trade because they afford a means of combining the capital and abilities of two or more persons.

Characteristics of a partnership

A *partnership,* as defined by the Uniform Partnership Act, is an association of two or more persons to carry on, as co-owners, a business for profit. It is a voluntary association, entered into by the parties without compulsion. Certain features of a partnership affect just the partners; other features affect the partners as well as others who are not members of the partnership. Let us examine some of these features.

Co-ownership of partnership property

All partners are co-owners of the assets of the partnership. For example, Dobbs and Sutter formed a 50-50 partnership to run a fuel oil business. The partnership owns two tank trucks of equal value. According to the co-ownership concept, each partner owns half of each truck, as well as half of the other assets of the firm.

Limited life

A partnership may be ended by the death or withdrawal of any partner. Other factors which may bring about the dissolution of a partnership include the bankruptcy or incapacity of a partner, the expiration of the period of time specified in the partnership agreement, or the completion of the project for which the partnership was formed.

Unlimited liability   Each partner is personally liable to creditors for all the debts the partnership incurs during his or her membership in the firm. When a new partner joins an existing firm, he or she may or may not assume liablity for debts incurred by the firm prior to admission. When a partner withdraws from a firm, he or she must give adequate public notice of withdrawal, or he or she may be held liable for debts the partnership incurs after withdrawal.

Mutual agency   Each partner can enter into binding contracts in the name of the firm for the purchase or sale of goods or services within the normal scope of the firm's business. When the partners agree among themselves to limit the right of any partner to enter into certain contracts in the name of the firm, this agreement is not binding on outsiders who are unaware of its existence.

Advantages of a partnership   Here are some advantages of the partnership form of business organization.

1. Partnerships offer opportunity to pool abilities and capital of two or more persons.

2. It is easy to form a partnership, the only requirement being an agreement or mutual understanding by the partners.

3. Legal restrictions are minimal. Although a partnership must have a legal purpose, there are no other limitations on types of business activities.

4. Federal income taxes are not levied against a partnership as an entity, although a partnership must file an information return (Form 1065), containing an income statement, balance sheet, and report of the distributive shares of income (the shares of the year's net income allocated to each partner). A partner has to pay taxes on his or her share of the net income, whether this share is taken out of the business or not.

Disadvantages of a partnership   Here are some disadvantages of the partnership form of business organization.

1. General partners (those who actively and publicly participate in transactions of the firm) have unlimited liability.

2. A partnership has limited life.

3. The actions of one partner are binding on the other partners; this relationship is known as mutual agency.

4. The raising of investment capital depends entirely on the partners themselves.

5. It is hard to transfer a partial or entire partnership interest to another person, as the transfer must be agreed to by all partners.

Partnership agreements

Although generally a partnership may be formed on the basis of an oral understanding, it is much better to have the partnership agreement based on a written contract. Although there is no standard form of partnership agreement, the following provisions are usually included.

- Effective date of the agreement
- Names and addresses of the partners
- Name, location, and nature of the business
- Duration of the agreement
- Investment of each partner
- Withdrawals to be allowed each partner
- Procedure for sharing profits and losses
- Provision for division of assets upon dissolution

Accounting entries for partnerships

The only difference between accounting for a sole proprietorship and accounting for partnerships is in the owners' equity accounts. Otherwise, the accountant uses the same types of assets, liabilities, revenues, and expenses that we have discussed before. But because there is more than one owner, it is necessary to have one capital account and one drawing account for each partner. As in the case of sole proprietorships, the capital accounts are involved only when there is a change in investments or when the Income Summary account and the Drawing accounts are closed.

Recording investments

The accountant makes a separate entry for the investment of each partner. All assets contributed by a given partner are debited to the appropriate asset accounts. If the partnership assumes liabilities, the accountant credits the proper liability accounts, and credits the partner's capital account for the net amount.

Let's take a case of recording initial investments in a partnership: Lucille D. Blane and Mary C. Reynolds decide to form a partnership for the operation of a jewelry store. Blane presently owns and operates Blane's Jewelry Store; she is contributing the assets and liabilities of her store to the new firm. Reynolds' investment is $20,000 in cash; the following is the entry to record this investment.

GENERAL JOURNAL   PAGE ___1___

	DATE		DESCRIPTION	POST REF.	DEBIT	CREDIT	
1	19– Feb.	2	Cash		20 0 0 0 00		1
2			Mary C. Reynolds, Capital			20 0 0 0 00	2
3			To record the original investment of				3
4			Mary C. Reynolds				4
5							5
6							6

Both partners have to agree on the equivalent monetary amounts at which Blane's noncash assets are to be recorded. Assume that Blane's Jewelry Store has the following account balances.

Cash	$ 2,900
Accounts Receivable	18,000
Allowance for Doubtful Accounts	200
Merchandise Inventory	20,400
Equipment	16,000
Accumulated Depreciation, Equipment	4,500
Notes Payable	1,600
Accounts Payable	8,400

Furthermore, $400 of the Accounts Receivable have been definitely ascertained to be uncollectible; the $400 should not be recorded on the books of the new partnership. Of the remaining $17,600 of Accounts Receivable, there is some doubt as to the collectibility of $500. The present appraised value of Blane's merchandise is $21,000. The present appraised value of Blane's equipment is $9,000. Accordingly, the accountant records Blane's investment as follows.

Feb.	2	Cash		2900 00	
		Accounts Receivable		17600 00	
		Merchandise Inventory		21000 00	
		Equipment		9000 00	
		Allowance for Doubtful Accounts			500 00
		Notes Payable			1600 00
		Accounts Payable			8400 00
		Lucille D. Blane, Capital			40000 00
		To record the original investment of			
		Lucille D. Blane			

The accountant debits Accounts Receivable for the face amount of the accounts taken over by the new partnership, and credits Allowance for Doubtful Accounts for the amount estimated to be uncollectible. Any customer accounts which are definitely uncollectible are excluded from those being taken over by the new business.

The accountant debits the new firm's Merchandise Inventory and Equipment accounts for the amount of their appraised present values. The accumulated depreciation is not recorded, because the appraised value represents the new book value for the partnership.

Additional investments

Now let's say that 8 months have gone by and the new partnership needs more cash. On October 1, the partners each invest an additional $4,000. The entry is as follows.

GENERAL JOURNAL   PAGE __28__

		DATE		DESCRIPTION	POST. REF.	DEBIT	CREDIT	
1		19–Oct.	1	Cash		8 0 0 0 00		1
2				Lucille D. Blane, Capital			4 0 0 0 00	2
3				Mary C. Reynolds, Capital			4 0 0 0 00	3
4				To record additional investments				4
5								5

At the end of the year, before the books are closed, the capital accounts of the partners will appear as shown here.

GENERAL LEDGER

ACCOUNT ___Lucille D. Blane, Capital___   ACCOUNT NO. ___301___

DATE		ITEM	POST. REF.	DEBIT	CREDIT	BALANCE DEBIT	BALANCE CREDIT
19–Feb.	2		J1		40 0 0 0 00		40 0 0 0 00
Oct.	1		J28		4 0 0 0 00		44 0 0 0 00

ACCOUNT ___Mary C. Reynolds, Capital___   ACCOUNT NO. ___303___

DATE		ITEM	POST. REF.	DEBIT	CREDIT	BALANCE DEBIT	BALANCE CREDIT
19–Feb.	2		J1		20 0 0 0 00		20 0 0 0 00
Oct.	1		J28		4 0 0 0 00		24 0 0 0 00

Drawing accounts

Drawing accounts of partners serve the same purpose as the Drawing account of the owner of a sole proprietorship. Debits to the Drawing accounts originate through transactions like those listed below.

- Withdrawal of cash by a partner, $200.
- Withdrawal of merchandise by a partner, $148.
- Partnership cash collected in behalf of the firm by a partner, but kept by the partner for personal use, $320.

Lucille D. Blane, Drawing			2	0	0	00								
Cash								2	0	0	00			
To record a cash withdrawal														
Mary C. Reynolds, Drawing			1	4	8	00								
Purchases								1	4	8	00			
To record a merchandise withdrawal at cost														
Lucille D. Blane, Drawing			3	2	0	00								
Accounts Receivable, S. Zurich								3	2	0	00			
S. Zurich, in full payment of account, the money retained														
by Blane														

From the accounting point of view, the last type of transaction isn't a good idea, but we mention it here because such things do, in fact, go on.

Division of net income or net loss

Recall that the closing entries for a sole proprietorship consist of the following steps.

1. Close the revenue accounts into Income Summary.

2. Close the expense accounts into Income Summary (the expense accounts do not include any payments to partners).

3. Close Income Summary into the Capital account by the amount of the net income or loss.

4. Close the Drawing account into the Capital account.

The only differences between closing entries for a partnership, as opposed to those for a sole proprietorship, pertain to steps 3 and 4. Instead of a single capital account and a single drawing account, in a partnership there are as many accounts of each type as there are partners. Income Summary is closed into the capital accounts by the amount of the net income or loss, and the drawing accounts are closed into the respective capital accounts.

Let's look at step 3, which deals with the division of net income. The partnership agreement should specify the arrangement for the division of net income. However, suppose the partnership agreement fails to do this. Then, from a legal standpoint, the partners should share any net income or loss equally. In actuality, partners may make any agreement they wish with respect to the division of net income or loss, as it is purely their own affair.

Partners may use any one of a number of alternative methods of sharing partnership earnings, or they may use a combination of methods. The variety of these methods reflects the differences in the values of services or investments contributed by individual partners. We shall discuss the methods listed at the top of the next page.

1. Division of income on a fractional-share basis
2. Division of income based on the ratio of capital investments
3. Division of income based on salary allowances
4. Division of income based on interest allowances

To illustrate the various methods, we shall look at two examples of each.
First, the partnership of Dodd and Easely has a net income of $48,000.
Second, instead of the net income of $48,000, the partnership of Dodd and Easely has a net loss of $2,000. We shall use the same balances of the capital and drawing accounts for each example, and consider that each method used for the division of net income represents a separate partnership agreement.

The balances of the capital accounts represent the partners' individual investments at the beginning of the year. The balances of the drawing accounts represent the total personal withdrawals during the year. These are shown by T accounts as follows.

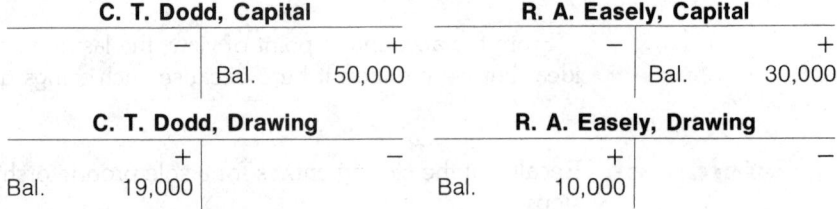

C. T. Dodd, Capital		R. A. Easely, Capital	
−	+	−	+
	Bal. 50,000		Bal. 30,000

C. T. Dodd, Drawing		R. A. Easely, Drawing	
+	−	+	−
Bal. 19,000		Bal. 10,000	

Division of income on a fractional-share basis

The simplest way to divide net income or loss is to allot each partner a stated fraction of the total. One can establish the size of the fraction by taking into consideration (1) the amount of investment of each partner, and (2) the value of services rendered by each partner. Assume that the partnership agreement stipulates that profits and losses are to be divided this way: three-fourths for Dodd and one-fourth for Easely.

The accountant may present a report of the division of net income as a separate statement, or record it on the income statement, immediately below Net income.

Net income of $48,000 If the accountant prefers to adopt the latter procedure, the division of net income would appear as follows.

Dodd and Easely			
Income Statement			
For year ended December 31, 19-			
Revenue from Sales:			
Net Income			48 0 0 0 00
Division of Net Income:	C.T. Dodd	R.A. Easely	Total
Fractional Share	36 0 0 0 00	12 0 0 0 00	48 0 0 0 00

The division of net income is recorded as a closing entry in step 3 of the closing procedure, whether or not the partner has withdrawn his or her share. The entry looks like this.

Income Summary	48 0 0 0 00	
C. T. Dodd, Capital		36 0 0 0 00
R. A. Easely, Capital		12 0 0 0 00

The entries for step 4, closing the drawing accounts into the capital accounts, are as follows.

C. T. Dodd, Capital	19 0 0 0 00	
C. T. Dodd, Drawing		19 0 0 0 00
R. A. Easely, Capital	10 0 0 0 00	
R. A. Easely, Drawing		10 0 0 0 00

Now let's see what these entries look like by means of T accounts, with steps 3 and 4 labeled.

Income Summary

(3) Closing	48,000	Bal.	48,000

C. T. Dodd, Capital

	−		+
(4)	19,000	Bal.	50,000
		(3)	36,000

C. T. Dodd, Drawing

	+		−
Bal.	19,000	(4) Closing	19,000

R. A. Easely, Capital

	−		+
(4)	10,000	Bal.	30,000
		(3)	12,000

R. A. Easely, Drawing

	+		−
Bal.	10,000	(4) Closing	10,000

Note that step 4 is the same for partnerships as for sole proprietorships.

Net loss of $2,000 The lower portion of the income statement is as shown at the top of page 598. (The parentheses around the totals indicate that the figures are minus numbers.)

Revenue from Sales:			
Net Loss			(2,000 00)
Division of Net Loss:	C. T. Dodd	R. A. Easely	Total
Fractional Share	(1,500 00)	(500 00)	(2,000 00)

Accordingly, the closing entries and posting to the ledger accounts look like this.

C. T. Dodd, Capital	1,500 00	
R. A. Easely, Capital	500 00	
Income Summary		2,000 00
To close net loss into the capital accounts		
C. T. Dodd, Capital	19,000 00	
C. T. Dodd, Drawing		19,000 00
To close the Drawing account		
R. A. Easely, Capital	10,000 00	
R. A. Easely, Drawing		10,000 00
To close the Drawing account		

Income Summary

Bal.	2,000	(3) Closing	2,000

C. T. Dodd, Capital

	−		+
(3)	1,500	Bal.	50,000
(4)	19,000		

C. T. Dodd, Drawing

	+		−
Bal.	19,000	(4) Closing	19,000

R. A. Easely, Capital

	−		+
(3)	500	Bal.	30,000
(4)	10,000		

R. A. Easely, Drawing

	+		−
Bal.	10,000	(4) Closing	10,000

When partners share net income on a fractional basis, this basis is often expressed as a ratio. So we could have expressed Dodd's three-fourths and Easely's one-fourth as a 3:1 (3-to-1) ratio.

When you list the division of net income as a ratio and want to turn the ratio into a fraction, do it this way. First add the figures; then use the total as the denominator of the fraction:

3:1 $\qquad$ (3 + 1 = 4) $\qquad$ ¾ and ¼

or (in the case of three partners):

5:3:1 $\qquad$ (5 + 3 + 1 = 9) $\qquad$ ⁵⁄₉ and ³⁄₉ and ⅑

or (in the case of four partners):

3:2:1:1 $\qquad$ (3 + 2 + 1 + 1 = 7) $\qquad$ ³⁄₇ and ²⁄₇ and ⅐ and ⅐

Division of income based on ratio of capital investments

Allocating earnings to partners on the basis of the amounts of their investment often works well for enterprises whose earnings are closely related to the amount of money invested, such as real estate ventures, cattle feeding operations, etc. Suppose that Dodd and Easely have agreed to share earnings or losses according to the ratio of their investments at the beginning of the year. Let's say that Dodd put in $50,000 and Easely $30,000. One can calculate their respective shares as follows.

Dodd	$50,000
Easely	30,000
Total	$80,000

$$\text{Dodd's share} = \frac{\$50,000}{\$80,000} = \frac{5}{8} \text{ or } .625 \ (62.5\%)$$

$$\text{Easely's share} = \frac{\$30,000}{\$80,000} = \frac{3}{8} \text{ or } .375 \ (37.5\%)$$

Net income of $48,000 When the partnership has a net income of $48,000, the accountant determines the distribution like this.

Dodd's share of earnings $\qquad$ $48,000 × ⅝ (or $48,000 × .625) = $30,000
Easely's share of earnings $\qquad$ $48,000 × ⅜ (or $48,000 × .375) = $18,000

The section of the income statement showing the division of net income looks like this.

Revenue from Sales:			
Net Income			48 0 0 0 00
Division of Net Income:	C.T. Dodd	R.A. Easely	Total
Capital investment ratio	30 0 0 0 00	18 0 0 0 00	48 0 0 0 00

The accompanying closing entries are as follows.

Income Summary	48 0 0 0 00		
C. T. Dodd, Capital		30 0 0 0 00	
R. A. Easely, Capital		18 0 0 0 00	
C. T. Dodd, Capital	19 0 0 0 00		
C. T. Dodd, Drawing		19 0 0 0 00	
R. A. Easely, Capital	10 0 0 0 00		
R. A. Easely, Drawing		10 0 0 0 00	

Net loss of $2,000 When the partnership has a net loss of $2,000, the accountant calculates the sharing of the loss as follows.

Dodd's share of the loss $2,000 \times \frac{5}{8}$ (or $2,000 \times .625) = \$1,250$

Easely's share of the loss $2,000 \times \frac{3}{8}$ (or $2,000 \times .375) = \$750$

The section of the income statement showing the division of net loss and the accompanying closing entries look like this.

Revenue from Sales:				
Net Loss				(2 0 0 0 00)
Division of Net Loss:		C.T. Dodd	R.A. Easely	Total
Capital investment ratio		(1 2 5 0 00)	(7 5 0 00)	(2 0 0 0 00)

C. T. Dodd, Capital	1 2 5 0 00	
R. A. Easely, Capital	7 5 0 00	
Income Summary		2 0 0 0 00
C. T. Dodd, Capital	19 0 0 0 00	
C. T. Dodd, Drawing		19 0 0 0 00
R. A. Easely, Capital	10 0 0 0 00	
R. A. Easely, Drawing		10 0 0 0 00

Note that the entries for step 4—closing the drawing accounts into the capital accounts—are always the same, regardless of whether the firm finishes the year with a net income or a net loss.

Division of income based on salary allowances

Salary allowances are purely allocations of net income, and are used as a means of recognizing and rewarding differences in ability and in the amount of time devoted to the business. *Salary allowances are different from payments to the partners, which are recorded in the drawing accounts.* They are different from remuneration to employees, which is recorded as Salaries or Wages Expense.

Suppose that Dodd and Easely have a partnership agreement which provides for yearly salaries of $12,000 and $8,000, respectively, with the remainder of the net income to be divided equally. It would also be possible to divide the remainder on the basis of the ratio of investments, or any other ratio agreed on by the partners.

Net income of $48,000   The Division of Net Income section of the income statement when there is a net income of $48,000 is as follows.

Revenue from Sales:			
Net Income			48 0 0 0 00
Division of Net Income:	*C.T. Dodd*	*R.A. Easely*	*Total*
Salary allowances	12 0 0 0 00	8 0 0 0 00	20 0 0 0 00
Remainder allocated equally	14 0 0 0 00	14 0 0 0 00	28 0 0 0 00
Net Income	26 0 0 0 00	22 0 0 0 00	48 0 0 0 00

Their accountant determines the allocation of the remainder as follows.

Net income	$48,000
Less amount allocated as salaries	
($12,000 + $8,000)	20,000
Remainder	$28,000

$$\text{Remainder} \div 2 = \frac{\$28,000}{2} = \$14,000$$

The closing entries are shown on top of page 602.

	Debit	Credit
Income Summary	48 0 0 0 00	
C. T. Dodd, Capital		26 0 0 0 00
R. A. Easely, Capital		22 0 0 0 00
C. T. Dodd, Capital	19 0 0 0 00	
C. T. Dodd, Drawing		19 0 0 0 00
R. A. Easely, Capital	10 0 0 0 00	
R. A. Easely, Drawing		10 0 0 0 00

Net loss of $2,000 When salary allowances are stipulated in the partnership agreement, they must be allocated (not necessarily paid) regardless of whether there is enough net income to take care of them.

Their accountant determines the remainder as follows.

Net Loss	$ 2,000
Add amount allocated as salaries	
($12,000 + $8,000)	20,000
Remainder	($22,000)

$$\text{Remainder} \div 2 = \frac{(\$22,000)}{2} = (\$11,000)$$

The income statements and closing entries are shown here and on the facing page.

Revenue from Sales:	C. T. Dodd	R. A. Easely	Total
Net Loss			(2 0 0 0 00)
Division of Net Loss:	C. T. Dodd	R. A. Easely	Total
Salary allowances	12 0 0 0 00	8 0 0 0 00	20 0 0 0 00
Excess of allowances over income allocated equally	(11 0 0 0 00)	(11 0 0 0 00)	(22 0 0 0 00)
Net Loss	1 0 0 0 00	(3 0 0 0 00)	(2 0 0 0 00)

R. A. Easely, Capital	3 0 0 0 00		
Income Summary			2 0 0 0 00
C. T. Dodd, Capital			1 0 0 0 00
C. T. Dodd, Capital	19 0 0 0 00		
C. T. Dodd, Drawing			19 0 0 0 00
R. A. Easely, Capital	10 0 0 0 00		
R. A. Easely, Drawing			10 0 0 0 00

After posting, the owners' equity accounts look like this.

Income Summary
Bal.	2,000	(3) Closing	2,000

C. T. Dodd, Capital
	–		+
(4)	19,000	Bal.	50,000
		(3)	1,000

C. T. Dodd, Drawing
	+		–
Bal.	19,000	(4) Closing	19,000

R. A. Easely, Capital
	–		+
(3)	3,000	Bal.	30,000
(4)	10,000		

R. A. Easely, Drawing
	+		–
Bal.	10,000	(4) Closing	10,000

As a result of the $2,000 net loss for the year, Dodd's capital account decreased by $18,000 (credit $1,000 and debit $19,000) and Easely's capital account decreased by $13,000 (debit $3,000 and debit $10,000).

Division of income based on interest allowances

Sometimes a partnership agreement stipulates an allowance for interest on the capital investment of the partners. This clause acts as an incentive for partners to not only leave their investments in the business but even to increase them. For example, suppose that Dodd and Easely, in addition to their salary allowances of $12,000 and $8,000, are allowed 8% interest on their capital balances at the beginning of the fiscal year, and that the remainder is to be divided equally. Interest allowances, like salary allowances, are just allocations of net income.

Net income of $48,000 The section of the income statement relating to the division of a $48,000 net income appears as follows.

Revenue from Sales:			
Net Income			48 0 0 0 00
Division of Net Income:	C.T. Dodd	R.A. Easely	Total
Salary allowances	12 0 0 0 00	8 0 0 0 00	20 0 0 0 00
Interest allowances	4 0 0 0 00	2 4 0 0 00	6 4 0 0 00
Remainder allocated equally	10 8 0 0 00	10 8 0 0 00	21 6 0 0 00
Net Income	26 8 0 0 00	21 2 0 0 00	48 0 0 0 00

The accountant figures out the remainder in the following way.

Net Income		$48,000
Less:		
Amount allocated as salaries		
($12,000 + $8,000)	$20,000	
Amount allocated as interest		
($4,000 + $2,400)	6,400	26,400
Remainder		$21,600

$$\text{Remainder} \div 2 = \frac{\$21,600}{2} = \$10,800$$

And the closing entries would look like this.

Income Summary	48 0 0 0 00	
C. T. Dodd, Capital		26 8 0 0 00
R. A. Easely, Capital		21 2 0 0 00
C. T. Dodd, Capital	19 0 0 0 00	
C. T. Dodd, Drawing		19 0 0 0 00
R. A. Easely, Capital	10 0 0 0 00	
R. A. Easely, Drawing		10 0 0 0 00

Net loss of $2,000 The accountant handles interest allowances the same way he or she handles salary allowances: Both must be allocated, regardless of whether there is enough net income to take care of them. The section of the income statement relating to the division of a $2,000 net loss appears as follows.

Revenue from Sales:				
Net Loss				(2 0 0 0 00)
Division of Net Loss:	C. T. Dodd	R.A. Easely	Total	
Salary allowances	12 0 0 0 00	8 0 0 0 00	20 0 0 0 00	
Interest allowances	4 0 0 0 00	2 4 0 0 00	6 4 0 0 00	
Excess of allowances over income				
allocated equally	(14 2 0 0 00)	(14 2 0 0 00)	(28 4 0 0 00)	
Net Loss	1 8 0 0 00	(3 8 0 0 00)	(2 0 0 0 00)	

Their accountant computes the remainder as follows.

Net Loss		$ 2,000
Add:		
Amount allocated as salaries		
($12,000 + $8,000)	$20,000	
Amount allocated as interest		
($4,000 + $2,400)	6,400	26,400
Remainder		$28,400

$$\text{Remainder} \div 2 = \frac{(\$28,400)}{2} = (\$14,200)$$

And the closing entries look like this.

R. A. Easely, Capital	3 8 0 0 00	
Income Summary		2 0 0 0 00
C. T. Dodd, Capital		1 8 0 0 00
C. T. Dodd, Capital	19 0 0 0 00	
C. T. Dodd, Drawing		19 0 0 0 00
R. A. Easely, Capital	10 0 0 0 00	
R. A. Easely, Drawing		10 0 0 0 00

After posting, the owner's equity accounts look like this.

Income Summary

Bal.	2,000	(3) Closing	2,000

C. T. Dodd, Capital

	−		+
(4)	19,000	Bal.	50,000
		(3)	1,800

C. T. Dodd, Drawing

	+		−
Bal.	19,000	(4) Closing	19,000

R. A. Easely, Capital

	−		+
(3)	3,800	Bal.	30,000
(4)	10,000		

R. A. Easely, Drawing

	+		−
Bal.	10,000	(4) Closing	10,000

Financial statements for a partnership

We have already talked about the way an income statement for a partnership should look, with the section on Division of Net Income inserted immediately below Net Income.

Changes in the balances of the partners' capital accounts are recorded in the statement of owners' equity. This is just like a statement of owner's equity for a sole proprietorship, except that there is a separate column for each partner.

	C. T. Dodd	R. A. Easley	Total
Dodd and Easely			
Statement of Owners' Equity			
For year ended December 31, 19___			
Capital, Jan. 1, 19___	50 0 0 0 00	30 0 0 0 00	80 0 0 0 00
Net Income for the year	26 8 0 0 00	21 2 0 0 00	48 0 0 0 00
	76 8 0 0 00	51 2 0 0 00	128 0 0 0 00
Less withdrawals during the year	19 0 0 0 00	10 0 0 0 00	29 0 0 0 00
Capital, Dec. 31, 19___	57 8 0 0 00	41 2 0 0 00	99 0 0 0 00

When a partner makes any additional permanent investment after the beginning of the fiscal period, the accountant records this right below the beginning balances of the capital accounts.

Partners have to pay federal income taxes on the basis of their distributive shares (their shares of net income) in the business. For example, the taxable income of C. T. Dodd is $26,800, even though he withdrew only $19,000. He lists $26,800 on his personal income tax return. The Internal Revenue Code decrees that details of the distributive shares of each partner must be recorded on a U.S. Partnership Return of Income (Form 1065).

Dissolution of a partnership

As we said earlier in this chapter, one of the disadvantages of a partnership is that it has a limited life. Any change in the personnel of the membership technically ends the partnership. When a partnership dissolves, the main visible result is a change in the names listed in the partnership agreement and a change in the division of net income. However, the routine transactions of the business go on as usual. For example, suppose that a partnership originally consists of A, B, and C. Then C withdraws his or her investment from the firm, and a new partnership emerges: A and B. During the transition, business is carried on as usual. In other words, in a dissolution, the original partnership is dissolved by either the sale of one partner's interest in the firm to a new partner, or the withdrawal of a partner, and the firm continues to operate as before.

Sale of a partnership interest

When a partner retires, he or she may sell his/her interest to a person outside the firm who is acceptable to the remaining partners. Let's say that at the end of a given year R. A. Easely has a capital balance of $31,760, and decides to sell his interest to P. E. Falkner for $40,000. The accountant makes the following entry to account for the transfer of ownership.

R. A. Easely, Capital	31 7 6 0 00	
P. E. Falkner, Capital		31 7 6 0 00
To transfer Easely's equity in the partnership to Falkner		

The difference between $40,000 and $31,760 represents a personal profit to *Easely,* not to the firm. There has been no change in the partnership's assets or liabilities, and consequently there is no change in the total owner's equity. However, remember that if the firm is to continue, Dodd (the other original partner) must be willing to accept Falkner as a new partner.

Withdrawal of a partner

The partnership agreement should provide for a set procedure to be followed when one of the partners withdraws. Such a procedure usually entails an audit of the books and a revaluation of the partnership's assets to reflect current market values.

*Partner
withdraws book
value of
his/her equity
after
revaluation*

Suppose that S. T. Hogan is retiring from the partnership of Gray, Hogan, and Insell. The partnership agreement stipulates that net income and net loss shall be shared on an equal basis; it also provides for an audit and revaluation of assets in the event that a partner retires. Here is the firm's balance sheet, immediately prior to the audit and revaluation.

Gray, Hogan, and Insell					
Balance Sheet					
September 30, 19___					
Assets					
Current Assets:					
Cash			28 0 0 0 00		
Accounts Receivable	8 0 0 0 00				
Less Allowance for Doubtful Accounts	5 0 0 00		7 5 0 0 00		
Merchandise Inventory			47 5 0 0 00		
Total Current Assets				83 0 0 0 00	
Plant and Equipment:					
Equipment			27 0 0 0 00		
Less Accumulated Depreciation			11 0 0 0 00	16 0 0 0 00	
Total Assets				99 0 0 0 00	
Liabilities					
Accounts Payable				7 0 0 0 00	
Owners' Equity					
R. L. Gray, Capital			46 0 0 0 00		
S. T. Hogan, Capital			24 0 0 0 00		
D. J. Insell, Capital			22 0 0 0 00	92 0 0 0 00	
Total Liabilities and Owners' Equity				99 0 0 0 00	

Then an accountant (usually from an outside firm) goes to work and audits the books and makes a fresh appraisal of the firm's assets. This audit and appraisal indicate that Merchandise Inventory is undervalued by $9,800, that Allowances for Doubtful Accounts should be increased by $200, and that Equipment is overvalued by $2,400. The accountant allocates the net difference between debits and credits to the partners' capital accounts, according to their basis for sharing profits and losses, as shown on the facing page.

	19— Sep.	30	Merchandise Inventory	9 8 0 0 00		1
2			Allowance for Doubtful Accounts		2 0 0 00	2
3			Equipment		2 4 0 0 00	3
4			R. L. Gray, Capital		2 4 0 0 00	4
5			S. T. Hogan, Capital		2 4 0 0 00	5
6			D. J. Insell, Capital		2 4 0 0 00	6
7			*To record the revaluation of the assets; net*			7
8			*increase in owners' equity is $7,200*			8
9						9
10						10
11						11
12						12
13						13

After the posting of the above entry, the owners' equity accounts look like this.

R. L. Gray, Capital		S. T. Hogan, Capital		D. J. Insell, Capital	
−	+	−	+	−	+
	Bal. 46,000		Bal. 24,000		Bal. 22,000
	Sept. 30 2,400		Sept. 30 2,400		Sept. 30 2,400

After the accountant has recorded the revaluation of the firm's assets, S. T. Hogan withdraws cash from the partnership equal to her equity, which leads to the following entry.

	Sep.	30	S. T. Hogan, Capital	26 4 0 0 00		1
2			Cash		26 4 0 0 00	2
3			*To record the withdrawal of S. T. Hogan*			3
4						4
5						5
6						6
7						7

Partner withdraws more than book value of his/her equity

Sometimes it happens that a partner may withdraw more cash than the amount of his or her capital account. There are two possible reasons for this: (1) The business is prosperous and shows excellent potential for growth. (2) The remaining partners are so anxious for the partner to retire that they are willing to buy him or her out.

In the firm of Gray, Hogan, and Insell, when Hogan announces that she's going to retire, Gray and Insell agree to pay her $27,000 for her interest in the partnership. Because the balance of her capital account after the revaluation is $26,400, the excess of $600 must be deducted from the capital accounts of the remaining partners, in accordance with their basis for sharing profits and losses. The entry appears at the top of page 610.

19— Sep.	30	S. T. Hogan, Capital	26 400 00	
		R. L. Gray, Capital	3 00 00	
		D. J. Insell, Capital	3 00 00	
		Cash		27 000 00
		To record the withdrawal of S. T. Hogan		

Partner withdraws less than book value of his/her equity

Sometimes a partner may be so anxious to retire that he or she is willing to take less than the current value of his or her equity just to get out of the partnership, or out of the business. In the firm of Gray, Hogan, and Insell, let's say that Hogan is willing to withdraw if she gets just $21,000 cash out of it all. Because the balance of her capital account after the revaluation is $26,400, the difference ($5,400) represents a profit to the remaining partners. The entry to record this is as follows.

19— Sep.	30	S. T. Hogan, Capital	26 400 00	
		R. L. Gray, Capital		2 700 00
		D. J. Insell, Capital		2 700 00
		Cash		21 000 00
		To record the withdrawal of S. T. Hogan		

Death of a partner

The death of a partner automatically ends the partnership, and his or her estate is entitled to receive the amount of his or her equity. Such a death makes it necessary to close the books immediately, so that the accountant can determine the firm's net income for the current fiscal period. Partnership agreements usually also provide for an audit and revaluation of the assets at this time. Then, after the accountant has determined the current value of the deceased partner's capital account, the remaining partners and the executor of the deceased partner's estate must agree on the method of payment. The journal entries are similar to those the accountant makes for the withdrawal of a partner. To be sure that they have enough cash to meet such a demand, partnerships often carry life insurance policies.

Liquidation of a partnership

A liquidation means an end of the partnership as well as of the business itself. This final winding-up process involves selling assets, paying off liabilities, and distributing the remaining cash to the partners. The closing entries are journalized and posted prior to the liquidation.

Occasionally it takes a long time to convert merchandise inventory and other assets into cash; on the other hand, things can also move quickly. One can never predict how long these liquidation operations may take. In the process, several things may happen. We shall discuss only two possibilities here, though you can find more complex situations set forth in more advanced books.

The accountant makes the necessary journal entries in four steps, as follows.

1. Sale of the assets, using the Loss or Gain from Realization account. The accountant debits this account for losses and credits it for gains. In this respect the account is comparable to the Cash Short and Over account discussed previously. The word *realization* refers to the sale of the assets for cash.

2. Allocation of loss or gain. The accountant closes the Loss or Gain from Realization account into the partners' capital accounts according to the profit and loss ratio. It must be closed as a separate account because it came into being after the regular closing entries had been recorded.

3. Payment of liabilities. The firm makes a final settlement with all creditors.

4. Distribution of remaining cash to the partners, in accordance with the balances of their capital accounts.

For example, in the partnership of Jacobs, King, and Lowell, the partners share profits and losses as follows: Jacobs, one-half; King, one-fourth; Lowell, one-fourth.

Let us now have a look at an abbreviated balance sheet for this firm.

Jacobs, King, and Lowell		
Balance Sheet		
June 30, 19___		
Assets		
Cash		10 000 00
Merchandise Inventory		20 000 00
Other Assets		40 000 00
Total Assets		70 000 00
Liabilities		
Accounts Payable		7 000 00
Owners' Equity		
R. C. Jacobs, Capital	27 000 00	
M. L. King, Capital	24 000 00	
C. C. Lowell, Capital	12 000 00	63 000 00
Total Liabilities and Owners' Equity		70 000 00

Assets are sold at a profit

Assume that the firm sells its merchandise inventory for $26,000, and the other assets for $48,000. Here are the journal entries to cover this.

	19—June	30	Cash	74 0 0 0 00		
1		30	Cash	74 0 0 0 00		1
2			Merchandise Inventory		20 0 0 0 00	2
3			Other Assets		40 0 0 0 00	3
4			Loss or Gain from Realization		14 0 0 0 00	4
5			Sold the assets at a gain			5
6						6
7		30	Loss or Gain from Realization	14 0 0 0 00		7
8			R. C. Jacobs, Capital		7 0 0 0 00	8
9			M. L. King, Capital		3 5 0 0 00	9
10			C. C. Lowell, Capital		3 5 0 0 00	10
11			To allocate the net gain to the partners'			11
12			capital accounts according to the profit			12
13			and loss ratio			13
14						14
15		30	Accounts Payable	7 0 0 0 00		15
16			Cash		7 0 0 0 00	16
17			To pay the claims of creditors			17
18						18
19		30	R. C. Jacobs, Capital	34 0 0 0 00		19
20			M. L. King, Capital	27 5 0 0 00		20
21			C. C. Lowell, Capital	15 5 0 0 00		21
22			Cash		77 0 0 0 00	22
23			To distribute the remaining cash to the			23
24			partners according to their account balances			24
25						25

The T accounts for the Cash and capital accounts look like this.

Cash					R. C. Jacobs, Capital			
	+		−			−		+
Bal.	10,000	(3)	7,000	(4)		34,000	Bal.	27,000
(1)	74,000	(4)	77,000				(2)	7,000

	M. L. King, Capital			
		−		+
(4)		27,500	Bal.	24,000
			(2)	3,500

	C. C. Lowell, Capital			
		−		+
(4)		15,500	Bal.	12,000
			(2)	3,500

Assets are sold at a loss: partners' capital accounts sufficient to absorb loss

Now suppose that Jacobs, King, and Lowell sell their merchandise inventory for only $16,000 and their other assets for $32,000. The journal entries would look like this.

	Date	Description	Debit	Credit
(1)	19— June 30	Cash	48 000 00	
		Loss or Gain from Realization	12 000 00	
		Merchandise Inventory		20 000 00
		Other Assets		40 000 00
		Sold the assets at a loss		
(2)	30	R. C. Jacobs, Capital	6 000 00	
		M. L. King, Capital	3 000 00	
		C. C. Lowell, Capital	3 000 00	
		Loss or Gain from Realization		12 000 00
		To allocate the net loss to the partners'		
		capital accounts according to the profit and		
		loss ratio		
(3)	30	Accounts Payable	7 000 00	
		Cash		7 000 00
		To pay the claims of creditors		
(4)	30	R. C. Jacobs, Capital	21 000 00	
		M. L. King, Capital	21 000 00	
		C. C. Lowell, Capital	9 000 00	
		Cash		51 000 00
		To distribute the remaining cash to the		
		partners according to their account balances		

The T accounts for the Cash and the capital accounts look like this.

Cash

	+		−
Bal.	10,000	(3)	7,000
(1)	48,000	(4)	51,000

R. C. Jacobs, Capital

	−		+
(2)	6,000	Bal.	27,000
(4)	21,000		

M. L. King, Capital

	−		+
(2)	3,000	Bal.	24,000
(4)	21,000		

C. C. Lowell, Capital

	−		+
(2)	3,000	Bal.	12,000
(4)	9,000		

Summary

A partnership is an association of two or more persons to carry on, as co-owners, a business for profit. Partnerships are used for professional and service enterprises as well as small merchandising and manufacturing firms. The main advantage of a partnership is that it makes possible the combining of people's abilities and investments to carry on a business. The main disadvantage is the unlimited liability assumed by each partner.

The accounting procedure for partnerships differs from that for sole proprietorships only in the owner's equity classification of accounts. Otherwise, partnerships have the same types of assets, liabilities, revenues, and expenses. On the income statement, after the net income is determined, the Division of Net Income section is added. The figures—representing the final allocations of net income to each partner—are used in the entry closing the Income Summary account into the capital accounts. The last step in the closing entries consists of closing each partner's drawing account into his or her capital account.

One can divide the net income for a partnership by any of the following methods (or a combination thereof): fractional-share basis, ratio of capital investments, salary allowances, and interest allowances.

A partnership ends whenever there is any change in the composition of its membership. The effect on the business may simply be a change in the members listed in the partnership agreement and in the capital accounts; or, at the other extreme, it may entail a breaking-up of the business. In the event of the death of one of the partners, the partnership agreement should provide for an immediate closing of the books and revaluation of the firm's assets.

Liquidation means going out of business, selling everything for cash, paying off liabilities in cash, and final withdrawals of partners' cash. The steps in the liquidation of a partnership are:

1. Sale of the assets for cash, using the Loss or Gain from Realization account.

2. Allocation of the Loss or Gain from Realization account to the partners' capital accounts.

3. Payment of liabilities.

4. Distribution of remaining cash to the partners.

Glossary

Co-ownership   A situation in which each party owns a fractional share of all the assets.

Dissolution   The ending of a partnership resulting from a change in the personnel of the membership, and the forming of a new partnership. The transition results primarily in changes in the capital accounts, with routine business being carried on as usual.

Distributive share   The share of the net income allocated to each partner.

General partner   One who has the right to take part in the management of a partnership and who has unlimited liability.

General partnership A partnership created for the conduct of a particular kind of business, such as a service, merchandising, or manufacturing business.

Limited partnership A partnership in which certain members contribute capital without assuming personal liability for the firm's debts beyond the amount of their investments.

Liquidation The ending of a partnership, involving the sale of the assets, payment of the liabilities, and distribution of the remaining cash to the partners.

Mutual agency Each partner may act as an agent of the firm, thereby committtting the entire firm to a binding contract.

Partnership An association of two or more persons to carry on, as co-owners, a business for profit.

Realization Conversion into cash, as happens in the case of the sale of assets.

Questions

1. What is meant by the concept of co-ownership of partnership property?

2. What do you consider to be the greatest advantage and the greatest disadvantage of the partnership form of business organization?

3. Is it possible for one partner to lose a greater amount than the amount of his or her investment in the partnership? Why?

4. Arno, Baker, and Collins are partners. Collins dies, and her daughter claims the right to take her mother's place in the partnership. Explain why Collins' daughter either does or does not have the right.

5. Rowe and Pound are considering forming a partnership. What do you consider to be the three most important factors to include in their partnership agreement?

6. How does a dissolution of a partnership differ from a liquidation of a partnership?

7. When assets other than cash are invested in a partnership by one of the partners, at what value are these assets recorded on the books of the partnership?

Exercises

Exercise 1 John Lodge, as his original investment in the firm of Lodge and Morris, contributes equipment that had been recorded on the books of his own business as costing $40,000, with accumulated depreciation of $26,000. The partners agree on a valuation of $18,000. They also agree to accept Lodge's Accounts Receivable of $20,000, collectible to the extent of 80%. Give the journal entry to record Lodge's investment in the partnership of Lodge and Morris.

Exercise 2 Stanfield, a partner in the firm of Reiman, Stanfield, and Taylor, sells her share in the partnership (capital balance of $36,000) to Brooks for $28,000. Assuming that Reiman and Taylor are willing to admit Brooks to the firm, give the entry on the firm's books to record the change in ownership. Does the withdrawal of Stanfield dissolve the firm?

Exercise 3 Adams and Bullock share profits and losses in the ratio of the balances of their capital accounts at the beginning of the year. The net income for a given year is $56,000, and the balances of the capital accounts for Adams and Bullock are $40,000 and $30,000, respectively. What is each partner's share of the net income?

Exercise 4 Newman is retiring from the partnership of Long, Martin, and Newman. The profit and loss ratio is 2:2:1. After the accountant has posted the revaluation and closing entries, the balances in the capital accounts are Long, $29,000; Martin, $24,000; and Newman, $14,000. Journalize the entries to record the retirement of Newman under each of the following unrelated assumptions.

a. Newman retires, taking $14,000 of partnership cash for her equity.

b. Newman retires, taking $16,000 of partnership cash for her equity.

Exercise 5 The partnership agreement of Abrams and Bower provides for salary allowances of $19,000 per year for Abrams and $17,000 per year for Bower. They share the remaining balances of net income on the basis of three-fifths for Abrams and two-fifths for Bower. Suppose that the net income amounts to $38,000; calculate the total share for each partner.

Exercise 6 Bauer is the senior partner of the partnership of Bauer, Chester, and Dawson. When Bauer dies, the firm's accountant conducts a revaluation of the assets. Research shows that the following assets are increased in value by these amounts: Merchandise Inventory, $22,000; Building, $62,000. The value of the asset Equipment is decreased by $6,000. Assuming that the partnership profit and loss ratio is 2:2:1, write the journal entry to show the revaluation of the assets prior to dissolution of the firm.

Exercise 7 Pearson and Quincy are partners who share profits and losses equally. The balances of their capital accounts are $60,000 and $80,000, respectively. When they liquidate their partnership, they sell the noncash assets and pay all their liabilities, leaving a balance of $94,000 in cash. What is the amount of the gain or loss on realization? How much cash should be distributed to each partner?

Exercise 8 The partners Gettman, Halley, and Ingram have a profit and loss ratio of 2:2:1. They decide to liquidate the firm and to sell off all their assets. After distribution of the firm's loss from realization, the credit balances of the capital accounts are as follows: Gettman, $62,000; Halley, $51,000; Ingraham, $57,000. The balance of Cash is $170,000. Write the entry the accountant would make on the books to record the distribution of cash.

Problems

Problem 22-1 The partnership of S. A. Dorsey, R. E. Elwell, and D. L. Ferguson has a net income of $92,850 for the current year. The balances in the capital accounts of the partners at the beginning of the year were $34,500, $39,000, and $48,000 respectively. At the end of the year the balances of the drawing accounts are $16,500, $19,800, and $18,000, respectively. The partnership agreement stipulates salary allowances as follows: Dorsey, $16,500; Elwell, $21,000, Ferguson, $18,000. The partnership agreement also allows interest of 10% on the balances of the capital accounts at the beginning of the year. The remainder (after salary and interest allowances) is divided equally among the three.

Instructions **1.** Prepare the section of the income statement for the current year which deals with division of net income.

2. Prepare the entries to record the closing of the firm's Income Summary and Drawing accounts.

3. Assuming a net income of $40,650, calculate the amount of the distributive share for each partner.

Problem 22-2 Donna Hess and Arta Downs, who are forming a partnership for an interior decorating business, plan to work full-time in the firm. Hess will make an initial investment of $30,000 and Downs, $45,000. They are considering the following plans for the division of net income.

a. Division in the same ratio as the balances of their capital accounts.

b. Interest of 10% on the balances of their capital accounts at the beginning of the year, and the remainder of the net income to be divided equally.

c. Salary allowances of $15,000 to Hess and $13,500, to Downs (according to value of services); interest of 8% on the balances of their capital accounts at the beginning of the year; and the remainder of the net income to be divided equally.

Instructions **1.** Using the form provided in the accounting stationery, record the distributive shares of net income for each of the partners, assuming (a) a net income of $45,000, and (b) a net income of $24,000.

2. Which plan is the fairest? Give reasons for your opinion.

Problem 22-3 Below and on page 618 are the account balances of Allman and Sharp as of December 31, the end of the current fiscal year, after adjusting entries have been posted.

Accounts Payable	$ 67,432
Accounts Receivable	53,438
Accumulated Depreciation, Equipment	45,380
Dennis A. Allman, Capital	60,000
Dennis A. Allman, Drawing	32,000
Allowance for Doubtful Accounts	1,842
Cash	3,658
Equipment	73,838
General Expenses (control)	14,646
Interest Expense	3,432
Merchandise Inventory	129,452
Notes Payable	20,000
Prepaid Insurance	720
Purchases	551,180

Purchases Discount	4,220	
Purchases Returns and Allowances	25,452	
Sales	700,490	
Sales Returns and Allowances	36,838	
Selling Expenses (control)	37,832	
Tracy C. Sharp, Capital	48,000	
Tracy C. Sharp, Drawing	24,000	

There were no changes in the partners' capital accounts during the year. The merchandise inventory at the beginning of the year was $141,234. The partnership agreement provides for salary allowances of $32,000 for Allman and $28,000 for Sharp and also stipulates an interest allowance of 9% on invested capital at the beginning of the year, with the remainder of the net income to be divided equally.

Instructions   **1.** Prepare an income statement for the year.

2. Prepare a statement of owner's equity for the year.

3. Prepare a classified balance sheet for the partnership at the end of the year.

Problem 22-4   The partnership of Lane, Morgan, and Shoemaker is to be liquidated as of April 30 of this year. The partners share profits and losses in the ratio of 2:2:1. The firm's post-closing trial balance looks like this.

Lane, Morgan, and Shoemaker		
Postclosing Trial Balance		
April 30, 19___		
Cash	53 7 4 0 00	
Merchandise Inventory	78 5 0 0 00	
Other Assets	60 6 0 0 00	
Accounts Payable		16 8 4 0 00
Marcia C. Lane, Capital		72 0 0 0 00
Rhoda A. Morgan, Capital		56 0 0 0 00
Ruth D. Shoemaker, Capital		48 0 0 0 00
	192 8 4 0 00	192 8 4 0 00

The firm's realization and liquidation transactions are as follows.

a. The merchandise inventory sold for $72,000, and the other assets sold for $56,000.

b. The accountant allocated the loss or gain from realization to the partners' capital acounts according to the profit and loss ratio.

c. The firm paid its creditors in full.

d. The firm distributed the remaining cash to the partners in accordance with the balances in their capital accounts.

Instructions   **1.** Record the balances in the selected ledger accounts.

2. Record the closing transactions in general journal form.

3. Post the entries to the ledger accounts.

Alternate problems

Problem 22-1A   The firm of C. C. Dobbs, L. E. Erickson, and M. C. Faris has a net income of $108,000 for this year. Balances in the capital accounts of the partners at the beginning of the year were $42,000, $46,500, and $54,000, respectively. At the end of the year, the balances of the drawing accounts are $21,000, $25,200, and $20,250, respectively. The partnership agreement stipulates salary allowances as follows: Dobbs, $21,000; Erickson, $25,500; Faris, $20,250. It also allows 10% interest on the balances of the partners' capital accounts at the beginning of the year. The remainder of the net income, after salary and interest allowances, is divided equally.

Instructions   **1.** Prepare the section of the income statement on the division of net income for the current year.

2. Prepare entries to close the firm's Income Summary and Drawing accounts.

3. Assuming that the net income of the firm is $45,000, calculate the amount of the distributive share for each partner.

Problem 22-2A   C. J. Sanders and D. L. Taylor, interior decorators, are forming a partnership. Both plan to work in the firm on a full-time basis. Sander's initial investment is $27,000, and Taylor's investment is $39,000. They are considering the following plans for the divison of net income.

a. Division in the same ratio as the balances of their capital accounts.

b. Interest of 9% on the balances of their capital accounts at the beginning of the year and the remainder of the net income to be divided equally.

c. Salary allowances of $18,000 to Sanders and $15,000 to Taylor (according to value of services), interest of 9% on the balances of their capital accounts at the beginning of the year, and the remainder of the net income to be divided equally.

Instructions   **1.** Using the form provided in the accounting stationery, record the distribution of net income for each of the partners, assuming (a) a net income of $33,000, and (b) a net income of $16,500.

2. Which plan is the fairest? Give reasons for your opinion.

Problem 22-3A The following are the account balances of Albertson and Smart as of December 31, the end of this fiscal year after adjusting entries have been posted.

Accounts Payable	$ 69,416
Accounts Receivable	58,964
Accumulated Depreciation, Equipment	46,820
Herman C. Albertson, Capital	64,000
Herman C. Albertson, Drawing	29,600
Allowance for Doubtful Accounts	2,148
Cash	3,742
Equipment	79,128
General Expenses (control)	14,212
Interest Expense	2,942
Merchandise Inventory	126,236
Notes Payable	16,000
Prepaid Insurance	690
Purchases	536,680
Purchases Discount	4,428
Purchases Returns and Allowances	25,690
Sales	684,836
Sales Returns and Allowances	35,872
Selling Expense (control)	35,562
Marilyn R. Smart, Capital	52,000
Marilyn R. Smart, Drawing	28,800

The merchandise inventory at the beginning of the year was $139,146, and there were no changes in the partners' capital accounts during the year. The partnership agreement provides for salary allowances of $31,200 for Albertson and $28,800 for Smart, and interest of 10% on invested capital at the beginning of the year, with the remainder of the net income to be divided equally.

Instructions

1. Prepare an income statement for the year.

2. Prepare a statement of owners' equity for the year.

3. Prepare a classified balance sheet at the end of the year.

Problem 22-4A The partnership of Lane, Morgan, and Shoemaker is to be liquidated as of September 30 of this year. The partners share profits and losses in the ratio of 2:2:1. The firm's post-closing trial balance is on the facing page.

The firm's realization and liquidation transactions are listed below and on page 622.

a. The merchandise inventory sold for $64,000, and the other assets sold for $48,000.

Cash	37	4	0	0	00											
Merchandise Inventory	67	2	4	0	00											
Other Assets	48	1	6	0	00											
Accounts Payable							15	7	2	0	00					
Marcia C. Lane, Capital							53	8	0	0	00					
Rhoda A. Morgan, Capital							43	6	8	0	00					
Ruth D. Shoemaker, Capital							39	6	0	0	00					
	152	8	0	0	00		152	8	0	0	00					

b. The accountant allocated the loss or gain from realization to the partners' capital accounts according to the profit and loss ratio.

c. The firm paid its creditors in full.

d. The firm distributed the remaining cash to the partners in accordance with the balances in their capital accounts.

Instructions   **1.** Record the balances in the selected ledger accounts.

2. Record the closing transactions in general journal form.

3. Post the entries to the ledger accounts.

23 Corporations: organization and capital stock

objectives

After you have completed this chapter, you will be able to do the following:
- Define a corporation.
- List at least two advantages and two disadvantages of a corporation.
- Journalize entries for the issuance of par-value stock.
- Journalize entries for the issuance of no-par stock.
- Journalize entries for the sale of stock on the basis of subscriptions.
- Prepare a balance sheet for a corporation, including Subscriptions Receivable, Organization Costs, Paid-in Capital accounts, and Retained Earnings.

THE THREE forms of business organizations are sole proprietorships, partnerships, and corporations. Although corporations are fewer in number, they account for more business transactions than the other two combined. Frequently a firm begins as a sole proprietorship or a partnership, and as it grows and prospers, it needs more investment capital. As a means of raising additional investment capital, the firm incorporates. In other cases, businesses are organized as corporations at the outset. Because of the predominance of corporations, everyone entering the business world should be familiar with the corporate form of organization, and its financial structure. We shall be dealing with profit corporations which issue stock and carry out business activities for the purpose of making profits and distributing the profits to their owners. Nonprofit corporations are those which do not issue stock or distribute profits, but carry out activities for charitable, educational, or other philanthropic purposes.

Definition of a corporation

In 1818 Chief Justice John Marshall defined a corporation as "an artificial being, invisible, intangible, and existing only in contemplation of the law."

A corporation indeed does act as an artificial legal being, deriving its existence from its charter. In every respect it is a separate legal entity, having a continuous existence apart from that of its owners, the stockholders. As an entity, a corporation may own property, enter into contracts, sue in the courts, be sued, and so forth.

Advantages of the corporate form

The corporation offers a number of advantages over the sole proprietorship and the partnership.

1. Limited liability. As a separate legal entity, a corporation is responsible for its own debts. All that a stockholder can lose is the amount of his or her investment. Since the stockholders are the owners, this is the most important advantage. On the other hand, the owners of sole proprietorships and partnerships are personally liable for the entire debts of the business.

2. Ease of raising capital. A corporation can accumulate greater amounts of investment capital than a sole proprietorship or partnership, because a corporation can sell stock. Some corporations have more than 1,000,000 stockholders. Sole proprietorships and partnerships are limited to the wealth of the few individual owners.

3. Ease of transferring ownership rights. Ownership rights in a corporation are represented by shares of stock, which can readily be transferred from one person to another without the permission of other stockholders. (Compare this with a partnership, in which the other partners have to give permission for changes in ownership in order for the business to continue.)

4. Continuous existence. The length of life of a corporation is stipulated in its charter; when the charter expires, it may be renewed. The death, incapacity, or withdrawal of an owner does not affect the life of a corporation, but such a circumstance would cause a partnership to be dissolved or liquidated.

5. No mutual agency. Stockholders do not have the power to bind the corporation to contracts, unless a given stockholder is an officer. Since owners need not participate in management, the corporation is free to employ the managerial talent it believes best to accomplish its objectives.

Disadvantages of the corporate form

The corporation also has a number of disadvantages.

1. Additional taxation. In addition to the usual property and payroll taxes, corporations must pay income taxes and charter fees. Since corporations are separate legal entities, they pay federal and state income taxes in their own names. Part of the corporation's net income goes to the stockholders in the form of dividends; this money is personal income to the stockholders, and consequently the stockholders have to pay personal income taxes on it. This is known as the *double taxation* of corporations, which represents their greatest disadvantage.

Charter fees (which are fees paid for the right of the corporation to exist) may be considered additional taxes, because they are paid to a state in return for the issuance of a charter.

2. Government regulation. Since states create corporations by granting charters, states can exercise closer control and supervision over corporations than over sole proprietorships and partnerships. States often regulate even the amount of net income that a corporation may retain, the extent to which it may buy back its own stock, and the amount of real estate it may own. By contrast, sole proprietorships need only have legal purposes; states impose no further regulations.

Forming a corporation

To organize a corporation, a person or persons must submit an application for a charter to the appropriate state official (corporation commissioner or secretary of state) of the state in which the company is to be incorporated. The application is called the *articles of incorporation*. Generally the application for the charter must at least include the several points of information listed at the top of the following page.

- Name and address of the corporation
- Nature of the business to be conducted
- Amount and description of the capital stock to be issued
- Names and addresses of the subscribers and the amount of stock subscribed by each
- Names of the promoters (or temporary officers) who will serve until the first meeting of the stockholders is held.

The application must be signed by three of the promoters. The articles of incorporation must be accompanied by a charter fee, based on the dollar amount of maximum stock investment, which is called the *authorized capital.*

When the state officials approve the articles of incorporation, these articles become the charter of the corporation. Shortly after receiving the charter, the stock subscribers hold an initial meeting, in order to elect an acting board of directors and formulate by-laws. The charter plus the by-laws provide the basic rules for conducting the corporation's affairs. Next, the directors meet to appoint officers to serve as active managers of the business. Then the corporation issues *capital stock certificates* to the subscribers who have paid in full. Since stockholders have now come into existence, at this point the stockholders elect a permanent board of directors.

The size of the corporation may vary as to number of stockholders and amounts of investment. It may be a small corporation with only three owners and a minimum investment of $1,000; or it may be a giant corporation, consisting of more than 1,000,000 owners, with an investment amounting to more than a billion dollars. In the small corporation, the three stockholders may also be the directors and officers. A corporation whose ownership is confined to a small group of stockholders is called a *close corporation.* A corporation whose ownership is widely distributed to a large number of stockholders is called an *open or public corporation.*

Organization costs

Let us suppose that a new corporation is forming, starting from scratch, and the organizers call in an accountant to set up the books. The accountant debits the costs of organizing the corporation—such as fees paid to the state, attorneys' fees, promotional costs, travel outlays, costs of printing stock certificates, and so on—to an account entitled Organization Costs. This account is classified as an *intangible asset.* The Intangible Assets account appears on the balance sheet as a separate category, below Plant and Equipment. The account, Organization Costs, is like a prepaid expense account, such as Prepaid Insurance, in that it will eventually be written off as an adjusting entry over a period of years. Organization costs are paid only once, although they benefit the corporation during its entire life; so it seems unfair to list them entirely as expenses of the first year. Income tax laws allow a company to write off its organization costs over a period of 5 years or more. The adjusting entry is a debit to Organization Cost Expense or Miscellaneous General Expense and a credit to Organization Costs.

Stock certificate book

One necessary element of organization costs is the printing of stock certificates. In a small corporation the certificates often have stubs attached, and certificates and stubs are bound in a stock certificate book, rather like a checkbook. The corporation issues the stock certificates only when the stockholder has paid for them in full. Each blank certificate must have written on it the name of the owner, the number of shares issued, and the date of issuance. The stub must show the name and address of the stockholder, the number of shares listed on the stock certificate, and the date of issuance. Both certificates and stubs are numbered consecutively.

When a transfer of ownership takes place, the stockholder surrenders the stock certificate to the corporation, and the corporation cancels it; the corporation also cancels the matching stub, and issues one or more new certificates in the place of these documents. This procedure enables the corporation to maintain an up-to-date record of the name of each stockholder and the number of shares owned by each. A corporation needs this information during the year, when it comes to paying out dividends.

The law requires large corporations whose stocks are listed on major stock exchanges to have independent registrars and transfer agents maintain their records of stock ownership. Banks and trust companies perform this service.

Structure of a corporation

The stockholders are the owners of the corporation; they delegate authority to the board of directors, which manages the corporation's affairs. (Generally the directors are also stockholders, although this is not always so.) The board of directors, in turn, delegates authority to the officers, who do the actual work of running the business. The officers themselves may also be members of the board of directors.

Dividends are the share of the corporation's earnings distributed to stockholders. The sources of dividends are the current year's net income after income taxes and the retained earnings of prior years.

Suppose the corporation issues some new stock. Each original stockholder then has the right to subscribe to additional shares, in proportion to his or her present holding. This is known as *preemptive right.* For example, assume that the corporation's new issue consists of 1,000 shares. The present amount of stock outstanding is 10,000 shares, of which Alice Brown owns 2,000. Her proportion of stock held to stock outstanding is one-fifth (2,000/10,000). Therefore she has the right to subscribe to 200 shares (one-fifth of 1,000 shares) of the new issue.

Stockholders' equity

The owner's equity in a corporation is called *stockholders' equity,* or *capital.* Just as in sole proprietorships and partnerships, the equity of the owners represents the excess of assets over liabilities. Of the five major classifications of accounts, the main difference with corporations occurs in the Stockholders' Equity classification, in which capital stock accounts replace owners' capital accounts, and Retained Earnings is used to record earnings plowed back into the business.

The following T accounts compare accounts for a sole proprietorship versus those for a corporation.

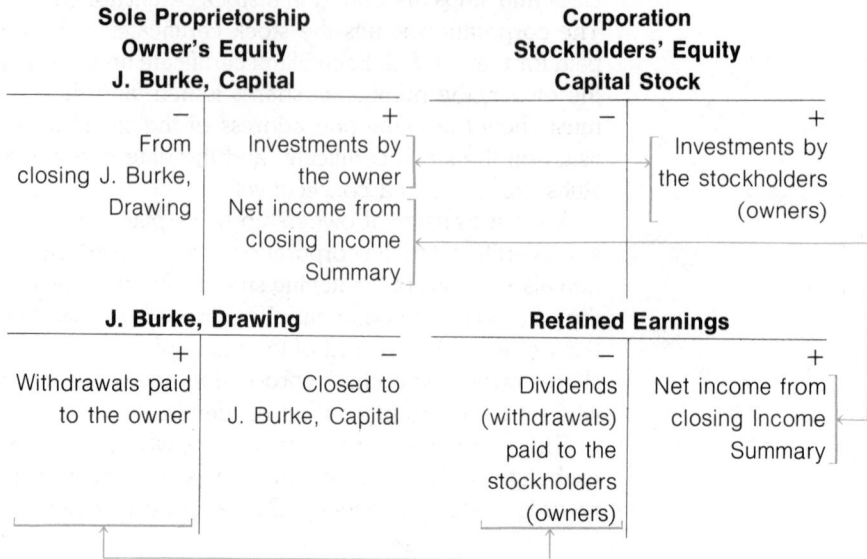

Balance of the capital account = Total of the balances of the capital stock and retained earnings accounts

Capital stock

Capital stock refers to shares of ownership in a corporation. *Authorized capital stock* is the maximum number of shares designated in the charter. *Issued* refers to the shares apportioned out to the stockholders. Stock that is actually in the hands of stockholders is called *outstanding stock*. Occasionally, a corporation may reacquire some of the stock it has issued by buying back its own stock or by receiving it as a donation from someone. This reacquired stock is known as *treasury stock;* consequently the number of shares that have been issued may differ from the number of shares outstanding. A more complete discussion of treasury stock is presented in Appendix B.

Classes of capital stock

In order to appeal to as many investors as possible, a corporation may issue more than one kind of stock, just as a manufacturer of refrigerators, say, makes different models in order to please different groups of potential buyers. The two main types of stock are *common* and *preferred*. Each type may have a variety of characteristics. Some may be *par-value stock,* in which a uniform face value of each share is printed on the stock certificates. Or some may be *no-par stock,* in which no value is printed on the stock certificates.

Common stock

When a corporation issues only one type of stock, it is called common stock, and may be either par or no-par stock. Holders of common stock have all the rights listed above, with voting privilege of one vote for each share of stock.

Preferred stock   Preferred stock is generally par-value stock, and is preferred in two ways: (1) the corporation pays dividends on preferred stock before it pays them on common stock, and (2) it pays them at a uniform rate. The dividend on preferred stock consists of a percentage of the par value of the stock. In the event that the corporation is liquidated, holders of preferred stock get paid off before holders of common stock. In most circumstances, however, holders of preferred stock do not have voting privileges. There are several specific types of preferred stock, so let's discuss each of them briefly.

Cumulative and noncumulative preferred stock   Suppose that a corporation has a bad year, and finds that it is not able to pay the dividend on its preferred stock. In this case the dividend is said to be *passed*. Stockholders who own *cumulative preferred stock* get to accumulate the dividends passed in former years (that is, the dividends in arrears). The corporation has to pay these dividends in full before it can pay any amount of dividends to common stockholders. If stockholders own *noncumulative preferred stock,* their dividends in arrears do not accumulate. In other words, if the corporation passes dividends once, they are gone forever. Since preferred stockholders naturally want a regular dividend, most preferred stock is cumulative.

Participating and nonparticipating preferred stock   Recall that the dividend on preferred stock consists of an established percentage of the par value of that stock. Some preferred stock, however, provides for the possibility of dividends in excess of this established amount; this kind of preferred stock is called *participating preferred stock*. Holders of participating preferred stock first get the regular dividend that is due them. Then the corporation allocates a stipulated amount to holders of its common stock. And *then* the stockholders who own participating preferred stock are allowed to participate or share in the extra earnings, which are distributed as cash dividends. The dividends of *nonparticipating preferred stock,* on the other hand, are limited to the regular rate. Most preferred stock is nonparticipating.

Issuing stock   Stock is issued when the buyer has paid for it in full or when the corporation has received noncash assets in exchange for its stock. Let us first discuss the issuance of par-value stock and then the issuance of no-par stock. [*Note:* A corporation may issue par-value stock at a figure equal to, above, or below its par value.]

Issuing stock at par for cash   There is a separate ledger account for each class of stock. The accountant records investments of cash as debits to Cash and credits to the stock accounts for the total amount of the par value. Later we shall deal with sales of stock in which the cash received is greater than or less than the par value of the shares issued. Remember that par value is the face value printed on each stock certificate. This designation of par value is a convenient means of dividing the corporation's capital into units, with the ownership of each unit known.

For example, the Dolliver Corporation is organized on July 16 with an authorized capital of 4,000 shares of $100-par preferred stock and 20,000 shares of $50-par common stock. On August 1 Dolliver issues 1,000 shares of preferred 8% stock at par and 10,000 shares of common stock at par. In general journal form, the entry looks like this.

	DATE		DESCRIPTION	POST REF.	DEBIT	CREDIT	
1	19— Aug.	1	Cash		600 000 00		1
2			Preferred 8% Stock			100 000 00	2
3			Common Stock			500 000 00	3
4			Issued 1,000 shares of preferred 8% stock at				4
5			par and 10,000 shares of common stock at par				5
6							6
7							7

GENERAL JOURNAL — PAGE 1

According to T accounts, the situation looks like this.

Cash		Preferred 8% Stock		Common Stock	
+	−	−	+	−	+
Aug. 1 600,000			Aug. 1 100,000		Aug. 1 500,000

The capital stock accounts (Preferred 8% Stock and Common Stock) are controlling accounts. The subsidiary ledger may consist of the stock certificate book, or it may be a supplementary record showing the name and address of each stockholder and the number of shares owned. This is known as a *stockholders' ledger*.

Issuing stock at par for noncash assets

Corporations often accept assets other than cash in exchange for their stock. The Dolliver Corporation received equipment, a building, and land from stockholders, in exchange for common stock, as we see below.

	DATE		DESCRIPTION	DEBIT	CREDIT	
1	Aug.	1	Equipment	6 000 00		1
2			Building	50 000 00		2
3			Land	10 000 00		3
4			Common Stock		66 000 00	4
5			Exchanged 1,320 shares of common stock			5
6			for equipment, building, and land			6
7						7
8						8

When a corporation accepts an asset other than cash, the accountant records the asset at its fair market value, in order to present an accurate balance sheet and have a realistic base on which to calculate future depreciation.

Now let's take the case of a corporation which gives shares of its stock to its promoters or organizers in exchange for their services in organizing the corporation. In this instance, the corporation receives the intangible asset, Organization Costs. Suppose that the Dolliver Corporation issues 100 shares of common stock to its organizers. The accountant handles it this way.

Aug.	1	*Organization Costs*		5 0 0 0 00			
		Common Stock			5 0 0 0 00		
		Issued 100 shares to the promoters in					
		exchange for their services in organizing					
		the corporation					

Issuing stock at a premium or discount

A newly organized corporation, such as the Dolliver Corporation, generally issues its stock at par. However, after the business has been operating for awhile, the directors may realize that they need additional investment capital. Perhaps the business has been so successful that they want to expand it. Or perhaps they need to cover losses suffered during the early years of the business. So the directors decide to issue some new stock. The present market price of the original stock affects the price they can secure for the new shares. The market price of the stock of a corporation is usually influenced by the following factors.

1. The earnings record, financial condition, and dividend record of the corporation

2. The potential for growth in earnings of the corporation

3. The supply of and demand for the money for investment purposes in the money market as a whole

4. General business conditions and prospects for the future

When a corporation issues stock at a price above par value, the stock is said to be issued at a *premium;* the premium is the amount by which the selling price of the new stock exceeds the par value. This premium price may be due to the fact that the corporation has been performing successfully in the past and has good prospects for growth in earnings in the future. Conversely, when a corporation sells its stock at a price below par value, the stock is said to be issued at a *discount;* the discount is the amount by which the selling price of the new stock falls below the par value. This discount price of stock may be due to the fact that the corporation incurred losses during its early period, or perhaps its prospects for the future are not too promising.

Premium on stock

When a corporation issues stock at a price *above* its par value, the accountant debits Cash or other noncash assets for the amount received, credits the stock account for the par value, and credits a premium account for the difference between the amount received and the par value.

Let's take an example. The Farragut Corporation issues 500 shares of $100-par preferred 9% stock at $103. In general journal form, the entry looks like this.

Cash		51 5 0 0 00	
Preferred 9% Stock			50 0 0 0 00
Premium on Preferred 9% Stock			1 5 0 0 00
Issued 500 shares at $103 per share			

According to T accounts, the entry looks like this.

Cash		Preferred 9% Stock		Premium on Preferred 9% Stock	
+	–	–	+	–	+
51,500			50,000		1,500
(500 shares			(500 shares		(500 shares
× $103 each)			× $100 each)		× $3 each)

In the case of par-value stock, the stock account contains only the total par value of the stock issued. One reason that buyers are willing to pay a premium for Farragut's 9% preferred stock is that the 9% rate may be higher than the current market rate for the same type of stock. For example, the rate of dividend on other stocks of companies having a comparable financial condition may be 8%.

Discount on stock

When a corporation issues stock at a price *below its par value,* the accountant debits Cash or other assets for the amount received, credits the stock account for the par value, and debits a discount account for the difference between the amount received and the par value.

Suppose that the Farragut Corporation issues 4,000 shares of $20-par common stock at $19. In general journal form, the entry is as follows.

Cash		76 0 0 0 00	
Discount on Common Stock		4 0 0 0 00	
Common Stock			80 0 0 0 00
Issued 4,000 shares at $19 per share			

According to T accounts, the entry looks like this.

Cash		Common Stock		Discount on Common Stock	
+	–	–	+	+	–
76,000			80,000	4,000	
(4,000 shares			(4,000 shares	(4,000 shares	
× $19 each)			× $20 each)	× $1 each)	

Again, as in the case of par-value stock, the accountant records in the stock account the total *par* value of the stock issued and treats the discount on the stock as a deduction from stockholders' equity, so it is a contra account.

The total par value of a corporation's stock represents its legal capital. In some states, the stockholders have a contingent liability for the amount of the discount, because the amount they paid for the stock does not cover the legal capital. Other states do not permit corporations to issue stock at a discount.

We use the fundamental accounting equation to review the placement of the accounts presented thus far.

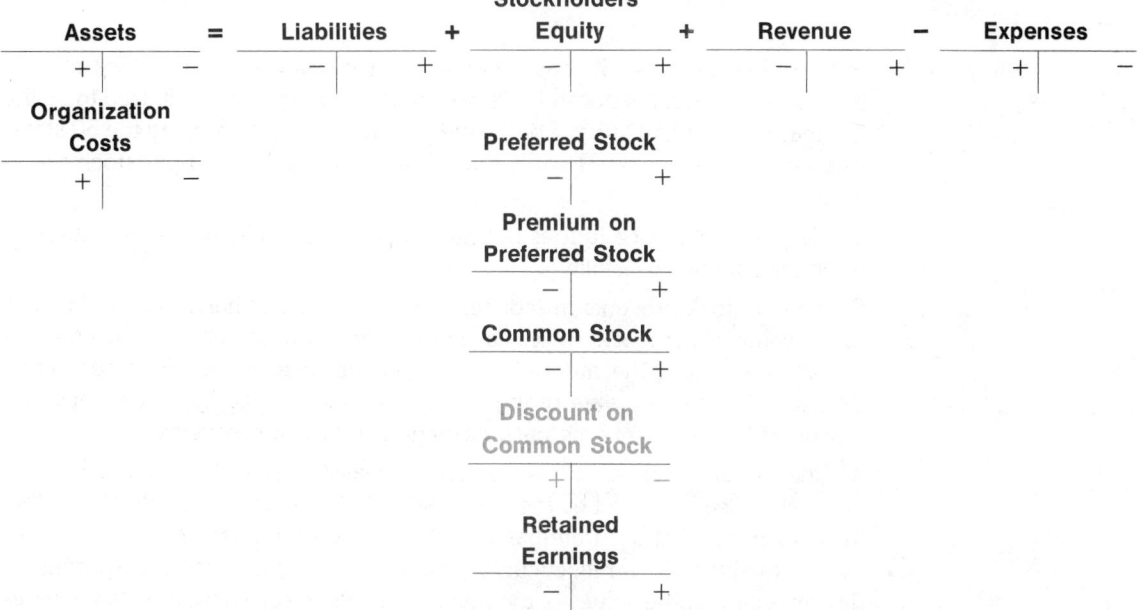

The Stockholder's Equity section of the balance sheet of the Farragut Corporation, showing the stock accounts, as well as the premium and discount accounts, would appear as shown here.

Stockholders' Equity				
Paid-in Capital				
Preferred 8% Stock,				
cumulative, $100 par (1,000 shares authorized,				
500 shares issued)	50 0 0 0 00			
Premium on Preferred 8% Stock	1 5 0 0 00	51 5 0 0 00		
Common Stock, $20 par				
(10,000 shares authorized, 4,000 shares issued)	80 0 0 0 00			
Less Discount on Common Stock	4 0 0 0 00	76 0 0 0 00		
Total Paid-in Capital		127 5 0 0 00		
Retained Earnings		45 0 0 0 00		
Total Stockholders' Equity			172 5 0 0 00	

Notice that the listing of the stock states the par value, the number of shares authorized, and the number of shares issued. The record also describes preferred stock as cumulative and participating; if the stock is noncumulative or nonparticipating, then the record doesn't mention the fact. This means that preferred stock is assumed to be noncumulative and nonparticipating, unless otherwise stated. Paid-in Capital is a main caption under Stockholders' Equity. Preferred stock, and related premium or discount accounts, are always listed before common stock. A corporation could also issue preferred stock at a discount and common stock at a premium.

No-par stock Preferred stock generally has a par value. However, common stock may or may not have one; if it doesn't, it is referred to as *no-par stock*. It used to be the law that all stock had to have par value. Today, corporations in all the 50 states can issue no-par stock. The main advantages claimed for no-par stock are as follows.

1. No-par stock, since it does not have a par value, may be issued without a discount contingent liability.

2. No-par stock prevents misconception on the part of naïve stockholders as to the value of the stock. In the case of par stock, investors might believe that the stock is worth the amount printed on the face of the stock certificate. Actually, the market value of the stock may differ markedly, due to ups and downs of the corporation's past earnings and future prospects.

3. The use of no-par stock results in more realistic values being placed on the noncash assets acquired by the corporation in exchange for stock. Recall that in order to present accurate balance sheets, the accountant records noncash assets at values which reflect current market prices. However, a corporation's directors can set the values of the noncash assets in such a way that sometimes balance sheets can carry distorted values. Stocks reported at such distorted values are referred to as *watered stocks*. The use of no-par stocks greatly reduces the possibility of distortions.

Stated value and no-par stock We have said that when all of a company's stock is of the par-value type, the par value of the shares represents the company's legal capital, which stockholders cannot withdraw. This law protects creditors. When various state legislatures passed laws permitting corporations to issue no-par stock, they tried to continue to protect creditors by stipulating that all or part of the amount the corporation receives for its no-par shares be exempt from withdrawal by stockholders, an amount known as the stock's *stated value*. The minimum stated value per share of no-par stock varies from state to state. In addition, in some states the board of directors of the corporation, if it wishes, may choose a stated value for the company's no-par stock that is higher than the minimum required by the state law.

Established amount of stated value

Augusta Modern Homes is located in a state that allows the board of directors of a corporation to designate a stated value for its stock. Accordingly, the board of directors of Augusta Modern Homes chooses a stated value of $25 per share for its common stock. On June 20, Augusta issues 1,000 shares at $28 per share, receiving cash. On September 10, it issues 1,000 shares at $30 per share, receiving cash. The accountant uses the account entitled Paid-in Capital in Excess of Stated Value to record the amounts of the excess over stated value.

The accountant's entries, in general journal form, are as follows.

19— June	20	Cash		28 000 00	
		Common Stock			25 000 00
		Paid-in Capital in Excess of Stated Value			3 000 00
		Issued 1,000 shares at $28 per share			

19— Sep.	10	Cash		30 000 00	
		Common stock			25 000 00
		Paid-in Capital in Excess of Stated Value			5 000 00
		Issued 1,000 shares at $30 per share			

According to T accounts, the entries look like this.

Cash			Common Stock			Paid-in Capital in Excess of Stated Value	
+	−		−	+		−	+
June 20 28,000				June 20 25,000			June 20 3,000
Sept. 10 30,000				(total stated)			(excess)
				Sept. 10 25,000			Sept. 10 5,000
				(total stated)			(excess)

Now let's compare the accounting for no-par stock with a stated value and the accounting for par stock: When a firm issues no-par stock with a stated value, the accountant substitutes the Paid-in Capital in Excess of Stated Value account for the premium account used for par-value stock. Although the pattern is similar, there is a definite distinction between par value and stated value. The corporation's charter stipulates the par value of its stock, and the corporation can change this value only with the approval of the state. On the other hand, the board of directors of a corporation can change the stated value of no-par stock by passing a resolution. In our problems involving no-par stock, however, we shall assume that there is an established stated value, as in our previous sample entries.

Some states have laws that require the entire proceeds from the issuance of no-par stock to be treated as stated value. This means that whatever the corporation gets for the stock, the accountant credits the amount to the stock account.

For example, on April 30 the Morrow Corporation issued 1,000 shares of no-par stock at $49 per share; on May 10 it issued an additional 1,000 shares at $51 per share. Morrow's accountant made the following entries in the general journal.

1	19— Apr.	30	Cash		49 0 0 0 00	
2			Common Stock			49 0 0 0 00
3			Issued 1,000 shares of no-par stock			
4						
5	May	10	Cash		51 0 0 0 00	
6			Common Stock			51 0 0 0 00
7			Issued 1,000 shares of no-par stock			

We've been talking about corporations that issue stock for which investors pay in full, either by giving cash or by giving noncash assets or promotional services. However, a corporation often sells its stock directly to investors on a subscription contract (installment) basis. This means that the investor enters into a contract with the corporation, promising to pay at a later date for a specified number of shares at an agreed price. The corporation agrees to issue the shares when the investor has finished paying for them in full.

The accountant records the amount of the subscription in the Subscriptions Receivable account, a current asset, and credits the par value or stated value of the stock to Stock Subscribed, a stockholders' equity account. The accountant then records the difference between the subscription price and the par value under either premium or discount, and the difference between the subscription price and the stated value under Paid-in Capital in Excess of Stated Value.

As the investor sends in payments, the accountant records them as debits to Cash and credits to Subscriptions Receivable. When the investor finishes paying for all the shares in full, the accountant records the issuance of the stock as a debit to Stock Subscribed and a credit to Common Stock or Preferred Stock. When corporations have investors who want subscriptions to both common and preferred stock, then the accountant uses separate accounts for each. We can best illustrate with some examples.

Subscription transactions: no-par stock The Reikert Manufacturing Corporation, a newly organized company, sets up its books with the following transactions involving its own stock.

May 1 Received subscriptions to 10,000 shares of common stock (stated value $10 per share) from various subscribers at $16 per share, with a downpayment of 50% of the subscription price.

June 1 Received an additional 30% of the subscription price from all subscribers.

July 1 Received an additional 20% of the subscription price from all subscribers; then issued the stock.

The general journal looks like this. The items in parentheses are just explanations.

	19—May	1	Subscriptions Receivable, Common Stock (10,000		
1			shares at $16 per share)	160 0 0 0 00	
2			Common Stock Subscribed		
3			(10,000 shares at $10 per share)		100 0 0 0 00
4			Paid-in Capital in Excess of Stated Value		
5			($160,000 − $100,000)		60 0 0 0 00
6			Received subscriptions to 10,000 shares at		
7			$16 per share		
8					
9		1	Cash (10,000 shares × $16 per share × .5)	80 0 0 0 00	
10			Subscriptions Receivable, Common Stock		80 0 0 0 00
11			Received 50% of the subscription of May 1		
12			on 10,000 shares		
13					
14	Jun.	1	Cash (10,000 shares × $16 per share × .3)	48 0 0 0 00	
15			Subscriptions Receivable, Common Stock		48 0 0 0 00
16			Received 30% of the subscription of May 1		
17			on 10,000 shares		
18					
19	Jul.	1	Cash (10,000 shares × $16 per share × .2)	32 0 0 0 00	
20			Subscriptions Receivable, Common Stock		32 0 0 0 00
21			Received 20% of the subscription of May 1		
22			on 10,000 shares		
23					
24		1	Common Stock Subscribed	100 0 0 0 00	
25			Common Stock (10,000 shares × $10 per share)		100 0 0 0 00
26			Issued 10,000 shares		

After the accountant has posted these transactions, the T accounts look like those shown at the top of the next page.

Cash

	+		−
May 1	80,000		
June 1	48,000		
July 1	32,000		

Common Stock

	−		+
		July 1	100,000
			(10,000 shares)

Subscriptions Receivable, Common Stock

	+		−
May 1	160,000	May 1	80,000
		June 1	48,000
		July 1	32,000

Common Stock Subscribed

	−		+
July 1	100,000	May 1	100,000
			(10,000 shares)

Paid-In Capital In Excess of Stated Value

	−		+
		May 1	60,000

Common Stock Subscribed represents the total par value or stated value of the shares subscribed. The accountant may consider it as a temporary account to handle shares which have been subscribed for, but not yet paid for in full. When the investors finish paying for all the shares, the accountant records the issuing of the stock by debiting the Stock Subscribed account and crediting the Stock account.

Subscription transactions: par-value stock The Fidelity Service Corporation, a newly organized company, has the following transactions involving its own stock.

June 15 Received subscriptions to 2,000 shares of preferred 9% stock ($100 par value) from various subscribers at $103 per share, with a down-payment of 40% of the subscription price.

July 1 Received 30% of the subscription price from all subscribers (2,000 shares).

July 15 Received 30% of the subscription price from subscribers to 500 shares, and issued 500 shares.

The general journal looks as follows. The items in parentheses are explanations.

	19— Jun.	15	Subscriptions Receivable, Preferred 9% Stock			
1						1
2			(2,000 shares at $103 per share)	206 0 0 0 00		2
3			Preferred 9% Stock Subscribed (2,000 shares at			3
4			$100 per share)		200 0 0 0 00	4
5			Premium on Preferred 9% Stock		6 0 0 0 00	5
6			Received subscription to 2,000 shares at			6
7			$103 per share			7
8						8
9		15	Cash (2,000 shares × $103 per share × .4)	82 4 0 0 00		9
10			Subscriptions Receivable, Preferred 9% Stock		82 4 0 0 00	10
11			Received 40% of the subscription of June 15			11
12			on 2,000 shares			12
13						13

14	Jul.	1	Cash (2,000 shares × $103 × .3)		61 8 0 0 00			14
15			Subscriptions Receivable, Preferred 9% Stock			61 8 0 0 00		15
16			Received 30% of the subscription of June 15					16
17			on 2,000 shares					17
18								18
19		15	Cash (500 shares × $103 per share × .3)		15 4 5 0 00			19
20			Subscriptions Receivable, Preferred 9% Stock			15 4 5 0 00		20
21			Received 30%, the final installment of the					21
22			subscription of June 15, on 500 shares					22
23								23
24		15	Preferred 9% Stock Subscribed		50 0 0 0 00			24
25			Preferred 9% Stock (500 shares × $100			50 0 0 0 00		25
26			per share)					26
27			Issued 500 shares					27
28								28
29								29
30								30
31								31
32								32

All this goes to show that Preferred 9% Stock Subscribed represents the total par value of the shares subscribed. It also points up the fact that a firm does not issue stock until the investor has paid for it in full. Since only 500 shares were paid for in full, the firm issued only 500 shares.

Controlling accounts and subsidiary ledgers

Because investors may finish paying for subscriptions at varying times, and because a firm issues stock only when the individual subscriber has paid in full, the firm's accountant has to maintain an account for each individual subscriber. As a result, the books exhibit the following relationships between controlling accounts and subsidiary ledgers.

Controlling Account	Subsidiary Ledger
Subscriptions Receivable, Preferred 9% Stock	Preferred 9% Stock Subscribers' ledger
Subscriptions Receivable, Common Stock	Common Stock Subscribers' ledger

These records are similar to the Accounts Receivable controlling account and the accounts receivable ledger.

The firm's accountant also has to keep an accurate record of the number of shares owned by each stockholder. Consequently, each stock account is a controlling account.

Controlling Account	Subsidiary Ledger
Preferred 9% Stock	Preferred 9% Stockholders' ledger
Common Stock	Common Stockholders' ledger

As we have said, a small corporation may use its stock certificate book as a subsidiary ledger. Naturally, the accountant must see to it that the information is complete, so that the company can declare and pay dividends correctly. Cash dividends are paid on outstanding stock only.

Illustration of a corporation balance sheet

In order to reinforce your understanding of the placement of the accounts introduced in this chapter, examine the balance sheet illustrated here. Because it covers so many of the concepts just discussed, you'll probably want to refer back to it in the future.

```
                          City Center Service
                             Balance Sheet
                             June 30, 19--

                                 Assets

Current Assets:
  Cash..................................................    $ 27,000.00
  Notes Receivable......................................      50,000.00
  Accounts Receivable...................  $419,000.00
    Less Allowance for Doubtful Accounts.    12,000.00     407,000.00
  Subscriptions Receivable, Preferred 9% Stock........      14,000.00
  Subscriptions Receivable, Common Stock.............       30,000.00
  Merchandise Inventory..............................      279,000.00
  Supplies...........................................        3,000.00
  Prepaid Insurance..................................          500.00
    Total Current Assets.............................                  $810,500.00
Plant and Equipment:
  Delivery Equipment.................................  $ 60,000.00
    Less Accumulated Depreciation....................    40,000.00   $ 20,000.00
  Store Equipment....................................  $ 82,000.00
    Less Accumulated Depreciation....................    19,000.00     63,000.00
    Total Plant and Equipment........................                    83,000.00
Investments:
  Friedman Equipment Company 8% Bonds................                    16,000.00
Intangible Assets:
  Organization Costs.................................                     8,000.00
Total Assets                                                          $917,500.00

                                Liabilities

Current Liabilities:
  Notes Payable......................................  $ 20,000.00
  Accounts Payable...................................    281,500.00
  Salaries Payable...................................      3,000.00
  Interest Payable...................................      1,000.00
Total Liabilities                                                     $305,500.00

                           Stockholders' Equity

Paid-in Capital:
  Preferred 7% Stock, $50 par (2,000 shares
    authorized and issued)...........................  $100,000.00
  Less Discount on Preferred 7% Stock................     1,000.00   $ 99,000.00
  Preferred 9% Stock, $50 par (4,000 shares
    authorized, 1,500 shares issued).................  $ 75,000.00
  Preferred 9% Stock Subscribed (500 shares).........    25,000.00
  Premium on Preferred 9% Stock......................     3,000.00    103,000.00
  Common Stock, no-par, stated value $10 per share
    (20,000 shares authorized, 14,000 shares issued)..  $140,000.00
  Common Stock Subscribed (2,000 shares).............    20,000.00
  Paid-in Capital in Excess of Stated Value..........    80,000.00    240,000.00
    Total Paid-in Capital............................               $442,000.00
Retained Earnings....................................                170,000.00
Total Stockholders' Equity...........................                             612,000.00
Total Liabilities and
  Stockholders' Equity...............................                            $917,500.00
```

Summary

A corporation is defined as "an artificial being, invisible, intangible, and existing only in the contemplation of the law." As a form of business organization, the corporation has the following advantages over a sole proprietorship or a partnership: limited liability, ease of raising capital, ease of transferring ownership rights, continuous existence, and no mutual agency. Its disadvantages are additional taxation and government regulation. The structure of the corporation is as follows: The stockholders elect the board of directors, and the board of directors appoints the officers to manage the corporation.

Capital stock may consist of two classes. (1) *Common stock* may be par value or no-par value. Holders of common stock get paid dividends after holders of preferred stock, and common stockholders usually have voting privileges. (2) *Preferred stock* frequently has par value. Stockholders who have preferred stock get paid a definite rate of dividend, and are paid before the holders of common stock, although they have no voting privileges. Preferred stock may be cumulative or noncumulative, participating or nonparticipating.

Glossary

Articles of incorporation   Application for a charter.

Authorized capital   The maximum number of shares that may be issued for each class of stock (common and preferred).

Capital stock   General term referring to shares of ownership in a corporation; subdivided into common stock and preferred stock.

Charter   Written right, issued by a state government, for a corporation to exist; approved articles of incorporation.

Close corporation   Having a relatively small group of owners.

Common stock   Stock whose owners are paid dividends after owners of preferred stock are paid (residual share); holders of common stock have voting privileges.

Corporation   "An artificial being, invisible, intangible, and existing only in contemplation of the law." As such, it is a separate legal entity.

Cumulative preferred   When a firm fails to pay dividends during certain lean years, these dividends may be said to accumulate; when the firm finally pays the accumulated dividends, holders of cumulative preferred stock must be paid these dividends before any dividends can be paid to holders of common stock.

Discount on stock   The deficiency by which the agreed price is less than the par value.

Dividends   Distributions of earnings of a corporation, in the form of either cash or additional shares of stock.

Double-taxation feature   The net income of the corporation is taxed, since the corporation is a separate entity; when the net income is then distributed as dividends to stockholders, it becomes part of the personal income of the individual stockholder, and is taxed a second time.

Intangible assets   A classification of assets including such accounts as Organization Costs, Patents, and Goodwill.

Issued stock   Stock issued by a corporation.

Legal capital   Minimum capital stock investment that a corporation must maintain; because it is legal capital, it is not subject to withdrawal by stockholders. This stipulation protects creditors.

Open corporation   A corporation having a large group of owners, ordinarily with shares traded on a stock exchange or in over-the-counter markets; also known as a public corporation.

Organization costs   The cost of organizing a corporation, such as fees paid to the state, attorneys' fees, promotional costs, travel expenses, costs of printing stock certificates, etc.

Outstanding stock   Stock actually in the possession of stockholders (issued stock less the number of shares reacquired by the company).

Paid-in capital   A caption in the balance sheet listed immediately under stockholders' equity. The paid-in capital section includes the stock accounts and their related premium or discount accounts.

Par value   Face value of stock, indicating amount per share to be entered in capital stock account.

Participating preferred   Holders of preferred stock share in any extra dividends distributed by the corporation after the regular dividend has been paid to holders of preferred stock and a stipulated dividend to holders of common stock.

Preemptive right   A stockholder who has a preemptive right, in order to maintain the same proportionate ownership in a corporation in the future as he or she does originally, has the privilege of subscribing to a new issue of stock in the same proportion as his or her present ownership.

Preferred stock   Dividends are paid to a holder of preferred stock at a regular rate, and before they are paid to a holder of common stock; the holder of preferred stock also has preference in the distribution of assets in the event of a liquidation.

Premium on stock   The amount by which the agreed price exceeds the par value.

Retained earnings   A stockholders' equity account representing capital generated by the corporation's earnings and which still remains in the firm.

Stated value   The amount per share of no-par stock which is recorded in the corporation's stock accounts; an amount designated by the law as being not subject to withdrawal by stockholders.

Treasury stock   A corporation's own stock which it has issued and which was at one time outstanding, and which the firm later reacquires, without intending to cancel.

Questions

1. In what respect is a corporation a separate legal entity?

2. List four advantages and two disadvantages of a corporate form of business organization over sole proprietorship and partnership forms. In your opinion, which is the greatest advantage and the greatest disadvantage?

3. List three types of organization costs. How is Organization Costs classified on a balance sheet? What eventually happens to Organization Costs?

4. If a corporation sells its stock at a premium, does the amount of the premium represent revenue to the firm?

5. In regard to common stock, what is the difference between par value and stated value?

6. What is a stock subscription?

7. What is the purpose of Common Stock Subscribed, and what happens to the account?

Exercises

Exercise 1 Describe the transactions recorded in the following ledger accounts of the Midwest Packing Company.

Cash					Common Stock	
(1)	206,000	(2)	5,000		(1)	200,000

Organization Costs					Premium on Common	
(2)	5,000				(1)	6,000

Exercise 2 The C. R. Smallwood Corporation is authorized to issue 30,000 shares of $50 par-value common stock. Record the following transactions in general journal form.

Jan. 16 Sold 6,000 shares of common stock at $51 per share, received cash.

21 Issued 2,100 shares of common stock in exchange for land and building valued at $20,000 and $90,000, respectively.

Feb. 25 Sold 2,000 shares of common stock at $52 per share, received cash.

Exercise 3 Pinecrest Estates, organized on February 7 of this year, was authorized to issue 700 shares of cumulative preferred 8% stock, $100 par value and 7,000 shares of common stock, $25 par value. Record in general journal form the following transactions, completed during Pinecrest's first year of operations.

Feb. 7 Sold 3,000 shares of common stock at par for cash.

7 Issued 70 shares of common stock to an attorney in return for legal services pertaining to incorporation.

May 6 Sold 500 shares of preferred stock at $101 per share; received cash.

Aug. 6 Issued 2,200 shares of common stock in exchange for land with a fair market value of $55,000.

Exercise 4 The outstanding stock of Carroll Development Corporation consists of 4,000 shares of preferred 6% stock, $100 par value and 12,000 shares of common stock, $50 par value. Carroll's board of directors declares a dividend of $80,000 for this year. How much of the dividend is allocated to holders of preferred stock and how much to holders of common stock?

Exercise 5 The Southwest Machine Tool Corporation is authorized to issue 100,000 shares of no-par common stock, $20 stated value. Record the following transactions in general journal form.

May   17 Sold 20,000 shares of common stock at $22 per share for cash.

June   8 Sold 10,000 shares of common stock at $21 per share for cash.

Exercise 6 The Northeast Tug and Barge Company has authorized capital consisting of 1,000 shares of cumulative preferred 7% stock, $100 par value and 10,000 shares of common stock, $25 par value. Record the following transactions in general journal form.

a. Received subscriptions to 600 shares of preferred 7% stock at $102 per share, with a downpayment of 50% of the subscription price.

b. Received 30% of the subscription price from all subscribers.

c. Received 20% of the subscription price from all subscribers, and issued the stock certificates.

Exercise 7 Describe the transactions recorded in the following ledger accounts of Finch Cedar Shingle Company, Inc.

Cash		Common Stock		Paid-in Capital in Excess of Stated Value	
(1) 14,000			**(1)** 10,000		**(1)** 4,000
(3) 14,800			**(5)** 20,000		**(2)** 6,000
(4) 11,200					

Subscriptions Receivable, Common Stock		Common Stock Subscribed	
(2) 26,000	**(3)** 14,800	**(5)** 20,000	**(2)** 20,000
	(4) 11,200		

Exercise 8 The M. C. Fleming Corporation's charter authorized it to issue 1,200 shares of $50-par-value preferred 6% stock and 12,000 shares of no-par common stock (stated value $10). The following balances are from the Balance Sheet columns of the work sheet.

Retained Earnings (credit balance)	$31,000
Common Stock Subscribed (2,000 shares)	20,000
Discount on Preferred 6% Stock	1,800
Common Stock	80,000
Preferred 6% Stock	50,000
Paid-in Capital in Excess of Stated Value	22,000

Prepare the Stockholders' Equity section of the balance sheet.

Problem 23-1 The Kendall Refrigeration and Air Conditioning Company, Inc., which was organized on May 7 of this year, has a charter which stipulates the following authorized capital: 3,000 shares of preferred 8% stock, $100 par value and 37,500 shares of common stock, $25 par value.

Kendall completed the following transactions during this year of operations.

May   6 Received subscriptions to 12,000 shares of common stock at $25 per share; collected 60% of the subscription price.

     12 Sold 1,200 shares of preferred 8% stock for $96 per share, receiving cash.

June 6 Subscribers to 12,000 shares of common stock paid an additional 20% of the subscription price.

July 6 Subscribers to 12,000 shares of common stock paid an additional 20% of the subscription price; Kendall issued the 12,000 shares of stock.

Aug. 3 Sold 600 shares of preferred 8% stock for $94 per share, receiving cash.

Sept. 11 Received subscriptions to 3,000 shares of common stock at $26 per share; collected 50% of the subscription price.

Oct. 19 Received subscriptions to 300 shares of preferred 8% stock for $97 per share; collected 20% of the subscription price.

Instructions Record the above transactions in general journal form.

Problem 23-2 Three people—Field, Purvis, and Tuttle—organized the Midwest Implement Company, Inc. The charter of this corporation authorizes capital consisting of 1,500 shares of preferred 7% stock, $50 par value and 15,000 shares of common stock, $10 par value.

Midwest Implement, during its first year of operations, completed the following transactions that affected stockholders' equity.

Mar. 1 Issued to Field 3,000 shares of common stock, at par, for cash.

      1 Bought equipment from Purvis for $39,000. Purvis accepted 3,900 shares of common stock in exchange for the equipment.

      1 Bought land and a building from Tuttle. It was agreed that the land would be valued at $14,250 and the building at $57,750. There is an outstanding mortgage on the property of $24,000, held by Commercial Savings and Loan Association. The corporation assumed responsibility for paying the mortgage. Tuttle accepted common stock at par for her equity.

      4 Paid an attorney $3,600 for paying state fees and for performing services needed for incorporating the firm.

      6 Issued 75 shares of common stock at par to Field for promotional services.

Apr. 9 Issued 600 shares of preferred 7% stock at $52 per share to investors for cash.

May 27 Issued 450 shares of preferred 7% stock at $51 per share to investors for cash.

Instructions **1.** Record the transactions in general journal form.

2. Post the entries to the following accounts: Common Stock, Preferred 7% Stock, Premium on Preferred 7% Stock.

3. Prepare the Stockholders' Equity section of the balance sheet as of December 31, the end of the first year of operations. Net income after taxes for the year was $36,000, and no dividends were declared during the year. As a result, Retained Earnings has a credit balance of $36,000.

Problem 23-3 The Woodward Bakery was organized on October 1 of this year with a charter providing for authorized capital as follows:

> 1,500 shares of preferred 8% stock, $50 par value
>
> 30,000 shares of no-par common stock ($5 stated value)

During the first year of operations, the Woodward Bakery completed the following transactions.

Oct. 2 Received subscriptions to 6,000 shares of common stock at $12 per share, collecting 30% of the subscription price.

  2 Bought equipment from Woodward, one of the promoters, for $36,000. Woodward accepted 2,000 shares of common stock in return for the equipment.

 14 Subscribers to 6,000 shares of common stock paid an additional 30% of the subscription price.

 16 Issued 150 shares of common stock to Woodward at $12 per share in return for promotional services valued at $1,800.

 20 Received subscriptions to 600 shares of preferred 8% stock at $53 per share, collecting 40% of the subscription price.

 23 Paid an attorney $1,960 for paying state fees and for performing services needed for incorporating the firm.

 30 Subscribers to 6,000 shares of common stock paid the remaining 40% of the subscription price; and Woodward Bakers then issued the 6,000 shares.

Nov. 5 Received subscriptions to 3,000 shares of common stock at $14 per share, collecting 50% of the subscription price.

 10 Subscribers to 600 shares of preferred 8% stock paid an additional 30% of the subscription price.

 16 Sold 150 shares of preferred 8% stock at $51 per share for cash.

 25 Subscribers to 3,000 shares of common stock paid the remaining 50% of the subscription price; the Woodward Bakery then issued the 3,000 shares.

Instructions Record the above transactions in general journal form.

Problem 23-4 The Pitts Sporting Goods, Inc., has an authorized capital of 1,500 shares of preferred 7% stock, $100 par value, and 15,000 shares of no-par common stock, stated value $20. The following account balances for the fiscal year ending December 31 of this year are taken from the Balance Sheet columns of the work sheet for the year.

Cash	$ 41,400
Equipment	138,000
Notes Payable	24,600
Preferred 7% Stock	120,000
Accounts Receivable	332,760
Accumulated Depreciation, Equipment	62,475
Land	45,000
Subscriptions Receivable, Preferred 7% Stock	7,650
Premium on Preferred 7% Stock	2,700
Merchandise Inventory	216,750
Building	192,000
Accounts Payable	281,460
Accumulated Depreciation, Building	30,900
Organization Costs	9,630
Allowance for Doubtful Accounts	10,380
Common Stock	180,000
Subscriptions Receivable, Common Stock	13,050
Preferred 7% Stock Subscribed	15,000
Common Stock Subscribed	30,000
Mortgage Payable (due February 1, 1989)	63,000
Paid-in Capital in Excess of Stated Value	52,500
Retained Earnings	126,000
Supplies	2,775

Instructions **1.** Determine the number of shares of preferred 7% stock subscribed and issued.

2. Determine the number of shares of common stock subscribed and issued.

3. Prepare a classified balance sheet.

Alternate problems

Problem 23-1A The Stewart Furniture Company, Inc., organized on April 9 of this year, has a charter that stipulates the following authorized capital.

6,000 shares of preferred 9% stock, $50 par value

30,000 shares of common stock, $20 par value

During the first year of its operations, the Stewart Company completed the transactions listed at the top of the next page.

Apr. 12 Received subscriptions to 9,000 shares of common stock at $20 per share, collecting 50% of the subscription price.

May 18 Sold 1,500 shares of preferred 9% stock for $49 per share, receiving cash.

June 12 Subscribers to 9,000 shares of common stock paid an additional 30% of the subscription price.

July 12 Subscribers to 9,000 shares of common stock paid an additional 20% of the subscription price; the Stewart Company then issued the 9,000 shares of stock.

Sept. 9 Sold 1,800 shares of preferred 9% stock for $48 per share, receiving cash.

Nov. 29 Received subscriptions to 1,500 shares of common stock at $21 per share, collecting 25% of the subscription price.

Dec. 18 Received subscriptions to 1,200 shares of preferred 9% stock for $49 per share, collecting 10% of the subscription price.

Instructions   Record the above transactions in general journal form.

Problem 23-2A   Three people—Barnhart, Foss, and Manuel—organized Juneau Excavation, Inc., with a charter providing for the following authorized capital.

> 1,500 shares of preferred 7% stock, $50 par value
>
> 15,000 shares of common stock, $10 par value

During its first year of operations, Juneau Excavation completed the following transactions that affected stockholders' equity.

Apr. 3 Issued 3,600 shares of common stock to Barnhart, at par, for cash.

4 Paid an attorney $3,975 for paying state fees and for performing services needed for incorporating the firm.

4 Bought equipment from Manuel for $42,900. Manuel accepted 4,290 shares of common stock in exchange for the equipment.

4 Bought land and a building from Foss. It was agreed that the land would be valued at $15,900 and the building at $48,750. There is an outstanding mortgage on the property of $28,500, held by Stone Federal Savings and Loan Association. The corporation assumed responsibility for paying the mortgage. Foss accepted common stock at par for his equity.

6 Issued 60 shares of common stock to Barnhart for promotional services.

May 4 Issued 450 shares of preferred 7% stock at $53 per share to investors for cash.

30 Issued 300 shares of preferred 7% stock at $52 per share to investors for cash.

Instructions   **1.** Record the above transactions in general journal form.

2. Post the entries to the following accounts: Common Stock, Preferred 7% Stock, Premium on Preferred 7% Stock.

3. Prepare the Stockholders' Equity section of the balance sheet as of December 31, the end of the first year of operations. Net income after taxes for the year was $34,350, and no dividends were declared during the year. As a result, Retained Earnings has a credit balance of $34,350.

Problem 23-3A The Middleton Nursery was organized on February 1 of this year, with a charter providing for the following authorized capital.

> 3,000 shares of preferred 7% stock, $25 par value
>
> 15,000 shares of no-par common stock, $15 stated value

During the first year of its operations, the Middleton Nursery completed the following transactions.

Feb. 1 Bought land from Middleton for $39,000. Middleton accepted 1,500 shares of common stock for the land.

2 Received subscriptions to 4,500 shares of common stock at $26 per share, collecting 40% of the subscription price.

3 Issued 75 shares of common stock to Middleton, at $26 per share, in return for promotional services.

5 Subscribers to 4,500 shares of common stock paid an additional 30% of the subscription price.

26 Paid an attorney $2,760 for paying of state fees and for performing services needed for incorporating the firm.

28 Received subscriptions to 750 shares of preferred 7% stock at $24 per share, collecting 20% of the subscription price.

28 Subscribers to 4,500 shares of common stock paid the remaining 30% of the subscription price; Middleton Nursery then issued the stock.

Mar. 6 Received subscriptions to 3,750 shares of common stock at $27 per share, collecting 50% of the subscription price.

14 Subscribers to 750 shares of preferred 7% stock paid an additional 40% of the subscription price.

20 Sold 300 shares of preferred 7% stock at $22 per share for cash.

26 Subscribers to 3,750 shares of common stock paid the remaining 50% of the subscription price; Middleton Nursery then issued the stock.

Instructions Record the above transactions in general journal form.

Problem 23-4A The Marshall Cycle Shop, Inc., has an authorized capital of 1,500 shares of preferred 8% stock, $100 par value and 15,000 shares of no-par common stock, stated value $20. The following account balances are from the Balance Sheet columns of the work sheet for the fiscal year ended March 31 of this year.

Cash	$ 44,940
Preferred 8% Stock	124,500

Equipment	144,675
Subscriptions Receivable, Preferrred 8% Stock	9,600
Accounts Payable	289,080
Common Stock Subscribed	45,000
Retained Earnings	139,500
Subscriptions Receivable, Common Stock	24,300
Building	198,000
Mortgage Payable (due January 1, 1989)	69,000
Paid-in Capital in Excess of Stated Value	56,250
Accounts Receivable	352,170
Accumulated Depreciation, Equipment	65,595
Notes Payable	27,300
Preferred 8% Stock Subscribed	25,500
Allowance for Doubtful Accounts	11,130
Organization Costs	10,680
Common Stock	180,000
Accumulated Depreciation, Building	40,350
Land	51,000
Merchandise Inventory	237,960
Supplies	2,880
Premium on Preferred 8% Stock	3,000

Instructions   **1.** Determine the number of shares of preferred 8% stock issued and subscribed.

2. Determine the number of shares of common stock issued and subscribed.

3. Prepare a classified balance sheet.

24

Corporations: taxes, dividends, and retained earnings

objectives

After completing this chapter, you will be able to do the following:
- Journalize entries for corporate income taxes.
- Journalize closing entries for a corporation.
- Complete a work sheet for a corporation.
- Journalize entries for the appropriation of Retained Earnings.
- Journalize entries for the declaration and issuance of cash dividends and stock dividends.
- Complete a corporate statement of retained earnings and a balance sheet, including the following types of accounts: Appropriated Retained Earnings, Stock Dividend Distributable, Dividends Payable, and Income Tax Payable.

CHAPTER 23 described the entries the accountant makes during the initial organization of a corporation. Now let's assume that the corporation is established, and turn our attention to the year-to-year entries for taxes, dividends, and retained earnings.

Procedure for recording and paying income taxes

Determining the net income of a corporation is simply a matter of

$$\text{Revenue} - \text{Expenses} = \text{Net Income}$$

One could compare most aspects of the revenue and expense accounts of a corporation to the revenue and expense accounts for sole proprietorships and partnerships. The net income of a sole proprietorship and the distributive shares of net income of a partnership are taxable as part of the owners' personal incomes. However, since the corporation is a separate legal entity, it must pay income taxes in its own name. Corporations are subject to federal income taxes; many states and cities also impose an income tax on them. We'll talk just about the income tax levied by the federal government. The same basic principles also apply to state and city income taxes.

In order to place corporations on a pay-as-you-go basis, the law requires most of them to estimate in advance the amount of their federal income taxes for the forthcoming fiscal year. The corporations then pay the estimated amounts in four installments during the year in which revenues are earned. The firm's accountant records each entry as a debit to Income Tax and a credit to Cash. The treatment of the Income Tax account is similar to that of an expense account, except that the accountant usually makes a separate entry closing Income Tax into Income Summary.

At the end of the fiscal year, after the corporation determines the exact amount of its income, it calculates the amount of the income tax. If the amount of income tax the corporation has paid in advance exceeds its tax liability for the year, the accountant debits the amount of the overpayment to Income Tax Paid in Advance, a current-asset account, and credits it to Income Tax. Usually, however, the amount of income tax paid in advance is less than the amount of the tax liability. In this case, the accountant debits the amount of the underpayment to Income Tax and credits it to Income Tax Payable, a current-liability account. The corporation may pay this liability in two equal installments: the first when the tax return is filed, $2\frac{1}{2}$ months after the close of the fiscal year, and the second 3 months later ($5\frac{1}{2}$ months after the close of the fiscal period). The entries are debits to Income Tax Payable and credits to Cash.

Income tax entries for a corporation: first year

Kansas City Restaurant Supply, Inc., begins operations on January 5. The corporation's fiscal year extends from January 1 through December 31. Its authorized capital consists of 200,000 of $20 par-value common stock. For the fiscal year, the corporation estimates that its net income will be $100,000 and that its income tax will be $40,000, as calculated below. Throughout this text, we shall assume that the federal corporation income tax rates are 22% of the first $25,000 of taxable income and 46% of the excess over $25,000.

$$\$25,000 \times .22 = \$\ 5,500$$
$$75,000 \times .46 = \underline{\ 34,500}$$
$$\underline{\underline{\$40,000}}$$

Here is the way the accountant for Kansas City Restaurant Supply records the payment of this tax.

Mar.	31	Income Tax		10 00 0 00	
		Cash			10 00 0 00
		Paid first quarterly installment of estimated			
		federal income tax for the year (one-fourth			
		of $40,000).			

Jun.	30	Income Tax		10 00 0 00	
		Cash			10 00 0 00
		Paid second quarterly installment of			
		estimated federal income tax for the year.			

Sep.	30	Income Tax		10 00 0 00	
		Cash			10 00 0 00
		Paid third quarterly installment of estimated			
		federal income tax for the year.			

1	Dec.	31	Income Tax	10 0 0 0 00		1
2			Cash		10 0 0 0 00	2
3			Paid fourth quarterly installment of estimated			3
4			federal income tax for the year.			4
5						5
6						6
7						7

At the end of the year, the accountant prepares a work sheet and determines that the net income of the corporation for the year is $120,000 ($980,000 in revenues minus $860,000 in costs and expenses). Since the estimated net income was $100,000, the additional amount of taxable income is $20,000 ($120,000 − $100,000). Consequently, the corporation owes the government additional income tax of $9,200 (.46 × $20,000). The following entry appears first as an adjusting entry on the work sheet.

1			*Adjusting Entry*			1
2	Dec.	31	Income Tax	9 2 0 0 00		2
3			Income Tax Payable		9 2 0 0 00	3
4			To record additional tax liability for this year.			4
5						5
6						6
7						7
8						8

The accountant now records the closing entries. In this illustration, to save time we have used "Revenues" to represent all temporary equity accounts having a credit balance, and "Expenses" to represent all accounts having a debit balance.

1			*Closing Entries*			1
2	Dec.	31	Revenues	980 0 0 0 00		2
3			Income Summary		980 0 0 0 00	3
4		31	Income Summary	860 0 0 0 00		4
5			Expenses		860 0 0 0 00	5
6		31	Income Summary	49 2 0 0 00		6
7			Income Tax		49 2 0 0 00	7
8		31	Income Summary	70 8 0 0 00		8
9			Retained Earnings		70 8 0 0 00	9
10						10
11						11
12						12
13						13
14						14

Now let's summarize the steps for the closing entries of a corporation.

1. Close revenue accounts into Income Summary.

2. Close expense accounts into Income Summary.

3. Close Income Tax into Income Summary, by the amount of the actual income tax for the year.

4. Close Income Summary into Retained Earnings, by the amount of the net income after income tax.

As we have said, the Retained Earnings account is classified as a stockholders' equity account, and consequently it is a permanent or real account, as opposed to a temporary-equity account. After the accountant has finished posting to the Retained Earnings account, if the account has a credit balance, it represents accumulated earnings. Conversely, if the Retained Earnings account has a debit balance, it represents a *deficit*. The accountant posts the entries for the year to the T accounts, as follows.

Cash				Expenses		
+		−		+		−
	Mar. 31	10,000	Bal.	860,000	Dec. 31 Clos.	860,000
	Jun. 30	10,000				
	Sep. 30	10,000				
	Dec. 31	10,000				

Income Tax				Income Tax Payable		
+		−		−		+
Mar. 31	10,000	Dec. 31 Clos.	49,200		Dec. 31 Adj.	9,200
Jun. 30	10,000					
Sep. 30	10,000					
Dec. 31	10,000					
Dec. 31 Adj.	9,200					

Revenues				Income Summary		
−		+	Dec. 31	860,000	Dec. 31	980,000
Dec. 31 Clos.	980,000	Bal.	980,000	Dec. 31	49,200		
				Dec. 31 Clos.	70,800		

Retained Earnings	
−	+
	Bal.
	Dec. 31 70,800

Income taxes are considered an expense necessary to conducting a business, and—as stated earlier—the accountant handles the Income Tax account similar to an expense account. However, it is common practice to make a separate entry closing Income Tax into Income Summary and not to include the amount for income tax with the total amounts for all the other expenses. The purpose of doing so is to make the amount of taxable income more evident from a quick analysis of Income Summary. Notice in the Income Summary T account illustrated above that the balance of the account prior to transferring the Income Tax balance is $120,000 ($980,000 − $860,000), the taxable income. If the amount of income tax was closed into Income Summary with all the other expenses, the amount of taxable income would not be as obvious.

Income tax entries for a corporation: second year

The next year begins with a carry-over of the income tax liability for the previous year. Kansas City Restaurant Supply estimates that its net income will be $110,000, and that the related income tax will be $44,600. The entries are shown here.

1	Mar.	15	Income Tax Payable	4600 00	
2			Cash		4600 00
3			Paid half of tax liability for last year, due 2½		
4			months after the close of the fiscal year.		
5					
6					
7					
8					
9					

1	Mar.	31	Income Tax	11150 00	
2			Cash		11150 00
3			Paid first quarterly installment of estimated		
4			federal income tax for the year (one-fourth		
5			of $44,600).		
6					
7					
8					
9					
10					
11					

1	Jun.	15	Income Tax Payable	4600 00	
2			Cash		4600 00
3			Payment of remaining half of tax liability for		
4			last year, due 5½ months after the close of		
5			the fiscal year.		
6					
7					
8					
9					
10					

1	*Jun.*	*30*	*Income Tax*			11	1	5	0	00											1
2			*Cash*									11	1	5	0	00					2
3			*Paid second quarterly installment of estimated*																		3
4			*federal income tax for the year.*																		4
5																					5
6																					6
7																					7
8																					8
9																					9
10																					10
11																					11
12																					12
13																					13

1	*Sep.*	*30*	*Income Tax*			11	1	5	0	00											1
2			*Cash*									11	1	5	0	00					2
3			*Paid third quarterly installment of estimated*																		3
4			*federal income tax for the year.*																		4
5																					5
6																					6
7																					7
8																					8
9																					9
10																					10
11																					11
12																					12
13																					13

1	*Dec.*	*31*	*Income Tax*			11	1	5	0	00											1
2			*Cash*									11	1	5	0	00					2
3			*Paid fourth quarterly installment of estimated*																		3
4			*federal income tax for the year.*																		4
5																					5
6																					6
7																					7
8																					8
9																					9
10																					10
11																					11

At the end of the year, the accountant determines the actual net income on the work sheet: $142,000. The net income in excess of the advance estimate is $32,000 ($142,000 − $110,000), and the amount of the adjustment for additional income tax is $14,720.

The second-year work sheet for Kansas City Restaurant Supply, Inc. is shown here.

ACCOUNT NAME	TRIAL BALANCE	
	DEBIT	CREDIT
Cash	3 4 9 0 00	
Accounts Receivable	106 6 8 0 00	
Allowance for Doubtful Accounts		1 8 2 0 00
Subscriptions Receivable, Common Stock	24 5 0 0 00	
Merchandise Inventory	180 5 0 0 00	
Prepaid Insurance	1 2 2 0 00	
Store Equipment	54 7 2 0 00	
Accumulated Depreciation, Store Equipment		27 2 5 0 00
Office Equipment	28 9 2 0 00	
Accumulated Depreciation, Office Equipment		8 4 1 0 00
Organization Costs	5 0 0 0 00	
Notes Payable		16 0 0 0 00
Accounts Payable		62 7 5 0 00
Common Stock		100 0 0 0 00
Common Stock Subscribed		20 0 0 0 00
Premium on Common Stock		2 4 0 0 00
Retained Earnings		69 0 0 0 00
Sales		1,062 0 0 0 00
Purchases	762 0 0 0 00	
Purchases Discount		4 8 0 0 00
Selling Expenses (control)	126 4 5 0 00	
General Expenses (control)	32 7 5 0 00	
Interest Expense	3 6 0 0 00	
Income Tax	44 6 0 0 00	
	1,374 4 3 0 00	1,374 4 3 0 00
Income Summary		
Interest Payable		
Income Tax Payable		
Net Income after Income Tax		

Kansas City

Work

For year ending

Restaurant Supply, Inc.

Sheet

December 31, 19—

ADJUSTMENTS DEBIT	ADJUSTMENTS CREDIT	INCOME STATEMENT DEBIT	INCOME STATEMENT CREDIT	BALANCE SHEET DEBIT	BALANCE SHEET CREDIT
				3 490 00	
				106 680 00	
	(e) 1 680 00				3 500 00
				24 500 00	
(b)189 880 00	(a)180 500 00			189 880 00	
	(f) 520 00			700 00	
				54 720 00	
	(c) 4 300 00				31 550 00
				28 920 00	
	(d) 2 760 00				11 170 00
				5 000 00	
					16 000 00
					62 750 00
					100 000 00
					20 000 00
					2 400 00
					69 000 00
			1,062 000 00		
		762 000 00			
			4 800 00		
(c) 4 300 00		130 750 00			
(d) 2 760 00					
(e) 1 680 00					
(f) 520 00		37 710 00			
(g) 120 00		3 720 00			
(h)14 720 00		59 320 00			
(a)180 500 00	(b)189 880 00	180 500 00	189 880 00		
	(g) 120 00				120 00
	(h) 14 720 00				14 720 00
394 480 00	394 480 00	1,174 000 00	1,256 680 00	413 890 00	331 210 00
		82 680 00			82 680 00
		1,256 680 00	1,256 680 00	413 890 00	413 890 00

When the accountant is completing the work sheet, he or she must give special treatment to the adjusting entry for the additional income tax. Before recording the adjustment for income tax, the accountant did the following.

1. Recorded and totaled the trial balance

2. Recorded all adjustments except the adjustment for income tax

3. Extended account balances into the Income Statement columns and tentatively determined the net income before taxes, as shown below. (The accountant's objective, naturally, is to determine the net income in advance, and then to calculate the exact amount of the income tax.)

ACCOUNT NAME	INCOME STATEMENT	
	DEBIT	CREDIT
Sales		1,062 0 0 0 00
Purchases	762 0 0 0 00	
Purchases Discount		4 8 0 0 00
Selling Expenses (control)	130 7 5 0 00	
General Expenses (control)	37 7 1 0 00	
Interest Expense	3 7 2 0 00	
Income Summary	180 5 0 0 00	189 8 8 0 00
	1,114 6 8 0 00	1,256 6 8 0 00
Net Income before Income Tax	142 0 0 0 00	
	1,256 6 8 0 00	1,256 6 8 0 00

4. The accountant calculates the additional income tax this way. (We present two methods; take your choice.)

Method 1

Actual net income	$142,000
− Estimated net income	110,000
Income not yet taxed	$ 32,000
× Tax rate (46%)	.46
Additional income tax	$ 14,720

Method 2

Income tax on net income of $142,000	
On first $25,000 ($25,000 × .22)	$ 5,500
On next $117,000 ($117,000 × .46)	53,820
Total income tax	$59,320
− Income tax already paid	44,600
Additional income tax	$14,720

5. The accountant records the adjusting entry of $14,720 in the Adjustments columns of the work sheet.

6. The accountant records the amount of the entire income tax in the debit column of the income statement, and completes the Income Statement columns by determining the net income after taxes: $82,680.

7. The accountant extends all remaining figures into the Balance Sheet columns, including Income Tax Payable and Net Income after Taxes, and completes the Balance Sheet columns.

Financial statements Here is an abbreviated income statement for the second year.

Kansas City Restaurant Supply, Inc.		
Income Statement		
For year ended December 31, 19–		
Revenue from Sales		
Sales	1,062 0 0 0 00	
Net Income before Income Tax	142 0 0 0 00	
Income Tax	59 3 2 0 00	
Net Income after Income Tax	82 6 8 0 00	

The balance sheet includes Income Tax Payable as a current liability, as well as the final balance of Retained Earnings. We'll be seeing a complete balance sheet later in this chapter.

Adjusting and closing entries

The next step in the accounting cycle is to take the adjusting entries and closing entries directly from the Adjustments columns of the work sheet.

19– Dec.		Account	Debit	Credit
		Adjusting Entries		
	31	Income Summary	180 5 0 0 00	
		Merchandise Inventory		180 5 0 0 00
	31	Merchandise Inventory	189 8 8 0 00	
		Income Summary		189 8 8 0 00
	31	Selling Expenses (control)	4 3 0 0 00	
		Accumulated Depreciation, Store Equipment		4 3 0 0 00
	31	General Expenses (control)	2 7 6 0 00	
		Accumulated Depreciation, Office Equipment		2 7 6 0 00
	31	General Expenses (control)	1 6 8 0 00	
		Allowance for Doubtful Accounts		1 6 8 0 00
	31	General Expenses (control)	5 2 0 00	
		Prepaid Insurance		5 2 0 00
	31	Interest Expense	1 2 0 00	
		Interest Payable		1 2 0 00
	31	Income Tax	14 7 2 0 00	
		Income Tax Payable		14 7 2 0 00
19– Dec.		**Closing Entries**		
	31	Sales	1,062 0 0 0 00	
		Purchases Discount	4 8 0 0 00	
		Income Summary		1,066 8 0 0 00
	31	Income Summary	934 1 8 0 00	
		Purchases		762 0 0 0 00
		Selling Expenses (control)		130 7 5 0 00
		General Expenses (control)		37 7 1 0 00
		Interest Expense		3 7 2 0 00
	31	Income Summary	59 3 2 0 00	
		Income Tax		59 3 2 0 00
	31	Income Summary	82 6 8 0 00	
		Retained Earnings		82 6 8 0 00

Income statement net income versus taxable income

In this illustration, we've been assuming that the accountant for Kansas City Restaurant Supply determined the income tax for the year as a matter of course by multiplying the corporation's net income for the year (as shown on the income statement) by the tax rate. The accountant maintained that the corporation's net income was its taxable income. Well, in real life, things aren't quite that simple. The net income shown on the income statement may differ quite a lot from the income reported for tax purposes. Here are some of the reasons why.

1. The depreciation method used for income statement purposes may differ from the method used for tax statement purposes. For example, the firm might use the straight-line method of depreciation for its income statement, but the declining-balance method (at twice the straight-line rate) for the tax statement.

2. A firm may include certain types of revenue in the income statement, but not in the tax statement. For example, in the income statement, the firm may count in the total of installment sales, but on the tax statement the firm may list only the cash actually received from installment sales (see Appendix C). Also, some items listed in the income statement, such as interest on state and municipal bonds, are not taxable; and some revenues, such as capital gains on the sale of property, are taxed at different rates.

3. A corporation may list certain types of expenditures as assets, and consequently not put them on the income statement, and on the tax statement list these same expenditures as expenses. For example, a company might not list expenditures for research and development on its income statement, whereas it would list them as expenses on the tax statement.

Appropriation of retained earnings

Since a corporation declares dividends out of its Retained Earnings, the *amount* of dividends is necessarily limited by the amount of Retained Earnings. However, rather than using the entire balance of Retained Earnings for cash or stock dividends (we'll discuss cash and stock dividends presently), the board of directors may wish to earmark part of Retained Earnings for some specific purpose. Let us say that the directors decide they want to provide for future expansion. So the board of directors passes a resolution, which is recorded in the minutes of a meeting, restricting or appropriating a certain amount of Retained Earnings for future expansion. The minutes of the meeting represent the source document for the accounting entry. For example, Kansas City Restaurant Supply, Inc., plans to erect its own building. To finance the project, it decides to restrict Retained Earnings for a total amount of $100,000, at the rate of $10,000 per year, for 10 years. So the accountant makes this type of entry at the end of each year, following the closing entries.

	1979 Feb.	5	Retained Earnings		10 0 0 0 00		
			Retained Earnings Appropriated for Building			10 0 0 0 00	
			To appropriate Retained Earnings, as ordered				
			by the board of directors in meeting of				
			Feb. 5, 1979.				

This appropriation of Retained Earnings does *not* represent a separate kitty or cash fund of $10,000. To accentuate this point, let us look at cash dividends: If we consider the Retained Earnings account as a well or reservoir from which cash dividends are declared, then this reservoir has dried up by $10,000. *If the corporation cannot declare and pay out these dividends, then the firm is* preserving its net assets, particularly cash.

At the end of the 10-year period, although there is *not* an actual $100,000 fund of cash, there is an additional $100,000 accumulated in net assets (assets minus liabilities). The corporation can now devise plans to convert the $100,000 increase in net assets into cash in order to put a downpayment on the building.

When the objective—buying or erecting the building—has been accomplished, the corporation no longer has to restrict Retained Earnings, so the accountant may make the following entry, reversing the ten previous entries.

	1989 Mar.	18	Retained Earnings Appropriated for Building		100 00 0 00		
			Retained Earnings			100 00 0 00	
			To return to Retained Earnings the balance in				
			the Retained Earnings Appropriated for				
			Building account, as ordered by the board of				
			directors in the meeting of Mar. 18, 1989.				

Here are some other examples of appropriated Retained Earnings accounts.

• Retained Earnings Appropriated for Plant Expansion (no specific objective stated)

• Retained Earnings Appropriated for Bonded Indebtedness (an obligation imposed by contract)

• Retained Earnings Appropriated for Self Insurance (self planning for casualty losses)

• Retained Earnings Appropriated for Inventory Losses (in the event of getting caught in a price drop)

• Retained Earnings Appropriated for Contingencies (in the event of a rainy day)

Each appropriated Retained Earnings account is labeled "Retained Earnings Appropriated for _____." Therefore the account Retained Earnings represents unappropriated retained earnings. These accounts appear in a statement of retained earnings, an illustration of which is shown on page 670.

Declaration and payment of dividends

A dividend is a distribution—of cash, shares of stock, or other assets—which a corporation makes to its stockholders. Dividends are allocated proportionately to persons who own stock, according to the number of shares they own, and according to whether the stock is preferred or common. We shall discuss three types of dividends: cash dividends, stock dividends, and liquidating dividends. Cash dividends and stock dividends reduce Retained Earnings; liquidating dividends reduce Paid-in Capital.

Cash dividends

The most usual form of dividends is dividends payable in cash. These ordinarily represent a share of the current earnings paid to the stockholders as a reward for their investment. The board of directors declares the dividends, and generally pays cash dividends up to a certain percentage of the firm's net income after income tax. The cash dividend is expressed as a specific amount per share—for example, $1.12 per share. A stockholder who owns 100 shares is thus entitled to $112.

Before a corporation can pay a cash dividend, three things must be in order.

1. Retained Earnings The company must have a sufficient balance in the unappropriated Retained Earnings account.

2. An adequate amount of cash A corporation may have earned large profits, but not all profits are in cash. For example, the revenue may be in the form of charge accounts, such as Accounts Receivable. Cash comes in only when the company receives payments from charge customers.

3. Formal declaration by the board of directors The payment of dividends, although it may be a matter of policy, is not automatic. The board of directors must pass the declaration in the form of a motion, and record it in the minute book. This minute book is the source document for the accounting entry.

Dividend dates

Three significant dates are involved in the declaration and payment of a dividend.

1. Date of declaration Date on which the board of directors votes to declare dividends. The entry recorded as of this date debits Retained Earnings and credits Dividends Payable.

2. Date of record Date as of which the ownership of shares is set. This date determines a person's eligibility for dividends, and ordinarily is about 3 weeks after the date of declaration.

3. Date of payment The date payment is made; on this date, the accountant debits the amount to Dividends Payable and credits it to Cash.

For example, on January 20, the board of directors of Kansas City Restaurant Supply declares a quarterly cash dividend of $.72 per share (5,000 shares × $.72 = $3,600) to stockholders of record as of February 11, payable on March 2. The entries, in general journal form, are as follows.

Jan.	20	Retained Earnings	3600 00			1
		Dividends Payable		3600 00		2
		To record declaration of quarterly cash				3
		dividend on common stock at the rate of $.72				4
		per share to stockholders of record as of Feb.				5
		11, payable Mar. 2, as ordered by board of				6
		directors in meeting of Jan. 20.				7

Mar.	2	Dividends Payable	3600 00			1
		Cash		3600 00		2
		Payment of quarterly dividend declared on				3
		Jan. 20 to stockholders of record as of				4
		Feb. 11.				5

Dividends Payable is classified as a current-liability account.

Stock dividends

A *stock dividend* is a distribution, on a pro rata (proportional) basis, of additional shares of a company's stock to the stockholders. In other words, the dividend consists of shares of stock rather than cash. One could describe it as a dividend payable in stock. Generally, stock dividends consist of common stock distributed to holders of common stock. Stock dividends are usually issued by corporations that plow back (retain) earnings in order to finance future expansion.

Suppose that the board of directors of Kansas City Restaurant Supply, Inc., declared a 20% stock dividend on October 11 to stockholders of record as of November 1, payable on November 16. The ledger sheet for the Common Stock account on October 11 looks like this in T account form.

Common Stock

	Bal. 100,000
	$20 per share
	(5,000 shares)

Number of shares in the stock dividend:
20% of 5,000 shares = 1,000 shares

The present market value of the shares is $23 per share. The entries, in general journal form, are as follows. (We have put in the calculations just by way of explanation.)

Oct.	11	Retained Earnings (1,000 shares × $23 each)	23 0 0 0 00		
		Stock Dividend Distributable (1,000 shares ×			
		$20 each)		20 0 0 0 00	
		Premium on Common Stock		3 0 0 0 00	
		To record the declaration of a 20% stock			
		dividend to stockholders of record as of Nov.			
		1, payable Nov. 16, as ordered by board of			
		directors in meeting of Oct. 11.			

Nov.	16	Stock Dividend Distributable	20 0 0 0 00	
		Common Stock		20 0 0 0 00
		Issuance of a stock dividend (1,000 shares)		
		declared on Oct. 11 to stockholders of record		
		as of Nov. 1.		

Stock Dividend Distributable is a stockholders' equity account, representing the total par value of the shares of stock to be issued. If the account is on the books at the time of the preparation of a balance sheet, the accountant lists it in the Paid-in Capital section, just below Common Stock.

The stock dividend—unlike the cash dividend—does *not* result in a reduction of assets, but merely reshuffles the stockholders' equity accounts. The stock dividend increases the Capital Stock accounts and decreases the Retained Earnings account, without making any change in the total stockholders' equity.

The stock dividend has no effect on the proportionate share of ownership of an individual stockholder. For example, Rosemary Baker owns 500 shares of a corporation's stock, which represents a one-tenth share in the corporation, since the total number of shares issued was 5,000. The corporation declares a 20% stock dividend. As her part of this dividend, she receives 100 shares (20% of 500 shares). Her total stock now amounts to 600 shares; the corporation's total stock is now 6,000 shares. Consequently, Rosemary Baker still has a one-tenth share in the ownership (600 shares/6,000 shares).

For accounting purposes, corporations make a distinction between a stock dividend of 25% or less (small) and a stock dividend of 26% or more (large). The above example represented a small stock dividend, in which the accountant debited Retained Earnings for the fair market value of the shares issued.

If the stock dividend had been a large one, the accountant would have debited Retained Earnings for the par or stated value of the shares to be issued.

Reasons for issuing stock dividends

In view of the fact that a stockholder's proportionate share or equity in a company does not change when the company issues a stock dividend, why does a corporation bother with stock dividends? Here are a few reasons.

1. Stock dividends appease stockholders by giving them paper to hold onto. The corporation can conserve its cash, and the stockholders feel partially satisfied. They didn't get cash, but at least they got something.

2. Stock dividends tend to reduce the market price of the stock. The supply of the stock increases with no immediate commensurate change in the demand for it. Stock with a lower price per share is more easily sold to the public.

3. Stock dividends enable stockholders to avoid income tax liability, since the recipients of stock dividends do not have to consider them as income, and therefore don't have to pay any income tax on them.

Liquidating dividends

A corporation pays *liquidating dividends* when either it is going out of existence or it is permanently reducing the size of its operations, so it returns to the stockholders all or a part of their investment. For example, in the situation shown here, a corporation has returned all stockholders' investment.

1		Common Stock		240 0 0 0 00	
2		Premium on Common Stock		10 0 0 0 00	
3		Cash			250 0 0 0 00
4		To end the business affairs of the corporation,			
5		the board of directors during meeting of Aug.			
6		12 authorized a 100% liquidation dividend.			
7					
8					
9					
10					
11					
12					
13					

Stock split   When there is a *stock split,* a corporation deliberately splits its stock, on the basis of its par or stated value, and issues a proportionate number of additional shares. For example, a corporation with 10,000 shares of $50 par value stock outstanding may reduce the par value to $25 and increase the number of shares to 20,000. If you own 200 shares before the split, you would own 400 shares after it. The company may accomplish the split in shares by calling in all the old shares and issuing certificates for new ones on a 2-for-1 basis; or it may issue an additional share for each old share. The accountant records a stock split by the following entry. (We list the par values by way of explanation.)

1	Common Stock ($50 par value)	400 0 0 0 00		
2	Common Stock ($25 par value)		400 0 0 0 00	
3	The board of directors have this day ordered			
4	a 2-for-1 stock split, increasing the out-			
5	standing shares from 10,000 to 20,000, and			
6	reducing the par value from $50 to $25.			

This 2-for-1 stock split reduces the market price per share by approximately half, thereby increasing the stock's salability, because it now costs less.

There is no change in Retained Earnings. The accountant changes the headings of the Capital Stock accounts in the ledger to show the new par or stated value per share, and revises the stockholders' ledger to show the new distribution of shares. (As an alternative, some accountants record stock splits with a memorandum entry.)

Minute book   We have said that the minute book is an important source document for any accounting entries involving the declaration of dividends and the appropriation of Retained Earnings. The minute book is just like the minute book of a club; it is a written, narrative record of all actions taken at official meetings. A corporation's minute book also contains all details relating to the purchase of plant and equipment, the obtaining of bank loans, the establishing of officers' salaries, etc.

Statement of retained earnings and a balance sheet for a corporation

In this chapter, we have discussed a number of possible situations that would affect the status of retained earnings within a given period of time. These changes are reported on a separate financial statement, called a *statement of retained earnings*. Generally, this statement would list only those items that represent significant changes. For example, in the statement of retained earnings of the Mid-State Distributing Company, shown here, specific appropriations for plant expansion and possible price declines are listed.

Mid-State Distributing Company				
Statement of Retained Earnings				
For year ended December 31, 19–				
Unappropriated retained earnings:				
Unappropriated retained earnings, Jan. 1, 19–	$112 700 00			
Add: Net income for the year	73 000 00	$185 000 00		
Less: Cash dividends declared	$ 20 000 00			
Stock dividends declared	39 500 00			
Transfer to Appropriation for Plant				
Expansion (see below)	4 000 00			
Transfer to Appropriation for Possible				
Price Declines (see below)	3 000 00	66 500 00		
Unappropriated retained earnings, Dec. 31, 19–			$119 200 00	
Appropriated retained earnings:				
Appropriated for Plant Expansion, Jan. 1, 19–	$ 16 000 00			
Add: Appropriation for the year (see above)	4 000 00			
Appropriated for Plant Expansion, Dec. 31, 19–		$ 20 000 00		
Appropriated for Possible Price Declines,				
Jan. 1, 19–	$ 15 000 00			
Add: Appropriation for the year (see above)	3 000 00			
Appropriated for Possible Price Declines,				
Dec. 31, 19–		18 000 00		
Retained earnings appropriated, Dec. 31, 19–			$ 38 000 00	
Total retained earnings, Dec. 31, 19–			$157 200 00	

So that you can better visualize the relationship of the statement of retained earnings to the balance sheet, the balance sheet for the Mid-State Distributing Company is illustrated below and is continued on page 672.

The accountant may use the account Paid-in Capital from Donation to record a situation in which the corporation receives a material gift. For example, the city of Loganville gives the Mid-State Distributing Company one acre of land, valued at $11,650, as an incentive to locate a processing plant there. The accountant for Mid-State debits Land and credits Paid-in Capital from Donation for $11,650 each.

Mid-State Distributing Company			
Balance Sheet			
December 31, 19–			
Assets			
Current Assets:			
Cash		6 4 2 0 00	
Accounts Receivable	163 3 9 0 00		
Less Allowance for Doubtful Accounts	4 2 9 0 00	159 1 0 0 00	
Subscriptions Receivable, Common Stock		3 5 0 0 00	
Merchandise Inventory		320 2 2 0 00	
Supplies		1 2 5 0 00	
Total Current Assets			490 4 9 0 00
Plant and Equipment:			
Equipment	80 7 6 0 00		
Less Accumulated Depreciation	26 7 5 0 00	54 0 1 0 00	
Building	160 0 0 0 00		
Less Accumulated Depreciation	78 0 0 0 00	82 0 0 0 00	
Land		40 0 0 0 00	
Total Plant and Equipment			176 0 1 0 00
Intangible Assets:			
Organization Costs		7 2 0 0 00	
Patents		7 0 0 0 00	
Total Intangible Assets			14 2 0 0 00
Total Assets			680 7 0 0 00
Liabilities			
Current Liabilities:			
Notes Payable	16 0 0 0 00		
Accounts Payable	85 6 9 0 00		
Income Tax Payable	9 2 0 0 00		
Dividends Payable	4 0 0 0 00		
Interest Payable	9 6 0 00		
Total Current Liabilities		115 8 5 0 00	
Long-term Liabilities:			
Mortgage Payable (due July 1, 19–)		54 0 0 0 00	
Total Liabilities			169 8 5 0 00

Stockholders' Equity				
Paid-in Capital:				
Preferred 7% Stock, $25 par (5,000 shares				
authorized and issued)	125 0 0 0 00			
Less Discount on Preferred 7% Stock	10 0 0 0 00	115 0 0 0 00		
Common Stock, no-par, stated value $10 per				
share (20,000 shares authorized, 16,000 shares				
issued)	160 0 0 0 00			
Stock Dividend Distributable (3,950 shares)	39 5 0 0 00			
Common Stock Subscribed (500 shares)	5 0 0 0 00			
Paid-in Capital in Excess of Stated Value	22 5 0 0 00	227 0 0 0 00		
Paid-in Capital from Donation		11 6 5 0 00		
Total Paid-in Capital		353 6 5 0 00		
Retained Earnings:				
Unappropriated Retained Earnings		119 2 0 0 00		
Appropriated:				
Appropriated for Plant Expansion	20 0 0 0 00			
Appropriated for Possible Price Declines	18 0 0 0 00			
Appropriated Retained Earnings		38 0 0 0 00		
Total Retained Earnings		157 2 0 0 00		
Total Stockholders' Equity			510 8 5 0 00	
Total Liabilities and Stockholders' Equity			680 7 0 0 00	

Summary

A corporation, since it is a separate legal entity, must pay a federal corporate income tax. Many state and local governments also levy income taxes on corporations. A corporation has to estimate the federal income tax it will have to pay for the forthcoming year, and pay it in advance in four quarterly installments. At the end of the year, when the corporation knows the exact amount of its net income, the company accountant makes an adjusting entry either for the amount of the additional tax owed or for the amount of the tax overpaid. Assume that additional tax is owed; in general journal form, the entries look like this.

	Income Tax	10 0 0 0 00	
	Cash		10 0 0 0 00
	Installments paid quarterly.		

	Adjusting Entry		
	Income Tax	9 2 0 0 00	
	Income Tax Payable		9 2 0 0 00

If the corporation owes additional taxes, it pays this account in two installments during the year following the taxable year. Here's what the entry for one payment would look like.

	Income Tax Payable	4 6 0 0 00	
	Cash		4 6 0 0 00
	Payment of additional tax liability.		

The steps in the closing process for a corporation are as follows.

1. Close revenue accounts into Income Summary.

2. Close expense accounts into Income Summary.

3. Close Income Tax into Income Summary.

4. Close Income Summary into Retained Earnings.

In completing the work sheet for a corporation, the accountant first determines the amount of the net income in the Income Statement columns. Next, the accountant backtracks to record the adjusting entry for income tax. Finally, he or she extends all the remaining current figures into the appropriate columns and completes the work sheet.

An appropriation of retained earnings is a restriction—or earmarking for a specific purpose—of the Retained Earnings account, making the amount unavailable for dividends. The entry in each case is a debit to Retained Earnings and a credit to Retained Earnings Appropriated for _____ (some specific purpose). The Retained Earnings account, by itself, is unappropriated.

The entries involving cash dividends are as follows.

	Retained Earnings		3 6 0 0 00			
	Dividends Payable				3 6 0 0 00	
	Declaration of cash dividends.					

	Dividends Payable		3 6 0 0 00			
	Cash				3 6 0 0 00	
	Payments of cash dividends.					

The entries involving stock dividends look like this.

	Retained Earnings (number of shares × market value per share		23 0 0 0 00			
	Stock Dividend Distributable (number of shares × par value or stated value per share)				20 0 0 0 00	
	Premium on Common Stock (or Paid-in Capital in Excess of Stated Value)				3 0 0 0 00	
	Declaration of a stock dividend.					

		Stock Dividend Distributable		20 0 0 0 00	
		Common Stock			20 0 0 0 00
		Issuance of a stock dividend.			

Glossary

Appropriation of retained earnings   Retained Earnings decreased for a specific purpose; this appropriation restricts the possibility of issuing cash and stock dividends.

Cash dividend   Distribution of corporation earnings to stockholders in the form of cash.

Deficit   Debit or negative balance in the Retained Earnings account.

Liquidating dividend   Distribution of corporation assets to stockholders in the final windup of the business.

Minute book   A written narrative of all actions taken at official meetings of the board of directors.

Stock dividend   Distribution of corporation retained earnings to stockholders in the form of shares of the corporation's own stock.

Stock split   A deliberate reduction of the par value or stated value of a corporation's stock and the issuing of a proportionate number of additional shares.

Questions

1. What is the difference between a stock dividend and a stock split?

2. Explain why an appropriation of retained earnings is not the same as setting aside cash?

3. How does a corporation dispose of a retained earnings appropriated account, such as Retained Earnings Appropriated for Building?

4. Why are stock dividends not considered to be taxable income to the receivers of the dividends?

5. If the Retained Earnings account has a debit balance, what is it called? How is it presented in the balance sheet?

6. What journal entry is made for cash dividends for the following dates: date of declaration, date of record, date of payment?

7. What are the journal entries to eliminate the following accounts: Income Tax Payable, Income Tax?

Exercises

Exercise 1 The Sherman Shoe Company has the following account balances pertaining to its common stock.

Subscriptions Receivable (1,000 shares)	$ 56,000
Common Stock, $50 par (8,000 shares issued)	400,000
Common Stock Subscribed (1,000 shares)	50,000
Premium on Common Stock	14,000

The board of directors declares a cash dividend of $5 per share. What is the total amount of the dividend?

Exercise 2 A corporation's balance sheet includes the following.

Preferred 6% Stock	$100,000
Preferred 6% Stock Subscribed	40,000
Subscriptions Receivable, Preferred 6% Stock	15,200
Discount on Preferred 6% Stock	1,400
Common Stock	160,000
Paid-in Capital in Excess of Stated Value	50,000
Retained Earnings (credit balance)	65,000

a. How much of the paid-in capital is the result of the preferred 6% stock?

b. How much of the paid-in capital is the result of the common stock?

c. What is the total stockholders' equity?

Exercise 3 Prepare the stockholders' equity section of the balance sheet from the following account balances.

Retained Earnings	$ 70,000
Subscriptions Receivable Preferred 9% Stock	20,000
Common Stock, $50 par (10,000 shares authorized)	300,000
Preferred 9% Stock, $100 par (500 shares authorized)	20,000
Premium on Common Stock	24,000
Preferred 9% Stock Subscribed	20,000

Exercise 4 The balance sheet of the Oliver Sheet and Tube Corporation gives the following information: Common Stock, $20 par (40,000 shares authorized, 32,000 shares issued), $640,000; Premium on Common Stock, $72,000; Retained Earnings, $184,000 (credit balance). When the market price of the stock is $28 per share, the

board of directors declares a 10% stock dividend. List entries to record a declaration of the dividend and issuance of the stock certificates.

Exercise 5   On December 31, the board of directors of Surfside Oyster Company, Inc., vote to appropriate $50,000 of the corporation's unappropriated retained earnings to Retained Earnings Appropriated for Plant Expansion. This is the fourth such appropriation, so it gives a balance of $200,000 in Retained Earnings Appropriated for Plant Expansion. On January 20, the corporation buys a warehouse for $194,000 (building, $166,000; land, $28,000), paying $74,000 down and financing the remainder on a mortgage note. Write the entries to record the following.

a. The appropriation of retained earnings on December 31

b. The purchase of the building and land

c. The release of $200,000 of the Retained Earnings Appropriated for Plant Expansion

Exercise 6   On December 31, the stockholders' equity of Northland Pottery Company, Inc., is as follows.

Paid-in Capital:			
Common Stock, no par, stated value $20 per			
share (20,000 shares authorized, 18,000 shares			
issued)	$360 000 00		
Paid-in Capital in Excess of Stated Value	61 000 00		
Total Paid-in Capital		$421 000 00	
Retained Earnings:			
Unappropriated Retained Earnings	$136 000 00		
Appropriated:			
Appropriated for Contingencies	70 000 00		
Total Retained Earnings		206 000 00	
Total Stockholders' Equity			$627 000 00

On December 31, when the stock was selling at $34 per share, the board of directors voted a 20% stock dividend, distributable on February 5, to stockholders of record on January 15. Give the entries to record the declaration and distribution of the dividend.

Exercise 7 Describe the entries recorded by letters in the T accounts below.

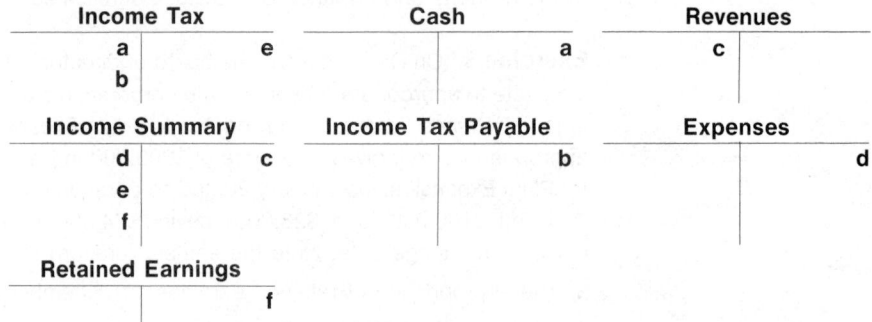

Income Tax		Cash		Revenues	
a	e		a		c
b					

Income Summary		Income Tax Payable		Expenses	
d	c		b		d
e					
f					

Retained Earnings	
	f

Exercise 8 The stockholders of Far North Exploration Company, Inc., donated 4,000 shares of no-par common stock to the corporation. Later the corporation sold the stock for $9 per share. Give the journal entries for the receipt of the stock and for the sale of the stock.

Problems _____

Problem 24-1 Some of the transactions of Waters and Marshall, Inc., during this fiscal year are as follows.

Mar. 11 Paid first installment on balance due on previous year's federal income tax, $7,500.

31 Paid $12,840 for the first quarterly installment of estimated federal income tax for this year.

June 12 Paid second installment of balance due on previous year's federal income tax, $7,500.

30 Paid $12,840 for the second quarterly installment of estimated federal income tax for this year.

July 15 Declared a cash dividend of $16,800 ($1.68 per share on 10,000 shares, $10 par value) to stockholders of record as of July 30, which is payable on August 10.

Aug. 10 Paid the cash dividend.

Sept. 20 Declared a 5% stock dividend on the common stock outstanding, to stockholders of record as of September 30, payable on October 10. Fair market value of stock, $14 per share.

30 Paid $12,840 for the third quarterly installment of estimated federal income tax for this year.

Oct. 10 Issued stock comprising the stock dividend.

Nov. 15 Declared a cash dividend of $17,640 ($1.68 per share on 10,500 shares) to stockholders of record as of November 30, payable on December 10.

Dec. 10 Paid the cash dividend.

Dec. 31 Recorded $14,640 additional federal income tax allocable to net income for the year.

31 The board of directors authorized the appropriation of retained earnings for plant expansion, $4,800.

Instructions   Record these transactions in general journal form.

Problem 24-2 The trial balance of the Gonzales Distributing Company, Inc., dated December 31 of this year, is as follows.

Gonzales Distributing Company, Inc.		
Trial Balance		
December 31, 19—		
Cash	7 020 00	
Notes Receivable	14 460 00	
Accounts Receivable	157 524 00	
Allowance for Doubtful Accounts		2 691 00
Subscriptions Receivable, Preferred 9% Stock	12 900 00	
Merchandise Inventory	280 110 00	
Prepaid Insurance	1 296 00	
Delivery Equipment	85 110 00	
Accumulated Depreciation, Delivery Equipment		16 095 00
Organization Costs	9 600 00	
Accounts Payable		73 149 00
Preferred 9% Stock ($100 par)		75 000 00
Preferred 9% Stock Subscribed		15 000 00
Premium on Preferred 9% Stock		3 300 00
Common Stock ($20 stated value)		150 000 00
Paid-in Capital in Excess of Stated Value		18 000 00
Retained Earnings		78 000 00
Sales		1,767 600 00
Purchases	1,343 010 00	
Purchases Discount		7 800 00
Selling Expenses (control)	198 945 00	
General Expenses (control)	56 100 00	
Income Tax	42 270 00	
Interest Income		1 710 00
	2,208 345 00	2,208 345 00

To reduce the number of accounts in the trial balance, Selling Expenses (control) is used in place of all selling expenses. Likewise, General Expenses (control) is used in place of all general expenses.

Data for the adjustments:

Merchandise Inventory, Dec. 31 (ending inventory), $288,285

Additional depreciation for the year amounts to $6,435; record depreciation expense under Selling Expenses (control).

Insurance expired during the year amounts to $771; record insurance expired under General Expenses (control).

Analysis of Accounts Receivable indicates $5,280 is uncollectible; record estimated bad-debt losses under General Expenses (control).

Accrued interest on Notes Receivable, $180

Additional income tax due for this year, $12,840

No dividends were declared during the year.

Instructions
1. Record the trial balance in the work sheet (leave two lines for General Expenses control) and complete the work sheet for the year.
2. Prepare an income statement.
3. Prepare a statement of retained earnings.
4. Prepared a classified balance sheet.

Problem 24-3 The Stockholders' Equity section of the balance sheet of the Murdock Lumber Company, Inc., as of December 31 is as follows.

Stockholders' Equity			
Paid-in Capital:			
Preferred 9% Stock, $100 par (3,500 shares authorized, 2,000 shares issued)	$200 000 00		
Premium on Preferred 9% Stock	8 000 00		
Common Stock, no par, stated value $20 a share			
(30,000 shares authorized, 16,000 shares issued)	320 000 00		
Paid-in Capital in Excess of Stated Value	160 000 00		
Total Paid-in Capital		$688 000 00	
Retained Earnings:			
Unappropriated Retained Earnings	$170 000 00		
Appropriated:			
Retained Earnings Appropriated for Expansion	36 000 00		
Total Retained Earnings		206 000 00	
Total Stockholders' Equity			$894 000 00

Some of the transactions that took place during the next year are:

Mar. 26 Declared the regular semiannual $4.50 per share dividend on the preferred stock and a $1.00 per share dividend on the common stock to stockholders of record on April 15, payable on April 21.

Apr. 21 Paid cash dividends declared on March 26.

28 Received subscriptions to 1,000 shares of common stock at $32 per share, collecting 60% of the subscription price.

May 15 Subscribers to 1,000 shares of common stock paid the remaining 40% of the subscription price; Murdock Lumber then issued the 1,000 shares.

Sept. 26 Declared the regular semiannual $4.50 per share dividend on the preferred stock and a $1.50 per share dividend on the common stock to stockholders of record on October 15, payable October 22.

Oct. 22 Paid cash dividends declared on September 26.

Dec. 21 Declared a 20% stock dividend on common stock outstanding to stockholders of record on January 15, payable January 21. Fair market value of the stock: $34.

31 After the accountant has closed all revenue, expense, and Income Tax accounts, the Income Summary account has credit balance of $136,000. Closed the Income Summary account.

31 Increased the appropriation for expansion by $18,000.

Instructions **1.** Enter in the ledger accounts the balances appearing in the Stockholders' Equity section of the balance sheet as of December 31.

2. Journalize entries in general journal form to record the transactions that occurred during the next year and post to the stockholders' equity accounts.

3. Prepare Stockholders' Equity section of balance sheet as of December 31 of the next year.

Problem 24-4 The account balances taken from the general ledger and statement of retained earnings for Meredith Mercantile, Inc., are as follows. Preferred 8% stock: 1,500 shares authorized, 1,200 shares issued. Common stock: 15,000 shares authorized, 10,200 shares issued.

Accounts Receivable	$189,540
Building	135,000
Mortgage Payable (due April 15, 1985)	63,000
Stock Dividend Distributable (930 shares)	13,950
Dividends Payable	7,200
Land	18,000
Accumulated Depreciation, Building	34,200
Notes Receivable	18,000
Preferred 8% Stock, $100 par, 1,500 shares authorized	120,000
Retained Earnings Appropriated for Plant Expansion	12,300
Income Tax Payable	21,900

Preferred 8% Stock Subscribed (300 shares)	30,000
Subscriptions Receivable, Preferred 8% Stock	15,150
Cash	8,730
Premium on Preferred 8% Stock	1,500
Paid-in Capital from Donation	18,750
Retained Earnings Appropriated for Inventory Losses	6,000
Merchandise Inventory	356,805
Equipment	69,900
Common Stock, $15 stated value, 15,000 shares authorized	153,000
Retained Earnings	114,600
Paid-in Capital in Excess of Stated Value	33,390
Accumulated Depreciation, Equipment	37,305
Accounts Payable	147,390
Allowance for Doubtful Accounts	6,930
Organization Costs	9,000
Prepaid Insurance	1,290

Instructions   Prepare a classified balance sheet dated December 31.

Alternate problems

Problem 24-1A   Some of the transactions of the Stillwell Overhead Door Corporation during this fiscal year are as follows.

Mar. 10 Paid installment of balance due on previous year's federal income tax, $22,470.

31 Paid $31,050 for the first quarterly installment of estimated federal income tax for current year.

June 14 Paid second installment of previous year's federal income tax, $22,470.

30 Paid $31,050 for the second quarterly installment of estimated federal income tax for this year.

July 18 Declared a cash dividend of $34,200 ($3.42 per share on 10,000 shares, $25 par value) to stockholders of record as of July 31, payable on August 12.

Aug. 12 Paid cash dividend.

Sept. 15 Declared a 10% stock dividend on common stock outstanding to stockholders of record as of September 28, payable October 8. Fair market value of stock: $40 per share.

30 Paid $31,050 for the third quarterly installment of estimated federal income tax for this year.

Oct. 8 Issued stock comprising stock dividend.

Nov. 18 Declared a cash dividend of $39,600 ($3.60 per share on 11,000 shares) to stockholders of record as of November 30, payable December 12.

Dec. 12 Paid cash dividend.

31 Recorded $21,960 additional federal income tax allocable to net income for the year.

31 The board of directors authorized the appropriation of retained earnings for plant expansion, $14,700.

Instructions   Record the above transactions in general journal form.

Problem 24-2A   The trial balance for Mooney Products Company, Inc., dated May 31 of this year, is as follows.

Mooney Products Company, Inc.		
Trial Balance		
May 31, 19–		
Cash	5 874 00	
Accounts Receivable	173 115 00	
Allowance for Doubtful Accounts		2 799 00
Subscriptions Receivable, Common Stock	39 000 00	
Merchandise Inventory	284 505 00	
Store Supplies	9 45 00	
Store Equipment	109 020 00	
Accumulated Depreciation, Store Equipment		17 430 00
Organization Costs	8 130 00	
Notes Payable		15 000 00
Accounts Payable		76 560 00
Preferred 8% Stock ($100 par)		60 000 00
Premium on Preferred 8% Stock		3 000 00
Common Stock ($20 stated value)		165 000 00
Common Stock Subscribed		45 000 00
Paid-in Capital in Excess of Stated Value		21 000 00
Retained Earnings		77 400 00
Sales		1,524 450 00
Purchases	1,093 650 00	
Purchases Discount		7 980 00
Selling Expenses (control)	201 456 00	
General Expenses (control)	57 399 00	
Interest Expense	2 310 00	
Income Tax	40 215 00	
	2,015 619 00	2,015 619 00

To reduce the number of accounts in the trial balance, Selling Expenses (control) is used in place of all selling expenses. Likewise, General.Expenses (control) is used in place of all general expenses.

Data for the adjustments:

Merchandise Inventory, May 31 (ending inventory), $291.330

Additional depreciation for the year amounts to $6,195; record depreciation under Selling Expenses (control).

Inventory of store supplies at May 31, $651; record the supplies used under Selling Expenses (control).

Analysis of Accounts Receivable indicates $5,235 is uncollectible; record estimated bad-debt losses under General Expenses (control).

Accrued interest on Notes Payable, $210

Additional income tax due for the current year, $14,130

No dividends were declared during the year.

Instructions
1. Record the trial balance in the work sheet (leave two lines for General Expenses control) and complete the work sheet for the year.
2. Prepare an income statement.
3. Prepare a statement of retained earnings.
4. Prepare a classified balance sheet.

Problem 24-3A The Stockholders' Equity section of the balance sheet of the Wells Motors, Inc., as of December 31 is as follows.

Stockholders' Equity			
Paid-in Capital:			
Preferred 9% Stock, $100 par (2,500 shares			
authorized, 1,500 shares issued)	$150 0 0 0 00		
Premium on Preferred 9% Stock	6 0 0 0 00		
Common Stock, no par, stated value $20 a share			
(20,000 shares authorized, 12,000 shares			
issued)	240 0 0 0 00		
Paid-in Capital in Excess of Stated Value	72 0 0 0 00		
Total Paid-in Capital		$468 0 0 0 00	
Retained Earnings:			
Unappropriated Retained Earnings	$140 0 0 0 00		
Appropriated:			
Retained Earnings Appropriated for Expansion	28 0 0 0 00		
Total Retained Earnings		168 0 0 0 00	
Total Stockholders' Equity			$636 0 0 0 00

Some of the transactions that took place during the next year are:

Apr. 12 Declared the regular semiannual $4.50 per share dividend on the preferred stock and a $1.25 per share dividend on the common stock to stockholders of record on May 1, payable on May 10.

May 3 Received subscriptions to 2,000 shares of common stock at $29 per share, collecting 70% of the subscription price.

10 Paid cash dividends declared on April 12.

28 Subscribers to 2,000 shares of common stock paid the remaining 30% of the subscription price; Wells Motors then issued the 2,000 shares.

Aug. 12 Declared the regular semiannual $4.50 per share dividend on the preferred stock and a $1.50 per share dividend on the common stock to stockholders of record on September 1, payable September 21.

Sept. 21 Paid cash dividends declared on August 12.

Dec. 29 Declared a 10% stock dividend on common stock outstanding to stockholders of record on January 16, payable January 28. Fair market value of the stock: $30.

31 After the accountant has closed all revenue, expense, and Income Tax accounts, the Income Summary account has a credit balance of $74,000. Closed the Income Summary account.

31 Increased the appropriation for plant expansion by $16,000.

Instructions **1.** Enter in the ledger accounts the balances appearing in the Stockholders' Equity section of the balance sheet as of December 31.

2. Journalize entries in general journal form to record the transactions that occurred during the next year and post to the stockholders' equity accounts.

3. Prepare Stockholders' Equity section of balance sheet as of December 31 of the next year.

Problem 24-4A Here are the account balances taken from the general ledger and statement of retained earnings for Eastgate Distributing Company, Inc. Preferred 8% stock: 1,500 shares authorized, 1,140 shares issued. Common stock: 30,000 shares authorized, 18,000 shares issued.

Prepaid Insurance	$ 1,440
Organization Costs	12,000
Allowance for Doubtful Accounts	8,460
Accounts Payable	169,140
Accumulated Depreciation, Equipment	51,300
Paid-in Capital in Excess of Stated Value	54,000
Retained Earnings	160,050
Common Stock, $15 stated value	270,000
Equipment	109,350
Merchandise Inventory	513,765
Retained Earnings Appropriated for Inventory Losses	12,600

Paid-in Capital from Donation	10,800
Premium on Preferred 8% Stock	3,000
Cash	13,065
Subscriptions Receivable, Preferred 8% Stock	18,360
Preferred 8% Stock Subscribed (360 shares)	36,000
Income Tax Payable	30,900
Retained Earnings Appropriated for Plant Expansion	24,000
Preferred 8% Stock, $100 par	114,000
Notes Receivable	18,900
Accumulated Depreciation, Building	93,600
Land	37,500
Dividends Payable	12,300
Stock Dividend Distributable (1,665 shares)	24,975
Mortgage Payable (due April 16, 1986)	72,900
Building	180,000
Accounts Receivable	243,645

Instructions   Prepare a classified balance sheet dated December 31.

Appendix B:
Treasury stock and retirement of stock

IN CHAPTER 23 we stated that treasury stock is the corporation's own stock that had been issued at one time and reacquired by the corporation at a later time. The corporation either bought back its own stock or received the stock from its stockholders as a donation. The reacquired stock is kept in the corporation's own treasury, and the stock may be resold at a later time. In this appendix, we shall present various transactions involving treasury stock. We shall also discuss the retirement of stock. When a corporation retires its own stock, it reacquires the stock for the purpose of permanently eliminating or canceling the stock.

Definition of treasury stock

Corporations óften reacquire shares of their own stock by buying them back in the open market. What the corporation is doing is putting its own stock back in its treasury, thereby reducing the stockholders' equity. Why does it do this? The corporation buys back its own stock for these reasons:

1. To have stock available to reissue to officers and employees under a bonus plan or employee stock-purchase plan.

2. To support the market value of the stock when it is unusually depressed.

3. To have shares available for exchanges of stock when the company acquires other companies.

Occasionally a corporation in poor financial condition may receive a donation of its own stock from its stockholders. The stockholders do this so that the corporation can sell the donated stock and thereby bring some badly needed new cash into the business. The reason is that the stockholders feel that it's wise to give up a little in order to save their investment.

There's a definite difference between treasury stock and unissued stock. *Treasury stock* is the company's own stock which it has issued previously, and which it reacquires; it has not canceled this stock. The company may hold treasury stock indefinitely. Although treasury stock is not entitled to share in cash dividends, it is ordinarily involved when there are stock dividends and stock splits. However, treasury stock has no voting rights, no preemptive right to share in new stock issues, and no right to share in the assets if the corporation should be liquidated. If treasury stock is reissued later at a price below its par or stated value, there is no contingent liability for the amount of the discount or deficiency of legal capital. In other respects it is similar to unissued stock.

Transactions involving treasury stock

When the company buys its own stock, the accountant debits the account Treasury Stock for the cost of the stock. The Treasury Stock account is a deduction from stockholders' equity. It is not an investment, because technically a corporation cannot own a part of itself. For purposes of accounting, one ignores the par or stated value, and the price at which the stock was originally issued. When the company resells its treasury stock, the accountant records it at the price paid for it, and either debits or credits the difference between the price paid and the selling price to an account titled Paid-in Capital from Sale of

Treasury Stock. For example, the paid-in capital of the Windsor Corporation is composed of common stock and premium on common stock, as follows: Common Stock, $50 par (10,000 shares authorized and issued), $500,000; Premium on Common Stock, $10,000. Retained earnings are $100,000. The corporation engages in the following transactions relating to its own stock.

1. Bought 500 shares of treasury stock at $60 per share.
2. Sold 100 shares of treasury stock at $65 per share.
3. Sold 100 shares of treasury stock at $58 per share.
4. Reissued 100 shares of treasury stock as a bonus to employees.
5. Received 120 shares from stockholders as a donation.
6. Sold the donated stock for $59 per share.

Here are the entries in general journal form.

		Debit	Credit
(1)	Treasury Stock	30 000 00	
	Cash		30 000 00
	Bought 500 shares of treasury stock at $60 per share		
(2)	Cash	6 500 00	
	Treasury Stock		6 000 00
	Paid-in Capital from Sale of Treasury Stock		5 00 00
	Sold 100 shares of treasury stock at $65 per share; the cost		
	was $60 per share		
(3)	Cash	5 800 00	
	Paid-in Capital from Sale of Treasury Stock	2 00 00	
	Treasury Stock		6 000 00
	Sold 100 shares of treasury stock at $58 per share; the cost		
	was $60 per share		
(4)	Bonus to Employees	6 000 00	
	Treasury Stock		6 000 00
	Reissued 100 shares of treasury stock as a bonus to employees		
	at cost		
(5)	Memorandum Entry: Received 120 shares of our stock from		
	stockholders as a donation		
(6)	Cash	7 080 00	
	Paid-in Capital from Donation		7 080 00
	Sold 120 shares of donated treasury stock at $59 per share		

When these entries are posted to the accounts, they will appear as illustrated here:

Cash			
+		−	
2	6,500	**1**	30,000
3	5,800		
6	7,080		

(An expense account)

Bonus to Employees			
+		−	
4	6,000		

(A stockholders' equity account)

Treasury Stock, Common			
+		−	
Cost of treasury stock purchased		Cost of treasury stock sold	
1 (500 shares)	30,000	**2** (100 shares)	6,000
5 Memo: Donation of 120 shares		**3** (100 shares)	6,000
		4 (100 shares)	6,000
		6 Memo: Sold 120 shares of donated treasury stock	

(A stockholders' equity account)

Paid-in Capital from Sale of Treasury Stock			
−		+	
Loss from sale of treasury stock		Gain from sale of treasury stock	
3	200	**2**	500

(A stockholders' equity account)

Paid-in Capital from Donation			
−		+	
		Gain to corporation	
		6	7,080

After the accountant makes these entries, the Stockholders' Equity section of the balance sheet would look like this.

Stockholders' Equity					
Paid-in Capital					
Common Stock, $50 par (10,000 shares authorized and issued, of which 200 shares are in the treasury)	500 0 0 0 00				
Premium on Common Stock	10 0 0 0 00	510 0 0 0 00		
Paid-in Capital from Sale of Treasury Stock		3 0 0 00		
Paid-in Capital from Donation		7 0 8 0 00		
Total Paid-in Capital		517 3 8 0 00		
Retained Earnings		100 0 0 0 00		
Total Paid-in Capital and Retained Earnings		617 3 8 0 00		
Less Treasury Stock (200 shares at cost)		12 0 0 0 00		
Total Stockholders' Equity			605 3 8 0 00

Retirement of stock

A corporation may buy shares of its own stock to be permanently canceled. This action is permissible if it does not jeopardize the interests of other stockholders or of creditors. For example, a company may buy preferred stock on the open market in order to reduce the prior-dividend advantage which holders of preferred stock have. This doesn't jeopardize the interests of the stockholders, because obviously they're willing to sell at the market price. A company may use this device to retire either preferred or common stock.

When a company buys stock in order to retire it, the company also cancels all the paid-in-capital accounts related to the shares. If there is a gain on the transaction (that is, if the firm is able to buy back the stock for less than the amount it originally sold it for), the accountant credits the gain to Paid-in Capital from Retirement of Stock; if there is a loss on the transaction (that is, if the firm has to pay more to buy back the stock than the amount it originally sold it for), the accountant debits the loss to Retained Earnings.

Gain on retirement of stock

The Saugus Sugar Corporation originally issued its $100 par-value preferred 9% stock at $102 per share, crediting the $2 premium to Premium on Preferred 9% Stock. Saugus later bought (for retirement) 100 shares at $98 per share. The entry to record the retirement, in general journal form, is as follows.

Preferred 9% Stock	10 0 00 00	
Premium on Preferred 9% Stock	2 0 0 00	
Cash		9 8 0 0 00
Paid-in Capital from Retirement of Stock		4 0 0 00
Purchased and retired 100 shares of preferred 9% stock at $98 per share.		

Loss on retirement of stock

Preferred stock is often *callable,* which means that the corporation can legally call it in at a specific price. This specific price, which is stipulated in the original contract of issue, is always in excess of the par value.

As an illustration: The Saugus Sugar Corporation has outstanding 1,000 shares of preferred 8% stock, par value $100, callable at $105 per share. The stock originally sold for $99 per share. Under the present market conditions, Saugus can issue 1,000 shares of preferred 6% stock, par value $100, at par, which will save dividends of $2,000 per year. The accountant for Saugus makes the following entry to retire the preferred 8% stock.

Preferred 8% Stock	100 0 0 0 00	
Retained Earnings	6 0 0 0 00	
Cash		105 0 0 0 00
Discount on Preferred 8% Stock		1 0 0 0 00
Purchased and retired 1,000 shares of preferred 8% stock at $105 per share.		

Problems

Problem B-1 Selected transactions involving treasury stock completed by the Forbes Corporation during this year are as follows.

Jan. 16 Bought 2,000 shares of own stock at $42 per share.

Mar. 19 Sold 1,000 shares of own stock at $46 per share.

Apr. 30 Received 1,400 shares from stockholders as a donation.

Nov. 21 Sold the donated stock for $40 per share.

Dec. 8 Sold 1,000 shares of treasury stock for $40 per share.

Instructions Record the above transactions in a general journal.

Problem B-2 The Sanchez Corporation has an authorized capital of 20,000 shares of $25 par-value common stock. Account balances are as follows.

Premium on Common Stock	$ 32,000
Treasury Stock (400 shares)	12,000
Organization Costs	4,000
Paid-in Capital from Donation	8,000
Retained Earnings	90,000
Income Tax Payable	26,000
Paid-in Capital from Sale of Treasury Stock	6,000
Common Stock	400,000

Instructions Prepare the stockholders' equity section of the balance sheet.

Problem B-3 The Schneider Corporation has a charter which stipulates the following authorized capital.

10,000 shares of preferred 7% stock, $40 par value

80,000 shares of common stock, $20 par value

During the current year, the Schneider Corporation completed the following transactions pertaining to its stock accounts.

Apr. 3 Received subscriptions to 1,000 shares of preferred 7% stock at $40 per share, collecting 50% of the subscription price.

June 16 Bought 900 shares of own common stock at $32 per share.

July 2 Subscribers to 500 shares of preferred 7% stock paid the remaining 50% of the subscription price; issued the stock.

Oct. 29 Acquired 1,000 shares of common stock for $26,000 from the estate of a deceased stockholder; retired the stock. The stock originally sold for $28 per share.

Dec. 20 Subscribers to 500 shares of preferred 7% stock paid an additional 25% of the subscription price.

Instructions Record the above transactions in a general journal.

*Corporations:
long-term
obligations*

objectives

After you have completed this chapter, you will be able to do the following:
* Journalize transactions involving the issuance of bonds at a premium or discount.
* Journalize adjusting entries for amortization of bond premiums and discounts and accrued interest payable.
* Journalize entries pertaining to the establishing of a bond sinking fund, the receiving of income from sinking fund investments, and the eventual payment of the principal of the bonds.
* Journalize transactions involving the redemption of bonds.

IN OUR discussions of corporations, we have assumed that the company got the money it needed for building and expansion by selling stock and retaining earnings. There's another possibility: A corporation can borrow money for a long period (5 to 40 years) by issuing bonds. For all practical purposes, one may consider a bond to be a long-term promissory note. A *bond issue*—the total amount which the corporation promises to pay—is subdivided into denominations of $1,000 or $5,000 each, with $1,000 the most common. You can get a better picture of bonds by comparing them with capital stock.

Bonds	Capital Stock
Bondholders are creditors; they receive interest, and are eventually repaid the principal.	Stockholders are owners; they receive dividends.
Bonds Payable is classified as a long-term liability account.	Capital stock is subdivided into Common Stock and Preferred Stock accounts, which are stockholders' equity accounts.
Interest paid on bonds is a valid expense which must be paid year after year. Otherwise, bondholders may initiate bankruptcy proceedings against the debtor corporation.	Dividends are distributions of net income, rather than expenses.
Interest is deductible as an expense before arriving at net income.	Dividends are not deductible before arriving at net income.

Classification of bonds

To appeal to investors, corporations have created a wide variety of bonds, each with slightly different combinations of characteristics, just as an automobile manufacturer offers different models with various combinations of accessories.

Term bonds All term bonds have the same term or time period, the entire issue of bonds coming due at the same time. For example, $1,000,000 worth of 10-year bonds issued January 1, 1976, all mature January 1, 1986.

Serial bonds Serial bonds have a series of maturity dates. *Example:* $1,000,000 worth of bonds issued March 1, 1976, may mature as follows.

$100,000 on March 1, 1981	$100,000 on March 1, 1986
$100,000 on March 1, 1982	$100,000 on March 1, 1987
$100,000 on March 1, 1983	$100,000 on March 1, 1988
$100,000 on March 1, 1984	$100,000 on March 1, 1989
$100,000 on March 1, 1985	$100,000 on March 1, 1990

Registered bonds When bonds are registered, the names of the owners are recorded with the issuing corporation. Title to such bonds is transferred when the bonds are sold, just as title to stock is transferred. The corporation pays interest by mailing checks to the registered owners.

Coupon bonds These derive their name from the interest coupons attached to each bond. The interest coupons are payable to bearer, in much the same manner as paper money is. The owners' names may or may not be listed for the amount of the principal. The illustration below shows the format of a coupon bond.

Atlas Corporation Bond $1,000, 20 years, 8% Payable semiannually, April 1 and October 1			
$40 Apr. 1, 1996	$40 Oct. 1, 1995	$40 Apr. 1, 1995	$40 Oct. 1, 1994
$40 Apr. 1, 1994	$40 Oct. 1, 1993	$40 Apr. 1, 1993	$40 Oct. 1, 1992
$40 Apr. 1, 1982	$40 Oct. 1, 1981	$40 Apr. 1, 1981	$40 Oct. 1, 1980
$40 Apr. 1, 1980	$40 Oct. 1, 1979	$40 Apr. 1, 1979	$40 Oct. 1, 1978
$40 Apr. 1, 1978	$40 Oct. 1, 1977	$40 Apr. 1, 1977	$40 Oct. 1, 1976

The corporation pays the interest every 6 months, and each coupon is worth $40. The owner of the bond clips the coupons as they become due, and deposits them with a regular commercial bank for collection.

Secured bonds When a bond is secured, it is covered or backed up by mortgages on real estate or by titles to personal property. It may be called a mortgage bond or an equipment trust bond. In case the corporation defaults in its payment of principal or interest, the bondholders, acting through a trustee, may take over the pledged assets.

Unsecured bonds An unsecured bond, also called a *debenture,* is one that is issued just on the corporation's credit standing. Such bonds usually succeed only when issued by financially strong firms.

A bond can have characteristics of all three classifications. For example, if a corporation issues 20-year mortgage bonds with coupons providing for the payment of interest, the bonds are term bonds, coupon bonds, and secured bonds.

A corporation which needs money on a long-term basis has the choice of raising the necessary funds by issuing (1) common stock, (2) preferred stock, or (3) bonds. Each choice has advantages and disadvantages. Since the holders of common stock control the corporation through their voting power, the choice of means of financing is up to them. Stockholders think about the pros and cons of bonds as follows.

Bonds offer these advantages:

1. The bond-issuing corporation has the prospect of earning a greater return on the money it raises than it has to pay out in interest. This is known as *leverage.* For example, if a firm can borrow money at an interest rate of 8% and use this cash in the business to earn a net income of 15% after taxes, then the additional earnings of 7% (15% − 8%) are available to pay dividends to the holders of common stock.

2. Interest payments are tax-deductible expenses.

3. Bondholders cannot vote, so common stockholders can retain control of the company's affairs.

On the other hand, these disadvantages have to be considered:

1. Bondholders are creditors of the corporation, so interest payments are fixed obligations. On the other hand, a corporation pays dividends only when it has enough money to do so.

2. The corporation must eventually pay the principal of the bonds it issues, but it does not have to repay the money it receives from issuing stock.

When a corporation is trying to decide whether to issue additional stock or to issue bonds, an important factor is estimated future earnings and the probable stability of these earnings. The advantages and disadvantages of issuing bonds become apparent in the following illustration.

Midwest Motor Freight, which has 40,000 shares of $50 par-value common stock outstanding, wishes to raise an additional $1,000,000 for expansion. Midwest is considering three possible ways of raising the money:

Plan 1 Issue an additional $1,000,000 of common stock, thereby increasing the total stock outstanding from 40,000 to 60,000 shares.

Plan 2 Issue $1,000,000 of 8% cumulative preferred stock.

Plan 3 Issue $1,000,000 of 7% bonds.

The table on pages 698–699 shows how Midwest Motor Freight would come out (1) if it had a yearly net income from operations of $420,000 and (2) if it had a yearly net income from operations of $60,000. (We assume that the federal corporation income tax is 50%.)

You can see that plan 3 offers the greatest advantage to the original holders of common stock, provided that the company's earnings are large enough to pay the bondholders and still leave a sizable share for the holders of common stock. When the company has a low level of earnings, plan 1 is most advantageous to the holders of common stock, because there are no prior claims of bondholders or preferred stockholders. The firm could use a combination of the three, but this would mean bigger underwriting or financing costs.

Accounting for the issuance of bonds

When a corporation issues bonds at face value, it records the transaction as a debit to Cash and a credit to Bonds Payable. Bonds Payable is a long-term liability account. If there is more than one bond issue, the company keeps a separate account for each. The listing in the balance sheet should identify the issue by stipulating its interest rate and due date.

Bonds sold at a premium

The corporation may receive a price for its bonds that is above or below their face value, depending on the rate of interest offered and the general credit standing of the company. If a corporation offers a rate of interest that is higher than the market rate for similar securities, investors may be willing to pay a premium for the bonds.

For example, on January 1, Dellroe Land Development Corporation issues $500,000 of 10%, 10-year bonds at 104, with interest payable semiannually, on June 30 and December 31. "104" refers to the price of the bonds; it is a percentage of the face value of the bonds, with the percent symbol omitted. This is how people record bond prices. In this example, $500,000 of bonds at 104 means 104% of $500,000 (1.04 × $500,000 = $520,000). [If $1,000,000 worth of bonds, say, had been sold at 106, the price received would have been $1,060,000 (1.06 × $1,000,000 = $1,060,000).] Dellroe's entry to record the sale of the bonds, in general journal form, is as follows.

	19– Jan.	1	Cash		520 0 0 0 00		
2			Bonds Payable			500 0 0 0 00	
3			Premium on Bonds Payable			20 0 0 0 00	

Common Stock now outstanding (40,000 shares)
Additional Common Stock, $50 par (20,000 shares)
Preferred Stock, 8%, cumulative
Bonds, 7%
Total Capitalization

Net Income from Operations (before income tax)
　Deduct: Bond interest expense
Net Income or Loss after bond interest
　Deduct: Federal and state income taxes (50%)
Net income after income taxes
　Deduct: Preferred dividends
Net income after income taxes and preferred dividends

Net income or loss per share of common stock

Premium on Bonds Payable represents the amount received over and above the face value of the bonds. The accountant lists Premium on Bonds Payable right below the bond account in the Long-term Liabilities section of the balance sheet. The corporation will write off or amortize Premium on Bonds Payable over the remaining life of the bond issue. The entries to pay the interest on the bonds, in general journal form, are shown here.

Jun.	30	*Interest Expense*		25 0 0 0 00		
		Cash			25 0 0 0 00	
		Made semiannual interest payment on bonds,				
		face value of $500,000, 10%.				

Dec.	31	*Interest Expense*		25 0 0 0 00		
		Cash			25 0 0 0 00	
		Made semiannual interest payment on bonds,				
		face value of $500,000, 10%.				

Adjusting entry for bonds sold at a premium

As we said, the company writes off or amortizes the Premium on Bonds Payable account over the remaining life of the bonds, which means debiting the account. The company uses Interest Expense as the offsetting credit. The entry appears as an adjusting entry, at the end of the fiscal period. It is first recorded

Net Income from Operations: $420,000			Net Income from Operations: $60,000		
Plan 1	Plan 2	Plan 3	Plan 1	Plan 2	Plan 3
$2,000,000	$2,000,000	$2,000,000	$2,000,000	$2,000,000	$2,000,000
1,000,000			1,000,000		
	1,000,000			1,000,000	
		1,000,000			1,000,000
$3,000,000	$3,000,000	$3,000,000	$3,000,000	$3,000,000	$3,000,000
$ 420,000	$ 420,000	$ 420,000	$ 60,000	$ 60,000	$ 60,000
0	0	70,000	0	0	70,000
$ 420,000	$ 420,000	$ 350,000	$ 60,000	$ 60,000	$ (10,000)
210,000	210,000	175,000	30,000	30,000	0
$ 210,000	$ 210,000	$ 175,000	$ 30,000	$ 30,000	$ (10,000)
	80,000			80,000	
$ 210,000	$ 130,000	$ 175,000	$ 30,000	$ (50,000)	$ (10,000)
$ 210,000	$ 130,000	$ 175,000	$ 30,000	$ (50,000)	$ (10,000)
60,000	40,000	40,000	60,000	40,000	40,000
shares	shares	shares	shares	shares	shares
$3.50 per share	$3.25 per share	$4.37 per share	$.50 per share	($1.25) per share	($.25) per share

in the Adjustments columns of the work sheet, like any other adjusting entry. (The calculation is recorded here purely as a means of explanation.)

			Adjusting Entries				
Dec.	31	Premium on Bonds Payable			20 00 00		
		Interest Expense ($20,000 ÷ 10 years)				20 00 00	

By T accounts, the entries look like this.

Cash

	+		−
Jan. 1	520,000	June 30	25,000
		Dec. 31	25,000

Bonds Payable

−		+
	Jan. 1	500,000

Interest Expense

	+		−
June 30	25,000	Dec. 31 Adj.	2,000
Dec. 31	25,000		

Premium on Bonds Payable

−		+
Dec. 31 Adj.	2,000	Jan. 1	20,000

In this illustration, we showed the amortization of the bond premium calculated by the straight-line method on an annual basis, which will also be used in the problems. As you can probably see, this is like calculating depreciation by the straight-line method. One can also record the amortization of the bond premium, just as one can record depreciation, on a monthly basis. It should be mentioned, however, that some corporations amortize premiums and discounts on bonds on the basis of present values, using present-value tables. This method is covered in advanced accounting courses.

After the accountant records the adjusting entry, the balance of Interest Expense is $48,000, representing the amount of the annual interest expense on the bonds, as follows.

Cash to be paid

Face value of the bonds	$500,000	
Interest (10 payments of $50,000 each)	500,000	$1,000,000
Less cash received		
Face value of the bonds	$500,000	
Premium on the bonds	20,000	520,000
Excess of cash to be paid over cash received		
(Interest expense for 10 years)		$ 480,000

$$\text{Interest expense per year} = \frac{\$480,000}{10 \text{ years}} = \$48,000$$

The adjusting entry reduces the balance of the Interest Expense account from $50,000 to $48,000. The accountant then closes Interest Expense into Income Summary in the amount of $48,000.

Bonds sold at a discount

When a corporation issues bonds that will pay a rate of interest that is less than the prevailing market rate of interest for comparable bonds, it sells its bonds at less than face value.

To demonstrate this, assume that on January 1, Plainview Dairy Products issues 6%, 20-year bonds with a face value of $100,000, at 96, with interest to be paid semiannually on June 30 and December 31.

	19– Jan.	1	Cash		96 0 0 0 00	
			Discount on Bonds Payable		4 0 0 0 00	
			Bonds Payable			100 0 0 0 00
			Sold 20-year bonds, 6%, dated Jan. 1, 19–,			
			at 96.			

Discount on Bonds Payable is a *contra-liability* account; it is listed on a classified balance sheet as a deduction from Bonds Payable. The entries, in general journal form, for the payment of interest are as follows.

	Jun.	30	Interest Expense		3 0 0 0 00	
			Cash			3 0 0 0 00
			Paid semiannual interest on bonds, face value			
			of $100,000, 6%.			

1	Dec.	31	Interest Expense			3 0 0 0 00			1
2			Cash				3 0 0 0 00		2
3			Paid semiannual interest on bonds, face value						3
4			of $100,000, 6%.						4
5									5

Adjusting entry for bonds sold at a discount

The corporation writes off or amortizes the Discount on Bonds Payable account, as it does the Premium on Bonds Payable account, over the remaining life of the bond issue, as an adjusting entry at the end of the fiscal period. Again, the accountant uses Interest Expense as the offsetting account in the adjusting entry. The adjusting entry, taken from the Adjustments columns of the work sheet, is as follows.

1			**Adjusting Entries**						1
2	Dec.	31	Interest Expense ($4,000 ÷ 20 years)			2 0 0 00			2
3			Discount on Bonds Payable				2 0 0 00		3
4									4
5									5

By T accounts, the entries look like this.

Cash				Bonds Payable	
+		−		−	+
Jan. 1 96,000		June 30 3,000			Jan. 1 100,000
		Dec. 31 3,000			

Interest Expense				Discount on Bonds Payable	
+		−		+	−
June 30 3,000				Jan. 1 4,000	Dec. 31 Adj. 200
Dec. 31 3,000					
Dec. 31 Adj. 200					

The adjustment for Discount on Bonds Payable results in an increase in the Interest Expense account. The following shows how this works out.

Cash to be paid

Face value of the bonds	$100,000	
Interest (20 payments of $6,000 each)	120,000	$220,000
Less cash received		
Face value of the bonds	$100,000	
Less discount on the bonds	4,000	96,000
Excess of cash to be paid over cash received		
(Interest expense for 20 years)		$124,000

$$\text{Interest expense per year} = \frac{\$124,000}{20 \text{ years}} = \$6,200$$

Accounting for the issuance of bonds **701**

The adjusting entry increases the balance of Interest Expense from $6,000 to $6,200. The accountant then closes Interest Expense into Income Summary in the amount of $6,200.

Illustration: bonds sold at a premium, whose interest payment dates do not coincide with end of fiscal year On March 1, Kolar Systems, Inc., issues $1,000,000 worth of 20-year, 9% bonds, at 103, dated March 1, with interest payable semiannually on September 1 and March 1. The corporation's fiscal year ends on December 31. A diagram of the dates looks like this.

Year 1		Year 2	
Bonds sold Mar. 1	Interest date Sept. 1	Interest date Mar. 1	Interest date Sept. 1
←——6 mos.——→	←— 4 mos.—→←2 mos.→←	——6 mos.——→	←—4 mos.—→

Since the date on which the interest has to be paid does not coincide with the end of the fiscal year, Kolar Systems has to make an adjusting entry for the accrued interest for the period from September 1 to December 31. The entries for the first year, in general journal form, are as follows.

	Mar.	1	Cash	1,030 0 0 0 00	
			Bonds Payable		1,000 0 0 0 00
			Premium on Bonds Payable		30 0 0 0 00
			Sold 20-year bonds, 9%, dated Mar. 1, at 103		

	Sep.	1	Interest Expense	45 0 0 0 00	
			Cash		45 0 0 0 00
			Paid semiannual interest on bonds		
			($1,000,000, 9%, 6 months).		

			Adjusting Entries		
	Dec.	31	Premium on Bonds Payable	1 2 5 0 00	
			Interest Expense ($30,000 x $\frac{10\ months}{240\ months}$)		1 2 5 0 00
		31	Interest Expense	30 0 0 0 00	
			Interest Payable		30 0 0 0 00
			($1,000,000, 9%, 4 months).		
			Closing Entry		
		31	Income Summary	73 7 5 0 00	
			Interest Expense		73 7 5 0 00

The amortization of the premium on December 31 is for only a part of a year. The next year, however, amortization will be for a full year. The adjusting entry for accrued interest on a bond is like the one for accrued interest on an interest-bearing note payable. The first-year entries look like this.

	Cash					Bonds Payable		
	+		−			−		+
Mar. 1	1,030,000	Sept. 1	45,000				Mar. 1	1,000,000

	Interest Expense					Premium on Bonds Payable		
	+		−			−		+
Sept. 1	45,000	Dec. 31 Adj.	1,250	Dec. 31 Adj.	1,250		Mar. 1	30,000
Dec. 31 Adj.	30,000	Dec. 31 Clos.	73,750					

	Income Summary					Interest Payable		
(Int. Exp.)	73,750	Closed				−		+
							Dec. 31 Adj.	30,000

Because the adjusting entry for accrued interest opened a new balance sheet account, Kolar's accountant has to make a reversing entry as of the first day of the next fiscal year. The reversing entry enables the accountant to make the regular entry for the payment of interest on March 1. The other entries for the second year are as follows.

			Reversing Entry		
	19– Jan.	1	Interest Payable	30 0 0 0 00	
			Interest Expense		30 0 0 0 00

	Mar.	1	Interest Expense	45 0 0 0 00	
			Cash		45 0 0 0 00
			Paid semiannual interest on bonds		
			($1,000,000, 9%, 6 months).		

	Sep.	1	Interest Expense	45 0 0 0 00	
			Cash		45 0 0 0 00
			Paid semiannual interest on bonds		
			($1,000,000, 9%, 6 months).		

				Adjusting Entries							
2	Dec.	31	Premium on Bonds Payable			1 5 0 0 00					2
3			Interest Expense					1 5 0 0 00			3
5		31	Interest Expense			30 0 0 0 00					5
6			Interest Payable ($1,000,000, 9%, 4 months)					30 0 0 0 00			6
8			Closing Entry								8
9		31	Income Summary			88 5 0 0 00					9
10			Interest Expense					88 5 0 0 00			10

The accountant brings forth the relevant T accounts from the previous year and posts them up to date.

Bonds Payable

−		+	
		Mar. 1	1,000,000

Premium on Bonds Payable

−		+	
Dec. 31 Adj.	1,250	Mar. 1	30,000
Dec. 31 Adj.	1,500		

Interest Payable

−		+	
		Dec. 31 Adj.	30,000
Jan. 1 Rev.	30,000	Dec. 31 Adj.	30,000

Interest Expense

+		−	
Sept. 1	45,000	Dec. 31 Adj.	1,250
Dec. 31 Adj.	30,000	Dec. 31 Clos.	73,750
Mar. 1	45,000	Jan. 1 Rev.	30,000
Sept. 1	45,000	Dec. 31 Adj.	1,500
Dec. 31 Adj.	30,000	Dec. 31 Clos.	88,500

Income Summary

(Int. Exp.)	73,750	Closed
(Int. Exp.)	88,500	Closed

Bond sinking fund

To provide greater security for bondholders, the bond agreement may specify that the issuing corporation make annual deposits of cash into a special fund—called a *sinking fund*—to be used to pay off the bond issue when it comes due. The company keeps the sinking fund separate from its other assets, and puts the cash deposited in the sinking fund to work by investing it in income-producing securities. When the bonds mature, the total of the annual deposits, plus the earnings on the investments, should add up to approximately the same as the face value of the bonds. The sinking fund may be controlled by either the corporation or a trustee—usually a bank.

When the corporation deposits cash in its sinking fund, it records the transaction as a debit to Sinking Fund Cash and as a credit to Cash. When the corporation or the trustee invests the sinking fund cash, the transaction is recorded as a debit to Sinking Fund Investments and a credit to Sinking Fund Cash, both of which are classified as investment accounts. When the corporation receives interest or dividend income on the investments, it debits Sinking

Fund Cash and credits Sinking Fund Income. Sinking Fund Income is classified as an Other Income account on the income statement.

For example, the Stevens Furniture Company issues $100,000 worth of 10-year bonds dated January 1, with the provision that at the end of each of the 10 years, it make equal annual deposits in a sinking fund. Stevens, which manages its own sinking fund, intends to invest this money in securities that will yield approximately 6% per year. Let us assume that, according to compound-interest tables, an annual deposit of $7,040 will accumulate to $100,000 in 10 years.

The following are a few of the many routine transactions that affect the sinking fund during the 10-year period.

Annual deposits of cash in bond sinking fund

Sinking Fund Cash	7 0 4 0 00	
Cash		7 0 4 0 00
Annual deposit in bond sinking fund, according to bond agreement.		

Purchase of investments (time of purchase and amount invested may vary)

Sinking Fund Investments	6 9 8 0 00	
Sinking Fund Cash		6 9 8 0 00
Bought $7,000 of Consolidated Steel 7% bonds at 99½, plus brokerage commission.		

Receipt of income from investments (interest and dividends are received at different times during the year)

Sinking Fund Cash	4 2 0 00	
Sinking Fund Income		4 2 0 00
Received interest and dividends on sinking fund investments.		

Sale of investments (investments may be sold and proceeds reinvested)

Sinking Fund Cash	18 6 2 0 00	
Sinking Fund Investments		18 4 0 0 00
Gain on Sale of Sinking Fund Investments		2 2 0 00
Sold sinking fund investments, yielding a profit of $220.		

Payment of bonds (cash available consists of sinking fund after sale of investments, with addition of last annual deposit, to bring sinking fund up to $100,000)

Bonds Payable		100 0 0 0 00	
Sinking Fund Cash			100 0 0 0 00
Paid bond obligation with sinking fund cash.			

Redemption of bonds

To protect itself against a decline in market interest rates, a corporation may issue *callable bonds.* Callable bonds give the corporation the right, as stipulated in the bond indenture or agreement, to redeem or buy back the bonds at a specified figure, known as the *call price,* which is ordinarily higher than the face value.

The Atlas Crockery Corporation issues $2,000,000 worth of 10%, 20-year, callable bonds, with a call price of 104. Later, interest rates in general go down. Under the new market conditions, Atlas could sell $2,000,000 worth of bonds at par, with an interest rate of 7%. It would pay Atlas to buy back the bonds, even though it would have to pay $2,080,000 for them ($2,000,000 × 1.04) and then turn around and issue new bonds at 7%. The annual savings in interest would amount to $60,000 (3% of $2,000,000). Even if a corporation's bonds are not callable, it may still buy its own bonds on the open market, if it can find any for sale.

When a corporation redeems its bonds at a price less than their book value, it realizes a gain. Conversely, if it redeems its bonds at a price that is more than their book value, it incurs a loss. The book value is the sum of the Bonds Payable account and the Premium on Bonds Payable (or Discount on Bonds Payable) account.

For example, Northeast Transit Company has $500,000 worth of callable bonds outstanding, with a call price of 105; there is an unamortized discount of $2,000. Northeast pays the interest up to date on December 31, and exercises its option of calling in or redeeming the bonds on the same date, December 31. The entry, in general journal form, is as shown at the top of the facing page. The loss represents the difference between the book value and the price paid (also determined by the difference between debits and credits).

Dec.	31	Bonds Payable		500 0 0 0 00			1
		Loss on Redemption of Bonds		27 0 0 0 00			2
		Cash			525 0 0 0 00		3
		Discount on Bonds Payable			2 0 0 0 00		4
		To record redemption of bonds, at 105					5

Recall that we said that even if a corporation's bonds are not callable, it can buy back the bonds, all of them, or as many as it can find on the open market. For example, the Seacoast Paper Company has $1,000,000 worth of 7% coupon bonds outstanding, on which there is an unamortized premium of $30,000. On July 15, Seacoast buys $100,000 (one-tenth of the original issue) of bonds in the open market at 97, plus 15 days' accrued interest. The entry, in general journal form, is as follows.

Jul.	15	Bonds Payable		100 0 0 0 00			1
		Premium on Bonds Payable		3 0 0 0 00			2
		Interest Expense ($100,000, 7%, 15 days)		2 9 1 67			3
		Cash			97 2 9 1 67		4
		Gain on Redemption of Bonds			6 0 0 0 00		5
		To record redemption of bonds at 97 plus					6
		accrued interest.					7

So, you can see that a redemption, in effect, cancels all or a portion of the Bonds Payable account, as well as the accompanying premium or discount. We shall list Gain on Redemption of Bonds (or Loss on Redemption of Bonds) in the income statement under the heading Other Income or Other Expense. If the gains or losses are of a significant amount, they are listed under the heading of Extraordinary Items, a classification of accounts appearing at the bottom of an income statement.

Balance sheet

The balance sheet of the C. K. Dill Company, Inc. shown on the following page is designed to show you how to place the accounts we've been talking about in this chapter.

```
                         C. K. Dill Company, Inc.
                              Balance Sheet
                            December 31, 19-

               Assets
Current Assets:
  Cash.........................            $ 12,000.00
  Notes Receivable.............              30,000.00
  Accounts Receivable          $220,000.00
    Less Allowance for Doubtful
    Accounts                      4,000.00  216,000.00
  Merchandise Inventory                     647,000.00
  Supplies                                    2,000.00
  Total Current Assets                                  $  907,000.00
Investments:
  Sinking Fund Cash                        $  5,000.00
  Sinking Fund Investments                   84,000.00
  Total Investments                                        89,000.00
Plant and Equipment:
  Equipment                    $222,000.00
    Less Accumulated Depr.        32,000.00 $190,000.00
  Building                     $180,000.00
    Less Accumulated Depr.        45,000.00  135,000.00
  Land                                        70,000.00
  Total Plant and Equipment                               395,000.00
Intangible Assets:
  Goodwill                                 $ 20,000.00
  Organization Costs                          8,000.00
  Total Intangible Assets                                  28,000.00
Total Assets                                            $1,419,000.00

               Liabilities
Current Liabilities:
  Accounts Payable                         $ 70,000.00
  Income Tax Payable                          8,000.00
  Dividends Payable                          12,000.00
  Total Current Liabilities                             $   90,000.00
Long-term Liabilities:
  6% Bonds Payable,
    due Dec. 31, 1980          $100,000.00
    Less Discount on Bonds
    Payable                       3,000.00 $ 97,000.00
  8% Bonds Payable,
    due March 31, 1992         $200,000.00
  Add Premium on Bonds Payable    2,000.00  202,000.00
  Total Long-term Liabilities                             299,000.00
Total Liabilities                                       $  389,000.00

               Stockholders' Equity
Paid-in Capital:
  Common Stock, $10 par
    (100,000 shares authorized,
    40,000 shares issued)      $400,000.00
  Premium on Common Stock       220,000.00
  Total Paid-in Capital                     $620,000.00
Retained Earnings:
  Appropriated
    For Plant Expansion         $100,000.00
  Unappropriated Retained
    Earnings                    310,000.00
  Total Retained Earnings                    410,000.00
Total Stockholders' Equity                              1,030,000.00
Total Liabilities and
  Stockholders' Equity                                  $1,419,000.00
```

Summary

A bond may be considered a corporation's long-term promissory note. A bond issue is usually subdivided into denominations of $1,000 and $5,000 each. Bondholders are creditors of the corporation; as such, they are entitled to interest payments, as well as repayment of the principal at maturity.

A bond is sold at a premium when the stated rate of interest is *higher* than the existing market rate of interest. A bond is sold at a discount when the stated rate of interest is *lower* than the existing market rate of interest. A corporation amortizes (writes off) premiums or discounts on bonds payable over the remaining life of a bond, beginning at the time the bond is sold. The amortization is recorded as an adjusting entry.

A bond sinking fund guarantees the security of the bondholders. A corporation redeems its bonds when it wishes to eliminate the debt, or to refinance the debt at a lower rate of interest.

Glossary

Amortization The systematic writing off of bond premium or discount.

Book value The sum of the Bonds Payable account (face value of the bonds) and the unamortized premium, or the difference between the amount of the Bonds Payable account and the unamortized discount.

Contra liability A deduction from a liability, such as Discount on Bonds Payable being a deduction from the balance of Bonds Payable.

Coupon bonds Bonds which have interest coupons attached to each bond. These coupons are payable to bearer and may be cashed on interest payment dates.

Debentures Unsecured bonds.

Discount Deficiency between the price received and the face value of a bond.

Extraordinary items Classification of accounts appearing at the bottom of an income statement, including gains or losses which do not recur with any regularity, such as gains or losses on redemption of bonds, gains or losses on the sale of long-term investments, fire losses, expropriation of property by a foreign government, major revaluation of a foreign currency, etc.

Indenture A bond agreement, or contract between the corporation and its bondholders.

Leverage Debt used as a lever to raise the owner's rate of return, earning income on borrowed money (as, for example, borrowing money at 8% and using it to earn a 15% rate of return).

Premium Excess between the price received and the face value of a bond.

Redeem Buying back or repurchasing bonds from bondholders.

Registered bonds Bonds whose owners' names are registered with the corporation that issued the bonds.

Secured bonds Bonds that are backed up by titles to property which may be claimed by the bondholders in the event that the issuing corporation does not fulfill its obligation.

Serial bonds Bonds of a particular issue that have a series of maturity dates.

Sinking fund   A special fund accumulated over the life of a bond issue, to enable the issuing corporation to pay off the bonds when they mature (come due).

Term bonds   Bonds of a particular issue which all have the same maturity date.

Unsecured bonds   Bonds which are backed only by the credit standing (good name) of the issuing corporation.

Questions

1. If the market rate of interest is higher than the rate of interest stated in the bond agreement, will the bonds be sold at a premium or a discount? Why?

2. How is the bond premium reported on the balance sheet?

3. What is the difference between term bonds and serial bonds?

4. What is the difference between a debenture and an indenture?

5. What are two definite obligations incurred by a corporation when it issues bonds?

6. What is a bond sinking fund, and what purpose does it serve?

7. How is a bond sinking fund classified on a balance sheet?

Exercises

Exercise 1   Suppose that a corporation sells $2,000,000 of 7%, 10-year bonds at 103. What is the amount of annual amortization of the premium?

Exercise 2   On January 2 of this year, a corporation issues $800,000 of 9%, 20-year bonds at 104. What is the net amount of interest expense for this year?

Exercise 3   On February 1 of this year, a corporation sold $2,000,000 of $7\frac{1}{2}$%, 10-year bonds at 97. The bonds were dated February 1, and the dates of interest payment are August 1 and February 1. Set forth entries to record the sale and the first interest payment.

Exercise 4   Determine the average annual interest cost on the following bond issue: $4,000,000, 9%, 20-year bonds at 94.

Exercise 5   Two companies are financed as follows.

	C. L. Thomas Inc.	C. N. Watkins Inc.
Bonds payable, 8% (issued at face value)	$ 400,000	$300,000
Preferred 9% stock, $100 par	100,000	400,000
Common stock, $100 par	1,000,000	800,000

Assuming a federal corporation income tax of 50%, determine for each company the earnings per share on common stock. Each company had an income of $150,000 before payment of bond interest and income tax.

Exercise 6 The Amalgamated Fishbait Corporation has outstanding $400,000 of 10-year sinking fund bonds. At the end of the ninth year after it has issued the bonds, the balance of Amalgamated's Sinking Fund Investments account is $370,000. List the entries to record the following.

a. The sale of the investments for $384,000

b. The final deposit in the sinking fund, bringing the balance of the account up to $400,000

c. The payment of the bonds

Exercise 7 The General Bicycle Corporation has the following account balances: Bonds Payable, $900,000; Premium on Bonds Payable, $27,000. As a step in redeeming the bond issue, General Bicycle buys $100,000 worth of its bonds on the open market at 96. Give the entry to record the redemption.

Exercise 8 Describe the entries recorded in the T accounts below.

Cash			
(1) 1,060,000	**(2)** 45,000		

Bonds Payable	
	(1) 1,000,000

Interest Expense			
(2) 45,000	**(4)** 2,000
(3) 15,000	**(5)** 58,000
	(6) 15,000

Premium on Bonds Payable	
(4) 2,000	**(1)** 60,000

Interest Payable			
(6) 15,000	**(3)** 15,000

Income Summary	
(5) 58,000	

Problems

Problem 25-1 During two consecutive years, the Metro Van and Storage Company, Inc., completed the following transactions.

Year 1

Jan. 2 Issued $1,500,000 worth of 20-year, $8\frac{1}{2}\%$ bonds, dated January 1 of this year at 99. Interest is payable semiannually on June 30 and December 31.

June 30 Paid semiannual interest on bonds.

Dec. 31 Paid semiannual interest on bonds.

    31 Recorded amortization of discount on bonds.

    31 Closed Interest Expense account.

Year 2

June 30 Paid semiannual interest on bonds.

Dec. 31 Paid semiannual interest on bonds.

    31 Recorded amortization of discount on bonds.

    31 Closed Interest Expense account.

Instructions Record the transactions in general journal form.

Problem 25-2 Sterling Printers, Inc., completed the following selected transactions.

Year 1

Mar. 1 Issued $750,000 of 20-year, 9% bonds, dated Mar. 1 of this year at 106. Interest is payable semiannually on Sept. 1 and Mar. 1.

Sept. 1 Paid semiannual interest on bonds.

Dec. 31 Recorded adjusting entry for accrued interest payable.

31 Recorded amortization of premium on bonds.

31 Closed Interest Expense account.

Year 2

Jan. 1 Reversed adjusting entry for accrued interest payable.

Mar. 1 Paid semiannual interest on bonds.

Sept. 1 Paid semiannual interest on bonds.

Dec. 31 Recorded adjusting entry for accrued interest payable.

31 Recorded adjusting entry for amortization of premium on bonds.

31 Closed Interest Expense account.

Instructions 1. Record the transactions in general journal form.

2. Post entries to the Interest Expense account. Label the appropriate entries in the ledger accounts as adjusting, closing, or reversing.

Problem 25-3 During two consecutive years, the Worthington Products Corporation completed the following transactions relating to its $9,000,000 issue of 30-year, 7% bonds, dated April 1 of the first year. Interest is payable on April 1 and October 1. The corporation's fiscal year extends from January through December 31.

Year 1

Apr. 1 Sold the bond issue for $8,730,000.

Oct. 1 Paid semiannual interest on bonds.

Dec. 31 Recorded adjusting entry for accrued interest payable.

31 Recorded adjusting entry for amortization of bond discount.

31 Deposited $115,500 in a bond sinking fund.

31 Closed Interest Expense account.

Year 2

Jan. 1 Reversed adjusting entry for accrued interest payable.

6 Bought various securities with sinking fund cash; cost, $108,630.

Apr. 1 Paid semiannual interest on bonds.

Oct. 1 Paid semiannual interest on bonds.

Dec. 31 Recorded receipt of $5,839.50 of income derived from sinking fund investments, depositing the cash in the sinking fund.

   31 Recorded adjusting entry for accrued interest payable.

   31 Recorded adjusting entry for amortization of bond discount.

   31 Deposited $169,950 in bond sinking fund.

   31 Closed Interest Expense account.

Instructions   **1.** Record the transactions in general journal form.

2. Post entries to the Interest Expense account and the Discount on Bonds Payable account. Label the appropriate entries in the ledger accounts as adjusting, closing, or reversing.

Problem 25-4   On May 1, Wilson Mall, Inc., whose fiscal year is the calendar year, issued $12,000,000 of 20-year, 9% bonds, dated April 1, with interest payable on April 1 and October 1. The following transactions pertain to the bond issue for the first two years.

Year 1

Apr. 1 Sold the bond issue for $12,120,000.

Oct. 1 Paid semiannual interest on bonds.

Dec. 31 Recorded adjusting entry for accrued interest payable.

   31 Recorded adjusting entry for amortization of bond premium.

   31 Deposited $240,000 in a bond sinking fund.

   31 Closed Interest Expense account.

Year 2

Jan. 1 Reversed adjusting entry for accrued interest payable.

   12 Bought various securities with sinking fund cash; cost, $231,900.

Apr. 1 Paid semiannual interest on bonds.

Jul. 1 Recorded receipt of $8,085 of income derived from sinking fund investments, depositing the cash in the sinking fund.

    8 Bought various securities with sinking fund cash; cost, $13,140.

Oct. 1 Paid semiannual interest on bonds.

Dec. 31 Recorded the receipt of $16,695 of income derived from sinking fund investments, depositing the cash in the sinking fund.

   31 Recorded adjusting entry for accrued interest payable.

   31 Recorded adjusting entry for amortization of bond premium.

   31 Deposited $300,000 in the bond sinking fund.

   31 Closed Sinking Fund Income account.

   31 Closed Interest Expense account.

1. Record the transactions in general journal form.

2. Post entries to the Interest Expense account and the Premium on Bonds Payable account. Label the appropriate entries in the ledger accounts as adjusting, closing, or reversing.

Alternate problems

Problem 25-1A During two consecutive years, the Roper Van and Storage Company, Inc., completed the following transactions.

Year 1

Jan.   1 Issued $750,000 worth of 20-year, 8% bonds, dated January 1 of this year at 98. Interest is payable semiannually on June 30 and December 31.

June 30 Paid semiannual interest on bonds.

Dec. 31 Paid semiannual interest on bonds.

     31 Recorded amortization of discount on bonds.

     31 Closed Interest Expense account.

Year 2

June 30 Paid semiannual interest on bonds.

Dec. 31 Paid semiannual interest on bonds.

     31 Recorded amortization of discount on bonds.

     31 Closed the Interest Expense account.

Instructions   Record the transactions in general journal form.

Problem 25-2A Shafer Printers, Inc., completed the following selected transactions.

Year 1

Apr.   1 Issued $1,500,000 worth of 20-year, 9% bonds, dated April 1 of this year at 104. Interest is payable semiannually on October 1 and April 1.

Oct.   1 Paid semiannual interest on bonds.

Dec. 31 Recorded adjusting entry for accrued interest payable.

     31 Recorded amortization of premium on bonds.

     31 Closed Interest Expense account.

Year 2

Jan.   1 Reversed adjusting entry for accrued interest payable.

Apr.   1 Paid semiannual interest on bonds.

Oct.   1 Paid semiannual interest on bonds.

Dec. 31 Recorded adjusting entry for accrued interest payable.

    31 Recorded adjusting entry for amortization of premium on bonds.

    31 Closed Interest Expense account.

Instructions **1.** Record the transactions in general journal form.

2. Post the entries to the Interest Expense account. Label the appropriate entries in the ledger accounts as adjusting, closing, or reversing.

Problem 25-3A During two consecutive years the Newport Development Corporation completed the following transactions related to its $8,000,000 issue of 25-year, 6% bonds, dated May 1 of the first year. Interest is payable on May 1 and November 1. The corporation's fiscal year extends from January 1 through December 31.

Year 1

May   1 Sold bond issue for $7,880,000.

Nov. 1 Paid semiannual interest on bonds.

Dec. 31 Recorded adjusting entry for accrued interest payable.

    31 Recorded adjusting entry for amortization of bond discount.

    31 Deposited $115,500 in a bond sinking fund.

    31 Closed Interest Expense account.

Year 2

Jan. 1 Reversed adjustment for accrued interest payable.

    4 Bought various securities with sinking fund cash; cost, $112,400.

May   1 Paid semiannual interest on bonds.

Nov. 1 Paid semiannual interest on bonds.

Dec. 31 Recorded receipt of $5,840 of income derived from sinking fund investments, depositing cash in sinking fund.

    31 Recorded adjusting entry for accrued interest payable.

    31 Recorded adjusting entry for amortization of bond interest.

    31 Deposited $172,000 in bond sinking fund.

    31 Closed Interest Expense account.

Instructions **1.** Record the transactions in general journal form.

2. Post entries to the Interest Expense account and the Discount on Bonds Payable account. Label the appropriate entries in the ledger accounts as adjusting, closing, or reversing.

Problem 25-4A On March 1, the Cincinnati Investment Corporation issued $9,000,000 worth of 25-year bonds, 9%, dated March 1, with interest payable March 1 and September 1. The corporation's fiscal year is the calendar year. The following transactions pertain to the bond issue for the first two years.

Year 1

Mar. 1 Sold bond issue for $9,045,000.

Sept. 1 Paid semiannual interest on bonds.

Dec. 31 Recorded adjusting entry for accrued interest payable.

31 Recorded adjusting entry for amortization of bond premium.

31 Deposited $162,000 in a bond sinking fund.

31 Closed Interest Expense account.

Year 2

Jan. 1 Reversed adjusting entry for accrued interest payable.

10 Bought various securities with sinking fund cash, $147,000.

Mar. 1 Paid semiannual interest on bonds.

July 1 Recorded receipt of $5,760 of income derived from sinking fund investments, depositing cash in sinking fund.

6 Bought various securities with sinking fund cash, $19,350.

Sept. 1 Paid semiannual interest on bonds.

Dec. 31 Recorded receipt of $6,660 of income derived from sinking fund investments, depositing cash in sinking fund.

31 Recorded adjusting entry for accrued interest payable.

31 Recorded adjusting entry for amortization of bond premium.

31 Deposited $194,400 in bond sinking fund.

31 Closed Sinking Fund Income account.

31 Closed Interest Expense account.

Instructions **1.** Record the transactions in general journal form.

2. Post entries to the Interest Payable account and the Premium on Bonds Payable account. Label the appropriate entries in the ledger accounts as adjusting, closing, or reversing.

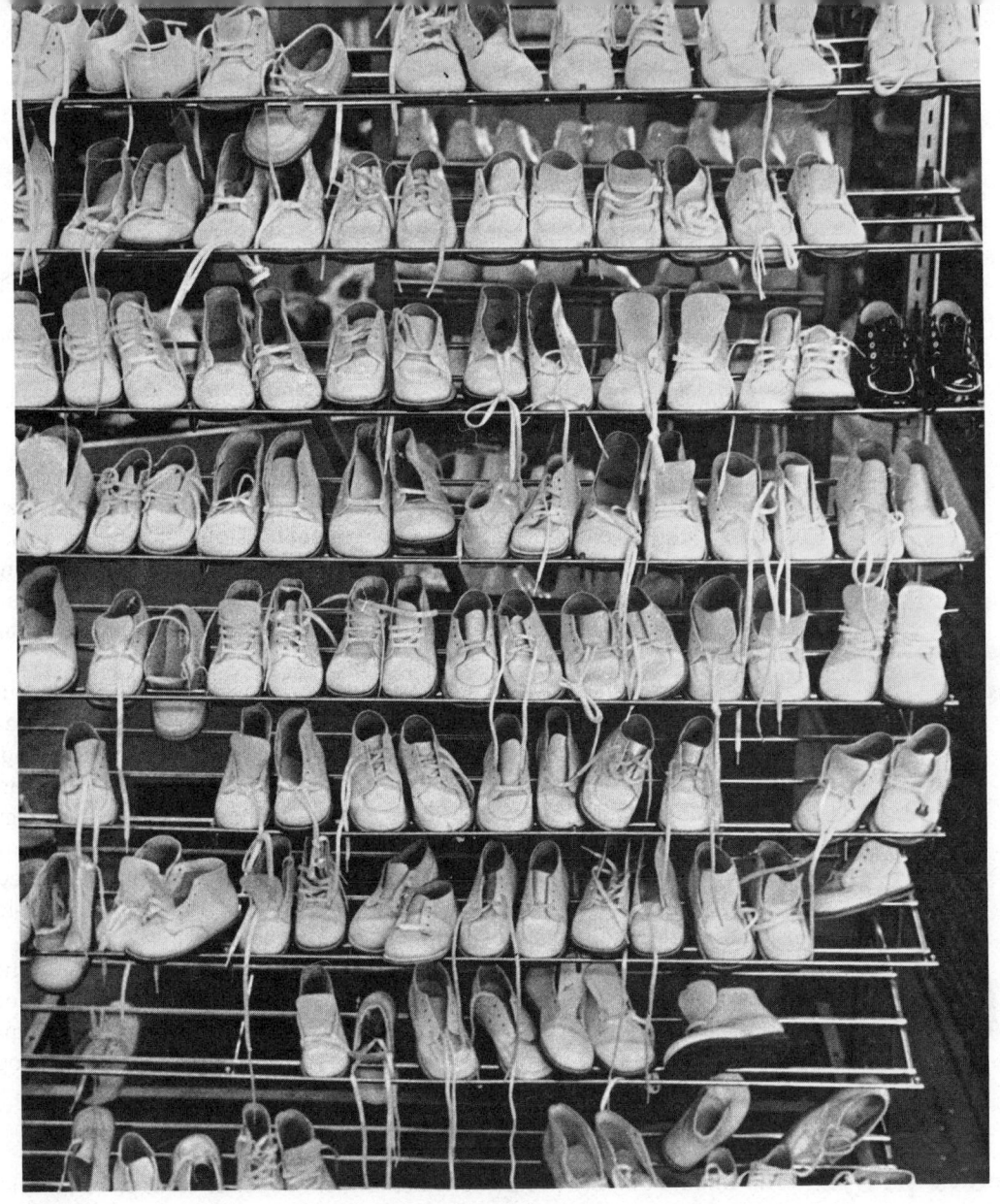

26 *Departmental accounting*

objectives

After completing this chapter, you will be able to do the following:
- Compile a departmental income statement extended through gross profit.
- Apportion operating expenses among various operating departments.
- Compile a departmental work sheet.
- Compile a departmental income statement extended through net income from operations.
- Compile a departmental income statement extended through contribution margin.

WHEN A COMPANY carries on a number of different business activities, the firm should be divided into a number of subdivisions or departments. This enables the company's management to delegate authority to departmental managers, who are held responsible for their respective departments, and to measure the profitability of each department. It is the element of profitability that we're going to discuss in this chapter.

Large companies have greater opportunities to use departmental accounting than small ones. However, even a small business—if it carries on more than one type of business activity—may benefit from departmental accounting. For example, the Whitehouse Company deals in insurance and property management, and accounts separately for insurance commissions and management fees. Sylvia and Irving Whitehouse, at the end of the fiscal year, can compare the profitability of each activity with the amount of time and attention they had to devote to it; this comparison may then form the basis for their decision to spend more time on one activity and less on the other.

For large business firms—those that engage in service, merchandising, or manufacturing—departmental accounting is a must. The accounting reports consist of several levels of income statements recorded on a departmental basis, and extended from sales through gross profit or net income from operations or contribution margin.

Gross profit by departments

The amount of gross profit of any department depends on its sales volume and its markup on the goods sold.

Net Sales − Cost of Merchandise Sold = Gross Profit

Gross profit, in the same context, consists of the items listed in the income statement shown at the top of page 719.

To determine the gross profit of a given department, one needs a separate departmental set of figures for each element entering into the gross profit. There are two methods of doing this.

1. Keep separate general ledger accounts for each item involved in gross profit, such as a Sales account for each department, a Sales Returns and

Revenue from Sales						
Sales						120 0 0 0 00
Less: Sales Returns and Allowances					6 0 0 0 00	
Sales Discount					3 0 0 0 00	9 0 0 0 00
Net Sales						111 0 0 0 00
Cost of Merchandise Sold						
Merchandise Inventory (beginning)					48 0 0 0 00	
Purchases				81 0 0 0 00		
Less: Purchases Returns and Allowances		4 0 0 0 00				
Purchases Discount		2 0 0 0 00		6 0 0 0 00		
Net Purchases					75 0 0 0 00	
Merchandise Available for Sale					123 0 0 0 00	
Less Merchandise Inventory (ending)					52 0 0 0 00	
Cost of Merchandise Sold						71 0 0 0 00
Gross Profit						40 0 0 0 00

Allowances account for each department, etc. Then record the balances of these accounts on the income statement.

2. Keep only one general ledger account for each item involved in gross profit, and apportion the balance to the various departments. For example, maintain one Sales account and one Sales Returns and Allowances account for the company, and in addition keep a breakdown of sales and sales returns for each department. Then record the figures for each department on the income statement.

Separate accounts by departments

Keeping separate accounts by departments yields the most accurate accounting data. One needs separate accounts for each department for Sales, Sales Returns and Allowances, Sales Discount, Purchases, Purchases Returns and Allowances, Purchases Discount, and Merchandise Inventory. *Example:* Action Enterprises has five departments, and uses five Sales accounts, five Sales Returns and Allowances accounts, five Sales Discount accounts, five Merchandise Inventory accounts, and so forth. The special journals contain columns for each departmental account, such as we see in the sales journal shown at the top of pages 720 and 721.

The accountant posts each total to a separate account, as indicated by the ledger account numbers. A company that has many departments and keeps a separate journal column for each may find that the journal becomes quite cumbersome in size. In a situation like this, it is better to post from the sales invoices directly to the departmental sales accounts. (This is like the process of posting from sales invoices described in Chapter 11.) Another alternative that firms use when they have many departments is to establish a controlling account in the general ledger and to record each department in a subsidiary ledger.

	DATE	INV. NO.		CUSTOMER'S NAME
1	19– Sep.	1	1698	Nancy Dolan
2		3	1702	Arthur Strachan
3		3	1704	Randy Sever
4				
5				
6				
7				

Maintaining one general ledger account

When a company keeps only one general ledger account for each item involved in gross profit, the accountant has to distribute the total amount among the various departments at the end of the accounting period. To do so, the accountant has to accumulate departmental information on supplementary records. *Example:* Martin's Grocery has a produce, a grocery, and a meat department. Martin's records sales by department, by having the checkout clerk punch them separately on the cash register. At the end of each day, the sales are recorded in a journal, taking the totals from the cash register tapes. Sales are also recorded on a departmental analysis sheet.

Businesses also use separate analysis sheets for sales returns, purchases, purchase returns, purchase discounts, etc. At the end of the accounting period, these analysis sheets give departmental breakdowns for each item.

Bookkeeping machines

Companies often use posting machines to record sales, purchases, cash receipts, or cash payments. They can program the machine to record in either a sales journal or departmental analysis sheet. For example, for each charge sale, the machine performs the following operations: prepares customer's invoice, posts to the customer's account, records the sale in the sales journal, and accumulates departmental sales totals.

Gross profit by departments

J. C. Holcomb Company, Inc., has two departments, A and B, and keeps separate accounts for each. The income statement for the fiscal year ending December 31, showing departmental reporting only up to the Gross Profit point, is on pages 722 and 723.

Net income from operations by departments

A company may extend departmental reporting of income to various points, such as Net Income from Operations, or Net Income. The J. C. Holcomb Company keeps separate accounts for each item that enters into gross profit, and does apportion the operating expenses between Gross Profit and Net Income from Operations to Department A or Department B on a logical basis. (We shall discuss this in detail presently.) For emphasis, let us look at the skeleton outline of the income statement, on the facing page.

POST. REF.	ACCOUNTS RECEIVABLE DEBIT	SALES CREDIT					
		DEPT. A	DEPT. B	DEPT. C	DEPT. D	DEPT. E	
✓	165 00	165 00					1
✓	376 00			376 00			2
✓	716 00		716 00				3
							4
	14 933 00	2 681 00	864 00	4 794 00	3 716 00	2 878 00	5
	(114)	(411)	(412)	(413)	(414)	(415)	6
							7

Departmentalized

Sales ⎱ Separate accounts or
— Cost of Merchandise Sold ⎰ analysis sheet
= Gross Profit
— Selling Expenses ⎱ Account balances
— General Expenses ⎰ are apportioned
= Net Income from Operations

Nondepartmentalized

+ Other Income
— Other Expense
= Net Income

Work sheet for departmental accounting

Recall once again the sequential steps of the accounting cycle: The accountant records the trial balance in the first columns of the work sheet, formulates and records the adjustments, completes the work sheet, and then uses the work sheet to prepare the income statement. The Income Statement columns of the work sheet for a company that keeps track of income by departments contain debit and credit columns for each department, as well as debit and credit columns entitled Nondepartmental, which includes Other Income and Other Expense accounts. The accountant, by the time she or he gets to the income statement, has already performed calculations concerning the apportionment of expenses, which are accordingly subdivided on the work sheet. A sample portion of the work sheet for the Holcomb Company is shown on pages 724–725. Various asset, liability, and owner's equity accounts are not shown, but they are included in the totals.

Income statement for departmental accounting

The income statement contains a set of columns for each department, as well as a set of columns for the combined total of all departments. On pages 726–727 is a more representative example of an income statement for the Holcomb Company than the one shown on pages 722 and 723, followed on page 728 by a discussion of the apportionment of operating expenses between the two departments.

		DEPARTMENT A	
Revenue from Sales			
Sales		560 000 00	
Less Sales Returns and Allowances		14 200 00	
Net Sales			545 800 00
Cost of Merchandise Sold			
Merchandise Inventory, Jan. 1, 19–		96 400 00	
Purchases	325 120 00		
Less: Purchases Returns and Allowances	9 580 00		
Purchases Discount	5 740 00		
Net Purchases		309 800 00	
Merchandise Available for Sale		406 200 00	
Less Merchandise Inventory, Dec. 31, 19–		110 000 00	
Cost of Merchandise Sold			296 200 00
Gross Profit			249 600 00
Operating Expenses			
Selling Expenses			
Sales Salary Expense			
Advertising Expense			
Depreciation Expense, Store Equipment			
Miscellaneous Selling Expense			
Total Selling Expenses			
General Expenses			
Office Salary Expense			
Rent Expense			
Utilities Expense			
Insurance Expense			
Bad Debts Expense			
Miscellaneous General Expense			
Total General Expenses			
Total Operating Expenses			
Net Income from Operations			
Other Income			
Interest Income			
Other Expenses			
Interest Expense			
Net Income			

Company, Inc.
Statement
December 31, 19—

	DEPARTMENT B		TOTAL		
1					
2	240 0 00 00		800 0 00 00		
3	5 8 00 00		20 0 00 00		
4		234 2 00 00		780 0 00 00	
5					
6	82 7 40 00		179 1 40 00		
7	167 8 90 00		493 0 10 00		
8	4 7 56 00		14 3 36 00		
9	3 2 74 00		9 0 14 00		
10	159 8 60 00		469 6 60 00		
11	242 6 00 00		648 8 00 00		
12	90 0 00 00		200 0 00 00		
13		152 6 00 00		448 8 00 00	
14		81 6 00 00		331 2 00 00	
15					
16					
17					
18			140 8 25 00		
19			17 6 00 00		
20			3 3 00 00		
21			4 2 70 00		
22				165 9 95 00	
23					
24			32 1 00 00		
25			16 4 00 00		
26			4 8 40 00		
27			4 4 00 00		
28			2 5 70 00		
29			9 20 00		
30				61 2 30 00	
31					227 2 25 00
32					103 9 75 00
33					
34					
35				3 6 24 00	
36					
37				2 4 00 00	1 2 24 00
38					105 1 99 00
39					
40					

Work sheet for year ended

ACCOUNT NAME	TRIAL BALANCE DEBIT	TRIAL BALANCE CREDIT	ADJUSTMENTS DEBIT	ADJUSTMENTS CREDIT
Accounts Receivable	82 040 00			
Allow. for Doubtful Accounts		862 00		(f) 2 570 00
Merchandise Inventory				
Department A	96 400 00		(b)110 000 00	(a)96 400 00
Department B	82 740 00		(d) 90 000 00	(c)82 740 00
Prepaid Insurance	5 540 00			(e) 4 400 00
Store Equipment	32 400 00			
Acc. Depr. Store Equip.		21 600 00		(g) 3 300 00
Sales				
Department A		560 000 00		
Department B		240 000 00		
Sales Ret. and Allowances				
Department A	14 200 00			
Department B	5 800 00			
Purchases				
Department A	325 120 00			
Department B	167 890 00			
Purchases Ret. and Allowances				
Department A		9 580 00		
Department B		4 756 00		
Purchases Discount				
Department A		5 740 00		
Department B		3 274 00		
Sales Salary Expense	140 825 00			
Advertising Expense	17 600 00			
Misc. Selling Expense	4 270 00			
Office Salary Expense	32 100 00			
Rent Expense	16 400 00			
Utility Expense	4 840 00			
Misc. General Expense	920 00			
Interest Income		3 624 00		
Interest Expense	2 400 00			
	1,471 864 00	1,471 864 00		
Income Summary			(a) 96 400 00	(b)110 000 00
			(c) 82 740 00	(d) 90 000 00
Insurance Expense			(e) 4 400 00	
Bad Debts Expense			(f) 2 570 00	
Depr. Expense, Store Equip.			(g) 3 300 00	
			389 410 00	389 410 00
Net Income (Loss) by Dep.				
Net Income				

	DEPARTMENT A INCOME STATEMENT		DEPARTMENT B INCOME STATEMENT		NONDEPARTMENTAL INCOME STATEMENT		BALANCE SHEET		
	DEBIT	CREDIT	DEBIT	CREDIT	DEBIT	CREDIT	DEBIT	CREDIT	
							82 04 00		2
								3 43 2 00	3
									4
									5
							110 00 00 00		6
							90 00 00		7
							1 1 4 0 00		8
							32 40 00 00		9
								24 90 00 00	10
									11
									12
		560 000 00							13
				240 000 00					14
									15
	14 20 0 00								16
			5 80 0 00						17
									18
	325 120 00								19
			167 890 00						20
									21
		9 5 80 00							22
				4 75 6 00					23
									24
		5 74 0 00							25
				3 27 4 00					26
	88 6 25 00		52 2 00 00						27
	10 3 36 00		7 2 64 00						28
	2 9 89 00		1 2 81 00						29
	22 4 70 00		9 6 30 00						30
	10 2 50 00		6 1 50 00						31
	3 0 25 00		1 8 15 00						32
	6 44 00		2 76 00						33
						3 6 24 00			34
					2 40 0 00				35
									36
	96 4 00 00	110 000 00							37
			82 7 40 00	90 000 00					38
	2 54 0 00		1 86 0 00						6
	1 7 99 00		7 71 00						40
	1 84 0 00		1 46 0 00						41
	580 2 38 00	685 3 20 00	339 1 37 00	338 0 30 00					42
	105 0 82 00			(1 1 07 00)		103 9 75 00			43
	685 3 20 00	685 3 20 00	339 1 37 00	339 1 37 00	2 4 00 00	107 5 99 00	1,118 7 61 00	1,013 5 62 00	44
					105 1 99 00			105 1 99 00	45
					107 5 99 00	107 5 99 00	1,118 7 61 00	1,118 7 61 00	46

		DEPARTMENT A		
1	Revenue from Sales			
2	Sales		560 000 00	
3	Less Sales Ret. and Allow.		14 200 00	
4	Net Sales			545 800 00
5	Cost of Merchandise Sold			
6	Merchandise Inv., Jan. 1, 19–		96 400 00	
7	Purchases	325 120 00		
8	Less: Purch. Ret. and Allow.	9 580 00		
9	Purch. Discount	5 740 00		
10	Net Purchases		309 800 00	
11	Merchandise Available for Sale		406 200 00	
12	Less Merchandise Inv., Dec. 31, 19–		110 000 00	
13	Cost of Merchandise Sold			296 200 00
14	Gross Profit			249 600 00
15				
16	Operating Expenses			
17	Selling Expenses			
18	Sales Salary Expense	88 625 00		
19	Advertising Expense	10 336 00		
20	Depr. Expense, Store Equip.	1 840 00		
21	Misc. Selling Expense	2 989 00		
22	Total Selling Expenses		103 790 00	
23	General Expenses			
24	Office Salary Expense	22 470 00		
25	Rent Expense	10 250 00		
26	Utilities Expense	3 025 00		
27	Insurance Expense	2 540 00		
28	Bad Debts Expense	1 799 00		
29	Misc. General Expense	644 00		
30	Total General Expenses		40 728 00	
31	Total Operating Expenses			144 518 00
32	Net Income (Loss) from Operations			105 082 00
33				
34	Other Income			
35	Interest Income			
36	Other Expense			
37	Interest Expense			
38	Net Income before Income Tax			
39	Income Tax			
40	Net Income after Income Tax			

#	DEPARTMENT B			TOTAL		
1						
2		240 000 00			800 000 00	
3		5 800 00			20 000 00	
4			234 200 00			780 000 00
5						
6		82 740 00			179 140 00	
7	167 890 00			493 010 00		
8	4 756 00			14 336 00		
9	3 274 00			9 014 00		
10		159 860 00			469 660 00	
11		242 600 00			648 800 00	
12		90 000 00			200 000 00	
13			152 600 00			448 800 00
14			81 600 00			331 200 00
15						
16						
17						
18	52 200 00			140 825 00		
19	7 264 00			17 600 00		
20	1 460 00			3 300 00		
21	1 281 00			4 270 00		
22		62 205 00			165 995 00	
23						
24	9 630 00			32 100 00		
25	6 150 00			16 400 00		
26	1 815 00			4 840 00		
27	1 860 00			4 400 00		
28	771 00			2 570 00		
29	276 00			920 00		
30		20 502 00			61 230 00	
31			82 707 00			227 225 00
32			(1 107 00)			103 975 00
33						
34						
35					3 624 00	
36						
37					2 400 00	1 224 00
38						105 199 00
39						47 588 00
40						57 611 00

Net income from operations by departments   **727**

One can readily identify some operating expense as belonging to a given department. For example, suppose that a salesperson makes sales in one department only; the accountant assigns that salesperson's salary or commission directly to that department. However, other operating expenses, such as Miscellaneous Selling Expense or Utilities Expense, cannot be restricted to one department, and must be divided between the departments on some equitable basis. Let's look at the operating expenses of the J. C. Holcomb Company and see what methods it uses to apportion them.

Sales salary expense   Holcomb allocates the salespersons' salaries to Department A or Department B according to the names on the payroll register, which lists each employee by department. Department A's share is $88,625; Department B's is $52,200.

Advertising expense   Holcomb advertises itself in three media: billboards, newspapers, and radio. The cost breakdown is like this:

Billboard advertising	$ 1,600
Newspaper advertising	9,600
Radio advertising	6,400
Total	$17,600

The billboard ads display the name of the company and tell where it is, but they don't advertise the products of Department A or Department B. Since no specific department is featured, Holcomb's accountant has to apportion the cost of these billboard ads according to gross sales, as follows:

Sales for Department A	$560,000
Sales for Department B	240,000
Total sales	$800,000

Department A's sales as a percent of total are

$$\frac{\$560,000}{\$800,000} = 70\%$$

Department B's sales as a percent of the total are

$$\frac{\$240,000}{\$800,000} = 30\%$$

Department A's share of cost of billboard advertising is

$$70\% \text{ of } \$1,600 = \$1,600 \times .7 = \$1,120$$

Department B's share of cost of billboard advertising is

$$30\% \text{ of } \$1,600 = \$1,600 \times .3 = \$480$$

Holcomb allocates the cost of its newspaper advertising according to the number of column inches each department uses. In a year, Holcomb buys 3,200 inches of newspaper advertising, divided according to departments, as shown at the top of the next page.

Ads for Department A are

$$1{,}920 \text{ column inches or } \frac{1{,}920}{3{,}200} = 60\%$$

Ads for Department B are

$$1{,}280 \text{ column inches or } \frac{1{,}280}{3{,}200} = 40\%$$

Department A's share of cost of newspaper advertising is

$$60\% \text{ of } \$9{,}600 = \$9{,}600 \times .6 = \$5{,}760$$

Department B's share of cost of newspaper advertising is

$$40\% \text{ of } \$9{,}600 = \$9{,}600 \times .4 = \$3{,}840$$

As for radio advertising, Holcomb again allocates cost to the two departments according to the amount of air time each department uses. In a year, Holcomb buys 1,250 minutes of radio time, divided according to departments, as shown here.

Ads for Department A are

$$675 \text{ minutes or } \frac{675}{1{,}250} = 54\%$$

Ads for Department B are

$$575 \text{ minutes or } \frac{575}{1{,}250} = 46\%$$

Department A's share of cost of radio advertising is

$$54\% \text{ of } \$6{,}400 = \$6{,}400 \times .54 = \$3{,}456$$

Department B's share of cost of radio advertising is

$$46\% \text{ of } \$6{,}400 = \$6{,}400 \times .46 = \$2{,}944$$

Here is a summary of Holcomb's allocation of advertising expense.

Expense	Department A	Department B	Total
Billboard advertising	$ 1,120	$ 480	$ 1,600
Newspaper advertising	5,760	3,840	9,600
Radio advertising	3,456	2,944	6,400
	$10,336	$7,264	$17,600

Depreciation expense, store equipment Holcomb keeps a plant and equipment ledger which notes the department in which each piece of equipment is located. The total year's depreciation of the equipment used in Department A is $1,840, and the total year's depreciation of the equipment used in Department B is $1,460.

Office salary expense People who work in the office of the Holcomb Company get paid a total of $32,100 per year. Holcomb apportions the amount of money which is paid in salaries to office workers on the basis of the amount of time the office personnel has to spend on each department. Holcomb's management estimates that 70% of the office force's time is devoted to Department A, and 30% to Department B.

Department A's share is 70% of $32,100 = $32,100 × .7 = $22,470
Department B's share is 30% of $32,100 = $32,100 × .3 = $9,630

Rent expense and utilities expense The Holcomb Company rents 40,000 square feet of floor space and allocates the expenses of rent and utilities on the basis of floor space occupied by each department, as follows. (Yearly expense for rent is $16,400; yearly expense for utilities is $4,840.)

Department A occupies 25,000 square feet or

$$\frac{25,000}{40,000} = 62.5\%$$

Department B occupies 15,000 square feet or

$$\frac{15,000}{40,000} = 37.5\%$$

Department A's share of rent is

62.5% of $16,400 = $10,250

Department B's share of rent is

37.5% of $16,400 = $6,150

Department A's share of utilities is

62.5% of $4,840 = $3,025

Department B's share of utilities is

37.5% of $4,840 = $1,815

In this case, for simplicity, we are assuming that all floor space is of equal value. However, when one is apportioning the rent expense in a multistory building, one has to take into account differences in the value of the various floors and locations.

Insurance expense Holcomb carries insurance policies to cover losses that might result from (1) damage to merchandise or equipment (annual cost, $3,600), and (2) injury incurred by customers while on the premises (annual cost, $800). The cost of the insurance on merchandise and equipment is based on the average cost of the assets held by each department. The average is equal to the cost of assets on hand at the beginning of the year plus the cost of assets on hand at the end of the year, divided by 2. The computations are shown at the top of the next page.

Item	Department A		Department B		Total
Merchandise Inventory					
Balance, Jan. 1	$ 96,400		$ 82,740		
Balance, Dec. 31	110,000		90,000		
Total	2)$206,400		2)$172,740		
Average	$103,200	$103,200	$86,370	$86,370	
Store Equipment					
Balance, Jan. 1	$ 19,440		$ 12,960		
Balance, Dec. 31	19,440		12,960		
Total	2)$ 38,880		2)$ 25,920		
Average	$ 19,440	19,440	$ 12,960	12,960	
Total		$122,640		$99,330	$221,970

Department A's percentage is

$$\frac{\$122,640}{\$221,970} = 55\%$$

Department B's percentage is

$$\frac{\$99,330}{\$221,970} = 45\%$$

Department A's share of property insurance is

$$55\% \text{ of } \$3,600 = \$1,980$$

Department B's share of property insurance is

$$45\% \text{ of } \$3,600 = \$1,620$$

The cost of liability insurance (in case of personal injury to customers) is based on sales. Using the same percentages as for billboard advertising, Holcomb apportions the cost of liability insurance as follows.

Department A's share of liability insurance is

$$70\% \text{ of } \$800 = \$560$$

Department B's share of liability insurance is

$$30\% \text{ of } \$800 = \$240$$

Here is a summary of the way Holcomb allocates its insurance expense.

Type of Insurance	Department A	Department B	Total
Property insurance	$1,980	$1,620	$3,600
Liability insurance	560	240	800
	$2,540	$1,860	$4,400

Bad debts expense, miscellaneous selling expense, and miscellaneous general expense Bad Debts Expense and the miscellaneous expense accounts vary according to the volume of sales. Accordingly, Holcomb apportions them on this basis, since volume of sales is a reasonable measure of the benefit each department derives from these accounts.

Item	Department A	Department B	Total
Bad Debts Expense	$1,799	$ 771	$2,570
Miscellaneous Selling Expense	2,989	1,281	4,270
Miscellaneous General Expense	644	276	920
	$5,432	$2,328	$7,760

Division of these expense accounts by department is as follows.

Department A's share of bad debts is

70% of $2,570 = $1,799

Department B's share of bad debts is

30% of $2,570 = $771

Department A's share of miscellaneous selling is

70% of $4,270 = $2,989

Department B's share of miscellaneous selling is

30% of $4,270 = $1,281

Department A's share of miscellaneous general is

70% of $920 = $644

Department B's share of miscellaneous general is

30% of $920 = $276

Contribution margin by departments

When a company breaks down its expense figures on a contribution-margin basis, its income statement gives the contribution each department makes toward the overhead expenses incurred on behalf of the business as a whole. One can divide operating expenses into two classes: (1) *direct expenses,* which are expenses incurred for the sole benefit of a given department and thus are under the control of the department head; (2) *indirect expenses,* which are expenses incurred as overhead expenses of the entire business and thus are not under the control of one department head. For example, Sales Salary Expense is a direct expense, since it is incurred purely for the benefit of one department. On the other hand, property tax on real estate is an overhead expense incurred for the business as a whole, and it is not directly chargeable to one department.

Some operating expenses may be partially direct and partially indirect. For example, Holcomb's Advertising Expense consisted partially of billboard advertising, which stressed the name and location of the company, and partially of newspaper advertising, which directly benefited separate departments of the company. So the part of the advertising budget that went to billboard advertising is an indirect expense, and the part that went to newspaper advertising is a direct expense. Costs of insurance on merchandise inventories and store equipment are a direct expense; costs of liability insurance are indirect or overhead expenses. When you are classifying an expense as being direct or indirect, use this rule of thumb: *If the department were not in existence, then the expense would not be in existence.* The expense must be directly related to the department.

Here is a skeleton outline of an income statement which emphasizes contribution margin.

> Sales
> — Cost of Merchandise Sold
> = Gross Profit
> — Direct Expenses
> = Contribution Margin
> — Indirect Expenses
> = Net Income from Operations
> + Other Income
> — Other Expense
> = Net Income

The income statement on pages 734–735 presents the same figures that we saw on pages 726–727 for the J. C. Holcomb Company, except that this time they are in the contribution-margin format. You will find it interesting to compare the two.

The meaning of contribution margin

Contribution margin means the contribution that a given department makes to the net income of the firm, and it is the most realistic portrayal of the profitability of a department. If the company does away with the department, the company's net income will decrease by the amount of the contribution margin. For example, in the case of the Holcomb Company, Department B had a contribution margin of $18,765; if Holcomb eliminated the department, its net income would be reduced by $18,765 (assuming that Holcomb didn't create a new department to take the place of Department B, or expand Department A to occupy the void).

In Holcomb's work sheet (see pages 724–725), in which operating expenses were apportioned to departments, Department B showed a net loss from operations of $1,107. Department B sustained this loss because it was assigned a number of indirect expenses. If Holcomb eliminated Department B, these indirect expenses would still exist and would therefore be assigned entirely to Department A, thereby accounting in part for the reduction in net income by $18,765 (the amount of the contribution margin).

		DEPARTMENT A	
Revenue from Sales			
Sales		560 000 00	
Less Sales Ret. and Allow.		14 200 00	
Net Sales			545 800 00
Cost of Merchandise Sold			
Merch. Inv., Jan. 1, 19–		96 400 00	
Purchases	325 120 00		
Less: Purch. Ret. and Allow.	9 580 00		
Purch. Discount	5 740 00		
Net Purchases		309 800 00	
Merchandise Available for Sale		406 200 00	
Less Merch. Inv., Dec. 31, 19–		110 000 00	
Cost of Merchandise Sold			296 200 00
Gross Profit			249 600 00
Direct Departmental Expenses			
Sales Salary Expense		88 625 00	
Advertising Expense		9 216 00	
Depr. Expense, Store Equip.		1 840 00	
Insurance Expense		1 980 00	
Bad Debts Expense		1 799 00	
Total Direct Depart. Expenses			103 460 00
Contribution Margin			146 140 00
Indirect Expenses			
Office Salary Expense			
Rent Expense			
Utilities Expense			
Adv. Expense (billboard)			
Insurance Expense (liability)			
Misc. Selling Expense			
Misc. General Expense			
Total Indirect Expenses			
Net Income from Operations			
Other Income			
Interest Income			
Other Expense			
Interest Expense			
Net Income			

Line	DEPARTMENT B			TOTAL		
1						
2		240 000 00			800 000 00	
3		5 800 00			20 000 00	
4			234 200 00			780 000 00
5						
6		82 740 00			179 140 00	
7	167 890 00			493 010 00		
8	4 756 00			14 336 00		
9	3 274 00			9 014 00		
10		159 860 00			469 660 00	
11		242 600 00			648 800 00	
12		90 000 00			200 000 00	
13			152 600 00			448 800 00
14			81 600 00			331 200 00
15						
16						
17		52 200 00			140 825 00	
18		6 784 00			16 000 00	
19		1 460 00			3 300 00	
20		1 620 00			3 600 00	
21		771 00			2 570 00	
22			62 835 00			166 295 00
23			18 765 00			164 905 00
24						
25						
26					32 100 00	
27					16 400 00	
28					4 840 00	
29					1 600 00	
30					800 00	
31					4 270 00	
32					920 00	
33						60 930 00
34						103 975 00
35						
36						
37					3 624 00	
38						
39					2 400 00	1 224 00
40						105 199 00

The usefulness of contribution margin

A company finds that income statements which show contribution margin are extremely useful when it comes to controlling direct expenses, because the company can hold the head of a given department accountable for expenses directly chargeable to the department. If the head of a department reduces direct expenses, this will have a favorable affect on the contribution margin.

A company that manufactures various products can also use the concept of the contribution margin to determine the profitability of a particular product. This, clearly, is one of the most important uses of the contribution margin.

Management can use an income statement portraying contribution margin as a tool for making future plans and analyzing future operations. Sometimes such an income statement may even cause a company to eliminate a department. For example, The Westcott Company has five departments; its net income for last year was $120,000, which is about the same as it has been for the past 4 years. Westcott's income statement, in which all operating expenses are apportioned to the various departments, shows that Department E has a net loss from operations of $9,000. In an abbreviated contribution-margin format, here are the results of the last fiscal year.

Item	Department E (only)	Departments A to D (only)	Total, Departments A to E	Total, Departments A to D (with E eliminated)
Sales	$120,000	$1,480,000	$1,600,000	$1,480,000
Cost of Merchandise Sold	72,000	880,000	952,000	880,000
Gross Profit	$ 48,000	$ 600,000	$ 648,000	$ 600,000
Direct Departmental Expenses	32,000	336,000	368,000	336,000
Contribution Margin	$ 16,000	$ 264,000	$ 280,000	$ 264,000
Indirect Expenses	25,000	135,000	160,000	160,000
Net Income (Loss)	($ 9,000)	$ 129,000	$ 120,000	$ 104,000

Now suppose that Westcott eliminated Department E. Because Department E's contribution margin amounts to $16,000, the net income of the entire firm would decrease by $16,000 ($120,000 − $104,000 = $16,000). Another factor Westcott has to consider is possible "spill-over sales" of Department E; that is, customers of Department E may also buy things in other departments.

Branch accounting

As a means of increasing sales and income, a firm may open branch operations in different locations. This applies to both merchandising and service enterprises. You can undoubtedly think of numerous examples of chain store outlets in retail fields, such as grocery stores, drug stores, and variety stores. Examples of branch operations in service fields are restaurants, dry cleaners, motels, and service stations.

With the increasing use of data processing equipment, the accounting for branch operations is generally performed (centralized) at the home office. The accounting system is similar to that for departmental accounting, with each branch being treated as a department.

Summary

Income statements, which are extended on a departmental basis from Sales through Gross Profit, are statements in which either a company keeps separate ledger accounts for each department as well as for each element in the Revenue from Sales section and the Cost of Merchandise Sold section, or a company keeps supplementary records of the departmental totals for each element.

A company may extend its income statements on a departmental basis from Sales through Gross Profit or Net Income from Operations or Contribution Margin. Skeleton outlines are as follows.

From Sales through Gross Profit

   Revenue from Sales
— Cost of Merchandise Sold ←   {Based on separate departmental accounts
= Gross Profit   {or supplementary analysis sheets
— Operating Expenses
= Net Income from Operations
+ Other Income
— Other Expenses
= Net Income

From Sales through Net Income from Operations

   Revenue from Sales
— Cost of Merchandise Sold ←   {Based on separate departmental accounts
= Gross Profit   {or supplementary analysis sheets
— Operating Expenses ←   {One ledger account for each expense apportioned to various departments
= Net Income from Operations
+ Other Income
— Other Expenses
= Net Income

In the above format, each department assumes a share of the overhead expenses.

From Sales through Contribution Margin

   Revenue from Sales
— Cost of Merchandise Sold ←   {Based on separate departmental accounts
= Gross Profit   {or supplementary analysis sheets
— Direct Departmental Expenses ←   {Expenses that are directly related to the department
= Contribution Margin
— Indirect Expenses
= Net Income from Operations
+ Other Income
— Other Expenses
= Net Income

In the last format, each department is responsible for only its own share of expenses, consisting of *direct* expenses. Contribution margin represents one department's contribution to the net income of the company as a whole, and gives the most realistic portrayal of the profitability (or lack of it) of the department. A company finds the concept of contribution margin useful in evaluating the present worth of a department, in planning for future operations, and in determining the profitability of a given product. Some operating expenses may be partially direct and partially indirect.

Glossary

Apportionment of expenses Allocating or dividing operating expenses among operating departments.

Contribution margin Gross profit of a department minus its direct expenses.

Direct expenses Expenses that benefit only one department.

Indirect expenses Overhead expenses that benefit the business as a whole.

Questions

1. In what ways may departmental accounting information be useful?

2. Assuming that operating expenses are to be allocated to various departments, what basis would you choose for the following expenses?

> Rent
> Depreciation of store equipment
> Office salaries
> Insurance

3. What is the difference between a direct and an indirect operating expense?

4. You have been employed as the new manager of a clothing store. Previously, the income statement listed total revenue and operating expenses only. The firm can be divided into two departments: clothing and shoes. You desire to know the gross profit for each department. What changes in the accounting system will be required?

5. Referring to the question above, what benefits do you expect to gain from the departmental information?

6. Department A has a positive contribution margin amounting to $35,000. What does this mean as far as the firm is concerned?

7. Concerning gross profit and contribution margin, why is contribution margin a more realistic portrayal of the profitability of a department?

Exercises

Exercise 1 The Newburn Drugstore occupies an area of 10,000 square feet. The departments and the floor space occupied by each are as follows.

Pharmacy	1,400 square feet
Camera supplies	600 square feet
Toiletries and cosmetics	6,500 square feet

Greeting cards	500 square feet
Receiving and storage	1,000 square feet

Newburn leases the building for $16,000 per year. Apportion the rent expense to the five departments.

Exercise 2 In the drugstore in Exercise 1, the pharmacy department has the following account balances.

Sales	$258,000
Purchases	138,000
Purchases Discount	3,000
Sales Returns and Allowances	6,000
Merchandise Inventory (beginning)	43,500
Purchases Returns and Allowances	4,500
Merchandise Inventory (ending)	39,000

Determine the amount of the gross profit.

Exercise 3 Lloyd's Shoe Store has annual expenses for salaries of office staff of $72,000, which it allocates to the various departments on the basis of gross sales for each department. Sales by department are as follows.

Women's shoes	$183,000
Girls' shoes	159,000
Accessories	18,000
Total	$360,000

Determine what share of the expense of office salaries each of the three operating departments should bear.

Exercise 4 For the shoe store in Exercise 3, the premium for public liability insurance is $360, and the premium for fire and theft insurance on the inventory is $540. The balances of the inventories at the end of the fiscal period are as follows.

Women's shoes	$60,000
Girls' shoes	45,000
Accessories	15,000

How much of the insurance costs should be allocated to each department, given that the public liability insurance is apportioned on the basis of gross sales, and the property insurance on the basis of the values of the ending inventories?

Exercise 5 The following figures apply to Milner and Porter's sporting goods department.

Sales	$492,000
Direct Departmental Expenses	104,000
Purchases	366,000
Purchases Returns and Allowances	6,000

Interest Expense	4,000
Sales Returns and Allowances	8,000
Merchandise Inventory (ending)	152,000
Indirect Expenses	62,000
Merchandise Inventory (beginning)	132,000

Determine the amount of the contribution margin.

Exercise 6 Peasley Hardware is considering eliminating its giftware department. If it does, the management feels that the indirect expenses and the level of operations in the other departments will not be affected. Here is information from Peasley's income statement for the fiscal year ended July 31, which is considered to be a typical year.

Item	Giftware Department	All Other Departments	Total of All Departments (Including Giftware)
Sales	$111,000	$843,000	$954,000
Cost of Merchandise Sold	72,000	594,000	666,000
Gross Profit	$ 39,000	$249,000	$288,000
Operating Expenses	45,000	166,500	211,500
Net Income (Loss from Operations	($ 6,000)	$ 82,500	$ 76,500

Peasley considers that $27,000 of the operating expenses of the giftware department are direct expenses. What is the contribution margin of the giftware department?

Exercise 7 For the hardware store in Exercise 6, prepare an income statement for the forthcoming year, assuming that Peasley discontinues the giftware department.

Exercise 8 The Stewart Pet Food Company has two departments: dog food and cat food. Their advertising expenses are as follows: billboard advertising (featuring the company name only), $5,400; brochures (10% of the space features the company name), $960. Sales for each department are as follows: dog food, $120,000; cat food, $80,000. How much of the $5,496 advertising expense featuring the company name would you allocate to the two departments, assuming that the expense is apportioned on the basis of sales?

Problems

Problem 26-1 The Stormy Mountain Ski Shop has two sales departments: ski equipment and clothing. Their accountant, after recording and posting all adjustments, including the adjustments for merchandise inventory, prepared the adjusted trial balance shown on the facing page.

Stormy Mountain Ski Shop

Adjusted Trial Balance

April 30, 19—

Cash	8 6 6 8 00	
Accounts Receivable	93 0 4 4 00	
Allowance for Doubtful Accounts		3 9 2 0 00
Merchandise Inventory, Ski Department	99 9 6 0 00	
Merchandise Inventory, Clothing	70 4 3 4 00	
Store Supplies	1 2 8 0 00	
Store Equipment	45 5 6 0 00	
Accumulated Depreciation, Store Equipment		29 5 2 0 00
Accounts Payable		61 2 7 4 00
F. L. Jeffries, Capital		164 0 0 0 00
F. L. Jeffries, Drawing	45 2 0 0 00	
Income Summary	113 4 3 6 00	99 9 6 0 00
	63 5 6 8 00	70 4 3 4 00
Sales, Ski Equipment		739 6 2 8 00
Sales, Clothing		514 2 8 0 00
Sales Returns and Allowances, Ski Equipment	13 6 4 0 00	
Sales Returns and Allowances, Clothing	11 5 9 2 00	
Purchases, Ski Equipment	623 4 4 8 00	
Purchases, Clothing	429 5 9 4 00	
Purchases Returns and Allowances, Ski Equipment		13 4 4 0 00
Purchases Returns and Allowances, Clothing		9 6 2 8 00
Purchases Discount, Ski Equipment		9 6 5 6 00
Purchases Discount, Clothing		7 9 7 6 00
Sales Salary Expense	53 6 8 0 00	
Depreciation Expense, Store Equipment	7 9 6 8 00	
Miscellaneous Selling Expense	4 5 2 00	
Office Salary Expense	24 0 0 0 00	
Rent Expense	11 2 0 0 00	
Utilities Expense	4 1 8 4 00	
Bad Debts Expense	6 3 2 00	
Miscellaneous General Expense	3 6 8 00	
Interest Expense	1 8 0 8 00	
	1,723 7 1 6 00	1,723 7 1 6 00

Instructions   Prepare an income statement to show gross profit for each department, net income from operations, and net income for the entire business. Beginning balances of merchandise inventories are as follows: ski equipment, $113,436; clothing, $63,568.

Problem 26-2   Northland Paint and Glass has two sales departments: a paint department and a glass department. Their accountant, after recording and posting all adjustments—including the adjustments for merchandise inventory—at the end of the fiscal year prepared the adjusted trial balance as shown on page 742.

Problems   **741**

Northland Paint and Glass

Adjusted Trial Balance

December 31, 19—

	Debit	Credit
Cash	11 280 00	
Accounts Receivable	104 640 00	
Allowance for Doubtful Accounts		5 680 00
Merchandise Inventory, Paint Dept.	160 672 00	
Merchandise Inventory, Glass Dept.	74 962 00	
Prepaid Insurance	1 968 00	
Store Supplies	1 596 00	
Store Equipment	128 440 00	
Accumulated Depr., Store Equip.		97 856 00
Accounts Payable		96 840 00
Sales Tax Payable		2 684 00
M.O. Clinton, Capital		223 890 00
M.O. Clinton, Drawing	48 000 00	
Income Summary	157 856 00	160 672 00
	72 448 00	74 962 00
Sales, Paint Department		952 000 00
Sales, Glass Department		408 000 00
Sales Ret. and Allow., Paint Dept	24 482 00	
Sales Ret. and Allow., Glass Dept	1 652 00	
Purchases, Paint Department	621 436 00	
Purchases, Glass Department	297 444 00	
Purchases Ret. and Allow., Paint Dept.		8 452 00
Purchases Ret. and Allow., Glass Dept.		2 592 00
Purchases Discount, Paint Department		11 768 00
Purchases Discount, Glass Department		8 560 00
Sales Salary Expense	243 564 00	
Advertising Expense	32 000 00	
Depr. Expense, Store Equip.	31 600 00	
Store Supplies Expense	1 212 00	
Miscellaneous Selling Expense	1 040 00	
Rent Expense	19 200 00	
Utilities Expense	7 200 00	
Insurance Expense	1 680 00	
Bad Debts Expense	4 400 00	
Miscellaneous General Expense	1 560 00	
Interest Expense	3 624 00	
	2,053 956 00	2,053 956 00

Merchandise inventories at the beginning of the year were as follows: paint department, $157,856; glass department, $72,448. The bases (and sources of figures) for apportioning expenses to the two departments are as follows.

Sales Salary Expense (payroll register): paint department, $136,676; glass department, $106,888

Advertising Expense (newspaper column inches): paint department, 1,200 inches, glass department, 800 inches

Depreciation Expense, Store Equipment (Plant and Equipment ledger): paint department, $23,284; glass department, $8,316

Store Supplies Expense (requisitions): paint department, $640; glass department, $572

Rent Expense and Utilities Expense (floor space): paint department, 5,000 square feet; glass department, 3,000 square feet

Insurance Expense (average cost of merchandise inventory, rounded off in dollars): paint department, $1,148; glass department, $532 (verify these figures)

Miscellaneous General Expense (volume of gross sales): paint department, $1,092; glass department, $468 (verify these figures)

Instructions Prepare an income statement by department to show net income from operations, as well as a nondepartmentalized one to show net income for the entire company.

Problem 26-3 The Fleming Jewelry Store has two departments: the jewelry department and the watch department. Their accountant prepares the trial balance shown on page 744, as of December 31, the end of the fiscal year.

Here are the data for the adjustments.

Merchandise inventories, December 31, the end of the fiscal period: jewelry department, $58,950; watch department, $40,050

Insurance expired, $615

Estimated uncollectible customer charge accounts (based on an analysis of accounts), $3,660

Depreciation of store equipment for the year, $7,290

Accrued salaries and commissions, $510

Accrued interest payable, $195

The bases for apportioning expenses to the two departments are as follows.

Salaries and Commissions Expense (time sheets): jewelry department, $44,550; watch department, $19,110

Advertising Expense (column inches of space): jewelry department, $7,920; watch department, $1,980

Depreciation Expense (equipment ledger): jewelry department, $5,028; watch department, $2,262

Rent Expense, Utilities Expense, Miscellaneous Expense, Bad Debts Expense, Insurance Expense (sales): jewelry, 60%; watch, 40%

Trial Balance

December 31, 19—

	Debit	Credit
Cash	9 2 1 0 00	
Accounts Receivable	60 1 8 0 00	
Allowance for Doubtful Accounts		1 5 9 0 00
Merch. Inv., Jewelry Department	62 1 0 0 00	
Merch. Inv., Watch Department	42 3 0 0 00	
Prepaid Insurance	8 7 0 00	
Store Equipment	26 9 4 0 00	
Accu. Depr., Store Equipment		12 1 6 5 00
Accounts Payable		58 1 1 0 00
R. C. Fleming, Capital		99 1 2 0 00
R. C. Fleming, Drawing	23 2 5 0 00	
Sales, Jewelry Department		180 0 0 0 00
Sales, Watch Department		120 0 0 0 00
Purchases, Jewelry Department	89 4 0 0 00	
Purchases, Watch Department	68 7 0 0 00	
Salaries and Commissions Expense	63 1 5 0 00	
Advertising Expense	9 9 0 0 00	
Rent Expense	10 8 0 0 00	
Utilities Expense	2 1 3 0 00	
Miscellaneous Expense	1 3 3 5 00	
Interest Expense	7 2 0 00	
	470 9 8 5 00	470 9 8 5 00

Instructions   Complete the work sheet.

Problem 26-4   On December 31, the end of the fiscal year, the Franklin Shoe Store has the following balances of revenue and expense accounts and merchandise inventory, after adjustments have been recorded. Franklin has two departments: women's shoes and men's shoes.

Sales, Women's Shoes			374 8 3 2 00
Sales, Men's Shoes			147 8 5 6 00
Sales Ret. and Allow., Women's Shoes	9 5 6 4 00		
Sales Ret. and Allow., Men's Shoes	4 0 1 2 00		
Merch. Inv., Women's Shoes	102 0 6 0 00		
Merch. Inv., Men's Shoes	43 5 6 4 00		
Purchases, Women's Shoes	223 9 4 8 00		
Purchases, Men's Shoes	86 6 4 8 00		
Purchases Ret. and Allow., Women's Shoes			5 2 8 0 00
Purchases Ret. and Allow., Men's Shoes			1 3 6 8 00
Purchases Discount, Women's Shoes			3 9 6 0 00
Purchases Discount, Men's Shoes			1 4 4 0 00
Sales Salary Expense	91 0 0 0 00		
Advertising Expense	8 2 2 0 00		
Depr. Expense, Store Equip.	6 4 0 0 00		
Bad Debts Expense	3 6 4 0 00		
Office Salary Expense	17 2 0 0 00		
Rent Expense	16 8 0 0 00		
Utilities Expense	2 4 8 0 00		
Insurance Expense	7 8 0 00		
Miscellaneous Selling Expense	7 4 8 00		
Miscellaneous General Expense	7 1 2 00		
Interest Expense	1 4 4 0 00		

The values of merchandise inventories on January 1 (beginning) are women's shoes, $95,640; men's shoes, $47,892.

Essential data for direct expenses (and sources of the figures) are as follows.

Sales Salary Expense (sales personnel work in one department only) is allocated as follows: women's shoes, $63,720; men's shoes, $27,280.

Advertising: newspaper advertising is allocated as follows: women's shoes, $6,560; men's shoes, $1,660.

Depreciation: Depreciation of store equipment is apportioned on the basis of the average cost of equipment in each department. The average cost of store equipment is women's shoes, $15,000; men's shoes, $5,000.

Bad Debts Expense: Department managers are responsible for granting of credit on sales made by their respective departments. Bad Debts Expense is allocated as follows: women's shoes, $2,592; men's shoes, $1,048.

Instructions   Prepare an income statement to show each department's contribution margin.

Problem 26-1A Eastern Appliance has two sales departments: household appliances, and radio and television. Eastern's accountant prepared this adjusted trial balance after all adjustments had been recorded and posted.

Cash	6 4 1 6 00	
Accounts Receivable	90 3 7 8 00	
Allowance for Doubtful Accounts		3 2 4 0 00
Merch. Inv., Appliance Dept.	172 2 3 8 00	
Merch. Inv., Radio and TV Dept.	136 3 9 0 00	
Store Supplies	1 0 2 8 00	
Store Equipment	39 3 4 0 00	
Accum. Depr., Store Equip.		25 5 3 6 00
Accounts Payable		95 9 7 0 00
L. C. Mendall, Capital		241 2 4 0 00
L. C. Mendall, Drawing	40 8 0 0 00	
Income Summary	157 2 3 2 00	172 2 3 8 00
	144 9 6 4 00	136 3 9 0 00
Sales, Appliance Department		747 1 1 8 00
Sales, Radio and TV Department		630 4 8 0 00
Sales Ret. and Allow., Appliance Dept.	14 2 8 2 00	
Sales Ret. and Allow., Radio and TV Dept.	12 9 5 2 00	
Purchases, Appliance Department	695 3 6 8 00	
Purchases, Radio and TV Department	487 3 5 4 00	
Purchases Ret. and Allow., Appliance Dept.		10 5 6 8 00
Purchases Ret. and Allow., Radio and TV Dept.		8 7 6 8 00
Purchases Discount, Appliance Dept.		13 6 8 2 00
Purchases Discount, Radio and TV Dept.		9 9 2 0 00
Sales Salary Expense	57 5 8 0 00	
Depr. Expense, Store Equip.	8 7 6 4 00	
Miscellaneous Selling Expense	3 5 2 00	
Office Salary Expense	11 7 6 0 00	
Rent Expense	9 6 0 0 00	
Utilities Expense	5 7 7 2 00	
Bad Debts Expense	4 8 4 00	
Miscellaneous General Expense	2 4 0 00	
Interest Expense	1 8 5 6 00	
	2,095 1 5 0 00	2,095 1 5 0 00

Instructions Prepare an income statement to show gross profit for each department, and net income from operations, as well as net income for the entire business. Beginning balances of merchandise inventories are: appliances, $157,232; radio-TV, $144,964.

Problem 26-2A Brewster Paint and Glass has two departments: a paint department and a glass department. Brewster's accountant prepares an adjusted trial balance at the end of the fiscal year, after all adjustments, including the adjustments for merchandise inventory, have been recorded and posted.

Brewster Paint and Glass		
Adjusted Trial Balance		
December 31, 19—		
Cash	9 652 00	
Accounts Receivable	93 780 00	
Allowance for Doubtful Accounts		5 240 00
Merch. Inv., Paint Dept.	168 284 00	
Merch. Inv., Glass Dept.	82 276 00	
Prepaid Insurance	1 680 00	
Store Supplies	1 524 00	
Store Equipment	107 364 00	
Accum. Depr., Store Equip.		83 620 00
Accounts Payable		77 360 00
Sales Tax Payable		2 568 00
C. E. Flanigan, Capital		180 888 00
C. E. Flanigan, Drawing	44 000 00	
Income Summary	165 520 00	168 284 00
	81 440 00	82 276 00
Sales, Paint Department		819 600 00
Sales, Glass Department		546 400 00
Sales Ret. and Allow., Paint Dept.	23 370 00	
Sales Ret. and Allow., Glass Dept.	3 432 00	
Purchases, Paint Department	530 204 00	
Purchases, Glass Department	344 254 00	
Purchases Ret. and Allow., Paint Dept.		9 236 00
Purchases Ret. and Allow., Glass Dept.		3 584 00
Purchases Discount, Paint Dept.		10 992 00
Purchases Discount, Glass Dept.		5 928 00
Sales Salary Expense	246 440 00	
Advertising Expense	28 000 00	
Depr. Expense, Store Equip.	26 872 00	
Store Supplies Expense	1 484 00	
Miscellaneous Selling Expense	1 360 00	
Rent Expense	16 000 00	
Utilities Expense	6 400 00	
Insurance Expense	1 800 00	
Bad Debts Expense	3 600 00	
Miscellaneous General Expense	1 640 00	
Interest Expense	5 600 00	
	1,995 976 00	1,995 976 00

Merchandise inventories at the beginning of the year were as follows: paint department, $165,520; glass department, $81,440. The bases for apportioning expenses and the sources of the figures are as follows.

Sales Salary Expense (payroll register): paint department, $149,600; glass department, $96,840

Advertising Expense (newspaper column inches): paint department, 1,200 inches; glass department, 800 inches

Depreciation Expense, Store Equipment (Plant and Equipment ledger): paint department, $19,232; glass department, $7,640

Store Supplies Expense (requisitions): paint department, $836; glass department, $648

Rent Expense and Utilities Expense (floor space): paint department, 5,000 square feet; glass department, 3,000 square feet

Insurance Expense (average cost of merchandise inventory, rounded off in dollars): paint department, $1,208; glass department, $592 (verify these figures)

Miscellaneous Selling Expense (volume of gross sales): paint department, $816; glass department, $544 (verify these figures)

Bad Debts Expense (volume of gross sales): paint department, $2,160, glass department, $1,440 (verify these figures)

Miscellaneous General Expense (volume of gross sales): paint department, $984; glass department, $656 (verify these figures)

Instructions Prepare an income statement by department to show net income from operations, as well as a nondepartmentalized income statement to show net income for the entire company.

Problem 26-3A The Oakland Jewelry Store has two departments: the jewelry department and the watch department. The trial balance, as of December 31, the end of the fiscal year, is shown on the facing page.

The data for the adjustments are as follows.

Merchandise inventories, December 31, the end of the fiscal period: jewelry department, $60,000; watch department, $36,000

Insurance expired, $585

Estimated uncollectible customer charge accounts (based on an analysis of accounts), $3,750

Depreciation of store equipment for the year, $7,230

Accrued salaries and commissions, $555

Accrued interest payable, $180

The bases for apportioning expenses to the two departments are as follows.

Salaries and Commissions Expense (time sheets): jewelry department, $45,540; watch department, $19,515

Advertising Expense (space): jewelry department, $7,680; watch department, $1,920

	Debit	Credit
Cash	9 3 0 0 00	
Accounts Receivable	59 4 0 0 00	
Allowance for Doubtful Accounts		1 5 6 0 00
Merch. Inv., Jewelry Dept	63 0 0 0 00	
Merch. Inv., Watch Dept	42 0 0 0 00	
Prepaid Insurance	9 0 0 00	
Store Equipment	27 3 0 0 00	
Accum. Depr., Store Equip.		12 2 1 0 00
Accounts Payable		58 0 8 0 00
L. O. Pender, Capital		99 4 2 0 00
L. O. Pender, Drawing	21 0 0 0 00	
Sales, Jewelry Department		180 0 0 0 00
Sales, Watch Department		120 0 0 0 00
Purchases, Jewelry Department	90 0 0 0 00	
Purchases, Watch Department	69 0 0 0 00	
Salaries and Commissions Expense	64 5 0 0 00	
Advertising Expense	9 6 0 0 00	
Rent Expense	10 8 0 0 00	
Utilities Expense	2 1 7 5 00	
Miscellaneous Expense	1 6 3 5 00	
Interest Expense	6 6 0 00	
	471 2 7 0 00	471 2 7 0 00

Depreciation Expense (equipment ledger): jewelry department, $5,061; watch department, $2,169

Rent Expense, Utilities Expense, Miscellaneous Expense, Bad Debts Expense, Insurance Expense (sales): jewelry department, 60%; watch department, 40%

Instructions   Complete the work sheet.

Problem 26-4A   The Frazier Shoe Store, after it has recorded adjustments, has the balances of revenue and expense accounts and merchandise inventories shown at the top of the next page for its two departments on December 31, the end of the fiscal year.

Sales, Women's Shoes									379	7	1	2	00
Sales, Men's Shoes									148	2	8	8	00
Sales Ret. and Allow., Women's Shoes	9	6	3	2	00								
Sales Ret. and Allow., Men's Shoes	4	3	6	8	00								
Merch. Inv., Women's Shoes	105	3	2	0	00								
Merch. Inv., Men's Shoes	45	9	6	0	00								
Purchases, Women's Shoes	224	2	8	0	00								
Purchases, Men's Shoes	86	5	8	0	00								
Purch. Ret. and Allow., Women's Shoes									3	2	9	6	00
Purch. Ret. and Allow., Men's Shoes									1	3	4	0	00
Purchases Discount, Women's Shoes									2	3	6	4	00
Purchases Discount, Men's Shoes									1	4	8	0	00
Sales Salary Expense	92	5	2	0	00								
Advertising Expense	8	4	0	0	00								
Depr. Expense, Store Equip.	6	4	0	0	00								
Bad Debts Expense	3	8	0	0	00								
Office Salary Expense	17	0	4	0	00								
Rent Expense	16	8	0	0	00								
Utilities Expense	2	5	2	0	00								
Insurance Expense		8	4	0	00								
Misc. Selling Expense		7	8	0	00								
Misc. General Expense		6	8	0	00								
Interest Expense	1	2	8	0	00								

The values of merchandise inventories on January 1 (beginning) are women's shoes, $97,420; men's shoes, $48,280.

Essential data for direct expenses (and sources of the figures) are as follows.

Sales Salary Expense (sales personnel work in one department only) is allocated as follows: women's shoes, $64,760; men's shoes, $27,760.

Advertising: Newspaper advertising is allocated as follows: women's shoes, $6,720; men's shoes, $1,680.

Depreciation: Depreciation of store equipment is apportioned on the basis of the average cost of equipment in each department. The average cost of store equipment is women's shoes, $15,000; men's shoes, $5,000.

Bad Debts Expense: Department managers are responsible for granting credit on sales made by their respective departments. Bad Debts Expense is allocated as follows: women's shoes, $2,736; men's shoes, $1,064.

Instructions Prepare an income statement to show each department's contribution margin.

Appendix C:
COD sales, layaway sales, and installment sales

IN THIS APPENDIX we shall talk about COD sales, layaway sales, and installment sales. We'll discuss COD and layaway sales briefly first, because they are relatively simple. However, in terms of volume, installment sales are by far the most important.

COD sales

COD sales (which means cash-on-delivery sales) enable a business firm to sell merchandise to customers who do not have established credit. The person who delivers the goods collects the cash from the customer at the time of delivery. This enables the seller to maintain control over the merchandise until cash is received. If the customer cannot pay, the delivering agent returns the goods to the seller.

The accounting procedure is straightforward: The seller prepares a sales invoice marked *COD* and encloses it with the merchandise to be delivered. If the customer pays, the seller then processes the sales invoice as if it had been a cash sale. Conversely, if the customer does not pay, the seller voids the sales invoice and returns the merchandise to stock. When this happens, the accountant lists the delivery charge as a debit to Delivery Expense and a credit to Cash.

Layaway sales

In the case of a *layaway sale,* also known as a *will-call sale,* the customer deposits some cash toward the purchase of a certain item, and the store puts it aside for the customer. The customer must pay the entire price (usually within a specified time) before the store will release the merchandise. If the customer does not complete the payments within the time allowed, she or he forfeits the money that has been paid. However, to preserve customer goodwill, the store often refunds the amount paid or allows it to be used as credit against future purchases.

Most customers do complete their payments on layaway sales; in this case, the store can go ahead and record the sale in the usual manner. For example, the Tall Men's Shop sells a coat on layaway to N. D. Webster. The coat costs $80, plus a $4 sales tax. Webster makes a deposit of $14 and then makes two additional payments, of $40 and $30. The entries, in general journal form, are as follows.

	Debit	Credit
Cash	14 00	
Accounts Receivable, N. D. Webster	70 00	
Sales		80 00
Sales Tax Payable		4 00
Layaway sale, initial deposit		

	Debit	Credit
Cash	40 00	
Accounts Receivable, N. D. Webster		40 00
Deposit received on layaway sale		

Cash			3 0 00						
Accounts Receivable, N. D. Webster							3 0 00		
Received final deposit on layaway sale, and released the									
merchandise.									

The Tall Men's Shop records these entries in the cash receipts journal. If the shop were to give Webster a cash refund, it would have to cancel the original sale.

Installment sales

Installment sales are common among retailers of automobiles, household appliances, electronic equipment, musical instruments, furniture, and jewelry. The installment plan is a sales arrangement by which the customer makes a cash down payment and gets possession of the merchandise in return for his or her promise to pay the rest of the money in small payments at regular intervals over a period of time. The written agreement between buyer and seller is known as a *conditional sales contract*. The seller keeps title to the merchandise, and will transfer title to the buyer on the condition that the buyer complete all the payments.

Accounting for installment sales

A firm may account for sales on the installment plan on either the accrual basis or the installment basis. Each method has its advantages, and both methods are widely used. Let us examine each in turn.

Accrual basis A firm which records installment sales on the accrual basis writes them up in the same manner as ordinary charge sales, that is, by debiting Accounts Receivable and crediting Sales. The accounting department makes a notation of the terms of the sale on the customer's individual account in the accounts receivable ledger.

In the event that the customer does not complete the payments, the seller repossesses the merchandise, and writes off the unpaid balance by debiting Allowance for Doubtful Accounts and crediting Accounts Receivable.

When the firm sells the repossessed merchandise again, it records this as a separate sale. For example, Monroe Jewelry Store sells a watch for $90 to F. Pierce, receiving a $30 cash down payment. Monroe records the transaction as follows.

Cash			3 0 00						
Accounts Receivable, F. Pierce			6 0 00						
Sales							9 0 00		
Sold Merchandise on account to F. Pierce.									

F. Pierce defaults on the payments, so Monroe Jewelry repossesses the watch, and writes off F. Pierce's account.

Allowance for Doubtful Accounts			60 00		
Accounts Receivable, F. Pierce				60 00	
Wrote off the account of F. Pierce as uncollectible and					
repossessed a watch.					

Monroe Jewelry then sells the repossessed watch for $27 cash.

Cash			27 00		
Sales				27 00	
Sold repossessed merchandise for cash.					

Installment basis When a company uses the installment basis, it assumes that each cash installment payment it receives is a partial recovery of the cost of the merchandise and a portion of the gross profit. In other words, the payment is a combination of part of the cost and part of the gross profit of the sale. For example, Ray's Used Cars sells a car for $800. The cost of the car is $600. The gross profit is $200 ($800 − $600). The gross profit as a percentage of the sale is 25% ($200/$800). If Ray's Used Cars collects $440 during the first year, the gross profit counted is $110 (25% of $440); if it collects the remaining $360 during the second year, the gross profit counted during that year is $90 (25% of $360).

The installment basis is acceptable for income tax purposes. Firms using this basis pay income tax only on the gross profit counted during the year in which they receive cash. In the case of the $800 sale by Ray's Used Cars, for income tax, the firm reports a gross profit of $110 during the first year (gross profit collected). The firm combines that $110 gross profit with the gross profits it collected during the year from other sales. Next it deducts its operating expenses to determine its net income. To find its income tax, it multiplys its net income by the tax rate.

Let's use this example to compare the installment basis with the accrual basis.

	Installment basis	Accrual basis
Gross profit reported for first year	$110	$200
Gross profit reported for second year	90	0

The types of goods sold on the installment basis are mainly the so-called consumer durables, often referred to as "big-ticket items." Since these items have distinguishing features, such as model numbers, serial numbers, etc., the firm is able to account for the cost of each item. This is similar to the system of accounting for perpetual inventories: When a firm buys merchandise, it debits Merchandise Inventory for the amount of the cost. When a firm sells merchandise, it credits Merchandise Inventory for the amount of the cost.

Companies have a special receivable account for their installment customers: *Installment Accounts Receivable.*

Illustration of an installment sale, beginning and ending in the same year, and paid in full On February 1, City Appliance Company sells a stereo set to Mary Connally for $260, with a down payment of $60, and four monthly payments of $50 each. The cost of the stereo set—that is, the amount that City Appliance paid for it—is $182. The entry, in general journal form, to record the sale is as follows.

19– Feb.	1	*Installment Accounts Receivable, Mary Connally*				
		(19–)		2 6 0 00		
		Merchandise Inventory			1 8 2 00	
		Deferred Installment Sales Income			7 8 00	
		To record installment sale of CJS stereo,				
		model 1619, cost $182.				

Note that Deferred Installment Sales Income shows City Appliance Company's gross profit on the sale. Ordinarily a company would use a sales journal that has special columns for each of the accounts listed. Installment Accounts Receivable is a controlling account. Note that the accountant lists the year in parentheses after each installment Accounts Receivable; this enables management to watch over installment credit.

When Mary Connally pays that $60 down payment, the accountant at City Appliance debits Cash and credits Installment Accounts Receivable. City Appliance handles later cash installment payments the same way, as follows.

Feb.	1	*Cash*		6 0 00		
		Installment Accounts Receivable, Mary Connally				
		(19–)			6 0 00	
		Downpayment on sale of CJS stereo, model				
		1619.				

Mar.	1	*Cash*		5 0 00		
		Installment Accounts Receivable, Mary Connally				
		(19–)			5 0 00	
		Payment on the sale of Feb. 1.				

Apr.	1	Cash						5 0 00							
		Installment Accounts Receivable, Mary Connally													
		(19—)									5 0 00				
		Payment on the sale of Feb. 1.													

May	1	Cash						5 0 00							
		Installment Accounts Receivable, Mary Connally													
		(19—)									5 0 00				
		Payment on the sale of Feb. 1.													

Jun.	1	Cash						5 0 00							
		Installment Accounts Receivable, Mary Connally													
		(19—)									5 0 00				
		Final Payment on the sale of Feb. 1.													

Ordinarily a merchant would write such entries in a cash receipts journal.

Now let us say that Mary Connally has completed all the payments. City Appliance makes an entry transferring the gross profit, based on the cash received on the contract during the year, from Deferred Installment Sales Income to Realized Installment Sales Income. The entry and corresponding T accounts are shown here.

Jun.	1	Deferred Installment Sales Income						7 8 00							
		Realized Installment Sales Income									7 8 00				
		Realized gross profit on the collections during													
		the year based on the installment sale to													
		Mary Connally.													

Installment Accounts Receivable

+		−	
Feb 1 260	Feb. 1	60
	Mar. 1	50
	Apr. 1	50
	May 1	50
	June 1	50

Cash

+		−
Feb. 1	60	
Mar. 1	50	
Apr. 1	50	
May 1	50	
June 1	50	

Merchandise Inventory

+	−
Feb. 1 182	

Deferred Installment Sales Income

−		+
June 1	78	Feb. 1	78

Realized Installment Sales Income

−	+
	June 1	78

Notice that Deferred Installment Sales Income has been canceled out. The accountant then closes the balance of Realized Installment Sales Income, representing the firm's gross profit on the transaction, into Income Summary.

Here is what the ledger card for City Appliance's installment accounts receivable ledger looks like.

	DATE		ITEM	POST. REF.	AMOUNT	DATE		EXPLANATION	POST. REF.	AMOUNT	BALANCE
			CHARGES					**PAYMENTS**			
	19– Feb.	1	CJS Stereo, model 1619, cost		2 6 0 00	19– Feb.	1	Downpayment		6 0 00	2 0 0 00
			$182.00, gross profit $78.00,			Mar.	1			5 0 00	1 5 0 00
			gross profit %, 30%, (78/260 =			Apr.	1			5 0 00	1 0 0 00
			.3 = 30%).			May	1			5 0 00	5 0 00
						Jun.	1			5 0 00	

Illustration of an installment sale, beginning in one year and ending the next year, and paid in full On October 15, City Appliance sells a refrigerator to Lester C. Jenks for $320, with a down payment of $110 and five monthly payments of $42 each. The cost of the refrigerator (that is, what City Appliance paid for it) is $240. Here are the entries, in general journal form, to account for the sale.

	DATE		ITEM		DEBIT	CREDIT	
1	19– Oct.	15	Installment Accounts Receivable, Lester C. Jenks				1
2			(19–)		3 2 0 00		2
3			Merchandise Inventory			2 4 0 00	3
4			Deferred Installment Sales Income			8 0 00	4
5			To record installment sale of Prentice				5
6			Refrigerator, model C118, cost $240.				6
7							7
8		15	Cash		1 1 0 00		8
9			Installment Accounts Receivable, Lester C.				9
10			Jenks (19–)			1 1 0 00	10
11			Downpayment on sale of Prentice				11
12			Refrigerator, model C118.				12
13							13

	DATE		ITEM		DEBIT	CREDIT	
1	Nov.	15	Cash		4 2 00		1
2			Installment Accounts Receivable, Lester C.				2
3			Jenks, (19–)			4 2 00	3
4			Payment on sale of Oct. 15.				4
5							5

	DATE		ITEM		DEBIT	CREDIT	
1	Dec.	14	Cash		4 2 00		1
2			Installment Accounts Receivable, Lester C.				2
3			Jenks (19–)			4 2 00	3
4			Payment on sale of Oct. 15.				4
5							5

			Adjusting Entry															
	Dec.	31	Deferred Installment Sales Income						4	8	50								
			Realized Installment Sales Income											4	8	50			
			Adjusting entry for realized gross profit on																
			collections during the year based on																
			installment sale to Lester C. Jenks (Gross																
			profit % = 80/320 = 25%; $194 × .25 =																
			$48.50).																

Note that, by the end of the year, Lester Jenks has paid City Appliance $194, which is his down payment of $110 plus two $42 payments.

The last entry, an adjusting entry made at the end of the fiscal year, accounts for the gross profit received on all installment contracts that are not paid in full. The accountant can gather the information from the ledger cards by multiplying the collections received for the year on each contract by the rate of gross profit on each item. If one does not use the specific percentage of gross profit on each sale, one can instead use an average percentage.

Here is the entry to close the revenue account, Realized Installment Sales Income.

			Closing Entry														
	19– Dec.	31	Realized Installment Sales Income						4	8	50						
			Income Summary											4	8	50	

At the end of the first year, Deferred Installment Sales Income has a credit balance of $31.50. Deferred Installment Sales Income will appear on the balance sheet under the caption of Deferred Credits, a liability category, written immediately above owner's equity.

During the first 3 months of the next year, Lester Jenks pays his three remaining installments. Then the accountant converts the remaining balance in Deferred Installment Sales Income into Realized Installment Sales Income. Here are the entries.

	19– Jan.	15	Cash						4	2	00						
			Installment Accounts Receivable, Lester C.														
			Jenks (19–)											4	2	00	
			Payment on the sale of Oct. 15, 19–.														

1	Feb.	14	Cash			4 2 00			1
2			Installment Accounts Receivable, Lester C.						2
3			Jenks (19—)				4 2 00		3
4			Payment on the sale of Oct. 15, 19—.						4
5									5
6									6

1	Mar.	14	Cash			4 2 00			1
2			Installment Accounts Receivable, Lester C.						2
3			Jenks (19—)				4 2 00		3
4			Payment on the sale of Oct. 15, 19—.						4
5									5
6									6

1	Mar.	14	Deferred Installment Sales Income			3 1 50			1
2			Realized Installment Sales Income				3 1 50		2
3			To record realized gross profit on collections						3
4			during the year on installment sale to						4
5			Lester C. Jenks (Gross profit % = 25%;						5
6			$126 \times .25 = $31.50).						6
7									7

The postings to the T accounts look like this.

Installment Accounts Receivable

+		−	
Oct. 15	320	Oct. 15	110
		Nov. 15	42
		Dec. 14	42
		Jan. 15	42
		Feb. 14	42
		Mar. 14	42

Cash

+		−
Oct. 15	110	
Nov. 15	42	
Dec. 14	42	
Jan. 15	42	
Feb. 14	42	
Mar. 14	42	

Deferred Installment Sales Income

−		+	
Dec. 15	48.50	Oct. 15	80
Mar. 14	31.50		

Realized Installment Sales Income

−		+	
Dec. 31		Dec. 31	48.50
Clos.	48.50		
		Mar. 14	31.50

Income Summary

Dec. 31		Dec. 31	48.50
Clos.	48.50		

Merchandise Inventory

+		−	
		Oct. 15	240

Illustration of an installment sale beginning in one year and defaulted 2 years later On December 5, City Appliance sells a color television set to Merle C. Sanford for $600, with a down payment of $60, and fifteen monthly payments of $36 each. The cost of the television set (to City Appliance) is $390. The entries are shown on the next two pages.

Date		Account	Debit	Credit	
19—Dec.	5	Installment Accounts Receivable, Merle C. Sanford			
		(19—)	600 00		
		Merchandise Inventory		390 00	
		Deferred Installment Sales Income		210 00	
		To record installment sale of Linton color			
		TV, model DF 912, cost $390.			
	5	Cash	60 00		
		Installment Accounts Receivable, Merle C.			
		Sanford (19—)		60 00	
		Downpayment on sale of Linton color TV,			
		model DF 912.			

Date		Account	Debit	Credit	
		Adjusting Entry			
Dec.	31	Deferred Installment Sales Income	21 00		
		Realized Installment Sales Income		21 00	
		Adjusting entry for realized gross profit on			
		collections during the year based on			
		installment sale to Merle C. Sanford (Gross			
		profit % = 210/600 = 35%; $60 × .35 = $21).			
		Closing Entry			
	31	Realized Installment Sales Income	21 00		
		Income Summary		21 00	

Date		Account	Debit	Credit	
19—Jan.	4	Cash	36 00		
		Installment Accounts Receivable, Merle C.			
		Sanford (19—)		36 00	

The last entry is repeated on February 5, March 5, April 2, May 3, June 6, July 6, August 5, September 10, October 12, November 21, and December 15.

Date		Account	Debit	Credit	
		Adjusting Entry			
Dec.	31	Deferred Installment Sales Income	151 20		
		Realized Installment Sales Income		151 20	
		Adjusting entry for realized gross profit on			
		collections during the year based on			
		installment sale to Merle C. Sanford (Gross			
		profit % = 35%; $432 × .35 = $151.20).			
		Closing Entry			
	31	Realized Installment Sales Income	151 20		
		Income Summary		151 20	

	19– Jan.	20	Cash					3 6 00						
1														1
2			Installment Accounts Receivable, Merle C.											2
3			Sanford (19–)									3 6 00		3
4			Payment on sale of Dec. 5, 19–.											4
5														5

After January of the second year after the sale, Merle Sanford stops making payments on the installment contract. Therefore on April 2 of that year, City Appliance repossesses the set. At this time, the wholesale value of the set is $40. The accountant for City Appliance first lists the installments collected during that year, and writes the entry as follows.

		19– Apr.	2	Deferred Installment Sales Income					1 2 60					
	1													1
	2			Realized Installment Sales Income									1 2 60	2
	3			To record realized gross profit on installment										3
	4			collected during the year, prior to the										4
	5			repossession based on installment sale to										5
	6			Merle C. Sanford ($36 × .35 = $12.60).										6
	7													7
(1)	8		2	Inventory of Repossessed Merchandise					4 0 00					8
(3)	9			Deferred Installment Sales Income					2 5 20					9
(4)	10			Loss on Repossession					6 80					10
(2)	11			Installment Accounts Receivable, Merle C.										11
	12			Sanford (19–)									7 2 00	12
	13			Repossessed Linton color TV, model DF 912,										13
	14			value of set $40.										14
	15													15

Note: A firm uses a separate account, Inventory of Repossessed Merchandise, to distinguish repossessed goods from new goods (Merchandise Inventory).

The numbers in parentheses indicate the suggested order for recording the debits and credits. Deferred Installment Sales Income and Installment Accounts Receivable, Merle C. Sanford, are cleared off the books by the last entry. If the debits are *less* than the credits, the difference represents a loss. Conversely, if the debits are *more* than the credits, the difference represents a gain. One can also view the above entry as a loss, since the debits to Inventory of Repossessed Merchandise and Deferred Installment Sales Income are not enough to clear the Installment Accounts Receivable account.

If the reverse had been true—that is, if the total of the debits to Inventory of Repossessed Merchandise and Deferred Installment Sales Income had been greater than the credit to Installment Accounts Receivable—the difference would have represented a gain on repossession. For example, suppose that the wholesale value of the set at the time of repossession had been $120; then the entry would have been as shown on the next page.

(1)	Apr.	2	*Inventory of Repossessed Merchandise*			1 2 0 00			
(3)			*Deferred Installment Sales Income*			2 5 20			
(2)			*Installment Accounts Receivable, Merle C.*						
			Sanford (19—)					7 2 00	
(4)			*Gain on Repossession*					7 3 20	
			Repossessed Linton color TV, model DF 912,						
			value of set, $120.						

Loss on Repossession is classified on the income statement as Other Expense; Gain on Repossession is classified as Other Income.

Here are T accounts to show City Appliance's $6.80 loss on the repossession.

Installment Accounts Receivable

+			−	
Dec. 5	600	Dec. 5	60
		Jan. 4	36
		Feb. 5	36
		Mar. 5	36
		Apr. 2	36
		May 3	36
		June 6	36
		July 6	36
		Aug. 5	36
		Sep. 10	36
		Oct. 12	36
		Nov. 21	36
		Dec. 15	36
		Jan. 20	36
		Apr. 2	72

Cash

+		−
Dec. 5	60	
Jan. 4	36	
Feb. 5	36	
Mar. 5	36	
Apr. 2	36	
May 3	36	
June 6	36	
July 6	36	
Aug. 5	36	
Sep. 10	36	
Oct. 12	36	
Nov. 21	36	
Dec. 15	36	
Jan. 20	36	

Merchandise Inventory

+		−	
		Dec. 5	390

Inventory of Repossessed Merchandise

+		−
Apr. 2	40	

Deferred Installment Sales Income

−		+	
Dec. 31	21.00	Dec. 5	210.00
Dec. 31	151.20		
Apr. 2	12.60		
Apr. 2	25.20		

Realized Installment Sales Income

−		+	
Dec. 31		Dec. 31	21.00
Clos.	21.00		
Dec. 31		Dec. 31	151.20
Clos.	151.20		
		Apr. 2	12.60

Income Summary

Closing		Dec. 31	21.00
Closing		Dec. 31	151.20

Loss on Repossession

+		−
Apr. 2	6.80	

You can see from the postings that all the accounts involved in the sale have now been canceled out.

Problems

Problem C-1 On March 15 of this year, James Robertson bought a suit from McAllister's Department Store on a layaway plan. The suit cost Robertson $144, plus $7.20 sales tax. Robertson made an initial deposit of $31.20 and then made two additional payments of $75 and $45 on March 30 and April 30.

Instructions Write the three entries pertaining to the layaway sale in general journal form omitting explanations.

Problem C-2 On June 14 of this year, Roger Gardner bought a trumpet on the installment plan from the Franklin Music Store, which led to the following transactions for Franklin's to record on its books.

June 14 Sold trumpet for $290 to Roger Gardner, agreeing to a down payment of $90 and four installments of $50 each. Cost of trumpet: $174.

14 Received down payment of $90 from Gardner.

July 12 Received $50 as first installment from Gardner.

Aug. 14 Received $50 as second installment from Gardner.

Sept. 16 Received $50 as third installment from Gardner.

Oct. 13 Received $50 as fourth and final installment from Gardner.

13 Recorded income realized on installment collections from Gardner.

Instructions Record the transactions in general journal form, omitting the explanations.

Problem C-3 The books of Goodall Hardware show the following transactions related to installment sales.

Year 1

Sept. 10 Sold a power saw to R. Francis, $320, on the installment plan, with a down payment of $80 and three installments of $80 each. Cost of power saw: $204.80. (gross profit % $= \dfrac{\$115.20}{\$320.00} = 36\%$)

10 Recorded down payment of $80 from Francis.

Oct. 9 Sold a lathe to C. L. Fenner, $364, on the installment plan, with a down payment of $84 and five installments of $56 each. Cost of lathe: $218.40. (gross profit % $= \dfrac{\$145.60}{\$364.00} = 40\%$)

9 Recorded down payment of $84 from C. L. Fenner.

11 Received $80 as first installment from R. Francis.

Nov. 5 Received $56 as first installment from C. L. Fenner.

12 Received $80 as second installment from R. Francis.

Dec. 9 Received $56 as second installment from C. L. Fenner.

Dec. 11 Received $80 as third and final installment from R. Francis.

11 Recorded the income realized on installments collected during the year from R. Francis.

31 Recorded as an adjusting entry the income realized on installments collected during the year from C. L. Fenner.

31 Closed the Realized Installment Sales Income account.

Year 2

Jan. 14 Received $56 as third installment from C. L. Fenner.

Feb. 10 Received $56 as fourth installment from C. L. Fenner.

Mar. 15 Received $56 as fifth and final installment from C. L. Fenner.

15 Recorded the income realized on installments collected during the year from C. L. Fenner.

Instructions **1.** Record these transactions in general journal form, omitting explanations.

2. Post the entries to the appropriate accounts.

Problem C-4 The books of the Hermanson Appliance store show the following transactions related to an installment sale.

Year 1

Oct. 21 Sold a dishwasher to A. C. Crocker, $339, on the installment plan, with a down payment of $39, and ten installments of $20 each. The cost of the dishwasher is $220.35.

21 Recorded down payment of $39 from A. C. Crocker.

Nov. 28 Received $30 as the first installment from A. C. Crocker.

Dec. 29 Received $30 as the second installment from A. C. Crocker.

31 Recorded as an adjusting entry the income realized on installments collected during the year, determined in the installment accounts receivable ledger, $17,589.63 (including $34.65 income realized on the installment sale to A. C. Crocker, using a 35% gross profit rate).

31 Closed the Realized Installment Sales Income account.

Year 2

Jan. 30 Received $30 as third installment from A. C. Crocker.

Mar. 20 Received $30 as fourth installment from A. C. Crocker.

June 28 Repossessed the dishwasher sold to A. C. Crocker. Recorded the income realized on installments collected during the year.

28 Recorded the repossession. The wholesale value of the dishwasher as of this date is $90.

Instructions **1.** Record the transactions in general journal form, omitting explanations.

2. Post the entries to the appropriate accounts.

27 Analyzing and interpreting financial statements

objectives

After you have completed this chapter, you will be able to do the following:
- Prepare a comparative income statement and balance sheet involving horizontal analysis.
- Prepare a comparative income statement and balance sheet involving vertical analysis.
- Compute the following: working capital, current ratio, quick ratio, accounts receivable turnover, merchandise inventory turnover, ratio of stockholders' equity to liabilities, ratio of value of plant and equipment to long-term liabilities, equity per share, rate of return on stockholders' equity, earnings per share of common stock, and price-earnings ratio.

AS WE SAID in Chapter 1, accounting is the process of analyzing, recording, summarizing, *and interpreting* business transactions. We are now ready to interpret the results: How does one draw conclusions from financial data that have been summarized in financial statements?

The financial condition of a company and the results of operations of business enterprises are of interest not only to owners, employers, and managers, but also to creditors, and to prospective owners and creditors. Everybody is interested in two aspects of an enterprise:

1. Its *solvency,* or its ability to pay its debts
2. Its *profitability,* or its ability to earn a reasonable profit on the owners' investment

This chapter will explain the techniques one uses to determine solvency and profitability.

Types of comparison

When one interprets any facts, one has to have something else to compare them with. In other words, a given set of facts by themselves is not significant. For example, if you are told that a certain corporation earned a net income of $56,000 during the past year, this figure by itself is not meaningful. Does this net income indicate a successful year, or a poor year? Does it compare favorably with other years, or unfavorably? Does it represent a reasonable return on sales and investment, or not? How does it compare with the net income of other firms in the same industry?

Thus you can see that a company's financial statements become meaningful only if you analyze them on a comparative basis. There are three useful bases for making such a comparison:

1. Statements of the same company for one or more prior years
2. Data for other companies in the same industry
3. Previously established standards or objectives

Comparative statements

A commonly used technique for analyzing and interpreting financial data is the preparation of comparative statements. Two types of analysis—horizontal analysis and vertical analysis—are commonly used.

Horizontal analysis

Horizontal analysis involves comparing the same item in a company's financial statements for two or more periods. As an illustration, let's look at the comparative income statement (below) and balance sheet (page 770) of City Builders' Supply Company, Inc., for 1982 and 1983.

City Builders' Supply Company, Inc.
Comparative Income Statement
For years ended December 31, 1983, and December 31, 1982

	1983	1982	Increase or Decrease Amount	Percent
Revenue from Sales				
Sales	$ 980,600.00	$860,000.00	$120,600.00	14.02
Less: Sales Ret. and				
Allowances	13,700.00	11,400.00	2,300.00	20.18
Net Sales	$ 966,900.00	$848,600.00	$118,300.00	13.94
Cost of Mdse. Sold				
Mdse. Inventory,				
Jan. 1	206,500.00	$138,700.00	$ 67,800.00	48.88
Purchases	817,100.00	645,700.00	171,400.00	26.54
Less: Purch. Ret. and				
Allowances	12,300.00	9,100.00	3,200.00	35.16
Mdse. Avail. for Sale	$1,011,300.00	$775,300.00	$236,000.00	30.44
Less: Mdse. Inventory,				
Dec. 31	353,600.00	$206,500.00	147,100.00	71.23
Cost of Mdse. Sold	$ 657,700.00	$568,800.00	$ 88,900.00	15.63
Gross Profit	$ 309,200.00	$279,800.00	$ 29,400.00	10.51
Operating Expenses				
Selling Expenses				
Sales Salary Expense	$ 114,650.00	$102,400.00	$ 12,250.00	11.96
Delivery Expense	17,700.00	13,700.00	4,000.00	29.20
Advertising Expense	7,900.00	6,900.00	1,000.00	14.49
Depr. Expense, Equip.	6,800.00	6,600.00	200.00	3.03
Store Supp. Expense	750.00	600.00	150.00	25.00
Total Selling Exp.	$ 147,800.00	$130,200.00	$ 17,600.00	13.52
General Expenses				
Office Salary Exp.	$ 33,440.00	$ 27,680.00	$ 5,760.00	20.81
Depr. Expense, Bldg.	14,200.00	14,200.00	0	0
Bad Debts Expense	6,200.00	5,400.00	800.00	14.81
Taxes Expense	6,100.00	5,200.00	900.00	17.31
Insurance Expense	1,100.00	1,000.00	100.00	10.00
Misc. Gen. Expense	860.00	720.00	140.00	19.44
Total Gen. Expenses	$ 61,900.00	$ 54,200.00	$ 7,700.00	14.21
Total Operating Exp.	$ 209,700.00	$184,400.00	$ 25,300.00	13.72
Net Income from				
Operations	$ 99,500.00	$ 95,400.00	$ 4,100.00	4.29
Other Expense				
Interest Expense	8,520.00	7,860.00	660.00	.08
Net Income before				
Income Tax	$ 90,980.00	$ 87,540.00	$ 3,440.00	3.93
Income Tax	36,840.00	35,500.00	1,340.00	3.77
Net Income after				
Income Tax	$ 54,140.00	$ 52,040.00	$ 2,100.00	4.04

Note that for each item the accountant first expressed the differences—that is, the increases or decreases of 1983 over 1982—in dollars, and then in percentages.

Take the increase in Sales, on the second line. Subtract Sales in 1982 from Sales in 1983.

$980,600	Sales for 1983
−860,000	Sales for 1982
$120,600	Increase of 1983 over 1982

To calculate the *percentage* of increase in Sales in 1983 over 1982, divide the dollar increase by the amount of Sales during the base year, 1982.

$$\frac{\$120,600}{\$860,000} = 860,000\overline{)120,600}^{\,.1402} = 14.02\%$$

Note: The expression *base year* means the year you are using as a basis for comparison.

As another example, take the increase in Sales Returns and Allowances in 1983 over 1982:

$13,700	Sales Returns and Allowances for 1983
−11,400	Sales Returns and Allowances for 1982
$ 2,300	Increase of 1983 over 1982

The percentage rate of increase is

$$\frac{\$2,300}{\$11,400} = 11,400\overline{)2,300}^{\,.2018} = 20.18\%$$

People appraising an income statement often use the percentage increase of net sales as a basis for comparison. In other words, they compare all other percentage changes with the percentage change in net sales, to see whether the other percentage changes are out of line. If net sales increased 13.94% from 1982 to 1983, other percentage changes should amount to approximately 13.94% also. If they vary considerably from 13.94%, they are out of line, and one should investigate to find the reasons for the difference.

Let's look at the main items on the income statement.

Item	Percentage Change
Net Sales	13.94%
Cost of Merchandise Sold	15.63%
Gross Profit	10.51%
Total Operating Expenses	13.72%
Net Income after Income Tax	4.04%

You can see that gross profit and net income after income tax are considerably out of line. Since gross profit is determined by subtracting Cost of Merchandise Sold from Net Sales, one should investigate the entire Cost of Merchandise Sold section of the income statement. This is a starting point in accounting for the comparatively small percentage increase in Net Income after Income Tax. The percentage changes of items in the Cost of Merchandise Sold section are as follows.

Item	Percentage Change
Merchandise Inventory, January 1	48.88%
Purchases	26.54%
Purchases Returns and Allowances	35.16%
Merchandise Inventory, December 31	71.23%

The merchandise inventory of January 1 was a carry-over from the previous year, but why the large increase in Purchases? Another thing: It costs a great deal to handle Purchases Returns and Allowances; why were so many more purchases returned in 1983 than in 1982? And look at the large increase in merchandise inventory at the end of the year; buying all that merchandise took a lot of cash. Also, with such a large increase in merchandise inventory, we would expect a larger increase in sales. Is the increase in sales large enough?

Now look at the balance sheet on page 770, which shows the comparison between 1982 and 1983. Again you will see the reason why changes are expressed in both dollars and percentages. Items showing either a large dollar change or a large percentage change stick out like a sore thumb. This time some minus totals show up. Look at the following items.

Item	Dollar Increase or Decrease	Percentage Increase or Decrease
Merchandise Inventory	$147,100	71.23%
Accounts Payable	42,600	146.90%
Cash	(19,100)	(49.35%)

Recall that the comparative income statement already exposed the jump in the Merchandise Inventory account. We should also consider the effects of changes in the balances of other related accounts. For example, the fact that Cash is down by 49% while at the same time Accounts Payable is up by 147% may indicate a pending financial crisis. In order to meet their bills, they may be forced to liquidate that big stock of merchandise by selling it off at cost, or even less. That 200% increase in Dividends Payable doesn't look good either. One point in their favor, though, is the decrease in Accounts Receivable. The increase in Allowance for Doubtful Accounts, although relatively small in amount, appears to be unreasonable.

City Builders' Supply Company, Inc.
Comparative Balance Sheet
December 31, 1983 and December 31, 1982

	1983	1982	Increase or Decrease Amount	Percent
Assets				
Current Assets				
Cash	$ 19,600.00	$ 38,700.00	$(19,100.00)	(49.35)
Accounts Receivable	76,700.00	81,400.00	(4,700.00)	(5.77)
Less: Allow. for Doubtful Accts.	3,300.00	2,600.00	700.00	26.92
Merchandise Inventory	353,600.00	206,500.00	147,100.00	71.23
Prepaid Insurance	2,000.00	2,100.00	(100.00)	(4.76)
Total Current Assets	$448,600.00	$326,100.00	$122,500.00	37.57
Investments				
Sinking Fund Cash	$ 4,100.00	$ 5,800.00	$ (1,700.00)	(29.31)
Sinking Fund Investments	61,700.00	59,400.00	2,300.00	3.87
Total Investments	$ 65,800.00	$ 65,200.00	$ 600.00	.92
Plant and Equipment				
Equipment	$ 88,600.00	$ 86,000.00	$ 2,600.00	3.02
Less: Accum. Depr.	41,000.00	34,200.00	6,800.00	19.88
Building	160,000.00	160,000.00	0	0
Less: Accum. Depr.	56,800.00	42,600.00	14,200.00	33.33
Land	40,000.00	40,000.00	0	0
Total Plant and Equipment	$190,800.00	$209,200.00	$(18,400.00)	(8.80)
Intangible Assets				
Organization Costs	3,000.00	4,000.00	(1,000.00)	(25.00)
Total Assets	$708,200.00	$604,500.00	$103,700.00	17.15
Liabilities				
Current Liabilities				
Accounts Payable	$ 71,600.00	$ 29,000.00	$ 42,600.00	146.90
Income Tax Payable	12,800.00	5,600.00	7,200.00	128.57
Dividends Payable	12,000.00	4,000.00	8,000.00	200.00
Salaries Payable	4,200.00	4,000.00	200.00	5.00
Total Current Liabilities	$100,600.00	$ 42,600.00	$ 58,000.00	136.15
Long-term Liabilities				
Bonds Payable, 6%, due Dec. 31, 1994	$100,000.00	$100,000.00	0	0
Less: Disc. on Bonds Payable	2,200.00	2,400.00	(200.00)	(8.33)
Total Long-term Liabilities	$ 97,800.00	$ 97,600.00	$ 200.00	.20
Total Liabilities	$198,400.00	$140,200.00	$ 58,200.00	41.51
Stockholders' Equity				
Paid-in Capital				
Common Stock, $100 par (4,000 shares authorized, 3,000 shares issued)	$300,000.00	$300,000.00	0	0
Premium on Common Stock	86,000.00	86,000.00	0	0
Total Paid-in Capital	$386,000.00	$386,000.00	0	0
Retained Earnings				
Appropriated				
Appropriated for Plant Expansion	$ 20,000.00	$ 12,000.00	$ 8,000.00	66.67
Unappropriated	103,800.00	66,300.00	37,500.00	56.56
Total Retained Earnings	$123,800.00	$ 78,300.00	$ 45,500.00	58.11
Total Stockholders' Equity	$509,800.00	$464,300.00	$ 45,500.00	9.80
Total Liabilities and Stockholders' Equity	$708,200.00	$604,500.00	$103,700.00	17.15

Vertical analysis   Another tool accountants can use to analyze financial statements is *vertical analysis*. To use this method, one needs to see, in a single statement, the relationship of component parts to the whole. In the case of an income statement, *the whole is net sales*. Although each percentage applies to one item only, one can quickly see the relative importance of each item in the statement. Let us look first at the comparative income statement (page 771) and then at the comparative balance sheet (page 772) for City Builders' Supply Company, Inc., this time arranged for vertical analysis.

```
                        City Builders' Supply Company, Inc.
                           Comparative Income Statement
                 For years ended December 31, 1983 and December 31, 1982
```

	1983 Amount	1983 Percent	1982 Amount	1982 Percent
Revenue from Sales				
Sales	$ 980,600.00	101.42	$860,000.00	101.34
Less: Sales Returns and Allowances	13,700.00	1.42	11,400.00	1.34
Net Sales	$ 966,900.00	100.00	$848,600.00	100.00
Cost of Merchandise Sold				
Merchandise Inventory, Jan. 1	$ 206,500.00	21.36	$138,700.00	16.34
Purchases	817,100.00	84.51	645,700.00	76.09
Less: Purchases Returns and Allowances	12,300.00	1.27	9,100.00	1.07
Merchandise Available for Sale	$1,011,300.00	104.59	$775,300.00	91.36
Less: Merchandise Inventory, Dec. 31	353,600.00	36.57	206,500.00	24.33
Cost of Merchandise Sold	$ 657,700.00	68.02	$568,800.00	67.03
Gross Profit	$ 309,200.00	31.98	$279,800.00	32.97
Operating Expenses				
Selling Expenses				
Sales Salary Expense	$ 114,650.00	11.86	$102,400.00	12.07
Delivery Expense	17,700.00	1.83	13,700.00	1.61
Advertising Expense	7,900.00	.82	6,900.00	.81
Depreciation Expense, Equipment	6,800.00	.70	6,600.00	.78
Store Supplies Expense	750.00	.08	600.00	.07
Total Selling Expenses	$ 147,800.00	15.29	$130,200.00	15.34
General Expenses				
Office Salary Expense	$ 33,440.00	3.46	$ 27,680.00	3.26
Depreciation Expense, Building	14,200.00	1.47	14,200.00	1.67
Bad Debts Expense	6,200.00	.64	5,400.00	.64
Taxes Expense	6,100.00	.63	5,200.00	.61
Insurance Expense	1,100.00	.11	1,000.00	.12
Miscellaneous General Expense	860.00	.09	720.00	.08
Total General Expenses	$ 61,900.00	6.40	$ 54,200.00	6.39
Total Operating Expenses	$ 209,700.00	21.69	$184,400.00	21.73
Net Income from Operations	$ 99,500.00	10.29	$ 95,400.00	11.24
Other Expense				
Interest Expense	8,520.00	.88	7,860.00	.92
Net Income before Income Tax	$ 90,980.00	9.41	$ 87,540.00	10.32
Income Tax	36,840.00	3.81	35,500.00	4.18
Net Income after Income Tax	$ 54,140.00	5.60	$ 52,040.00	6.13

When you arrange an income statement for vertical analysis, you express each item's figure as *a percentage of net sales*. In other words, you divide the total for each item by the total of net sales. Here's how that works.

Gross Profit % = Gross Profit ÷ Net Sales

$$\text{Gross Profit \% (1983)} = \frac{\$309,200}{\$966,900} = .3198 = 31.98\%$$

$$\text{Gross Profit \% (1982)} = \frac{\$279,800}{\$848,600} = .3297 = 32.97\%$$

Net Income from Operations % = Net Income from Operations ÷ Net Sales

$$\text{Net Income from Operations \% (1983)} = \frac{\$99,500}{\$966,900} = .1029 = 10.29\%$$

$$\text{Net Income from Operations \% (1982)} = \frac{\$95,400}{\$848,600} = .1124 = 11.24\%$$

City Builders' Supply Company, Inc.
Comparative Balance Sheet
December 31, 1983 and December 31, 1982

	1983		1982	
Assets	Amount	Percent	Amount	Percent
Current Assets				
Cash	$ 19,600.00	2.77	$ 38,700.00	6.40
Accounts Receivable	76,700.00	10.83	81,400.00	13.47
Less: Allow. for Doubtful Accts.	3,300.00	.47	2,600.00	.43
Merchandise Inventory	353,600.00	49.93	206,500.00	34.16
Prepaid Insurance	2,000.00	.28	2,100.00	.35
Total Current Assets	$448,600.00	63.34	$326,100.00	53.95
Investments				
Sinking Fund Cash	$ 4,100.00	.58	$ 5,800.00	.96
Sinking Fund Investments	61,700.00	8.71	59,400.00	9.83
Total Investments	$ 65,800.00	9.29	$ 65,200.00	10.79
Plant and Equipment				
Equipment	$ 88,600.00	12.51	$ 86,000.00	14.23
Less: Accumulated Depreciation	41,000.00	5.79	34,200.00	5.66
Building	160,000.00	22.59	160,000.00	26.47
Less: Accumulated Depreciation	56,800.00	8.02	42,600.00	7.05
Land	40,000.00	5.65	40,000.00	6.62
Total Plant and Equipment	$190,800.00	26.94	$209,200.00	34.61
Intangible Assets				
Organization Costs	3,000.00	.42	4,000.00	.66
Total Assets	$708,200.00	100.00	$604,500.00	100.00
Liabilities				
Current Liabilities				
Accounts Payable	$ 71,600.00	10.11	$ 29,000.00	4.80
Income Tax Payable	12,800.00	1.81	5,600.00	.93
Dividends Payable	12,000.00	1.69	4,000.00	.66
Salaries Payable	4,200.00	.59	4,000.00	.66
Total Current Liabilities	$100,600.00	14.21	$ 42,600.00	7.05
Long-term Liabilities				
Bonds Payable, 6%, due Dec. 31, 1984	$100,000.00	14.12	$100,000.00	16.54
Less: Discount on Bonds Payable	2,200.00	.31	2,400.00	.40
Total Long-term Liabilities	$ 97,800.00	13.81	$ 97,600.00	16.15
Total Liabilities	$198,400.00	28.01	$140,200.00	23.19
Stockholders' Equity				
Paid-in Capital				
Common Stock, $100 par (4,000 shares				
authorized, 3,000 shares issued)	$300,000.00	42.36	$300,000.00	49.63
Premium on Common Stock	86,000.00	12.14	86,000.00	14.22
Total Paid-in Capital	$386,000.00	54.50	$386,000.00	63.85
Retained Earnings				
Appropriated				
for Plant Expansion	$ 20,000.00	2.82	$ 12,000.00	1.99
Unappropriated	103,800.00	14.66	66,300.00	10.97
Total Retained Earnings	$123,800.00	17.48	$ 78,300.00	12.95
Total Stockholders' Equity	$509,800.00	71.99	$464,300.00	76.81
Total Liabilities and				
Stockholders' Equity	$708,200.00	100.00	$604,500.00	100.00

Net Income after Income Tax % = Net Income after Income Tax ÷ Net Sales

$$\text{Net Income after Income Tax \% (1983)} = \frac{\$54,140}{\$966,900} = .0560 = 5.60\%$$

$$\text{Net Income after Income Tax \% (1982)} = \frac{\$52,040}{\$848,600} = .0613 = 6.13\%$$

One could also interpret the percentages as shown here.

1983

For every $100 in net sales, gross profit amounted to $31.98.
For every $100 in net sales, net income from operations amounted to $10.29.
For every $100 in net sales, net income after income tax amounted to $5.60.

1982

For every $100 in net sales, gross profit amounted to $32.97.
For every $100 in net sales, net income from operations amounted to $11.24.
For every $100 in net sales, net income after income tax amounted to $6.13.

Again we see the relative importance assumed by Purchases (84.51% of Net Sales) and Merchandise Inventory (36.57% of Net Sales). In the selling-expense category, the percentage score of Sales Salary Expense declined slightly. Advertising Expense as a percentage of Net Sales remained the same. (Is that necessarily a good sign?)

When you perform a vertical analysis of a comparative balance sheet, you express each item's figure as *a percentage of total assets,* or as a percentage of total liabilities and owners' equity, which is the same figure. For example, suppose you want to find the percentage of total assets represented by Cash, Accounts Receivable, and Merchandise Inventory.

$$\text{Cash \%} = \text{Cash} \div \text{Total Assets}$$

$$\text{Cash \% (1983)} = \frac{\$19,600}{\$708,200} = .0277 = 2.77\%$$

$$\text{Cash \% (1982)} = \frac{\$38,700}{\$604,500} = .0640 = 6.40\%$$

$$\text{Accounts Receivable \%} = \text{Net Accounts Receivable} \div \text{Total Assets}$$

$$\text{Accounts Receivable \% (1983)} = \frac{\$73,400}{\$708,200} = .1036 = 10.36\%$$

$$\text{Accounts Receivable \% (1982)} = \frac{\$78,800}{\$604,500} = .1304 = 13.04\%$$

$$\text{Merchandise Inventory \%} = \text{Merchandise Inventory} \div \text{Total Assets}$$

$$\text{Merchandise Inventory \% (1983)} = \frac{\$353,600}{\$708,200} = .4993 = 49.93\%$$

$$\text{Merchandise Inventory \% (1982)} = \frac{\$206,500}{\$604,500} = .3416 = 34.16\%$$

One could also interpret the above percentages as follows.

1983

For every $100 in total assets, $2.77 is in the form of Cash.
For every $100 in total assets, $10.36 is in the form of Accounts Receivable.
For every $100 in total assets, $49.93 is in the form of Merchandise Inventory.

1982

For every $100 in total assets, $6.40 was in the form of Cash.
For every $100 in total assets, $13.04 was in the form of Accounts Receivable.
For every $100 in total assets, $34.16 was in the form of Merchandise Inventory.

These percentages accentuate City Builders' Supply's poor status with respect to Cash and Merchandise Inventory, as well as their favorable status with respect to Accounts Receivable. Other items that strike a warning note are

- The percentage value of plant and equipment declined during 1983.

- The percentage value of Accounts Payable more than doubled during 1983.

Our illustrations show full income statements and balance sheets. But sometimes accountants give financial statements in condensed form, and put the details in supporting schedules. In this case, the figures are taken from the supporting schedules, and the percentages are worked out the same way.

Trend percentages

One may also use percentages to indicate trends or general directions that become evident only when one makes a comparison covering a period of years. Here is the way to calculate the percentages.

1. Select a representative year as the base year.

2. Label the base year 100%.

3. Express all other years as percentages of the base year.

Let us say that you have been able to cull the following figures from the income statements for City Builders' Supply for 1979 through 1983.

Item	Year				
	1979	**1980**	**1981**	**1982**	**1983**
Net Sales	$714,200	$782,380	$806,400	$848,600	$966,900
Cost of Merchandise Sold	466,150	519,180	540,300	568,800	657,700
Gross Profit	248,050	263,200	266,100	279,800	309,200

You establish 1979 as the base year, and calculate the trend percentages for Net Sales by dividing the Net Sales of each year by the Net Sales for 1979.

$$\text{For 1980:} \quad 714{,}200\overline{)782{,}380} = 1.0954$$

$$\text{For 1981:} \quad 714{,}200\overline{)806{,}400} = 1.1290$$

$$\text{For 1982:} \quad 714{,}200\overline{)848{,}600} = 1.1881$$

$$\text{For 1983:} \quad 714{,}200\overline{)966{,}900} = 1.3538$$

You determine trend percentages for Cost of Merchandise Sold and Gross Profit in the same way. Here are the results, with the percentages rounded off to the nearest whole number.

Item	Year				
	1979	1980	1981	1982	1983
Net Sales	100%	110%	113%	119%	135%
Cost of Merchandise Sold	100%	111%	116%	122%	141%
Gross Profit	100%	106%	107%	113%	125%

Observe that over the 5-year period, the trend of Net Sales is upward. However, Cost of Merchandise Sold is also going up, but at a more rapid rate. In other words, over the 5 years, Cost of Merchandise Sold increased faster than Net Sales, resulting in smaller increases in Gross Profit. This is fine if it's the company's plan to achieve a greater volume of sales accompanied by more moderate profits. But if this shrinking Gross Profit is *not* consistent with company policy, then it may be a sign that the company is not passing along its increased costs to its customers.

Industry comparisons

Vertical analysis, using percentage figures, is very useful when you wish to compare the figures for one company with the average figures for the given industry. Such comparisons are often referred to as *common-size statements*, since one expresses all items as percentages of a common base. Again, for the income statement, the common base is net sales. Net sales is set at 100%, and all other items are expressed as a percentage of net sales. For example, trade and marketing associations gather information and publish common-size statements.

Analysis by creditors and management

Because management is vitally interested in increasing the company's solvency and profitability, managers are concerned with all types of analytical tools and techniques. Because creditors want assurance of being repaid for credit extended, they are concerned first with the company's solvency, and second with its profitability.

How do short-term creditors and management analyze an enterprise?

Bankers and other short-term creditors are primarily interested in the *current* position of a given firm: Does the firm have enough money coming in to meet its current operating needs and to pay its current debts promptly? (*Current,* to them, means one year; this is consistent with the way accountants refer to "current assets" and "current liabilities.") Let us use as an example some calculations derived from the comparative financial statements of City Builders' Supply for 1982 and 1983.

Working capital

As we stated previously, *working capital* is the excess of current assets over current liabilities. One determines the working capital for City Builders' Supply as shown atop the following page.

$$\text{Working capital} = \text{Current assets} - \text{Current liabilities}$$
$$\text{Working capital (1983)} = \$448{,}600 - \$100{,}600 = \$348{,}000$$
$$\text{Working capital (1982)} = \$326{,}100 - \$42{,}600 = \$283{,}500$$

City Builders Supply has $348,000 of capital available to work with during 1983 versus $283,500 of capital available to work with during 1982.

Current ratio

The relationship of a company's current assets to its current liabilities is known as its *current ratio*. One arrives at this figure by dividing current assets by current liabilities.

$$\text{Current ratio} = \frac{\text{Current assets}}{\text{Current liabilities}}$$

$$\text{Current ratio (1983)} = \frac{\$448{,}600}{\$100{,}600} = 4.5{:}1$$

$$\text{Current ratio (1982)} = \frac{\$326{,}100}{\$42{,}600} = 7.7{:}1$$

A firm's current ratio reveals its debt-paying ability. City Builders' Supply's current ratio of 4.5:1 in 1983 indicates that there is $4.50 of cash coming in within a year from now for every dollar City Builders' Supply has to pay out within a year. But they were better off in 1982, because that year they had $7.70 coming in within the year for every dollar to be paid out within the year.

From the points of view of bankers and other credit grantors, the adequacy of a company's current ratio depends on what type of business the firm is in. The minimum ratio for a merchandising business is generally 2 to 1—higher if the firm's type of merchandise is subject to abrupt changes in style. But a public utility, which has no inventories other than supplies, is considered solvent even if its current ratio is less than 1 to 1. Due to the stability of the product involved in the building-supply business, a ratio of 4.5 to 1 for City Builders' Supply is satisfactory. (*Note:* If the company has changed inventory-valuation methods from one year to another—for example, if it has switched from FIFO to LIFO—a correction should be made in the costs of merchandise inventories; otherwise there is no common base for making a comparison.)

Quick ratio

The relationship of a company's current assets that can be quickly converted into cash to its current liabilities is known as its *quick ratio* or *acid-test ratio*. Quick assets are cash, notes receivable, net accounts receivable (that is, accounts receivable less allowance for doubtful accounts), interest receivable, and marketable securities. You don't count inventories and prepaid expenses because they are further removed from conversion into cash than other current assets are. You determine the quick ratio by dividing quick assets by current liabilities.

$$\text{Quick ratio} = \frac{\text{Quick assets}}{\text{Current liabilities}}$$

$$\text{Quick ratio (1983)} = \frac{\$19,600 + (\$76,700 - \$3,300)}{\$100,600} = \frac{\$93,000}{\$100,600} = .92 : 1$$

$$\text{Quick ratio (1982)} = \frac{\$38,700 + (\$81,400 - \$2,600)}{\$42,600} = \frac{\$117,500}{\$42,600} = 2.76 : 1$$

City Builders' Supply's quick ratio of .92:1 in 1983 indicates that there are 92 cents in cash coming in quickly—without involving the liquidation of inventory—for every dollar they have to pay out within a year. For 1982, there was $2.76 that they could realize quickly for every dollar they had to pay out within a year.

A quick ratio of 1 to 1 is normally considered satisfactory. Therefore the quick ratio for City Builders' Supply exposes a precarious short-term financial position. One has to consider this quick ratio in conjunction with the company's working capital and its current ratio. Although working capital and current ratio are two indicators of a firm's ability to meet its current obligations, they don't reveal *the composition of its current assets*—a very important factor.

Relationship of each current asset to total current assets

Suppose that you are asked to find out the proportionate positions of each item in the list of current assets of City Builders' Supply. Your first step is to compile a schedule of each current asset as it relates to total current assets, as shown in the illustration below.

	December 31, 1983		December 31, 1982	
	Amount	Percent	Amount	Percent
Current Assets				
Cash	$ 19,600.00	4.37	$ 38,700.00	11.87
Accounts Receivable (net)	73,400.00	16.36	78,800.00	24.17
Merchandise Inventory	353,600.00	78.82	206,500.00	63.32
Prepaid Insurance	2,000.00	.45	2,100.00	.64
Total Current Assets	$448,600.00	100.00	$326,100.00	100.00

As an example, the percentage of cash to total current assets is calculated like this:

$$\frac{\$19,600}{\$448,600} = .0437 = 4.37\%$$

We have already commented on the large increase in the proportion of merchandise inventory (it was 63% of current assets in 1982, but amounts to 79% of current assets in 1983). This change, coupled with the decline in the cash position (12% of current assets for 1982, only 4% of current assets for 1983), reinforces the message we got from the decline in the quick ratio, indicating that the firm may have a hard time paying its current debts.

Since money tied up in accounts receivable does not yield any revenue, any firm tries to collect accounts receivable promptly and to keep them at a minimum. It can use the cash it gets from collection of accounts receivable to reduce bank loans, or to take advantage of cash discounts. This reduces the amount of interest expense it has to pay, and the cost of the merchandise it buys. Prompt collection also reduces the risk of loss from bad debts.

Accounts receivable turnover   Accounts receivable turnover is the number of times charge accounts are turned over (or paid off) per year. A turnover implies a sale on account followed by payment of the debt in cash. One computes this by *dividing net sales on account by average net accounts receivable*. If possible, use the average of the monthly balances of accounts receivable, since this allows for seasonal fluctuations. If you haven't got figures for monthly balances, use the average of the balances at the beginning and the end of the previous year. Combine notes receivable from customers with accounts receivable. Here's how it looks for City Builders' Supply.

$$\text{Accounts receivable turnover} = \frac{\text{Net Sales on Account}}{\text{Average Accounts Receivable (net)}}$$

$$\text{Average Accounts Receivable} = \frac{\text{Beginning Accounts Receivable} + \text{Ending Accounts Receivable}}{2}$$

$$\text{Accounts receivable turnover (1983)} = \frac{\$773,020}{\dfrac{\$78,800 + \$73,400}{2}} = \frac{\$773,020}{\$76,100} = 10.16 \text{ times/yr.}$$

$$\text{Accounts receivable turnover (1982)} = \frac{\$678,880}{\dfrac{\$58,400 + \$78,800}{2}} = \frac{\$678,880}{\$68,600} = 9.90 \text{ times/yr.}$$

The beginning balance of Accounts Receivable during 1982 ($58,400) appeared on the 1981 balance sheet.

You can also use the figure for accounts receivable turnover to determine the number of days that the receivables were on the books. Calculate this by dividing 365 days by the turnover figure.

$$\text{Year (1983)} = \frac{365 \text{ days}}{10.16 \text{ times per year}} = 35.93 \text{ or } 36 \text{ days}$$

$$\text{Year (1982)} = \frac{365 \text{ days}}{9.90 \text{ times per year}} = 36.87 \text{ or } 37 \text{ days}$$

So it took an average of 1 day less in 1983 to collect accounts receivable than it did in 1982. This reduction represents a slight improvement in collections for City Builders' Supply. Since the company's credit terms are net 30 days, 36 or 37 days is reasonable.

Merchandise inventory turnover   Merchandise inventory turnover is the number of times a company's average inventory is sold during a given year. One calculates this by *dividing Cost of Merchandise Sold by average Merchandise Inventory*. Here is the calculation for City Builders' Supply.

$$\text{Merchandise inventory turnover} = \frac{\text{Cost of Merchandise Sold}}{\text{Average Merchandise Inventory}}$$

$$\text{Average Merchandise Inventory} = \frac{\text{Beginning Merchandise Inventory} + \text{Ending Merchandise Inventory}}{2}$$

$$\text{Merchandise inventory turnover (1983)} = \frac{\$657,700}{\dfrac{\$206,500 + \$353,600}{2}} = \frac{\$657,700}{\$280,050} = 2.35 \text{ times/yr.}$$

$$\text{Merchandise inventory turnover (1982)} = \frac{\$568,800}{\dfrac{\$138,700 + \$206,500}{2}} = \frac{\$568,800}{\$172,600} = 3.30 \text{ times/yr.}$$

If possible, one should use the average of the monthly balances of Merchandise Inventory (add them and divide by 12). The figure for merchandise inventory turnover varies depending on the type of product involved. One can compare the figure for merchandise inventory turnover for one company with figures for the rest of the industry, and thus use it as a test of merchandising efficiency. Each turnover yields a gross profit or markup to the company. Note that there has been a serious decline in the rate of merchandise inventory turnover for City Builders' Supply. This is something to watch.

One may also use the figure for the merchandise inventory turnover to determine the number of days that the merchandise was kept in stock. One calculates this the same way one calculates accounts receivable turnover, by dividing 365 days by the turnover figure.

$$\text{Year (1983)} = \frac{365 \text{ days}}{2.35 \text{ times per year}} = 155 \text{ days}$$

$$\text{Year (1982)} = \frac{365 \text{ days}}{3.30 \text{ times per year}} = 111 \text{ days}$$

Note that City Builders' Supply's merchandise remained in stock 44 days longer in 1983 than it did in 1982. This surely calls for an investigation of their sales and purchasing practices.

In addition to yielding a higher gross profit, rapid merchandise inventory turnover has other advantages: The money invested in the inventory is tied up for a shorter period of time; storage costs are lower; there is less risk of spoilage (if the merchandise is perishable); there is less risk of change in demand (if the merchandise is affected by changes in style or in business conditions).

How do long-term creditors and management analyze an enterprise?

Long-term creditors include mortgage holders and bondholders. Whenever specific property has been pledged or mortgaged, they have first claim on the property in the event that the company cannot keep up its payments. Even in the case of debentures (unsecured bonds), the bondholders have a prior claim to the general assets of the company, a claim that takes precedence over that of the stockholders. Management is concerned with the company's taking care of its present obligations, as well as preserving its credit standing, and hence its ability to borrow in the future.

Ratio of stockholders' equity to liabilities When we speak of the ratio of stockholders' equity to liabilities, we are talking about the ratio of the stockholders' investment to the creditor's equity.

In calculating any ratio, we mean the ratio *of* something *to* something else. When we write the ratio as a fraction, we put the *of* part in the numerator and the *to* part in the denominator. Look at this calculation for City Builders' Supply.

$$\text{Ratio of Stockholders' Equity to Liabilities (1983)} = \frac{\$509,800}{\$198,400} = 2.57:1$$

$$\text{Ratio of Stockholders' Equity to Liabilities (1982)} = \frac{\$464,300}{\$140,200} = 3.31:1$$

In 1983, for every $2.57 of stockholders' investment, the creditors have loaned $1. City Builders' Supply's ratio of stockholders' equity to liabilities shows a significant decline since 1982, from 3.31:1 to 2.57:1. Creditors like to see a high proportion of stockholders' equity, because stockholders' equity, or owners' equity, acts as a buffer in case the company has to absorb losses. Also, if owners have a good-sized investment, they think twice before they are willing to assume large risks.

Ratio of plant and equipment to long-term liabilities There is another factor that provides a margin of safety to mortgage holders and bondholders—the ratio of the value of a firm's total plant and equipment to its long-term liabilities. In addition, this ratio indicates the potential ability of the enterprise to borrow more money on a long-term basis. Let's look at the calculation for City Builders' Supply.

$$\text{Ratio of Plant and Equipment to Long-term Liabilities} = \frac{\text{Plant and Equipment}}{\text{Long-term Liabilities}}$$

$$\text{Ratio of Plant and Equipment to Long-term Liabilities (1983)} = \frac{\$190,800}{\$97,800} = 1.95$$

$$\text{Ratio of Plant and Equipment to Long-term Liabilities (1982)} = \frac{\$209,200}{\$97,600} = 2.14$$

In 1983 there is $1.95 book value of plant and equipment for every dollar of long-term liabilities. But in 1982, there was $2.14 book value of plant and equipment for every dollar of long-term liabilities. So this figure, too, is less favorable.

As we have seen, a firm's creditors and managers may use eight devices to determine the financial position of a firm:

• working capital
• current ratio
• quick ratio
• relationship of each current asset to total current assets
• accounts receivable turnover
• merchandise inventory turnover

- ratio of stockholders' equity to liabilities
- ratio of plant an equipment to long-term liabilities

Analysis by owners and management

In addition to being concerned about the solvency and the profitability of a company, the owners, as well as the managers, are also vitally interested in the value and return on investment in the company. In many cases the owners are the managers. However, in other situations, managers are employed by the owners. What diagnostic tools do they use to determine the financial health of their company?

Equity per share

When you examine the annual report of a corporation, you encounter the term *equity per share*—also referred to as *book value per share*. If a corporation has only one class of common stock outstanding, one determines the equity per share by dividing the total stockholders' equity by the number of shares of stock issued. Here are the calculations for City Builders' Supply.

$$\text{Equity per share} = \frac{\text{Total stockholders' equity available to a class of stock}}{\text{Number of shares issued and outstanding}}$$

$$\text{Equity per share (1983)} = \frac{\$509,800}{3,000 \text{ shares}} = \$169.93 \text{ per share}$$

$$\text{Equity per share (1982)} = \frac{\$464,300}{3,000 \text{ shares}} = \$154.77 \text{ per share}$$

When there are shares of preferred stock outstanding, one must deduct the liquidation value, including any dividends in arrears on cumulative preferred stock before one arrives at the stockholders' equity available to holders of common stock. (Remember that in the event of a firm's liquidation, holders of preferred stock are paid before holders of common stock.)

Note: The term *equity per share* does *not* mean the cash value or market value of a share, but the amount that would be distributed per share of stock *if* the corporation liquidated without incurring any expenses, gains, or losses in selling its assets and paying its liabilities. The equity per share increases as a firm retains net income after taxes. This concept of equity per share is important in contracts involving the sale of stock. For example, a large stockholder might obtain an option to buy the shares of small stockholders at the value of the equity per share as of a certain future date.

Rate of return on common stockholders' equity

The main reason why a corporation exists is to earn a net income for its stockholders. Therefore the rate of return on the common stockholders' equity is important as a means of measuring how good or bad the investment is. One can determine this rate by dividing the net income (after taxes) available to holders of common stock by the *average value* of their equity. On the following page is the calculation for City Builders' Supply.

$$\text{Rate of return on common stockholders' equity} = \frac{\text{Net income available to common stock}}{\dfrac{\text{Beginning common stock equity} + \text{ending common stock equity}}{2}}$$

$$\text{Rate of return on common stockholders' equity (1983)} = \frac{\$54,140}{\dfrac{\$464,300 + \$509,800}{2}} = \frac{\$54,140}{\$487,050} = .1112 = 11.12\%$$

$$\text{Rate of return on common stockholders' equity (1982)} = \frac{\$52,040}{\dfrac{\$422,100 + \$464,300}{2}} = \frac{\$52,040}{\$443,200} = .1174 = 11.74\%$$

This isn't much of a decline. However, management should look into the matter to uncover the possible causes. Again, one begins by looking hard at merchandise inventory, particularly since in this case it represents 49.93% of total assets.

Earnings per share of common stock

You often see earnings per share of stock listed in financial columns of newspapers. If a corporation has no preferred stock outstanding, you compute the earnings per share of common stock by dividing net income (after taxes) by the number of outstanding shares of common stock. When there is preferred stock, you have to deduct any dividends on preferred stock before arriving at the amount available to common stock (again, as you recall, because dividends on preferred are paid before those on common). Here is the calculation of earnings per share of common stock for City Builders' Supply.

$$\text{Earnings per share of common stock} = \frac{\text{Net income available to common stock}}{\text{Number of shares of common stock outstanding}}$$

$$\text{Earnings per share of common stock (1983)} = \frac{\$54,140}{3,000 \text{ shares}} = \$18.05$$

$$\text{Earnings per share of common stock (1982)} = \frac{\$52,040}{3,000 \text{ shares}} = \$17.35$$

Any big change during the year in the *number* of shares outstanding naturally has a vital effect on the amount of earnings per share. That's why a company must disclose any information relating to stock dividends and stock splits.

Price-earnings ratio

The *price-earnings ratio* is a measure commonly used to determine whether the market price of a corporation's stock is reasonable. The way you calculate the price-earnings ratio of a company's stock is to divide the market price per share by the annual earnings per share. Let's say that the market price of a share of common stock of City Builders' Supply at the end of 1983 is $132, and that at the end of 1982 it was $120. Here is how you figure out the price-earnings ratio.

$$\text{Price-earnings ratio} = \frac{\text{Market price per share}}{\text{Earnings per share}}$$

$$\text{Price-earnings ratio (1983)} = \frac{\$132.00}{\$18.05} = 7.3 = 7.3:1$$

$$\text{Price-earnings ratio (1982)} = \frac{\$120.00}{\$17.35} = 6.9 = 6.9:1$$

What is called reasonable for a price-earnings ratio varies from one industry to another. Stocks quoted in the Dow Jones Average have usually had around a 15:1 price-earnings ratio. Corporations which have shown a large continued growth in earnings over a period of years may have a ratio of more than 30:1.

You may also use the price-earnings ratio in this manner: If the acceptable price-earnings ratio for a given stock is 15:1 and if the earnings per share equal $2.50, it follows that the maximum reasonable price you ought to pay for it is $37.50 (that is, $2.50 × 15). But what if the stock is selling for only $20? You may well consider it to be undervalued.

Summary

A great many people are vitally interested in the financial condition and results of operations of a business enterprise: owners, managers, creditors, prospective owners and creditors, and employees. The status of an enterprise depends on its solvency and profitability. Comparative financial statements are useful in making a line-by-line comparison of items over a period of years.

These statements are compiled using horizontal or vertical analysis. Trend percentages indicate trends or general directions that may become apparent only when one makes a comparison over a period of years. The base year is set at 100%. Industry comparisons, or common-size statements, are also useful, in that a person can compare items in the financial statement of one company with the same items in the financial statements of other companies of similar size which produce the same kind of product or service.

The management of a business uses many yardsticks to analyze and interpret financial statements. Short-term creditors and management use the following techniques.

$$\text{Working capital} = \text{Current assets} - \text{Current liabilities}$$

$$\text{Current ratio} = \frac{\text{Current assets}}{\text{Current liabilities}}$$

$$\text{Quick ratio} = \frac{\text{Cash} + \text{Receivables} + \text{Marketable securities}}{\text{Current liabilities}}$$

$$\text{Accounts receivable turnover} = \frac{\text{Net Sales on Account}}{\text{Average Accounts Receivable}}$$

$$\text{Merchandise inventory turnover} = \frac{\text{Cost of Merchandise Sold}}{\text{Average Merchandise Inventory}}$$

Long-term creditors and management use the following ratios.

$$Ratio\ of\ Stockholders'\ Equity\ to\ Liabilities = \frac{Stockholders'\ Equity}{Liabilities}$$

$$Ratio\ of\ Plant\ and\ Equipment\ to\ Long\text{-}term\ Liabilities = \frac{Plant\ and\ Equipment}{Long\text{-}term\ Liabilities}$$

Owners and managers use the following measures.

$$Equity\ per\ share = \frac{Total\ stockholders'\ equity\ available\ to\ a\ class\ of\ stock}{Number\ of\ shares\ issued\ and\ outstanding}$$

$$Rate\ of\ return\ on\ common\ stockholders'\ equity = \frac{Net\ income\ available\ to\ common\ stock}{Average\ common\ stock\ equity}$$

$$Earnings\ per\ share\ of\ common\ stock = \frac{Net\ income\ available\ to\ common\ stock}{Number\ of\ shares\ of\ common\ stock\ outstanding}$$

$$Price\text{-}earnings\ ratio = \frac{Market\ price\ per\ share}{Earnings\ per\ share}$$

Glossary

Accounts receivable turnover The number of times charge accounts are paid off per year; a turnover is a sale on account and subsequent repayment.

Acid-test ratio Same as quick ratio.

Base year The year used as a basis for comparison.

Common-size statements Financial statements using vertical analysis expressed as percentages showing average figures for the whole industry for companies of similar size that produce the same product or service.

Horizontal analysis Comparing the same item in the financial statements of an enterprise for two or more periods.

Liquidate To wind up the affairs of a business by paying off the creditors and selling the assets for cash.

Merchandise inventory turnover The number of times the merchandise inventory is turned over per year; a turnover is the purchase and subsequent sale of merchandise.

Quick assets Assets consisting of cash, receivables, and marketable securities.

Quick ratio Quick assets divided by current liabilities.

Vertical analysis Portraying items in financial statements as percentages (or proportional parts) of a given item on the same financial statement.

Working capital The excess of current assets over current liabilities.

Questions

1. What is the difference between a firm's solvency and its profitability?

2. In regard to comparative income statements, what is the difference between horizontal analysis and vertical analysis?

3. A firm has a gross profit percentage consisting of 34%. What does this mean?

4. What is a common-size statement?

5. Why is a high merchandise inventory turnover considered to be a benefit to a firm?

6. Which of the following types of business firms would you anticipate having a high merchandise inventory turnover?

A supermarket   A bakery

A jewelry store   A camera store

An art gallery

7. What does a decrease in the accounts receivable turnover rate indicate as far as a firm is concerned?

Exercises

Exercise 1 Calculate the percentages of increase and decrease for the following unrelated items.

Item	1983	1982
Cash	$40,500	$38,250
Notes Receivable	21,000	24,000
Equipment (net)	91,500	99,000
Retained Earnings	57,000	48,000

Exercise 2 Using the following revenue and expense data, prepare a comparative income statement expressing each item for both 1983 and 1982 as a percentage of sales. Comment on the results.

Item	1983	1982
Sales (net)	$1,050,000	$900,000
Cost of Merchandise Sold	810,000	675,000
Selling Expenses	142,500	135,000
General Expenses	31,500	30,000
Income Tax	30,000	27,000

Exercise 3 Calculate trend percentages for the following items, and comment on the trends. Use 1980 as the base year.

Item	1980	1981	1982	1983
Sales (net)	$600,000	$660,000	$726,000	$774,000
Cost of Merchandise Sold	360,000	423,000	480,000	492,000
Merchandise Inventory	63,000	69,000	78,000	90,000

Exercise 4 The items shown atop the following page are taken from the financial statements of the Strong Company.

Item	1983	1982
Sales (net on account)	$900,000	$800,000
Cost of Merchandise Sold	680,000	640,000
Merchandise Inventory (at end of year)	140,000	132,000
Accounts Receivable (at end of year)	121,200	104,000

All sales are on a credit basis. Compute the following for 1983.

a. Percentage of gross profit

b. Accounts receivable turnover

c. Merchandise inventory turnover

Exercise 5 The following items are from the balance sheet of the Stanley Company.

Cash	$144,000
Marketable Securities	62,000
Accounts Receivable (net)	472,000
Merchandise Inventory	168,000
Prepaid Expenses	6,000
Accounts Payable	240,000
Notes Payable	22,000
Salaries Payable	2,000

Compute the following.

a. Working Capital

b. Current ratio

c. Quick ratio

Exercise 6 The following items are taken from the financial statements of the Morgan Company. All sales are made on account.

Sales (net on account)	$2,400,000
Total Assets	3,200,000
Total Liabilities	1,200,000
Net Income	192,000
Average Accounts Receivable	500,000
Average Merchandise Inventory	340,000
Gross Profit	700,000

Compute the following.

a. Accounts receivable turnover

b. Merchandise inventory turnover

c. Rate earned on total assets

d. Rate earned on stockholders' equity

Exercise 7 The following items are from the balance sheets of the D. C. Michaelson Company as of December 31, 1983 and December 31, 1982.

Item	1983	1982
Current Assets:		
Cash, Marketable Securities, and Receivables (net)	$240,000	$216,000
Merchandise Inventory	360,000	312,000
Total Current Assets	$600,000	$528,000
Current Liabilities	$300,000	$240,000

Calculate the following for each year and comment on the company's comparative financial position.

a. Working capital

b. Current ratio

c. Quick ratio

Exercise 8 The Stockholders' Equity section of the balance sheet of the Barkley Corporation is as follows.

Stockholders' Equity		
Paid-in Capital:		
Common Stock, $10 par (50,000 shares authorized, 40,000 shares issued)	400 0 0 0 00	
Premium on Common Stock	120 0 0 0 00	
Total Paid-in Capital	520 0 0 0 00	
Retained Earnings	280 0 0 0 00	
Total Stockholders' Equity		800 0 0 0 00

Net income (after tax) for the year is $128,000. The present market price of the stock is $48 per share. Determine the following.

a. Equity per share

b. Earnings per share

c. Price-earnings ratio

d. Rate of return on stockholders' equity

Problems

Problem 27-1 During 1983 Robert's Shoe Store put on a big sales promotion campaign that cost $10,000 more than it usually spent for advertising. Atop page 788 we see the condensed comparative income statement for the fiscal years ended December 31, 1982 and December 31, 1983.

		1983	1982
Revenue from Sales:			

Robert's Shoe Store

Comparative Income Statement

For years ended December 31, 1983 and December 31, 1982

	1983	1982
Revenue from Sales:		
Sales	427 6 8 0 00	324 0 0 0 00
Less: Sales Returns and Allowances	35 0 4 0 00	24 0 0 0 00
Net Sales	392 6 4 0 00	300 0 0 0 00
Cost of Merchandise Sold	223 0 2 0 00	177 0 0 0 00
Gross Profit	169 6 2 0 00	123 0 0 0 00
Operating Expenses:		
Selling Expenses	74 8 9 6 00	60 4 0 0 00
General Expenses	22 0 8 0 00	19 2 0 0 00
Total Operating Expenses	96 9 7 6 00	79 6 0 0 00
Net Income from Operations	72 6 4 4 00	43 4 0 0 00
Other Expense	7 5 0 00	6 0 0 00
Net Income	71 8 9 4 00	42 8 0 0 00

Instructions   Using horizontal analysis, prepare a comparative income statement for the 2-year period. Round off percentages to the nearest whole percent (two decimal places).

Problem 27-2   Use the comparative income statement for Robert's Shoe Store.

Instructions   Using vertical analysis, prepare a comparative income statement for the 2-year period. Round off percentages to the nearest whole percent (two decimal places).

Problem 27-3   The year-end financial statements of Steiner Sales Company are presented on pages 789 and 790.

Instructions   Determine the following, showing the figures you used in your calculations (round off to two decimal places).

1. Working capital

2. Current ratio

3. Quick ratio

4. Merchandise inventory turnover

5. Number of days merchandise inventory kept in stock

6. Rate earned on stockholders' equity

7. Earnings per share of common stock

Steiner Sales Company, Inc.			
Income Statement			
For year ended December 31, 1982			
Revenue from Sales:			
Sales			705 0 0 0 00
Cost of Merchandise Sold:			
Merchandise Inventory, Jan. 1, 1982	114 0 0 0 00		
Purchases	460 2 0 0 00		
Merchandise Available for Sale	574 2 0 0 00		
Less: Merchandise Inventory, Dec. 31, 1982	121 8 0 0 00		
Cost of Merchandise Sold		452 4 0 0 00	
Gross Profit		252 6 0 0 00	
Operating Expenses:			
Selling Expenses (control)	139 0 5 0 00		
General Expenses (control)	69 3 0 0 00		
Total Operating Expenses		208 3 5 0 00	
Net Income from Operations		44 2 5 0 00	
Other Expense:			
Interest Expense		7 8 0 0 00	
Net Income before Income Tax		36 4 5 0 00	
Income Tax		8 2 5 0 00	
Net Income after Income Tax		28 2 0 0 00	

Balance Sheet

December 31, 1982

Assets				
Current Assets:				
Cash		17 2 5 0 00		
Notes Receivable		6 0 0 0 00		
Accounts Receivable (net)		80 5 5 0 00		
Merchandise Inventory		121 8 0 0 00		
Prepaid Expenses		2 1 0 0 00		
Total Current Assets			227 7 0 0 00	
Plant and Equipment:				
Delivery Equipment (net)		77 1 0 0 00		
Store Equipment (net)		46 8 0 0 00		
Office Equipment (net)		13 6 5 0 00		
Total Plant and Equipment			137 5 5 0 00	
Total Assets			365 2 5 0 00	
Liabilities				
Current Liabilities:				
Notes Payable	3 0 0 0 00			
Accounts Payable	32 2 5 0 00			
Total Current Liabilities		35 2 5 0 00		
Long-term Liabilities:				
Mortgage Payable (due June 30, 1993)		120 0 0 0 00		
Total Liabilities			155 2 5 0 00	
Stockholders' Equity				
Common Stock, $10 par (10,000 shares authorized				
and issued)		150 0 0 0 00		
Retained Earnings		60 0 0 0 00		
Total Stockholders' Equity			210 0 0 0 00	
Total Liabilities and Stockholders' Equity			365 2 5 0 00	

Problem 27-4 The condensed comparative income statement of the Lawrence Produce Corporation is presented atop the facing page.

Instructions 1. Express the income statement data in trend percentages.

2. Comment on any significant relationships revealed by the percentages.

Lawrence Produce Corporation
Comparative Income Statement
For years ended December 31, 1981, 1982, 1983 (thousands of dollars)

	1981	1982	1983
Sales (net)	9 3 0 0 00	10 2 0 0 00	11 4 0 0 00
Cost of Merchandise Sold	6 6 0 0 00	7 4 4 0 00	8 4 4 5 00
Gross Profit	2 7 0 0 00	2 7 6 0 00	2 9 5 5 00
Operating Expenses:			
Selling Expenses	1 3 9 5 00	1 4 1 3 00	1 5 8 1 00
General Expenses	9 1 5 00	9 3 0 00	9 3 0 00
Total Operating Expenses	2 3 1 0 00	2 3 4 3 00	2 5 1 1 00
Net Income before Income Tax	3 9 0 00	4 1 7 00	4 4 4 00
Income Tax	1 7 1 00	1 8 3 00	1 9 5 00
Net Income after Income Tax	2 1 9 00	2 3 4 00	2 4 9 00

Alternate problems

Problem 27-1A During 1983 Roger's Family Shoe Store put on a big sales promotion campaign that cost $19,200 more than it usually spent for advertsiing. Here is the condensed comparative statement for the fiscal years ended December 31, 1982 and December 31,1983.

Roger's Family Shoe Store
Comparative Income Statement
For years ended December 31, 1983 and December 31, 1982

	1983	1982
Revenue from Sales:		
Sales	470 5 6 0 00	346 0 0 0 00
Less Sales Returns and Allowances	36 4 0 0 00	26 0 0 0 00
Net Sales	434 1 6 0 00	320 0 0 0 00
Cost of Merchandise Sold	278 1 6 0 00	195 2 0 0 00
Gross Profit	156 0 0 0 00	124 8 0 0 00
Operating Expenses:		
Selling Expenses	89 9 6 0 00	69 2 0 0 00
General Expenses	22 4 4 0 00	20 4 0 0 00
Total Operating Expenses	112 4 0 0 00	89 6 0 0 00
Net Income from Operations	43 6 0 0 00	35 2 0 0 00
Other Expenses	5 6 0 00	4 0 0 00
Net Income	43 0 4 0 00	34 8 0 0 00

Instructions Using horizontal analysis, prepare a comparative income statement for the 2-year period. Round off percentages to the nearest whole percent (two decimal places).

Problem 27-2A Use the comparative income statement for Roger's Family Shoe Store.

Instructions Using vertical analysis, prepare a comparative income statement for the 2-year period. Round off percentages to the nearest whole percent (two decimal places).

Problem 27-3A The year-end financial statements of Lambert Distributing Company, Inc., are presented below and on the facing page.

Lambert Distributing Company, Inc.		
Income Statement		
For year ended December 31, 1982		
Revenue from Sales:		
Sales		810 0 0 0 00
Cost of Merchandise Sold:		
Merchandise Inventory, Jan. 1, 1982	120 0 0 0 00	
Purchases	504 6 0 0 00	
Merchandise Available for Sale	624 6 0 0 00	
Less: Merchandise Inventory, Dec. 31, 1982	132 9 0 0 00	
Cost of Merchandise Sold		491 7 0 0 00
Gross Profit		318 3 0 0 00
Operating Expenses:		
Selling Expenses (control)	168 7 5 0 00	
General Expenses (control)	82 9 5 0 00	
Total Operating Expenses		251 7 0 0 00
Net Income from Operations		66 6 0 0 00
Other Expense:		
Interest Expense		11 4 0 0 00
Net Income before Income Tax		55 2 0 0 00
Income Tax		16 3 5 0 00
Net Income after Income Tax		38 8 5 0 00

Lambert Distributing Company

Balance Sheet

December 31, 1982

Assets			
Current Assets:			
Cash		21 300 00	
Notes Receivable		6 000 00	
Accounts Receivable (net)		77 700 00	
Merchandise Inventory		132 900 00	
Prepaid Expenses		1 800 00	
Total Current Assets			239 700 00
Plant and Equipment:			
Delivery Equipment (net)		74 550 00	
Store Equipment (net)		46 350 00	
Office Equipment (net)		14 100 00	
Total Plant and Equipment			135 000 00
Total Assets			374 700 00
Liabilities			
Current Liabilities:			
Notes Payable	3 600 00		
Accounts Payable	50 700 00		
Total Current Liabilities		54 300 00	
Long-term Liabilities:			
Mortgage Payable (due June 30, 1998)		115 200 00	
Total Liabilities			169 500 00
Stockholders' Equity			
Common Stock, $10 par (10,000 shares authorized and issued)		150 000 00	
Retained Earnings		55 200 00	
Total Stockholders' Equity			205 200 00
Total Liabilities and Stockholders' Equity			374 700 00

Instructions Determine the following, showing the figures you used in your calculations (round off to two decimal places).

1. Working capital
2. Current ratio
3. Quick ratio
4. Merchandise inventory turnover
5. Number of days merchandise inventory in stock
6. Rate earned on stockholders' equity
7. Earnings per share of common stock

Problem 27-4A Here is the condensed comparative income statement of the Kinnamon Corporation.

Kinnamon Corporation			
Comparative Income Statement			
For years ended December 31, 1981, 1982, 1983 (thousands of dollars)			

	1981	1982	1983
Sales (net)	16 00 0 00	17 6 0 0 00	20 0 0 0 00
Cost of Merchandise Sold	11 4 0 0 00	12 8 0 0 00	15 0 0 0 00
Gross Profit	4 6 0 0 00	4 8 0 0 00	5 0 0 0 00
Operating Expenses:			
Selling Expenses	2 3 6 8 00	2 5 5 4 00	2 6 8 8 00
General Expenses	1 5 6 0 00	1 5 6 0 00	1 5 7 2 00
Total Operating Expenses	3 9 2 8 00	4 1 1 4 00	4 2 6 0 00
Net Income before Income Tax	6 7 2 00	6 8 6 00	7 4 0 00
Income Tax	2 9 8 00	3 0 4 00	3 3 0 00
Net Income after Income Tax	3 7 4 00	3 8 2 00	4 1 0 00

Instructions 1. Express the income statement data in trend percentages.

2. Comment on any significant relationships revealed by the percentages.

28 *Statement of changes in financial position*

objectives

After you have completed this chapter, you will be able to do the following:
- Demonstrate an understanding of the nature and purpose of a statement of changes in financial position.
- Demonstrate how to collect and organize data to be used in a statement of changes in financial position.
- Prepare a statement of changes in financial position.

FIRST, let us review the basic financial statements that have been presented.

Income statement Portrays the results of operations of an enterprise during a fiscal period (revenue minus expenses)

Statement of owner's equity Portrays the changes that have taken place in the owner's investment during a fiscal period (beginning investment plus net income minus withdrawals or dividends)

Balance sheet Portrays the financial condition or position of an enterprise at the end of a fiscal period (status of assets, liabilities, and owner's or stockholders' equity)

In this chapter, we introduce another major financial statement, the statement of changes in financial position. According to the Accounting Principles Board of the AICPA, this statement should be presented along with the other principal financial statements.

Financial position

Financial position is frequently measured by the excess of a firm's current assets over its current liabilities. This excess is also defined as the firm's working capital. In other words, as we stated previously *working capital equals current assets minus current liabilities*. Recall that current assets represent cash or other items that can be converted into cash within one year, and current liabilities represent debts that must be paid within one year. As a result working capital is the excess of the amount coming in within one year (collectible) over the amount going out within one year (payable), or the amount of capital that the firm has available to work with or use.

> If current assets increase, then working capital increases.
> If current assets decrease, then working capital decreases.
> If current liabilities increase, then working capital decreases.
> If current liabilities decrease, then working capital increases.

Statement of changes in financial position

The statement of changes in financial position explains in detail how working capital has changed between the beginning and the end of the fiscal period. Some accountants refer to the statement of changes in financial position as being the "where got, where gone" statement of working capital. The statement is also referred to as a statement of sources and applications of funds; in this case, "funds" are interpreted broadly to mean working capital. At any rate, we are concerned with changes in current assets and current liabilities, as opposed to changes in cash only. This concern is due to the fact that in a typical operating cycle the majority of business transactions are completed on a credit basis, as shown here:

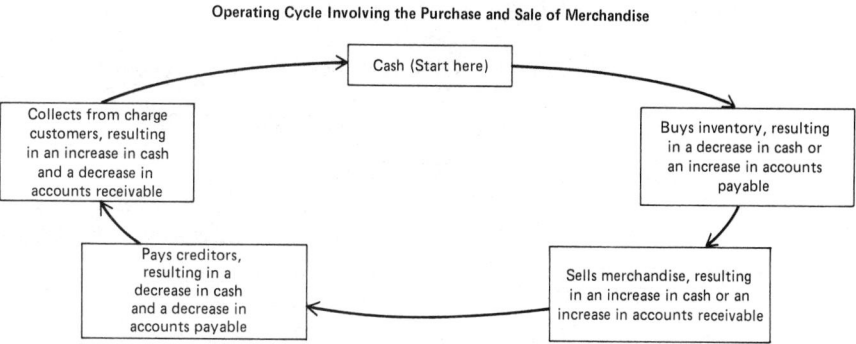

Operating Cycle Involving the Purchase and Sale of Merchandise

We will demonstrate how to prepare a statement of changes in financial position through three illustrations.

First illustration Suppose that J. Jenkins started a business, Jenkins Company, on January 1 by originally investing $50,000 in cash. Also assume that later during the year Jenkins invested an additional $10,000 in cash. In abbreviated form, the financial statements of the business at the end of the year (December 31) are presented below and on the following page.

Jenkins Company		
Income Statement		
For year ended December 31, 1983		
Sales (net)		85 000 00
Cost of Merchandise Sold:		
Purchases (net)	62 000 00	
Less Merchandise Inventory Dec. 31	14 000 00	
Cost of Merchandise Sold		48 000 00
Gross Profit		37 000 00
Operating Expenses		
Wages Expense	10 000 00	
Rent Expense	5 000 00	
Depreciation Expense, Equipment	3 000 00	
Miscellaneous Expense	2 000 00	
Total Expenses		20 000 00
Net Income		17 000 00

Jenkins Company
Statement of Owner's Equity
For year ended December 31, 1983

J. Jenkins, Capital, January 1		50 000 00
Additional Investment, July 1		10 000 00
Total Investment		60 000 00
Add: Net Income for the year	17 000 00	
Less: Withdrawals during the year	12 000 00	
Increase in Capital		5 000 00
J. Jenkins, Capital, December 31		65 000 00

Jenkins Company
Comparative Balance Sheet
December 31, 1983

	END OF YEAR	BEGINNING OF YEAR
Assets		
Current Assets:		
Cash	11 000 00	50 000 00
Accounts Receivable	18 000 00	
Merchandise Inventory	14 000 00	
Total Current Assets	43 000 00	50 000 00
Plant and Equipment:		
Equipment	30 000 00	
Less Accumulated Depreciation	3 000 00	
Total Plant and Equipment	27 000 00	
Total Assets	70 000 00	50 000 00
Liabilities		
Current Liabilities:		
Accounts Payable	5 000 00	
Owner's Equity		
J. Jenkins Capital	65 000 00	50 000 00
Total Liabilities & Owner's Equity	70 000 00	50 000 00

In preparing a statement of changes in financial position, these steps should be followed:

1. Determine the amount of the change in working capital between the beginning of the year and the end of the year. In this example, since this is the first year of operations, the working capital at the beginning of the year happens to be the original investment. The working capital at the end of the year is based on the year-end balance sheet. The change in working capital is calculated like this:

Beginning of year		**End of year**		
Current assets:		Current assets:		
Cash	$50,000	Cash	$11,000	
Total current assets	$50,000	Accounts Receivable	18,000	
Less current liabilities	0	Merchandise Inventory	14,000	
Working capital	$50,000	Total current assets		$43,000
		Less current liabilities:		
		Accounts Payable		5,000
		Working capital		$38,000

Changes in working capital:	
Working capital (ending)	$38,000
Less working capital (beginning)	50,000
Decrease in working capital	$12,000

2. On scratch paper, prepare a schedule of increases and decreases in the current asset and current liability accounts, and verify the amount of the change in working capital determined in Step No. 1, $12,000.

Change in Current Accounts	Balance at End of Year	Balance at Beginning of Year	Increase or (Decrease) in the Account	Increase or (Decrease) in Working Capital
Increase (decrease) in current assets:				
Cash	$11,000	$50,000	($39,000)	($39,000)
Accounts Receivable	18,000	0	18,000	18,000
Merchandise Inventory	14,000	0	14,000	14,000
Increase (decrease) in current liabilities:				
Accounts Payable	5,000	0	5,000	(5,000)
Net increase (decrease) in working capital				($12,000)

At this point, the answer has now been verified, a $12,000 decrease in working capital.

On the following page we present a statement of changes in financial position, and next we shall discuss the individual sections of the statement. You will recognize that we are again verifying the amount of the change in working capital.

Jenkins Company

Statement of Changes in Financial Position

For year ended December 31, 1983

Sources of Working Capital:			
Operations during the Year:			
Net income	17 000 00		
Add expenses not requiring decreases in working capital			
Depreciation Expense, Equipment	3 000 00	20 000 00	
Additional investment by owner		10 000 00	
Total Sources of Working Capital		30 000 00	
Uses of Working Capital:			
Purchase of equipment	30 000 00		
Withdrawals by owner	12 000 00		
Total Uses of Working Capital		42 000 00	
Decrease in Working Capital		12 000 00	
Changes in Components of Working Capital:			
Increases (decreases) in Current Assets:			
Cash	(39 000 00)		
Accounts Receivable	18 000 00		
Merchandise Inventory	14 000 00	(7 000 00)	
Increases (decreases) in Current Liabilities:			
Accounts Payable	5 000 00	5 000 00	
Decreases in Working Capital		12 000 00	

Sources of working capital

As you know, revenue minus expenses equals net income. Regarding the income statement, revenue is in the form of either an increase in cash or an increase in accounts receivable, both resulting in an increase in working capital. Expenses are in the form either of a decrease in cash or an increase in accounts payable, both resulting in a decrease in working capital. Therefore, net income represents an increase or source of working capital. *Net income will always be a source of working capital,* and it is merely a matter of recognizing it.

In the income statement, depreciation was deducted from revenue to arrive at net income. However, unlike the other expenses like Wages Expense, Rent Expense, and Miscellaneous Expense, *the Depreciation Expense was not paid to anyone.* In other words, depreciation did not cost the firm any cash, nor did it result in an additional liability during the year. Therefore, the amount of the depreciation taken should be added to the amount of working capital generated by the firm's operations during the year.

If the additional investment by the owner was in the form of cash, the entry would be a debit to Cash and a credit to Capital. This transaction results in an increase in working capital, because a current asset account is increased without a corresponding increase in a current liability account.

Uses of working capital

If the purchase of equipment was recorded as a debit to Equipment and a credit to Cash, this transaction results in a decrease in working capital, because a current asset was decreased without a corresponding change in a current liability. If the transaction was recorded as a debit to Equipment and a credit to Accounts Payable, there would also be a decrease in working capital, because a current liability was increased without a corresponding increase in a current asset.

A withdrawal by the owner is recorded as a debit to Drawing and a credit to Cash. This transaction results in a decrease in working capital, because a current asset was decreased without a corresponding change in a current liability.

Please observe that all of the transactions listed above have one thing in common:

One side of the transaction (debit or credit) involves a current asset or current liability, and the other side of the transaction (debit or credit) involves a noncurrent asset or noncurrent liability.

For example:

Bought equipment for cash, $30,000		
(Debit) Equipment (noncurrent account)	30,000	
(Credit) Cash (current account)		30,000
Bought equipment on account, $30,000		
(Debit) Equipment (noncurrent account)	30,000	
(Credit) Accounts Payable (current account)		30,000
Owner withdrew cash for personal use, $12,000		
(Debit) J. Jenkins, Drawing (noncurrent account)	12,000	
(Credit) Cash (current account)		12,000

Changes in components of working capital

On scratch paper you have previously prepared a schedule of increases and decreases in current asset and current liability accounts. This schedule is used as a basis for the lower part of the official statement of changes in financial position.

Second illustration The abbreviated financial statements of Sanders Corporation are presented below and on the facing page.

Sanders Corporation
Income Statement
For year ended December 31, 1984

Revenue:		
Sales (net)		900 000 00
Cost of Merchandise Sold:		
Merchandise Inventory, January 1, 1983	128 000 00	
Purchases (net)	698 000 00	
Merchandise Available for Sale	826 000 00	
Less Merchandise Inventory, December 31, 1984	126 000 00	
Cost of Merchandise Sold		700 000 00
Gross Profit		200 000 00
Operating Expenses:		
Wages Expense	103 200 00	
Depreciation Expense, Building	8 000 00	
Depreciation Expense, Equipment	5 200 00	
Bad Debt Expense	3 000 00	
Supplies Expense	2 000 00	
Miscellaneous Expense	4 000 00	
Total Operating Expenses		125 400 00
Net Income from Operations		74 600 00
Other Expenses:		
Interest Expense		15 000 00
Net Income		59 600 00

Sanders Corporation
Statement of Retained Earnings
For year ended December 31, 1984

Retained Earnings, January 1, 1983		50 400 00
Add: Net income for the year	59 600 00	
Less: Dividends declared	47 400 00	
Increase in Retained Earnings		12 200 00
Retained Earnings, December 31, 1984		62 600 00

Sanders Corporation
Comparative Balance Sheet
December 31, 1984

	END OF YEAR	BEGINNING OF YEAR
Assets		
Current Assets:		
Cash	30 000 00	19 200 00
Accounts Receivable	32 000 00	38 000 00
Less Allowance for Doubtful Accounts	1 100 00	1 200 00
Merchandise Inventory	126 000 00	128 000 00
Supplies	4 000 00	4 000 00
Total Current Assets	190 900 00	188 800 00
Plant and Equipment:		
Equipment	116 800 00	100 000 00
Less Accumulated Depreciation	24 400 00	19 200 00
Building	320 000 00	320 000 00
Less Accumulated Depreciation	24 000 00	16 000 00
Land	80 000 00	80 000 00
Total Plant and Equipment	468 400 00	464 800 00
Total Assets	659 300 00	653 600 00
Liabilities		
Current Liabilities:		
Notes Payable	9 000 00	8 000 00
Mortgage Payable (current portion)	16 000 00	16 000 00
Accounts Payable	66 800 00	78 400 00
Wages Payable	900 00	800 00
Total Current Liabilities	92 700 00	103 200 00
Long-Term Liabilities		
Mortgage Payable	184 000 00	200 000 00
Total Liabilities	276 700 00	303 200 00
Stockholders' Equity		
Common Stock, $100 par (4,000 shares authorized,		
3,200 shares issued)	320 000 00	300 000 00
Retained Earnings	62 600 00	50 400 00
Total Liabilities and Stockholders' Equity	659 300 00	653 600 00

Step 1 Determine the amount of the change in working capital between the beginning and the end of the year.

	1984	1983
Current assets	$190,900	$188,800
Less current liabilities	92,700	103,200
Working capital	$ 98,200	$ 85,600

Increase in working capital 1984 over 1983 = $12,600 ($98,200 − $85,600)

Step 2 On scratch paper, prepare a schedule of increases and decreases in the current asset and current liabilities accounts.

Change in Current Accounts	1984	1983	Increase or (Decrease) in the Account	Increase or (Decrease) in Working Capital
Increase (decrease) in current assets:				
Cash	$ 30,000	$ 19,200	$10,800	$10,800
Accounts Receivable (net)	30,900	36,800	(5,900)	(5,900)
Merchandise Inventory	126,000	128,000	(2,000)	(2,000)
Supplies	4,000	4,800	(800)	(800)
Increase (decrease) in current liabilities:				
Notes Payable	9,000	8,000	1,000	(1,000)
Mortgage Payable (current portion)	16,000	16,000	—	—
Accounts Payable	66,800	78,400	(11,600)	11,600
Wages Payable	900	800	100	(100)
Increase in working capital				$12,600

As mentioned previously, the above schedule is used to complete the changes in the components of working capital section (second part) of the statement of changes in financial position, as shown on the facing page.

In making up the sources and uses section of a statement of changes in financial position, we can consider net income to be a regular item that is added to the sources of working capital; conversely, a net loss would be deducted. Depreciation expense is always added to the sources of working capital. Finally, cash dividends (either declared or paid) or withdrawals are always listed as uses of working capital. In other words, net income, depreciation and dividends are regular recurring items, and it is simply a matter of spotting them in the financial statements.

Concerning the possible other items, such as an additional investment, a purchase of equipment, a payment of the principal of a mortgage, etc., the clues to detecting these transactions are found in the changes in the balances of the non-current accounts (plant and equipment, long-term liabilities, and stockholders' equity). Next, we look into the specific accounts in the ledger and possibly trace the transaction back to the journal to determine why the transaction took place as well as its effect upon working capital. For example, in the

Sanders Corporation												
Statement of Changes in Financial Position												
For year ended December 31, 1984												
Sources of Working Capital:												
Operations during the Year:												
Net income	59	6	0	0	00							
Add expenses not requiring decreases in working capital:												
Depreciation Expense, Building	8	0	0	0	00							
Depreciation Expense, Equipment	5	2	0	0	00							
Sale of common stock	20	0	0	0	00							
Total Sources of Working Capital						92	8	0	0	00		
Uses of Working Capital												
Purchase of equipment	16	8	0	0	00							
Decrease in mortgage payable	16	0	0	0	00							
Declaration of cash dividend	47	4	0	0	00							
Total Uses of Working Capital						80	2	0	0	00		
Increases in Working Capital						12	6	0	0	00		
Changes in Components of Working Capital:												
Increases (decreases) in Current Assets:												
Cash	10	8	0	0	00							
Accounts Receivable	(5	9	0	0	00)							
Merchandise Inventory	(2	0	0	0	00)							
Supplies	(	8	0	0	00)	2	1	0	0	00		
Increases (decreases) in Current Liabilities:												
Notes Payable	1	0	0	0	00							
Mortgage Payable (current portion)	–	–	–	–	–							
Accounts Payable	(11	6	0	0	00)							
Wages Payable		1	0	0	00	10	5	0	0	00		
Increase in Working Capital						12	6	0	0	00		

case of the Sanders Corporation, the following changes took place in the balances of the noncurrent accounts between the beginning of the year (or end of the previous year) and the end of the year.

- *Equipment increased from $100,000 to $116,800.* If we examine the ledger account for Equipment, and, upon tracing the transaction back to the journal, we find that the original entry was a debit to Equipment and a credit to Accounts Payable. You recognize that the transaction resulted in a decrease in working capital.

- *Mortgage Payable decreased from $200,000 to $184,000.* If we examine the ledger account for Mortgage Payable, and, upon tracing the transaction back to the journal, we find that the original entry was a debit to Mortgage Payable and a credit to Cash. You recognize that the transaction resulted in a decrease in working capital.

- *Common Stock increased from $300,000 to $320,000.* If we examine the ledger account for Common Stock, and, upon tracing the transaction back to the journal, we find that the original entry was a debit to Cash and a credit to Common Stock. You recognize that the transaction resulted in an increase in working capital.

- *Retained Earnings increased from $50,400 to $62,600.* Upon examining the ledger account, you recognize the net income being added to the account and dividends being deducted from the account. The information for net income and dividends is also shown in the statement of retained earnings.

Broad concept of financing and investing activities

The Accounting Principles Board of the American Institute of Certified Public Accountants held that the statement of changes in financial position should list all the important aspects of transactions involving financing and investing even though current assets or current liabilities are not involved. For example, bought a building and issued a mortgage; entry, debit Building and credit Mortgage Payable. Another example, received land and issued common stock; entry, debit Land and credit Common Stock. On a statement of changes in financial position, using this broad concept of financing activities, the issuances of the mortgage and common stock would be listed as sources of working capital, and the acquisition of the building and land would be listed as uses of working capital. In these cases, the sources cancel out the uses; and there is no net change in the amount of working capital. Further discussion of specific situations involving the broad concept of financing and investing activities will be left to more advanced accounting texts.

Working capital— a restatement

At this point, now that you are acquainted with the statement of changes in financial position, let us restate the possible sources and uses of working capital. Some accountants refer to the working capital as funds (in the inclusive sense, cash or items closely related to cash, such as current assets minus current liabilities).

Sources

Current operations—net income plus expenses not reducing working capital, such as depreciation

Long-term liabilities—borrowing on a long-term basis resulting in an increase in current assets: example, issuing bonds for cash (debit Cash and credit Bonds Payable)

Sale of noncurrent assets—for cash or other current asset: example, sale of equipment for cash (debit Cash and credit Equipment)

Sale of capital stock—for cash or other current asset: example, issue common stock for cash (debit Cash and credit Common Stock)

Uses

Purchase of noncurrent assets—for cash or on a short-term basis: example, buy equipment on account (debit Equipment and credit Accounts Payable)

Repayment of long-term liabilities—such as mortgage or bonds: example, retired (redeemed) bonds, paying cash (debit Bonds Payable and credit Cash)

Bought back (canceled) outstanding stock—bought back our own preferred stock, paying cash (debit Preferred 8% Stock and credit Cash)

Declaration of a cash dividend—results in an increase in a current liability: example, declared a cash dividend to be paid in thirty days (debit Retained Earnings and credit Dividends Payable)

Third illustration

The comparative balance sheet of the Foley Corporation at December 31, 1984 and the preceding year appears on the following page in condensed form.

An examination of the income statement and the statement of retained earnings, as well as the ledgers and journals, reveals the following additional information pertaining to this year.

a. Net income (no extraordinary items), $42,000.

b. Depreciation expense: equipment, $12,000; building, $21,000.

c. Bought equipment, $10,000, paying cash.

d. Retired $20,000 of bonds, paying $20,000 in cash.

e. Sold common stock ($10,000 par value) receiving $12,000 in cash.

f. Declared cash dividends, $26,000.

Step 1 Find the amount of the change in working capital.

	1984	1983
Current assets	$320,000	$294,000
Less current liabilities	85,000	90,000
Working capital	$235,000	$204,000

Increase in working capital = $31,000 ($235,000 − $204,000)

Foley Corporation
Balance Sheet
December 31, 1984

Assets	1984	1983
Current Assets:		
Cash	30 000 00	22 000 00
Accounts Receivable (net)	96 000 00	82 000 00
Merchandise Inventory	191 000 00	186 000 00
Prepaid Insurance	3 000 00	4 000 00
Total Current Assets	320 000 00	294 000 00
Plant and Equipment:		
Equipment	150 000 00	140 000 00
Less Accumulated Depreciation	(58 000 00)	(46 000 00)
Building	330 000 00	330 000 00
Less Accumulated Depreciation	(80 000 00)	(59 000 00)
Land	60 000 00	60 000 00
Total Plant and Equipment	402 000 00	425 000 00
Total Assets	722 000 00	719 000 00
Liabilities		
Current Liabilities:		
Accounts Payable	50 000 00	60 000 00
Dividends Payable	26 000 00	22 000 00
Salaries Payable	9 000 00	8 000 00
Total Current Liabilities	85 000 00	90 000 00
Long-term Liabilities:		
Bonds Payable	100 000 00	120 000 00
Total Liabilities	185 000 00	210 000 00
Stockholders' Equity		
Common Stock, $100 par	400 000 00	390 000 00
Premium on Common Stock	46 000 00	44 000 00
Retained Earnings	91 000 00	75 000 00
Total Stockholders' Equity	537 000 00	509 000 00
Total Liabilities and Stockholders' Equity	722 000 00	719 000 00

Step 2 Prepare a schedule of increases and decreases in current asset and current liability accounts. Verify the amount of the change in working capital, $31,000.

Change in Current Accounts	1984	1983	Increase or (Decrease) in the Account	Increase or (Decrease) in Working Capital
Increase (decrease) in current assets:				
Cash	$ 30,000	$ 22,000	$ 8,000	$8,000
Accounts Receivable (net)	96,000	82,000	14,000	14,000
Merchandise Inventory	191,000	186,000	5,000	5,000
Prepaid Insurance	3,000	4,000	(1,000)	(1,000)
Increase (decrease) in current liabilities:				
Accounts Payable	50,000	60,000	(10,000)	10,000
Dividends Payable	26,000	22,000	4,000	(4,000)
Salaries Payable	9,000	8,000	1,000	(1,000)
Increase in working capital				$31,000

Foley Corporation

Statement of Changes in Financial Position

For year ended December 31, 1984

Sources of Working Capital:		
Operations during the Year:		
Net income	42,000.00	
Add expenses not requiring decreases in working capital:		
Depreciation Expense, Equipment	12,000.00	
Depreciation Expense, Building	21,000.00	
Sale of common stock	12,000.00	
Total Sources of Working Capital		87,000.00
Uses of Working Capital:		
Purchase of equipment	10,000.00	
Retirement of bonds payable	20,000.00	
Declaration of cash dividends	26,000.00	
Total Uses of Working Capital		56,000.00
Increase in Working Capital		31,000.00
Changes in Components of Working Capital:		
Increases (decreases) in Current Assets:		
Cash	8,000.00	
Accounts Receivable	14,000.00	
Merchandise Inventory	5,000.00	
Prepaid Insurance	(1,000.00)	26,000.00
Increases (decreases) in Current Liabilities:		
Accounts Payable	(10,000.00)	
Dividends Payable	4,000.00	
Salaries Payable	1,000.00	(5,000.00)
Increase in Working Capital		31,000.00

Summary

The statement of changes in financial position is considered to be a major financial statement. Financial position represents the excess of current assets over current liabilities (working capital). Therefore, a change in financial position is in reality a change in the amount of working capital between the beginning and the end of a fiscal period.

An increase in current assets represents an increase in working capital; on the other hand, an increase in current liabilities represents a decrease in working capital.

Steps in the formulation of the statement of changes in financial position:

1. Calculate the amount of working capital at the beginning and the end of the fiscal period; next, find the amount of the difference.

2. Prepare a schedule of increases and decreases in current asset and current liability accounts. Verify the amount of the net increase with the amount of the difference in working capitals determined in Step No. 1.

3. Prepare the sources-and-uses-of-working-capital-section of the statement of changes in financial position. First, record the usual items, such as net income (before extraordinary items), depreciation, and withdrawals or declarations of cash dividends. Next, investigate changes in the noncurrent assets and noncurrent liabilities to see if these changes resulted in an increase or decrease of working capital. Verify the final increase or decrease in working capital with the amounts determined in Step No. 1.

4. Prepare the changes-in-components-of-working-capital section of the statement of changes in financial position, using as a basis the schedule of increases and decreases in current asset and current liability accounts previously prepared in Step No. 2.

Sources and uses of working capital

Sources	Uses
(where got—increases in working capital)	*(where gone—decreases in working capital)*
Sale of goods and services (for cash or another current asset)	Purchase of merchandise (for cash or current liability)
Depreciation expense	Payment of expenses (in cash or current liability)
Owners' investments (in cash or another current asset)	Buying of plant and equipment (for cash or current liability)
Long-term borrowing	Payment of long-term debt
Sale of plant and equipment (for cash or another current asset)	Withdrawals, or declarations of dividends (in cash or current liability)

To verify your understanding of the possible sources and uses of working capital, think of possible transactions that affect working capital. Note that the sale of goods and services (sources of working capital), the purchase of merchandise (use of working capital), and the payments of expenses (use of working capital) are all taken care of in the income statement. Depreciation is an exception because it is a noncash expense.

Glossary

Statement of changes in financial position A financial statement that explains in detail how working capital has changed between the beginning and end of the fiscal year.

Working capital The excess of a firm's current assets over its working capital.

Questions

1. What are the principal sources of working capital? What are the principal uses of working capital?

2. What information is contained in a statement of changes in financial position that is not readily apparent in the other financial statements?

3. Why does an increase in a current liability result in a decrease in working capital?

4. Why is depreciation expense considered to be a source of working capital?

5. What are the necessary sources of information for the preparation of a statement of changes in financial position?

6. Why are noncurrent accounts examined to expose changes in working capital?

7. If a business changed its depreciation method from straight-line to sum-of-the-years'-digits, what would be the effect on working capital?

Exercises

Exercise 1 From the following account balances, determine the amount of the working capital:

Notes Payable	$ 2,000
Equipment	12,000
Accounts Receivable	9,000
J. Rankin, Capital	19,000
Cash	6,000
Allowance for Doubtful Accounts	1,000
Accounts Payable	5,000

Exercise 2 What is the amount of the increase or decrease (if any) in working capital of each of the following transactions, considered individually?

a. Bought equipment on account, $600.

b. Issued 1,000 shares of common stock for $12 per share ($10 par), receiving cash.

c. Issued a $4,000, 60-day note to a creditor in settlement of a charge account.

d. Received $5,000 from charge customers to apply on account.

e. Sold merchandise on account, $900 (cost $600).

Exercise 3 Equipment costing $14,000, having an accumulated depreciation of $14,000, is discarded. A junk dealer agreed to remove and dispose of the equipment in exchange for any salvage rights. How does this transaction affect working capital?

Exercise 4 For each of the following firms, compute the amount of the increase or decrease in working capital due to operations and transactions.

	A	B	C
Net income (loss) from operations	$20,000	($60,000)	$140,000
Depreciation of plant and equipment	3,000	9,000	20,000
Retired (bought back) bonds payable			60,000
Sold equipment (at cost) for cash		4,000	

Exercise 5 What is the amount of the increase or decrease (if any) in working capital as a result of each of the following transactions.

a. Declared a 10% stock dividend on $500,000 of par value common stock outstanding.

b. Purchased bonds for retirement, $2,000,000, at 102. The bonds were originally sold at 100.

c. On January 1, land costing $300,000 was purchased for $100,000 cash down payment plus four installments of $50,000 due every six months on June 30 and December 31.

Exercise 6 For the current year, a company reported a net loss of $11,000 on its income statement and an increase of $5,000 in working capital on its statement of changes in financial position. Explain the seeming contradiction between the net loss and the increase in working capital.

Exercise 7 From the following list of transactions completed by Florida Sea Tours during 19—, prepare a statement of changes in financial position for the year.

a. Florida Sea Tours reported net income of $300,000 for the year.

b. Made payments on the mortgage principal of $100,000.

c. Borrowed $60,000 in cash from the bank, payable in six months.

d. Bought deck chairs on account, $30,000, payable in three months.

e. Depreciation recorded for the year, $120,000.

f. Cash dividends declared and paid, $50,000.

Exercise 8 The net income after taxes reported on the income statement of Wilson Corporation for the current year ended December 31 is $80,000. Adjustments required to determine the amount of the increase in working capital provided by operations, as well as some other data used for the year-end adjusting entries, are described below. Prepare the sources-of-working-capital section of the statement of changes in financial position.

a. Wages accrued but not yet paid, $2,000.

b. Depreciation expense, $20,000.

c. Interest accrued on notes receivable, $1,000.

d. Income tax accrued but not yet paid, $3,000.

Problems

Problem 28-1 Harrow Corporation has the following balances of current asset and current liability accounts at the end of the year.

Item	End of Year	Beginning of Year
Cash	$ 52,500	$ 51,500
Notes Receivable	30,000	26,000
Accounts Receivable (net)	71,000	73,000
Merchandise Inventory	146,000	167,500
Prepaid Insurance	5,800	5,500
Accounts Payable	65,000	61,200
Income Tax Payable	10,000	8,000
Dividends Payable	30,000	24,000
Wages Payable	7,600	9,200

Instructions

1. Determine the difference in working capital between the beginning and the end of the year.

2. Prepare the "Changes in components of working capital" section of the statement of changes in financial position.

Problem 28-2 The comparative balance sheet of the Matthews Company at June 30 of this year, and the preceding year appears below in condensed form.

Assets	THIS YEAR	PRECEDING YEAR
Cash	22 0 0 0 00	24 6 0 0 00
Accounts Receivable, (net)	32 1 0 0 00	30 9 0 0 00
Merchandise Inventory	83 4 0 0 00	86 2 0 0 00
Supplies	2 7 0 0 00	3 1 0 0 00
Equipment	98 0 0 0 00	72 4 0 0 00
Accumulated Depreciation, Equipment	(42 0 0 0 00)	(36 5 0 0 00)
Total Assets	196 2 0 0 00	180 7 0 0 00
Liabilities and Owner's Equity		
Accounts Payable	47 3 0 0 00	38 9 0 0 00
Mortgage Payable (current portion)	— — — —	4 0 0 0 00
Mortgage Payable	— — — —	16 0 0 0 00
D.R. Matthews, Capital	148 9 0 0 00	121 8 0 0 00
Total Liabilities and Owner's Equity	196 2 0 0 00	180 7 0 0 00

Additional data for this year obtained from the income statement, the statement of owner's equity, and from an examination of the noncurrent asset and noncurrent liability accounts in the ledger are as follows.

a. Net income (no extraordinary items) reported on the income statement, $46,100.

b. Depreciation reported on the income statement, $5,500.

c. Additional equipment purchased for cash, $25,600.

d. The mortgage note was not due for five years, but the term permitted earlier payment without penalty.

e. Withdrawals by Matthews during, the year, $19,000.

Instructions

1. Determine the difference in working capital between the beginning and the end of the year.

2. Prepare the ''Changes in components of working capital'' section of the statement of changes in financial position.

3. Complete the statement of changes in financial position for year ended June 30.

Problem 28-3 The comparative balance sheet of the Jackson Corporation at December 31 of this year and of the preceding year appears below in condensed form.

Assets	THIS YEAR	PRECEDING YEAR
Cash	16 0 0 0 00	14 8 0 0 00
Accounts Receivable (net)	49 4 0 0 00	42 6 0 0 00
Merchandise Inventory	93 4 0 0 00	90 7 0 0 00
Prepaid Insurance	1 4 0 0 00	1 6 0 0 00
Equipment	72 0 0 0 00	72 0 0 0 00
Accumulated Depreciation, Equipment	40 0 0 0 00	34 0 0 0 00
Building	98 0 0 0 00	98 0 0 0 00
Accumulated Depreciation, Building	24 0 0 0 00	21 0 0 0 00
Land	10 0 0 0 00	10 0 0 0 00
Total Assets	276 2 0 0 00	274 7 0 0 00
Liabilities and Stockholders' Equity		
Notes Payable	3 0 0 0 00	5 5 0 0 00
Accounts Payable	21 0 0 0 00	35 0 0 0 00
Dividends Payable	32 0 0 0 00	30 0 0 0 00
Common Stock, $10 par	150 0 0 0 00	140 0 0 0 00
Premium on Common Stock	2 0 0 0 00	—
Retained Earnings	68 2 0 0 00	64 2 0 0 00
Total Liabilities and Stockholders' Equity	276 2 0 0 00	274 7 0 0 00

Additional data for this year obtained from the income statement, the statement of retained earnings, and from an examination of the noncurrent asset and noncurrent liability accounts in the ledger are as follows.

a. Net income (no extraordinary items) reported on the income statement, $36,000.

b. Depreciation of equipment reported on the income statement, $6,000.

c. Depreciation of building reported on the income statement, $3,000.

d. Issued 1,000 additional shares of common stock for $12 per share, receiving cash.

e. Declared cash dividends, $32,000.

Instructions

1. Determine the difference in working capital between the beginning and end of the year.

2. Prepare the section of the statement of changes in financial position entitled, changes in components of working capital.

3. Complete the statement of changes in financial position for year ended December 31.

Problem 28-4 The comparative balance sheet of the Bagwell Corporation at December 31 of this year and the preceding year appears below in condensed form.

Assets	THIS YEAR	PRECEDING YEAR
Cash	36 000 00	44 000 00
Notes Receivable	3 000 00	4 000 00
Accounts Receivable (net)	60 000 00	55 400 00
Merchandise Inventory	140 000 00	126 000 00
Supplies	6 000 00	5 000 00
Equipment	69 000 00	69 000 00
Accumulated Depreciation, Equipment	42 000 00	28 000 00
Building	100 000 00	90 000 00
Accumulated Depreciation, Building	36 000 00	32 000 00
Land	30 000 00	30 000 00
Total Assets	360 600 00	358 900 00
Liabilities and Stockholders' Equity		
Accounts Payable	41 000 00	47 000 00
Income Tax Payable	4 000 00	3 100 00
Salaries Payable	2 000 00	2 400 00
Preferred 8% Stock, $100 par	80 000 00	90 000 00
Common Stock, $100 par	160 000 00	160 000 00
Premium on Common Stock	6 400 00	6 400 00
Retained Earnings	67 200 00	50 000 00
Total Liabilities and Stockholders' Equity	360 600 00	358 900 00

Additional data for this year obtained from the income statement, the statement of retained earnings, and from an examination of the noncurrent asset and noncurrent liability accounts in the ledger are as follows.

a. Net income (no extraordinary items) reported on the income statement, $44,700.

b. Depreciation of equipment reported on the income statement, $14,000.

c. Depreciation of building reported on the income statement, $4,000.

d. Cash dividends of $27,000 were paid during the year.

e. An addition to the building was constructed at a cost of $10,000, paid in cash.

f. One hundred shares of preferred stock were repurchased and canceled at a cost of $105 per share.

Instructions **1.** Determine the difference in working capital between the beginning and end of the year.

2. Complete the entire statement of changes in financial position for year ended December 31 (with the two sections in proper order).

Alternate problems

Problem 28-1A Everett Corporation has the following balances of current asset and current liability accounts at the end of the year.

Item	End of Year	Beginning of Year
Cash	$ 63,400	$ 60,000
Notes Receivable	32,000	33,000
Accounts Receivable	74,000	77,000
Merchandise Inventory	154,000	156,500
Prepaid Insurance	6,200	6,000
Accounts Payable	68,000	65,800
Income Tax Payable	11,000	10,000
Dividends Payable	30,000	28,000
Wages Payable	8,100	8,300

Instructions **1.** Determine the difference in working capital between the beginning and the end of the year.

2. Prepare the "Changes in components of working capital" section of the statement of changes in financial position.

Problem 28-2A The comparative balance sheet of the Mathison Company at June 30 of this year and the preceding year appears on the facing page.

Additional data for this year obtained from the income statement, the statement of owner's equity, and from an examination of the noncurrent asset and noncurrent liability accounts in the ledger are as follows.

Assets	THIS YEAR	PRECEDING YEAR
Cash	26 5 0 0 00	27 2 0 0 00
Accounts Receivable (net)	33 4 0 0 00	32 1 0 0 00
Merchandise Inventory	84 6 0 0 00	82 4 0 0 00
Supplies	3 2 0 0 00	3 5 0 0 00
Equipment	96 4 0 0 00	80 4 0 0 00
Accumulated Depreciation, Equipment	(41 0 0 0 00)	(38 5 0 0 00)
Total Assets	203 1 0 0 00	187 1 0 0 00
Liabilities and Owner's Equity		
Accounts Payable	44 6 0 0 00	42 2 0 0 00
Mortgage Payable (current portion)	4 8 0 0 00	4 8 0 0 00
Mortgage Payable	18 0 0 0 00	20 0 0 0 00
D.L. Mathison, Capital	135 7 0 0 00	120 1 0 0 00
Total Liabilities and Owner's Equity	203 1 0 0 00	187 1 0 0 00

a. Net income (no extraordinary items) reported on the income statement, $37,600.

b. Depreciation reported on the income statement, $2,500.

c. The principal of the mortgage was reduced by $2,000.

d. Additional equipment purchased for cash, $16,000.

e. Withdrawals by Mathison during the year, $22,000.

Instructions 1. Determine the difference in working capital between the beginning and the end of the year.

2. Prepare the "Changes in components of working capital" section of the statement of changes in financial position.

3. Complete the statement of changes in financial position for year ended June 30.

Problem 28-3A The comparative balance sheet of the Hanson Corporation at December 31 of this year and of the preceding year appears below in condensed form.

Assets	THIS YEAR	PRECEDING YEAR
Cash	19 0 0 0 00	17 6 0 0 00
Accounts Receivable (net)	51 5 0 0 00	50 8 0 0 00
Merchandise Inventory	94 1 0 0 00	92 4 0 0 00
Prepaid Insurance	1 5 0 0 00	1 4 0 0 00
Equipment	75 0 0 0 00	75 0 0 0 00
Accumulated Depreciation, Equipment	44 0 0 0 00	38 0 0 0 00
Building	100 0 0 0 00	100 0 0 0 00
Accumulated Depreciation, Building	32 0 0 0 00	24 0 0 0 00
Land	14 0 0 0 00	14 0 0 0 00
Total Assets	279 1 0 0 00	289 2 0 0 00
Liabilities and Stockholders' Equity		
Notes Payable	6 0 0 0 00	4 0 0 0 00
Accounts Payable	24 9 0 0 00	28 0 0 0 00
Dividends Payable	36 0 0 0 00	34 0 0 0 00
Common Stock, $20 par	160 0 0 0 00	150 0 0 0 00
Premium on Common Stock	8 0 0 0 00	7 5 0 0 00
Retained Earnings	44 2 0 0 00	65 7 0 0 00
Total Liabilities and Stockholders' Equity	279 1 0 0 00	289 2 0 0 00

Additional data for this year obtained from the income statement, the statement of retained earnings, and from an examination of the noncurrent asset and noncurrent liability accounts in the ledger are as follows.

a. Net income (no extraordinary items) reported on the income statement, $14,500.

b. Depreciation of equipment reported on the income statement, $6,000.

c. Depreciation of building reported on the income statement, $8,000.

d. Issued 500 additional shares of common stock for $21 per share, receiving cash.

e. Declared cash dividends, $36,000.

Instructions **1.** Determine the difference in working capital between the beginning and end of the year.

2. Prepare the "Changes in components of working capital" section of the statement of changes in financial position.

3. Complete the statement of changes in financial position for year ended June 30.

Problem 28-4A The comparative balance sheet of the Hanover Corporation at December 31 of this year and the preceding year appears below in condensed form.

Assets	THIS YEAR	PRECEDING YEAR
Cash	16 0 0 0 00	27 0 0 0 00
Notes Receivable	5 4 0 0 00	15 0 0 0 00
Accounts Receivable (net)	40 0 0 0 00	62 0 0 0 00
Merchandise Inventory	108 5 0 0 00	104 3 0 0 00
Supplies	7 0 0 00	8 0 0 00
Equipment	66 0 0 0 00	66 0 0 0 00
Accumulated Depreciation, Equipment	20 0 0 0 00	8 0 0 0 00
Building	120 0 0 0 00	100 0 0 0 00
Accumulated Depreciation, Building	42 0 0 0 00	36 0 0 0 00
Land	40 0 0 0 00	40 0 0 0 00
Total Assets	334 6 0 0 00	371 1 0 0 00
Liabilities and Stockholders' Equity		
Accounts Payable	43 0 0 0 00	61 0 0 0 00
Income Tax Payable	5 0 0 0 00	4 7 0 0 00
Salaries Payable	3 2 0 0 00	3 0 0 0 00
Preferred 8% Stock, $100 par	100 0 0 0 00	120 0 0 0 00
Common Stock, $50 par	170 0 0 0 00	170 0 0 0 00
Premium on Common Stock	4 4 0 0 00	4 4 0 0 00
Retained Earnings	9 0 0 0 00	8 0 0 0 00
Total Liabilities and Stockholders' Equity	334 6 0 0 00	371 1 0 0 00

Additional data for this year obtained from the income statement, the statement of retained earnings, and from an examination of the noncurrent asset and noncurrent liability accounts in the ledger are as follows.

a. Net income (no extraordinary items) reported on the income statement, $23,200.

b. Depreciation of equipment reported on the income statement, $12,000.

c. Depreciation of building reported on the income statement, $6,000.

d. An addition to the building was constructed at a cost of $20,000, paid in cash.

e. Two hundred shares of preferred stock were repurchased and canceled at a cost of $103 per share.

f. Cash dividends of $21,600 were paid during the year.

Instructions   **1.** Determine the difference in working capital between the beginning and end of the year.

2. Complete the entire statement of changes in financial position for year ended December 31 (with the two sections in proper order).

29 *Manufacturing accounting*

objectives

After you have completed this chapter, you will be able to do the following:
- Complete a work sheet for a manufacturing enterprise.
- Prepare financial statements for a manufacturing enterprise.
- Journalize adjusting entries for a manufacturing enterprise.
- Journalize closing entries for a manufacturing enterprise.

IN EARLIER chapters we have dealt with accounting procedures mainly as they apply to service and merchandising enterprises. Now let us turn to another type of business operation: manufacturing.

All the accounting principles we have discussed up to now pertain to manufacturing concerns as well as to service and merchandising firms. But in addition, manufacturers have special procedures to account for manufacturing costs. In this chapter we shall discuss the way manufacturers determine the total cost of goods manufactured during each accounting period. To acquaint you with the end results, during the early part of the chapter we shall present financial statements of a manufacturer. These statements will enable you to understand the function of the work sheet and its relationship to the financial statements. You may consider this chapter to be an introduction to accounting for manufacturing operations. The discussion of cost accounting systems is beyond the scope of this text.

Comparison of income statements for merchandising and manufacturing enterprises

Manufacturing and merchandising companies have the same type of revenue accounts. However, a merchant buys goods in a finished condition, and later sells the goods at a higher price in the same condition; a manufacturer buys raw materials, transforms them into finished goods, and later sells the finished goods.

To show you how the two compare, portions of an income statement for a merchandising firm and portions of an income statement for a manufacturing firm are shown below and on the next page.

A Merchandising Company				
Income Statement				
For year ended December 31, 19–				
Sales (net)			2,000 0 0 0 00	
Cost of Merchandise Sold:				
Merchandise Inventory, Jan. 1	400 0 0 0 00			
Purchases (net)	1,200 0 0 0 00			
Merchandise Available for Sale	1,600 0 0 0 00			
Less Merchandise Inventory, Dec. 31	250 0 0 0 00			
Cost of Merchandise Sold		1,350 0 0 0 00		
Gross Profit		650 0 0 0 00		

Atlas Manufacturing Company
Income Statement
For year ended December 31, 19—

Sales (net)			2000 0 0 0 00
Cost of Goods Sold:			
Finished-goods Inventory, Jan. 1	400 0 0 0 00		
Cost of Goods Manufactured	1200 0 0 0 00		
Goods Available for Sale	1600 0 0 0 00		
Less Finished-goods Inventory, Dec. 31	250 0 0 0 00		
Cost of Goods Sold			1350 0 0 0 00
Gross Profit			650 0 0 0 00

Determining the cost of goods sold

The main difference in accounting for a merchandising firm and for a manufacturing firm lies in determining the cost of goods (or merchandise) sold.

Merchandising Firm	**Manufacturing Firm**
Beginning Merchandise Inventory	Beginning Finished-goods Inventory
+ Purchases (net)	+ Cost of Goods Manufactured
= Merchandise Available	= Goods Available
− Ending Merchandise Inventory	− Ending Finished-goods Inventory
= Cost of Merchandise Sold	= Cost of Goods Sold

A manufacturing concern refers to its products as *goods;* a merchandising concern refers to its inventory as *merchandise.* Cost of Goods Manufactured for a manufacturer is the equivalent of Net Purchases for a merchandiser.

Statement of cost of goods manufactured

The statement of cost of goods manufactured accompanies and supports the income statement. An illustration involving the Atlas Manufacturing Company is shown on page 824.

The accountant must naturally always prepare the statement of cost of goods manufactured before the income statement, in order to incorporate Cost of Goods Manufactured in the income statement.

Elements of manufacturing costs

No matter what type of product a manufacturer makes, the three elements that make up the cost of the goods manufactured are *raw materials used, direct labor,* and *factory overhead.* These three elements are discussed in the following paragraphs.

Raw materials used

Raw materials used consist of the materials that enter directly into—and become a part of—the finished product. The delivered cost of these materials is the figure one enters opposite "Raw Materials Used." For example, if you are manufacturing pencils, for raw materials you need wood, lead, paint, an eraser, and a metal band. Raw materials are also called *direct materials.*

Atlas Manufacturing Company				
Statement of Cost of Goods Manufactured				
For year ended December 31, 19—				
Goods-in-process Inventory, Jan. 1				130 0 0 0 00
Raw Materials:				
Raw-materials Inventory, Jan. 1		90 0 0 0 00		
Raw-materials Purchases (net)		230 0 0 0 00		
Cost of Raw Materials Available for Use		320 0 0 0 00		
Less Raw-materials Inventory, Dec. 31		100 0 0 0 00		
Cost of Raw Materials Used		220 0 0 0 00		
Direct Labor		565 0 0 0 00		
Factory Overhead:				
Indirect Labor	120 0 0 0 00			
Supervisory Salaries	110 0 0 0 00			
Heat, Light, and Power	42 0 0 0 00			
Depreciation Expense, Factory Equipment	32 0 0 0 00			
Depreciation Expense, Factory Building	25 0 0 0 00			
Repairs and Maintenance	24 0 0 0 00			
Factory Insurance Expired	22 0 0 0 00			
Factory Supplies Used	14 0 0 0 00			
Miscellaneous Factory Costs	16 0 0 0 00			
Total Factory Overhead		405 0 0 0 00		
Total Manufacturing Costs			1,190 0 0 0 00	
Total Cost of Goods in Process in Period			1,320 0 0 0 00	
Less Goods-in-process Inventory, Dec. 31			120 0 0 0 00	
Cost of Goods Manufactured			1,200 0 0 0 00	

Direct labor

Direct labor consists of the wages paid to factory employees who work—with machines or hand tools—directly on the materials, to convert them into finished products. The manufacturer debits the Direct Labor account for the gross wages of those who work directly on the raw materials. The cost of direct labor varies directly with the level of production.

Factory overhead

Factory overhead consists of manufacturing costs (other than raw materials used and direct labor) which cannot be traced directly to products being manufactured. A manufacturer uses Factory Overhead as a controlling account. The specific titles of accounts in the Factory Overhead ledger vary from company to company, with the exact accounts depending on the nature of the company and the information desired. In our illustration, the accounts in the Factory Overhead ledger are: Indirect Labor; Supervisory Salaries; Heat, Light, and Power; Depreciation of Factory Equipment; Depreciation of Factory Building; Repairs and Maintenance; Factory Insurance Expired; Factory Supplies Used; and Miscellaneous Factory Costs.

Indirect labor is the cost of labor of those people who keep the plant in operation, rather than directly working on production. *Examples:* mill-wrights, maintenance workers, timekeepers, etc.

Factory supplies used reveals the cost of materials used to keep the plant in operation (oil, grease, etc.). These items are also called *indirect materials*.

Other items that may be included in Factory Overhead are: workmen's compensation insurance, payroll taxes on wages of factory employees, taxes on factory building and equipment, taxes on raw materials and goods-in-process inventories, patents written off, and small tools written off.

Balance sheet for a manufacturing firm

The ending balances of a manufacturing firm's inventory accounts appear in the Current Assets section of the balance sheet, as shown here. On the following pages is a work sheet that is discussed immediately afterwards.

```
                    Atlas Manufacturing Company
                            Balance Sheet
                          December 31, 19-

             Assets
Current Assets:
  Cash                                          $ 14,000.00
  Notes Receivable                                50,000.00
  Accounts Receivable            $180,000.00
    Less Allowance for Doubtful
    Accounts                        6,000.00     174,000.00
  Raw-materials Inventory                        100,000.00
  Goods-in-process Inventory                     120,000.00
  Finished-goods Inventory                       250,000.00
  Prepaid Insurance                                3,000.00
  Factory Supplies                                 2,000.00
  Total Current Assets                                          $  713,000.00
Plant and Equipment:
  Factory Equipment              $360,000.00
    Less Accumulated Depr.        250,000.00    $110,000.00
  Office Equipment              $ 62,000.00
    Less Accumulated Depr.         45,000.00      17,000.00
  Factory Building              $500,000.00
    Less Accumulated Depr.        275,000.00     225,000.00
  Land                                           100,000.00
  Total Plant and Equipment                                       452,000.00
Total Assets                                                   $1,165,000.00

             Liabilities
Current Liabilities:
  Notes Payable                                 $ 40,000.00
  Accounts Payable                                82,000.00
  Income Tax Payable                              16,000.00
  Dividends Payable                               12,000.00
  Total Current Liabilities                                    $  150,000.00
Long-term Liabilities:
  Bonds Payable
  (due Dec. 31, 1985)                                             300,000.00
Total Liabilities                                              $  450,000.00

             Stockholders' Equity
Paid-in Capital:
  Common Stock, $10 par
    (50,000 shares authorized,
    30,000 shares issued)         $300,000.00
  Premium on Common Stock          100,000.00
  Total Paid-in Capital           $400,000.00
Retained Earnings                  315,000.00
Total Stockholders' Equity                                        715,000.00
Total Liabilities and
  Stockholders' Equity                                         $1,165,000.00
```

ACCOUNT NAME	TRIAL BALANCE		ADJUSTMENTS	
	DEBIT	CREDIT	DEBIT	CREDIT
Cash	14 000 00			
Notes Receivable	50 000 00			
Accounts Receivable	180 000 00			
Allowance for Doubtful Accounts		2 500 00		(l) 3 500 00
Raw-materials Inventory	90 000 00		(b)100 000 00	(a)90 000 00
Goods-in-process Inventory	130 000 00		(d)120 000 00	(c)130 000 00
Finished-goods Inventory	400 000 00		(f)250 000 00	(e)400 000 00
Prepaid Insurance	25 000 00			(i) 22 000 00
Factory Supplies	16 000 00			(j) 14 000 00
Factory Equipment	360 000 00			
Accum. Depr., Factory Equipment		218 000 00		(g)32 000 00
Office Equipment	62 000 00			
Accum. Depr., Office Equipment		40 000 00		(k) 5 000 00
Factory Building	500 000 00			
Accum. Depr., Factory Building		250 000 00		(h)25 000 00
Land	100 000 00			
Notes Payable		40 000 00		
Accounts Payable		82 000 00		
Dividends Payable		12 000 00		
Bonds Payable		300 000 00		
Common Stock		300 000 00		
Premium on Common Stock		100 000 00		
Retained Earnings		214 900 00		
Sales (net)		2,000 000 00		
Raw-materials Purchases	230 000 00			
Direct Labor	565 000 00			
Indirect Labor	120 000 00			
Supervisory Salaries	110 000 00			
Heat, Light, and Power	42 000 00			
Repairs and Maintenance	24 000 00			
Miscellaneous Factory Costs	16 000 00			
Selling Expenses (control)	300 000 00			
General Expenses (control)	143 500 00		(l) 3 500 00	
			(k) 5 000 00	
Interest Expense	18 000 00			
Income Tax	63 900 00		(m)16 000 00	
	3,559 400 00	3,599 400 00		

form continued on
pages 828–829

| STATEMENT OF COST OF GOODS MANUFACTURED | | INCOME STATEMENT | | BALANCE SHEET | |
DEBIT	CREDIT	DEBIT	CREDIT	DEBIT	CREDIT
				14 000 00	
				50 000 00	
				180 000 00	
					6 000 00
				100 000 00	
				120 000 00	
				250 000 00	
				3 000 00	
				2 000 00	
				360 000 00	
					250 000 00
				62 000 00	
					45 000 00
				500 000 00	
					275 000 00
				100 000 00	
					40 000 00
					82 000 00
					12 000 00
					300 000 00
					300 000 00
					100 000 00
					214 900 00
			2,000 000 00		
230 000 00					
565 000 00					
120 000 00					
110 000 00					
42 000 00					
24 000 00					
16 000 00					
		300 000 00			
		152 000 00			
		18 000 00			
		79 000 00			

	Debit	Credit
Manufacturing Summary	(a)90 000 00	(b)100 000 00
	(c)130 000 00	(d)120 000 00
Income Summary	(e)400 000 00	(f)250 000 00
Depr. Expense, Factory Equipment	(g)32 000 00	
Depr. Expense, Factory Building	(h)25 000 00	
Factory Insurance, Expired	(i) 22 000 00	
Factory Supplies Used	(j) 14 000 00	
Income Tax Payable		(m)16 000 00
	1,207 500 00	1,207 500 00
Cost of Goods Manufactured		
Net Income		

Work sheet for a manufacturing firm

You have seen that the three financial statements of a manufacturing firm are (1) a statement of cost of goods manufactured, (2) an income statement, and (3) a balance sheet. Since the purpose of a work sheet is to enable the accountant to prepare the necessary financial statements, it follows that the work sheet must have a set of columns for each financial statement. For a manufacturer, this means extra columns for the statement of cost of goods manufactured.

Let us examine the work sheet for Atlas Manufacturing Company, shown on pages 826–827 and atop these two pages.

Note: In the Trial Balance columns, all accounts representing manufacturing costs have debit balances, just as expense accounts have debit balances. Now look at the adjusting entries for inventories. (We are assuming that Atlas uses a physical inventory system.) A manufacturer's inventory, like a merchandiser's inventory, involves two steps: (1) The accountant takes off (or closes off) the beginning inventory. (2) The accountant adds on the ending inventory. However, in manufacturing accounting, there are three inventories involved: Raw-materials, Goods-in-process, and Finished-goods.

Since Raw-materials and Goods-in-process Inventory appear in the statement of cost of goods manufactured, the accountant adjusts them using the Manufacturing Summary account. Since Finished-goods Inventory appears in the income statement, the accountant adjusts it using the Income Summary account. Finished-goods Inventory for a manufacturing firm is equivalent to Merchandise Inventory for a merchandising firm. By T accounts, the adjusting entries are as follows.

Raw-materials Inventory			Manufacturing Summary		
+		−	(a)	90,000	(b) 100,000
Bal. 90,000	(a)	90,000	(c)	130,000	(d) 120,000
(b) 100,000					

Goods-in-process Inventory		
+		−
Bal. 130,000	(c)	130,000
(d) 120,000		

90 0 0 0 00	100 0 00 00									
130 0 00 00	120 0 00 00									
		400 0 0 0 00	250 0 0 0 00							
32 0 0 0 00										
25 0 0 0 00										
22 0 0 0 00										
14 0 0 0 00										
						16 0 0 0 00				
1,420 0 0 0 00	220 0 0 0 00									
	1,200 0 0 0 00	1,200 0 0 0 00								
1,420 0 0 0 00	1,420 0 0 0 00	2,149 9 0 0 00	2,250 0 0 0 00	1,741 0 00 00	1,640 9 0 0 00					
		100 1 0 0 00			100 1 0 0 00					
		2,250 0 0 0 00	2,250 0 0 0 00	1,741 0 0 0 00	1,741 0 0 0 00					

Finished-goods Inventory				Income Summary			
+		–		(e)	400,000	(f)	250,000
Bal.	400,000	(e)	400,000				
(f)	250,000						

The other adjustments are like the ones we have already seen. Note the transferring of the figures in the Adjustments columns to the remaining columns of the work sheet. Just as the accountant transfers the figures on the Income Summary line into the Income Statement columns as separate figures, he or she also transfers the four figures on the Manufacturing Summary lines into the Cost of Goods Manufactured columns as separate figures, like this.

ACCOUNT NAME	ADJUSTMENTS		ADJUSTED TRIAL BALANCE		STATEMENT OF COST OF GOODS MANUFACTURED	
	DEBIT	CREDIT	DEBIT	CREDIT	DEBIT	CREDIT
Manufacturing Summary	(a)90 0 0 0 00	(b)100 0 0 0 00	90 0 0 0 00	100 0 0 0 00		
	(c)130 0 0 0 00	(d)120 0 0 0 00	130 0 0 0 00	120 0 0 0 00		
Income Summary	(e)400 0 0 0 00	(f)250 0 0 0 00			400 0 0 0 00	250 0 0 0 00

On the work sheet, the accountant transfers the cost of goods manufactured ($1,200,000, the difference between the debit and credit totals in the Statement of Cost of Goods Manufactured columns) from the Statement of Cost of Goods Manufactured columns to the Income Statement debit column (consider it to be the equivalent of Net Purchases for a merchandising firm), as shown atop the following page.

ACCOUNT NAME	STATEMENT OF COST OF GOODS MANUFACTURED		INCOME STATEMENT	
	DEBIT	CREDIT	DEBIT	CREDIT
	1,420 0 0 0 00	220 0 0 0 00		
Cost of Goods Manufactured		1,200 0 0 0 00	1,200 0 0 0 00	
	1,420 0 0 0 00	1,420 0 0 0 00		

Accounting cycle for a manufacturing firm

In this discussion of accounting for a manufacturing firm, we have presented the financial statements first, so that you could see the desired end results. Since you were familiar with the statement of cost of goods manufactured, you recognized that the accountant also listed each item appearing on the statement in the work sheet, in the columns labeled Statement of Cost of Goods Manufactured. Similarly, the accountant listed each item that appeared on the income statement in the work sheet, in the columns labeled Income Statement.

To fix the steps in your mind in the proper sequence, let us state the steps in the manufacturer's accounting cycle.

1. Journalize the transactions.
2. Post the ledger accounts.
3. Prepare a trial balance.
4. Determine the adjustments.
5. Complete the work sheet.
6. Prepare the financial statements.
7. Journalize and post adjusting entries.
8. Journalize and post closing entries.
9. Prepare a post-closing trial balance.

Adjusting entries

After the manufacturer's accountant has assembled the information, he or she records the adjustments in the Adjustments columns of the work sheet, just as the accountant for a merchandising firm does. Here is the information (identified by letter) for the adjustments, as shown on the work sheet for the Atlas Manufacturing Company.

(a) and (b) Cost of the ending raw-materials inventory, $100,000
(c) and (d) Cost of the ending goods-in-process inventory, $120,000
(e) and (f) Cost of the ending finished-goods inventory, $250,000
(g) Depreciation of factory equipment, $32,000
(h) Depreciation of factory building, $25,000
(i) Expired factory insurance, $22,000
(j) Cost of the factory-supplies inventory, $2,000
(k) Depreciation of office equipment, $5,000
(l) Estimated uncollectible accounts, $6,000

(m) Income tax, $79,900 (based on a net income before income tax of $180,000; the accountant determined this by completing the income statement columns of the work sheet without including income tax).

The accountant journalizes the adjusting entries.

	19— Dec.		*Adjusting Entries*					
2		31	Manufacturing Summary	90 0 0 0 00				2
3			Raw-materials Inventory			90 0 0 0 00		3
4								4
5		31	Raw-materials Inventory	100 0 0 0 00				5
6			Manufacturing Summary			100 0 0 0 00		6
7								7
8		31	Manufacturing Summary	130 0 0 0 00				8
9			Goods-in-process Inventory			130 0 0 0 00		9
10								10
11		31	Goods-in-process Inventory	120 0 0 0 00				11
12			Manufacturing Summary			120 0 0 0 00		12
13								13
14		31	Income Summary	400 0 0 0 00				14
15			Finished-goods Inventory			400 0 0 0 00		15
16								16
17		31	Finished-goods Inventory	250 0 0 0 00				17
18			Income Summary			250 0 0 0 00		18
19								19
20		31	Depreciation Expense, Factory Equipment	32 0 0 0 00				20
21			Accumulated Depreciation, Factory Equipment			32 0 0 0 00		21
22								22
23		31	Depreciation Expense, Factory Building	25 0 0 0 00				23
24			Accumulated Depreciation, Factory Building			25 0 0 0 00		24
25								25
26		31	Factory Insurance Expired	22 0 0 0 00				26
27			Prepaid Insurance			22 0 0 0 00		27
28								28
29		31	Factory Supplies Used	14 0 0 0 00				29
30			Factory Supplies			14 0 0 0 00		30
31								31
32		31	General Expenses (control)	5 0 0 0 00				32
33			Accumulated Depreciation, Office Equipment			5 0 0 0 00		33
34								34
35								35
1		31	General Expenses (control)	3 5 0 0 00				36
2			Allowance for Doubtful Accounts			3 5 0 0 00		37
3								38
4		31	Income Tax	16 0 0 0 00				39
5			Income Tax Payable			16 0 0 0 00		40

Closing entries

Now we come to the steps one must take in performing the closing entries for a manufacturer.

1. Close the costs that appear in the statement of cost of goods manufactured into the Manufacturing Summary account.

2. Close the Manufacturing Summary account into the Income Summary account (by the amount of the cost of goods manufactured).

3. Close the revenue accounts into the Income Summary account.

4. Close the expense accounts into the Income Summary account.

5. Close the Income Tax account into the Income Summary account.

6. Close the Income Summary account into the Retained Earnings account (by the amount of the net income after income tax).

19– Dec.		*Closing Entries*		
	31	*Manufacturing Summary*	1,200 0 0 0 00	
		Raw-materials Purchases		230 0 0 0 00
		Direct Labor		565 0 0 0 00
		Indirect Labor		120 0 0 0 00
		Supervisory Salaries		110 0 0 0 00
		Heat, Light, and Power		42 0 0 0 00
		Repairs and Maintenance		24 0 0 0 00
		Miscellaneous Factory Costs		16 0 0 0 00
		Depreciation Expense, Factory Equipment		32 0 0 0 00
		Depreciation Expense, Factory Building		25 0 0 0 00
		Factory Insurance, Expired		22 0 0 0 00
		Factory Supplies Used		14 0 0 0 00
	31	*Income Summary*	1,200 0 0 0 00	
		Manufacturing Summary		1,200 0 0 0 00
	31	*Sales (net)*	2,000 0 0 0 00	
		Income Summary		2,000 0 0 0 00
	31	*Income Summary*	470 0 0 0 00	
		Selling Expenses (control)		300 0 0 0 00
		General Expenses (control)		152 0 0 0 00
		Interest Expense		18 0 0 0 00
	31	*Income Summary*	79 9 0 0 00	
		Income Tax		79 9 0 0 00
	31	*Income Summary*	100 1 0 0 00	
		Retained Earnings		100 1 0 0 00

Here are the T accounts for Manufacturing Summary and Income Summary, labeled so that you can readily identify the accounts recorded.

Manufacturing Summary

Raw-materials Inventory, Jan. 1	90,000	Raw-materials Inventory, Dec. 31	100,000
Goods-in-process Inventory, Jan. 1	130,000	Goods-in-process Inv., Dec. 31	120,000
Raw-materials Purchases	230,000	Closing	1,200,000
Direct Labor	565,000	(To Income summary)	
Indirect Labor	120,000		
Supervisory Salaries	110,000		
Heat, Light, and Power	42,000		
Repairs and Maintenance	24,000		
Miscellaneous Factory Costs	16,000		
Deprec. Expense, Factory Equip.	32,000		
Deprec. Expense, Factory Bldg.	25,000		
Factory Insurance Expired	22,000		
Factory Supplies Used	14,000		
	1,420,000		1,420,000

Income Summary

Finished-goods Inventory, Jan. 1	400,000	Finished-goods Inventory, Dec. 31	250,000
(From Manufacturing Summary)	1,200,000		

Determining the value of ending inventories

We have been talking about the fact that a manufacturer has to record the costs of the ending inventories for (1) raw materials, (2) goods in process, and (3) finished goods. The manufacturer lists these costs first in the Adjustments columns of the work sheet, and then carries the figures forward into the financial statements. Let us now consider each inventory separately, because each poses a slightly different set of problems.

Raw-materials inventory

The items that go to make up the raw-materials inventory are in the same form they were in when the manufacturer bought them; nothing has been done to them yet. So the accountant first ascertains the quantities on hand and the unit costs, then determines the values of the inventories. The value of the ending inventories may be calculated by either FIFO, LIFO, or weighted-average method. One may also use the lower-of-cost-or-market rule. All these involve the periodic taking of inventories.

As an alternative, a manufacturer may keep *perpetual inventories,* which provide a continuous or running balance of the firm's inventory. A firm that uses perpetual inventories, when it buys raw materials, immediately debits Raw-materials Inventory for the cost of these materials. When the materials are put into production, the manufacturer credits Raw-materials Inventory for the cost of the materials used. The same debiting and crediting process goes on in the Goods-in-process Inventory and the Finished-goods Inventory accounts, as these raw materials go through the manufacturing process. If a company keeps perpetual inventories, it verifies the balance of the account periodically by physically counting the goods on hand. Any discrepancy that exists can be handled by an adjusting entry. If there is no discrepancy, then the company does not need to make an adjusting entry involving the inventory.

Goods-in-process inventory

How does one calculate the cost of the goods-in-process inventory? We have seen that the cost of manufacturing any product consists of (1) *raw materials used,* (2) *direct labor expended,* and (3) *factory overhead.* Therefore the manufacturer should keep a record of the amount and cost of raw materials placed in production. The manufacturer should also keep a record of the cost of direct labor expended on the ending goods-in-process inventory.

The third item, factory overhead, consists of a group of accounts such as Heat, Light, and Power; Repairs and Maintenance; and Miscellaneous Factory Costs; to name a few. So the manufacturer cannot calculate the *exact* cost of factory overhead involved in the ending goods-in-process inventory, and must therefore estimate this cost. The firm does this by using a percentage of the direct labor cost involved in the ending inventory. The reasoning here is that, since factory overhead is closely related to the level of production, and since the level of production varies directly with the amount of direct labor, the cost of factory overhead should be regarded as a percentage of direct labor. For example, Heat, Light, and Power is part of factory overhead, and varies directly with the level of production.

One may determine the percentage figure for factory overhead from the most recent statement of cost of goods manufactured. The factory overhead rate for the Atlas Corporation is as follows.

$$\text{Factory overhead rate} = \frac{\text{Factory overhead}}{\text{Direct labor}} = \frac{\$405,000}{\$565,000} = .72 = 72\%$$

Summary

The same accounting principles that govern the accounts of service and merchandising enterprises also govern those of manufacturing companies. The additional element that enters into the accounting for manufacturing firms is the determination of the cost of goods manufactured.

The balance sheet includes the balances of the inventory accounts under the heading of Current Assets.

We presented the financial statements first to show you how the accounts introduced here for a manufacturer are recorded on the work sheet. Each figure appearing in the statement of cost of goods manufactured also appears in the columns labeled Statement of Cost of Goods Manufactured; likewise, each figure appearing in the income statement also appears in the columns labeled Income Statement.

In making the adjusting entries, the accountant adjusts the inventories appearing in the statement of cost of goods manufactured (raw materials and goods in process) into the Manufacturing Summary account, and adjusts the inventories appearing in the income statement (finished goods) into the Income Summary account.

In making the closing entries, the accountant first closes all manufacturing-cost accounts into the Manufacturing Summary account. Next the accountant closes Manufacturing Summary (now representing the cost of goods manufactured) into the Income Summary account. All other adjusting and closing entries are handled in the usual manner.

The manufacturer determines the costs of the goods-in-process and finished-goods inventories by adding the cost of the raw materials used, the cost of the direct labor, and the estimated cost of factory overhead, which is figured as a percentage of the cost of direct labor. For an example, refer to the table below. In our illustration of the Atlas Manufacturing Company, we established the rate for factory overhead as being 72% of direct labor.

Item	Goods in Process	Finished Goods
Raw materials used	$ 49,200 00	$103,090 00
+ Direct labor	40,000 00	83,000 00
+ Factory overhead (72% of direct labor)	28,800 00	59,760 00
	$118,000 00	$245,850 00

Glossary

Direct labor   Wages paid to factory employees who convert the raw materials into finished products.

Direct materials   Delivered cost of raw materials used in manufacturing products.

Factory overhead   All manufacturing costs except raw materials used and direct labor. Examples: heat, light, and power; repairs and maintenance; indirect labor; indirect materials.

Indirect labor   That portion of work performed by workers who keep the plant in operation—such as factory maintenance workers, timekeepers, etc.—rather than workers who are directly occupied with production, considered to be part of factory overhead.

Indirect materials   Factory supplies, such as oil, grease, cleaning fluids, etc., considered to be part of factory overhead.

Raw materials   Delivered cost of materials (also called direct materials) to be used in producing the finished goods.

Questions

1. What inventory accounts appear in the chart of accounts of a manufacturing company?

2. What are the three major elements involved in manufacturing costs?

3. Which inventories appear in the statement of cost of goods manufactured?

4. In a work sheet, why is cost of goods manufactured entered in the Statement of Cost of Goods Manufactured Credit and the Income Statement Debit columns?

5. What is the purpose of the Manufacturing Summary account?

6. What inventory of a manufacturing firm is handled the same way as the merchandise inventory of a merchandising firm?

7. List five accounts that you would consider to be factory overhead costs.

Exercises

Exercise 1 From the following balances, determine the cost of the raw materials used.

Raw-materials Purchases	$1,680,000
Raw-materials Inventory, May 31	200,000
Raw-materials Inventory, May 1	120,000

Exercise 2 Prepare a statement of cost of goods manufactured, using any of the following balances you need.

Raw-materials Purchases	$1,680,000
Raw-materials Inventory, May 31	200,000
Raw-materials Inventory, May 1	120,000
Goods-in-process Inventory, May 1	600,000
Finished-goods Inventory, May 31	320,000
Direct Labor	2,400,000
Goods-in-process Inventory, May 31	800,000
Factory Overhead	1,800,000
Finished-goods Inventory, May 1	360,000

Exercise 3 From the data in Exercise 2, determine the percentage of factory overhead. Assume that the cost of the goods in process on May 31 is $800,000, comprising raw materials of $240,000 and direct labor of $320,000. How much is the factory overhead? Verify the figure by means of the percentage of factory overhead.

Exercise 4 From the following balances, determine the cost of goods manufactured.

Cost of Goods Sold	$1,700,000
Finished-goods Inventory, April 1	400,000
Finished-goods Inventory, April 30	300,000

Exercise 5 From the following, calculate the cost of the ending goods-in-process inventory, which contains the following three elements.

Raw materials used	$180,000
Direct labor	200,000
Factory overhead (85% of direct labor)	?

Exercise 6 The Statement of Cost of Goods Manufactured columns and the Income Statement columns of the work sheet for the Brown Manufacturing Corporation

for the year ended December 31 are as follows. Brown's beginning inventory of raw materials is $30,000; its beginning inventory of goods in process is $144,000. Prepare a statement of cost of goods manufactured.

ACCOUNT NAME	STATEMENT OF COST OF GOODS MANUFACTURED		INCOME STATEMENT	
	DEBIT	CREDIT	DEBIT	CREDIT
Sales				1,350 000 00
Raw-materials Purchases	240 000 00			
Direct Labor	600 000 00			
Indirect Labor	12 000 00			
Heat, Light, and Power	6 000 00			
Miscellaneous Factory Costs	3 000 00			
Selling Expenses (control)			127 500 00	
General Expenses (control)			52 500 00	
Income Tax			150 000 00	
Manufacturing Summary	30 000 00	45 000 00		
	144 000 00	150 000 00		
Income Summary			120 000 00	135 000 00
	1,035 000 00	195 000 00		
Cost of Goods Manufactured		840 000 00	840 000 00	
	1,035 000 00	1,035 000 00	1,290 000 00	1,485 000 00
Net Income			195 000 00	
			1,485 000 00	1,485 000 00

Exercise 7 Prepare an income statement for the Brown Manufacturing Corporation. Beginning inventory of finished goods is $120,000.

Exercise 8 Journalize the closing entries for the Brown Manufacturing Corporation.

Problems

Problem 29-1 The statement of cost of goods manufactured for the Atkinson Manufacturing Company is as shown on page 838.

Instructions 1. Journalize the adjusting entries for the Raw-materials Inventory and the Goods-in-process Inventory.

2. Journalize the closing entries for manufacturing costs.

3. Post the entries to the Manufacturing Summary account.

4. Journalize and post the entry to close the Manufacturing Summary account.

Statement of Cost of Goods Manufactured

For year ended June 30, 19–

Goods-in-process Inventory, July 1			240000 00
Raw Materials:			
Raw-materials Inventory, July 1		500000 00	
Raw-materials Purchases (net)		780000 00	
Cost of Raw Materials Available for Use		1280000 00	
Less Raw-materials Inventory, June 30		530000 00	
Cost of Raw Materials Used		750000 00	
Direct Labor		1200000 00	
Factory Overhead:			
Indirect Labor	220000 00		
Supervisory Salaries	190000 00		
Depreciation Expense, Factory Equipment	130000 00		
Heat, Light, and Power	38000 00		
Depreciation Expense, Factory Building	37600 00		
Repairs and Maitenance	28400 00		
Factory Supplies Used	24000 00		
Factory Insurance Expired	17600 00		
Property Tax on Factory Building	14400 00		
Miscellaneous Factory Costs	12800 00		
Total Factory Overhead		712800 00	
Total Manufacturing Costs			2662800 00
Total Cost of Goods in Process during the Period			2902800 00
Less Goods-in-process Inventory, June 30			520000 00
Cost of Goods Manufactured			2382800 00

Problem 29-2 The trial balance of the Atwood Products Corporation as of December 31 of this year is shown on the facing page.

You are given the following information for the adjustments.

a. Year-end inventories: raw materials, $43,000; goods in process, $63,400; finished goods, $69,250.

b. Allowance for Doubtful Accounts to be increased by $800 (debit General Expenses (control).

c. By taking an inventory, the management finds that $2,000 of factory supplies were used during the year.

d. Estimated depreciation of factory machinery, $8,750.

e. A study of the company's insurance policies shows that $1,200 of factory insurance expired during the year.

Atwood Products Corporation

Trial Balance

December 31, 19–

	Debit	Credit
Cash	4 2 0 0 00	
Accounts Receivable	35 8 0 0 00	
Allowance for Doubtful Accounts		1 4 5 0 00
Raw-materials Inventory	45 0 0 0 00	
Goods-in-process Inventory	71 3 0 0 00	
Finished-goods Inventory	68 2 0 0 00	
Prepaid Factory Insurance	1 8 0 0 00	
Factory Supplies	3 0 0 0 00	
Machinery	84 0 0 0 00	
Accumulated Depreciation, Machinery		42 0 0 0 00
Accounts Payable		29 3 0 0 00
Common Stock		100 0 0 0 00
Paid-in Capital in Excess of Stated Value		20 0 0 0 00
Retained Earnings		72 0 0 0 00
Sales		638 7 5 0 00
Raw-materials Purchases	70 0 0 0 00	
Direct Labor	209 7 0 0 00	
Indirect Labor	79 9 0 0 00	
Heat, Light, and Power	16 0 0 0 00	
Machinery Repairs	9 0 0 0 00	
Selling Expenses (control)	139 9 5 0 00	
General Expenses (control)	60 0 5 0 00	
Income Tax	5 6 0 0 00	
	903 5 0 0 00	903 5 0 0 00

f. Accrued direct labor, $300; accrued indirect labor, $100; accrued sales commissions, $100.

g. Additional income tax, $6,200.

Instructions **1.** Prepare a work sheet.

2. Prepare a statement of cost of goods manufactured.

3. Prepare an income statement.

Problem 29-3 On the following page are the columns that reflect the statement of cost of goods manufactured and the income statement in the work sheet of the Farber Specialty Products Company, Inc., as of December 31, the end of the fiscal year. Their beginning inventory of raw materials is $138,240; their beginning inventory of goods in process is $248,800.

ACCOUNT NAME	STATEMENT OF COST OF GOODS MANUFACTURED DEBIT	CREDIT	INCOME STATEMENT DEBIT	CREDIT
Sales				2,999 920 00
Sales Returns and Allowances			24 800 00	
Sales Discounts			23 600 00	
Selling Expenses (control)			358 980 00	
General Expenses (control)			145 720 00	
Raw-materials Purchases	769 000 00			
Direct Labor	965 800 00			
Indirect Labor	221 240 00			
Heat, Light, and Power	53 960 00			
Factory Supervision	53 900 00			
Rent, Factory	32 000 00			
Machinery Repairs	31 800 00			
Depreciation Expense, Machinery	31 680 00			
Factory Supplies Used	12 400 00			
Factory Insurance Expired	7 600 00			
Small Tools Written Off	2 520 00			
Miscellaneous Factory Costs	1 360 00			
Loss on Disposal of Equipment			17 200 00	
Interest Expense			13 600 00	
Income Tax			104 160 00	
Manufacturing Summary	138 240 00	143 200 00		
	248 800 00	252 980 00		
Income Summary			362 800 00	373 440 00
	2,570 300 00	396 180 00		
Cost of Goods Manufactured		2,174 120 00	2,174 120 00	
	2,570 300 00	2,570 300 00	3,224 980 00	3,373 360 00
Net Income after Income Tax			148 380 00	
			3,373 360 00	3,373 360 00

Instructions

1. Prepare a statement of cost of goods manufactured.
2. Prepare an income statement.
3. Journalize the adjusting entries for the inventories.
4. Journalize the closing entries.

Problem 29-4 On the facing page are adjusting and closing entries that appear on the books of the Baker Sash and Door Corporation at the end of the fiscal year, June 30.

Instructions Prepare a statement of cost of goods manufactured for the year.

	DATE		DESCRIPTION	POST REF.	DEBIT	CREDIT	
1	19— Jun.	30	*Adjusting Entries*				1
2		30	Manufacturing Summary		130 05 0 00		2
3			Raw-materials Inventory			130 05 0 00	3
4							4
5		30	Raw-materials Inventory		117 73 5 00		5
6			Manufacturing Summary			117 73 5 00	6
7							7
8		30	Manufacturing Summary		166 11 0 00		8
9			Goods-in-process Inventory			166 11 0 00	9
10							10
11		30	Goods-in-process Inventory		159 63 0 00		11
12			Manufacturing Summary			159 63 0 00	12
13							13
14			*Closing Entries*				14
15		30	Purchases Discount		5 76 0 00		15
16			Manufacturing Summary			5 76 0 00	16
17							17
18		30	Manufacturing Summary		1431 79 5 00		18
19			Raw-materials Purchases			355 05 0 00	19
20			Direct Labor			733 41 0 00	20
21			Indirect Labor			73 11 0 00	21
22			Supervision			104 22 0 00	22
23			Depreciation Expense, Machinery			75 00 0 00	23
24			Depreciation Expense, Factory Building			30 00 0 00	24
25			Heat, Light, and Power			21 30 0 00	25
26			Repairs and Maintenance			19 18 5 00	26
27			Property Tax Expense, Machinery			2 77 5 00	27
28			Property Tax, Expense, Factory Building			3 30 0 00	28
29			Factory Supplies Used			10 30 5 00	29
30			Factory Insurance Expired			2 70 0 00	30
31			Miscellaneous Factory Costs			1 44 0 00	31
32							32
33		30	Income Summary		1444 83 0 00		33
34			Manufacturing Summary			1444 83 0 00	34
35							35
36							7

Alternate problems

Problem 29-1A The statement of cost of goods manufactured for the Cramer Manufacturing Company is as shown on the following page.

Cramer Manufacturing Company																			
Statement of Cost of Goods Manufactured																			
For year ended June 30, 19–																			

Goods-in-process Inventory, July 1										80	0	0	0	00
Raw Materials:														
Raw-materials Inventory, July 1				136	0	0	0	00						
Raw-materials Purchases (net)				197	5	0	0	00						
Cost of Raw Materials Available for Use				333	5	0	0	00						
Less Raw-materials Inventory, June 30				130	0	0	0	00						
Cost of Raw Materials Used				203	5	0	0	00						
Direct Labor				291	0	0	0	00						
Factory Overhead:														
Indirect Labor	54	2	0	0	00									
Supervisory Sales	38	0	5	0	00									
Depreciation Expense, Factory Equipment	36	0	0	0	00									
Depreciation Expense, Factory Building	10	9	0	0	00									
Heat, Light, and Power	9	3	0	0	00									
Repairs and Maintenance	7	2	0	0	00									
Factory Supplies Used	6	9	5	0	00									
Factory Insurance Expired	3	8	0	0	00									
Property Tax on Factory Building	3	7	5	0	00									
Miscellaneous Factory Costs	3	5	5	0	00									
Total Factory Overhead				173	7	0	0	00						
Total Manufacturing Costs									682	2	0	0	00	
Total Cost of Goods in Process for Period									748	2	0	0	00	
Less Goods-in-process Inventory, June 30									87	5	0	0	00	
Cost of Goods Manufactured									660	7	0	0	00	

Instructions

1. Journalize the adjusting entries for the Raw-materials Inventory and the Goods-in-process Inventory.

2. Journalize the closing entries for manufacturing costs.

3. Post the entries to the Manufacturing Summary Account.

4. Journalize and post the entry to close the Manufacturing Summary account.

Problem 29-2A The trial balance of the Gardner Manufacturing Corporation as of December 31 of this year is shown on the facing page.

Gardner Manufacturing Corporation

Trial Balance

December 31, 19–

	Debit	Credit
Cash	4 3 5 0 00	
Accounts Receivable	34 7 0 0 00	
Allowance for Doubtful Accounts		1 3 5 0 00
Raw-materials Inventory	45 8 0 0 00	
Goods-in-process Inventory	71 0 5 0 00	
Finished-goods Inventory	69 2 0 0 00	
Prepaid Factory Insurance	2 1 0 0 00	
Factory Supplies	3 0 0 0 00	
Machinery	85 5 0 0 00	
Accumulated Depreciation, Machinery		43 2 0 0 00
Accounts Payable		27 4 5 0 00
Common Stock		100 0 0 0 00
Paid-in Capital in Excess of Stated Value		25 0 0 0 00
Retained Earnings		68 3 3 0 00
Sales		645 7 0 0 00
Raw-materials Purchases	69 9 5 0 00	
Direct Labor	210 6 4 0 00	
Indirect Labor	80 7 3 0 00	
Heat, Light, and Power	16 2 0 0 00	
Machinery Repairs	9 8 0 0 00	
Selling Expenses (control)	141 7 1 0 00	
General Expenses (control)	59 3 7 5 00	
Income Tax	6 9 2 5 00	
	911 0 3 0 00	911 0 3 0 00

You are given the following information for the adjustments.

a. Year-end inventories: raw materials, $42,700; goods in process, $64,200; finished goods, $70,350.

b. Estimated depreciation of factory machinery, $9,250.

c. A study of the company's insurance policies shows that $1,550 of factory insurance expired during the year.

d. Allowance for Doubtful Accounts to be increased by $775 (debit General Expenses (control).

e. Accrued direct labor, $360; accrued indirect labor, $120; accrued sales commissions, $140.

f. By taking an inventory, the management finds that $1,900 of factory supplies were used during the year.

g. Additional income tax, $5,900.

Instructions   **1.** Prepare a work sheet.

2. Prepare a statement of cost of goods manufactured.

3. Prepare an income statement.

Problem 29-3A   Here are the columns reflecting the statement of cost of goods manufactured and the income statement in the work sheet of the Cunningham Machine Products Corporation as of December 31, the end of the fiscal year. Their beginning inventory of raw materials is $142,920; their beginning inventory of goods in process is $253,400.

ACCOUNT NAME	STATEMENT OF COST OF GOODS MANUFACTURED DEBIT	STATEMENT OF COST OF GOODS MANUFACTURED CREDIT	INCOME STATEMENT DEBIT	INCOME STATEMENT CREDIT
Sales				3016480 00
Sales Returns and Allowances			25200 00	
Sales Discounts			24000 00	
Selling Expenses (control)			373900 00	
General Expenses (control)			147220 00	
Raw-materials Purchases	764000 00			
Direct Labor	973800 00			
Indirect Labor	221680 00			
Heat, Light, and Power	55240 00			
Factory Supervision	53860 00			
Rent, Factory	36000 00			
Machinery Repairs	35840 00			
Depreciation Expense, Machinery	34760 00			
Factory Supplies Used	9800 00			
Factory Insurance Expired	7200 00			
Small Tools Written Off	2480 00			
Miscellaneous Factory Costs	1300 00			
Loss on Disposal of Equipment			16000 00	
Interest Expense			15200 00	
Income Tax			104100 00	
Manufacturing Summary	142920 00	147640 00		
	253400 00	265680 00		
Income Summary			369200 00	385200 00
	2592280 00	413320 00		
Cost of Goods Manufactured		2178960 00	2178960 00	
	2592280 00	2592280 00	3253780 00	3402080 00
Net Income after Income Tax			148300 00	
			3402080 00	3402080 00

Instructions 1. Prepare a statement of cost of goods manufactured.

2. Prepare an income statement.

3. Journalize the adjusting entries for the inventories.

4. Journalize the closing entries.

Problem 29-4A Below are adjusting and closing entries that appear on the books of the Daniels Marine Products Company at the end of the fiscal year, June 30.

Instructions Prepare a statement of cost of goods manufactured for the year.

	19— Jun.				
1			*Adjusting Entries*			1
2		30	Manufacturing Summary	133 1 5 5 00		2
3			Raw-materials Inventory		133 1 5 5 00	3
4						4
5		30	Raw-materials Inventory	135 9 2 7 00		5
6			Manufacturing Summary		135 9 2 7 00	6
7						7
8		30	Manufacturing Summary	169 2 3 0 00		8
9			Goods-in-Process Inventory		169 2 3 0 00	9
10						10
11		30	Goods-in-process Inventory	175 2 6 0 00		11
12			Manufacturing Summary		175 2 6 0 00	12
13						13
14			*Closing Entries*			14
15		30	Purchases Discount	6 3 1 5 00		15
16			Manufacturing Summary		6 3 1 5 00	16
17						17
18		30	Manufacturing Summary	1192 3 0 5 00		18
19			Raw-materials Purchases		382 4 4 0 00	19
20			Direct Labor		509 1 9 0 00	20
21			Indirect Labor		57 7 2 0 00	21
22			Supervision		87 9 6 0 00	22
23			Depreciation Expense, Machinery		63 0 0 0 00	23
24			Depreciation Expense, Factory Building		36 0 0 0 00	24
25			Heat, Light, and Power		19 2 3 0 00	25
26			Repairs and Maintenance		14 5 2 0 00	26
27			Property Tax Expense, Machinery		1 9 0 5 00	27
28			Property Tax Expense, Factory Building		2 7 6 0 00	28
29			Factory Supplies Used		14 2 0 5 00	29
30			Factory Insurance Expired		1 8 0 0 00	30
31			Miscellaneous Factory Costs		1 5 7 5 00	31
32						32
33		30	Income Summary	1177 1 8 8 00		33
34			Manufacturing Summary		1177 1 8 8 00	34
35						35

Index

A

ABA number 183, (*def.*) 203
Accelerated depreciation 535, (*def.*) 547
Account (*def.*) 11
  chart of 76–77, (*illus.*) 76, (*def.*) 86, 385–386
  classification of 40, 77, 383–386
  clearing of 125
  contra 101, 111, (*def.*) 114, 392
  contra-liability 700, (*def.*) 709
  controlling 276, (*def.*) 285
  four-column (*illus.*) 77
  for merchandising enterprises 269–270
  mixed 107, (*def.*) 114
  numbering of 76–79, (*def.*) 86, 274, 385–386
  real 134, (*def.*) 136
  separated by department 719
  temporary-equity 131, (*def.*) 136, 386, 396
  T form of 41, 43–46, (*illus.*) 53, (*def.*) 57
  uncollectible 465–490
  See also specific account titles
Accountant, rules for 2–3
Account Distribution section 561, (*illus.*) 562
Accounting 2, (*def.*) 11
  accrual basis of 150–151, 167, (*def.*) 170, 753–754
  allowance method of 467–476, (*def.*) 483
  branch 736–737
  career opportunities in 3–4
  cash basis of 150–151
  cash-receipts-and-disbursements basis of 151
  for COD sales 752
  compared to bookkeeping 3
  consistency in 501–502
  departmental 718–737
  fields using 3
  five processes of 2
  for installment sales 753–762
  for issuing bonds 697–704
  for lawyers 166
  lay person's need for 4
  for manufacturing 822–835
  for merchandise enterprises 267–292, 294–320
  modified cash basis of 151
  for Notes Payable account 410–432
  for Notes Receivable account 441–458

  for partnerships 592–596
  payroll 215–266
  for professional enterprises 150–180
  for service enterprises 6–148
  for valuation of inventories 492–506
  for valuation of plant and equipment 528–548
  voucher system of 558–576
Accounting cycle 96–97, (*def.*) 114, 124
  for manufacturing firms 830–833
Accounting process, steps in 68, 96
Accounting system, EDP 505
Accounts Payable account 7
  changing to Notes Payable account 417–418
  in chart of accounts 76
  journalizing 71–72, 74
  order in classified balance sheet 383
  posting 83
Accounts payable ledger 300–302
Accounts Receivable account 22, (*def.*) 29
  aging 470–472
  analysis of 778–779
  book value of 469, (*def.*) 483
  in chart of accounts 76
  as controlling account 276
  for dishonored notes receivable 444–445
  estimating bad debts on basis of 470–475
  for installment sales 755
  journalizing 71, 74
  order in classified balance sheet 383
  patient's ledger record and 153–154
  posting 83
  posting from sales journal 274
  schedule of 276
Accounts Receivable Debit and Sales Credit column 273
Accounts receivable ledger 276–280, (*illus.*) 278
  posting credit memorandums in 281
Accounts receivable turnover 778, (*def.*) 784
Accrual basis of accounting (*def.*) 170
  compared to installment basis 754
  for installment sales 753–754
  use of combined journal with 167
  versus cash basis 150–151
Accrued interest
  on notes payable 425–426, (*def.*) 432
  on notes receivable 451–452, (*def.*) 458

Purchases (contd.)
  net 378, (def.) 396
  recording at net amount 573–575
Purchases account 270, 297
  closing 388, 389
Purchases Discount account 270
Purchases journal 298–300
Purchases Returns and Allowances account 270, 297, 302–305, (def.) 310, 566–568
Purchasing department 294
Purchasing procedures 294–298

Q

Quarter (def.) 255
Quarter-of-a-month periods (def.) 255
Quick assets (def.) 784
Quick ratio 776–777. (def.) 784

R

Rate of interest 411, (def.) 432
Rate of return, on common stockholder's equity 781–782
Ratio of cost value to retail value 520
Raw materials (def.) 835
Raw-materials inventory 833–834
Raw-materials used 823
Real account 134, (def.) 136
Retained Earnings account as 655
Realization (def.) 615
Realized Installment Sales Income account 756
Record of original entry 68
Redemption of bonds 706–707
Registered bonds 695, (def.) 710
Rent Expense account
  in chart of accounts 76
  closing into Income Summary account 127
  journalizing 73
  posting 84
Report form 11
Repossession, merchandise, accounting for 761–762
Restrictive endorsement 184, (def.) 204
Retail business 271, 326
Retail method, of estimating value of inventories 516–520
Retail value, ratio to cost value 520
Retained Earnings account (def.) 642
  appropriation of 664–668, (def.) 675
  deficit (def.) 675
  as real account 655

Retirement of stock 691
Returns
  purchases 302–305, (def.) 310, 567–568
  sales 280, (def.) 285
Revaluation, and partnership dissolution 608–609
Revenue 18, (def.) 30
  in accrual and cash basis 150–151
  in chart of accounts 76–77
  in fundamental accounting equation 40
  in income statement 26
  net income balance 104
  other income 380
  from sales 377
  in trial balance 55
  unearned, adjustments for 353–355
  unearned, in classified balance sheet 384
Revenue accounts
  closing 386
  posting 120, 130
  in work sheet 98
Revenue expenditures (def.) 548
  in plant and equipment costs 536
Reversing entry (def.) 396
  for accrued interest 426
  for bonds 703
  for merchandise enterprises 390–393

S

Salaries and wages (def.) 219
  accrued 103, (def.) 114
  adjusting entry for 251
  calculating 221
  reversing entry for 392
Salaries Payable account 227, 251
Salary allowances, income division by 601–603
Sales
  accounting for 267–292
  COD 752
  estimating bad debts as percentage of 474–476
  installment 753–762
  layaway 752–753
  matching bad debts losses with 467
  net (def.) 396, 768, 775
  revenue from 377
Sales account 270
  closing 386, 389
Sales contract, conditional 753
Sales discount (def.) 285
Sales Discount account 270, 327
Sales invoices 271

Vertical analysis (*contd.*)
   for industry comparisons 775
Voucher (*illus.*) 561, (*def.*) 576
   canceling or altering 566–568
   characteristics of 559–560
   correcting 571–572
   due date 561
   filing of 565–566
   number for 560
   preparation and approval of 560–562
   record (*def.*) 576
   situations requiring special treatment by 566–572
Vouchers register 563
Vouchers Payable account 562–563
Voucher system (*def.*) 576
   of accounting 558–576
   and expenses 562–563
   as management tool 572
   objectives of 558–559
   used with net amount system 573–575

W

Wage amd Tax statement (Form W-2) (*illus.*) 244
Wages (*def.*) 219
   adjusting entry for 251
   calculating 219–220
Wages Expense account
   adjusting entries for 102, 103
   in chart of accounts 76
   closing into Income Summary account 127
   journalizing 75
   posting 84
   reversing entry for 390–392

Wages Payable account
   in classified balance sheet 384
   reversing entry for 390–392
Weighted average cost method 499, (*def.*) 506
   compared to other methods 501
   to determine raw-materials inventory 833
   with perpetual inventories 504
Wholesale business 271, 326–327
Will-call sale 752. *See also* Installment sales
Withdrawal 24, (*def.*) 30
Withholding, income tax 222–224, 242–246
Working capital (*def.*) 397, 784
   amount available 796
   analysis by creditors and management 775–776
   changes in 796–811
   in classified balance sheet 384–385
   sources of 800–801, 807, 810
   uses of 801, 807, 810
Working papers. *See* Work sheet
Workmen's compensation insurance 250–251, (*def.*) 255
Workmen's compensation laws 219, (*def.*) 229
Work sheet (*illus.*) 97, 97–98, 108, 109
   adjustments recorded in 105
   closing entries from 131–132
   for corporations 658–661, (*illus.*) 658–659
   for manufacturing enterprises (*illus.*) 826–827, 827–830
   for merchandising enterprises 358–362, (*illus.*) 360–361
   for professional enterprises 160–163
Write-off method of accounting for bad debts 477–480
W-2 form (*illus.* 244